GISSING: THE CRITICAL HERITAGE

THE CRITICAL HERITAGE SERIES

GENERAL EDITOR: B. C. SOUTHAM, M.A., B.LITT. (OXON.)
Formerly Department of English, Westfield College, University of London

---

For a list of books in this series see the back end paper

GISSING

THE CRITICAL HERITAGE

Edited by
PIERRE COUSTILLAS
Professor of English, University of Lille
and
COLIN PARTRIDGE
Associate Professor, University of Victoria, British Columbia

ROUTLEDGE & KEGAN PAUL: LONDON AND BOSTON

First published 1972
by Routledge & Kegan Paul Ltd
Broadway House, 68–74 Carter Lane,
London EC4V 5EL and
9 Park Street,
Boston, Mass. 02108, U.S.A.

Library of Congress Catalog Card Numbers: 72–81444

ISBN 0 7100 7367 4

Printed in Great Britain
by Richard Clay (The Chaucer Press), Ltd.,
Bungay, Suffolk

General Editor's Preface

The reception given to a writer by his contemporaries and near-contemporaries is evidence of considerable value to the student of literature. On one side we learn a great deal about the state of criticism at large and in particular about the development of critical attitudes towards a single writer; at the same time, through private comments in letters, journals or marginalia, we gain an insight upon the tastes and literary thought of individual readers of the period. Evidence of this kind helps us to understand the writer's historical situation, the nature of his immediate reading-public, and his response to these pressures.

The separate volumes in *The Critical Heritage Series* present a record of this early criticism. Clearly for many of the highly-productive and lengthily-reviewed nineteenth- and twentieth-century writers, there exists an enormous body of material; and in these cases the volume editors have made a selection of the most important views, significant for their intrinsic critical worth or for their representative quality—perhaps even registering incomprehension!

For earlier writers, notably pre-eighteenth century, the materials are much scarcer and the historical period has been extended, sometimes far beyond the writer's lifetime, in order to show the inception and growth of critical views which were initially slow to appear.

In each volume the documents are headed by an Introduction, discussing the material assembled and relating the early stages of the author's reception to what we have come to identify as the critical tradition. The volumes will make available much material which would otherwise be difficult of access and it is hoped that the modern reader will be thereby helped towards an informed understanding of the ways in which literature has been read and judged.

B.C.S.

Contents

Preface

The intention of the editors has been to present much of the worthwhile commentary published between 1880, the year of George Gissing's first novel, and 1912. The latter date is a convenient demarcation: Gissing had been dead for nine years, a younger generation of writers, such as James Joyce and D. H. Lawrence, had begun to appear, and Virginia Woolf's perceptive article (No. 191) is a milestone in appreciation of Gissing's work. A perspective on the further development of his critical reputation during the twentieth century may be gained from *Collected Articles on George Gissing*, edited by Pierre Coustillas (Frank Cass, London, 1968).

The editors' intention, therefore, has been to record the contemporary responses to Gissing's works at the time of publication. These responses indicate the prejudices and judgments of an age, the minor controversies which can becloud or enhance a new publication, and the intellectual structures which—sometimes profoundly, sometimes pretentiously—are raised by efforts at interpreting writing as varied in range and quality as that of George Gissing.

The items discovered in the preparation of this book point towards a correction to the conventional image of the man and his critical reputation. This accepted image has been of a writer either neglected in his lifetime or the recipient of innumerable vicious attacks. Although verbal assaults were made both on his subject-matter and on his fictional method, there was also a considerable number of very fair assessments penned by contemporary reviewers. Despite journalistic facility and an imprecise critical terminology, many late Victorian commentators perceived Gissing's strengths; he may have offended their reading habits, but they struggled to overcome their distaste by trying to effect a balance between his literary strengths and weaknesses. Gissing's reputation benefited from such sympathetic notices and cautious critical commentaries. The credit lies with some much-maligned late Victorian reviewers, a selection of whose labours is presented here.

Acknowledgments

The editors wish to acknowledge the help provided by the following institutions: Bibliothèque Nationale, Boston Public Library, British Museum and Newspaper Library, Manchester Public Library, New York Public Library.

Individuals who have kindly suggested items for inclusion are Jean Cazemajou (University of Bordeaux), Roger Laufer (Monash University) and Martha Vicinus (Indiana University).

Dr David Thatcher (University of Victoria) and Mrs Hedda Thatcher have generously co-operated in translating the article by Eduard Bertz.

The courtesy of permitting the editors to reprint short extracts from volume II of *The Letters of James Joyce*, edited by Richard Ellman, has been extended by Messrs Faber and by the Viking Press Inc.

The editors would also like to thank Professor Quentin Bell and Mrs Angelica Garnett for kind permission to reproduce 'The Novels of George Gissing', by Virginia Woolf, *The Times Literary Supplement*, January 1912.

All possible care has been taken to trace ownership of the selections included and to make full ackowledgement for their use.

Preparation of this book has been expedited by the secretarial assistance of Mrs Paula Kelch (University of Victoria) and of Mme Hélène Coustillas to whom the editors make grateful acknowledgment.

Finally, a grant from the Canada Council facilitated travel, research and editorial consultation in the latter stages of preparing this book: gratitude for this generous consideration is expressed.

Introduction

I

Writing with pungent irony in 1891 George Gissing put into the mouth of one of his least likeable characters a sentiment which may possess an autobiographical strain: 'I'm like poor Jackson, the novelist, who groaned to me once that for fifteen years the reviewers had been describing his books as "above the average". In whatever I have undertaken the results were "above the average", and that's all. This is damned poor consolation for a man with a temperament like mine!' (*Denzil Quarrier*, ch. VI).

Throughout his life Gissing's relations with professional critics were at all times uneasy and his posthumous work, baffling in its variety, did nothing to lessen their ambiguity. From his very first novel he was aware of the gulf that lay between his own conscious intentions and those which the impressionistic reviewer attributed to him. Most of his novels of the 1880s and early 1890s (to 1892 with *Born in Exile*) involved him in more or less open warfare with publishers, publishers' readers, editors or critics. The number and diversity of taunts and criticisms levelled at his first books would have daunted and reduced to silence more than one novelist. His difficulties with Bentley and James Payn are well known—*Mrs Grundy's Enemies* and *Clement Dorricott* have disappeared and *A Life's Morning*, written in 1885 and issued in 1888, only achieved publication on condition that a happy ending should be tacked on to it.[1] He was accused of excessive realism, of dreariness, of pessimism (such epithets as 'gloomy' and 'depressing' recur with irritating frequency in the writings of his British reviewers), of presenting life undramatically, of choosing unsavoury subjects. Nothing of this was unknown to him. His reactions ranged from partial yielding dictated by hunger to private anger and public protest. Until his reputation was established with an élite of readers and he commanded a position of comparative strength, he went through alternatives of haughty resistance to publishers' dictates and concessions made to an influential publisher's reader like Meredith or to a shilly-shallying Philistine like George Bentley.

It must be admitted that his temperament was difficult to please and that his own estimate of his work varied considerably. Even before he had seen the first review of his first novel, *Workers in the Dawn*, he was aggressively defiant of all opposition and was convinced that, given the subject-matter and his treatment of the story, the book was bound to be misinterpreted. His open letter (No. 1) has the tone of dignified revolt. Conversely, a sympathetic, intelligent notice would lead to sudden enthusiasm which never lasted very long. On the whole, the attitude to his critics was one of marked disagreement and he occasionally took the trouble to develop objections and refute the arguments of his censors. In this respect his long letter to Morley Roberts (No. 89) is a significant example. After *Demos*, he begged his publishers—Smith, Elder at the time—to cease sending him press cuttings about his books, 'to stop that horror', and for half a dozen years he did not paste a single cutting in the *ad hoc* album, which he had bought hopefully in 1880. His *Commonplace-Book*, which documents the origins of *The Private Papers of Henry Ryecroft*, has a scathing section on reviewing ending with a list of 'journalistic imbecilities'. Similarly, he indulged in not a few verbal assaults on critics in his unpublished diary and in his correspondence. Perhaps some summary of his fluctuating feelings is conveyed in *The Whirlpool* (1897). The morning after her first public recital Alma eagerly inspects newspaper notices. One speaks of her as 'a lady of some artistic promise' and comments on her nervousness. She thinks: 'Nervous! Why, the one marvellous thing was her absolute conquest of nervousness' (p. 315). Other criticisms harmonized 'in their tone of compliment' and 'all agreed that her "promise" was exceptional'. At a later date she reviews these same published comments: 'It was significant that the musical critics whose opinion had any weight gave her only a word or two of cautious commendation; her eulogists were writers who probably knew much less about music than she, and who reported concerts from the social point of view.' Alma considers the symbolic act of casting all the items into the fire but in a complex of feelings finally compromises: 'Long years hence, would it not be a legitimate pride to show these things to her children? A misgiving mingled with the thought, but her reluctance prevailed. She made up a parcel, wrote upon it, "My Recital, May 1891", and locked it up with other most private memorials' (pp. 372–3).

A similar complex of feelings characterized Gissing's attitude to his critical reception: he was legitimately annoyed not only by narrow-minded and bigoted judgments, but also by excessive praise smacking of flattery or pointing to a lack of critical acumen. For instance, James

Payn's clumsy, repentant tribute (No. 87) displeased him as much as Israel Zangwill's overblown encomiums.[2] Nor did he approve unreservedly the general surveys of his work which appeared after 1887 and with greater frequency from the mid-1890s onwards. Only tactfulness prevented him from openly carping at those articles by Morley Roberts or H. G. Wells reprinted in the present volume (Nos 75 and 113). When he thought that misinterpretation was becoming frankly disobliging, as when Wells commented on the political views expressed in *The Whirlpool*, he ventured to put his friend right in a wearily apologetic manner. All his personal writings tend to show that he had little faith in the capacity of his contemporaries to understand his books, artistically or ideologically. Journalists as a body he distrusted and when he came to write down his opinion of contemporary criticism in *An Author at Grass*, it was not an encouraging one: there was, he thought, not a single sound and genial English literary critic 'in admitted and justified authority'. And of reviewing he wrote: 'On the whole, is any sort of human work so incompetently performed? Is any other kind of artisan so regularly paid in sterling coin for manufacture so valueless, and often so harmful?'[3]

Because of his difficult beginnings, so painful to such a sincere and devoted artist, he never quite rid himself of his (at best) distant attitude to the various classes of people who handle a book after it has left a writer's study in manuscript form. William Morris Colles, his sole literary agent from 1893 to 1898, learnt through experience that he had to deal with an exacting author whose novels and short stories were not to be treated like those of any tradesman of letters; Arthur Henry Bullen, who was both Gissing's friend and publisher during the writer's middle period, also quickly realized that he had to do with a rather touchy and self-respecting writer. Towards the end of his short life Gissing readily admitted that he had done without popularity for twenty years, claiming as a consequence the right to please himself first, regardless of the opinions and counsels of literary agents, publishers' readers and critics. He ultimately saw himself as a novelist with a small, but tenaciously faithful public, regarded by publishers with a mixture of respect and contempt, but supported by a minority of unknown reviewers emotionally devoted to his cause (No. 191).

This image is not untrue, but it needs some additional touches. Gissing read but a small part of the criticism dealing with his work from 1880 to 1903, and a remarkably small part during the years from 1887 to 1892 and from 1896 to 1903. The bulk of what came under his notice, voluntarily or not, he deemed unintelligent and/or jejune. Today with the advantage of retrospect, we can picture his position in the literary world of his time in a clearer, more balanced way. While acknowledging that some of the criticism passed upon his work was downright hostile, if not insulting, and the majority of it tepid or reluctantly appreciative, we realize that right from his first book there were reviewers who valued his art and criticism of life, emphasizing his strong points and responding sympathetically to his sense of a personal mission—a mission more and more widely recognized in recent years. The *Academy*'s vibrant homage (No. 157) reflected the opinion of a fraction of the reading public that was not entirely unvocal. Contemporaries like Edmund Gosse, Walter Besant, Henry Norman, Allan Monkhouse, Justin McCarthy and Thomas Seccombe gave Gissing more than one shout of support even though, as was the common practice at that time in dailies and weeklies, they did not sign their contributions.

Further, his books, at least after *Demos*, were far more widely reviewed than has been assumed by later critics. For the twenty-eight titles ranging from *Workers in the Dawn* to *The House of Cobwebs*, there have been unearthed about 850 reviews, eighty per cent of which (omitting all general surveys of Gissing's work to 1906) constitutes the critical reaction in Britain. It can be confidently asserted that any further search on both sides of the Atlantic, would increase the figure at least by half—a claim based on the fact in his publishers' records that some forty or fifty copies of each title were sent for review to the London and provincial press. Broadly speaking, the critical response increased in bulk as time went on. Yet the increase was by no means steady. Short novels like *Sleeping Fires* and *The Paying Guest*, published within a month during the winter of 1895/6, naturally roused little curiosity in literary columns although they enjoyed substantial sales. They belonged to low-priced series launched just after the collapse of the three-decker and their publishers relied mainly on sales from railway bookstalls. Again, a volume of short stories like *Human Odds and Ends* was neglected by critics and so was the costly travel book *By the Ionian Sea*, few copies of which seem to have been sent out to the press by Chapman & Hall. These exceptions nevertheless fail to invalidate the statement that the later volumes received more critical attention than his first. Gissing's best-known titles were among those that produced the most copious comments: *Demos* (a controversial story on the then burning question of socialism), *New Grub Street* (which made the literary world convulse), *In the Year of Jubilee* and *The Whirlpool* (with their vivid, thought-laden depiction of the new middle class in expanding London and its suburbs), the highly praised study of Dickens and the autumnal *Private Papers of Henry Ryecroft*, whose success would have been hard to predict. Yet, it is significant that his light-hearted attempt at striking a comic vein in *The Town Traveller* set in motion a flow of praise and evaluation, social and literary, whereas such an outstanding novel of ideas as *Born in Exile* was either disregarded or reviewed slightingly by some of the leading journals.

An eagle-eyed all-knowing critic surveying the history of Gissing criticism in 1906, after the publication of his posthumous collection of short stories, *The House of Cobwebs*, would have noted the growing consideration granted by reviewers to his work; there was a group of whole-hearted admirers in the forefront but also a small band of hostile critics like Stephen Gwynn and Arthur Symons who tended to grow more vociferous and active after his death. By this time the dramatic alternative of glory versus neglect was almost painfully obvious.

2

Gissing's works never enjoyed a vast circulation. His earnest tone, his cheerless view of human affairs alienated the vast majority of lowbrow novel-readers who would not allow themselves to be depressed by their reading and who strongly adhered to the view that a novel must be entertaining and conclude on a happy note. During the first two-thirds of his career the diffusion of his stories was handicapped by the usual circulating library system involving publication in three volumes. Until 1894, all his novels, with the sole exception of *Denzil Quarrier* (1892), were written with a view to publication in that form and the number of copies printed did not exceed 1,000, a proportion of them being often remaindered. His poorest sales were those of his first novel, published at his own expense, with 277 copies printed and 49 sold six months after publication while his best-selling title was *New Grub Street*, his only three-decker to have run into a second edition in that form.

The next stage was that of the 6*s*. one-volume edition, part of which could be sold to some colonial library and retailed at a substantially lower price. The number of copies of *Demos* for the 6*s*. edition was 1,000 but Smith, Elder thought it wise to reduce the figure to 750 for

The Nether World, an additional 1,500 being sold to Petherick of Melbourne for his Colonial Library. The last stage, at least for the novels issued by that firm was that of the half-crown cloth-bound and 2*s*. 'yellowback' editions, with printings of a few thousand copies. When, as in the case of *Eve's Ransom* (1895) and *The Whirlpool* (1897), the book was first published at 6*s*. and was thus intended to be bought instead of borrowed through the libraries, the circulation of Gissing's books naturally increased although not in a spectacular way. For instance, Lawrence & Bullen twice printed 2,000 copies of *The Whirlpool* in April and May 1897 but the sales afterwards stagnated and it is doubtful whether more than 6,000 copies of this novel ever circulated in Britain and the colonies before the First World War. When Gissing passed from Lawrence & Bullen to Methuen in 1898, then to Chapman & Hall in 1901, his books in the 6*s*. form still did not sell more than a few thousand copies. His only volume which really conquered the public at large was the last one that appeared in his lifetime, *The Private Papers of Henry Ryecroft*; Constable claimed to have disposed of 64,000 copies by 1939. However, when sixpenny reprints became the fashion in the 1900s, some other titles were also widely diffused. *The Town Traveller*, *The Crown of Life*, *The Unclassed*, *Our Friend the Charlatan*, *Will Warburton* and *New Grub Street* sold in thousands, as indeed did *The Odd Women* and *Born in Exile* in Nelson's red-covered Sevenpenny Series after 1907 and 1910 respectively. Neither the interwar years nor the years after 1945, all characterized by a number of new editions and reprints, witnessed a deep change in the situation. In the United States, where the scale of popularity of his books was about the same as in Britain, the two most popular volumes were *New Grub Street* and *The Ryecroft Papers* which enjoyed prolonged success in the Modern Library.

Considering the comparatively small appeal of his work to the average English and American reader, it is not surprising that only a few of his books first broke into print in serial form. Gissing was aware of the dangers of such publication—Dickens offered a notable instance and warning—and he did not wish to write down to the requirements of the editors of the leading periodicals. Besides, neither William Morris Colles nor James B. Pinker proved very efficient in placing his later books with periodicals. Colles failed signally with *The Town Traveller* which for once had been composed especially for serial publication, and Pinker marked time in his negotiations, which made Gissing impatient and led to his giving up all attempt to serialize

The Crown of Life and *Our Friend the Charlatan*. However, there is no doubt that he reached many readers through periodicals and dailies: between 1888 and 1903 *A Life's Morning* appeared in the *Cornhill*, *Demos* was reprinted in the *Manchester Weekly Times*, *Eve's Ransom* was first issued in the *Illustrated London News* and both *By the Ionian Sea* and *The Ryecroft Papers* in the *Fortnightly Review*. But this form of publication, which was financially rewarding, probably earned him a larger public abroad than in his own country. Six of his books were published serially in Russia, two in France, one in Austria-Hungary and one in Japan.[4] A further element of paradox is discerned if it is realized that his most popular novel in this form, *Eve's Ransom* (1895), was also, in both senses of the word, one of his slightest. Serialized in London, Paris and Moscow, it enjoyed the further distinction of being translated in volume form in France and Holland. Had Gissing known of this, he would have laughed at the incapacity of some editors and translators to distinguish between pikes and minnows. But he would have appreciated being read in translations, provided they were good. He was of the opinion that serial publication, whether complete or not, had no great weight with serious readers, who invariably judged a novel from its edition in book form. He also believed that his reputation abroad would ultimately react in a favourable manner upon his reputation in his native country; however, he did not live to see his sudden rise to fame in Japan. The main stages of his lasting reputation in that country have been retraced by Shigeru Koike in his well-known essay currently available in *Gissing East and West* (Enitharmon Press, London, 1970). The first breakthrough on Japanese territory was made in July 1909 when the Tokyo review *Shumi* printed extracts of *The Ryecroft Papers*; they were the prelude to innumerable Japanese editions of the whole book in English, in Japanese or with facing bilingual texts. There is no doubt that more copies of this pseudo-biography have been sold in Japan itself in one form or another than in the rest of the world, even though recently the same book has run through eight Italian editions within a few years. And Gissing's short stories have similarly known in Japan a popularity that no one in England or America would dream of associating with Gissing's name, but this popularity has engendered a very small amount of critical appraisal apart from the worthy little volume by Masanobu Oda.

The criteria by which Gissing's literary production was judged in the thirty-odd years covered in the present anthology and indeed up to the present day were many, chaotic and contradictory. In his role of mediator between author and public one reviewer may deprecate a book for reasons which, in the eyes of another reviewer, can only lead to a favourable verdict. A personal impressionistic approach, with a personal explicit frame of reference, was the rule. Sympathy with, or antipathy against, the author's view of life dictated or at least coloured the reviewer's judgment. The degree of artistic consciousness on the part of the critic, his own opinion of the novel's respectability as a genre also affected his assessment. However, some salient features appear in novel-reviewing as practised in the late Victorian and Edwardian periods. When Gissing began to write, the status of fiction was still a controversial matter and there is no doubt that the novel even by the end of the century was not unanimously accepted as a 'serious' art-form—quite apart from being placed on the same level as drama and poetry. The mediocrity of Victorian drama, when contrasted with the better part of Victorian fiction, emphasizes the difficulty of the situation for contemporary novelists. In 1892 William Archer, the literary critic and translator of Ibsen, could ask leading novelists of the day why they did not write plays. Gissing's reply clearly expresses the poor esteem in which he held the contemporary theatre; he accused it of commercialism and of pandering to the low taste of the average theatre-goer; in contrast, he asserted his elevated notion of the novelist's art.[5]

The open letter concerning *Workers in the Dawn* had earlier set the tone: his own standards were placed high—which accounts for the harsh view he took of his own fiction in retrospect. In the 1880s the novel's function, as understood by responsible critics, was both to instruct and to entertain. More conservative publishers, like George Bentley, were highly conscious of their role as self-appointed guardians of national morality; they feared the reactions of critics and circulating libraries alike. Gissing's first published novel doubtless suffered several rejections because of its comparative immaturity, but also and mainly on account of the boldness of its subject. *Mrs Grundy's Enemies* was ultimately put aside by Bentley after it was set in print and the author had been paid for fear reviewers would declare it a sin and a shame. When Gissing later submitted *The Unclassed* to the same publisher, he received in return a long sermonizing letter, together with a copy of the reader's report. Bentley objected to 'a prostitute being represented as good and noble and pure', adding that 'it does not appear to me wholesome, to hold up the idea that a life of vice can be lived without loss of purity and womanly nature. . . . I doubt the means you adopt, and I think your book might familiarize some with a condition of things best not dwelt upon.'[6]

A Victorian critic of the 1880s expected the novel to offer intellectual entertainment, stimulate a reader's imagination and yet direct its ideas into morally acceptable paths. A novelist's liberty was thus inevitably restricted; if he was to please his judges, he had to avoid issues which might transform the moral garden into a free-thinking wilderness. It was a novelist's duty to seek to improve his reader, but he must not be too serious as 'improvement' was to be achieved through means both grave and gay. Gravity alone would not have been suitable; tears had to be followed by laughter. The recipe had been given by eighteenth-century novelists and most successfully applied by Dickens. Problem-novels usually incurred the disfavour of reviewers, the genre being deemed an improper vehicle for the discussion of current political, social, religious or philosophical issues. As a rule, novelists thought differently, and the public, piqued by curiosity, disregarded the critics' dictum. James Payn, in his capacity as Smith, Elder's reader, took a strong stand against the novel with a purpose; he pressed Gissing to write less serious novels and repeatedly objected to his pessimism until Gissing, relying on his growing reputation and tired of being catechized, tried his chance with more liberal publishers.[7] The cultural and moral climate was, however, to change appreciably in the 1890s and even more in the 1900s. The naughtiness of the yellow 1890s and the decadent spirit prevailing at the time are only the more showy manifestations of the general hankering after change. Gissing himself acknowledged the advent of the new era ironically in his preface to the second edition of *The Unclassed* (No. 12).

Critics had a number of casually expressed criteria by which they measured a novel's merits. Perhaps central was the view of the novelist as a *creator* of personages; having taken upon himself this godlike function, his responsibility was to breathe 'soul' into his creations. This 'soul', by definition, would imply an edifying and exemplary influence over readers. As mediator-guardians of fictional, but influential, 'souls', reviewers watched carefully an author's portrayal of character, his development of plot, the modulations of his ending, and his deviations from an easily readable style. A prose which chose a middle way between latinized periods and journalese was advocated: Gissing received warnings occasionally against a tendency in both directions. Similarly Gissing was found deficient in the endings he gave to his novels and the dramatic tensions of his plots. In his early books, until

Denzil Quarrier (1892), he sometimes remembered reviewers' complaints, but it was in a novelette he failed to publish, *All for Love*, that he made the most extensive concessions—indeed so extensive that a modern reader may well wonder whether this story, *à la* Wilkie Collins, was not intended as a satire of current critical criteria. Questioning of prevailing criteria invariably provoked discussions of realism, which Gissing tackled, as early as 1884, in a letter to the *Pall Mall Gazette*. He appealed to his fellow novelists' artistic consciences and, quoting from Thackeray's preface to *Pendennis*, lamented that since the death of Fielding, 'no writer of fiction among us has been permitted to depict to his utmost power a man';[8] Gissing was promptly assaulted on the front page of *Punch* (No. 11). The epithet 'realistic' was to be frequently applied to his work, usually in a half-derogatory way, but Gissing was sensitive enough to this aspect of the art of fiction to express his opinion publicly twice—in *Isabel Clarendon* (vol. i, pp. 229–30) and in his article defining 'The Place of Realism in Fiction'. In the latter he asserted:[9]

> Realism . . . signifies nothing more than artistic sincerity in the portrayal of contemporary life; it merely contrasts with the habit of mind which assumes that a novel is written 'to please people', that disagreeable facts must always be kept out of sight, that human nature must be systematically flattered, that the book must have a 'plot', that the story should end on a cheerful note, and all the rest of it.

Gissing's tone leaves no doubt about his attitude to the critical criteria. A survey of contemporary evaluations of his work may both clarify and justify this attitude.

3

THE STRUGGLE FOR RECOGNITION: THE EARLY NOVELS (1880–90)

An impassioned, rough-hewn manifesto striking wildly at Victorian social evils and shams, *Workers in the Dawn*, greatly perturbed contemporary reviewers. Some of the leading journals and newspapers, like the *Saturday Review* and the *Pall Mall Gazette*, preferred to ignore the book. Others poured contempt upon it. For instance the *Whitehall Review* (15 July 1880), after noting mistakenly that the volume seemed intended to expose the evils of irreligion and drunkenness, dismissed it summarily as follows: 'It is seldom that a series of less amusing puppets have been exhibited on the fictional stage.' The *World* (16 October 1880) was still more scornful: 'The story would treat of high life and of low. Its pictures of the former are untrue and vulgar, and the latter unnecessarily coarse and profane; and the whole is as feeble a history of nauseous people and unsavoury things as can well be.' Gissing was further accused by the *Graphic* (19 June 1880) of having written a plotless novel, and of carrying the art of padding to such an extent that he might well divert his perseverance to another channel. As for the workers mentioned in the title the reviewer thought that 'we fain would hide [their doings] from the gaze of the gentler members of our families'.

Exception was taken to the choice of the subject, which was pronounced too dark and painful (*Athenaeum*, No. 2), to the squalid and shocking scenes (*Illustrated London News*, 31 July 1880), to the attack upon the Church of England (*Court Circular and Court News*, 19 June 1880) and to the satire of the upper middle class (Saintsbury in the *Academy*, No. 4). The book as a work of art also gave rise to some adverse criticism. In an otherwise not unfair notice the *Daily News* (29 July 1880) deplored the 'often illiterate' style which was 'redeemed only by its intensity of earnestness'. The plot was disapproved of as being too rambling or non-existent.

Yet the author's merits did not go unacknowledged. The *Athenaeum* (No. 2) admitted that the story offered a striking picture of working-class life, and that its author possessed 'considerable readiness and fluency of style'; the *Weekly Dispatch* (15 August 1880) stressed the truthfulness and force of the scenes described, though it made the common enough remark that 'it is one of the functions of art to make plain by contrast, and to introduce into even the darkest picture enough light to show up the darkness'. It further conceded that the author's motives were admirable. Saintsbury, despite his dislike of both setting and ideology, declared that the book 'leaves on the mind a certain "obsession" . . . which merely insignificant work never produces'. Above all, the *St. James's Gazette* (28 August 1880), the *Manchester Examiner and Times* (No. 5) and the *Spectator* (No. 6) realized that the novel, despite its inevitable imperfections contained promise of some first-rate work. It is interesting to note that at least three reviewers were reminded of *Alton Locke* (No. 5, together with the *St. James's Gazette* and the *Court Circular*) and that the Manchester critic sensed the influence of a greater name than Kingsley's. Neither these perceptive appraisals nor Frederic Harrison's generous encouragements prevented *Workers in the Dawn* from falling into prolonged oblivion. Gissing later came to disclaim this first novel, omitting it from the list of his work. At some unknown date, but doubtless in the 1890s, he attempted to revise it only to give it up after the first volume. Today, its finest critic remains Robert Shafer, editor of the second edition (Doubleday & Doran, 1935).

Gissing's second published story should have been *Mrs Grundy's Enemies* but, as has been mentioned, Bentley eventually became aware of the subject's boldness and of its treatment; he decided against publication after the story had reached proof stage. The novelist was pursuing his investigation of what he later called 'the nether world' and was making himself a solid reputation (with publishers' readers, so far nearly as numerous as readers *tout court*) for choosing unsavoury themes and disregarding social and moral taboos. *The Unclassed* confirmed him in this tradition. Fortunately, Chapman & Hall's reader was George Meredith, and Meredith, however different his inspiration and themes may have been from Gissing's until 1884, could appreciate and recommend novels that were of sterling value, even if they violated decorum. His response to *The Unclassed* (No. 7 a and b), was nearly as enthusiastic as Gissing's own response to Meredith's novels.[10] Not so were magazine editors when they received review copies. As the author remarked in 1895 (No. 12) the book, portraying a prostitute reclaimed to an honest life by love, was very nearly killed by a conspiracy of silence. Only eight reviews of the first edition have been found, two of them so belated as to have no possible consequence on the sales. Reviewers held the book at arm's length. Some phrases they used reflect their guarded approach. The *Evening News* (No. 8) entitled its front-page one-column article 'A Novel for Men'; the *Morning Post* (7 August 1884) paid a brief homage to the artistic value of the story but concluded that it is 'a grave error to treat subjects of this nature in the form of a novel, since they involve the consideration of details clearly unfit for general perusal'; the *Daily Telegraph* (21 August 1884) after a prudish allusion to the heroine—'a woman . . . raising herself from ignominy by force of character'—wished the author could exhibit better judgment in the selection of his next subject; lastly, the *Graphic* (No. 10) seemed relieved in finding 'dull' a novel which might have been unwholesome.

That *Workers in the Dawn* had already been forgotten by 1884 is testified by the fact that only one reviewer, in the *Daily News* (19 October 1885) happened to mention it. He did so glowingly: 'A novel written a few years ago by Mr George Gissing, *Workers in the Dawn*, was so remarkable for power and a certain intensity and gloom of pessimistic philosophy that it made a permanent impression on those who met with it.' This critic must have been singularly liberal-minded in order to declare of the author: 'The knife with which he probes the wound is sometimes roughly handled, but it is held by one who well knows what he is doing.' Doubtless an upholder of realism, he saw in the happy ending of *The Unclassed* something closer to 'the prerogative of the romancer than to the probabilities of real life'. The comments on the literary aspect of the book were quite contradictory. Those in the *Athenaeum* (28 June 1884) amounted to such an unfair slating that it triggered off in Gissing a hostility that was never to abate, for the very good reason that it was fostered by not a few other grossly biased appraisals. With squeamish delicacy, the reviewer declared he would concentrate on the book's merits 'from the strictly technical point of view of fiction'. In turn were pilloried the construction of the story, the movements of the characters, the style ('singularly bald and abrupt') and the female characters. The *Evening News* (No. 8) had practically declared the contrary three days earlier, praising the subject and the 'felicity of craftsmanship', the style ('unpretentious and clear') and the study of character ('never superficial, and at times really penetrating'). The *World* (30 July 1884) made no effort to conceal its aversion to the story, yet admitted that the author 'has told it strongly; he is not commonplace; and he is, I think, sincere.' A similar verdict was rendered by the *Spectator* (31 January 1885) and by the *Daily Telegraph* (21 August 1884), which had the further merit of pointing to what was already one of the writer's major themes, in our time commented upon by Asa Briggs and Raymond Williams: 'Mr Gissing realizes how cruel is the solitude of great cities to the friendless, and the unique sorrows of the lonely and poor in the busy haunts of men find in him an eloquent exponent.' Until *The Ryecroft Papers* and *Veranilda*, the mental and moral solitude of an individual at odds with his environment was to remain dramatized in his work; it was a conflict, as Gissing saw it, inevitably sharpened by a shortage of money, and measurably softened by financial adequacy.

Although *The Unclassed* received but scant attention in the press and was ultimately banned from Mudie's Library, it won the praise of some leading novelists and critics. Besides Meredith, Hardy was known to hold it in high esteem; William Sharp and Oswald Crawfurd among others demanded that it should be reprinted. In the 1890s casual allusions in print to the story were not infrequent and the main obstacle to surmount soon became the author's reluctance to revive work which he regarded as youthful and romantic. In writing, on the suggestion of his friend Eduard Bertz, a short preface to the second edition (No. 12), Gissing seems to have borne in mind the *Spectator*'s remark that 'the symbolical means she [the heroine] adopts of wiping out her degraded past is almost absurdly fanciful'. He shortened the scene of Ida Starr's midnight bathing, but contrary to many subsequent statements by Morley Roberts and his followers, he let the symbol stand, being content to refer to the idealism of youth.

Apparently, the more prudish subscribers to Mudie's Library had not been alone in finding *The Unclassed* offensive. It is tempting to interpret the scurrilous attack on Gissing in *Punch* (No. 11) as a reprimand not only for his courageous statement in the *Pall Mall Gazette* of December 1884 but also for his boldness in publishing this novel. A liberalization in the moral atmosphere between the mid-1880s and the mid-1890s, noted in the 1895 preface, was amply illustrated by the reception, in both England and America, of the novel in its trimmed form. Thus, the London *Literary World* (3 January 1896), remarked in a glowing notice that '*The Unclassed* reads as very mild stuff when compared to some of the stories that have succeeded it.' The *Daily Chronicle* (No. 13) and the *Speaker* (4 January 1896) were both anxious to exculpate Gissing from the charge of uncleanliness and to vindicate the choice of his subject, the first of these papers offering a valuable comparison with the major works of the early 1890s. Not all reactions, however, were as generous and friendly. The *World* (12 February 1896), for one, condemned the book as an unpalatable production typical of 'an era of sex-problems and Hill-topism'.[11] American reception is fairly exemplified by the comments of the *Buffalo Courier* (No. 14). R. F. Fenno, the New York publisher, advertised the book as 'George Gissing's greatest story', printing in the July 1896 issue of the *Literary News* an impressive number of commendatory judgments. The volume in paper-bound form was for a time one of the 'leading sellers' on the American market.

After *The Unclassed*, Gissing wrote *Isabel Clarendon*, which was recast into two volumes on George Meredith's advice, *A Life's Morning*, *Demos* and *Thyrza*. Here the order of publication may obscure the progress of Gissing's art and ideas. The appearance of *A Life's Morning* was delayed until James Payn could find space for it as a serial in the *Cornhill*, and *Isabel Clarendon* was slow in appearing because of Chapman's dilatory methods and of the commercial necessity to have *Demos* in libraries and bookshops while the socialist demonstrations were in the forefront of political news. Partly in order to avoid publishing two novels within a few months of each other, partly with a view to exploiting public curiosity about a novel on socialism in days of socialist agitation, *Demos* was issued anonymously. The wildest guesses were made concerning its authorship, the names of Gladstone and Mrs Oliphant being suggested among others. On the whole the book was very favourably reviewed in England, and its detractors, as could be expected, consisted mainly in left-wing liberals incensed by the author's bias against socialism. The *Manchester Guardian* (29 July 1886) wrote in sarcastic vein:

> The Radicals of *Demos* are very cheap persons; indeed the *beaux rôles* are for the sons of the gentry and for their daughters. All comes right in the end; the most gentlemanlike of men wins the most gentlewomanlike of women, and at a time the bad behaviour of the popular party is but a remembrance of sorrow that serves as a foil to present joy.

The reviewer added in a tone of pique: 'A political novel must be first rate or nothing, as champagne must either sparkle or be thrown away.' The *Daily Chronicle* (22 May 1886) printed a short politico-literary notice savouring of spitefulness, which was as controversial as the novel itself: 'The author of *Demos,* though successful enough with personal incidents has not grasped either the reality or the romance of Socialism.' Conversely, more conservative journals applauded the book frantically. The *Scottish Review* (No. 19) and the *St. Stephen's Review* (17 April 1886) provide good examples of this passionate response to the political aspect of the novel. As in the case of *Workers in the Dawn*, several comparisons were made with earlier novels in the same vein, *Alton Locke* in particular. Gissing's picture of socialism elicited opposite appreciations—the *Athenaeum* (No. 16) and the *World* (28 April 1886) declared it old-fashioned, more characteristic of Parson Lot than of Hyndman's Social Democratic Federation, which was indeed but partially true, whereas the *St Stephen's Review*, which thought the book was a first novel, guaranteed its fidelity to life.

Short of agreeing with the author's political credo, most reviewers acknowledged his familiarity with working-class life (Nos 15 and 17) and his grasp of psychology. The humblest lower-class characters, especially the women and among them old Mrs Mutimer, were often selected for praise. From this novel dates a general tendency to point out Gissing's unusual ability to portray female characters. Probably because the book's subject coincided with current political news, the literary achievement was a topic of comparatively little attention. One comes across many general statements—*Public Opinion* (2 April 1886) called the book 'a novel of remarkable power and finish', and the *Queen* (31 July 1886) described it as 'ably written'—but the technique of the narrative was practically ignored. The *Guardian* (No. 18), for instance, confessed to being fascinated by the analysis of Richard Mutimer's modest library but missed the opportunity to point out the intellectual implications of the device regarding the author's chosen values. The *Daily News* seems to have been the only journal to consider the artistic aspect of the story, regretting the slow beginning, recalling Algernon in *Rhoda Fleming* apropos of 'Arry Mutimer and stressing the irony resulting from the contrast between the refined literary dilettante in socialism and his more down-to-earth comrades.

The little we know of the American reactions shows that they ranged from the trivial and insulting (*Nation*, 1 July 1886)[12] to the substantial and perceptive (No. 20). Gissing's writings were then absolutely unknown across the Atlantic and so they remained almost until the mid-1890s for *Isabel Clarendon*, *Thyrza*, *New Grub Street* and *Born in Exile* were not issued by American firms in his lifetime and his other books had very limited sales. So had *Isabel Clarendon* when it came out in Britain. With this novel began the rolling fire of epithets like 'pessimistic', 'gloomy' and 'depressing' levelled by British reviewers. This time the approach of critics was of necessity literary. Gissing, after *The Unclassed*, had been experimenting and the novelty of *Isabel Clarendon* disturbed some readers attached to the traditional, explicit, painstaking rendering of life associated with three-volume fiction. Half the reviewers complained about the supposed deficiency in movement or incident or about the unconventional ending which failed to indicate plainly the fate of all the characters. The *Graphic* (2 October 1886), the *Saturday Review* (No. 25), the *Illustrated London News* (10 July 1886) and the *Guardian* (No. 26) harped on the former point. The *St. James's Gazette* (5 June 1886) exclaimed childishly that this was hardly fair story-telling. The *Scotsman* (No. 23) and the *Academy* (No. 24) were particularly embarrassed by the Jamesian ending, and Kingcote's introvert, morbid character was not adequately perceived through the rose-coloured spectacles of most reviewers. Ada Warren, one of Gissing's first 'new women', displeased the *Morning Post* (28 July 1886), but enchanted James Ashcroft Noble (No. 24).

Despite these negative points, characterization was vastly praised, even though some of the characters failed to please. The book was admitted to have a certain freshness; the vernal influence of Meredith and the atmosphere of *The Vicar of Wakefield*, round about Mr Vissian, suggested comparisons. The *Academy* paid Gissing a distinct compliment in 'recommending [his book] heartily to that cultivated class of readers who seek in fiction what Mr Matthew Arnold says is to be found in good poetry—a "criticism of life" '.

However, no reviewer was aware that this was Gissing's fourth published novel. Only one (*Spectator*, 23 October 1886) referred to *The Unclassed* and the other two stories were absolutely ignored. With *Thyrza* the situation changed and the *Pall Mall Gazette* published the first survey of Gissing's works (No. 32), followed about a year later by *Murray's Magazine* (No. 33), in which Edith Sichel attempted, much to the novelist's dislike, to classify him as a philanthropist. *Thyrza* won the quasi-unanimous encomiums of critics, but some of these still had difficulty in believing that 'George Gissing' was not like George Sand, George Eliot and John Oliver Hobbes, of the feminine gender (No. 28). The story's gentleness and delicate pathos not unreasonably led to this assumption; it decidedly addressed itself to the weaker side of the average reviewer. Even the *Athenaeum* (No. 27) surrendered to its power of seduction, surpassed though it was in admiration by the *Whitehall Review* (No. 28). Most notices stressed the excellence of the popular scenes and able characterization, especially that of minor figures like Totty Nancarrow (*Spectator*, 25 June, and *Graphic*, 6 August 1887) or Lydia Trent (*Court Journal*, 7 May 1887). The idealization of the heroine was often noted but only *The Times* (21 May 1887) referred to it regretfully, opining that 'it would have been better to make Thyrza a more natural and fleshly plebeian'. The sentimentality of the tale mollified the critical power of most reviewers, who predicted for the book a greater success than it was in fact to enjoy, even though it ran to several reprints in the twenty years following original publication. The *Publishers' Circular* (4 July 1891) acclaimed the second edition as unreservedly as the first. The *Guardian* (No. 31) jibbed a little at Bunce's atheistic views, but yielded ultimately as did *Public Opinion* (13 May 1887) which concluded its account of the story in typically Victorian fashion: 'The novel is an exceedingly good one, and fixes the reader's attention from beginning to end.' Although no one openly said so, the delight given by the narrative also proceeded from the realization that here was a writer who could depict sordid realities without raking the mud which Zola and his school were so fond of stirring under a reader's nose. The *Saturday Review* (17 October 1891) on the appearance of the one-volume edition (1891) warned Gissing against an excess of sentiment, assuredly a danger to which he was open occasionally, as in *The Crown of Life*. In a cool analysis of the book, *The Times* drew the author's attention to a technical flaw which was removed in the second edition: 'In the third volume, an entirely minor plot, with entirely fresh characters (we mean the Emersons) is opened up to the distraction of the reader' (21 May 1887).

Thyrza was to remain Gissing's only moderately optimistic working-class story. *A Life's Morning* followed it in order of publication and he watched the serialization in 1888 with increasing uneasiness. This time the reviewers of the novel in book form were most likely pacified by the happy ending, which could hardly have been forecast by the middle of the narrative. The appraisals ran very much on the same lines as those of *Thyrza*, with some interesting differences. Thus, the *Pall Mall Gazette* (12 December 1888) after noticing 'the effective and cleverly drawn contrast between two types of feminine character', Beatrice Redwing and Emily Hood, ventured to remark that

> Mr Gissing's gentlemen are never equal to his working men; in attempting to make them refined he only succeeds in making them feeble, and it makes us regret that he does not confine himself to that class of life which he knows so intimately, and has described with such skill and fidelity in *Demos* and *Workers in the Dawn*. On the other hand, as a study of feminine nature, *A Life's Morning* is perhaps the most successful of all Mr Gissing's works.

The book's realistic scenes were accepted because of the tragic tension in the story of the Hood family and also on account of some comic relief, favourably alluded to by the *Manchester Guardian* (10 December 1888). Yet the *Guardian* (No. 37), organ of the Anglican Church, could bring itself to accept neither Emily as a character nor the story's moral. Some disagreements also occurred with regard to the style which was praised by the *Whitehall Review* (13 December 1888), but criticized for a certain tendency to ponderousness by the *Athenaeum* (No. 35), the *Daily Telegraph* (25 December 1888) and the *Court Journal* (No. 36). Few literary allusions were made about the situation or treatment of the main themes, and even then not those one would naturally expect. The *Manchester Guardian* reviewer was reminded of George Eliot and Henry James, while the *Spectator* (No. 38) mentioned Baring-Gould's *Mehalah*. Thomas Seccombe later suggested Meredith's *The Ordeal of*

Richard Feverel, but no one thought fit to name *Wuthering Heights* or *Jane Eyre* which Gissing had doubtless in mind when delineating the fiery character of Dagworthy and the occupation of Emily. The change in the winding up of the narrative with Emily going to the altar instead of dying from heart failure passed almost unnoticed. *Public Opinion* (7 December 1888) even affirmed that 'the novel is thoroughly holding to the end.' Only the *Scottish Review* (April 1889) spotted the flaw—the unsatisfactory disappearance of Beatrice, which is somewhat out of character, and the 'inevitable marriage'. One cannot help regretting that the title should have been deprived of the ironical ring it would have assumed if Emily Hood had not been resuscitated by what Morley Roberts called 'Payn and poverty'.

With *The Nether World*, his greatest and darkest proletarian novel, Gissing moved towards naturalism, but would not continue this progress towards sexual explicitness—an attitude noted by a reviewer in the *Standard* (17 June 1889): 'While he runs Zola close as a realist, his thoughts and language are as pure as those of Miss Yonge herself.' The book was too frank in dealing with the appalling living conditions of the London proletariat to please everyone. A reaction of disgust can be read in not a few contemporary notices: *Vanity Fair* (22 June 1889) thought some of the scenes 'so graphically described as to be positively revolting'; at the end of a vibrant eulogy, the *Glasgow Herald* (22 April 1889) admitted after quoting the motto on the title page: 'There is no denying the beauty of Mr Gissing's flower, but what a revolting *fumier* it is!' The relentless picture of the urban underworld, hateful as it was to some reviewers for political, religious or literary reasons, brought about some grossly unfair, if not positively abusive, judgments. The *Daily Chronicle* (6 May 1889), for example, delivered itself of this singular opinion: 'The author of *Demos* evidently does not know the real working man, and he is so inartistic as to describe a popular outing at the Crystal Palace in the same terms as a drunken orgie of one of London's slums.' And the *Athenaeum* (27 July 1889) improved upon this critical impercipience by the comment: 'To gain enough superficial knowledge of the poor to draw harrowing pictures of their condition, even with plenty of details, is exceedingly easy; but to dive into their real thoughts and ways requires not only exceptional opportunities, but an exceptional gift of dealing with them'; the review ended with the lowbrow suggestion that 'a touch of humour, which Mr Gissing does not seem to possess, would have done much to relieve the weariness which *The Nether World* forces upon the reader'.[13] The

Church weekly (No. 42) and one of the Anglican pontiffs, F. W. Farrar (No. 43), resented the book's truthfulness which implicitly cast a slur upon Christianity and its futile, paternalistic solution to the misery of the poor—philanthropy; but the *Guardian* tried to do the story greater justice than Farrar who used it as a peg on which to hang his views on social problems. The *Guardian*, in its accounts of Gissing's novels not infrequently deplored that he did not advocate the Christian remedy for the evils described, and could never quite admit of social reality when it was unsightly or mentally disturbing. In the present case, it mistook angry indignation for 'cynical contempt'.

Not a few reviewers tried to comfort themselves with the thought that after all Gissing exaggerated. The *Pall Mall Gazette* (4 June 1889) paid homage to the ruthless descriptions of lower-class life, to the pathos of the story and to its unflagging interest, but wondered whether it was a wise thing to rouse in a reader 'a feeling of crushing impotence, a sense of deepest guilt in possessing any of the common foods of life', without indicating a remedy. The *Graphic* (15 June 1889) was less honest because it mixed social with literary values:

> *The Nether World* keeps the reader at one deadly level of depression. . . . Its being so well written, and with such thoughtfulness, knowledge, and conviction, intensifies the gloom of the inevitable deduction that there is no use in effort for ourselves or for others, and that misery is very much a matter of fatalism. We all know by this time how the very poor live; and there is little benefit in fresh descriptions unless they are given for some other reason than to create despair. . . . No good ever yet came out of pessimism, and never will; and on that ground, if on no other, it would stand condemned.

Thereupon, the critic indulged in an access of wishful thinking and pronounced the story improbable and hardly to 'be recommended to readers in search of either profit or pleasure, despite its graphic power'. The New York *Nation* (No. 44) did not go as far but its reviewer, also, sought refuge and solace in the thought that Gissing had darkened his picture.

The value of the novel on both the documentary and artistic planes was nonetheless recognized by a number of journals, even some of those with a circulation mainly among fashionable society. The *Morning Post* (27 May 1889) expressed unstinted admiration for Gissing's realism as did the *Court Journal* (No. 40) and the *Whitehall Review* (No. 41). *Public Opinion* (12 April 1889) called Clem Peckover 'a creation' and thought the relations between Clara Hewett and her father were unfolded in a masterly manner.

How firm and clear a touch Mr Gissing has for delineating the annals of the London poor. . . . There is much humour and fun in the book, too, as well as pathos, and here and there a deeper note of true, not mock, tragedy. The description of a bank holiday at the Crystal Palace is excellent. Those who can appreciate a realism quite on the Dickens plan, but without the perpetual farce that takes one's attention off the hideousness of London poverty, will find plenty of it in these three volumes, which cannot fail to add much to the growing reputation of the writer.

Gissing was then being discovered in France, where *Demos* was being translated, in Russia, where one Zotov commented very favourably on *Demos*, *The Unclassed* and *A Life's Morning* (*Nablyudatel*, 15 November 1889) and also in Germany. Bertz's article on his friend's work (No. 45), of which he had intimate knowledge, was the first to encompass the whole of the novelist's production and to rise above the particular issues of a particular novel. Bertz places his subject within a historical and European framework and he discovers a coherence, unity and prime motive in the total work. The piecemeal criticism of most of the novels in English periodicals appears narrow-minded and almost pedestrian in comparison with Bertz's capacity to view Gissing's seven books *en bloc*—and in their diversity. The parallel with Hogarth, inspired by a careful reading of the first two novels and fostered by conversations Bertz had with Gissing in their common period, is at once suggestive and adequate; he obviously knows not only his writer but also the ethical and cultural climate in which the latter is working. He sees him much as we do nowadays—a dedicated artist with a frustrated sense of beauty, convinced that 'the brutishness of the degenerate masses is clearly connected with the ugliness which constantly surrounds them'. Lastly, Bertz pertinently stresses such manifest elements of Gissing's position as his hostility to the industrial system and his hatred for the inhumanity of the modern social structure.

The Nether World—an anguished cry uttered after the youthful death of his wife Nell—was the last of his working-class stories and also represented some relief of the tension he had known since the dramatic Manchester episode. Gissing never returned to the study of lower-class life. His next novel, influenced by a first visit to Italy, anticipated a new vein in his writing; *The Emancipated* did little to increase his fame and met with a cool reception from the majority of critics, few of whom were sufficiently liberal to appreciate this dramatization of a Puritan North-country girl's emancipation. It further incurred the by now familiar charge of pessimism (Nos 47 and 48). Gissing's sanely ambiguous attitude to emancipation, veiled in discreet irony, puzzled some critics, and even produced some self-contradictions, like that of the *Morning Post* (30 April 1890) reviewer who reproached the author with having written a novel with a purpose, yet deplored that he had failed to take sides. The heroine, Miriam Baske, was disliked by the *Guardian* (28 May 1890) on aesthetic-moral grounds and by *Vanity Fair* (19 April 1890). The latter journal voted the Neapolitan setting poetic and truthful, although the *Manchester Guardian* (2 January 1894) disagreed when reviewing the second edition. The book's literary aspect received little attention until reissued in England in 1893 and in America in 1895. Of interest are the two very different notices printed by the *Spectator*. The first (21 June 1890)—a skimpy, indifferent estimate thrown into a column of 'Current Literature', which had incensed Gissing because it omitted to mention that he was the author of several novels—contrasts with a lengthy, if biased, analysis (No. 50) of the theme of emancipation. Between the appearance of these notices Gissing had shortened his work for the one-volume edition but both English and American critics seemed to have still found it slow in movement. It was, however, the ambiguity of the writer's message that irritated contemporary reviewers. A good deal of unseemly prejudice was given free play as well as some misunderstanding of the author's aims. The New York *Nation* (16 February 1896) wrote[14]

> Though not indifferent to the charm of southern landscape his pen cannot express it. His descriptions are dry and chill, suggestive of phylloxera in the vineyards and frost upon the oranges. He perceives the softening effect of Greek art and Latin manners on British prejudice and self-sufficiency, but does not succeed in transforming the stern patroness of a dissenting chapel in Bartles . . . either into a gay figure symbolic of intellectual freedom, or a gracious, kind and honorable woman.

All in all, *The Emancipated* failed to receive its due; the public had come to regard Gissing as the portrayer, with Walter Besant, of the lower orders of society and could not readjust its sights after a single book on an altogether different subject. Soon a new phase was to begin in the writer's personal life. His second marriage heralded fresh inspiration. Hitherto he had most often been referred to as 'the author of *Demos*'; now he became for a decade 'the author of *New Grub Street*'.

A FOOTING GAINED: THE MIDDLE YEARS (1890–7)

New Grub Street could not leave the literary world indifferent. The book was widely read, reviewed, alluded to and it provoked a literary quarrel in the columns of the writers' professional journal (Nos 60 and 61). For the first time, it was evident that Gissing possessed, even if he had previously been unaware of the situation, a band of ardent followers, some among his fellow writers, who were prepared to take up the pen in order to vindicate his realistic view of existence and testify to its accuracy. Gissing was felt to be a force, and approval or disapproval of his image of literary life had in it something personal; some articles gave the impression of being addressed as much to the author as to the public for whom they were intended. Superlatives poured on to the printed page. The *London Figaro* (13 June 1891) styled the story 'in some respects the most powerful . . . he has written', the *Guardian* (27 May 1891) his best bit of work since *Thyrza* and the *Daily Graphic* (13 April 1891) described Gissing as 'one of the cleverest of the younger novelists'. There were also some readers who found it his most dismal book. Objections, naturally, were plentiful—that it was neither art nor life (No. 59), that the range of literary types was 'neither complete nor even widely representative' (*Pall Mall Gazette*, 1 June 1891), that the selfish heroine should eventually be rewarded at the expense of the unselfish one (*Vanity Fair*, 9 May 1891), that the whole story depended on a confusion between the material and the spiritual wages for artistic work (*Manchester Guardian*, 14 April 1891), that by his selection of grim subjects Gissing was endangering his claim to rank among the first of rising novelists (No. 54), etc., etc. But there was an abundance of testimonies bringing further grist to Gissing's mill, like that of the *Court Journal* (No. 53). The *Saturday Review* (No. 56), after taking exception to the new picture of Grub Street, thought it well to publish a notice of the novel reaching a different conclusion (No. 57). The *National Observer* (9 May 1891) aptly noted that the real theme was money, on which subject the *Guardian* (27 May 1891) was prompted to spur its rickety Christian hobby-horse with the platitude that money does not lead to happiness.

Reluctant as some critics were to recognize the truthfulness of the literary life as depicted by Gissing in one of his gloomiest and satirical moods, they felt no hesitation in placing *New Grub Street* in the front rank of his production. The rich gallery of characters earned him much praise, but the arrangement of the plot received no special attention.

One reviewer stressed the clever, lifelike use of dialogue, while one or two others thought it too 'shoppy'. This is indeed one of the most interesting aspects of the book to the modern reader. Here are discussed in a vivid manner, by characters whose voices have the ring of a recording from life, the professional and cultural problems that loomed large in Gissing's sensitive brain—the advent of the first generation educated under Forster's Education Act of 1870, the development of a popular press aiming at the millions of 'quarter-educated', the growing commercialization of the literary profession with the expansion of the society weeklies and monthlies, the appearance of the literary agent—often a failed writer—to sell the literary goods at the highest obtainable price. Recent introductions to the book by John Gross and Bernard Bergonzi have examined these points. It is also relevant to notice that, in the same year as *New Grub Street* was published, professional writers in Britain were absorbing the effect of the new American Copyright Act. Both the novel and the Act (the provisions of which Gissing at once tried to take advantage of) were new accretions for professional consciousness, as evidenced by the discussions of both in the *Author*.

Denzil Quarrier, written after *Born in Exile* but issued before, is an extensive reshuffling of a discarded novelette, *All for Love*, once composed with a view to serialization.[15] Even in its new form, the story shows Gissing in a minor key. Its reduced length caused the *World* (24 February 1892) to place it above *The Nether World* and *New Grub Street*, but this judgment went counter to the general opinion. The *Chicago Tribune* (No. 63), in which Gissing had once published his first short stories, faithfully expressed the general opinion, declaring that 'promising a story as it is, [it] affords but a partial test of its author's capacity'. The *Daily Chronicle* (No. 64), which hitherto had given him the cold shoulder, suddenly waxed enthusiastic and became one of his keenest and most constant supporters, whereas the *Bookman* (March 1892) was at pains to demonstrate that while the first chapter foreshadowed a tragedy of character, the story turned out to be a tragedy of circumstances. The two main aspects of the narrative—political and feminist—received unequal attention and diverging appreciation. The *Bookman*, the *Athenaeum* (9 April 1892) and *The Times* (No. 66) praised the electioneering scenes, which the *Illustrated London News* (28 May 1892) deemed 'little more than passable'. As one would expect, the *Guardian* (No. 67) recoiled at the description of the matrimonial entanglement and the tragic suicide of Lilian, but there were signs that public opinion was becoming more liberal and tolerant (No. 65). On the artistic plane, the story also gave rise to all sorts of jarring comments. For one thing, Glazzard's Judas-like figure appeared unlikely to some (*The Times*, No. 66, and *Academy*, 9 April 1892), but quite plausible to others (*Saturday Review* and *Illustrated London News*). The plot was warmly commended by the *Whitehall Review* (19 March 1892) and the *Daily Chronicle*, but uncharitably run down by the *Graphic* (23 April 1892). As usual, the critical reception of the book offered one example of slanderous attack. H. D. Traill accused the author in the *New Review* (March 1892) of presenting pictures 'vulgarly exaggerated in line, and in colour of a crude violence to set the teeth on edge'. In reporting this to his brother, Gissing betrayed some impatience: 'To this man I should reply in Sam's words: "You lie, and you know you lie." Whatever my fault, it is not crudeness of colouring—as I think you will agree; least of all in this particular book, where the tone is kept studiously sober.'[16] He must have found the comparisons with Meredith and Dickens (Nos 64 and 66) more dignified and rewarding; besides, the impression on readers of the *New Review* must have been counteracted in the May number by Edmund Gosse's mention of *Denzil Quarrier* as one of 'the praiseworthy novels of the moment'.

The character of Godwin Peak in the next novel, *Born in Exile*, was inadequately appreciated, as was the novel as a whole. In recent years Jacob Korg and Walter Allen have brought to light several dimensions of the story which the 1892 reviewers overlooked completely.[17] Again some abuse was thrown at the writer by the *Saturday Review* (No. 71), the *Pall Mall Gazette* (1 July 1892) which said the material was of the slenderest but cleverly worked up, and, on the appearance of the second edition, by the *Glasgow Herald* (9 March 1893) which equated Gissing with Mrs Gummidge. However, the terrible earnestness of the tone, the intellectual distinction of the philosophical-religious debate with which the dialogue is fraught and Peak's own stature definitely impressed critics. The *Speaker* (No. 68) commended the characterization and acknowledged Gissing's power in evoking an overpowering atmosphere, but of course disliked his pessimism. Peak was a masterly and original creation but he conveyed some doubtful feelings. The *Westminster Review* (November 1892) pronounced him 'unsympathetic', the story 'ugly' and the theme 'ungrateful'. George Cotterell (No. 74) remarked more worthily that the cleverness of the book was attested by the fact that Peak neither forfeits the reader's sympathy nor wins his admiration, and the *Graphic* (23 July 1892) made the prophetic observation that Peak would become an even more common type in the next generation. The *Guardian* (No. 73) whined a little because Gissing's view of life did not correspond to its Christian *image d'Epinal*: 'The hard, dusty highway of life, trodden by all these people without hope and without faith, is a more distressing spectacle than the author probably meant to make it, and the hero approaches a Napoleonic ideal of cynical self-seeking.' The most illuminating responses, after all, were perhaps that of the *Daily Chronicle* (No. 70), which not unjustifiably pointed to a temporary tendency on Gissing's part to use pedantic diction, together with that of *The Times* (No. 72), which saluted the minor characters. Only the people who knew the author personally could realize what the book signified to him. Eduard Bertz and Morley Roberts (No. 75) were among these.

The subject of *The Odd Women* had been announced in *Denzil Quarrier*. From his very first book Gissing had been interested in the changing status of the Victorian woman and he was a living example—and victim—of the effects that the combined idealization of and contempt for woman could have on men emotionally unbalanced. *The Odd Women*, like *Demos*, was a problem-novel whose appearance was well-timed. The feminine press could not be indifferent to it but the reactions varied very much according to the degree of emancipation of the reviewer, as can be seen from those appreciations in the *Queen* (3 June 1893), arrogantly hostile to 'the shrieking sisterhood', the *Woman's Herald* (22 June 1893), which declared that 'no novel perhaps . . . has treated more exhaustively and more adequately the whole position of women', and in the *Illustrated London News* (No. 81). A virtue of Gissing's book was that it presented a variety of emotional relationships and so reflected a gamut of attitudes to marriage. Noting this, the *Spectator* (27 May 1893) stressed Gissing's 'eager intentness of vision', a characteristic of all his most genuinely inspired novels, like *Workers in the Dawn*, *The Nether World*, *New Grub Street* and *Born in Exile*. The *Pall Mall Gazette* reviewer (No. 79) must have had this in mind when admitting that '*The Odd Women* is a great vindication of realism from the charge of dulness', an impression echoed by the *Boston Beacon*.[18] However Gissing's methods still met with very strong opposition from the traditionalist reviewers. More than ever appeared the epithets 'pessimistic', 'gloomy' and 'depressing'. The *Academy* (24 June 1893) would not grant that Gissing's scenes were typical, the *Review of Reviews* (July 1893) recalled Zola's 'sordid realism' and the

Speaker (14 October 1893) regretted that the book 'should assume a somewhat dogmatic and polemical air, inconsistent with the true aims of fiction'. Yet the last-named journal could not help admiring the female characters of this 'powerful and thoughtful book'. The *dramatis personae* called forth nothing but compliments and, when some reservations were made, as in the *Saturday Review* (No. 77), they seem to have been dictated by irritation at the type of person described rather than at the delineation of it. The construction of the story and the style elicited some negative remarks, which their authors unfortunately kept from illustrating. On the whole, the book certainly enhanced Gissing's reputation; No. 80 is an instance among others of very favourable American response. Comments went on steadily in his lifetime and the passage of time has given the book a documentary aspect which twentieth-century critics have unreservedly acknowledged.

In the Year of Jubilee, its successor, also focused on the woman question but examined it from the cultural rather than the economic angle. Gissing so brilliantly analysed the new suburban society, then in a state of patent vulgarization, that he hurt many susceptibilities. When critical admiration was expressed—that is in most cases—it was expressed more and more loudly, with increasing conviction. *New Grub Street*, *The Odd Women* and the novel under review all tackled contemporary issues with a vigour which penetrated the professional complacency of reviewers, forcing them to take sides. Among the opponents were those who felt they had to protest against a scathing picture of the social class among which their journal recruited its readers (*World*, 19 December 1894), those who shied at the hero's revolutionary views on marriage (*Daily News*, 27 December 1894, and *Guardian*, 3 April 1895, more than ever out of touch with Gissing's unvarnished fiction), and those who objected to the theme and/or to its treatment. Among the latter should be mentioned the *National Observer* (19 January 1895) with its view that the material used by the writer was unsuitable for a work of art, a typical complaint made by the same paper about *The Odd Women*:

> Mr Gissing may have come across such people as the Lords, such people as the Frenches, such people as the Morgans, and the Barmbys, such a man as Lionel Tarrant. But why spend time, why expend talent, in their dissection, their exposition? . . . A work of art it certainly cannot be called, for it can give no one, unless he be a hater of humanity, pleasure. . . . The fictionist must give us something to sympathize with, or one toils through his pages with distaste or even with indignation.

More carefully pondered and worded was the attack in the *Spectator* (No. 88), Gissing's rejection of which is of crucial interest (No. 89).

On the other hand, the massive eulogistic response to *In the Year of Jubilee* promoted Gissing to the front rank of living English novelists. The *Athenaeum* relented temporarily (No. 85), James Payn (No. 87) paid tribute to a writer he still was unable to understand, L. F. Austin (No. 84) observed portentously that Gissing was 'one of the few novelists to take the trouble to have a view of life', and he emphasized what differentiated him from the mass of fiction-writers. Such popular papers as *To-Day* (12 January 1895) and the London *Literary World* (4 January 1895) also joined rather loudly the chorus of acclaim. William Sharp in the *Academy* (2 March 1895) proclaimed that Gissing had at last come into his inheritance. The New York *Nation* (No. 90) provided an example of intelligent American reaction, as did the *New York Times* (28 July 1895) which declared that Gissing was in fashion. Indeed he was, even though the sales of his books made no spectacular forward leap. General surveys of his work were becoming fairly common on each side of the Atlantic and the selection of them reprinted here (Nos 82, 95 and 104) are an index to the phenomenon. His place and stature were being recognized. Editors wanted his portrait, publishers did not have enough of his work; his short stories found space in magazines whose editors would have spurned a manuscript from him two years before.

The three one-volume novels of unequal value that followed resulted from the revolution in the book trade subsequent to the collapse of the venerable three-decker. In general, *Eve's Ransom* puzzled most critics and failed to satisfy completely even those most sympathetic to Gissing's cause; *Sleeping Fires* gave rise to little constructive criticism and *The Paying Guest* was imperfectly appreciated, apart from the revelation of a comic Gissing upon whom reviewers pounced with alacrity. It was felt with some relief that *Eve's Ransom* was pleasantly free from problems and from the tension and harsh tone prevailing in most of the author's recent works, but the subtle irony of both title and situations, much as had been the case with *The Emancipated*, was too rarely noticed. The *Daily Chronicle* (No. 92) may be regarded as an exception in this respect. Praised by *Woman* (1 May 1895) and by George Cotterell (No. 93), Eve appeared so enigmatic to some reviewers that one of them, in Pyrrhic fashion, pronounced her 'decidedly too deep for Mr Gissing'.[19] It was indeed his new narrative method, adapted to a short, brisk tale, which perturbed censors like the critic in the *National*

Observer (18 May 1895) who was disappointed by the size of the book and the narrator's easy manner; they feared he might try to produce too slight stories too quickly. *Sleeping Fires* indicated that their apprehension was not unjustified. The London *Literary World* (17 January 1896) launched a new warning: 'Judging from Mr George Gissing's contribution to the "Autonym Library", *Sleeping Fires* by name, this author's time for respite has come.' H. G. Wells (No. 96) wondered whether his *confrère* had studied Mrs Hungerford or Mr Norris! Yet there were readers who welcomed Gissing's capacity to be 'tolerably cheerful when he likes' and his passing from the atmosphere of suburbia to that of Greece (*Glasgow Herald*, 2 January 1896). George Cotterell (No. 98) discerned in the booklet 'a note of hope, of acquiescence, in the higher destiny of man', and *The Times* critic (22 February 1896) extolled his use of the Greek setting. Apropos of *In the Year of Jubilee*, he had sighed for the days when Gissing wrote about the lower class and idealized some figures in it. Now it was left to *Woman* (5 February 1896) to ask for another *Nether World*—'that was a masterpiece'.

The Paying Guest surprised commentators even more. A jocose Gissing all of a sudden ceased to be a contradiction in terms and all the press apparently, except the *Sketch*, rejoiced to find between two covers bearing his name an unsparing description of his accredited milieu in a tone of pure comedy. Had it been commissioned to please H. G. Wells the book could not have been more appropriately planned and written. The note of condescension, later to be felt in *The Town Traveller*, was absent and, neither matter nor manner being irksome, critics rivalled each other in their choice of flattering epithets. The *Daily News* (No. 100) and the *Academy* (No. 102) are two instances of this contagion. The *Publishers' Circular* (1 February 1896), the *Weekly Sun* (19 January 1896) and the *Globe* (22 January 1896) would testify to similar delight. America, on the whole, resisted the temptation to puff a slender volume into a big book, and the New York *Book Buyer* (March 1896), which was not amused, fell into another extreme when it wrote that 'this sort of tale seems to us about as worthy as an intaglio carving in putty'.

Gissing read some of the reviews of these short novels, which he had agreed to write as he was glad rather than otherwise to see the tradition of three volumes break down; besides, the offers made to him were financially alluring. But he was not deceived by the weight which at least the last two of them would carry with posterity. He promised himself he had for ever finished with these popular series, and he kept his word. *The Whirlpool*, his next work, was his most ambitious book since *Born in Exile*, also one of his best by any standards. No story from his pen had been hitherto so widely reviewed; often the accounts of it became veritable articles. And its philosophy of existence shocked in many quarters. The old objections were revived—against the realism and oppressiveness of the ambiance (*Morning Post*, 22 April 1897), against the so-called unsympathetic approach to human nature (*Sketch*, 5 May 1897), against the godless world depicted (*Guardian*, 4 August 1897). There were also new ones, especially in the American press—unfairness to women (*Nation*, 26 May 1898), mediocrity of craftsmanship, very limited inspiration and ineffective realism (*New York Times*, 23 April 1898). Abuse assumed a more virulent form; the New York *Critic* (No. 110) likened Gissing to a public scourge. Even more than with *In the Year of Jubilee*, reviewers divided into two sides. For some the book was a masterpiece, a triumph (Nos 106, 108, 109), for others it was a downright falsification of life (*Nation*), a cynical, dismal story spun out by a humourless Thackeray (William Morton Payne in the Chicago *Dial*, 1 August 1898).

Various valuable points were discussed: the Zolaesque title and social scope of the story, the supreme importance of life's little trivialities as reflected in the narrative, the sense of fatalism, symbolized by the image of a whirlpool, the satire of *fin-de-siècle* weaknesses and shortcomings, the slavery of leading characters to their temperament and the role of money dominating life. Gissing's characterization wrung admiration from some of the most reluctant readers: the *National Observer* (24 April 1897) found Alma 'delineated with extraordinary skill' and the *Scotsman* (12 April 1897) applied nearly the same phrase to all the personages, as did the *Glasgow Herald* (15 April 1897). Greenough White, in the July number of the *Sewanee Review* devoted a long, thoughtful article to the well-observed modernity of the restless dozen central figures.[20]

The book was thought important enough by three leading American novelists for them to review it. Hamlin Garland (*Book Buyer*, February 1898) warmly approved of Gissing's vivid and earnest realism; he emphasized the central part played by money, but saw in Cyrus Redgrave, 'the inevitable seducer', an element of unreality, a concession to convention in a 'dignified study of modern English life'. Henry James (No. 112) paid homage to Gissing's 'saturation', but the technique of *The Whirlpool* and other novels did not satisfy him. Harold

Frederic, in a recently identified contribution to the *Saturday Review*[21] thought that Zola's method was foreign to Gissing's talent. In England H. G. Wells profited by the opportunity to publish a detailed survey of Gissing's works, not free of serious misinterpretations, especially on the question of imperialism (No. 113). From *The Whirlpool* also dated Henry-D. Davray's nearly systematic review of the writer's novels in the influential *Mercure de France*. Davray admitted his prejudice towards the Zolaesque framework of the story and jibbed at the author's harshness to womankind, but he summed up his impressions as follows: '*The Whirlpool* est un livre considérable, où s'affirme un effort énorme, un grand talent, et une puissante valeur d'écrivain.' His conclusion was fair enough: 'M. Gissing est l'un des jeunes romanciers anglais desquels on espère le plus, encore que ses huit ou dix livres déjà publiés aient exaspéré bien des gens, fatigué beaucoup d'autres, et enthousiasmé un grand nombre.' Gissing had now a small public in America and he numbered a few scattered devotees on the Continent. In the year of the Diamond Jubilee, his name had also a precise significance in his own country.

NEW PATHS AND OLD: THE LAST ACHIEVEMENTS (1897–1903)

Until 1897, except for the people who read his short stories in periodicals, Gissing was exclusively a novelist. From that date onwards, he appeared as a short story writer (*Human Odds and Ends*), a Dickens critic with two volumes on Dickens and an essayist—*By the Ionian Sea* and *The Private Papers of Henry Ryecroft*. Because his dark, realistic tales of modern life had never been largely accepted, a notable proportion of critics, delighted to discover a less austere man and a writer who, contrary to expectation, could appreciate optimistic literature, was tempted to overvalue his later, non-fictional books, at the expense of his true life's work. This trend of criticism remains to the present day.

Generally, *Human Odds and Ends* (1897) aroused the usual responses to realism and pessimism, but Gissing's talent for short fiction did not pass unnoticed (No. 115). The *Sketch* (24 November 1897) was gratified by the 'growing ease and grace of his style'. 'For condensed force and fitting effectiveness Mr Hardy and Mr Kipling are the masters of this kind of writing in England; but one can now name Mr Gissing in the next breath after [them] without irreverence.' The *Bookman* (No.

116) percipiently recorded an evolution towards pity, and *Literature* (11 December 1897) a distinct vein of comedy and pathos, whereas *The Times* (No. 117), in an ironical notice, felicitously described Gissing in this collection as the 'biographer of the unfortunate'. The volume also called forth some horrified remarks from the stand-offish and prudish reviewers of the *World* (1 December 1897) and the *Guardian* (19 January 1898). The former predicted: 'The most resolutely cheerful readers will, we imagine, collapse under the gloom, the bitterness, and, we must add, the sordidness of these plain tales from the depths of vulgar and unlovely experience.' The latter, although unexpectedly friendly to Gissing's art, revealed the extent of its snobbery by calling 'Lord Dunfield' impertinently odious because it enacts the ruffianly revenge of a love-lorn peer of the realm. The tragic tale entitled 'A Day of Silence' was perceptively selected by several commentators as the best.

The massive reviewing of *Charles Dickens, a Critical Study* was almost unanimously approbatory. Articles, leaders and notices sang the merits of Gissing's congenial approach to his subject because he was neither blind to Dickens's serious artistic shortcomings (which it was then the fashion to magnify in intellectual circles) nor niggard of praise for his aptitude to create immortal characters. The five items selected here reflect the contemporary conviction on both sides of the Atlantic that no finer study of Dickens had so far appeared. Special mention was often made of the study of Mrs Gamp, of the satirical portraiture, of the influence of the theatre on the novels. Gissing, much to his public's delight, was even capable of humour. His book may be regarded as a tribute to a writer whose influence on his work had manifested itself, particularly in *Workers in the Dawn* and *Thyrza*; it was also tangible evidence of the conflict in him between his heart, which went out to Dickens the man, and his brain, to which Dickens's notion of the artist, at his desk or in public, was fundamentally alien. After this book, as testified by No. 122, the question of Gissing's pessimism became more than ever a matter for discussion. 'Ah! If he would only bask in the sunshine and forget the shadows!' critics moaned. *The Whirlpool* was recalled and, Rolfe's exclamations being misread, it was imagined, until *The Crown of Life* refuted the notion, that Gissing had turned imperialist.

The Town Traveller revived the ephemeral hopes roused by *The Paying Guest* and the study of Dickens that he might ultimately cultivate a more sanguine outlook on life. The *Pall Mall Gazette* (No. 123),

Spectator (3 September 1898), *Morning Post* (No. 124) and *Guardian* (No. 126) all exemplify the same desire. But Gissing had written this novel as a farce and, like Zola with *Le Rêve*, he intended it as a humorous reply to a challenge. He had based a part of his plot on a contemporary *cause célèbre*, the Druce–Portland case, concerning the disappearance of a peer, and had introduced into the other part of the plot the then popular craze for missing-word competitions (No. 123). He had never enjoyed writing the story but he quickly came to dislike it and went to the length of asking some of his close friends not to read it. The book provided most reviewers with rollicking mirth as they glanced socially downwards at Gammon, the 'traveller' and Polly Sparkes, the programme-seller: each was thought to be admirably portrayed and Gissing's depiction of the cockney world marvellously true to life. Briskness of narrative, freshness of conception and the conveyed vitality of such characters won Gissing a new audience seeking in a novel nothing more than a few hours' easy entertainment. The *Glasgow Herald* (10 September 1898) thought that he had done nothing better and that nothing better of the kind had been done since Dickens. The affair of the missing peer was assuredly less admired than the Gammon–Polly–Parish intrigue but the fantasy and exuberance of it all inclined everyone to indulgence. Very few commentators realized that Gissing ran some risk in such one-dimensional writing and the *Westminster Gazette* (30 August 1898) was apparently the only newspaper to warn him against the danger of caricature. Naturally enough there were some journals, like *Vanity Fair* (8 September 1898), *Daily Mail* (13 September 1898) and the Boston *Literary World* (18 February 1899) which expressed their preference for Gissing's old, grave manner, but their attitude implied no dislike for a novel which has been viewed since its publication as an interesting period piece. It was felt by the London *Literary World* (7 October 1898), which had staunchly supported since the early 1890s the author's more serious pictures of the lower and middle classes, that Gissing had turned a somersault. The satirical painting of Christopher Parish, the pitiable clerk who wins the missing-word competition and Polly's hand therewith, created a temporary commotion among his peers (Nos 128 and 129); the record of the ensuing discussion is admittedly of greater social than literary interest but reveals a fascinating, if somewhat pathetic, response to the novel.

Gissing needed no warning. Even before *The Town Traveller* was in the bookshops, he was planning *The Crown of Life*, a novel as solid and thoughtful as *Born in Exile* or *The Whirlpool.* Externally, a love-story on the pattern of *Sleeping Fires,* the volume was primarily concerned with the problem of international peace at a time when war was threatening in South Africa. For commercial reasons, the British publisher, Methuen, postponed publication until the autumn of 1899 and the book's immediate relevance was abruptly superseded. Unlike its more superficial predecessor little critical justice was accorded it. Britain had become the prey of a nationalistic fever which contaminated most of the press and Gissing's novel was not judged according to its intrinsic merits, but according to political criteria. The article in *Literature* (No. 133) is a characteristic petulant reception at the hands of an imperialist reviewer. Morley Roberts, in the *Review of the Week* (No. 130), mainly confined himself to the literary analysis of the book, but, as a disciple of Kipling and a partisan of physical force, he also disagreed with Gissing's message of peace and fraternity among peoples. The *St. James's Gazette* (No. 132), *Manchester Guardian* (7 November 1899), *New York Tribune* (No. 131) and Melbourne *Book Lover* (No. 134) emphasized some salient features which dailies like the *Pall Mall Gazette* (11 November 1899) and *Daily Chronicle* (10 November 1899) did not see, or refused to see, because the hero's views on the Empire vexed them. The book's construction satisfied neither the *Publishers' Circular* (4 November 1899), which thought the plot lacked cohesion and that characters were too numerous, nor the *Manchester Guardian*; but the *Saturday Review* (2 December 1899) could discover nothing wrong with either structure or characters:

> We find what we are accustomed to in a novel by Mr Gissing: a strong story, a profusion of secondary characters, distinct, clear-cut types; the sinister Hannaford with his collection of bloodstained war-relics, his wife who has grown to loathe him, Olga the neurotic daughter, Kite the anaemic artist of genius, Miss Bonnicastle the vigorous designer of advertiser posters.

The story is full of the appeasing, ennobling influence of Gabrielle Fleury, to whom it owes much of what the *Manchester Guardian* called 'a broad and philosophical humanity', already discernible in *The Whirlpool.* Meredith (No. 7d) was undoubtedly sensitive to this aspect of *The Crown of Life*, but in his eyes the heroine, Irene Derwent, must have been lacking in some of the basic ingredients he tried to infuse in his own protagonists—namely blood, brain and spirit. James Joyce's response (No. 189) to this novel as well as to *Demos* proceeds from a notion of literature that was irreconcilable with Gissing's. The articles by Arnold Bennett (No. 135) and Jane H. Findlater (No. 136), coming just after Gissing's publication of a novel about the upper class, are significant in that they reveal the value persistently attached to his working-class novels a decade after he had abandoned this subject area.

The quasi-simultaneous publication in book form of *Our Friend the Charlatan* and *By the Ionian Sea* confirmed and enlarged Gissing's reputation. The press, whether English or American, enthused. Elizabeth Lee also welcomed the novel in *Das Litterarische Echo* (July 1901). A few sour notes sounded by Stephen Gwynn and A. Macdonell were drowned in the chorus of praise. Gwynn in the *Fortnightly* (July 1901) asserted that Gissing had 'an appalling talent for the portrayal of unattractive characters' and that '[his] was an anaemic country of no illusions'. Macdonell voiced an unreasonable request in the *Bookman* (August 1901): he would have liked a more candid authorial approach to Dyce Lashmar, the charlatan, with fewer drawing-room scenes and more electioneering scenes. On the contrary, a society weekly like the *World* (3 July 1901) strongly approved the book:

> It is not merely entertaining and clever; by its ruthless exposure of low motives, unworthy aims, and petty methods of 'playing the game', it impresses some vital truths respecting the real and mock values of life. From the purely literary point the workmanship commends itself by thoroughness of plan, strong individuality, the restriction of persons to the artistic needs of the design, and the consistent evolution of the charlatan's motives, acts, and self-approval.

'Clever' and 'skilful' were the epithets to which reviewers most often resorted in order to convey the general impression produced by the story: the title greatly appealed to American reviewers,[22] and the psychological insights were invariably praised even when it was observed that the writer succeeded more in the handling of ideas than in the building of characters. *Literature* (No. 140) and the French *Revue* (15 August 1901) made suggestive allusions to Meredith's Sir Willoughby Patterne, whereas *The Times* (No. 142) saw in old Lady Ogram a Dickensian character. Henry Harland (No. 139) placed Gissing between Turgenev and Zola.

Appreciation of the author's intellectual agility and satirical ability was increased when a reviewer, as in the *Academy* (Nos 141 and 144), was able to discover at the same time Gissing's talent in the narration of his Southern Italian travels and his aesthetic and moral preoccupations. *Literature* (No. 145) admitted to a discovery which might lead to a reconsideration of much past criticism: 'Mr Gissing has been known as a novel writer and a critic. We are not sure that he has not equal claims to distinction as a classical scholar.' The *Guardian*'s confession (No. 146) was even more candid and would have caused the author to smile wryly had he read it; he would have been surprised to hear that this paper numbered him among its friends. The *Athenaeum* (27 July 1901), however, obtusely regarded this de luxe edition as a mere guide-book. Two of the articles (Nos 148 and 149) that followed attempted to define some specific trends of his past work while Morley Roberts placed him within a general European framework, ancient and modern. The notices of Forster's *Life of Dickens*, abridged and revised by Gissing, tended to spread the now widely acknowledged idea that Gissing was a Dickens scholar but he disowned any such pretension. The *Life* contained a number of fresh paragraphs and judgments from his pen, but no one has yet thoroughly evaluated the extent of his abridgment and additions.

The publication of *The Private Papers of Henry Ryecroft* was the summit of Gissing's career as his contemporaries saw it. British reviewers hailed the book as his masterpiece and widened the rift between the two tendencies among critics to regard him either first and foremost as a novelist or as a born essayist and scholar whom untoward circumstances had made a writer of fiction. In the United States some reviewers (Grace E. Martin, No. 161, is an instance) frowned at the old-fashioned framework of a pseudo-diary edited by a friend; because of its anti-democratic, anti-scientific philosophy and its plea for individual retreat from urban bustle the book was more coolly received, but there were some ardent apologists. Only three or four journals in England passed unflattering comments. The *Morning Post* (5 March 1903) thought it essentially commonplace and the *Publishers' Circular* (28 March 1903) 'a little mawkish and not a little boring', adding that 'we are tired of tired people and the lazy life of sentimentalists'. About the *Spectator* notice (14 March 1903), Gissing enquired of his agent Pinker if he could 'form any conjecture as to why [it] treated *Ryecroft* slightingly in half a dozen lines of small type'.[23] The *Athenaeum* review (No. 155) made him indignant but he had learnt by this time that no fair criticism of his work could be expected from this journal.

The nine reviews reprinted here reflect the range of interests found in Ryecroft's meditations and reminiscences. They appealed to people as a self-revelation, as *By the Ionian Sea* had done in 1901. The last sentence of this book with its expression of yearning for the world of antiquity, which had been frequently quoted in notices, was now readily associated with Ryecroft; in addition a pathetic image formed itself of the man who had written the powerful novels of urban working-class and middle-class life in a milieu altogether alien to his sympathies. The new image of Gissing (he being equated rather uncritically with Ryecroft) was substituted for the old one of a man interested only in the dreary depiction of the seamy side of nineteenth-century civilization. The 'testamentary dignity' noted by the *Academy* (No. 157) invited critics to throw a backward glance upon his twenty novels and to consider his last volume as the coping-stone of an edifice hitherto examined only from the outside. 'A Daniel among the hollyhocks,' the *Outlook* entitled its review (31 January 1903). 'The book of a poet upon whom the present age of sensation rarely obtrudes,' wrote the *Daily Mail* (3 February 1903), 'a paean to contentment and a leisured life.' The recollections of Grub Street days, the bookish flavour, the autumnal atmosphere, the elaborate style and above all the wisdom with which the book is instinct filled reviewers with delight. They were frequently impelled to rapturous exclamations and paraphrase rather than analytical criticism: Gissing's most carefully wrought work unfortunately produced little immediate criticism of comparable subtlety.

POSTHUMOUS WORKS AND AFTERMATH (1904–12)

At his death Gissing left one 'romance of real life', *Will Warburton*, and a historical novel set in sixth-century Italy, *Veranilda*; he had been working on the latter at odd moments since 1897 although it had been in his mind since he left college. He had wished *Veranilda*, of which he had great hopes, to appear before *Will Warburton*, and his literary executors adhered to this wish. Between his death on 28 December 1903, when *The Ryecroft Papers* were in their fourth impression, and the publication of *Veranilda* nine months later, several appreciations of his personality and work were printed in the English and American press. Nathaniel Wedd's contribution (No. 162) stresses the central arguments underlying all Gissing's work from *Workers in the Dawn* to *The Ryecroft Papers*: the spread of culture as a prerequisite to reformation of society and the incompatibility of culture with poverty. But it is only fair to add that Gissing devoted some of his best studies to the deterioration, through England's accession to wealth, of whatever culture was extant. There is a link between Bertz's early article (No. 45), Wedd's and the unsigned piece in the *Atlantic Monthly*. After *By the Ionian Sea* and *The Ryecroft Papers* it became easy to realize that Gissing had 'a passionate love of beauty', that 'in his analysis of the ugly there was always an implied contrast with the beautiful'. Bertz, whose intimate knowledge of the author can be reckoned an exceptional privilege, had pointed to this crucial notion long before in 1889.

Veranilda combined the two aspects of Gissing—classical scholar and novelist. It brought about a literary quarrel, both private and public, even before it was issued.[24] H. G. Wells's preface, which was rejected and replaced by Frederic Harrison's tamer and shorter piece (No. 164), offended the author's family not only because it referred to his life in an objectionable manner but also because it tried to promote the book at the expense of the social novels. In this respect, it foreshadowed the volume's critical reception in the autumn and winter of 1904. Harrison had also extolled *Veranilda* and belittled the stories of modern life; he therefore made almost inevitable the division of critical responses into two sharply contrasted groups. Nos 165 to 169 offer an alternative series of agreement and disagreement with Harrison's position, together with his disappointment (No. 170) at being contradicted, sometimes in a rough manner (No. 169). The response to the novel proper is an excellent index to the subjectivity of criticism: for instance, what the *Scotsman* (6 October 1904) regarded as a lively, colourful work, the New York *Critic* (No. 172) found lacking in all Gissing's best qualities and the *Speaker* (22 October 1904) termed 'poor and jejune'. The *Morning Post* (28 September 1904) called attention to the excellent 'portrayal of the ecclesiastical and religious life of the time, when the feud between Catholics and Arians divided men even more deeply than race hostilities and so often cloaked private enmities', and the *New York Tribune Weekly Review* (18 February 1905) praised the story-telling and harmony of subject and form:

He tells [the story] with an old-fashioned dignity and deliberation, with a kind of quiet fervor that lends a glow to his pages, yet never threatens the integrity of the atmosphere of stateliness which we associate with ancient Rome. He had so absorbed himself in the spirit of antiquity that when he came to write his book he found himself as much at ease in realizing the life of the past as though it were the life of the present. . . . There is nothing here of the flamboyant scene painting which has done so much to discredit the modern novel of old Rome. But there is, instead, a breadth of style in the handling of his pictures in their main relations, as there is a delicacy of touch in his treatment of the details, by which, as the story moves on, the imagination is taken captive.

Perhaps it was unfortunate that the merits of *Veranilda* could not be assessed without reference to Gissing's other novels. Some voices made themselves heard from the Continent. Elizabeth Lee in *Das Litterarische Echo* (15 November 1904) and Henry-D. Davray in the *Mercure de France* (15 January 1905) concurred in saying that prominent as were the qualities of *Veranilda*, they could not make us forget 'the poet of the realistic novels'.[25] In this light also Jane H. Findlater (No. 173) and Allan Monkhouse (No. 174) saw Gissing at the end of 1904. Both writers had been attentive to the development of his art and ideas for ten or fifteen years and their interpretation of him is of more than historical interest. Together with C. F. G. Masterman (No. 180) they contributed to checking for a while the threatening critical imbalance in favour of the non-fictional works. Masterman's view was that of left-wing Christian liberalism and, as such, is as worthy of attention as the response of Blatchford's *Clarion*, the widely read organ of anti-religious socialists.[26]

With *Will Warburton* commentators who had disdained the resuscitation of Romans and Goths were glad to find again what they called 'the true Gissing'. The *Evening Standard* (23 June 1905) led: '*Will Warburton*, which comes without promise or laudation of any kind, serves as an argument in favour of the more popular impression of Gissing's talent. Here, in the mean streets of London, he is really at home.' Edward Garnett (No. 178) shared this opinion. Like the *Morning Leader* (No. 175), *Spectator* (1 July 1905) and *Saturday Review* (No. 179), he pointed to the greater mellowness which had been noticeable since *By the Ionian Sea* and most conspicuously in the Monte Cassino chapters of *Veranilda*. The book suggested comparison with *New Grub Street* but in making this comparative evaluation *The Times Literary Supplement* (No. 176) and the *Athenaeum* (No. 177) reached opposite conclusions. *Will Warburton* was doubtless fuller of the milk of human kindness, although later critics have preferred *New Grub Street*. St John Adcock, sensing a danger that future historians of literature should establish a mistaken hierarchy of values among Gissing's novels, ventured to make a retrospect which shows insight into the relations of the writer and his time (*Bookman*, August 1905):

Some of his critics used to reprove him for his gloomy views of life, as if it were desirable that all novelists should be of the same optimistic temperament and monotonously regard the world from the same standpoint: they were continually urging him to be less depressing, to look more on the brighter side of things, to write more hopefully, seeming to think, indeed that the only right thing for him, as a sincere artist, to do was to write of humanity not as he saw it but as they saw it; and I have often read with wonder their wonderings at his perversity in choosing sombre themes and writing of them sombrely.

The *Publishers' Circular* (9 December 1905) had been one of these siren voices, so it was no marvel that for the reviewer in this weekly, *Will Warburton* was 'a great advance on his previous works of the same class'. The truth was that the mellowing of Gissing's tone, his 'extraordinary poignancy of feeling' and the 'almost painful tenderness' characteristic of his late works,[27] which Adcock imagined to be a concession to public taste, were the consequence of premature ageing and persistent ill-health. Like Will Warburton, he had acquired a quality alien to youth—that of resignation.

The volume of short stories which concluded the posthumous publications was generally regarded as quite a new facet of Gissing's art. Arthur Waugh (No. 184) recalled flatteringly *Human Odds and Ends* but Noel Ainslie, author of three novels and like Waugh a past acquaintance of Gissing, thought *The House of Cobwebs* could not compare with it (*Gentleman's Magazine*, June 1906).[28] By 1906 some details of Gissing's private life had been rumoured about and H. Hamilton Fyfe in the *Evening News* (18 June 1906) and Davray in the *Mercure de France* rightly indicated the autobiographical value of 'A Lodger in Maze Pond'. Once more the only sour note came from the *Athenaeum* (7 July 1906) which in a hasty, misinformed review dealt a final blow: 'He was an intellectual observer painfully toiling with brushes the use of which he hardly understood.' Other critics, with the possible exception of the New York *Outlook* (1 September 1906), made some attempts, however brief, to define Gissing's art in the short story. The *Daily Telegraph* (18 May 1906) evoked Charles Lamb in connection with all the bookish allusions in 'Christopherson' and the title story, and remarked that 'the Gissing of *The Ryecroft Papers* is here, with the technique of Henry James and the heart of a warmer author'. The *Spectator* (26 May 1906) rejoiced that this volume did not reveal the usual weakness of posthumous volumes—inferior work withheld by the writer's self-criticism. 'In point of workmanship, observation, and the philosophy of life which they set forth [these stories] show him at his best and his sanest.' The social categories represented—very nearly the nobodies examined in No. 148—illustrated the solidarity of the unsuccessful. As with *Will Warburton*, the *Guardian* (25 July 1906) noted a more humane strain—although the stories were in fact written over the last ten years of Gissing's life. The most successful tales were generally thought to be 'Christopherson', 'The Scrupulous Father' and 'A Poor Gentleman'.

By 1906 rising writers looked upon Gissing as a man of the previous generation. This might imply respect in the manner of H. Hamilton Fyfe or William Barry (*Bookman*, July 1906); it might imply a mixture of admiration and dissatisfaction as is conveyed by D. H. Lawrence's brief references in his letters or absolute rejection (No. 189). There were also those critics like Paul Elmer More and Virginia Woolf, who felt strongly attracted to his work and were attempting to bring out the essence of his contribution to the late nineteenth-century novel. Theirs was the perspective of the literary historian and evaluator: the steady passing of time was already permitting such a perspective.

4

THE CRITICAL TRADITION FROM 1912 TO THE PRESENT DAY

The year 1912 was a crucial one in Gissing studies. It saw the quasi-simultaneous publication of two books that were destined to be equally influential but equally disastrous—a fictionalized biography by Morley Roberts entitled *The Private Life of Henry Maitland* and Frank Swinnerton's critical study. Both works were so biased that they provoked literary squabbles in England and America. Roberts's shapeless, inaccurate tale, fastening on the less attractive aspects of his friend's life, did much harm to Gissing's memory, even though it was intended, by a strange aberration, as an apology. Swinnerton's appraisal was a youthful attempt at demolishing work of which he understood neither the deep human interest nor the literary value. Thomas Seccombe aptly referred to it, in a review, as an 'able deprecation' but Swinnerton's arguments were later examined and rejected by A. Rotter in *Frank Swinnerton und George Gissing. Eine Kritische Studie* (1930) and Ruth Capers McKay in *George Gissing and His Critic Frank Swinnerton* (1933). By 1922 May Yates had already discussed in a small book entitled *George Gissing: An Appreciation* his art and personality. The following year Madeleine Cazamian devoted part of *Le Roman et les Idées en Angleterre* (vol. i) to a detailed enquiry into his reactions to science and its human consequences.

During the interwar period Morley Roberts continued publishing occasional articles as he had done since his contribution to the *Novel*

Review (No. 75). In the *Bookman's Journal* (19 December 1919) he asked 'What is a classic?' He concluded:

A classic is a book of known descent with known descendants. . . . George Gissing, I believe, answers to both tests. His descent is obvious; his moulding influences were the best modern literature of England and France, while his knowledge of the classics, though not that of a great scholar, served him perpetually as a guide and a stimulus. All these exerted their power on him, and begot his work, influenced though it was by his abnormal surroundings and his deprivations. That he has begotten other work may be doubted by some. It may be denied by the very men who still feel his influence. But those who look about the modern world of literature will observe, if they have any perceptions of the critic, that he still lives in other men's books.

In the late 1920s Roberts wrote a series of introductions to the five novels of his friend once issued by Smith, Elder and reconstituted the image of Gissing struggling against the dictates of publishers and circulating libraries. It was also Roberts's idea that Gissing contributed 'to raise the general standard of ordinary English prose. He always aimed at clarity, and rarely if ever missed it. Yet, all the same . . . he was no born writer of fiction.'[29]

This was an impression that Samuel Vogt Gapp's *George Gissing, Classicist,* helped to reinforce. Gapp thoroughly documented the extent of his subject's classicism and its influence on his life and writings. 'With me,' Gissing had written in 1886, 'it is a constant aim to bring the present and the past near to each other, to remove the distance which seems to separate Hellas from Lambeth.' Stanley Alden, before the publication of this letter, had argued that Gissing was a humanist, interested in the problems of modern man—a natural being in an artificial environment—rather than a realist like Zola,[30] and Virginia Woolf, in an article often reprinted, stressed that he was one of the few novelists who cared to make their characters think:[31]

His books . . . owe their peculiar grimness to the fact that the people who suffer most are capable of making their suffering part of a reasoned view of life. . . . Hence when we have finished one of Gissing's novels we have taken away not a character, not an incident, but the comment of a thoughtful man upon life as life seemed to him.

Besides Gapp's volume, the interwar years saw the appearance of a number of special studies on Gissing and the social question, his feminine portraiture and his indebtedness to French naturalism. Most of the works were still in print in the 1920s and 1930s and the publication of several volumes of uncollected short stories, selections and correspondence gave rise to a number of articles that made correlations between his art and his life. When, on the issue of the last volume of short stories in 1938, Q. D. Leavis submitted Gissing to her scrutiny, she felt able to praise only *New Grub Street*, placing this novel above all others. The very common critical tendency of the interwar period was to picture Gissing as inextricably entangled in the paraphernalia of the Victorian novel and to treat him as a necessarily minor novelist.

The 1940s witnessed the efforts of a new generation to reinterpret his work. George Orwell, an eager Gissingite, wrote several stimulating articles, defending him against ill-founded charges and stressing his apology for the individual, his hatred of poverty and his fundamental honesty. William Plomer wrote sympathetically in introductions to new editions and more subdued estimations were proposed by V. S. Pritchett and Walter Allen. The 1950s marked the beginning of a scholarly approach to Gissing. A bulk of unpublished letters and diaries had by this time reached institutional libraries, and thoroughly documented criticism became possible. John D. Gordan's catalogue, compiled for the 1953 New York Gissing exhibition, revealed to the public a mass of hitherto inaccessible material. The catalogue and exhibition constituted an appropriate, though unintended reply to an excellent article by Russell Kirk, entitled 'Who Knows George Gissing?', published in 1950. In that same year, Jacob Korg started a series of contributions which are sure to leave a deep mark on the subsequent approach to the subject, and Mabel Collins Donnelly hastily produced in 1954 the first biography since *The Private Life of Henry Maitland* (1912). Portions of her book were soon superseded by Korg's critical biography (1963) which, though severe to some of Gissing's novels, did the service of putting them within a scholarly perspective of late Victorian literary achievement.

Interest in Gissing since the late 1950s has substantially benefited from the marked renascence of Victorian studies; important volumes of correspondence, with Wells, Bertz and Gabrielle Fleury, have fostered biographical, critical and bibliographical research. Many novels have been reprinted, though only a few at reasonable prices. Solid critical editions have at last begun to appear. A steady stream of theses, often followed by pertinent articles, has flowed from English and American scholars. The 1970s are to see the publication of several biographies, critical studies and bibliographies, together with some fresh appraisals of individual novels. Such continuing, developing work in progress demonstrates the end of earlier prejudices against Gissing's pessimism and his art—prejudices which, as this collection shows, characterized but did not dominate the critical reception accorded him in his lifetime. Gissing's writings remain a source of fascination for literary critics and social historians—adequate testimony of a complex consciousness in which art, social conscience and philosophic ruminations vibrantly unite. The years have amply reinforced the tentative statement made in 1902 (No. 148) that even Gissing's least sympathetic critics must admit 'that he stands apart and that he stands for something'.

NOTES

1 The nerve-racking negotiations with Bentley concerning *Mrs Grundy's Enemies* and *Clement Dorricott* have been examined by Royal A. Gettmann in *A Victorian Publisher* (Cambridge University Press, 1960); those with Smith, Elder and their reader James Payn are related in Morley Roberts's fictionalized biography of Gissing, *The Private Life of Henry Maitland* (Nash, 1912, new editions 1923, 1958).

2 *Pall Mall Magazine*, July 1893, 442.

3 'An Author at Grass', *Fortnightly Review*, 1 May 1902, 917–19. This extract comes from a section which was not reprinted in the revised version that appeared in book form. Some years before, when William Blackwood offered to send complimentary copies of his magazine containing 'A Victim of Circumstances' to acquaintances on the press, he replied: 'I am in the happy position (for an author) of knowing not a single reviewer, nor person of journalistic influence' (28 December 1892, National Library of Scotland).

4 See *Cornhill Magazine*, January–December 1888; *Manchester Weekly Times*, 20 July 1889–1 February 1890; *Illustrated London News*, 5 January–30 March 1895; and *Fortnightly Review*, 1 May–1 October 1900 and May 1902–February 1903. *Demos, Thyrza, A Life's Morning, The Nether World, New Grub Street* and *Eve's Ransom* were serialized in Russia; *New Grub Street* and *Eve's Ransom* in France; *New Grub Street* in Austria-Hungary and *The Private Papers of Henry Ryecroft* in Japan.

5 'Why I don't Write Plays; XV: Mr George Gissing', *Pall Mall Gazette*, 10 September 1892, 3.

6 4 January 1884. B.M. Add. MSS 46,644.

7 See his last letter to Payn, 10 August 1891, in *The Rediscovery of George Gissing*, John Spiers and Pierre Coustillas, National Book League, London, 1971, 81.

8 'The New Censorship of Literature', 15 December 1884, 2.

9 *The Humanitarian*, July 1895, 14–16. This article was reprinted in *Selections Autobiographical and Imaginative from the Works of George Gissing*, Cape, London, 1929, 217–21.

10 Recorded in *Letters of George Gissing to Members of his Family* (1927), 155, 156 and 170–2.

11 The allusion was to the Hill-top novels of Grant Allen, author of *The Woman Who Did* (1895).

12 'In the opinion of the anonymous author of *Demos* there apparently is no merit in being brief. The story of English socialism, as *Demos* purports to be, is extremely tedious, and is only superficially concerned with socialism. It is mechanically put together, without life or interest; and is so far from being a genuine Tendenz novel that it seems to have fulfilled its end in getting published.'

13 The New York *Critic* (6 July 1889) similarly tottered on the brink of absurdity: 'It was with real curiosity that the reviewer picked up *The Nether World* by George Gissing. Here was an opportunity to enlarge one's information. But it did not take long to discover that the book contained nothing uncommon either in material or intent, and that its title was a symbolic covering for what appeared cruel and puzzling to the author in the world that is.'

14 Contrast this with the *Dial* (1 November 1895): 'The background of Southern Italy cast[s] a sort of glamour over the pages', and the *Saturday Review* (20 January 1894): 'Miriam gradually emancipates herself, in a shame-faced furtive sort of way that is cleverly suggested in the course of the story, and at the same time with unexaggerated force.'

15 *All for Love* was published for the first time in *George Gissing. Essays and Fiction*, edited with an introduction by Pierre Coustillas, Johns Hopkins Press, Baltimore and London, 1970.

16 Letter to Algernon Gissing, 6 March 1892, Berg Collection.

17 See Jacob Korg, 'The Spiritual Theme in *Born in Exile*', in *From Jane Austen to Joseph Conrad*, edited by Rathburn and Steinmann, University of Minnesota Press, 1959, and in *Collected Articles on George Gissing*, edited by Pierre Coustillas, Frank Cass, 1968.

18 Quoted in the *Literary News*, May 1893, 149, and in the *Dial*, 16 July 1893, 26.

19 *Nation* (New York), 11 July 1895, 32.

20 Reprinted in *Collected Articles on George Gissing*.

21 10 April 1897, 363. See Monteiro, George, 'Harold Frederic: An Unrecorded Review', *Papers of the Bibliographical Society of America*, First Quarter 1969, 30–1. The authorship of the review, however, had been made quite clear by a letter from H. G. Wells to Gissing published in their 1961 volume of correspondence.

22 See No. 143, Boston *Literary World* (1 August 1901, 115), *Literary News* (September 1901, 260).

23 Letter of 4 April 1903 (Berg Collection).
24 See P. Coustillas, 'The Stormy Publication of Gissing's *Veranilda*', *The Bulletin of the New York Public Library*, November 1968, 588–610.
25 Elizabeth Lee, *Das Litterarische Echo*, 15 November 1904, 273.
26 See *Clarion*, 8 January 1904, 3 and 25 March 1904, 3.
27 *New York Tribune Weekly Review*, 8 July 1905, 11.
28 On the identification of the anonymous reviewer, see *Gissing Newsletter*, December 1967, 1–3.
29 Morley Roberts, 'George Gissing', *Queen's Quarterly*, Autumn 1930, 617–32.
30 'George Gissing, Humanist', *North American Review*, September 1922, 364–77. Reprinted in *Collected Articles on George Gissing*.
31 Introduction to the Travellers' Library edition of *By the Ionian Sea* (1933), 13.

NOTE ON THE TEXT

The materials printed in this volume follow the original texts in all important respects. Lengthy extracts from the writings of George Gissing have been omitted in most cases; however, whenever they are central to the reviewer's or critic's argument they have been retained. Indications of the omitted quotations are given, so that a reader may refer to Gissing's original texts. Typographical errors in the reviews and articles have been silently corrected, and factual errors made by reviewers have received brief comment in headnotes or footnotes.

WORKERS IN THE DAWN

June 1880

1. Gissing on his own book

8 June 1880

No sooner was *Workers in the Dawn* published than it created embarrassment in Gissing's native town. On hearing of the situation from his brother Algernon, the author wrote to him two letters, a private one, in which he said he was sorry for 'all these complications', and an open letter intended for circulation among the likely readers of the novel in Wakefield. The latter is reproduced here from *Letters of George Gissing to Members of His Family*, ed. Algernon and Ellen Gissing (1927), pp. 73–4.

In view of the very kind efforts being made by some of your Wakefield friends to procure a circulation for *Workers in the Dawn*, I think it is better that I should send you a few lines (relative to the book) which I should like you to show to any interested in the matter. The book in the first place is not a novel in the generally-accepted sense of the word, but a very strong (possibly *too* plain spoken) attack upon certain features of our present religious and social life which to *me* appear highly condemnable. First and foremost, I attack the criminal negligence of governments which spend their time over matters of relatively no importance, to the neglect of the terrible social evils which should have been long since sternly grappled with. Herein I am a mouthpiece of the advanced Radical party. As regards religious matters, I plainly seek to show the nobility of a faith dispensing with all we are accustomed to call religion, and having for its only creed belief in the possibility of intellectual and moral progress. Hence it follows that I attack (somewhat savagely) the modern development of Ritualism, which, of course, is the absolute antithesis of my faith.

In doing all this, I have been obliged to touch upon matters which will be only sufferable to those who read the book in as serious a spirit as mine when I wrote it. It is *not* a book for women and children, but for thinking and struggling *men*. If readers can put faith in the desperate sincerity of the author, they will not be disgusted with the book; otherwise it is far better they should not read it.

I write this in order to relieve you personally from any unpleasantness which may ensue upon the introduction of my book to Wakefield, and you would do me a service if you could show this to such as have manifested the least interest in the matter. I fear it is the fate of many men to incur odium by their opinions, but the odium is only cast by those who cannot realize the sincerity of minds differently constituted from their own.

2. Unsigned review, *Athenaeum*

12 June 1880, 758

To Gissing's knowledge, as well as to ours, this was the first printed critical reaction to *Workers in the Dawn*. He commented on it in a letter of 15 June 1880 to his brother Algernon:

> The critics are unprincipled vagabonds, on the whole. He of the *Athenaeum* knows very little indeed of the spirit of my book, and his knowledge of the latter may be gauged by his twice calling poor old Tollady a 'book-seller'. Then what in the name of conscience does the fellow mean by calling Gresham a 'Skimpolian cynic'? I imagine the likeness between him and Harold Skimpole, in *Bleak House*, is something which it requires special critical acumen to discover. Yet Bertz and I agree that it is rather an attractive review. Above all, the critic does me the justice of believing in my sincerity, and even says that the book may do good. I believe it will. But he treats it too much as if it were a mere polemical pamphlet, and not a *work of art*, as which, of course, I desire it to be judged. We shall see what other reviewers have to say. Such a long review in the *Athenaeum* is rather a compliment

(*Letters of George Gissing to Members of His Family*, p. 74).

Whether the light which illumines Mr Gissing's hero and heroine be that of dawn or twilight may be a matter of opinion, but some people think the social difficulties of over-population and pauperism may be redressed by rousing the passions of the poor, and others that religion may be usefully replaced by an amalgam of Schopenhauer, Comte, and Shelley. To both these opinions our author is an enthusiastic subscriber. So much being premised as to the point of view, it may be added that he has done his subject the justice of sparing no graphic detail of the miseries of the vicious and the poor, and that the result is a striking and, let us hope, a useful picture. Though he is not quite a master of what he would probably decline to call the Queen's English, he has considerable readiness and fluency of style, much power of vituperation, and an honest partisanship. He has fallen into the error, common to most polemical novelists, of making the horns and tail of his *bête noire* so very grotesque as to take from the seriousness of the contest. To make the enemy so weak as to exclude the possibility of comparison with the friend, to divide all the clergy, for instance, into knaves or fools, only outrages the reader's common sense, and gives him reason to suspect that argument has been wisely avoided. These are commonplaces to a really educated man, but it is possible there may be some excuse in this respect for the ardour of a novice. Such a moral impossibility as Mr Whiffle the curate can impose upon no one; and a man capable of drawing a woman so nearly excellent as Helen Norman would probably not have made the mistake of contrasting her so unworthily, had it not been for some social inexperience. Helen is an ideal Comtist, full of the enthusiasm of humanity which is the best part of her prophet's teaching. Her love for Arthur, the strange *protégé* of the old bookseller—who has been taken from the gutter and bred by kindly and, indeed, religious heathens in the fiercest school of politics, a training which sits oddly upon his gentle and rather feeble nature—is well drawn, and she rises to what is clearly thought to be an extraordinary pitch of virtue when she declines to become the mistress of the man she loves. On the whole, she has a serious and sweet nature, she is as zealous for the poor as many another woman of very different opinions, and though she does not seem to give much reason for them, she adopts her views after at least acquainting herself with the names of a good many foreign authors. Of the minor personages it is unnecessary to speak; with the exception of a kind of Skimpolian cynic and his daughter (for whom Helen might have done more), they are differentiated by the strength of their opinions rather than by any positive contrasts of character. They most of them come to bad ends. The bookseller dies in poverty, pressed by a hard and unjust creditor; the fiercest radical goes mad and burns himself alive; Arthur's wife dies of drink and prostitution; and her husband, who has deserted her in despair, is driven, on hearing of the death of Helen, his ideal woman, to die what Aristotle thought the death of a coward in the waters of Niagara Falls.

3. Frederic Harrison: Letter to George Gissing

22 July 1880

When, a few weeks after publication, Gissing had reached the conclusion that his publisher Remington was doing very little to promote *Workers in the Dawn*, for the publication of which the author had paid £125, he boldly wrote to Frederic Harrison, the leader of English Positivists, sending him a copy. The influence of Auguste Comte on the heroine, Helen Norman, is expounded at some length in vol. i, ch. 14, 'Mind-Growth', which consists in extracts from the young lady's diary. Gissing's turning to Harrison was something of an act of despair since, by his own admission, no reader had so far understood the spirit in which the book had been written. While he readily acknowledged that his story was a *Tendenz-Roman*, he protested against the reviewers' preconceived notion that this was incompatible with the qualities of a work of art. Gissing ended his appeal to Harrison, dated 9 July 1880, with these words: 'To Comte I owe in the largest measure the enthusiasm to which I have given here expression, and it was by your writings, sir, that I first was led to Comte. I am thus indebted to you for guidance at an important stage of my intellectual development, and, were it only to give some utterance to my gratitude, I am glad to have found this opportunity of addressing you' (unpublished letter, Carl H. Pforzheimer Library). Harrison's reply is reprinted from *Letters of George Gissing to Members of His Family*, pp. 77–9.

My Dear Sir,

There can be no doubt as to the power of your book. It will take rank amongst the works of great rank of these years. I have not yet finished it, and I cannot yet make up my mind as to its place as a work of true art. It belongs to a school of which I know nothing, and which I hold at arm's length, at least I think so. I am no critic, and very rarely read a modern romance, and I especially hate the so-called realism of Zola. But your painting of dark life seems to me as good as his, and to have a better social purpose—at least I hope so. I am, as I say, very little experienced in judging fiction, and I make no pretensions to judge at all work so full of power both in imagination and in expression as your story. It has most deeply stirred and impressed me by its creative energy. And I cannot wait till I have read it coolly, and felt it as a whole, before I write to you. It kept me out of bed a large part of last night—I took it up after my work—and that is what very few books have done for many years.

There cannot be the smallest doubt about its power, and power of almost every kind that fiction admits. But as you ask my opinion I will be frank. I do not pretend to offer either advice or criticism, your work is far above anything I could do in that way, if I wished. And I do not wish. But I will tell you what I feel about it—as yet—before finishing it. I am not sure that the social and moral aim is sufficiently sincere, or rather sufficiently strong, to justify the deliberate painting of so much brutality. Perhaps it is. I have not yet read enough to see what your moral and social aim exactly is. I am the last person who ought to pretend to judge such a book, for I loathe books of the 'Assommoir' class and never open them, nor indeed modern fiction except on rare occasions. Your book therefore goes against all my sympathies in art, so that my admiration for its imaginative power is wrung from me. Whether prostitutes, thieves, and debauchees talk as you make them talk in the night-houses of the Haymarket, I do not know, nor wish to know. It is possible that they are introduced to good purpose. I will try to see it.

But I will not trouble you further with my present half-instructed feeling. That is a personal matter with me, and cannot be of any value. I think I know enough of romances to say this—that you may be sure of your book eventually proving a literary success. There are scenes, I am sure, which can hold their ground with the first things in modern fiction. The circulating libraries will be very shy of it. I do not think girls ought to read it at all. But men of insight will very soon discover its power. I will myself take care that one or two such read it, and I will urge my own opinion on the editor of more than one literary review. I never presume to 'review' books, as the picking out of scraps, and the saying of smart things about them, is called. And if I did review the book publicly, I might say many things which the author would not like. But you may be quite sure of this—your book cannot be lost sight of. Do not be in a hurry. Books like that are not often written in England, though they sometimes are in France. You will be neglected for a few months, abused for two or three, and in six have a distinct (but not altogether tranquil) reputation. Such is the opinion of an avowed ignoramus in these matters.

If after this letter, which I have not sought to make pleasant, you care to make any further communication to me, I shall on my side be very willing to know more of you. I am one of those Goths, fanatics, or prigs, as we are sometimes called, who think much less of artistic or literary power, than of the objects for which it is used, the principles with which it is associated, and the character of those who possess the gifts of the angry fairy. I have written enough to show you that anything you choose to tell me of yourself, your views and aims, will deeply interest me. I write from the country, and I am going next week to another part of the country. I shall return to London in August, and I shall like to meet you there, if you care to meet me after this frank letter of mine.

I am, yours very truly,
Frederic Harrison

P.S.—To show you that I do not write in any unfriendly way I will repeat to you three criticisms or remarks made on the book by my wife, whose judgment in fiction I trust far more than my own.

1. There is enough stuff in the book to make six novels.
2. The finer type of London workman has never been so truly drawn.
3. Where are the 'Workers in the Dawn'?

You had better regard what I have said as premature till I know more of your work and of you.

4. George Saintsbury, *Academy*

31 July 1880, xviii, 76–7

Saintsbury (1845–1933), the distinguished literary critic and historian, had still to achieve his reputation at the time he wrote this sympathetic review.

Mr Gissing is one of those persons for whom the heart of the sensitive reviewer feels a certain sorrow. His book is in every sense an extravagant one. He has got into his head the very common notion that social order as at present established is the root of all evil, and he writes a long (a very long) novel to illustrate this notion. Nearly all his people of the upper class are foolish or wicked, and nearly all those of the lower are wretched and wronged. Yet, oddly enough, the bad ends to which nearly all, rich and poor, come are occasioned almost in every single instance by some personal error or folly which it is difficult to connect with the social system at all. Nor has Mr Gissing been fortunate enough to make his portraits, at all events in the case of the upper classes, in the least life-like. Yet when the necessary and important deductions have been made for all these shortcomings, there remains something to be said for the author. He possesses sincerity, which is a great thing, and imagination which is a greater. Although any reader of some little experience will know that his pictures are partly false and partly exaggerated, yet his book leaves on the mind a certain 'obsession'—there is no word for it in English, though neither thing nor term is specially or properly French—which merely insignificant work never produces. It ought to be mentioned, perhaps, that *Workers in the Dawn* is not exactly intended for the well-known young ladies whose bread is cut in the equally well-known *tartines*. There is nothing in the least unclean in Mr Gissing's handling of his subjects, but in his choice of them he is more adventurous than is usual with the English novelist.

5. Unsigned review, *Manchester Examiner and Times*

15 September 1880, 3

On seeing this long appraisal of his book Gissing exulted and urged his brother to buy a copy of the paper (postcard to Algernon Gissing, 17 September 1880).

The appearance of a novel of more than average merit by an unknown author is not too common to leave the reviewer without excuse for expressing his gratification thereon when he enjoys the exceptional experience; and the novel before us is only inadequately described when it is defined by this hackneyed phrase. Mr Gissing is, we believe, a young man, and no one who reads his book will require to be told that he is a young author. The faults of his work are apparent enough; and they are not least notable in the lack of constructive skill; but far more striking than the short-comings is the power displayed, the ability to portray and discriminate character, the vivid and graphic descriptive sketches of life in the London slums, and the intense pathos which often quickens the reader's interest in incidents unattractive in themselves. Then we are never allowed to forget the author's almost overwhelming earnestness. He enters so thoroughly into the varied emotions of the principal characters that we often wonder in reading even the improbable incidents—and the story abounds with such—whether the author is not sketching from the experience of some one he has personally known. His boldness is fettered by no scruples; he deals with the gravest subjects, and with the most difficult and delicate phases of modern social life; but the utterance of the most outspoken divergence from received opinion never suggests irreverence, and the most realistic pictures of vice and degradation are never open to the charge of licentious description. We are at a loss to determine whether Mr Gissing shares the opinions of his hero and heroine, both of whom rise into the serene air of sweetness and light above the mists of such superstitions as Christianity at a very early age. The lady was scarcely

17 when she chanced to find Strauss's *Life of Jesus*, and before she was 20 she had satisfied herself by a severe course of theological and metaphysical study at Tübingen, by a close examination of the Positive philosophy and of modern Pessimism, that the human hope of immortality was nothing but a pretty fancy, and that the belief in an all-wise Providence was illogical and unscientific. But she is a beautiful soul, spotless, and only undeserving of the name by which some of her friends called her because she was sympathetic to a degree that Pallas Athenae never was. She devoted her time and her fortune to the amelioration of the poor, and this not merely by means which Miss Octavia Hill would approve, but by daring the dangers of such haunts of vice as would try the courage of the boldest and most philanthropic of men. The hero, if less immaculate, is more human, and his experience is much more varied. He, too, escapes entirely from the trammels of religious and theological superstitions, and faces cheerfully the issues involved in a belief that there is nothing for us but this world, and that the scheme of man's regeneration must be completed in the sphere of what is known to his material senses. Yet the moral of their life and death is not in harmony with the aspirations of the 'advanced.' Their scheme is an utter failure, and more than once at the moment of agony with both of them there is an unconscious appeal to an unknown power. Their aims are unattained, they feel the anguish of despair, each of them utterly fails to reclaim one who is near and dear from degradation and infamy. The lady dies lonely and broken hearted, and the hero, after having seen to his own satisfaction courses of duty in labour and sacrifice, and hopes of amelioration by devotion to art, throws himself down the falls of Niagara, and ends life a miserable failure. Then there is a man of the world, who is utterly indifferent to either religion or philosophy, who, having no principle to guide him, succumbs to temptation, and is guilty of a most dishonourable conspiracy against the young man he had promised to befriend. And we find it equally difficult to determine whether Mr Gissing shares the opinion of the very excellent working men who advocate social changes as the means of elevating the working classes. He certainly guards himself against responsibility for the more extravagant doctrines by setting forth arguments against them, and we are disposed to think that there is no more powerful moral in the novel than that involved in the fall of the lost girl whom the young hero most injudiciously marries. Mr Gissing, indeed, perhaps unconsciously, intensifies the lesson of the doctrine that the elevation of a class is only

possible by the reformation of its individuals. The girl is presented to us in the midst of temptation, but with the power of choice. The good is set before her, she knows its value; she has no doubt about the impropriety of her conduct, but she allows her appetites and passions to rule, and, not once or twice, she falls. Yet even at her lowest depths we are reminded that there is a possibility of restoration; but it is equally clear that this can only be exercised by a firm determination to resist. Friendly counsels will do much, example and sympathy more, but because she will not herself walk in the way pointed out as the only road to happiness she falls lower and lower.

We will not attempt to give an outline of the plot of this remarkable novel; but we ought to say that though the author himself probably thought of calling attention to serious problems in the first place, and of interesting his readers by the adventures of the characters in the second, his story will be found attractive even to the ordinary novel reader. They will probably skip many pages which will specially interest another class of readers, those in which occur the impossible long speeches and the discussions on philosophy, ethics, art, &c. The story is too long, but though there are many more characters than were required for its proper development, we are never confused by the crowd; every one has its distinct individuality, and, with few exceptions, some distinct object to serve. We should extend this notice far beyond the ordinary limits if we referred to one-tenth of the passages we marked in reading *Workers in the Dawn*. In the character and career of the hero there is a certain resemblance to *Alton Locke*, and the outspoken statements and vigorous style also remind us of some passages in that story. But in the narrative of Arthur Golding's early years, his escape from the clergyman's home, his flight to London, and the wonderfully pathetic story of his life in the slums, his experience as a shopboy, his education under difficulties—in our opinion the most dramatic and successful portion of the story—the influence of a greater than Kingsley is suggested. But here, as anywhere in the book, we are as little disposed to question the author's originality as his power. Mr Gissing seems to have been a student of many systems, and his knowledge of some of the subjects discussed or referred to in his novel must of necessity be superficial. He has great facility in writing, a dangerous fluency indeed, and there is scarcely a chapter that does not suggest haste; but the wonder is that with such a design the errors of taste and style and construction are not more numerous. If the author shares to any great extent the artistic instincts of his hero, he will not require to be told that he must curb his powers and learn the expediency of restraint, and we have no doubt he will. He has written one of the most painful stories we have read for a long time, but assuredly one which emphatically offers a promise of something great.

6. Unsigned review, *Spectator*

25 September 1880, liii, 1226–7

In a postcard to his brother Algernon, dated 26 September 1880, Gissing qualified this review as 'important'. When Algernon had read it George passed this comment on it:

> The *Spectator* was unjust in many respects, most outrageously so, however, in saying that in describing the life of Mr Gresham, Mr Norman, Mr Waghorn, and the well-to-do people, I was describing something I had never seen. *All* the reviewers take me for a working-man, I fancy, tho' a careful reading of my book would show such a supposition to be grossly absurd. Why, it is the *other* kind of life that I have had to make a study of—the low, not the middle-class life. And, say what they like, *all* my well-to-do characters are natural enough. But they will not confess the likeness. They are willing enough to admit that I have drawn blackguards well when those blackguards are of the poorer classes; the existence of blackguards elsewhere they won't recognize. 'O Scribes and Pharisees, hypocrites!'

(*Letters of George Gissing to Members of His Family*, p. 81).

Whether Mr Gissing does or does not ultimately attain a high place in imaginative literature, there is no doubt that *Workers in the Dawn* is a very powerful work. So powerful are its best parts, that they amply make amends for the ludicrous ignorance and deep-seated prejudice displayed in the delineation of character and description of life, where character and life are unknown by personal experience to the author.

Unfortunately, it is the world of poverty and misery, and the dark side of human nature, with which Mr Gissing is best acquainted. Vice, with the dire effect it produces on human beings, both physically and morally, when generation after generation lives and dies without a hope, or even wish for anything better, is drawn with terrible reality.

The story is one of much pathos. A man of good position falls, through drink and vice, into the depths of poverty; and dying early, his son Arthur, the hero of the book, is found by Mr Norman, a clerical friend of his father's in his college days, in a low lodging-house in the slums of London. The child is taken home to the country rectory to be brought up, but civilisation has no charm for him, and the memory of his dead father calls him back to the scenes and haunts in which he had spent the few happy moments that he could remember. He runs away to London, and his history, as he is tossed about from one associate to another, until he finds a home and a friend in a kindly old printer, makes the chief interest of the earlier part of the book. Meanwhile, the reader is introduced to Mr Whiffle, a curate of Mr Norman's, and to his son Augustus, who ultimately develops into the villain of the story; to the Greshams, friends of Mr Norman's, and to his daughter, Helen, all of whom play a more or less prominent part in Arthur's life. It is in the delineation of these characters that Mr Gissing shows how limited his observation has been, and how little diffident he is in describing what he has not observed. Hardly one line that deals with them is true to nature, and the pictures he draws of the Clergy of the Church of England, whom he hates with a rabid hatred, become simple caricatures, and go far to spoil a work that otherwise is very strong indeed. It would have been wiser if the author could have kept in bounds a cynicism that refuses to see any good in institutions which he does not understand, and with which he has no sympathy. The heroine, too, is a more or less impossible creation. Gifted with great beauty and rare intelligence, and left rich through the death of her father, Helen Norman, at the age of nineteen, devotes herself entirely to a life spent among the back-streets and alleys of London. Such enthusiasm is of course far from impossible, but Mr Gissing has drawn Helen Norman as exchanging, before the age of twenty, by close thought and reading, an earnest Christianity for an equally earnest atheism; and to paint such a woman as Helen as never for one moment feeling her heart quail before the hopeless misery and still more hopeless task of dealing effectually with such misery, shows the author to be very young and totally inexperienced in the reactions and heartburnings that to a nature so cultured and sympathetic are inevitable.

But we have no wish to dwell on the weaknesses of the book. To any one who has come across the dark sides of life, the truth of the picture drawn is unquestionable. No attempt is made to gloss over the hardening effect of poverty and vice. Mr Gissing does not try to hide the depths to which human nature can fall, when generations of brutality and ignorance have done their worst. That the reasons he gives for the state of things are open to criticism does not undo the fact that the disease is there, and needs strong remedies. If his remedies are Quixotic, it will not help the matter to ignore the want of enthusiasm on the part of the educated classes to deal with questions which may be difficult to solve, but which will, nevertheless, go on asserting themselves until they are dealt with. Those whose lives are passed among scenes such as those drawn in *Workers in the Dawn* may be forgiven, if to them Communism presents an easy and alluring cure for evils that are intensely real, and we cannot wonder if it is difficult for the poor to believe that such evils are not caused directly by the selfishness and inertia of the rich. That this is the case, we do not say, and no doubt education and a large-minded legislation may in time produce a radical change in the condition of the poor; but that the poor themselves should lay the *cause* at the door of class differences is only natural, when it can be shown with such real force how almost impossible it is for individuals to raise themselves whilst bound down by the vice and ignorance of their immediate surroundings. How well Mr Gissing recognises this is shown in the description of Carrie, whom the hero marries, in an enthusiasm of pity and love produced by the wrongs she has suffered at the hands of one of a higher class. Her downward career, and the impossibility of evoking a spark of sustained effort to resist it, are very strikingly painted, and the effect produced on Arthur is painfully true to nature. Under the combined sense of hopelessness and finding himself deceived in the woman for whom he has sacrificed his career, he gives up the struggle, and allows himself to drift for a season into evil courses, and the inevitable consequences they would produce in a character like Arthur's. In all this we feel we are dealing with real flesh and blood, and not with any mere creation of fancy. Arthur's gradual awakening to the fact that he has married a woman whom it is impossible to raise, and who drifts steadily and surely into drink and deception, is given with great delicacy and skill. His struggle between loyalty to the false wife and love for the ideal in Helen is extremely pathetic. We are made to realise clearly the duplex nature of Arthur,—one side keenly appreciative of all possible happiness, the other aspiring to be governed by the highest motives of the soul. A large part of the strength of the book lies in the author drawing no moral. Where he paints actual life, he allows the inevitable flaws in all characters to assert themselves to the full. This is least true of Helen Norman. In her an attempt is made to draw ideal perfection, and in consequence she is at bottom passionless and unreal; but in Arthur, genius and noble desire are very cleverly shown blended with irresolution and weakness, which prevent his mastering adverse circumstances, and hamper and eventually destroy his life.

Some of the most telling descriptions of the book are those of people and scenes that have little to do with Arthur's history. The description of the Pettindund ménage is one of these. Possessed of rather more means than their immediate neighbours, the object nearest to their heart is the yearly festival of Christmas, when they may give themselves for a week together to one prolonged scene of horrible gluttony and drink. For this purpose they screw and pinch for months, that the money so saved may be expended regally when the time of rejoicing shall have arrived, while side by side with horrors such as these is brought out the utter want of sympathy and kindness that such excesses tend to produce in the poor. With an exceedingly low standard of morality for themselves, if one outside their immediate circle should, through greater poverty or temptation fall below it, people of the Pettindund class will always be found ready to cast a stone, and there is nothing that has been said against the working-class, but can find a counterpart in words and actions ascribed to some of them by Mr Gissing. Every now and then, however, he lets a gleam of brightness into the picture, but with the effect of making the shadows more dark. The simple kindliness of Mr Tollady, and the calm strength of Will Noble almost raise a hope of individual effort touching the sore; but these characters only serve to show how want of opportunity and absence of power inevitably tend to make such efforts futile and unproductive.

That the tone of the book should be pessimist, and the end of Arthur despair, is only natural from an author whose creed is atheism, and whose sympathies are keenly alive to the sins and sorrows of the human race. His heroine, moulded on Strauss, and finding in Darwin and Comte the sustenance and comfort that her life of self-sacrifice requires, is saved from any possible reaction by an early death at two-

and-twenty. The best Mr Gissing can do for the Church of England is to make her clergy sceptics, and to give them Horace for their Prayer-book; and though he is more merciful to Dissent, and, in the person of Mr Hatherley, gives us a pleasant sketch of genuine earnestness, Mr Gissing has evidently no idea of the real strength and beauty of Christianity. How little he understands the large part that Christianity has played in the cause of civilisation, or the extent of what it has accomplished in ameliorating the position of the poor, is very evident, and his ignorance of its moral standard is equally displayed by the motives and principles that he imagines are countenanced and commended by Christians.

7. George Meredith on Gissing

1884, 1885, 1897, 1899

Meredith and Gissing first met on 13 February 1884 after Gissing had submitted *The Unclassed* to Chapman & Hall for whom Meredith acted as manuscript reader. The identity of the 'reader' was not revealed on that occasion. From July 1895, when the two novelists met again at a dinner of the Omar Khayyám Club, to May 1899 when Gissing settled in France, they saw each other at intervals at Box Hill. Occasional correspondence between them continued until Gissing's death.

(*a*) Extract from a letter of Gissing to his brother Algernon, 14 February 1884, about *The Unclassed:* 'Chapman says his reader has scarcely ever spoken so strongly of a MS.' (Unpublished part of letter, Yale.)

(*b*) Extract from a letter of Gissing to his brother Algernon, 31 October 1885, about *Isabel Clarendon*: 'Meredith tells me I am making a great mistake in leaving the low-life scenes; says I might take a foremost place in fiction if I pursued that. Well, the next will in some degrees revert to that, though it will altogether keep clear of matter which people find distasteful. I shall call it *Demos* and it will be rather a savage satire on working-class aims and capacities.' (*Letters of George Gissing to Members of His Family*, p. 172.)

(*c*) Extract from a letter of Meredith to Gissing, 17 September 1897: 'Come as early as convenient. I will tell you my impression of *The Whirlpool*, a work of strength, well weighed and delivered.' (*The Letters of George Meredith*, ed. C. L. Cline (1970), 1278.)

(*d*) Extract from Edward Clodd's unpublished diaries, 8–9 April 1899. When Gissing informed Meredith he contemplated writing a novel set in sixth-century Rome, Meredith remarked: 'You may have histories, but you cannot have novels on periods long ago. A novel can only truly reflect the minds of men and women around us and after all, in depicting the present, we are dealing with the past which is enfolded in it.'

(*e*) Extract from Edward Clodd's unpublished diaries, 28 October 1899: '[Meredith] liked Gissing's *Crown of Life* except the closing chapter; says he should not bury himself in Switzerland because his works come of observation and are not of the imaginative order. The novelist must live with his creations.'

(*f*) Extract from a letter of Meredith to Gissing, 31 October 1899, about *The Crown of Life:* 'I have enjoyed the book, for the story, the writing and the reflections. Irene is my love. I complain that you drop her midway for too long a space, and when she is recovered she is not moving. I speak plainly because you have given me a right to her.' (*The Letters of George Meredith*, ed. C. L. Cline (1970), 1339.)

THE UNCLASSED

June 1884

Revised edition, November 1895

8. Unsigned review, *Evening News*

25 June 1884, 1

The review, occupying a full column, was significantly entitled 'A Novel for Men'. Gissing read it but has left no written comment.

Mr George Gissing is a daring man to choose such characters and situations to represent as are to be found in his latest novel, *The Unclassed.* To choose for heroine a girl who makes her livelihood contentedly enough by the saddest of callings, and for hero a man who has, like too many men of our time, questioned and speculated away all he ever possessed of principles of morality or duty, is daring enough; but at any rate it is possible to adopt the treatment familiarised by the Abbé Prévost in *Manon Lescaut* or by Dumas *fils* in the *Dame aux Camélias.* Mr Gissing, however, original in this as in other respects, shuns sentimentality and courts the serious consideration of the difficult moral problems his subject supplies, and we are bound to say that this confidence in his own power to deal successfully with exceedingly delicate materials is justified by the result now before us. The whole book is rich in situations and in interest. The study of character is never superficial, and at times really penetrating. The style is unpretentious and clear; and although Mr Gissing neither writes, nor professes to write, *virginibus puerisque*, yet to the thoughtful reader anxious to see life thoroughly, and to see it whole, *The Unclassed* contains nothing that will give offence, and much that will repay perusal. It would be interesting to compare the treatment of a similar theme by any living

French author with Mr Gissing's serious and sincere work—work which is absolutely free either from pruriency or prudery, being in fact, and in the best sense, English. The point of view reminds us of De Quincey's in that touching episode of the poor street-walker, whose charity and unselfishness are a bright spot in *The Confessions of an Opium-eater.* The story opens in Miss Rutherford's School in Lisson-grove, where Ida Starr, the heroine of the book, has just struck down with her slate another girl who had provoked her past endurance, by casting in her teeth that her mother is a bad woman, and gets her living on the streets. The taunt is only too true, though the fact is unknown to Ida. The scene between mother and daughter when Miss Rutherford's letter comes, and, on the mother asking her daughter why she has to leave, Ida tells of her violence and the cause of it, is truly pathetic. The child's look of love and proud confidence intensifies the unhappy mother's anguish, whose dread is that if the child knew how her mother got her living she would cease to love and respect her. The bitterness with which this bread of poverty and shame is earned, and the survival of intense motherly affection and watchful care for the child that she may have a good education, and that no breath of evil may sully her young mind, are touchingly described, and will give to many readers a very different notion of the 'unfortunate' class to any they have had before. Ida's mother dies, and she is left to make her way as best she may. As might be expected, the best she can do is little, and she lives a miserable life, first as drudge in an eating-house, then as servant in wretched places where she is starved and bullied, till at last worn out, she succumbs to the desire of escaping in any way from her misery, and becomes the mistress of a young man, son of the lady in whose house she had last served. From this the descent is not only easy but almost inevitable to the kind of life which causes her to meet, one night in Pall Mall, Osmond Waymark, the hero, if hero he can be called, of the story. The account of the genuinely platonic friendship between this artistic and Bohemian writer and the beautiful but fallen girl is exceedingly fresh and life-like. We will not spoil the story by describing the plot, which is worked out with considerable skill, and in which the interest is unflagging, and by no means confined to the principal characters. The study of Waymark's feeling for Ida Starr and for Maud Enderby simultaneously, will interest the psychologist as well as the ordinary reader. The descriptions of Litany-lane and Jubilee court show knowledge of the slums and skill in portraying the types found there. There is a terrible realism in much of the writing dealing with the life that festers and decays morally and physically in the rookeries which, in large numbers, are still the disgrace of London. Perhaps the most weird of the dwellers in Jubilee court is the creature known as Slimy, a hideous caricature of humanity, whose death has about it features of special horror. Waymark, who is employed by the owner, Abraham Woodstock, to collect the rents, finds in Slimy a most interesting if repulsive study. One day, on coming up to Slimy's room, Waymark sees signs of something amiss. Slimy, lifting a huge club, quietly tells him he will knock him down like a bullock unless he remains quiet, and then carefully ties him to hooks driven firmly into the floor. Then he takes the satchel in which is contained the money already collected, and last of all declares his intentions. 'Fifty year,' he says,

> 'an' not one 'appy day. Money means 'appiness, an' them as never 'as money 'll never be 'appy, live as long as they may. Well, I went on a-sayin' to myself, 'Ain't I to 'ave not one 'appy day all my life?' An' it come to me all at once that money was to be 'ad for the trouble o' takin' it—money an' 'appiness. A pound ain't no use, nor yet two pound, nor yet five pound. There's a good deal more than five pound 'ere now, Mr Waymark. What d'you think I'm going to do with it? I'm a-goin' to drink myself dead. That's what I'm agoin' to do, Mr Waymark.'

And the Caliban of the slums is as good as his word. Mr Gissing has succeeded in lifting the veil from the life of a section of the world of London concerning which serious novelists have too long kept silence, and he has done his work with so much good feeling and good taste that no reader will be offended, while all will be the richer for some authentic information, much needed in these days of social reform, when the refuge and the reformatory are stupidly set to cure what might easily be prevented, at least in great part. Mr Gissing is thoroughly acquainted with the main subject on which he writes, but while we thank him for the data, we regard the inferences which he frames into a philosophy of life as altogether erroneous. When, for instance, he touches Christianity, it is, though we doubt not he writes in perfect good faith, to travesty it. Again, the notion that the mind of a prostitute can remain pure and unsullied in the midst of her profession is simply contrary to fact, however well it may fit in with this or that theory. On the other hand, we fail to see how any objection can be taken to the theory that love can save the streetwalker from her life of degradation, and even purify her heart from the pollution of the past. In Mrs Oliphant's *Wizard's Son* a young man is saved from a life of vice by the power of love awakened in him by a pure and good woman; and the book has been deservedly lauded for its high purpose by the daily and weekly press. Mr Gissing substitutes a young woman for a young man, and, though we are instituting no comparison between him and Mrs Oliphant, surely deserves the same treatment. To sum up: it is in choice of subject, as well as in felicity of craftsmanship, that the strength of a novelist is shown, and in both respects Mr Gissing has deserved well of the reading public. At the same time, it must be said that a more complete power of seeing, and a stronger grasp than Mr Gissing possesses, might have made a permanent and valuable work of art out of the materials that have been employed in *The Unclassed.*

9. Arthur R. R. Barker, *Academy*

28 June 1884, xxv, 454

Gissing remarked on the following review in a letter to his brother dated 29 June 1884: 'A much fairer notice [than in the *Athenaeum*] was in the *Academy*,—a thing which surprised me. The writer speaks very plainly of what the story deals with, and goes on to say that there is promise of good work. . . . I wanted you to be sure that I am quite skin-hardened. I know precisely the value of my work, and can read very calmly these adverse reviews. There will be more of them yet' (Berg Collection, New York Public Library).

The author—or rather authoress, for the work plainly shows a female hand—of *The Unclassed* has written a tale of lower middle-class life in London in the manner of M. Zola or his disciples. We say in the manner, for the manner of the *naturaliste* school is to give sufficient prominence to the shadows of life to produce a picture of powerful effect. The spirit of the modern French realists differs in no way from that of generations of French writers in every branch of literature, who have ever sought to feed the emotional craving for the *sel gaulois* (read the English 'dirt') on one pretext or another. The spirit of *The Unclassed* is not the spirit of Zola, as the book is not prurient; but the manner of the book is realistic to a degree which will shock many readers. For the rest, the author has not sufficient control over her imagination to bring her characters and incidents into thorough harmony with nature. The story abounds with situations in which verisimilitude is sacrificed for effect. And, while on this subject, we may remark that a long-continued platonic attachment between a normal young man—even of aesthetic tastes—and a London prostitute is an incident hardly within the range of probability, to say the least. The drawing of the characters, though unequal, is in parts very vigorous, and shows a capacity which may be expected to reward its cultivation with good fruit.

10. Unsigned review, *Graphic*

13 September 1884, xxx, 286

The *Graphic* was an illustrated London weekly, in format and appearance much like the *Illustrated London News*. Gissing saw this review of *The Unclassed:* a cutting was pasted in his album of press clippings.

It is not at all easy to deal with *The Unclassed.* As its title indicates, it treats of persons and subjects which have been by general consent excluded from English fiction. Not that Mr Gissing has made any attempt to make sensational capital out of his subject—nobody need fear in him a pioneer of the school of M. Zola. He is earnestly full of the idea that no class is really very black, or indeed, anything less than very white, and he has therefore sketched some fancy portraits of very high-minded, but otherwise ordinary young persons, and then labelled them as he pleases. It is difficult to say to what order of readers *The Unclassed* appeals. Certainly not to unwholesome appetites for the realistic, because it is as tame and flavourless as the purest water, while the nature of its subject will certainly repel the majority. If it be intended to do good, as we suppose is the case, Mr Gissing must be content with congratulations on his good intentions. He has decidedly made a profound mistake in imagining that fiction is either a right or a practical instrument for giving effect to them. He was bound to be either unwholesome or dull; and, to his credit be it said, he has chosen the latter alternative.

11. Unsigned, 'Gissing the Rod', *Punch*

3 January 1885, lxxxviii, 1

After reading George Moore's attack on the circulating libraries entitled 'The New Censorship in Literature' (*Pall Mall Budget*, 12 December 1884) which Moore concluded by remarking that 'at the head . . . of English literature sits a tradesman', Gissing had ventured to give his own view in a letter to the editor of the newspaper. He asked whether it would not be better to recognize 'that the course of literature is really directed by the men who make literature' (*Pall Mall Gazette*, 15 December 1884, 2, and *Pall Mall Budget*, 19 December 1884, 12–13). Gissing's letter attracted the attention of *Punch*, edited at the time by Francis Cowley Burnand, author of *Gaiety Burlesques*. The humorous journal poured scorn upon what it regarded as another foolish discussion about contemporary novel-writing. Gissing attributed the outburst to Burnand himself. 'My sole feeling was one of surprise,' he wrote to his brother; 'it did not interrupt my work for an hour. I am getting very used to abuse in the place of criticism' (from a letter dated 2 January 1885, *Letters of George Gissing to Members of His Family*, p. 151).

We have but now laid our hand upon a few days' old number of the *Pall Mall Gazette* which containeth a piece of wisdom so entirely monumental, that it well deserves to be 'aere perennius'—which we would render, for the moment, into 'longer-lived than its own brass.' It has nothing to do with the conduct of that bright and many-sided journal, be it said, but merely with a Correspondent who has at least the courage of his opinions in signing his name . . .—the great Mr George Gissing. Humbly we own that we never heard his name before, though it seems suggestive of a kind of guttural German embrace performed by the nationaliser of the Land. But Gissing should be known. This is what Gissing writes:—

One of the most painful confessions in literature is that contained in the preface to *Pendennis*, where Thackeray admits that 'since the author of *Tom Jones* was buried no writer of fiction among us has been permitted to depict to his utmost power a man,'—on penalty, be it understood (by Gissing) of a temporary diminution of receipts. If this be not a tradesman's attitude, what is? Let novelists be true to their artistic conscience, and the public taste will come round. In that day there will be no complaint of the circulating libraries. It is a hard thing to say, but Thackeray, when he knowingly wrote below the demands of his art to conciliate Mrs Grundy, betrayed his trust; and the same thing is being done by our living novelists every day.

O ye demigods and little Gissings, did anybody ever hear the like of this? Not all the water of Gissingen can do much for anybody who openly prays that the public taste may 'come round' again to the open coarseness of *Tom Jones*; the vice of an age as much as our age has its own, which Thackeray, one of the cleanest-minded writers who ever lived, points out in that same preface to be happily out of date. All the world knows what that preface meant, save and except Gissing, who thinks that Thackeray's artistic conscience suggested Dirt, and his art demanded it, but that he was afraid of losing money by it!! Had he but been true to his conscience and his tastes, his receipts would have gone up in time, for Gissing would have bought his books. But Thackeray betrayed his trust (ye gods! Thackeray!) by being sweet and pure, though it is a 'hard thing to say.' It should have been not only hard but impossible, Gissing. As for our living novelists, they are disgusting Gissing by 'doing the same every day.' Well, they are, Gissing; and speaking with some knowledge of them, we do not altogether regret it. We regret that Gissing cannot get the reading he likes, except by going back to more conscientious days; and we do not wholly love Mrs Grundy. But we like her taste in books better than Gissing's. We will do all we can to help you to your desired celebrity, Gissing, though we care not to be gissing who can have brought you up. Praised be the gods for thy foulness, Gissing! but also that, as we fondly hope, there are not very many like thee.

12. Gissing's Preface to the second edition of *The Unclassed*

October 1895

Despite its cool reception by professional critics in 1884, *The Unclassed* had made a deep impression on the minds of some reviewers and readers. In the next ten years the book was occasionally referred to in literary journals. Thomas Hardy was known to hold it in high esteem. After serious hesitation, Gissing yielded in September 1895 to his publisher's request to reprint it in a revised form. From the 8th to the 13th of that month, he went through his novel and cut it by one-third. For a comparison of the two versions, see Joseph J. Wolff, 'Gissing's Revision of *The Unclassed*', *Nineteenth-Century Fiction*, June 1953, 42–51. This preface to the new edition was written at the suggestion of Eduard Bertz.

This book was written and sent forth a long, long time ago. Judge of its antiquity from the fact that the original publishers were afraid to think what they had done—that editors, for the most part, were unwilling to have the book noticed in their columns—and that the few readers into whose hands it fell (some of them intelligent people) drew aside to make known in whispers their condemnation or their praise.

The date was 1884—a long time ago.

Nowadays, the theme and its presentment will, at worst, be 'matter for a flying smile.' It will be recognised as the work of a very young man, who dealt in a romantic spirit with the gloomier facts of life.

Revising this early effort, the author has been glad to run his pen through superfluous pages, and to obliterate certain traces of the impertinent Ego. But the narrative remains what it was, and should be read as narrative pure and simple. Romance has no moral, and youth may be pardoned its idealism.

With regard to the title, which has sometimes been misunderstood, I should like to say that by 'unclassed' I meant, not, of course, *déclassé*, nor yet a condition technically represented by the heroine. Male and female, all the prominent persons of the story dwell in a limbo external to society. They refuse the statistic badge—will not, like Bishop Blougram's respectabilities, be 'classed and done with.'

G.G.

13. Unsigned review, *Daily Chronicle*

2 December 1895, 3

Henry Norman, literary editor of the *Daily Chronicle*, was a friend of Gissing's. He may have written this review. Gissing read it and recorded the fact in his Diary, but made no comment.

In a foreword of considerable pertinence and point, Mr Gissing hints that this book was regarded as a little over-daring, even immoral, on its publication eleven years ago. And he remarks upon the change in public and publishers' opinions since then. It is very true that the world has grown more lenient, has lent a more willing ear to those authors who have refused to speak well of it, has had to listen to many a frank statement of its misdeeds, so much so that the unlettered are in danger of concluding that nothing is any longer held improper to be written or to be said. We are therefore sometimes compelled to assert that there is such a thing as the 'immoral' novel, the novel no one should write and no one should publish—and we hold this to be the novel which gives an untrue, a partial, or an insincere view of life. The thing which is true or sincerely written—though it be not agreeable reading—must not be counted immoral, though it is of course not necessary, as Aristotle reminded us, to tell everything that is true. But this latitude implies after all no such wide license to the novelist. In this book we have the story of some young men and some young women of the 'unclassed'—that is, belonging to no distinct or defined class of society, and because it is written by Mr Gissing the story is an interesting one. There is Osmond Waymark, of mounting spirit and grand dissatisfaction of soul; and Julian Casti, a poet of the pestle and mortar, as was Keats aforetime, only his fate is sadder than Keats's, for he married from pity and heroism his cousin, one Harriet Smales, and was by her driven to his death, and there is Maud Enderby, a shadowy creature hardly of this world; and finally, there is the heroine, Ida Starr, at eighteen a street-walker in the Strand. How Ida leaves this life for love of Osmond Waymark and how Waymark treats her is told in the book, but the propriety or impropriety that should have puzzled the original publisher eleven years ago is whether Mr Gissing's Ida is a genuine, a possible character. If a character of such purity and beauty can exist in such surroundings, then the book is in no sense immoral. If, on the other hand, the author imagines a woman-soul of such lovely quality, and arbitrarily and for 'the purposes of fiction' places her in such surroundings, then, in so far, is the book immoral, because untrue. Therein certainly lies the real point as to whether the original publisher was justified in his timidity or not: for us, the book as a whole interests because it is one of the earliest works of a man who has now taken his place among our premier novelists. Those who have felt on reading *New Grub Street*, *The Odd Women*, *In the Year of Jubilee*, and some recently published sketches which might be called the grey lights on life, will like to see how the author envisaged things when no measure of success had come to him. They will find little difference in his attitude. There is the same sense of fatalism; the same recognition of the forces in society which crush—nearly always—the individual; the same pale but constant hope which threads, like a strand of silver, the dark web of Mr Gissing's pessimism. They will see the same sympathy, intellectual and rational rather than instinctive and cordially human, with the less fortunate of human kind; the same faithful record of the gyves of squalor. Over all is cast a veil of romance which Mr Gissing has since burnt in the white flame of realism; romance which was in him more imitative than natural. For the young writer, in his crudest moments of originality, is ever imitative in a small degree. From *The Unclassed* to his later work, the change is all gain; what picked him out from his fellows is all there still, and his gifts have only mellowed and grown. It is difficult, in running over the names of Mr Gissing's novels, to remember that he is still a very young man—as fine novelists go—that he has a dozen years' advantage of his equals, that life has much more, has many different things to show him. It will soon be two years since he wrote a novel. Already he has painted London poor and London lower middle-class society as has no one else. He may be said to have patented the type of eager, ardent-souled young man at war with his surroundings, and he knows and can write things about women—both harsh and kind things—which his brother novelists have so far never come to learn. So we are waiting. We read and place *The Unclassed*—actually with one of his best-drawn, most convincing characters, Harriet Smales, within its pages—upon our shelves, and we look out for what is coming. For all questions of moral and immoral are settled as regards Mr Gissing's work; all that he sees he sees true, and he writes with a sincerity as assured as his own future. He is done with Ida Starrs and with 'Thyrzas'—he will give us no more of these; but no man need turn in shame from the romantic dream or vision of his youth. True to life they may not have been; but they were lovely dreams and pure.

14. Unsigned review, *Buffalo Courier*, as reprinted in the *Literary News*

July 1896, 205

George Gissing's novels usually treat of some social problem, but one would not say that they are of the morbid kind. One gets the idea rather that his purpose is to show that the debased and the exalted have like longings, like aspirations, like souls. In his novel of *The Unclassed*, the heroine is an outcast who is led by her love for a man who has unselfishly befriended her to turn from her old life and to undergo hardship and privation to win his esteem. He, knowing all the circumstances of her life, grows to love her and in the end marries her. Thus, the heroine is something like Tess, but the hero is not an Angel Clare. Neither of the characters is typical. The life led by such a woman as Ida Starr speedily destroys strength of character and refinement. To preserve them argues a rare nature—one of the most opposing qualities. But the principal idea in the book, though it is not obtruded in Sarah

Grand's brutal fashion, is that a man risks no more in marrying a woman that has fallen from grace than a woman risks in the very common case of marrying a man who has repeatedly yielded to temptation. The book is written with fine skill, the characters are drawn with power, and are quick with life, and one obtains an inkling of the struggle of the 'odd women' in London. George Gissing has made a scientific study of men and women and their relation to the artificial life of the end of the nineteenth century. He is fearless and true, but he has kept the element of hope and lets his readers share it with him. All his stories teach by their influence the great lesson of self-conquest and self-sacrifice. In these days of wild writing about the new woman, her sphere and her mission, it is good to read a dispassionate statement on the woman question.

DEMOS

March 1886

15. Unsigned review, *The Times*

3 April 1886, 5

As soon as he saw this review of *Demos* (which had been published anonymously) in *The Times*, Gissing sent a postcard to his brother, scribbling a few exultant words. He was gratified to find long quotations, one of them the description of Manor Park Cemetery. In this connection, it is worth noting John Morley's reaction as transcribed in a letter from Gissing to his brother. Gissing was quoting from a letter by Morley to Frederic Harrison: 'I have been reading *Demos*. Is it Gissing's? I suppose so. There is some masterly work in it. One page, that describing the East End graveyard—contains a passage which is one of the most beautiful in modern literature. And there is genius throughout' (*Letters of George Gissing to Members of His Family*, p. 185).

If a tale of Socialism does not find abundance of readers it is not because the times are not ripe for it. This remarkable novel presents the great social problem in a striking garb. If the author's treatment is rather superficial and his philosophy unsatisfactory, we must put it down to the exigencies of modern fiction and the unsatisfying nature of his subject. In brooding passion, in philosophy, in literary power of contrasting the lot of the rich and the poor—not to speak of its want of a moral—*Demos* does not aspire to vie with *Alton Locke*, but it tells a story more practical, and of more brightness and variety. Nor is the book wanting in eloquent passages and pathetic episodes which show it to be written by one who has a burning sympathy with the toiling poor. For pathos, take Emma Vine, the seamstress, sitting at the bed-side of her dying sister Jane, comforting her with cheerful face while her own heart is riven with woe at her lover's desertion, and trying to conceal the news which will cut short the sufferer's life; for eloquence, take the following, upon Jane's burial-place:

[Here the description of Manor Park Cemetery is quoted.]

But *Demos*, though a tale of English Socialism, is not a Socialistic novel. Perhaps it would pique curiosity more deeply if it were. Sometimes the author seems to preach the doctrines of Saint-Simon, and sometimes to scoff at them. Not until the third volume do we learn the standpoint of the writer from the lips of the Rev. Mr Wyvern, whom without undue presumption we may take to represent him. Mr Wyvern, we are told, was once a badly paid curate, working in a wretched parish. The sight of the misery around him made him a Socialist. But now he has 'outgrown it.' His old zeal only lingers in the form of tolerance. He 'can enter into the mind of a furious proletarian as easily as into the feeling which you (the aristocratic Hubert Eldon) represent.' He is now content that the world should in substance remain as it is. . . .

This comfortable doctrine has, as the author perceives, this awkwardness, that it withdraws from its professors all motives for furthering social 'progress.' The Rev. Mr Wyvern accepts progress as an inevitable law of our nature. He says:

Every one of these poor creatures has a right to curse the work of those who clamour progress, and pose as benefactors of their race.

We quote at some length these uncommon, if not original, views, because they are the key to much that is halting and inconclusive in the book. *Demos* does not appeal powerfully to the senses or the reason in favour of either Socialism or private property; it hardly presumes to weigh the claims of either.

[Here follows an outline of the first part of the novel.]

In one way the characterization of the chief actors is inconclusive. To put a great question in issue in a work of fiction, the representatives of the opposing causes ought to possess equal probity, which is not so here. Socialists might protest against setting up a selfish egoist to do battle in their name. 'Put a Saint-Simon, a Proudhon, or a Karl Marx in his place,' they might say, 'and let us then see whether an example of disinterestedness might not be set to mankind.' But *Demos* only purports to present us with a few realistic samples of modern Socialism.

It would be rash to assert that Mutimer and other supporters of the *Fiery Cross* or the *Tocsin* are less sincere or more likely to be spoilt by good fortune than the Socialist agitator as we actually know him in public life. If *Demos* suggests a practical moral, it is that the modern Socialist is insincere. But on the general problem we get but negative results, leading us nowhere, and sadly bidding us despair of the future of the human race.

16. Unsigned review, *Athenaeum*

10 April 1886, 485

Gissing pasted the review in his album of press cuttings, but made no comment in his correspondence.

The reader of *Demos* will learn very little about English socialism of the modern kind, as it has been expounded in public squares and private drawing-rooms. The author does not seem to have gone to contemporary professors of the mystery, or even to socialist newspapers and magazines, in order to put the case as scientifically as it is capable of being put. *Demos* might have been written by the author of *Alton Locke* and of *North and South*, or of *Shirley*, so far as the freshness of its ideas on popular discontent or industrial mutiny is concerned. This is a little disappointing in 'a story of English socialism' at the present day; and a second disappointment is found in the fact that weak and vicious people are chosen as the exponents of ideas which the author intends to demolish, whilst the opposite ideas are maintained by persons of refinement and good feeling. This is a blemish in point of art and a weakness in point of persuasion. The true artist would have drawn one or two captivating, or at any rate interesting, socialists, and would have tempered the necessary catastrophe with sundry amenities and compensations; and in so doing he would have taught a more serviceable lesson and written a more attractive and lifelike story. What has been said will indicate the lines on which *Demos* has been constructed, and within those lines it is a really able and vigorous romance. Though the hero is by no means true to his principles, he does in some measure secure and retain the interest of the reader. We sympathize with his good intentions at the outset and with his misfortunes at the close; but we are never allowed to think him much of a hero, or particularly strong, or consistent, or even intelligent. There are many types of character in the book, most of them fairly well drawn, and the author has some power in depicting tender and pathetic scenes. Three conspicuous examples of this are afforded in the treatment of Richard Mutimer's desertion of his sweetheart, in the lamentations of his mother over the curse of wealth, and in the tragic circumstances of Mutimer's own death.

17. Unsigned review, *Spectator*

10 April 1886, lix, 486–7

In a letter dated 15 April 1886 to his sister Ellen, Gissing remarked: 'Smith & Elder send me all the reviews, and I have now a good batch of them—some serious, some imbecile. The *Spectator* review is admirably written' (*Letters of George Gissing to Members of His Family*, p. 178).

This is a novel of very considerable ability, though it falls short of the highest power. It is evidently written by a man who has a very intimate knowledge of the working classes, and not a little sympathy with them, though his own bias would appear to be aristocratic and aesthetic, rather than democratic and scientific. Nothing can be more skilful than the sketch of the artisan family round whose fortunes the story of the book revolves. The chief character is very powerfully drawn, and though it is by no means a heroic character in any sense of the word,—for the fibre of his mind is essentially commonplace and poor, —there is in him a pathetic unconsciousness of the depth of his own insincerities, a power of recovery from them such as that complete unconsciousness often implies, and, again, a large mixture of coarse virtues, which render the sketch of Richard Mutimer a very striking and original creation. His mother, too, with her narrow, complaining, and almost dumb integrity, her pitiable misery when she finds her family so enriched that she is completely separated from them by the new wealth, her inarticulate wrath when her eldest son breaks his engagement with the girl to whom he was betrothed, and her complete inability to adapt herself, even passively, to circumstances of any novel kind, is a very powerful picture of the nature which works in a particular groove, and will not bear taking out of that groove. The weak, pretty daughter, and the worthless, blackguard son, are less careful, but hardly less truthful studies,—the whole making up probably a fair moral average for families of the type intended,—a type, of course, neither of the lowest nor of the highest kind. But if the other figures in this tale of English Socialism had been anything like as powerfully sketched as these, the book would be one of the highest order of ability. As it is, we can hardly say so much for it as that. Undoubtedly, its ability is considerable. The sketch of the one or two Socialist meetings which the author has occasion to describe, of the style of Socialist literature, and of the conversation of Socialist agitators, shows an intimate knowledge of that field of action, though anything but a favourable bias towards it. But when the author comes to delineate middle-class life, his touch is far less powerful. Mr and Mrs Westlake are shadows, and the latter is a shadow who, if she could not have been made more than a shadow, should hardly have been introduced at all. It is a mistake to describe a poetess in whose kiss the heroine finds the bliss of an intoxicating rapture, when the author cannot show you even vaguely the nature of the enchantment intended. Again, Mrs Eldon and her son, the clergyman, Mr Wyvern, and even Mrs Waltham, are by no means powerful sketches; while of the heroine, Adela Waltham,—who afterwards marries the Socialist hero of the tale,—we can only say that she misses the mark at which the author aims, though it is quite evident that with a very few touches more, with a very little deeper insight into the kind of character intended, she might have become one of the most attractive heroines in modern fiction. As it is, the author hesitates, in his picture of her, between a merely refined nobility and true spiritual devotedness of character, opening with the one, and apparently deviating into the other. We suspect that he means to paint a character which begins in faith, and losing faith, drops into mere faithfulness to her own early ideal, without that confidence in Divine help and guidance which could alone have sustained such faithfulness at the highest point. But he either shrinks from directly conveying this loss of purpose and faith, or else his imagination has failed him. It is certain that Adela Mutimer's character seems to waver between two different standards of moral aim, one of them mainly religious, the other, one of mere moral consistency and refinement. The total effect is, therefore, hazy, and falls short of what the reader is led to expect. Of the middle-class figures decidedly the best is Alfred Waltham, the combative Radical, who loves contradiction so dearly that he adopts views without any very serious conviction, which in later life he has to drop.

[Here follows an example of Waltham's conversation.]

The sketch of Alfred Waltham is by far the best, outside the region of the working class, in the book. But then, it is within the region of the working class that the unique power of the book shows itself.

Unquestionably, both Richard Mutimer and Emma Vine are drawn with real power; and in the latter you have the nobleness of disinterested love, painted with as truthful and sympathetic a touch as if the writer's sympathies were wholly democratic, instead of being, as they certainly are, aristocratic. She is so much more real than Adela Waltham, that we could wish his drift had enabled the author to make Emma Vine, and not Adela Waltham, his heroine. There is a power in the picture of her mute patience, of her constancy, of her devotion to the dying sister and her little niece and nephew, of her uncomplainingness when she is deserted, and her power over the drunkard who is so willing to leave her children to Emma's care, which makes us regret the change of scene whenever the author carries his story away from Emma and her sewing-machine, to the sorrows of the more refined and hazier Adela.

Richard Mutimer is well painted from beginning to end. His acute ignorance, his keen vanity, his moral obtuseness, his conventional earnestness, his fundamental good nature, the ease with which he deceives himself, his great capacity for ignoring and half-forgetting his own baser acts, and the easy good intentions which crop up again, almost before he has completely abandoned his most disgraceful designs, his love for his frivolous sister, his secret reverence for his refined wife, his wish to convince her of his noble aims, even when he is perfectly aware that she has only just succeeded in saving him from deliberate crime,—all these characteristics are painted with a power which makes Richard Mutimer, the Socialist leader, a real and living figure.

What the story needs, besides a more vividly painted heroine, is some spiritual and intellectual background with which the dream of Socialism can be contrasted. We supposed, at first, that Mr Wyvern,—who clearly resembles one of George Eliot's agnostic clergymen,—such a one as Mr Irvine, for example, in *Adam Bede*,—was intended to furnish us with this higher ideal of life and duty. But Mr Wyvern soon falls into the background, and we have nothing but Hubert Eldon's dreams of art and Mrs Westlake's dreams of poetry, to set over against Richard Mutimer's coarse and hesitating philanthropic selfishness or selfish philanthropy. Aestheticism appears to be the only alternative in the author's mind for the materialistic ideal in the realisation of which his Socialist hero so miserably fails. *Demos* is the book of a pessimist with no belief in the power of what are called progressive ideas, but also with little or no spiritual faith which might prove a higher motive-power than that of which equality and fraternity are the favourite watch-cries.

18. Unsigned review, *Guardian* (London)

14 April 1886, xli (1), 544

In the letter quoted in the previous headnote, Gissing ranked this review as the next best after that in the *Spectator*, adding: 'It is rather amusing to find myself praised in the Church organ' (MS. misquoted in the volume of Gissing's letters to his family).

Demos: a Story of English Socialism, is a very clever study of a not very beautiful phase of artisan life. If there were no other good thing in the book besides the description in the first volume of Richard Mutimer's library we should like everybody who has ever played with ideas of working-class education to read it for the sake of that description. Everybody has been telling us lately what we *ought* to read. The author of *Demos* has thought it worth while to tell us what the advanced artisan *does* read:—

[The quotation, from ch. 5, which follows, listing such authors as Malthus, Robert Owen, Thomas Paine and Voltaire, has obvious ironic connotations in the reviewing context of this 'Church organ'.]

The character of Richard Mutimer, artisan, socialist, demagogue, and capitalist, is worked out from first to last in admirable consistency with this description of his mental constitution. He has virtues—moral and practical—and plenty of intelligence of a hard and useful kind. When we make his acquaintance as an artisan in his own family and among his own class, we form a favourable opinion of him. When accident puts money and power into his hands, his defects of imagination, of tenderness, of refinement, become glaring faults. By the influences of prosperity he is moreover led into one or two distinct breaches of honour—of which the worst is his casting off of the girl he was engaged to marry. But he does not lose all integrity. Possessed of wealth, he loyally devotes his money to the cause of democracy, and starts mining works on his estate upon thorough-going socialistic principles. When the works are in full operation, the discovery of a missing will ousts him from possession. House, lands, and money pass into the hands of an aristocratic idealist, who razes the socialistic settlement to the ground, and restores the reign of nature; and Richard Mutimer, after some further ups and downs, is killed by a mob. It is certainly a fault of the novel that it is too strongly coloured by sordid and painful elements. It would, however, be most unfair to give the impression that all the interest of the book depends upon skill in delineating the unbeautiful. One must wish, indeed, that at least one man's character had been as elaborately worked out on noble and sympathetic lines as are those of Mutimer and his associates on unsympathetic lines. Much more, for instance, might have been made of the interesting and original character of Mr Wyvern, the vicar of the parish where the works are set up; and Hubert Eldon, the aristocrat, is a great deal too sketchy. Mr Westlake, the cultivated socialist, is a very pleasant gentleman, but absolutely unpractical; and his wife Stella is the least intelligible character in the book, though apparently the one to which the author attaches the most profound significance. Stella apart however, the women's characters are strong, original, and beautiful enough to redeem the book from the charge of being too grim. We only wish Adela, the wife first of Richard Mutimer and afterwards of Hubert Eldon, had been allowed to finish her career without its being said of her that she had 'achieved her womanhood' in the moment of accepting her second husband. As she has been perfectly womanly throughout—in courage, purity, faith, and loyalty—the phrase is either meaningless cant or a weak denial of better sense that has gone before. Nothing can be clearer or more commendable than the moral of the story as a whole; which may be stated shortly as an illustration of the importance of keeping the two great commandments of Christianity in their proper order. Mr Wyvern and Adela both cordially recognise the identity of the principle of socialism with that of the injunction to love our neighbour as ourselves: they only refuse to allow it precedence of the yet higher commandment. The deterioration of Mutimer's character is the obvious consequence of his denial of the higher commandment. Socialism passes through a sort of 'Jesuitism' into egotism, and all the finer charities of life are crushed out, though his broad loyalty to his cause is not seriously impaired. Hubert Eldon is a creature of refined instinct, and his point of view is done full justice to by the vicar when he says, 'You, being you, I approve'—in answer to the young man's question as to his opinion of the wholesale destruction of his predecessor's works. But of Mr and Mrs Westlake and the honours accorded to them, we do not know quite what to make. Stella is very sweet and beautiful, and her poetic faith in the people is touching and inspiring. But if the people are what the author of *Demos* shows, and if Mr Wyvern is right as to what is best for the world, then Adela's 'womanhood' would have been better 'achieved' under other auspices than those of this visionary pair. We are not at all sure that a fourth volume might not in strict consistency show Adela travelling also to the goal of egotism—*her* route being the fairer but not less fatal one of aestheticism.

19. Unsigned review, *Scottish Review*

April 1886, 328–30

The *Scottish Review* was a conservative journal of the serious kind then in its seventh half-yearly volume. It ceased publication during the Boer War. The five Gissing novels which appeared under the Smith, Elder imprint were reviewed in it, but the author does not seem to have been aware of any of these notices.

Demos has reached us too late to occupy the prominent place due to so powerful and important a publication. It is a book not only to read, but to mark, learn, and inwardly digest; a most thorough exposure of that most transparent of shams, so called 'Socialism', pitiless in its calm completeness, and total absence of any animus, or trace of personal feeling. The author keeps himself entirely out of sight; he deals with a class which it is abundantly evident he well knows, and tells his story with straightforward vigour and directness, and but little attempt at literary polish, and leaves it to point its own moral. By the simple means of truthful portraiture, he shows that the motive force which underlies a fiery crusade on behalf of the oppressed wage-earning class is a selfishness as absolute as any which has helped to produce the evils against which it declaims. The lowest, most ignorant classes, are to be roused to a ruinous attack of brute force upon capital, for, in spite of specious assurances, that is where it must end, nominally for their own benefit, really, that by their means their leaders may obtain wealth, notoriety, or whatever else may be the object of their vulgar personal ambition.

Richard Mutimer is, perhaps unconsciously, at least at first, a sham from first to last—a sham revealed by that crucial test, the sudden acquisition of wealth; for there is no greater fallacy than a belief a man's character is changed by his becoming suddenly wealthy. The change simply brings out what is in him, by removing restraints imposed by less independent circumstances. Mutimer, the zealous champion of the oppressed wage-earning class, become a capitalist, professes to devote his wealth to the benefit of 'the Propaganda'; is by no means a specially lenient master; is feverishly anxious for vulgar applause, and personal prominence, and in order to associate himself more closely with the class he has denounced, is guilty of the meanest treachery. The sudden collapse of his fortune is evidently just in time to prevent it from being withdrawn from the service of 'the cause', and devoted to more personal uses. There is keen irony in two incidents in the course of the story. First, in the evident willingness of Mutimer, the man born and bred as a mechanic, to commit a felony, rather than give up his own possession of that capital which he had denounced as an iniquitous thing; while his wife, one of the hateful upper class, will willingly face the life of a mechanic's wife in London, in order that justice may be done. Second, in the final catastrophe coming to pass through Mutimer, back in his old character as a social agitator, inciting a large number of the working class to invest their savings in just one of those schemes which would be impossible but for the existence of that accumulated capital which he has spent his life in denouncing.

'Arry Mutimer is significant in evidence of how soon the socialist millennium would find itself face to face with a dangerous class, well instructed by its teaching in the advantage of the application of brute force to the acquisition of prosperity.

On the whole, *Demos* appears to us one of the most valuable publications we have seen for a long time, and should its full significance come home to the class of which it treats, we only hope the writer may never find himself recognized in 'Commonwealth Hall', or any other seminary for the diffusion of the doctrine of universal brotherhood.

20. Unsigned review, *New York Daily Tribune*

9 May 1886, 10

Reprinted in the *Literary News*, June 1886, 174.

In the United States, *Demos* was published by Harper & Brothers as No. 522 in their Franklin Square Library. As in the English edition the author's name was not revealed. The *New York Daily Tribune* headed its review: 'A Conservative Novel—Socialism and Romance'.

This book has caused a stir in English literary circles, and not without reason. It is a powerful story on a subject just now of general interest. It exhibits a remarkable knowledge of the habits of thought and action of the British working classes, and also of the *bourgeoisie* or middle class.

[Here follows a summary of the story.]

Incidentally much light is thrown upon English socialism. It is seen in several aspects. There is the so-called socialism of the working classes, which is represented as little else than a willingness to go to assembly rooms and listen to ranting speakers, whose abuse of capitalists tickles the ears of the audience, without suggesting to them any change in their habits of life. After these speeches they adjourn to the public houses, and over a social glass criticize the orators freely, laughing among themselves at the revolutionary sentiments, and not affecting to regard them as anything but claptrap. The conservatism of the British working man is well illustrated, and the completely superficial character of his dalliance with socialist doctrines. Then there is the philosophic socialism of Mr Westlake (possibly meant to represent William Morris), who edits a socialist journal of a semi-aesthetic character, and has a young wife whose exalted ideas fascinate every one, but are at the same time thoroughly unpractical. Finally, there is the small band of extremists, who swear by the *Tocsin*—a sheet of the *Freiheit* type, which approves assassination, advises the working men to 'arm', and indulges in all the incendiarism that can be ventured upon without incurring an indictment. The *Tocsin* is read with a certain relish, for your British working man likes plenty of savor in all his food, both physical and intellectual, and whether eating pickled whelks at a street stall, or purveying his Sunday literature, he insists on hot and spicy provender—pepper and vinegar in abundance.

So he reads the *Tocsin* and approves the hard names it applies to the 'bloated capitalists'. But when it comes to leaving the work that brings him his weekly wages, in order to parade about the streets or to get in collision with the police, this lukewarm socialist will none of it. . . .

The story . . . is full of sound reflection and vivid description. But it is essentially English in the thought that underlies it. *Demos* teaches the immutability of class distinctions, and, consequently, the futility of the socialist, nay, of the democratic movement. It is not the lack of knowledge, of education, that wrecks the Mutimers. It is the want of that subtle, indefinable superiority of character which is assumed to be incapable of attainment save through generations of higher culture. . . .

The philosophy of *Demos* is in fact an old-fashioned Tory one. It is uttered by Hubert Eldon and Vicar Wyvern very plainly toward the end of the book. It involves the belief that modern progress is all wrong; that the masses are really not unhappy at all; that possessing lower sensibilities and desires and aptitudes, they can enjoy life quite as much as their social betters do; that work and wages sufficient should satisfy them, and would but for the pernicious chatter of philanthropic and socialist writers; that the really unfortunate class to-day consists of those who are educated beyond their positions and opportunities, and fitted to appreciate all that wealth can procure, are doomed to hopeless poverty.

In that, the story is a protest against democratic progress quite as much as a picture of the socialist movement in England. It is written with rare force and still rarer depth of reflection. It exhibits, with pitiless clearness, many of the evils which seem inseparable from modern civilization. But at bottom it is an expression of that conservatism which makes the background of revolution, and at the same time the writer is too clearsighted not to recognize the uselessness of remonstrance, the inevitable advent of the coming change.

21. Julia Wedgwood, *Contemporary Review*

August 1886, l, 294–6

Frances Julia Wedgwood, a friend of Robert Browning, was a writer on contemporary social and religious subjects who achieved a small prominence in the intellectual life of her time, because among other issues of her strenuous objections to vivisection.

If the moral colouring of fiction be a faithful reflection of that which pervades the life of its time, we should say that this must be overshadowed in our day by some influence that brings into sharp relief whatever is perplexing, disappointing, and bitter. Perhaps the fact that the novels before us present for the most part a dark view of life might to some minds suggest the opposite view: it is the young who love tragedy, it is those who know nothing of actual, who delight to dwell on the description of imaginary, woe. Still the tone of fiction does on the whole form an index to what we may call the *spirits*, as distinct from the *spirit*, of a particular time, and so far as it goes we must allow that it bears witness to some influence depressing to ours. It is the chill, and not only the storm of life which we feel here; love is disappointing, not only disappointed; life is arduous, sordid, full of anxiety; poverty is crushing, wealth is corrupting. And while the shadows of earth are more visible than they were, the light of heaven is less visible; this world, while it is more naked than it was, is not more beautiful, and the other world is faint and dim. . . .

[A paragraph discussing *Hurrish, A Study* by the Hon. Emily Lawless follows.]

Demos is more ambitious, and more disappointing. It is less pathetic, though not wholly without pathos, and its characteristic is cleverness rather than power. Yet it has much of all that the ordinary novel-reader demands—plot, dialogue, and to a great extent character; and the writer has one great artistic advantage for treating his subject—his sympathies and his opinions run in different channels. He knows and sympathizes with the working class, while his opinions, we should say, are Conservative. The artist should always have his sober sense on one side, and his feelings on the other—that combination of Jacobite sympathies and eighteenth-century opinion which gives Scott his steadiness of hand and firmness of touch, being the typical instance of their union. But the opinion and feeling are not blended here in the same catholic union; the sympathy sometimes fails, the opinions are indistinct, and yet give too much colouring to parts of the story. Several of the subordinate figures are drawn vigorously; the vulgar young Radical strikes us as clever, and the Socialist's mother and sister are distinct and lifelike. But power fails where it is most needed. The chivalric figure—it is thus that we presume the heir whose fortune is delayed by a lost will is intended to impress the reader—is a mere flat wash; and the democrat, though more distinct, is fitfully drawn, and seems hardly the same at first and last. The most touching character is the sempstress, the first love of the Socialist hero, deserted on his accession to wealth, in whose room at last, when pursued by a howling mob, he seeks shelter and finds death; and the impression she leaves on the mind somewhat relieves the hard and dreary feeling with which one closes the book. Its lack is conviction. The plans of the Socialist are, we are made to feel, mere poisonous error; but his rival has no plans at all, and merely wishes to undo what he has done. If we are invited to contemplate a problem, we should feel there is a solution somewhere. Surely the moral of *Demos* does not need preaching. Are there not enough indolent and luxurious *nouveaux riches* who waste their money on no mistaken efforts to benefit their brethren?

ISABEL CLARENDON

June 1886

22. Unsigned review, *St. Stephen's Review*

3 July 1886, 23

As his publisher (Chapman & Hall) sent him no reviews of *Isabel Clarendon*, Gissing saw only a few notices. He pasted four in his album of cuttings; he had gathered twenty-one for *Demos*.
The *St. Stephen's Review* had very strong conservative tendencies; it had recently acclaimed *Demos*, seeing in its author a man of conservative temperament and anti-socialist conviction.

Isabel Clarendon by George Gissing, is as much like *The Basilisk* as *The Mysteries of Udolpho* is like the *Ordeal of Richard Feverel.* Mr Gissing is evidently a great admirer of the greatest of our living novelists, but George Meredith is not a writer who permits of imitation, his wit is too incisive, his imagination too subtle. Yet Mr Gissing has succeeded in writing a most excellent story and in sketching a man of the type of Kingcote, given as a careful study of an abnormal psychologic development. The man whose extreme sensitiveness has rendered him utterly indolent can never be a pleasing person, but he is scientifically accurate. Debarred from joining in what the world calls its pleasures, they yet receive full heritage of its misfortunes. That Kingcote should have fallen in love with a woman like Isabel Clarendon, who is a perfect woman, but a woman of society all the same, is only natural, and that he should have afterwards found that she was quite incapable of appreciating his passion of feeling for his agonies is equally true to that phase of mental growth which Mr Gissing has laid himself out to follow. Isabel Clarendon I have called a perfect woman. She is lovable, queen-like, and beautiful, but she is weak, the creature of her environment, and when she meets Kingcote, though she loves him better than she has ever loved any one before, his super-subtle flame of love doesn't satisfy her, and she learns to forget him. Women must have passion, and can forgive jealousy, but they must understand the one and feel the other. Kingcote's burning words, coming from the spiritual side of the man, excited by love, fell upon the animal side of a woman in love. So the novel ends sadly, as it should do. It is a most delicate piece of work, and the minor characters are all as carefully drawn as those of hero and heroine. All may not feel the scientific truth which the story of *Isabel Clarendon* illustrates, but all will acknowledge that the novel is thoroughly readable, and far beyond the average.

23. Unsigned review, *Scotsman*

8 July 1886, 7

The *Scotsman* was a liberal daily founded in 1817 which regularly devoted columns to discussions of literature. All but four of Gissing's books were reviewed in it from 1880 to 1906.

No one who read *Isabel Clarendon* will hesitate to pronounce it the work of a man who is something more than a clever writer. Mr Gissing brings a fresh and original mind into the field of fiction. He does not follow the beaten track. His plot, if it may be called a plot, is not of any of the fashionable patterns. We are not sure that, as a mere story, *Isabel Clarendon* gains by this. Those who read novels for the story only may, in fact, be warned off the ground. Events do not take the course that the habitual novel reader would predict or desire, and the narrative simply stops like that of an epic, and is not nicely rounded off and finished according to the recognised and on the whole excellent practice of novel-writers. The reader wishes that characters and events had turned out differently, and when he gets to the end there are several points on which his interest and curiosity are not satisfied. For all that the story is possessed of an interest which to those who can enjoy an original study of character will be absorbing. From a dramatic point of view this is one of the freshest and most powerful fictions by a new writer that has appeared for a long time. Kingcote, who is the Hamlet of the tragedy, is a remarkable study of a mind of peculiarly fine fibre afflicted with a fatal morbid taint, which, in spite of the amiability, nobleness, and even active goodness which distinguish him, makes his life a misery to himself and others. Isabel is a less peculiar, but singularly perfect representation. Her passion for Kingcote seems at first sight inexplicable both in its genesis and its endurance, till her history and position are well considered, when it will appear a master-stroke of art. Every character is distinctive. Ada Warren ranks with the two just mentioned in importance and felicity, but the more ordinary persons are admirably fitted to their parts and are each as true as life. We cannot particularise further; but we have no hesitation in saying that this is a drama in the form of a novel which will repay not only perusal but study.

24. James Ashcroft Noble, *Academy*

10 July 1886, xxx, 24

James Ashcroft Noble, a journalist and critic, was the author of *Morality in English Fiction* (1887), *The Sonnet in England, and other essays* (1893) and *Impressions and Memories* (1895).

Many mournful memories conspire to prevent one from opening with very high expectations of pleasure a book with an unfamiliar name on the title-page; but *Isabel Clarendon* has none of the ordinary characteristics of a first novel. Mr George Gissing, who is apparently a new writer, must in his time have filled a good many waste-paper baskets with his tentative efforts, for there is nothing amateurish in the story by which he introduces himself to the novel-reading world. *Isabel Clarendon* is above all things a mature book; and such faults as it has are the faults of a man who has deliberately formulated certain principles of art, not of one who fumbles on without any principles at all and describes the process as 'writing under inspiration'. Mr Gissing is probably, like Gautier, rather contemptuous of inspiration, and his book has not a single character or a single situation which is not clearly the outcome of laborious and intelligent study. In following the practice of Mr Henry James by leaving nearly all the threads of his story hanging loose at the end of the second and last volume, I cannot help thinking, with due humility, that he is mistaken. I cannot escape from the old-fashioned opinion that if a man sets himself to write a story it should *be* a story with a fore-ordained and inevitable close, which leaves behind it a sense of imaginative satisfaction. But writers like Mr James and Mr Gissing think otherwise; so their readers must needs be content with the goods the gods provide. In *Isabel Clarendon* there is certainly ample material for contentment. It is impossible to be quite sure that one understands the nature of the hero, Bernard Kingcote, whose capacity for self-torment seems to have in it a touch of insanity. But, without understanding, one can recognise the sympathetic subtlety of the portraiture; and the character of Ada Warren, which presents fewer difficulties, is an imaginative triumph. Indeed, the book has so much interesting matter that one would like to linger over the enjoyable things which it contains; but this is impossible, so I must regretfully content myself with recommending it heartily to that cultivated class of readers who seek in fiction what Mr Matthew Arnold says is to be found in good poetry—a 'criticism of life.'

25. Unsigned review, *Saturday Review*

10 July 1886, lxii, 58

Mr George Gissing resembles the father of the doll's dressmaker in at least one point, which, let us hasten to say, is not his fondness for 'three-pennorth rum.' He is 'man talent.' Unluckily, however, his judgment by no means equals his talent. Nothing can exceed his scorn of barbarians who have the healthy tastes of Englishmen for fighting and bodily exercise, and pursuing the birds of the air and the beasts of the field, unless it be his indulgent contempt for the female counterparts of the said barbarians, whether their tastes lead them to matins or Captain Marryat. Mr George Gissing is advanced, agnostic, anti-optimist, antagonistic to social conventions, *omne quod incipit in a*, in short. His heroine is a young lady who remarks 'I am an Atheist' to a total stranger. His hero is one of the dyspeptic persons who, instead of going into a monastery, as in former days (where at least they plagued nobody but each other), mope and moan about the world without the pluck to do or the power to enjoy anything. He himself (the author, not the hero) has a fondness for formulating the most delightfully positive aphorisms. 'Fearlessness is generally equivalent to lack of imagination,' 'The demonstrative affectionateness which is a proof of incapacity for deeper emotions,' and so forth. In short, Mr Gissing would appear to have read George Eliot to his wounding, and more modern chatterers on Socialism and the Supernatural and so forth to his hurt. Yet, as we have said, he is a man of talent, and even of considerable talent. Not only does he write well, but he has no small power of interesting the reader—power which is all the more remarkable in that his characters, as may be guessed from what has been said already, not unfrequently verge on the preposterous, and that the actual story which he has to tell is of the thinnest possible kind, almost thin enough to satisfy Mr Henry James or Mr Arthur Hardy. That a person with neither means, connexions, nor energy of any kind, having attracted the favour, or rather the caprice, of a woman of more amiability than passion, and very much addicted to the vanities of this present world, will not keep her affection if he does not strike while the iron is hot may be said to be a proposition likely to commend itself beforehand to the most humble intellects; and the same may be said of another proposition—to wit, that a frivolous and selfish man of the world will not be constant, either when he is poor to a pretty girl who has no fortune, or when he is rich to an ugly one whose fortune is more than likely to pass from her. Yet such interest of the story kind as the book has consists solely in the establishment of these indubitable verities. Its action is very limited, and it closes with a new beginning in the shape of a broad hint that the two deserted ones are going to console themselves and each other. On the other hand, as a study of character it is almost equally inconclusive. The jilted hero is, as has been said, a wofully feeble vessel; and, as Mr Gissing either does not see or does not care to express the humorous as well as the sentimental view of his character, the result is anything but satisfactory. Isabel Clarendon, the incarnation of amiable selfishness, is an ambitious attempt, with some good touches about her, but somehow or other wanting the breath of life; and Ada Warren, the atheistic and ugly young person of vast undeveloped capacities in the way of intellect, goodness, and even beauty, is shown as little more than a very crude child, whose absurdities and ill manners are just excusable on the score of a constitutional pain in her temper and a rather false position. And yet the book is decidedly interesting in its way. With a good shaking Mr Gissing might do much.

26. Unsigned review, *Guardian* (London)

15 September 1886, xli (2), 1364

Mr Gissing's novel is a strange compound of force and weakness. It has one woman's character—that of Isabel Clarendon, whose name is the title of the book—which is a masterpiece of invention and execution. It sounds like a paradox to say so, and yet it is true that both the charm of this woman and the originality of the study depend on the fact that the character is after all an essentially commonplace one. She is a very nice woman, with nothing extraordinary about her. She does wrong, and owns it humbly; she has plenty of intelligence, but no genius; she has affections, but is not passionate; she has a conscience, but not a morbid one. Everybody admires her; all men worship her. She craves for love; she likes admiration, but she does not flirt. She has prejudices, and she knows they are prejudices, and tries to conquer them without succeeding. She fears poverty, and marries unworthily to escape from it; but after all she is not a worldly woman—only a coward. And all this is worked out with a delicate, affectionate carefulness which makes this one character a delightful feature in the book. To set against it, however, there is a background of plot which is exceedingly unpleasant. Moreover the story is told in a manner against which we must protest very strongly. It is, in truth, only half told—some of the most important circumstances are only hinted at, the relations between the characters who are brought together in the story are left uncertain, and the imagination of the reader is kept constantly strained in unpleasant directions. Of course this sort of reserve has always one reason: the author fears that he will outrage the reader's taste if he states his plot in plain and full language. But the compromise does not really get over the difficulty. To those readers who can follow the suggestions, a story hinted is as good—or rather as bad—as told; to those who only imperfectly understand, it is almost sure to be worse. In any case a book so written must stand condemned as a work of art; confusion of purpose is not more surely fatal to effect in composition than uncertainty of interpretation is to enjoyment. Much of what we have said about the plot, we would apply also to the philosophical tendency of the book. That Mr Gissing does not look at the problems of life from the orthodox point of view is clear. It is not clear, however, what is his point of view. There is a note of despair in most of the reflective passages, and one character, an interesting young woman called Ada Warren, declares herself an atheist. She is very disagreeable and very plain at the beginning, but in time she develops into good looks and greatness of character. The heroic part in the book is given to her, and she does one act of noble unselfishness; but the process by which her better self grows is not made very intelligible, nor do we feel at all sure how far Mr Gissing approves of her. Does he mean us to understand that atheism is the last word of human wisdom and that it is a word of despair though not of sin? If so, he would have done better to make his meaning clearer. There is a great deal of skill in the construction of the subordinate characters in the story, and the conversations are well managed. The morbid man who is too fastidious to live in society and too weak to live alone is a particularly clever study, but he is rather too large for the story.

THYRZA

April 1887

27. Unsigned review, *Athenaeum*

7 May 1887, 605

Gissing wrote to his sister Ellen after reading the following account of his novel: 'In the *Athenaeum* you will see a notice; they put me at the head of novels of the week. Thank heaven, I shall not be obliged to see other reviews. Is it conceivable that a man or woman could write weaker and more uncritical stuff than this? Such a being must lack, not only brains, but common feeling. But then these people do not read the books in reality; they haven't time' (unpublished letter, 7 May 1887, Berg Collection, New York Public Library).

He returned to the subject a week later: 'Bertz writes that *Thyrza* cannot possibly be popular, because it has no plot. I myself thought and said the same, yet look at the amazing first sentence of the *Athenaeum* review. Nay, there is no understanding it. The quotation on the title page is from the glorious idyllist Theocritus. It means "But we heroes are mortals, and being mortals, of mortals let us sing." Alas, how little these reviewers comprehend (apprehend, I should say), of my real meaning. In truth I think of very little but Art, pure and simple, and all my work is profoundly pessimistic as far as mood goes. Never mind, if I live another ten years, there shall not be many contemporary novelists ahead of me, for I am only beginning my work' (from a letter to his sister Ellen, 14 May 1887, *Letters of George Gissing to Members of His Family*, p. 193).

There is much more of a plot in *Thyrza* than there was in Mr Gissing's last story, *Demos*. The plan of one is not altogether dissimilar from the plan of the other: we have in each an enthusiastic man attempting for himself and others to work out the higher life under unfavourable circumstances, and in both cases the cares or joys of the world prevent the growth of the good seed. In addition Mr Gissing has repeated one or two of his old characters, and has perhaps drawn unconsciously from Arthur Donnithorne his humble friend Adam. Be this as it may, he has been conscientious over his work, and has written a very good story indeed. That is to say, the plot, though elaborate, is consistent and well proportioned; his heroine and most of her friends are distinct persons, animated by thoroughly natural feelings; and his effects are produced in a perfectly legitimate manner. Thyrza Trent is a child of nature sadly out of her element in the narrow streets of Lambeth; she beats herself against her bars, and receives more than one ugly bruise. As a matter of fact, every one of Mr Gissing's characters receives ugly bruises; not one escapes without painful experiences and sobering chastisements. The three volumes are full of disillusions, and many readers will consider some of the incidents needlessly sombre; but in power and pathetic treatment the novel is above the average.

28. Unsigned review, *Whitehall Review*

12 May 1887, 20

This conservative periodical, which had attacked *Workers in the Dawn* but paid homage to *Demos*, published the following appreciation under the title 'A Novel of the People'.

The anonymous author of *Demos* emerged, some time since, from behind the veil which he was pleased to draw around his name proper, and stands confessed in the present day as a certain Mr George Gissing. Whether this be his own name or one chosen for publishing purposes will doubtless transpire in course of time. He has certainly no reason to be ashamed of allowing the world at large to become possessed of all particulars concerning himself that concerns the public, for his powers are very far above the average, and we must welcome him as a very promising recruit in the literary ranks. Before dealing with *Thyrza* at full length we would like to relieve ourselves publicly of the firm conviction that 'George Gissing' is of the feminine gender, in spite of his swashing and martial outside, but, if we are mistaken, we offer humble apologies, at the same time that we intend to rest on our conviction until we have very good proof afforded us of its truth or the reverse. *Thyrza* is a story of one of the 'people'. A dweller in the East End, making her living at lining hats, mixing with her own order, who in real life are not conspicuous for refinement, yet Thyrza is as lovely as a houri, and as well-mannered (indeed better-mannered than some) as a duchess. The story of her life is a distressful one, because it is so marred by untoward circumstance, and she goes from one trouble to another until the reader feels that the release which awaits her is as merciful as it is abrupt and ill-conceived. The book as a whole is profoundly imbued with despondency—the despondency, however, of a thoughtful and cultured mind—and it is full of the gloom which a study of real life must ever cast on him who studies it. It deals, as all Mr Gissing's books have hitherto dealt, to some extent with a social phase which has seen a wide development among us of late years, and that is the attempt to bring two opposite classes of people into more friendly and intimate relations with each other. But of late years the subject has been treated as a matter for patient research, and the dwellers in the West have penetrated into the East, doing some good, and a vast deal of harm. Among the good may be counted such books as this one of Mr Gissing's, which is doubtless the result of experience poetised by the hand of genius. It does not deal with the lowest class of all, but more especially with the men and women of the working-class, whose wits have been sharpened by long struggle, and whose senses have been alert from childhood in that keenest of competitions—the winning of the daily bread. Chance introduces these recipients to books, the contents of which are accepted by the sharpened wits and the alert senses, and so a smattering of education is secured which ripens into knowledge, and blossoms into attainments that rise to the surface and make their mark sooner or later. Of such men Gilbert Grail in Mr Gissing's book is an excellent example, and it is perhaps due to her acquaintanceship with him that Thyrza is so very much above the average of the East-end hat-liner. The love element of the story is all worked at cross-purposes, and on the principle of I love thee, thou lovest some one else, he loves her for a time; and, while the common-sense reader argues that it is remarkably true to life, the romantic reader will find fault with the crooked ways into which love twists itself in Mr Gissing's hands. The book depends on no ingenuity of plot or exciting incidents for the success which undoubtedly it is but it is a finished piece of work, both as a novel of remarkable character studies and as a narrative. Mr Gissing writes gracefully and in good taste, with plenty of vigour and strength of a most promising kind. We have few novelists in the present day who outrival him in quiet power and intensity, or who can approach his perfectly level method of thought and feeling.

29. Unsigned review, *Saturday Review*

11 June 1887, lxiii, 847–8

The same journal gave a further favourable review of *Thyrza* when, after the success of *New Grub Street,* Smith, Elder issued a second revised edition in one volume. In this later review (17 October 1891, lxxii, 450) Gissing was warned against 'an excess of sentiment or a too-rose-coloured view of the society he described'. That he should be regarded for once as an optimist rather amused him.

Thoughtful novels have to be very good to achieve success. Therefore, Mr George Gissing, who now declares himself to have been responsible for *Demos,* a thoughtful novel which attracted a good deal of attention a year or so ago, is a noticeable recruit in the select ranks of the particular industry now under consideration. Every page of *Thyrza* is thoughtful; but there is also a good deal in it that is attractive, and very much that is powerful. The hero is named Walter Egremont, and he is a prig *comme il y en a peu*. His father had been a workman; but he made a fortune, and brought up Walter as a gentleman. The consequence was that the young man spent his time in weighing his own soul (and finding it wanting) and his money in pedantic schemes for the improvement of other people. This brought him into relations with Thyrza, a weak-bodied and weak-minded working-girl. Her soul was a very sponge for softness and expansiveness, and consequently it turned out thoroughly unpractical, and burst its earthly shackles at an early period, much to the advantage of the society in which she moved. This society was that of the respectable slums to the south of Westminster Bridge Road (a road which appears to the superficial observer to run north and south, but in reality runs east and west), and Mr Gissing either knows by experience, or intuitively divines, quite as much about it as George Eliot did about English Jews. His description may be faithful or it may not, but it is wonderfully vivid and picturesque. Thyrza, being engaged to Egremont's principal workman *protégé*, falls desperately in love with Egremont, and he with her, though he does not avow his passion. Great complications and profound though high-toned misery naturally ensue, and form the groundwork of the story. The plot might have been compassed by any one of a thousand living authors; but the crowd of people incidentally introduced are admirable. Egremont, his workman friend, whom he unwittingly betrays, and his associates generally, have a great many discussions about how they can best do each other good; but Mr Gissing, like a shrewd observer, brings their machinations to nought, and the more they meddle with other people's affairs the greater grief they come to. This is as it should be and as it would be, and Mr Gissing deserves credit for it. Eventually a marriage is arranged between Egremont and a pleasant young lady, whose principal weakness is being, and having for some years been, in love with him. It is more than he deserves, and it is particularly irritating that he by no means adequately appreciates his good fortune. Naturally enough, there are a few affectations of language to be found in the book. 'Quieten' is not English, any more than 'The sweet lips that so passioned for his.' These errors are worth censuring because they are deliberate. Probably no one alive is entitled to make new verbs intentionally; certainly Mr Gissing is not. There is a great deal of good stuff in the book, but it is almost exclusively among the thoughtless poor of Lambeth. An old atheist, and his courtship of (and by) a rattle-pated Roman Catholic workgirl, are particularly pleasing; and there is a clever sketch of a modern member of Parliament. In one scene of Egremont's Mr Gissing rises to genuine tragedy. This is where Thyrza's two lovers meet for the first time after the collision of their affections, and it is a really good bit of work. There is no disputing that Mr Gissing has unusual ability.

30. Unsigned review, *Murray's Magazine*

June 1887, 864

This monthly publication had been launched in January of the same year.

This is a no less remarkable book than *Demos*, and though there are fewer stirring incidents, the characters are truer to life and inspire more sympathy. The interest of the story is concentrated in Lambeth, where Thyrza lives, a lonely factory girl whose 'cabin'd ample spirit' yearns for a fuller life. There are touches of great pathos and beauty in the description of her love for the young idealist, who, in his attempt to raise the working man by the gift of a library, becomes the cause of sorrow and uprooting. The lives and surroundings of the hard-working poor are described with rare insight and vividness, and therein lies Mr Gissing's especial power. It is a grey world that he draws; but if his tone is somewhat morbid, it is redeemed by the earnestness and force with which he writes.

31. Unsigned review, *Guardian* (London)

3 August 1887, xlii (2), 1161

Thyrza is in many ways a very striking book. Mr Gissing has succeeded in laying before his readers a very lifelike picture; the characters are well and vividly drawn, and the story is full of interest throughout. The conversations are good and never drag, and there is enough humour to lighten the book and make it extremely readable. The hero is a young man named Egremont, who has inherited a share in a large manufactory in Lambeth. He is an enthusiast, and resolves to devote his life to improving the social and intellectual condition of the working classes in Lambeth; for this purpose he forms various schemes, such as the giving of lectures, a free library, &c. In the course of these he comes across one Gilbert Grail, a grave, clever, thoughtful man, whose work lies all day at a candle factory, and who with difficulty snatches a few hours at night for reading. Egremont selects him as librarian, and Grail thereupon asks the heroine Thyrza, who, with her sister Lydia, lives in the same house, and works at a hat factory, to marry him. She is quite young, and though she does not love him, she admires and reverences him, and consents. Then comes the catastrophe. Egremont and Thyrza meet and fall in love with each other. Nothing is said, but each separately realises what has happened. Egremont goes abroad, hoping on his return to find Thyrza married to Grail, and Thyrza, feeling that the marriage is impossible to her, runs away from home, and finds a place in a shop. There she falls ill, and is eventually found by Mrs Ormonde, a charitable lady, who is a friend of Egremont's. Grail, having by some ill-natured gossip discovered how the matter stands, resigns the librarianship, and all Egremont's hopes of reforming Lambeth come to an end. It is arranged between him and Mrs Ormonde that he shall go to America for two years, during which time she undertakes that Thyrza shall be educated, and if at the end of that period he is still of the same mind he is to ask her to marry him. This conversation is overheard by Thyrza, who is accordingly buoyed up during the two years by the hope of marrying Egremont, and she thinks only of fitting herself to be his wife. He returns at the appointed time, but his love for Thyrza is gone. Still he considers that he is bound in honour to her; but when Mrs Ormonde tells him that Thyrza is happy without him, he receives the news with relief, and makes no attempt to see her. Thyrza when she realises this gives him up, and finally dies. The plot is intricate, and there are many side developments and incidents, besides a great number of other characters; these, however, in almost every case directly affect the story, and up to the end of the second volume we have no fault to find with the construction of the book, except that the incident on which the whole turns—namely, Thyrza's overhearing the conversation between Mrs Ormonde and Egremont, seems to us hardly worthy of the position which the author gives to it. But in the third volume we have an entirely new episode, and two new characters, Harold Emerson and his wife, are introduced, who are made much too prominent; in fact, the third volume, with the exception of two or three scenes of considerable power, is distinctly inferior to the other two. Thyrza and her strong, sensible, faithful sister Lydia remind us to some extent of Effie and Jeanie Deans, but they are by no means copies. Thyrza is a beautiful creation; the pathos of her character, and the description of her pure, passionate nature concentrating itself in love for Egremont is admirably done. She is a distinct addition to the heroines of fiction. Mr Gissing knows the poor of London well, and it is depressing to find that he takes for granted an almost universal indifference to religion amongst the men. We notice by-the-bye that although he often mentions the Roman Catholic Church and 'chapel,' he never once alludes to any Anglican Church except Westminster Abbey, and that is for the historical not the religious associations. It is not easy to make out what is Mr Gissing's own opinion in the matter, or whether he sympathizes with the efforts made by Egremont and Grail to meet the indifference to, and in some cases the hatred of, Christianity with lectures and dissertation on the 'beauty' and 'profound spiritual significance of the Christian legend.' But whether he sympathizes with this mode of meeting unbelief or not, he at any rate acknowledges its failure. Bunce, the good, upright, but unbelieving artisan, with his hatred of Christianity, founded, as usual, on gross ignorance and misconception, is not likely to be impressed by a man who urges him to take 'what good there is in Christianity,' that is, the beauty and aesthetic part of it, and 'have nothing to do with the foolish parts'—i.e. the dogmas. But whatever Mr Gissing's religious opinions may be, there is no doubt that he has written a very good and interesting novel, and has considerably raised his reputation as an author.

32. 'George Gissing as a Novelist', *Pall Mall Gazette*

28 June 1887, 3

Gissing declined to send this article to his relatives at Wakefield as it displeased him in many respects, although it was obviously intended as high laudation. On 10 July 1887 he commented in a letter to his brother: 'Poor stuff said to be written by Stead.' *Letters of George Gissing to Members of His Family*, p. 197.

William Thomas Stead, a prolific writer on political and religious subjects, was to become the editor of the *Review of Reviews* at its inception in 1890.

It was, apparently, through his publisher, George Smith, that Gissing heard of the supposed authorship of this article.

The publication of *Thyrza* has definitely revealed to the public the authorship of *Demos*, although for readers of George Gissing's earlier works the identity of the writer can hardly have been an unfathomable mystery. For *Demos* emphatically displays all the qualities which distinguished *Workers in the Dawn* and *The Unclassed* from the ordinary three-volume novel of the day, and it is unspoiled by many of the defects of its predecessors. It is equal to them in vivid description, in courageous presentation of truth, in profound and sympathetic knowledge of the lives of the London poor; it surpasses them in artistic completeness and in literary finish. As a novelist George Gissing has undoubtedly advanced in his art; but it is not as a novelist, in the narrow sense of the word, but as a social reformer and as an eager student of social life, that he occupies so important a place among living writers. For putting aside *Isabel Clarendon*, which seems to us curiously inferior to his other work, and leaving *Thyrza* for later consideration, the three novels mentioned above may all be classed as books with a purpose. Let not the intending reader take alarm at this definition. It is not a case of unwelcome moral platitudes being dragged in when least required, or of an impossible story specially invented for the elucidation of the author's favourite hobby. They are novels with a purpose, in the same sense as Balzac's *Comédie Humaine* are novels with a purpose. They are dramatic expositions of modern life in all its pathos and often in all its hideousness, left to point its own inevitable moral. *Workers in the Dawn* and *Demos* both deal with different aspects of that ever-present problem, the condition of our working classes. *The Unclassed* deals with a subject which most novelists deem advisable to leave untouched, but which the author rightly believes cannot possibly be left on one side, if any truthful picture is to be given of city life. Ladies in their drawing-rooms may persistently shut their eyes to what they prefer to ignore, but the position of their fallen sisters is brought every hour of the day before the eyes of the working classes, and on the whole Mr Gissing is to be congratulated on the manner in which he has fulfilled his task. No one, had they never extended their acquaintance with London beyond that small section familiarly spoken of as the West-end, could doubt the truth of his descriptions, and for those who possess some knowledge of the localities he describes, the accuracy is only the more striking.

The main interest of Mr Gissing's novels lies, however, in his conception of human character, with its capacities for freedom and development. And here it is impossible not to observe a decided falling off in his belief in human perfectibility. *Workers in the Dawn* and *The Unclassed*, painful as they often are in their vivid realism, are yet pervaded by an unshaken hope in better days to come. It is not the men and women, it is the social system which is to blame. As long as men like Samuel Tollady and William Noble are to be met with why need we despair? As long as women like Ida Starr can raise themselves by dint of sheer courage and unselfish love from degradation to virtue, no one will deny that all good results may be hoped for. But in *Demos* it is far otherwise. The reader lays down the volume with a feeling of pained disappointment. He has been expressly told that 'Richard Mutimer represented too favourably, to make him anything but an exception, the best qualities his class can show.' And what is the result? Having unexpectedly inherited a large fortune, Mutimer throws over the girl he was engaged to marry, entirely fails to appreciate and almost ill-uses the wife he selects, relinquishes by degrees all his best principles, and, though maintaining outwardly his political beliefs, relapses at last into a mere blustering demagogue. Is the British workman 'at his best' so little capable of using the gifts of fortune with wisdom and moderation, or would Mr Gissing have us believe that the possession of wealth is inevitably productive of gross selfishness even in superior natures? No hope is to be gathered from *Demos* for the future of the English working man, and it is just because no one can doubt that the author has studied long and earnestly the socialistic problem, that the feeling of depression at his conclusions is so strong.

Will Mr Gissing's ultimate reputation as a novelist be raised by his latest work, *Thyrza*? We almost fear not. It will no doubt be pronounced by the ordinary subscriber to Mudie as much the pleasantest of his books, but the pleasantness has been obtained by the sacrifice of much of the individuality. It is a much slighter story than its predecessors: Thyrza Trent is a Lambeth working girl, very delicately drawn, even idealized, we should say, were not the idealization of his characters so foreign to Mr Gissing's habit. She breaks off her marriage with a man in her own class of life, owing to a frantic passion for Walter Egremont, a young man of philanthropic proclivities; Thyrza waits patiently and hopefully through a probationary period of two years, during which the lovers are bound not to meet, only to find at the end her own love more ardent than ever, while Egremont's has faded away. Although social questions occupy a secondary place in *Thyrza*, the tendency, as in *Demos*, is towards despondency. Gilbert Grail's life is only saddened by his keen intellect and literary tastes in hopeless struggle against the exigencies of daily manual labour, and Egremont's well-meant endeavours to brighten the lives of his fellow men end in abject failure. For the first time, too, the author displays a tendency towards the Christianizing of his characters, who until now have invariably been of an advanced freethinking type; thus, whereas Helen Norman found consolation in a broad acceptation of the doctrines of Comte, Lydia Trent is helped to happiness by a regular attendance at chapel. It would be premature to conclude that Mr Gissing's own religious views have undergone considerable modification, but it will be interesting to observe the theological tone of his next novel.

An important point in the estimation of a man's creative talent is the amount of success with which he delineates his female characters. In the present case the success is only partial: some, indeed, are charmingly conceived and drawn; others, like Isabel Clarendon, Helen Norman, and even Adela Mutimer, sadly want a vivifying touch, and the sketches of Society damsels are hopelessly unreal. The truth is that Mr Gissing's secret is not so much imaginative power as knowledge, coupled with dramatic expression, and this fact becomes obvious whenever he strays on to unfamiliar ground. Moreover, he never shows us the humorous side of life; throughout he takes life seriously, and it is only due to his talents to judge his writing in the same spirit. There is no English novelist of the present day better qualified to speak in the name of the English working classes; the study of his books is both a pleasure and a profit to the reader and we sincerely hope that in his future work Mr Gissing will confine himself to those phases of life with which he is familiar, and that there will be no falling off from the very high standard of excellence attained in *Demos*.

33. Edith Sichel on Gissing, *Murray's Magazine*

April 1888, 506–18

Edith Sichel (1862–1914) was an amateur memorialist and literary critic, mainly remembered for a few works on the French Renaissance. Provided with ample means, she could indulge in reviewing, essay-writing and philanthropy as so many hobbies. When she published the following article, 'Two Philanthropic Novelists: Mr Walter Besant and Mr George Gissing', she was still unknown. Gissing read her article on its appearance with a mixture of pleasure and irritation—pleasure to see his works the subject of a long article and placed alongside those of Besant, a writer of established standing, irritation because Miss Sichel had avoided all *literary* criticism. In his correspondence with his relatives he denied that his books were merely monochromatic, mentioning Totty Nancarrow (*Thyrza*), the Westlakes and Letty Tew (*Demos*). *He* did not pass abruptly from buffoonery to seriousness, as Besant did. Edith Sichel had expected to be thanked for her efforts but, when a year had passed and no token of gratitude from Gissing had reached her, she chose to wring some reaction from the author by writing to him through his publishers. There followed an interesting correspondence on literary subjects in which he sharply rejected the idea that he wrote with a philanthropic motive. His masters, he said, were the novelists of France and Russia. The only English contemporaries whose work in the field of fiction he cared for were Meredith and Hardy.

On Edith Sichel, see *Old and New*, by the same, with an introduction by A. C. Bradley (Constable, London, 1917) and *Edith Sichel: Letters, Verses, and Other Writings*, dedicated to her friends by Emily Marion Ritchie and printed for private circulation, 1918.

Nowadays everybody is turning their attention to that many-headed monster Demos. Even Mrs Grundy is shaking her poke-bonnet and muttering that the times are out of joint. Trafalgar Square, on the one hand, is flooded with demonstrations; Belgravia, on the other, broaches theories after dinner over its port wine—or even from its sofas. Amateur Philanthropy has become as fashionable as Amateur Theatricals have hitherto been.

Now, although this may have its absurd side, as is indeed necessary with any dilettantism, we cannot but own that the tendency is good. We are at any rate awake. Self-interest—the only true alarum for the majority, alas!—has roused us, and we see that some attempt at solution of social problems is necessary to our safety. Hence, the philanthropic atmosphere which is gradually spreading from the slums of St George's-in-the-East to the very halls of My Lord and Lady Dives, has penetrated into every region of daily life, and more especially into literature. We have had the Historical Romance, the Mystic Romance, the Social Romance, the Psychological Romance; it has remained for the present day to give us the Philanthropic Romance. It must yet be seen whether such Romance will answer its purpose. To us, at least, it seems more probable that the public will take its ugly lesson of hometruths in the form of a pleasing tale, which has no pretensions to be personal, than in the direct and dull shape of long statistics. And if the novel can thus succeed in turning people's thoughts and energies towards undeniable evils, without sensationalizing them, it will indeed have fulfilled a mission which has not been attempted since the days of *Aurora Leigh*.

True, we have had Mrs Gaskell and Charles Dickens, both of whom described the poorer classes with master-pens; but Dickens, in so doing, confined himself to the exposure of particular abuses, and beyond this, had little or no purpose of their mental improvement. *Oliver Twist* was certainly not written to induce reform amongst thieves, and theatrical effect is often his sine quâ non; whilst Mrs Gaskell, who possessed all the purpose, confined it to the interests of the Manchester millfolk, wrote of what she knew, and only solved such problems as came beneath her eye—thus leaving a purely local and temporary answer to purely local and temporary questions. It must also be added that even Mrs Browning's task was easier than the latter-day novelists'. She was a poet, writing in poetic form, and possessing all the advantages offered by that form. For in poetry, when difficulties loom around, we are relieved by beauty of diction and imagery, and are often carried away by the loveliness of those indefinite ideas and ideals which the poet alone is allowed to give as a cure for minute, statistical evils, such as really need the most practical and specific remedies.

These remedies the novelist, who has not the protection of poetry, is supposed to provide. He is exposed on the dead-level of bald prose, and has no refuge anywhere, so that every vagueness, let alone inaccuracy, is at once eagerly spied out by the argus-eye of popular criticism, and brought home to him without loss of time. Every honour is therefore due to the spirits who have attempted a labour beset with so many hardships, however incomplete the result; and it is with all gentle courtesy and absolute humility that we approach the work of the two leaders of this genus of Romance—Walter Besant and George Gissing.

They may be considered as representatives of the two schools of Philanthropy—the Optimistic and the Pessimistic—Besant taking the former, and Gissing the latter point of view. It will be interesting for a moment to inquire which method, according to their own showing, proves the most effective. This is the easier as their mise-en-scène is much the same. They neither of them, as a rule, describe the lowest of the low. Besant generally prefers the hardworking sempstresses and day-labourers of the East-End. Gissing keeps to the artisan and better sort of work-girl in Lambeth, Holloway, or the like. They are thus far in accord that they both acknowledge this class to be the best material to work upon, and both preach that prevention is better than cure. Strangely enough, too, they see many of the same good qualities in this material, and it is mainly in their view of the possibilities of the qualities that their difference consists—the difference of long and short sight, of focus rather than of the eye itself. But this is large enough to fix a great gulf betwixt them and to hinder all further resemblance.

Let us take the two most characteristic novels of each of these men, and briefly sketch their plot and result. *All Sorts and Conditions of Men*, and *The Children of Gibeon*, are perhaps Besant's—*Thyrza* and *Demos* Gissing's most typical stories. We will begin with *All Sorts and Conditions of Men*.

Angela Messenger, a student from Nuneham and the heiress of a huge brewery, wishes to use her wealth and learning for the good of the people, and on leaving Cambridge, where she has studied the Social Sciences, she takes lodgings in a boarding-house at Stepney Green and lives there *incognita*, conceiving that her only chance of helping those below her is to live as they do. The same mode of life has simultaneously been pressed upon a young man, Harry Goslett by name, and the adopted son of a lord. When the story takes place, the lord thinks fit to reveal to him the real facts of his parentage, and tells him that he adopted him as an experiment, and took him away from his home for that purpose. His father had been a common serjeant, and had married a woman of his own class. On learning this, Harry determines to give up the luxury which is not his birthright, and to live and work amongst his brethren. He finds shelter beneath the same roof as Angela, who gives herself out as a dressmaker, and he becomes her *aide-de-camp* and the furtherer of all her plans. Angela begins by forming a dressmakers' association, supposed to be self-supporting and cooperative, but in reality maintained by fictitious orders from 'Miss Messenger.' She takes a house in which they work, ventilates, adorns, and amplifies it—prepares a gymnasium and a tennis-ground, and forms an evening club of entertainment, where, with Harry's help, she teaches music and dancing. In a short time this *regime*, together with improved diet, produces marvellous effects. The girls without exception grow refined, both outwardly and inwardly, and Angela and Harry, believing that culture and pleasure will do away with all spiritual ill, and that association (which according to them is the end of these means) will abolish physical evil, end not only by matrimony, but by planning the Palace of Delight which is built out of her fortune. This institution is intended to embrace every sort of pastime and instruction; it is a small world, including technical schools, schools of all sorts (in connection with board-schools), dancing-rooms, concert-rooms, theatres, statue and picture-galleries, industrial exhibitions—every pleasure in short which can be imagined, and some of which may indeed now be seen in the People's Palace, built in the Mile-End Road, on much the same site as here planned. The book winds up with the opening ceremony.

The Children of Gibeon is merely a variation on the same theme, except that it more specially demonstrates the wrongs done to the sempstresses. In this case, an aristocratic lady adopts the daughter of a laundress and a burglar, and brings her up entirely *incognita* with her own daughter, so that nobody—not even the girls themselves—knows which is which, though the story of the adoption is common property. She also sends the plebeian's brother Claude to the University, and invites him to her house when her daughters are twenty, merely saying he is the brother of one of them. After this the former plot repeats itself. One of the girls is sensitive and artistic, and shrinks from the life of the poor, though why Mr Besant should oppose the artist's nature to the philanthropist's remains questionable. The other, Beatrice, feeling sure she is the adopted girl, becomes fired with the notion of life with her brethren, and goes to live in the East-End, in the same house as three sempstresses (one her supposed sister), whom she gradually conciliates, though they are at first hostile. Claude constitutes himself her protector, and shares her ideas. When the two girls come of age their parentage is revealed to them. Beatrice turns out to be the real and Viola the adopted daughter, and the curtain drops on the marriage of Claude with Beatrice, and their withdrawal to the scene of her former labours, where they resolve to live, and to consecrate life to philanthropy. We leave them and Mr Besant, all delightfully certain that they can reform the ills that flesh is heir to, by means of a 'Brotherhood of Labour,' a 'Sisterhood for the Protection of Workwomen,' a 'Street Committee for Sanitary Improvements,' and an 'Earthly Tract Society' for the diffusion of pamphlets inducive to culture.

Now let us turn to Mr Gissing's books. Here we have a very different picture. Solomon gave us to understand that there was no new thing under the sun; but Mr Gissing does not even allow us the sun to be under. He is mentally colour-blind, and whereas Mr Besant paints in perpetual *couleur-de-rose*, Mr Gissing revels in the blues. His descriptions, his thoughts, his characters, abounding as they do in power, are one and all monochromic without relief.

In *Thyrza* a young man named Egremont, a strong Idealist, whose father was a self-made man, but who had himself received a University education, conceives great theories for the regeneration of the people, with whom the factory possessed by his father in Lambeth puts him in easy relations. Wishing to realize these theories, he begins by taking a room and there lecturing on English Literature, and afterwards on Modern Thought. He has amongst his audience every specimen of the most intelligent artisan; but about the only man on whom he makes lasting impression is one Gilbert Grail, a workman with a passion for reading, to whom Egremont's teaching seems of real value. Grail is reserved, proud, and intelligent, as men of his class are, but eventually becomes intimate with his lecturer, and aids him in all his philanthropic plans, espcially in the arrangement of a Free Library, on which Egremont was then expending most of his energy. Just at this time Grail becomes engaged to Thyrza, a work-girl who lives with her devoted sister Lyddy in the same house as himself.

This Thyrza is certainly an exception amongst her fellows, which is perhaps accounted for by the fact that her mother was a teacher. At any rate, she possesses the typical artist nature, with a glorious voice with which to express it. Fiery, impressionable, thirsting for love, she accepts Grail's offer of marriage rather from respect than affection.

Egremont meanwhile settles Gilbert's pecuniary prospects by making him his librarian at the new library, where he and his wife are to live. Not long before the day fixed for their wedding, Egremont sees Thyrza at the library for the first time. This is the beginning of sorrow. In spite of his struggles, and against his will, he falls in love with her, and she with him. She breaks off her engagement with Grail, who, by reason of his education and of all the gentle instincts it has engendered, feels his trouble as no common man could. He has always felt the cruelty of a fate which gave him the passion for learning, and at the same time tied him down to mere manual labour; but now he is more bitter than ever. Thyrza, meanwhile, in despair at her conduct, disappears, thinking this kindest to Gilbert. The passion which has grown up in her heart seems to her inevitable; her truthful, impulsive nature makes the tie of marriage with Grail a disloyal impossibility, whilst her refined instincts and intense temperament make sorrow prey doubly upon her also. She finds work as a servant in an eating-house, hides her whereabouts, falls dangerously ill, and is eventually discovered by Mrs Ormonde, a philanthropic lady and a friend of Egremont's, who has known his story throughout. When Thyrza gets well, she separates her from her belongings, and trains her for a singer, hoping to make her forget her love in work. As for Egremont, his lectures had all failed long before this affair—the audience had dropped off, and Grail alone had remained—Grail, whom he had only succeeded in making more unhappy. His library having now also failed, as Gilbert of course resigns his post, Egremont retires to America, and grows less morbid in the backwoods. He has given his word to Mrs Ormonde to keep away from Thyrza for a certain number of years, and keeps his promise. At the end of that time his passion has cooled. Misled by the philanthropic lady, who acts from the best motives, he believes that Thyrza has forgotten him, and he marries an old friend—a scholarly icicle with a great many 'motives,' and jogs through life contented, but never quite happy. Thyrza has all this time kept faithful to him, and dies of a broken heart. Grail withdraws in utter misery to Battersea, and the only person who is eventually happy is the unselfish Lyddy, Thyrza's more commonplace sister, who is strong in plain action, not in intellect, and who marries the man she cares for. We shut the book, convinced that, according to Mr Gissing, any effort is failure, idealism a lovable folly, the practical philanthropist an impossibility, pleasure for the poor a false existence, only bringing them still lower, and culture, above all, an irretrievable mistake.

Demos is just as saddening, if not more so. It is written to prove the errors of Socialism and the impracticability of equality. Mutimer, a Socialistic workman, comes by an accident into a large estate, and marries a lady—a girl in the neighbourhood, who is persuaded into the match by a worldly mother. Mutimer is a shrewd, clever man with a strong will, who was eminent so long as he stayed in his own class, and whilst the necessity for work subjugated his brutal instincts and uneducated thirst for power. But his good star waned when he came into his property and deserted the work-girl, to whom he was originally engaged, for a well-born wife. Socialism he only uses as a means to push himself; and although he forms model works and a model village community on his estate, and spends thousands on them, it is only to bring him into Parliament. The book exists to prove this, and to unfold the degrading misery of his wife, who is daily exposed to his coarseness and incongruous habits of thought and life; also to demonstrate the ruin of the rest of his humble family by their sudden acquisition of wealth. He eventually falls a victim to his own cause. The Socialists begin to mistrust and hate him, and end by hounding him to death. He is pursued by the mob, and takes refuge, horribly mutilated and half dead, in the house of his quondam love, where he dies disgracefully. His wife ends by marrying a man whom she had loved before her first marriage, and the last scene again leaves us with the depressing feeling that there is no such thing as success or happiness in the world, let alone the fitness of things, and that every other man is moved to action by self-interest pure and simple.

'We are interesting,' says the author in this book, 'in proportion to our capacity for suffering, and dignity comes of misery nobly borne.' 'We are interesting,' says every one of Mr Besant's books, 'because we can enjoy ourselves, if our capability of happiness be properly developed.' Both have caught hold of a half-truth—one writes to prove the success, the other the failure of Idealism. The one wanders out with all the hopes of an intelligent child, and loses himself in the vague, satisfied as a rule, by rosy mists and melodious generalities. The other is hemmed in by a throng of hideous facts, and, not being tall enough to see beyond them, sinks to the earth crushed by utter despair. The one is the literary progressionist, the latter-day Oedipus, who has found the answer to the Sphinx's riddle; the other is the thorough Conservative, who being powerless to prevent the 'progress' to which he ascribes all the ills of the world, has nothing better left him than to sit and bewail them—the more zealously that he is presumably, at present, a convert from the Radicalism of youth. Starting from such opposite standpoints, although both of them have the same feelings and therefore wish for the same end, their minds are so different that the means that each proposes for this end, lie as widely as possible apart. Gissing has but one—the Tory ideal—the re-establishment of a Lilliputian Feudal System adapted to the needs of the nineteenth century. 'Let us,' says he, in the person of Mr Wyvern in *Demos*,

'effect the substitution of human relations between employer and employed for the detestable "nexus of cash payment." That is only a return to the good old order, and it seems to me that it becomes more impossible every day. . . . I denounce the commercial class, the *bourgeois*, the capitalists, call them what you will, as the supremely maleficient, the intellect of the country is poisoned by their influence. They it is indeed who are oppressors; they grow rich on the toil of poor girls in London garrets, and of men who perish prematurely to support their children. . . . What is before us? Evil. . . . Progress will have its way and its path will be a path of bitterness. . . . Two vices are growing among us to dread proportions—indifference and hatred. The one will let poverty anguish at its door, the other will hound on the vassal against his lord. . . . Let us raise our voices, if we feel impelled to do so at all, for the old simple Christian rules, and do our best to get the educated by the ears.'

Nor can he tell us how to arrive at the means that he thus recommends. Being himself, as far as his books reveal him, devoid of any conviction, even the conviction of doubt, he fails to give us any solution, or to offer us either the guidance or the confidence which he lacks himself. We feel more inclined to try and comfort him than to receive any explanation of life from him. It seems indeed as if, in hopeless confusion and tossed on the unstable waves, yet abhorring compromise, he wrote rather to make himself clear to himself and as a personal relief, than for any altruistic purpose.

Now let us turn to Besant and hear what he has to say on these topics. Popular Radicalism he opposes with all his might, fathoming the fallacies of the demonstrative demagogue with a strong sense, curiously diverse from the dreamy indefiniteness of so much of his work. It is only literary Radicalism, if we may so call it—the Radicalism of social theories and political generalities, rather than the localized rules and scientific formulae of practical politics—which he advocates. Listen to the speech, in *All Sorts and Conditions of Men*, which Harry Goslett makes at a working-man's club in answer to a certain demagogue called Dick Coppin.

'Whether the House of Lords, or the Church, or the Land Laws stand or fall, that, my friends, makes not the difference of a penny-piece to any single man among us. . . . It comes of your cursed ignorance. . . . You think that Governments can do anything for you. Has any Government ever done anything for you? Never—never—never. Because it cannot. Does any Government ask what you want—what you ought to want? No. Can it give you what you want? No. . . . Whatever you want, *you must do for yourselves*. . . . Now then, what do we want?'

He then continues with a list of the measures which he considers certain to produce reform. 1. Local Government. 2. Cheap food. 3. Improved houses, of which the working-men themselves should be the inspectors. 4. Improved Board School education (which Goslett declares has hitherto been all 'Kings of Israel' and 'spelling'), and the sending of their 'own men to the School Boards to get that thing done.' 5. Pleasure (for says he, 'You can't play music, nor sing, nor paint, nor dance—you can do nothing'), and the substitution of holidays at different times for the set Bank Holidays. 6. Co-operation for the improvement of the women's wages and condition.

Now this is all very well; and doubtless the measures suggested by Mr Besant would produce, if not the perfect cure he seems to anticipate, at any rate considerable improvement. But although association, to which he *does* definitely point as a potent aid, already within popular power, would doubtless go far to better the wages and hours of working-women, or even to produce the alterations in holiday-making which he deems so important, still it would hardly affect the laws of commerce and of population, on which the price of food is really based—or the fact of over-population which governs competition. Nor could it create the appreciation of the 'pleasure' provided, which is the real essence of pleasure. For you may have as many concerts, picture-galleries, and standard play-houses as you like, but if the appreciative feeling be not there, the pleasure can no more exist than sound for a stone-deaf person. But when we ask how we are to reach these goals, our Oedipus can give no other clue than the aforementioned association—nothing more practical than a Brotherhood of Labour, to include both men and women as workers, and to control work and wages alike—further forbidding the men to marry under thirty and the women under twenty-five; not to speak of the Earthly Tract Society and the Street Committee which we have before mentioned. And when these are established, 'there will come,' he hopefully writes, 'a time—one sees it already in the close future—when the pickpocket shall find no home anywhere and the burglar no place to store his swag and keep his "jemmy," when all evil-doing shall be driven out of the land, and faith, goodness, charity, hope, and the love of beauty and the desire for art shall spring up like flowers in the sunny month of June, and the men shall at last join hands, and shall swear by the living God—the women shall no longer be robbed and wronged.'

But this is hardly sufficient answer to such facts as he mentions in connection with the proposed institutions.

'Elevenpence-halfpenny a day and fourpence for the workbook, which you can get for a penny outside, and if you dare to complain they make it sixpence. There's machine-work and shirts at a penny apiece; we can get twopence a dozen for the button-holes; there's bottle-washing for five shillings a week, and cigar-making for the same. There's the dust-yards and the sifting at a shilling a day.'

These are rigid details which require rigid measures, alas! and not only generous dreams from our armchairs, over our evening fire; for it is thus that Mr Besant always seems to us to be writing—from out the midst of a cozy haze of blue tobacco-smoke, and in a study adorned by Apollos and Venuses, Michael Angelos and olive-green books, together with all the suggestive appliances of a modern culture. Mr Gissing, on the contrary, writes from a back-alley reeking with putrid vapours, strewn with blackened orange-peel and resounding with hideous din, so that he cannot even hear the voice of Nineteenth Century consolation. The one worships culture for all men, and cries out that nobler pleasures should be provided for the poor; the other declares that 'universal education . . . works most patently for growing misery . . . Its results affect all classes and all for the worse'; whilst his 'heart bleeds for the class created by the mania for education, and consisting of those unhappy men and women whom unspeakable cruelty endows with intellectual needs, whilst refusing them the sustenance they are taught to crave.' As for pleasure, he says: 'Go along the poorest street in the East-End of London and you will hear as much laughter, witness as much gaiety, as in any thoroughfare of the West—laughter and gaiety of a miserable kind—I speak of it as relative to the habits and capabilities of the people.' It is curious to remark here, that the pessimism of Mr Gissing, which allows him to believe in none but the blackest of futures, causes him at the same time and from sheer hopelessness to accept the present with much more resignation than the optimistic Mr Besant, who sees a golden time coming, but meanwhile takes the gloomiest view of popular happiness as it exists at this minute. But this is perhaps the case with every optimist and pessimist—for whereas the former, who is perpetually living in radiant plans, must necessarily be perpetually crushed by reality, and thrown into corresponding depths; the latter, knowing no help for matters but blind endurance, has no refuge but philosophy, and sits down, with the quiescence of a man who waits patiently by the wayside because he sees no end to his journey.

Here again both these authors seize half a truth, and both, consequently, become guilty of half a falsehood. This one-sidedness, which weakens all their work, seems due to a certain want of proportion which is common to both of them, and which may be called lack of humour in its largest sense. Without this last-named faculty, a heart-whole view of life is a sheer impossibility, and we therefore find that Mr Gissing writes us a realistic jeremiad, whilst Mr Besant gives us a Bowdlerized Whitechapel—a family edition of the East-End, which is wholesome for our hopes, but often not so true a picture as the other.

Meanwhile these two agree strangely in some things: in their hostile mistrust of politics, for instance; above all, they unite in believing that Religion, as they separately understand the word (though both use it to express an earnest and defined conviction of some sort), will alone redeem the working-classes: that their ruin lies in their having lost this, and in their growing indifference and consequent incapability of action. But whilst Mr Besant prays for the new creed and for Comte's edition of Christianity, Mr Gissing invokes the old letter and the old spirit—for others, even if not for himself.

Indeed, the main difference between them lies in the fact that Mr Gissing looks for salvation from the upper, and Mr Besant from the lower classes. This naturally affects their whole view of things, and more especially of the working-man and the philanthropist. In the former, and the possibilities within him, Mr Besant is, as we have seen, an ardent believer. Mr Gissing, on the contrary, regards the faults of the working-classes as radical differences and positive evils, not merely as undeveloped germs and negative good. 'The fatal defect in working-people,' he writes, 'is absence of imagination. Half of the brutal cruelties perpetrated by uneducated men and women are directly traceable to lack of the imaginative spirit, which comes to mean lack of kindly sympathy.' Now lack of imagination is a solid fault, which cannot be changed in the individual, but which it will take centuries of patient effort to influence, and whilst the last-named author asserts the absence of any sympathies, Mr Besant is assuring us that it is only when we educate these non-existent sympathies that we shall certainly find Utopia.

We detect the same tone with regard to their relation towards the philanthropist. Talking of Dalmaine, the self-interested, pushing politician in *Thyrza*, Gissing observes: 'These men are the practical philanthropists, and to sneer at them is very much the same as to speak contemptuously of the rain-shower which aids the growth of the corn.' In the ardent worker and in personal influence he has no faith, and only looks for success from such efforts as spring from the hope of personal advancement.

On the other hand, 'Let us all go and live in the East-End,' sings Mr Besant, who holds this out to us as his second panacea—the complement of association. But he forgets that we have ties at home as well as abroad, and that if we all lived in the East-End, the West would be empty, whilst an already terribly overcrowded neighbourhood would become still more overcrowded; he does not see that trade would die, that culture, conversation, ideas, and literature would sicken for want of proper surroundings, and of that variety of topics on which they live; above all, that we should have no fresh air-current to carry Eastwards. He forgets that philanthropy means love of mankind, not of one particular section of mankind; that the rich have claims on us as well as the poor, and that the higher duty often lies in a proper combination of both elements. Modern asceticism differs from mediaeval asceticism, in so far as it takes for its end the redemption of humanity instead of personal salvation; but a convent life is not confined to four walls. We may be monks and nuns in the midst of a crowd, and none the less narrow than those of old, because our cells live within us, instead of our living within them.

But no critic of any tone, however insignificant (indeed, the more insignificant he is, the more imperative would seem his obligation) can end nowadays without a final lunge at the fault which he has made his monopoly in an author, and which is probably his own besetting sin. We will therefore repeat that this *idée fixe* of Mr Besant's seems again to spring from that same lack of proportion which causes extreme views both in him and Mr Gissing, and makes them blind themselves to the sensible safety of the Via Media. They should examine how far they allow their own natural favouritism for pet theories to block up their horizon. Mr Gissing's resolute wailing is surely disproportionate, and though no one could accuse Mr Besant of too much lamentation, still unfounded ecstasies are also want of symmetry, and persistent glee about non-existent joys is not sense of humour.

Mr Gissing, who starts by telling us that he 'concerns himself with facts,' and that 'the great fact of all is the contemptibleness of average humanity,' does doubtless hold the most courageous position, for he faces, nay, he over-faces truth. It is a diseased truth which he gives us, devoid of sweetness and devoid of faith and hope. Happily morbidity is not the reality of life, and we feel that there is a weakness about the eyesight which can only see 'contemptibleness' in that 'average humanity' which is, after all, composed of most of our friends and relations, even though, in this case, the failing springs not from pride, but from despondency.

Mr Besant, on the other hand, continually gallops away from truth, on a very high horse indeed, or hides it from himself in a pink-silk veil. But it is fair to him to say that this foible does not arise from cowardice, but from a humane shrinking from the realising of other people's sorrow, and from an intense need of faith in his fellow-creatures. He is indeed the best to work upon—the best in ideal, though Gissing be the best in fact; and if we could only join his aims, his buoyancy and his elastic power of planning, to the latter's love of truth, of facing the worst without flinching and of describing what he sees, we might perhaps find at least the alpha of the Sphinx's enigma. Meanwhile, whilst we remember the truth of Mr Gissing's pictures, we will not say with him that 'to sleep is better than to wake; and how should we who live bear the day's burden, but for the promise of death?' We will rather dream our dream, in the conviction that it will gladden our realities, as music the fight, and we will believe with Mr Besant, that 'There are so many joys within our reach; there are so many miseries which we can abolish . . . we shall all together continually be thinking how to bring more sunshine into our lives, more change, more variety, more happiness.'

A LIFE'S MORNING

November 1888

34. Unsigned review, *Saturday Review*

1 December 1888, lxvi, 650

It is some years now since Mr George Gissing began to write novels in which the vigour of individual thought attracted as much as the tone of bitter and defiant pessimism repelled. Perhaps the repulsion outmeasured the attraction; for Mr Gissing's books, though they have a reputation, are scarcely popular. They probably never will be as long as the common taste is for the sweet and smooth. It has been laid down as an axiom that the man who says he likes dry champagne will say anything. It is a true saying of many men, and perhaps of all women. The tonics Mr Gissing administered to the social world, which he saw so plainly to be sick, were bitter enough to wry the palate. He found things wrong, and he used the rough side of his tongue to say so. Time has apparently softened the asperity—which, indeed, never was cynical. *A Life's Morning* has a great deal of the melancholy of Mr Gissing's former books, but it has a wider sense of beauty and a broader feeling of human possibilities. The style is tense; and, though Mr Gissing is an entirely original thinker and writer, one notices here and there the influence, for good, of Mr George Meredith, and the example, for ill, of George Eliot. Some of the sentences in this novel might be quotations from *Theophrastus Such*. The value of the story, however, lies in the noble conceptions of character given in the two women who play unequal parts in their influence on Wilfrid Athel, who is intended to represent modern youth in its most intellectual aspect. Emily Hood is drawn with all the care and power of which the author is capable, and this is saying very much, to represent the ideal of pure womanhood. Her name is 'written in starlight.' Beatrice Redwing is a striking contrast to her—rich in beauty, youth, and wealth, genius, and social rank; and when the crisis comes, most readers will think

Beatrice rises in self-sacrifice above her rival. Mr Gissing will have to submit, we imagine, to the verdict of most of his realistic readers that Beatrice is the prize better worth winning than the lonely, faded, poverty-struck, humiliated governess; and that when Wilfrid gave up Beatrice, his position in Parliament and the fashionable world, the 'phantasmagoric drawing-rooms,' for solitude with Emily, he was abandoning realities to walk with his head in the 'starlight,' where Emily's name was written. Yet there may be some who will not think so, and will believe the author has proved his case. The 'phantasmagoric drawing-rooms' is a very illustrative phrase in Mr Gissing's philosophy. To these Beatrice would speed away to shine among the brightest 'from praying by the bedside of a costermonger's wife.' And why should she not? And why should a drawing-room full of educated men and women be more phantasmagoric than a costermonger's squalid room? After all, the classes have souls to be saved as well as the masses. Mr Gissing's sympathies are intensely with the poor, the weak, and the suffering; and it is almost with surprise one notes his concession of true nobleness of spirit to a girl who has fourteen thousand a year and who shines in drawing-rooms. A few minor characters move round the three central figures, minor only in the sense that all cannot play leading parts. Some of the pleasantest scenes are devoted to the excellently drawn matron, Mrs Baxendale, the Athel interior, and the lamentations of the unfortunate Mrs Hood. Mr Gissing in these regions permits more free play to the humour he possesses, but which he keeps too rigidly apart in general from his views of life. The episode of the disgrace and death of Emily's father is in itself a tragedy; and the struggle in the moral nature of Dagworthy, Emily's dangerous lover, with its result in his permanent degradation, is perhaps too strongly described for artistic effect. It seems in its intensity to throw the hero's figure into shadowiness. We will not, however, quarrel with an author for being too uniformly impressive in his delineation of character, though a lighter touch in ordinary narrative would be pleasant as a background. To speak of 'the parks, where fashion's progress circles to the "Io Triumphe" of regardant throngs' seems to soar a little above the level of Rotten Row.

35. Unsigned review, *Athenaeum*

8 December 1888, 770

Two days before the following notice appeared Gissing wrote to his friend Bertz:

> Never yet have I known this paper do a generous thing, whilst the mean ones that have come under my notice are innumerable. Again and again I have said to Roberts that I was astonished at its persistency in narrow malice; he observes the same characteristic. I cannot but wonder what clique of men can be responsible for such an ignoble line of conduct. Scarcely ever do they give hearty praise to any book, save those written by two or three authors whom it is the *fashion* to praise. It must be managed by a very small corporation of very silly fellows. And, by the bye, earnestly I implore you not to tell me what it says about my book

(*The Letters of George Gissing to Eduard Bertz*, ed. Arthur C. Young, (1961), 20–1).

Except for a tendency to wordiness and an occasional heaviness of touch, *A Life's Morning* is excellent, both as regards incident and characterization. Mr Gissing understands the value of contrast, and he is equally at home in depicting the angularities of Lancashire life and the graceful repose of a handsomely appointed establishment in the South. His characters do not remain stationary, but are developed both from within and without as the narrative goes on. And as the characters grow so does the interest of the plot, which abounds in strong situations. There is little doubt, however, that the work would have gained by condensation as regards dialogue, description, and commentary. For Mr Gissing is somewhat prone to moralizing, and though he is always thoughtful and intelligent, and occasionally acute, he is loath to say a plain thing in a plain way, and exhibits an unfortunate predilection for ponderous Latinisms which would have irritated the late Mr Barnes. Such affectations of style are to be regretted in a writer who holds a high view of the functions of a novelist, and is obviously animated by a sincere sympathy for all that is best in human nature.

36. Unsigned review, *Court Journal*

29 December 1888, 1516

Undeniably clever and full of somewhat ostentatious theorising upon deep problems of human nature, yet not by any means lacking in the purely human interest which must be conspicuous in the pages of a popular novel, Mr George Gissing's new story, *A Life's Morning*, will certainly find many and avid readers among those who prefer a novel which asks for some exercise of their intellectual powers, and affords food for thought, besides gratifying the taste for an interesting piece of mere fiction. Despite a rather marked tendency towards the use of pedantic diction, Mr Gissing tells an effective story in an interesting fashion; and although the hero is a young gentleman who by the time of his going to school was able to write letters home in a demotic which would not, perhaps, have satisfied Champollion or Bruzsch, but which were sufficiently marvellous to his schoolfellows, and the heroine a woman of an almost equal passion for culture, we find, to our joy, that these learned folk are very human, after all, when once the all-conquering passion comes upon the scene. It is a little alarming at first to be confronted with a hero who has not yet left Balliol, and still finds that his despair is the universality of his interests, whose subject is the study of humanity, who yearns to know everything that man has done or thought or felt, who is, in a word, smitten with an insatiable greed of knowledge, and is man enough to ask, 'Might one not learn more in one instant of unreflecting happiness than by toiling on to a mummied age, only to know in the end the despair of never having lived?' Needless to say the hero, Wilfrid Athel, who rhapsodizes in this fashion, is very young; and needless, also, perhaps, to add that he finds his 'instant of unreflecting happiness' in the love of a woman. The heroine, Emily Hood, is an unconventional character, ably drawn; and Beatrice Redwing is a fine type of noble, beautiful, self-sacrificing womanhood. Other interesting people flit through the author's pages, the course of true love runs roughly enough, and the inevitable element of the tragic is duly introduced. But it is rather for its thoughtful, but not too deep, philosophising and its unconventionality throughout that *A Life's Morning* will be read; and as it is far above the average novel in merit, we trust that it will find wide favour.

37. Unsigned review, *Guardian* (London)

23 January 1889, xliv (1), 136

Mr George Gissing is a novelist who may be counted upon for much that is true to human nature, much that is original, not a little that is beautiful, and a general effect of grim, despairing effort after one does not exactly know what. All these things are to be found in his latest work, *A Life's Morning*. But let no one go to the book in search of the fresh exhilaration of spirits which should belong to the morning of life as well as to the morning of the day. There are two heroines in the story, and each in different ways shows herself made of heroic stuff. And there is one hero—not, in our opinion, heroic at all. Wilfrid Athel is the only son of an English country gentleman, who has made a romantic marriage of the nature of a *mésalliance* in youth; but, having lost his wife, has committed no further indiscretion, and become with advancing years all that a conventional English country gentleman should be. His widowed sister, Mrs Rossall, lives with him, and Wilfrid shows himself the son of his father by falling in love with Emily Hood, the governess of Mrs Rossall's twin daughters. The great fault of the book is that Emily Hood is not an attractive person. The author intends her to be such; he attributes to her beauty, refinement, soul, dignity, virtue, and charm. But he fails to make her live; she remains a catalogue of imputed qualities, and cannot, therefore, justify to the reader the passion of the two men who lose their hearts to her. The other woman, Beatrice Redwing, is, on the contrary, very living, and in her case strong attraction is easier to understand. But here again the author has gone wrong. Beatrice is a creature of fine, impulsive temperament, capable of caprice and folly, but kept straight by finer instincts of unselfishness and principles of religion. Mr Gissing treats all the parts of her character with a sort of cynical impartiality which suggests that the restraining principles are only caprice in another form. The incident upon which Mr Gissing has chosen to make his plot turn is so miserably sordid that it seems to contaminate the whole book. We cannot escape from its depressing influence, and the series of tragic events which follow it affect us like readings from the 'Police News.' The character of Richard Dagworthy, the manufacturer, in whose office Emily's father is a clerk, is the strongest, and in that sense the best in the book. His wooing, coarse and unscrupulous as it is at some points, carries our sympathy as Wilfrid Athel's never can. One feels that if Emily could have married him it would have been the beginning of a nobler life for him, and a more real and human one for her. To sum up, the book is very clever and very dismal. Mr Gissing writes as he always does, in the strenuous manner of a man who has something to teach us. But we fail to find any other moral in his book, but that life is a hopeless and degrading coil for all who have not the means of culture; and that the means of culture are wealth, power, and worldly position.

38. Unsigned review, *Spectator*

9 February 1889, lxii, 204

In *A Life's Morning*, as in the book last considered, we have an illustration of the Second Commandment in the shape of an innocent daughter suffering vicariously for a blameworthy father; and the two works resemble each other also in making study of character their primary object. Yet though the object is the same, the manner of treating it differs widely. For in *A Life's Morning*, motives are exhaustively gone into and examined, instead of merely glanced at from the outside; the sketches are not lightly outlined, but painted in laboriously with a multiplication of touches that occasionally produces the heaviness liable to result from over-elaboration; the prevalent tint is rather sombre than cheerful; existence is seen to be a serious, often painful, and not at all humorous affair, affording ample food for reflection, but little or none for laughter. And though Mr Gissing's performance may be the result of more thought and care than that of Mr Christie Murray,* and display talents of a deeper and more solid nature, we doubt its being as much approved of as the other by the majority of readers.

* Author of *The Weaker Vessel*, a drawing-room comedy which had been earlier considered by the reviewer as clever, entertaining and irremediably superficial.

The most interesting part in it is that relating to the struggle that takes place between the heroine and a rich mill-owner, who is desperately enamoured, and bent upon marrying her, notwithstanding her own strong aversion to the arrangement. 'Amongst vulgar conceptions of the befitting is the self-immolation of daughters (not of sons) on their parents' behalf,' says the author. And the mill-owner being quite of that opinion, gets her father into his power, and forces upon her the odious necessity of choosing between the ruin and dishonour of a tenderly loved father, or saving him by means of a hateful marriage. This is a dilemma in which so many previous heroines of fiction have been studied, that it is not possible to convey very much freshness to the inevitable self-communings and arguments *pro* and *con* which have to be gone through before the decision is finally arrived at; and the amount of interest excited by Emily Hood in so hackneyed a situation, says much for the writer's skill. The male figure most worthy of notice is that of the aforesaid mill-owner, whose rough, forceful individuality, and fierce, violent love, making him cruel to its very object, somewhat remind us of Elijah in *Mehalah*. The legitimate hero, Wilfrid, is a tame, insipid young gentleman, so far from being good enough for the two exceptionally gifted and attractive girls who fall in love with him, as to make us wonder whether the author intended him to exemplify the truth of the old saying that kissing goes by favour.

THE NETHER WORLD

April 1889

39. Introduction to *The Nether World*

Colonial Edition, 1890

The Introductory Note signed 'P.R.' appeared in the colonial edition which E. A. Petherick & Co. issued early in 1890, pp. iii–vi. Gissing had no knowledge of it.

The Roman satirist assures us that

> Want is the scorn of every wealthy fool;
> And wit in rags is turned to ridicule,

and we all know that conventionally poverty is neither poetical nor picturesque, except contemplated in a picture or in a foreign land, decked out in the trickery of a strange garb. The writer who could take up the exposition of low-type industry, who could interest us in real working men and women and the idlers, and worse than idlers, who hang on to the skirts of the industrious poor, and are the real causes of the main parts of the squalor and vice that we see around us; the writer who could eliminate the inherent pathos, the poetry and the humour, that lie latent in what has been termed in the newspapers 'horrible London', and who could show us the true humanities—as Carlyle would understand it—underneath dirt, rags, and repulsive looks, must needs be a strong and clear-visioned and sympathetic soul himself. In the book to which this serves for Preface, we have unmistakable evidence of the presence of a prose Dante of the contemporary poor, whose sombre mood is veined and relieved by a delicate appreciation of all that really preserves the struggling London industrial poor from absolute despair and utter moral shipwreck.

The 'Nether World', in Mr George Gissing's realistic romance of workaday London in the unlovely and monotonous regions of Clerkenwell, relates, of course, to the Inferno of grinding poverty; and in the typical case of John Hewett and his family, we feel ourselves faced by realities, not the abstractions of a socialistic way of regarding poverty as the mere doctrinaire does. Clara Hewett, indeed, cradled in want, a work girl, and once a barmaid, is a distinct creation, and at the same time a subtle and wholesome revelation of the craving for ladyhood that is inherent in some natures, however low their birth, or sordid their material surroundings. Clara and her inward strivings after an ideal of her own, her terrible trials and final misfortune, and her ultimate fate, must be counted as a crowning achievement; while in her relations to her father Mr Gissing has evinced a mingled delicacy and strength and a true insight into the real, not the merely imaginary, workings of the human heart, which carries the reader on from page to page in an absorbing sympathy which is born out of the overpowering realism of this remarkable book. John Hewett, indeed, with his rugged virtue, his friendship for Sidney, in some sort the workaday hero of the more sentimental part of the story, and his determination to marry a girl on whom the stigma of imprisonment rested, is a remarkable character. Equally so is grandfather Snowdon, returned from the Antipodes with a fortune which he will not avow, and his pet theory for educating his neglected and ill-treated grandchild Jane—a slave in a house let out to working people—into the discerning, sympathetic, lady administrator of really effective relief to the poor. But how much more than this we have! Is not poor Pennyloaf—corruption of Penelope in Clerkenwell, where the final 'e' is not pronounced—as comic as aught in Dickens, and yet woful withal as poor 'Jo' of *Bleak House*? In 'Clem', the bold, sensuous, selfish, callous, and physically beautiful London factory girl, we have a portrait true and distinct as Zola ever drew, and entirely devoid of the needless offensiveness wherewith the French master of Realism overloads his life-delineations. Mrs Peckover's lodging-house stands out to the full as distinct as any interior in *The Old Curiosity Shop*, and Jane Snowdon is an affecting study in real child life. The tragedy of Grace Danvers is grim as anything of the kind in *Bleak House*, while Eagles, the hoary malcontent of Clerkenwell Green, who, long before there existed a Financial Reform Almanack, represented the work in his own person, is, like all the rest of the *dramatis personae*, a study from the life.

Then 'Sam' is intensely comic, and quite as distinct a type as Dick Swiveller, while the way in which the irony of circumstance frustrates enthusiasm, even when combined with sterling worth and apparent means, is a true stern lesson read out of the destinies of real men and women. Satire is lavishly mingled with these long and fact-filled annals of the poor; but it is the satire that Humanity loves to use, sword-like, to carve out better terms for the suffering and the oppressed. Touches of real affection too gleam golden-like through the generally selfish and sordid atmosphere wherein most of the characters move and have their being, and go far to humanize much that is otherwise grim and terrible, Rembrandt-like, with a great horror of darkness. Mr Gissing writes with a fearless fidelity to what *is*, and the pathos and passion, wherein the book is so rich, arise out of the exigencies of the narrative, and are not simply grafted on certain prearranged situations. If to reproduce Nature herself is the higher form of literary art, then is Mr Gissing a great artist indeed, and apart from the rich fund of entertainment furnished by an exceedingly interesting narrative, we have much in the book which must rebuke many among us, while presenting from the Nether World of contemporary life many problems of life which are pressing with increasing urgency for solution. In a word, *The Nether World*, besides being a deeply interesting human story, has powerful claims on all who think and feel for their poorer brethren, and as a novel 'with a purpose' has deep significance for all classes of Philanthropists.

40. Unsigned review, *Court Journal*

27 April 1889, 590

It is a tragic, heartbreaking picture, yet not without gleams of hope, which Mr George Gissing paints in his vigorous and realistic story, *The Nether World*. The world in question is that terrible underworld of London, in which exist abject poverty, dumb, miserable despair, the elements of crime, revolution, all that horde of dreadful possibilities which sometimes flit across the brain of society and terrorise it into fitful and fruitless charity. Mr Gissing takes his readers to Clerkenwell—that hive of toiling and moiling human beings, where perhaps the strangest paradoxes in all the working world are to be found; where one man deals in diamonds on the first floor, while in the basement another dies of starvation, and overhead young human animals spend the proceeds of labour in bestial drunkenness culminating in brutal violence. We find ourselves indeed in a 'nether' world—a world the habits, customs, language, hopes, fears, crimes, of which are all so far removed from the smooth surface of well-bred, well-fed society, that we seem to have been suddenly transported, not to another postal district of the metropolis, but to some horrible region of damned souls, such as a modern Dante might imagine as the final punishment of the most degraded types of humanity. We move, shuddering, with the author, through an atmosphere fetid with all the abominations of life in the slums. The writer is sufficiently realistic for us to easily fill in the blanks which he must perforce leave. Yet, terrible as is the picture of depravity which he paints, he gives us also some clever studies which go to prove that even in this 'nether world' pure lives are led, noble ambitions cherished, heroic sacrifices not unknown, obscure martyrdoms bravely borne—by no means rare. The story, although brimful of human interest and possessing an adequate plot, is first and foremost a study—faithful and daringly graphic—of life as it is in a world of which society sometimes hears, but of which it knows perilously little. Mr Gissing's realistic book is one to be read and read again. It contains a terrible warning, but also more than a grain of hope. Its pathos is very true, its tragedy grimmest of the grim, but through its pages run the golden threads of love, purity and nobility of motive, though the lesson of the book will rather be gathered from its pictures of utter poverty and its consequent temptation, degradation and crime. Society knows something of 'slumming'; let it read Mr Gissing's book and it will learn more of that terrible underworld which has obviously been the subject of the author's close and sympathetic study. John Hewett and his poor, patient wife, Clara Hewett, the ambitious, ill-starred Sidney Kirkwood, sweet Jane Snowdon, Clem Peckover, and 'Pennyloaf', are distinct creatures of which Dickens himself would not have been ashamed, and, as with the Master of this school of fiction, broad human charity is the keynote of the book throughout. Mr Gissing's shoulders may yet grow broad enough for the hitherto unappropriated mantle of the great novelist. We shall await his next work with exceptional interest.

41. Unsigned review, *Whitehall Review*

4 May 1889, 19

This review was entitled 'George Gissing's Wholesome Novel'.

The Nether World—a world which no one understands so well as Mr Gissing; a world with which he has the very keenest sympathy; a world of darkness, of sorrow, of vice, of never-lifting blackest fog, of direst want, and bitterest suffering. This is the 'Nether World' of which Mr Gissing writes, in which he places the characters of his story, and from which he never once wanders throughout the course of it. And all this of which he writes so clearly and keenly is surging and heaving under the other life of ease and luxury, of wanton waste, and wilfullest squandering which is led by those whom an accident of birth has placed in the upper world. 'But for God's grace, there goes Richard Baxter!' said that thorough-going old Calvinist, as he saw a man led out to execution, and it is this feeling which prompts Mr Gissing to do what he can for his suffering fellows. Such books as this one do an infinitude of good: they depict human life and human suffering with its marvellous power of endurance in true colours. There is no affectation, no prudishness; no glossing over the horrors of whole families penned in one room; of the circumstance which makes those who are 'born in God's image' resemble the brute beast of earth in everything save power of speech, and yet there is nothing degrading and disgusting, nor anything to revolt those fine 'susceptibilities' of which we of the upper world are so proud, and which we use merely as a cloak for the selfishness and enervation bred of comfort and luxury, in this wonderful story of life amongst the sweater's victims. Mr Gissing devotes his time to a study of this life, and his energies in trying to better it, and to bring home to the rich the reality of 'how the poor live.' There is an immense amount of good done in the present day by philanthropists and others, but so far as it has gone it is only like the pebble wall the child erects on the beach in the innocent hope of stopping the flow of the tide. Mr Gissing's story is a sad one, because it is so terribly true, and we rise from a perusal of his book with a load at our hearts and a feeling of hopelessness, such as Hercules must have felt when called upon to cleanse the Augean stables. And as far as we can see at present there is no Hercules now living, albeit writers of Mr Gissing's stamp resemble him somewhat.

42. Unsigned review, *Guardian* (London)

29 May 1889, xliv (1), 845

It is interesting to contrast this notice of the novel in the official Anglican weekly with the declamatory use made of the novel by Dean Farrar in No. 43.

Mr Gissing's new book again takes us to East London, and introduces us to a crowd of characters ranging from the skilled artisan downwards. It is, of course, interesting and well written; but it has not the power of *Demos* nor is there any character which, like the heroine in *Thyrza*, stands out conspicuously by beauty and individuality above the rest. Sidney and Jane, though meant, no doubt, to be the flowers which, according to Mr Gissing's motto, justify the description and analysis of the rank and corrupt soil in which they grow, are rather colourless, uninspiring figures, good indeed, high-souled, and helpful to those around them, but described without the touch of genius which often marks Mr Gissing's studies of character. On the other hand, the minor personages in *The Nether World* are drawn with all the author's usual force and vigour. Old Hewett and his son Bob, Clem Peckover, Pennyloaf, and the Byasses are all additions to Mr Gissing's grim and depressing gallery of portraits from East London, where they, or their like, may be found in numbers; and they are described with absolute and relentless truth. The quality which distinguishes the author's books from others which describe the London poor is this truth of delineation. He never for a moment idealises his characters; he sees with keenness, perhaps he almost exaggerates, the coarseness of their vices, their lives, their very amusements; and he describes them with what is sometimes almost brutal accuracy. The account of Bank Holiday at the Crystal Palace, for instance, is unnecessarily crude and painful; the want of refinement in the people seems simply to irritate Mr Gissing. It is possible, indeed, that Mr Gissing might not find the amusements of the upper classes a subject for unmitigated admiration; but at any rate this description of the people has in it more of cynical contempt than of sympathy and insight. The book is rather diffuse, the stories of many lives are interwoven, and sometimes the thread of the main story, that of Jane Snowdon, is lost. But the events and characters are so real that interest never flags, for doubtless if the veil were lifted from the lives of the poor in East London they would be found to resemble very nearly those of the persons in *The Nether World.* The most pathetic part of the book is the history of 'Pennyloaf.' Mr Gissing is tender enough to his poor, oppressed women, and draws them with true delicate touches of infinite pity.

43. F. W. Farrar, *Contemporary Review*

September 1889, lvi, 370–80

Frederick W. Farrar, the Archdeacon of Westminster, was a prominent figure in London cultural and religious circles. He was an occasional contributor to the leading reviews and wrote various books of a religious character which enjoyed considerable success. Gissing found his article poorly and coldly written (Diary, 15 September 1889) and made this comment in a letter to Bertz: 'Yes, I have read Farrar's article. To tell you the truth, it struck me as a little insulting; the tone was so very much *de haut en bas*. Only an English cleric would be capable of writing about a book, and never once mentioning the author's name' (*The Letters of George Gissing to Eduard Bertz*, p. 75).

It is not my purpose to review the novel of which the title stands at the head of this paper. I have never been a Reviewer. I have none of the gifts which enable so many Reviewers with consummate skill to be blind to great merits and lynx-eyed to minute errors and misprints. The merits of any book worthy of the name invariably loom larger before me than its faults. If it is animated by a noble and serious purpose I read it with the sole desire to gain what I can from it, and I leave its errors and limitations to be pointed out by others, who will, perhaps, revel in the sense of their own superiority in the contemptuous condemnation of books of which they could not have written a single page. So many of the purest and grandest works of genius with which the world has ever been enriched have been trampled upon by anonymous arrogance, and have continued uninjured their beneficent influence, still 'adding sunlight to daylight by making the happy happier;' and so many books, radically useless and unworthy, have been heralded into life with flourishes of trumpets and indiscriminate praise —only to die before the year is over—that I for one will have as little as possible to do with praising books which are foredoomed to failure, or sneering at books which, whatever may be their imperfections, fulfil in any measure the aims which the authors have set before themselves, and may increase the knowledge or hallow the aspirations of those who read them.

Of the author of *The Nether World* I know nothing, and his previous novel, *Demos*, has left no strong impression on my mind. But his present work is so sombre and earnest in its terrible realism that it will not easily be forgotten by any serious thinker.

And this realism gives to it a far deeper significance than at all belongs to it as a novel. It is well fitted to bring the careless, the indolent, the selfish, the luxurious face to face with problems which it will be impossible for Government or Society much longer to ignore. Those problems make some of us feel as if the splendour and prosperity of the nation were built upon the slopes of a volcano, neither extinct nor even slumbering, but which gives signs, from time to time, that not many years hence it may burst into terrible eruption.

I have called the book realistic, but happily it is an English book, and the reader will find in it none of that leprous naturalism which disgusts every honourable reader in the works of Zola and his school. There is nothing in it which is loathly, nor malignant, nor cynical, though it deals throughout with the ruin and shipwreck of human existence, the catastrophe and horror of hopeless degradation. But as a picture the book is unutterably sad, because it is so disastrously true. I do not know from what personal familiarity the writer may have derived his intimate knowledge of the conditions of artisan and pauper life in the dingiest purlieus of great cities; but after thirteen years, in which I have been made familiar with the condition of things which it describes I can bear witness that not one element of disaster is overcoloured, not one touch of wretchedness exaggerated. It is on this ground that I venture to call attention to the book, in order that the rich and the noble may get to know something of the world which lies beneath their feet, and may lay to heart the awful significance of the facts which are here revealed.

The characters of the book are all typical. Thoroughly natural and individual, they yet represent whole classes to be found in the lower strata of society. There is the young woman, who, with every crude and tigerish element of animalism in her nature uncorrected by a single civilizing influence, develops into a monster of ferocity and cunning. There is the youth—strong, clever, good-looking, intensely egotistical —who, without religion and without a conscience, becomes step by step a felon and a brute. There is the married woman who has taken to drink, whose room is decorated with old pledge-cards of total abstinence which she has repeatedly violated, who is assaulted and beaten into an unrecognizable mass of bruises by the husband whom she has driven to desperation, and whom she consigns to prison; who is then deserted by him; who, with her eyes open to her fate, drenches herself with thick, drugged, stupefying beer, whenever she can beg, borrow, or steal twopence; and who is dragged hell-wards, daily, by the flaming fiend of habit. There is the needle-girl, with her helplessness, her nerveless imbecility, her utter ignorance, her dolorous prettiness, her thriftless marriage, her half-starved children dying about her like flies. The writer chooses for the motto of his book the sentence of Renan, 'La peinture d'un fumier peut être justifiée pourvu qu'il y pousse une belle fleur; sans cela le fumier n'est que repoussant.' These grievous specimens of humanity are foils to two characters—a working man and a working girl—who, although they are unable to emerge from the misery through whose muddy and shoreless tide they have to swim for their very lives, yet retain to the last their moral nobleness.

No less true to fact are the pictures of the scenes in the midst of which these characters move and have their being. Readers may here learn something of the indescribable tyranny often exercised in low houses over the little slaveys-of-all-work. They may begin to realize the chronic misery of an artisan with a superfluous number of rickety and ill-conditioned children, who have no prospect before them but that of low lives from hand to mouth, ground to the very dust by the depression of poverty, and finding in the streets a burning fiery furnace of every temptation to careers of squalor, recklessness, and sin. They will see how facile is the descent to Avernus of many poor families; at how fearful and accelerated a pace they may, even with the best intentions, go all down hill, because they have the glaring incentives to drunkenness always at their doors—incentives fearfully potent to seduce even the sober and the self-respecting when the leaden waves of despair begin to close over their heads. They will see placarded as it were before their eyes the incidents which, to some of us, are already so painfully familiar—a 'respectable' funeral, with its hideous concluding wassail of beer and gin; the sort of food—ill-cooked, unwholesome, and unsatisfying—which the people and their children eat; the picture of a street-fight between two women, tearing each other till their cheeks run with blood, amid volleys of oaths and obscenity from the leering, jeering, blighted, dehumanized crowd of men and girls and hobbledehoys, who gloat over the spectacle with an exhilaration more detestable than that of the ancient spectators of a gladiatorial show.

They may contemplate the history of a soup-kitchen, and the way in which paupers of the lowest class regard the soft 'philanthropy' of their richer neighbours. They will spend a day's honeymoon with a pair who marry within a few shillings of destitution, and the expenses of whose coarse holiday compel them next morning to pawn their wedding ring. And these are but fragments of the manifold initiation into the lives of the neglected and improvident poor.

[Here follows the description of the Bank Holiday spent at the Crystal Palace: it is selected for quotation by Dean Farrar as 'it is one of the least painful.']

What is the object, it may be asked, of painting such scenes, such characters—such conditions of society, and of human life reduced to its barest and blankest elements of spiritual death, of moral atrophy, of physical degradation?

If the object only were to provide amusement for a passing hour, or to stimulate by new sensations the jaded appetite of the novel-reader;—or if the object only were to furnish a terrible exhibition for a cold and insulting curiosity—it would be worthy of the severest reprobation.

If, again, it were the purpose of those who describe this triumph of the fraud and malice of the devil and man, to foster in our minds the deadening pessimism which makes men acquiesce in the dogma that this is the worst of all possible worlds—it would be an unhealthy and misdirected object.

Nor should we protest less distinctly against any notion that such realistic pictures are excusable only on the plea of Art for Art's sake. That 'such things are' is not, in itself, an adequate excuse for dragging them into publicity. That a dunghill exists, or that a beggar's foot is dirty, is no sufficient reason for painting them. Nature herself protests within us against the revelation of her horrors, the laying bare of her sores. 'We are bound to reticence,' says George Eliot, 'most of all by that reverence for the highest efforts of our common nature, which commands us to bury its lowest fatalities, its invincible remnants of the brute, its most agonizing struggles with temptation, in unbroken silence.' There is nothing which militates against this canon in truthful pictures of the evil elements which defile the outmost waves of civilization in our great cities, if those pictures be treated in a pitiful and noble spirit. In touching on the tragedies of the country Wordsworth wrote—

The generations are prepared, the pangs,
The eternal pangs are ready; the dread strife
Of poor Humanity's afflicted will
Struggling in vain with ruthless destiny.

It is true, alas! that the lives of the slums show us a tragedy in all its pathos without any of its dignity, and a low comedy with all its vulgarism but none of its fun. But we do not contemplate it as a scenic effect, nor as though we were like the gods of Epicurus, careless of the world. We look on it that we may not be content to hide ourselves from the sufferings of our kind, but that we may feel their reality and aim at their alleviation. Millions of us read the accounts of the horrors in Whitechapel. If we do so out of a morbidly aesthetic delight in the thrill and shudder of horror which they cause, we do ill. If, after reading them, we only shrug our shoulders and fold our hands, in callous acquiescence in that which is supposed to be inevitable, we do ill. If we read them with a sense of humiliation, a sense of something like personal guilt in the fact that they should go on in the midst of us, a sense of terrible fellowship in the sufferings of those whom we see suffer, we may rise purified and stimulated to nobler efforts by their perusal; and then, in reading them, we do well. . . .

The author of the book of which the title stands at the head of this paper has little or nothing to impress upon us as to the nature of the remedy. In one passage he says, with unconcealed irony: 'To humanize the multitude two things are necessary—two things of the simplest kind conceivable. *In the first place, you must effect an entire change of economic conditions: a preliminary step of which every tiro will recognize the easiness.* Then you must bring to bear on the new order of things the constant influence of music.' This leaves us terribly at sea, and even Professor Huxley's guidance becomes of little immediate practical service. 'Cultivate their intelligence and sense of dignity,' he says; 'give them higher aspirations than those which could be gratified by their common vices, and they would improve the houses of their own accord.' The national education Act of 1870 was meant to cultivate their intelligence. It is the daily and hourly effort of the clergy, in their parishes, and by agencies without number, to give them higher aspirations. Yet the tide of vice and pauperism seems to roll on with ever deeper and ever muddier waters as the number of the unemployed becomes more and more unmanageable. The gin palaces are still the prolific curse of all the most squalid neighbourhoods, and the rotting rookeries in which infamous generations of harlots and felons have herded together remain unimproved and undestroyed.

Is there, then, no remedy? Is this deepening curse to continue until the pit swallows it? Let me say at once that there is no new remedy, no miraculous remedy, no remedy of instantaneous efficacy. As our most eminent living statesman told us long ago, 'It is against the ordinance of Providence, it is against the interests of man, that immediate reparation should be possible when long-continued evils have been at work. For one of the greatest safeguards against misdoing would be removed if at any moment the consequences of misdoing could be repaired.' We must, therefore, accustom ourselves to the repetition and reinforcement of old and simple principles, and we must rely for deliverance, not upon new and startling propositions, but upon simple fidelity to acknowledged truths. . . .

44. Unsigned review, *Nation* (New York)

20 February 1890, 160

The Nether World is another effort to put the problem of the poor before us. The crowded neighborhoods of East London, with which Mr Besant has made us familiar, appear in a different aspect, although the street corners and the trades are unchanged. The 'Nether World' is a dreadful place, where there are no happy surprises such as Mr Besant permits his readers, when the possibility of romance slowly dissipates in the dun-colored atmosphere of economic hopelessness. In the attempt to give an outline of the story, we are struck by the inadequacy of the ordinary critical vocabulary. We cannot say that we are introduced to the characters—we fall afoul of most of them. Longer acquaintance seems only to add to the gloomy sum total of their undesirable natural endowment and its unremunerative spiritual development. The author ought in justice to be relieved of any intention of writing a pleasant story, but it may be questioned whether he meant to give so strongly the impression that in the nether world the only force that can be counted on is the tendency to sag. In the production of this impression the resources of a powerful literary method have been employed. There is little of the sketchy work with which the problems of our time are often detailed in fiction: everything here is stalwart, robust, not to be eluded, not to be whiffed away by impatient distaste, nor ignored by lofty preoccupation. There is darkness that can be felt, and crime that goes to make up statistics, and neither lends itself to a distinctively aesthetic impression. It is terribly real, terribly painful. The imagination of the reader cannot, like most of the people whose bad fortune he follows, find refuge in 'the public' and a taste for drink.

A narrative method nearly as minute as that of Scott, inferences as baldly put as if by a statistical expert, produce a reaction at last. Perhaps the best result of this realism is the question left now and then in a reader's mind, Is there really any nether world? Do not Sidney Kirkwood and Jane Snowdon, with their self-denying lives and steadfast ideals, redeem it all? But even if not, one is tempted to ask whether the avowed realism of the result has not occasionally deepened the shadows of description too much. The writer of this notice happened to be in St John's Square on the day of the great popular demonstration in Regent's Park when the crowd was gathering, and neither surroundings nor people made an impression of hopeless sordidness. The dignity of the past was not unmatched by something very like it in the present. 'The people' were often deformed, oftener toil-worn and prematurely old, but 'the people' were often sturdy and resolutely content. Three college professors from the United States found no difficulty, even at such a time, in establishing relations of intelligent sympathy with the worst-dressed and the worst-featured of the swarming crowds: a common humanity had not been buried far below the surface even by years of toil and trouble in the nether world. The place that holds all sorts and conditions of men cannot, after all, be a world apart.

But there is one effect of this realism greatly needed in the popular consideration of the questions involved. It is the steady emphasis of the fact that these are literally living troubles; that they cannot be settled by logic nor yet by the decisions of a critical moment—they must be haltingly lived out and established by slow years in bone and nerve. Moreover, this story touches upon a difficulty often unrecognized or eluded by writers of science and fiction—the poor do not, as a matter of course, become possessed of a missionary spirit in proportion as they are more highly organized and better able to maintain themselves. They long to get out of it all, but points of departure are rarely attractive places in a logical, aesthetic, or moral sense. And when they accept the task of living in better spirit the life about them, existence is still a puzzle, still sad to them, though neither so mad nor so bad as that of their neighbors. The characters depicted in *The Nether World* may be roughly divided into two classes—those who do as they like and are wretched, and those who do as they ought and are not happy. But, cramped as has been the outlook for all, the latter have managed to smuggle in an ideal. It is not necessary to ask for the sources of supply. In plain life, perhaps, people rarely go back of the every-day virtues, patience, charity, long-suffering. For them possession does away with the need of philosophy. The author's realism gives expression to much that is menacing in our time. It calls our attention sharply, almost roughly, to our ill-discharged brotherhood. But however much of blunder and sin may be laid to our charge, this final victory of the ideal spares us the sight of humanity spoiled and imbruted. 'Where they abode it was not all dark. Sorrow certainly awaited them, perchance defeat in even the humble aims that they had set themselves; but at least their lives would remain a protest against those brute forces of society which fill with wreck the abysses of the nether world.'

45. Eduard Bertz on Gissing, *Deutsche Presse*

November 1889

Bertz, who had known Gissing since 1878, published this article under the title 'George Gissing: ein Real-Idealist'. It appeared in three instalments, 3 November 1889, 357–9; 10 November 1889, 366–7; 17 November 1889, 374–5. The *Deutsche Presse* was the organ of the German Society of Authors, and Bertz was Secretary of the Society.

Gissing commented in a letter to his friend dated 14 December 1889: 'I need not say that the article pleased and gratified me enormously. I can quite understand the approval with which it has met, as a piece of literary work. You have omitted no single point which I could have wished to see mentioned. Of course it is the writing of a friend, but then there has never been a lack of the other kind of criticism' (*The Letters of George Gissing to Eduard Bertz*, p. 86).

The article has been translated by David and Hedda Thatcher.

At a time when our literary critics (at any rate those who do not deny to literature its natural right of development) are hailing Russian, French, Scandinavian and Danish authors as representatives of a realism reflective of the spirit of our times, an error is being propagated that English literature is still going over the same old ground. Yet the more perceptive observer would find it incredible that a sense for what is most valid in the modern movement should not be felt at all in the land of Shakespeare. Of course, English literature is still largely dominated by a puritan aesthetic which acts as a moral watchdog over the literary family: whatever fails to conform to its rigid prescriptions is rejected with all the arrogant pride of narrow-mindedness. Hence the novels being produced in such quantities in England today do not dare to break with the old tradition. It says all the more for the power and importance of one man's mind when he can open up new paths on his own and, despite the conspiracy of dictatorial mediocrities, is able to break the petrified rules and gain recognition from the truly discriminating. George Gissing's novels have won him such acclaim.

Realism, of course, is nothing new in English literature. Since the middle of the eighteenth century a vein of realism has run through it. For what is realism if not that sense of the simple truth of nature which imbued the poetry of a Burns, a Cowper, a Wordsworth with imperishable life? And if we looked for the origin of the realistic novel we might well find it in England: for Fielding created it. That it has managed to maintain its position right up to modern times, even though it lacked the popularity of its sentimental counterpart, is demonstrated by one great writer: Thackeray.

It is really a false assumption to think that the demand for realism is a recent one. Since literature began, realism, except for occasional periods of eclipse, has been tacitly accepted as the highest law of art. Obedience to this law revealed the master, disobedience betrayed the bungler. The rise of modern English literature dates from the death of Pope, when an outmoded classicism gave way to a naturalistic poetry derived from actual life. Since then, realism has never quite lost its prestige, although it was in the nature of things that a great mass of ordinary, unthinking, semi-literate readers would come to the fore and adopt it as their preferred literary mode. Even these bat-like creatures, whose spiritual shortsightedness had predisposed them to favour the puppeteer Richardson, could not deny Fielding's impact once they had been exposed to him. Phantoms gave up their right to exist in literature —real people were in demand.

The great stream of modern English novels is not characterised by an absence of realistic method but by its restricted use. For there is neither a qualitative nor a quantitative difference between the new realism and the old. What the modern novel requires is an extension of subject-matter, in depth as well as in breadth; it seeks after new themes; it observes the soul's activity from a higher point of view and extends the boundaries of what is aesthetically permissible because of its interrelation with the general spirit of the modern age. Scientific and social development has entered a new phase. Men's minds are in a state of oppression and ferment: the rapid growth of a new world-vision is overshadowing the old. How could we expect literature to lag behind these universal changes? It has to incorporate the great problems of our time—that is its proper task. George Gissing has recognised this task as no other English novelist has done.

What typifies our modern society is, above all, the struggle for emancipation on the part of the lower classes. To study the essence of this phenomenon in the forms it assumes, its modes of operation and its aims (particularly in its relations to the upper classes), is the necessary task of the modern novel of manners. This is the material which clamours for artistic expression in the hands of any modern author whose heart has been wrung by the loud cries of protest he hears today. It is with this in mind that Gissing sketches out in *The Unclassed*, the second of his seven novels to appear to date, his artistic programme. He puts it in the mouth of a young fellow-writer who represents one of the most characteristic aspects of his own attitude:—

'I begin to see my way to magnificent effects: ye gods, such light and shade. The fact is, the novel of every-day life is getting worn out. We must dig deeper, get to untouched social strata. Dickens felt this, but he had not the courage to face his subjects; his monthly numbers had to lie on the family tea-table. Not *virginibus puerisque* will be my book, I assure you, but for men and women who like to look beneath the surface, and who understand that only as artistic material has human life any significance.'

However, to write a good modern novel requires more than lending a sensitive ear to the clamorous contradictions of the age. Juvenal's example might well produce a satirist or a critic of society, but it cannot create an artist—something more than *saeva indignatio* is needed to animate a genuine work of art. The power of artistic creation is not possible unless there is delight in the subject for its own sake—a full appreciation of its poetic significance, however shocking it may be in real life. That Gissing clearly recognises this essential principle is already evident in a remark he makes about Hogarth (whose realism has much in common with his own artistic approach) in the novel mentioned above (*The Unclassed*).

We talk of his aims in choosing these subjects; we call him a social reformer, a moralist. That is only an accident of his work, and so far as he himself believed in such an aim he was deficient in self-consciousness. Suppose for a moment that his pictures could have been so miraculously efficient as to lead to a social revolution. Think you he would have rejoiced in the destruction of Gin Lane? Never believe it! No more sketchings on the thumb-nail, no more artist's rapture in view of a group of vilest humanity, no more glorious effects of filth and outrage! Hogarth would have sunk into despondency, and died cursing the work of his own hands.

This should naturally be taken *cum grano salis*, but it contains a characteristic truth. Gissing does not write to a thesis. He observes the common people in their brutalised condition; he shares their suffering and their anger; he tries to understand them, and seeks to grasp the causes of their social distress. He accords paramount importance to tone, for it is tone that makes his works artistic. His significance, then, lies not so much in his choice of subject but in his artistic handling of it—he is, first and foremost, an artist.

(To be continued)

It is precisely for this reason that his novels have the same powerful impact as Hogarth's pictures: as genuine social tragedies they effect in the reader a catharsis through the simple power of truth. In a long essay in the *Contemporary Review* on Gissing's latest novel *The Nether World* (a significantly ambiguous title), Archdeacon Farrar, speaking from many years' experience, testifies that it pictures corruption without over-colouring and misery without exaggeration. That is why, he says, he would like to call the public's attention to the work—'the moral world in the lower streets of our great cities is a fearful chaos, and unless we can improve it a catastrophe is surely at hand.'

Gissing does not write with this purpose in mind; any effect his books may have in the direction of reform can be ascribed to his artistic realism, which naturally springs from an intimate knowledge of the conditions he describes. No English writer has ever known the English people, the English working classes, better than George Gissing; none has been able to portray it so masterfully, so graphically. In knowledge of human beings, in depth of psychological insight, in precision and truth to life of characterisation, he ranks with Thackeray and far surpasses Dickens.

Besides their realistic delineation of the lower social classes another parallel can be drawn between Gissing and Hogarth. Coleridge used to remark on the 'beautiful faces of the women' in Hogarth's pictures; never, he says, does Hogarth's satire stifle that love for beauty which belongs to him as an artist. Indeed, that the painter of the ugly should have sought out the laws of the beautiful and believed he had discovered its characteristic features, is not without a deeper significance. For Gissing the cult of beauty is a religion in an even higher sense—indeed, the highest religion. Other like-minded writers have escaped from the world of ugly reality into an ideal world and averted their gaze from whatever repugnant things offended their eyes and hearts. Gissing, on the other hand, cannot turn aside from human misery; it fascinates him. Its horrors penetrate his soul and compel him to capture in words what has shaken him to the very core. His realism derives from the contrast between the actual and the ideal. And that is why he cannot be content with merely depicting the ugly—this contrast is found even in his books. If any emphatic teaching is to be extracted from them, it is to urge us to cultivate beauty and combat ugliness in the world. The vicar in *Demos*, to some extent a spokesman of the author's own vision, reads to his young friends from Plato's *Phaedrus* Socrates' prayer for 'inner beauty': this very prayer is used by Gissing to epitomise the aspirations of his hero in a later novel. In Gissing's view, this striving for inner beauty develops from a response to external beauty. The brutishness of the degenerate masses is clearly connected with the ugliness which constantly surrounds them.

Ordinary reality is thus used by the novelist as a backcloth against which nobility of soul can stand forth. He is a realist, but there is no contradiction between realism and idealism—quite the opposite: to achieve an organic connection between the two is perhaps the highest aim of art. There is no higher idealism than a sincere striving for truth. But it is absolutely vital, if realism and idealism are not to weaken each other through interaction, that each remains faithful to itself. They can only do this in a strong, courageous, noble soul. George Gissing is such a realist of the ideal.

However, he does not restrict himself to showing us how the noble element struggles against the common ground in which it has its roots: as a realist it is his painful task to show us how, in most cases, the noble suffers crushing defeat in this struggle. For this is the awareness to which his sense of truth, his study of reality, his contemplation of the nature of human hopes have led him. His is a deeply pessimistic view of the world and his final word to us is—resignation. As always, the deepest pessimism is the child of the purest idealism.

(To be continued)

This pessimism alone would prevent him from becoming a doctrinal writer, but one must also note his artistic objectivity which sees two sides to every question and lifts him above all partisan feeling. Nevertheless his criticisms of our society are harshly severe. He hates the modern industrial system with its ruthless competition and struggle of man against man; he hates with a white-hot hatred the inhumanity of our social structure. There is a pronounced aristocratic trait in his character which stems from his spiritual thirst for beauty—every contact with the common inspires him with feelings of aversion. But his sense of justice remains unimpaired. 'Might is right' is the governing law of our social life; the weak lie in the dust, downtrodden, living like beasts in their misery. Insofar as cause and guilt can be equated, the rich and the powerful are to blame; *they* are responsible for the degenerate condition of the poverty-stricken masses. Gissing lets the facts speak for themselves, and the facts speak eloquently. Farrar is quite right: this is the way to provoke conscience.

The most striking and characteristic thing about this knowledgeable and acutely perceptive observer of the working classes whose spirit and voice he renders with superb truth, is that he is a man of mature and extensive culture. Equally well versed in philosophy and literature, he relaxes from his creative work by communing with the great spirits of the classical past, especially the writers and thinkers of Greek and Roman antiquity whose work he reads in the original languages. This is so important for an understanding of him because it explains the contradiction, encountered in all his books, between the dreary, apathetic existence of the dehumanised beasts of burden in modern industrial society and that radiant freedom expressed by the highest contemporary aesthetic culture. His vision is wide-ranging and cosmopolitan: he is completely devoid of shortsighted national pride and those other prejudices which possess the vast majority of the insular British, to whom the surrounding sea is like the Great Wall of China. To say his mind is of the richest, his philosophy sharply individual, is simply to pay him his due. Everything he writes bears the stamp of individuality; it impresses itself on his compact style in which there is no room for verbosity.

Every thoughtful reader will perceive the high seriousness, the moral elevation, of his mind. There is little scope for humour in his writings, but he does possess a sense of humour, a virtue he thinks indispensable in any person deserving of our esteem. The passages in which he deals with human foibles in a humorous vein are, without exception, eminently successful. But in a temperament as profound and passionate as his we could hardly expect anything but high seriousness to predominate!

In fact a deep passion lies at the root of his being. It pervades the religious earnestness of his approach to love, any profanation of which hurts his sensibility, especially the profanation of a loveless marriage. The only difference, he once said, between the woman who sells herself by authority of the church and the one who spends her life under the streetlamps is the degree of immorality in each case. He imagines the great artist Nature bent upon the creation of a soul which contains, in the purest perfection, all the elements of feeling which are in turn essential to the ideals of virgin, wife and mother—this is his ideal of womanhood. That woman should occupy a high position in the work of a writer who thinks in this manner needs no further comment; there is no more sympathetic or understanding judge of the female heart: a whole gallery of typical female figures in every moral shade from black to white gazes out at us from his books.

Not yet thirty-two, George Gissing is still a young man. No artist is born a master of his craft, and his first novel, *Workers in the Dawn* with which he began his literary career in 1880, was not a faultless production. But already at this time the sinewy strength and passionate intensity of his descriptions and the vividness of his creative imagination were admired, even by those unaware of just how young he was. Since then Gissing has progressively developed and become more profound; with every new book he has evinced a greater maturity, a more refined artistic sensitivity, a deeper knowledge of the human soul, a mellower judgement. Perhaps he has yet to reach the peak of his creative achievement—he admits himself that everything he has done to date is the work of an apprentice. But that should not prevent us from recognising him even now as the most original and significant phenomenon in contemporary English fiction.

As I will shortly be publishing a full-length essay on him, there is no need to enumerate his works individually here. I will only mention those novels of his which have gained the widest circulation. *Demos: A Story of English Socialism* appeared in 1886, anonymously in the first edition (as in the Tauchnitz edition); all subsequent editions, however, carry his name.* Authorised German and French translations of this book will, I am told, be issued this year. Apart from its excellent character development, the novel is remarkable for its dramatically moving plot; the theme gives it not only human but also sociological interest. There is a harsher juxtaposition here than in his other books between a people, the iconoclastic masses struggling for liberation, and the spirit of aristocratic conservatism which finds in the cultivation of beauty the reward of a liberal education. It lies in the nature of the theme that the first should suffer defeat; any other outcome would have been unrealistic and historically false, for it is clear from the outset that the author sides with the forces which uphold civilisation. Despite

* The second English edition, published in one volume in November 1886, was also anonymous.

this, he is most successful in his characterisation of ordinary men and women which, achieved with masterly skill, shows his deep and genuine sympathy for the sufferings of the oppressed.

This is even truer of his later novels, particularly *Thyrza* (1887) and *The Nether World* (1889). His pessimism allows little prospect of any victory for justice and humanity, but he is not one of those who condone evil on account of its power and measure the validity of ideals according to the success they achieve. 'Are we to range ourselves on the side of evil,' he asks, 'because we despair of being able to defeat it?' There is a heroic ring to the conclusion of his last book; the idealist cannot surrender; he is too proud for that, despite his sense of utter hopelessness. We feel ourselves raised to the level of tragic exultation; the noble is victorious in defeat. The concluding words of Gissing's most recent novel express the fundamental thought which runs, in increasingly refined form, through all his works; they are 'a protest against those brute forces of society which fill with wreck the abysses of the nether world.'

THE EMANCIPATED

March 1890

46. Unsigned review, *Illustrated London News*

19 April 1890, xcvi, 498

The *Illustrated London News* was a sixpenny magazine reporting mainly topical matters and carrying short articles of a general nature. It usually published a serial story and occasional short stories. When Clement King Shorter became its editor, Gissing was frequently requested to contribute.

It will be readily understood that the title of Mr Gissing's novel is meant to signify an attempt to illustrate, by a story of modern social and domestic life, some likely effects of a recent intellectual movement altering the standards of faith and duty. Much part of the vague apprehensions that are frequently expressed on this score, as if serious forethinking on questions of religion and morality were necessarily attended with licentious conduct, might be spared, to a candid and charitable judgment, by recognizing the possibility of earnest minds which have deliberately quitted the orthodox position having found other valid sanctions for imperative rules of just and virtuous conduct. As a novelist thoughtfully observing and describing the actual processes of mental change going on at the present time, the author of *Demos*, *Thyrza* and *The Nether World* is not called upon to denounce or to commend those tendencies which every preacher, moral essayist, or professional guide, on one side or the other, undertakes to estimate from the didactic standpoint. Speculative truth can never be safely disposed of by a work of fiction, designed either to show the practical bad consequences of holding erroneous views, or, conversely, to exhibit noble personal characters uninjured by the reception of heterodox opinion. The better we know mankind as they really are, the more easily do we perceive that very good men and women can long entertain the most absurd beliefs, and that some who zealously maintain what seems to be the right doctrine are nowise superior in spirit or in behaviour.

The precise ground and range of those views which Mr Gissing intends to represent in operation among the chief personages of his story, calling them *The Emancipated*, cannot be identified with any set of opinions hitherto acknowledged as prevailing in respectable English society. There are some people who have left off going to church, or who, like Mrs Baske, after her Neapolitan experiences and her studies of art and literature, give up the Dissenting Chapel at Bartles; there are some who admit a sceptical criticism of the historical Scriptures, and who do not conceive of Inspiration, or of Revelation, from the orthodox point of view. If such persons are to form a class ironically called *The Emancipated*, or sincerely considering themselves to be so, there is still no warrant for ascribing to them an injurious affinity with other persons who have lax notions about marriage, who have no sense of honour, fidelity, or integrity, who deny all moral responsibility, who are selfish, idle, profligate, and deceitful. Mr Reuben Elgar, the brother of Mrs Baske, is a sheer blackguard of the latter description, whereas she, educated in a narrow puritanism, becomes wisely tolerant and gentle, devoting the leisure of her widowhood to a liberal self culture, and finally marries the high-minded, conscientious, sagacious Mallard, a type of stern veracity, and rigorous honesty, equally one of the 'Emancipated' class. We fail to see that in the behaviour and lives of these persons, or of Cecily Doran, the youthful beauty and heiress, who imprudently runs away with Elgar from her guardian and her aunt, and becomes the happy wife of a dissolute scoundrel, there is any common ground of action furnished by their opinions concerning the Church and the Bible. Ross Mallard is as good a man, and Miriam Baske as good a woman, before and after the change of opinion in the mind of the latter, as one would be likely to meet in any sect of religionists; Cecily, a charming, generous, enthusiastic girl, afterwards sorely tried by a vicious husband, is scrupulously faithful to conjugal duty. If they had all remained punctual churchgoers, and had never read a word of modern science or philosophy, it does not appear manifest that their conduct in domestic and social relations would have been much better than it was. On the other hand, such a man as Elgar, an utter egotist, a base sensualist, with vanity enough to affect lofty sentiments and win the admiration of ignorant young women, a reckless spendthrift, libertine, and gambler, wasting his friends' money, excusing himself by gross falsehoods, idling away his manhood, inveigling an orphan heiress, then treating his wife with cool neglect, and sinking into the coarsest kind of vulgar vice, is not the product of 'advanced thought' in our age. His stale and hollow pretext that 'one cannot help being what one is', and that there is no moral responsibility, no merit or blame, for what one does, has in all ages been the natural sophistry of self-indulgence, and often compatible with the profession of a reputed orthodox creed.

It does not appear, therefore, how, or from what obligations of morality, any of these different characters are 'emancipated'; and in the case of Mallard and Cecily, at any rate, there are no signs of a reaction from earlier religious impressions. They have, from independent reflection, and by force of ideal or spiritual aspiration, reached a high standard of life: Mallard is a hero of constancy in unselfish friendship; she is a dignified martyr of misplaced womanly affection, still preserving her true self-respect. Miriam Baske, indeed, emerges by intellectual culture from the ignorant prejudices which forbade her to appreciate Greek sculpture and Italian painting, to enjoy music, poetry, and the drama, and to look with toleration on the manners of foreign nations. She is emancipated also from the harshness, the Pharisaic pride, the personal jealousy, which had been fostered by her individual position as the notable patroness of a petty sectarian congregation in an obscure provincial town. None of these examples would seem to have any significance in estimating the value of those controversies, theological and philosophical, critical or scientific, to which reference is made or implied in some passages of the dialogue. The story is one of independent personal characters, mutually influencing each other, of sympathies and antipathies, mistaken interpretations of behaviour, one deplorable act of rashness on the part of an innocent girl, its expiation by severe distress, and some pathetic scenes of patient suffering, with the touching death of Madeline Denyer, at whose bedside Cecily almost forgets her own private sorrow. Regarded in this light, Mr Gissing's latest work is one of his best, and we commend it to discriminating readers.

47. G. Barnett Smith, *Academy*

19 April 1890, xxxvii, 263

George Barnett Smith, a biographer of Gladstone, was the author of many books on historical and literary subjects.

If it were not for a certain undercurrent of pessimism running through his work, Mr George Gissing would take high rank among writers of fiction. While it is no part of a novelist's duty to inculcate that everything happens for the best in this best of all possible worlds, neither should he close his eyes to the fact that there is a good deal of substantial happiness to be obtained here below. *The Emancipated* is notable for the number of broken or marred lives it depicts. People are emancipated from false ideas of religion, from false principles of art, from the thraldom of false love; and, indeed, all through the story one character or another is in process of emancipation of some kind. . . .

The novel is unquestionably clever, and well worth reading. If a little overcharged with misery, it is at any rate suggestive and striking in parts. It is the production of a man who can think, and who can express himself with unconventional force and freedom.

48. Unsigned review, *Saturday Review*

21 June 1890, lxix, 772

Mr George Gissing has earned a position for himself among contemporary novelists by his vivid portraiture of low London life. The subject, except for those who have accepted the doctrine of the French realists that nothing can be too repulsive for artistic description, is a depressing one, and we congratulate the author of *The Nether World* on having made his escape into an atmosphere which, if not exhilaratingly fresh, is at least less burdened with miasmatic horrors than that to which he has on some former occasions condemned his readers and himself. The 'Emancipation' with which his latest story deals is, generally, the breaking away of several young people from the creeds, tastes and prejudices of their early training. The moral appears to be that, narrow, foolish and vulgar as such creeds and prejudices may be, the young people who desert them mostly come to grief. The heroine of the tale, Miriam Baske, is the widow of a narrow-minded Dissenter, and deeply impregnated with Methodistic Calvinism. Under the wholesome influence of Neapolitan scenery, agreeable surroundings, sensible friends and a strong-minded artist-lover, she shakes off the trammels of her childhood's belief, and abandons her project of building a Baptist chapel in favour of some less sectarian form of charity, retaining, however, even in her more genial phase, a disagreeable tinge of Puritanic acerbity. Reuben Elgar, her brother, is less fortunate. He too has become enlightened, and regards the irrational bigotry of his childhood's religion with contempt and disgust. But stripped of these commonplace but wholesome safeguards, he abandons himself to the conduct of his emotions; and, as his tastes are not severely stoical, he begins with running away with a pretty young wife, and ends in a dingy paradise of music-halls and ballet-girls. A third and more interesting case of emancipation is Cecily Doran, who has the misfortune to lose her heart to her friend's dissolute brother, and learns by rough and disagreeable experience that young gentlemen of strong feelings and ill-regulated minds make exceedingly bad husbands. She, too, had started in Puritanic surroundings, but had passed into a more genial phase of life in the guardianship of Mrs Lessingham, a lady of cosmopolitan tastes, who thinks that the proper way to bring up girls is to let them see the world, know its dangers, and tread among its enjoyments with a fearless foot. Cecily Doran, accordingly, under the guidance of this indulgent chaperon, has travelled about Europe wherever beauty, art, and culture are to be found, and is panoplied, her credulous custodian imagines, against the temptations which beset the inexperienced novice. She has, unfortunately, remained woman enough to lend a too credulous ear to the promptings of young Elgar's infectious passion; and, when circumstances do not lend themselves propitiously to favour the young lover's wishes, cuts the difficulty by a runaway match. A sturdier growth of intellectual freedom is exhibited by Mallard, an eccentric artist, who exhibits praiseworthy fortitude in his suppression of the attachment which he secretly cherishes for his ward, Cecily Doran; a passion which, it is needless to say, the young lady only aggravates by her unsuspicious good-nature to a friend whom she imagines too old and too crabbed to allow of romance. He finds his reward ultimately in the hand of Mrs Baske. Mr and Mrs Spence, a refined and cultivated couple, who have abandoned business and wealth for art and Italy, and who devote themselves to 'emancipating' Mrs Baske, complete the more important *dramatis personae* of a story which, as it is set in a framework of pretty Italian scenery, has, it will be seen, ample scope for interesting and effective scenes. All would be, to our taste, more interesting and effective were the story told at less inordinate length, and if the author could contrive to produce the desired result by a few happy strokes rather than by an elaboration of detail, which lapses not unfrequently into prosaic minuteness. There are, however, readers with plentiful leisure and patient temperament who will, no doubt, follow the evolution of Mr Gissing's drama with interest and satisfaction, and will condone its somewhat tardy process in consideration of the care and thoughtfulness which have obviously been devoted to the work. But if Mr Gissing aspires to popularity he must condescend to human infirmity by endowing some, at least, of his *dramatis personae* with those graces of character which conduce to attractiveness, and inspire the reader with feelings of interest and affection. Novels, no less than poems, should obey the Horatian mandate to be 'sweet.' Mr Gissing's pages abound in light rather than sweetness, and neither of his heroines appeals very forcibly to our goodwill or makes us in the least disposed to envy the lovers who are destined to enjoy their companionship for the rest of a lifetime.

49. Unsigned review, *Westminster Review*

September 1890, 333–4

The Emancipated is a remarkable novel, but, like too much of the best contemporary fiction, its perusal is more calculated to give pain than pleasure. Many evidences of close observation lie scattered over the three volumes; but it is the observation of morbid symptoms rather than of healthy life. Mr Gissing's men and women are not simple enough to be satisfied with merely living, they must perpetually watch themselves live; they are as it were for ever feeling their own pulse. The author, too, is never tired of examining their symptoms mental and moral, and he lays his diagnosis before his readers at wearisome length. But his fundamental error, which in a degree vitiates the accuracy of his view of life, is that he mistakes mere evanescent surface currents of thought and feeling for real and profound modifications in human nature. He takes too seriously such phrases as 'the modern ideal of life', 'the altered relation of the sexes', 'the complex modern woman', etc. It is, perhaps, the inevitable fate of lesser men to be taken by these passing shows of things, while none but the very greatest pierce to the permanent underlying realities—the central core of humanity, which remains for ever the same, or alters so slowly that, as with the hour-hand of a watch, we cannot discern its onward movement. Therefore it is that while writers of yesterday are already out of date, Shakespeare's heroes and heroines are as true to life now as they were when he created them—in all essentials as much of our day as of his. Indeed the brightest and prettiest thread that runs through Mr Gissing's rather sombre web is but a nineteenth century version of 'the taming of the shrew'. Miriam Baske, the heroine of the episode in question, is, no doubt, intended to be regarded as one of 'the emancipated', because, having been reared in 'the strictest sect of the Pharisees', she gradually, amid fresh scenes and new influences, shakes off the sectarian yoke. But, in truth, she does but exchange one yoke for another. It is love—not reason—that conquers her fierce spiritual pride; and finally, she blissfully yields to the somewhat Petruchio-like wooing of a rugged, masterful, but sterling man, and becomes a happy wife. The really 'emancipated' women in the story, one and all, make shipwreck of their lives—apparently, in direct consequence of their emancipation. It is hard to divine how far Mr Gissing's sympathies go with the doubting, questioning, self-analysing turn of mind, types of which, he has laboured, not unsuccessfully, to set before us; but, whether designedly or not, the moral suggested by his book is that, if advancing civilisation implied the definite multiplication of such unrestful and tormented beings as most of those who figure in his pages, one would, to use Professor Huxley's forcible words, 'hail the advent of some kindly comet which would sweep the whole affair away.'

50. Unsigned review, *Spectator*

11 August 1894, lxxiii, 183–4

This was a belated review of the second edition (revised) published by Lawrence & Bullen late in 1893. The *Spectator* had earlier given a dull, unperceptive account, which Gissing had found offensive, of the three-volume edition. See Introduction.

Inasmuch as absence of order means chaos, and licence cannot be averted without the aid of restraint, it is evidently necessary for society to be governed by laws of some kind. But as it is important for its members to know whether the claim to obedience should be respected as uttered by the voice of the Creator, or distrusted as emanating from no higher authority than Mrs Grundy endeavouring to impose fetters without good reason, therefore it behoves people to remember that there is a motive for everything if only they can find it, and to examine boldly into the origin of the laws now in force in order to ascertain whether they are produced by inherent and unalterable conditions of the human race, or due solely to conventionality and prejudice. And the interest attached to the views upon this and other branches of the subject of emancipation of so clever a person as the writer of *The*

Emancipated, entitles the work to more attention than the reading public might otherwise be inclined to bestow upon it.

What Mr Gissing treats of principally is emancipation from old-fashioned ideas respecting religious belief, male superiority, and the greater moral latitude allowed to men than women; and it is note-worthy that, in dealing with the matter, he seems to regard it as affecting women only, without ever mentioning any possible influence it may have upon his own sex also. Religious devotion, for instance, is spoken of as the ordinary resource of a woman who is denied the 'natural solace' (this apparently refers to matrimony) 'of her need to taste the happiness of submission to a stronger than herself;' and when Miriam, at first a strict Puritan, lapses into religious indifference, and becomes unhappy, she can only be restored to peace of mind by the 'strong human hand' of a husband. But what use or comfort religion might be to men is never alluded to at all, and the author appears to consider it solely as a sort of *pis-aller* for spinsters,—an ingredient in life which man is too divine to require, though it may perhaps come in handy for woman if she is unfortunate enough to be unsubjected to male control. As Miriam exemplifies the effect of emancipation in mature years, so in Cecily's career is shown the result of it in early training. The 'Heavenly Twins' themselves could hardly desire doctrines more advanced than those of the aunt by whom she is brought up; for this lady condemns the old-fashioned system of education, which she defines to be 'not so much the imparting of knowledge as the fostering of special ignorances,' and boasts that she has helped her niece 'to see things as they *are*, not as moral teachers would like them to be, and as parents make-believe to their girls that they are indeed.' Educated on these enlightened lines, Cecily, falling in love with a good-for-nothing scamp of whom her aunt does not approve, has no hesitation about running away and risking her reputation by travelling alone with him from Naples to London to be married. When by degrees her eyes have been opened to his worthlessness, and her love for him is killed, she is fired to revolt at not having 'an equal freedom to exercise all her powers, to enrich her life with experiences of joy,' even though 'she asked no liberty to be vile as he made himself.' In a position of this kind, a woman of the old education, we are told, 'readily believes that it is not to experiences of joy, but of sorrow, that she must look for her true blessedness; her ideal is one of renunciation; religious motive is in her enforced by what she deems the obligation of her sex;' but Cecily, on the contrary, who is of the emancipated order, and whilst still a girl 'threw for ever behind her all superstitious and harassing doubts,' has no such consolation; she resents bitterly being bound to one who acknowledges no mutual bond, and is, in virtue of his sex, practically free; and, realising for the first time that the unequal hardships of a woman's lot are not chargeable only to society since she is limited by inexorable laws of nature, Cecily is moved to a passionate indignation that would obviously have ended in departure from paths of moral rectitude had there been a lover to tempt her astray,—which fortunately there was not.

However much Mr Gissing may approve of emancipation, its outcome, as exhibited in his various characters, is not very attractive. And his whole tone leads to the inference that whilst he would hesitate about agreeing with David that 'the fool hath said in his heart there is no God,' he would endorse cordially all texts enjoining the submission of women to men, whom he regards as so immeasurably the superior of the two, as to render vain all female efforts to escape from thraldom. But such a verdict in favour of the author's own sex reminds one forcibly of Aesop's fable where the lion, looking at a statue of a man strangling a lion, says, 'That is your version of the story; let us be the sculptors, and for one lion under the feet of a man you shall have twenty men under the paw of a lion;' and one wonders if the fable's moral, that men are but sorry witnesses in their own cause, may not apply also to *The Emancipated.* Considered as a treatise on the particular subject dealt with, the book deserves to be read; but as a work of fiction it is by no means equally satisfactory, for there is a prevailing lack of lightness and 'go' that makes one think an emancipated world would be a dreary place to live in; and novel-readers in general are not likely to relish the substitution of mental analysis and reveries for plot and incident,—of which there are absolutely none. We are somewhat surprised, by-the-bye, to find nothing said as to the desirability, or otherwise, of encouraging emancipation of thought in any direction where emancipated ideas can have no practical effect (as in respect of laws that are by the nature of things unalterable), for this question seems to us to be decidedly pertinent to Mr Gissing's theme.

51. Unsigned review, *Critic* (New York)

22 February 1896, 123

This is a review of the first American edition, published by Way & Williams, Chicago.

If the thoughts and emotions of Mr Gissing's characters are not thoroughly understood, it will be from no lack of explanation and description. He is not content to allow his reader to interpret their speech and action: he is a perpetual chorus, telling what is meant by the developments of the story, and pointing out the special significance of each one. Even when we suppose ourselves entirely familiar with the few creatures who make their entrances and exits upon his stage; even when we have advanced to the third act of the tragi-comedy, we are carried back now and then to the beginnings of things, and made to review in detail the early history of some of the moving figures. Nothing is told by suggestion, everything is overladen with detail. The labor this necessitates weighs heavily upon the mind of the reader, and it would require infinite leisure and patience to read the book from cover to cover. Yet the judicious, who know what to omit, will be rewarded for taking it up. The conversations are capital as a rule—simple, natural, often clever without apparent effort, and sometimes impassioned, with a thoroughly modern reserve. Mr Gissing is observant, earnest and astute, but he is not yet an artist. Like many of the contemporary novelists he cares but little for plot, combining with that indifference a strange blindness to the immense value of construction. In itself, plot is, indeed, a matter of comparatively little consequence—a slight thing, which may become typical or elemental in the handling. Yet the plot of this novel is sufficiently well selected. It is the fact that it rambles on without definite plan that operates so seriously to its disadvantage. It is not only condensation that the book needs, but design and system and the effective accentuation of progress. In the drawing of his characters Mr Gissing is much more successful, though he holds them somewhat too securely in bondage, and will not allow one quite to forget that they are puppets.

Nevertheless, Mr Gissing is seriously to be reckoned with, not as one of the elect, but as an intellectual force which may some day make itself felt. The title he gives to his novel is quite as applicable to himself, for his events are not the traditional events of romance, his characters not the conventional heroes and heroines. Reuben Elgar is a clever creation of a most unpleasant type, and the inevitableness of his final downfall is skilfully suggested throughout the book. The only wonder is that so vitally weak a man could have fascinated Cecily Doran; but that anomaly only makes the story more true to life. The intercourse between the two in the first ardor of their passion, and afterwards in the various stages of its gradual collapse, is the most successful work in the book—the most condensed and vivid and suggestive. Like Richard Feverel in a way, Cecily represents the failure of a system of education: the apparently successful attempt to evolve a modern, rational, enlightened woman ends in an elopement of the most romantic and foolish character. With the inevitable disappointments that follow, this is a brilliant piece of work. In Mallard, Mr Gissing deals with a more difficult character, which he makes less convincing. In the first half of the book Mallard is handled with much cleverness, but later one loses him, somehow. And throughout the story the author never quite loses self-consciousness. As a whole, however, *The Emancipated* has quality and force enough to make one thoughtfully consider some of the tendencies of our own manner of life.

NEW GRUB STREET

April 1891

52. Unsigned review, *Whitehall Review*

18 April 1891, 19–20

Mr Gissing's newest literary triumph is a singularly skilful piece of work, and proves how true a prophetic vision was ours when, on reading his first book a few years ago, we proclaimed him to be a man of no mean parts, with a great future, if he never deviated from the course he was commencing to hew for himself in the path of fame. Since then he has never disappointed us, and each fresh work he has published has been better and stronger than the one which preceded. In *New Grub Street* we perceive the same masterly and original analysis of character, and the same truth of description, as in the other remarkable stories he has told us. He has a profound and intense sympathy with the lives and the sufferings of men and women, a wonderful insight into their hearts and souls, and an almost unparalleled directness of speech in expressing what most authors fail to convey—a sense of perfect reality. Critics and the public will grumble that the book is sad, morbid, gloomy; well, so is life, or at least that phase of life of which Mr Gissing writes. The book is one long, desolate tragedy—the tragedy of helpless human nature in its struggle with the great forces of the universe. It is so sad because it is so real. Mr Gissing points out with a truthful and realistic force what every sensible person cannot fail to recognise—that it is not the man who aims nobly who succeeds; that when punishment follows wrongdoing, it is not as retribution. The teaching of the whole book is that it is as well to follow duty, but on the clear understanding that no reward is the result. The motive-forces of the book are:—Life, which suffers so much, and has no respite until death steps in to help; faith, which dies hard, after an agonising struggle against circumstance; love, which gives all, and gains nothing in return. And to these motive-forces Mr Gissing has given expression in a wonderful manner. The hard and painful literalness of poverty; the results of a combat with poverty on the varied natures of the characters: these are the trenchant themes on which he discourses so eloquently and ably. No matter how the world at large may judge this book, Mr Gissing has made with *New Grub Street* an addition to contemporaneous 'literature' which will be appreciated far and wide by readers of culture, refinement and taste. For those who cannot appreciate the genius which created, and the talent which perfected, such men and women as Amy and Edwin Reardon, Marian Yule and her father, and Jasper Milvain and his sisters, we have nothing but profound pity. There is a touch applied by the incidental reference in the third volume to an unsuccessful doctor, which the greatest writers of our, or any other, day might have envied. The man or woman who cannot appreciate, or who stoops to depreciate, such a book as *New Grub Street*, may surely be an object of pity to all who can enjoy this wonderfully clever, yet intensely sad, tragedy.

53. Unsigned review, *Court Journal*

25 April 1891, 710

Very clever and very painful is Mr George Gissing's latest, *New Grub Street*. Mr Gissing always writes well, and it is therefore invariably a pleasure to read his books; but in the present case this pleasure is discounted not only by the depressing nature of his theme, but by the irresistible conviction that much of the author's pessimism and many of his incidents and inferences are only too likely to be true. The book is one long study of literary failure on the part of men of genuine ability and scholarly requirements, and of pecuniary success in the same calling by a man whose style is flashy, attainments mediocre, and principle conspicuous by its absence. Disappointment, failure, grinding poverty, sordid struggle, misery, illness, affliction, self-slaughter—these are the lot of most of the denizens of New Grub-street, while social success, the love of a beautiful woman, professional reputation and monetary value, come to the man who makes but a trade of literature, who is mean, selfish, crafty, caddish to a degree, and whose literary work is of the most meretricious, catchpenny style. The ordinary reader of circulating library fiction will probably not care to read Mr Gissing's three volumes, despite their occasional glimpses of love interest; but those who are in the literary world, and know something of the struggles, the ambition—worthy and unworthy—the despair, the fitful triumphs, all the pains and penalties and few prizes of the literary life of unknown men, all the cruelty inflicted—intentionally or unintentionally—by malicious or careless reviewers, all the heart-rending anxieties and occasional gleams of happiness which come to a conscientious worker in the field of contemporary literature, will read *New Grub Street* with an intense interest, augmented by the recognition of an unexaggerated truth of some at least of its sad pictures. Discouraging to the last degree to all but writers who have made a name, and who are not prepared to sacrifice their literary conscience, if they possess one, and follow Jasper Milvain's example of writing simply to make money, *New Grub Street* may answer a good purpose if, in addition to interesting those who are already in the literary arena, it should dissuade or even terrify aspirants from rushing heedlessly into an already hopelessly overcrowded calling, in which successes are rare, and failures, both deserved and undeserved, the rule.

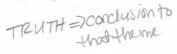

54. Unsigned review, *World*

29 April 1891, 28

Gissing transcribed part of the opening sentence of this review and commented: 'Now here is twaddle! How can a man endanger such a claim by mere choice of subject? He may endanger the vulgar *recognition* of his claim' (George Gissing's *Commonplace Book*, ed. Jacob Korg (1962), 55).

Why does not some influential friend of Mr George Gissing point out to him how greatly, by his selection of grim subjects, which he treats after the most depressing fashion, he is endangering his otherwise indubitable claim to rank among the first of rising novelists? Step by step he advances in his art. *Demos* was clever, *The Nether World* was better, and *New Grub Street* is best of all: but the low key in which they one and all are pitched, the desperate gloom of pessimism and poverty in which their action takes place, the hopeless unrelieved misery which pervades their pages, will undoubtedly prevent their author from achieving the amount of popularity, which is due to his talent, his experience, and his excellent English.

55. L. F. Austin, *Illustrated London News*

2 May 1891, xcviii, 571

Louis Frederic Austin was one of the more intelligent and conscientious literary journalists writing at the end of the nineteenth century. He was a regular contributor to the *Illustrated London News* and the *Sketch*, discussing Gissing and his works in various publications. The novelist saw him several times at meetings of the Omar Khayyám Club. See *The Book of the Omar Khayyám Club*, London, 1910.

Gissing recorded the existence of the following review in his Diary but made no comment.

It is probable that Mr George Gissing's remarkable novel, *New Grub Street*, will not remove certain popular conceptions about the lives of professional writers. Mr Gissing presents his subject in extremely sombre colours. One of his chief characters is a novelist who is shattered by misfortune, and made hopelessly incapable of work. Edwin Reardon sits for hours with his manuscript in front of him, unable to write a line. What could be more decisive proof to the practical mind of the irresponsibility of the literary faculty? Another character is a scholarly drudge who compiles articles which nobody reads, and snarls at his family during meals. A third produces a realistic novel about a grocer, and commits suicide. A fourth gives lessons in the art of novel-writing, and is saved from the prevailing squalor by a windfall in the shape of the editorship of a chatty journal. A fifth, who declines to be conscientious, because it is a luxury he cannot afford, succeeds by combined meanness and audacity in making an independent position in the world of journalism. A sixth is a girl who sets her heart upon the journalist, and is thrown aside when he finds that she is not a stepping-stone in his fortunes. Every one of these portraits is painted with surprising skill and relentless fidelity to the general scheme of sordid struggle. In this Grub Street nobody is able to earn sufficient money for a bare subsistence, except the journalist, who, after living on his mother's slender purse while he learns his trade, picks up a livelihood with the greatest toil, and crowns his achievements by marrying a widow with ten thousand pounds. Jasper Milvain's candid selfishness, which is by no means displeasing in every respect, or unaccompanied by good-nature, will probably strike many readers as overdrawn. The whole story, with its consistent note of pessimism from first to last, its total indifference to romance, its universal envelope of poverty, its intensely painful analysis of failure, will be repugnant to all who hold that the true aim of the artist is to represent the beautiful and to idealise the facts of common life. Mr Gissing sees nothing but a fight for existence, and the defeat of nearly all the combatants. The picture is doubtless true within its limits. Life is extremely hard for a great number of the workers in the ever-growing army of writers. The blood and tears which built the Pyramids have left as little trace of anguish as the shelves of the British Museum Library. But Mr Gissing's Grub Street is likely to create as grave a misconception in the minds of his readers as that with which Thackeray charged Pope. A literary man's existence is not the unrelieved despair which is painted in this novel. Youthful poets do not tread on roses, like Bulwer Lytton's Leonard Fairfield, and sucking barristers who turn to journalism are not all as fortunate as Arthur Pendennis. But a journalist of Jasper Milvain's capacity does not usually take a year to earn twenty or thirty pounds, and the average lives even of regular book-makers do not exhibit such concentrated seaminess as Alfred Yule's. There is a little sunshine even in Grub Street, and, if anyone feels any interest in its denizens after reading Mr Gissing, he may be assured that they do not all live on tea and dripping, and disbelieve in immortality.

But, gloomy as this book is, the very grimness of its hostility to common illusions is a refreshment to the jaded reader of the average novel. There is power in every line. The growth of Amy Reardon from romantic belief in struggling genius to the mature worldliness of a comfortable drawing-room is a notable feat in the development of character. But will Mr Mudie's subscribers relish the process? If so, English novelists may venture to draw from life.

56. Unsigned commentary, *Saturday Review*

2 May 1891, lxxi, 524–5

Gissing read this article, entitled 'New Grub Street', together with the review of his book printed in the same periodical a week later and reproduced as No. 57. He was amused to find that the second appraisal somehow contradicted the first, and remarked on the situation satirically in a letter to Bertz dated 17 May 1891 (*The Letters of George Gissing to Eduard Bertz*, pp. 124–5). See also his letter to Algernon Gissing dated 21 May 1891 in *Letters of George Gissing to Members of His Family*, p. 319.

Old Grub Street was poverty-stricken, but it was neither hopeless nor joyless. The children of this stony-hearted stepmother were merry enough, no doubt, in spite of Mr Pope, for their quarrel with him made them conspicuous, and they must have known that there was not in all their quivers so leaden a shaft but it pierced Pope's mail, and rankled in his vanity. Great men have sojourned in Grub Street; they have admitted that it was grubby; but even Dr Johnson does not say that it was permanently gloomy. This chief of literary hacks did his work, which was usually job-work, and took his pay, and grumbled not, but consistently spoke well of the booksellers. In brief, of old time Grub Street was a section of human life on a low level, but the sun shone into the garrets. English Mimis and Musettes were visitors not unknown; Hope abode in it, and sometimes Fortune arrived with fame or a modest competence in her hands. At worst the work done was work in letters, and, toilsome and precarious as it might be, of letters it had the charm and the consolation.

New Grub Street, according to Mr Gissing, in his novel of that name (Smith & Elder), is a very much worse, much more miserable, place than Grub Street the old. The borders and marches of this quarter of the town are ill defined, but perhaps we may describe Grub Street as the territory inhabited by the men and women whose pens win their bread. If that be topographically correct, Carlyle and Thackeray, Leigh Hunt and Dickens, were all of the parish where Mr Gissing's characters take their fortunes in such sorry cheer. It is, perhaps, a modern virtue to see everything in black, to abstain from wit, from humour, from gaiety, as strictly as many people abstain from alcoholic drinks. But this was not the manner of the great men whom we have named, nor of the small men in these old days. Like Philip Firmin's friend, they sang—

> And for this reason,
> And for a season,
> Let us be merry before we go!

It is a common belief that even modern Grub Street knows this carol and is not always of a sombre mood. Are there no cakes nor ale, nor any midnight chimes in Grub Street the new? Is life one unbroken and embittered pursuit of the five-pound note? Are there no men poor, but young and light of heart, in the literary parish? We cannot believe that all the parishioners are gloomy failures, conscientious *ratés*. Nay, many of us have tarried by the tables of Grub Street, and have been content with its cowheel and its porter. The entire population does not consist of worthy 'realistic' novelists, underpaid and overworked on one side, and of meanly selfish and treacherous, but successful, hacks on the other. If we understand Mr Gissing's theory of the literary life among the rank and file, he thinks that genius, or even conscientious talent, is in a way repressed, is driven into work of a low kind for the sake of bread-and-butter, while the hodmen of letters who do their hodmen's duties successfully and with acceptance are persons destitute of soul. But may we not argue that what these worthies perform is what nature has fitted them to perform; and that, though they would give ten years of their lives to possess genius and employ it, still they admire, and do not envy, its possessors? Nature has not made it possible for us all to be pessimistic novelists, however greatly we may desire it. As Dr Johnson's friend said, he who had tried to be a philosopher, 'somehow cheerfulness would break in,' and that is fatal. Then the others, the noble laborious failures—it is possible that they are not all men of genius. They may have miscalculated their strength, and vanity may have had much to do with their discomfiture. On the whole, we do not feel convinced by Mr Gissing that Grub Street is such a very ill habitation. The natives can forget their woes, and are not for ever brooding over unfavourable reviews, and on ways of hitting back at their adversaries—usually at the wrong man. They think of many things, they talk of many things, besides 'shop'; indeed, if Grub Street is restricted to its profession, there is not matter enough in it to found a novel on. It is like trying to write a novel of University life. The field is too narrow; the fiction is starved. Reviews, cheques, accepted articles, rejected articles, padding, hack-work in general, is not good 'stock' for a novel, and gives an ill flavour to men's loves and lives. But Mr Gissing, we think, has made this flavour much too strong. Even in Grub Street the fog sometimes lifts, and in the window gardens of the natives you may see blossoming the herb Pantagruelion. But it never blossoms in the windows of those who are unlucky enough to think that they are neglected and under-estimated. This is the besetting sorrow or besetting sin of artists of all kinds in and out of Grub Street. From this embittering error that we may all be delivered, *Beate Francisce, ora pro nobis!*

57. Unsigned review, *Saturday Review*

9 May 1891, lxxi, 551

See headnote to No. 56.

The dwellers in *New Grub Street* as drawn by Mr George Gissing, are neither wholly saints nor wholly sinners; and it is this very complexity of their characters which, as the story develops, keeps our interest almost painfully alive. Jasper Milvain, of the facile pen and the yet more facile conscience, Edwin Reardon and Harold Biffen, the unpractical dreamers, even the worldly and apparently heartless Amy Reardon—all are instinct with life, not the lay figures of the ordinary three-volumed novel. The book is almost terrible in its realism, and gives a picture, cruelly precise in every detail, of this commercial age. The degradation of art by the very necessity of its 'paying its way' is put forward with merciless plainness. The bitter uselessness of attempting a literary career unless you are prepared to consult the market, and supply only that for which there is a demand, forms a sort of text for the book. Art for Art's sake is foredoomed to financial failure. Granting that it is possible to make too much of the pessimistic side of literature in the nineteenth century, still Mr Gissing has produced a very powerful book. He is full of clever touches on literary and social matters, and estimates to a nicety the literary pabulum which the general public enjoys. 'The people who read women's papers are irritated by anything that isn't glaringly obvious—the art of writing for them is to express vulgar thoughts and feelings in a way that flatters vulgar thinkers and feelers.' Of a truth, mankind as a whole adores the commonplace. Again, 'I would have a paper addressing itself to the quarter-educated, that is to say to the great new generation which is being turned out by the Board schools, the young men and women who can just read, but are incapable of sustained attention.'

58. Unsigned review, *Spectator*

30 May 1891, lxvi, 764

Mr George Gissing has never written a more vigorous or a more depressing story than *New Grub Street*. As will be inferred from the title, it deals with the lower grades of life in the world of contemporary literature and journalism, and had the author cared to follow the present fashion of imitative clap-trap nomenclature, he might have called his book 'In Darkest Bohemia.' What makes the novel so unrelievedly melancholy is not so much the prevalence of an atmosphere of sordid misery, though this undoubtedly has its effect in lowering the spirits of the reader; it is the persistent dramatic and narrative vigour with which Mr Gissing embodies his conception of a world in which the man of genius, learning, or fine literary skill is pushed to the wall or trampled under foot, while his rival, with nothing but a poor surface cleverness, made effective by dogged, unsensitive, unscrupulous pushing, triumphantly reaches the goal of success. The old Grub Street of

Pope's day was bad enough, in all conscience, but we really prefer it to the new Grub Street of Mr Gissing's pages. In the former there was much that was revolting, but there was also something of *camaraderie* and good-fellowship, of brotherly kindness and charity; in the latter nothing is heard but the one cry, 'Every man for himself, and the devil take the hindmost.' It is difficult to say whether we are more depressed by the slow torture which in various ways crushes the life out of Edwin Reardon, Alfred Yule, and Harold Biffen, or by the snaky wrigglings, each of which brings Jasper Milvain nearer to his paradise of pounds, shillings, pence, and fame. It seems to us that here, as elsewhere, Mr Gissing holds a brief for pessimism, and that his story is, in essence, an *ex-parte* statement; but the force and impressiveness of the statement are unmistakable. The chapters which deal with the relations between the unpractical genius Reardon and his practical wife; the story of Yule and his daughter; the description of Biffen's rescue of his precious manuscript from the burning lodging-house, are all master's work; and there is not in the whole book a single page which lacks the force of a relentless realism. *New Grub Street* is, in short, a novel which many may fail to enjoy, but which few competent critics can fail to admire, even if they admire under protest.

59. Unsigned review, *Murray's Magazine*

June 1891, 855–6

'I want to deal with the essentially unheroic, with the day-to-day life of the vast majority of people who are at the mercy of paltry circumstances.' This literary aim, which Mr Gissing puts into the mouth of one of his characters, is clearly his own object in his latest work. His characters are for the most part emphatically unheroic, and the one or two who by their ideals and aspirations rise above the common herd are the victories of miserably sordid conditions. Throughout the three closely-written volumes there is little or no relief from the monotone of poverty, failure, ineffectual struggle, and ignoble success. Where our sympathy is awakened, as with Marian, Reardon and Biffen, we are called on to suffer; only when our contempt is aroused, as with Jasper Milvain, are we allowed to congratulate. We would fain believe that this powerful picture of the strain and stress of literary and journalistic competition is painted in too sombre colours, and that life is less relentless than realism. This, of the book as a whole; taken separately, the characters are drawn with vigorous, life-like touches. Each stands out from the canvas in strong and well-defined individuality; but in the relentless setting of 'paltry circumstances' they are allowed little freedom of action, and are constrained by conditions as painful as they are unpicturesque. Deeply interesting as the book is, we feel that it is not Art, and we trust that it is not Life.

60. Walter Besant, on *New Grub Street*, *Author*

1 June 1891, vol. ii, No. 1, 15

The *Author* was the official organ of the Society of Authors and Besant was its editor. His contribution appeared under the title 'Notes and News'. Gissing commented on Besant's article and that by Andrew Lang (see No. 61) in a letter to Bertz dated 20 July 1891:

> You will notice how very imperfectly Besant has understood the book. His description of Reardon is ludicrous. Then again, you will find that Lang makes a mistake which proves that he has not read the story with anything like serious attention. These things are natural enough. Such overworked men *cannot* read books with close thought; they only skim even those which they think interesting (*The Letters of George Gissing to Eduard Bertz*, p. 128).

He held Besant in poor esteem and invariably referred to the *Author* in deprecatory terms. On 7 August, he begged Bertz not to return the three numbers of this journal he had forwarded, asserting they were valueless to him (p. 129).

Mr George Gissing ought to be publicly thanked for introducing to the world a form of literary life which has long been known to all who have penetrated into the by-ways and slums of this many-sided calling. He presents to us several well defined and by no means uncommon types. There is the young man of literary aspirations who rashly attempts to make of letters his livelihood, encouraged by the success of a single first novel. He has no education to speak of; he has no knowledge of society; he has no personal experiences; he has no travel. In fact, he is absolutely devoid of any equipment except a true feeling for Art, and a burning desire to succeed. He cannot succeed. It is not possible for such a man to succeed. He fails dismally, and he dies. In real life such a man would not die. He would sink lower—lower—

until he became the wretched drudge and hack of a penny novelette publisher, which is Malebolge itself. Next, there is the young man who looks about him, sees what will pay, and how men get on in the literary profession. He enters upon his work with the intention of succeeding, and he does succeed. In real life such a man might succeed in the way indicated, but not quite so easily. He becomes an Editor. Now, one of the chief requisites in a modern Editor is that he should know many men, and belong to certain social circles. This young man, with no social position, would certainly not be made an Editor quite so easily. On the other hand, his career illustrates the advantages to be derived from accepting the existing conditions, and trading upon them. But the truest, saddest figure in the book is that of the old *littérateur*, a critic of the former school, who hangs on to letters, getting more and more soured every day, having a paper accepted now and then, doing a stroke of work here and another there, living a life of absolute dependence upon publishers and Editors, whose work nobody wants, whose whole history has been one of humiliations, disgusts and disappointments, who waits humbly on publishers and hopes for their 'generosity.' Truly, as his daughter says, his is a loathsome profession. It is the utter degradation of letters; it is Grub Street with us still. But he degrades his profession still more for he meditates constantly upon the pride of being the Editor of a literary journal, and his only thought, in that capacity, is how he will tear and rend his brother writers. 'I will show them,' he says, 'I will show them how to scarify.' Yes, that is still the thought of certain authors. As it was in the days of Churchill, so it is now. Because a man follows the calling of letters, he must, by other followers of that profession, be slated, scarified, torn to pieces. Every other profession has its unwritten laws of decency and politeness. That of literature, none. I do not suppose that Mr Gissing's book can become popular, but from my own knowledge I can testify to its truth. I know them all, personally,—two or three of each—Mr Yule—Jasper—Edwin—and the fidelity of Mr Gissing's portraits makes me shudder.

61. Andrew Lang and Walter Besant, *Author*

1 July 1891, vol. ii, No. 2, 43–4, 51

Andrew Lang (1844–1912) was a best-selling writer of remarkable versatility—poet, anthropologist (his books on folklore involved him in much controversy), Greek scholar, historian, biographer, translator, essayist, critic, novelist and author of fairy tales. It was probably as a novelist that he was least successful. Gissing regarded him as a sort of Jasper Milvain and disliked his personality. Lang's reply to Besant, entitled 'Realism in Grub Street', shows how much he viewed life through rose-coloured spectacles. Besant, however, would not acknowledge himself beaten although, on the whole, he gave his contemporaries the impression, like his opponent, of being utterly committed to a sanguine view of life.

(*a*) Andrew Lang: Grub Street is the mother of all of us 'd——d literary fellows,' whether we dwell on the first floor or in the attics. Even these eminences were not disenchanted, when we were twenty, M. Béranger says; and why should Mr Gissing try to disenchant the whole eligible district? I would be understood to speak with all respect of Mr Gissing's *New Grub Street*; it is not his fault, but his misfortune, that he sees everything in black. This is the burden of what is queerly called 'Realism.'

One reads in reviews about Mr Gissing's 'poignant realism,' but is it real at all? To myself it seems a perverted idealism, idealism on the seamy side. In Grub Street there are many mansions; they are not all full of failure, and envy, and low cunning, and love of money, and hatred of success. In the *Author* of June, a writer says that he 'can testify to the truth' of the 'New Grub Street.' He is unlucky enough to know people like Mr Gissing's characters, and the fidelity of the portraits makes him shudder. I also am a dweller in Grub Street, but am so fortunate as not to know anybody who resembles these unhappy *ratés*. I do not know the man of comparative genius, with no health, and with an unsympathetic wife. I do not know the impudent and half-educated speculator in 'literature.' I do not know—I wish I did—the gentleman who wants to write on Diogenes Laertius, a delightful subject, and I hope, when he does write that essay, he will clear up the passage about the Megarian historian and Homer.

Willamowitz is too speculative, though decidedly ingenious; but Mr Yule is not here. I want to talk Diogenes Laertius and kindred pedantries with him in vain. However, it is not to be questioned that persons like Jasper and Mr Yule and Edwin may exist, or may have existed; so may Lucien de Rubempré. They may be 'real,' but then they are not everybody. They are not the whole population of Grub Street. There are good fellows there, poor, plucky, contented. Them, at least, I have known, and no picture of Grub Street is real which leaves them out. In Miss Braddon's excellent story, 'The Doctor's Wife,' there is a denizen of Grub Street, Mr Sigismund Smith, a penny novelist. He has humour, and good humour; he likes his trade, and there are many worse trades. The Muses have not given it to me to write a good penny novel; would that they had. It is an enviable art. What is much of Balzac, but glorified penny novel? Well, nobody calls Miss Braddon a realist, but Sigismund Smith is as 'real' as these envious failures, these evil successes. He is not recognised as real, because he is jolly. There are plenty of jolly people in Grub Street, only Realism averts her blue spectacles from them. As to 'scarifying,' what nonsense is talked about it! It is only a battle with snowballs at most. Let some gentleman have his fling at me, let me have my fling at him, if I like; 'it is such easy writing.'

Who is a penny the worse? In some paper I read, for example, that Mr Robert Buchanan has been calling me a Cockney somewhere. That, surely, is 'scarifying'? Perhaps the snowball would hurt if it hit. But it seems to go a little wide; and, if I choose, I can bowl at Mr Buchanan's manly legs. Does he play cricket in a kilt? It seems to me that, in Grub Street, we cry out a great deal for very little hurt. This 'scarifying' is not so bad as what Apollo did to Marsyas. Our skins, however thin, are left to decorate our persons.

In real life, the unlucky hero of Mr Gissing would have had a devoted wife, who believed in her husband's genius; but to give him such a wife would not be Realism. It would be romance, or something improper of that kind. There are depths a good deal deeper in Grub Street than Mr Gissing has chosen to sound. He might have been much more realistic, and yet have been not untrue, except by the suppression of the other side of the truth.

(*b*) Walter Besant: Mr Andrew Lang offers a few remarks on Mr Gissing's 'Grub Street'. So much the better for Mr Gissing's book, which should become in greater demand, even though the writer says he knows no such residents in Grub Street. He touches also on sundry questions rising out of the book, especially on the great Art of Scarifying. 'It is only', he says, 'a battle with snowballs at most.' The ordinary fellow who writes, thinskinned, morbid, sensitive, fails to rise to the height of caring no more for the Scarifier than for the boy who throws a snowball. It is, however, pleasant for him to feel that he ought to receive blows of the bludgeon, or the rasping of the harrow with so much tranquillity. He envies the man who can; for himself, it is beyond him, even if he knows that he shall get the chance of hitting back again—which does not too often happen; he writhes, he groans, he swears. And it is small comfort to him that another man stalks in silent dignity as careless of bludgeon, and rake, and harrow, as if they were no more than light and feathery snowballs.

62. Unsigned review, *New York Tribune Illustrated Supplement*

20 March 1898, 17–18

The *New York Tribune* did much to promote Gissing's works in the United States. The following review was obviously written in the hope of inducing an American firm to publish *New Grub Street.* However, it was not until 1903 that Gissing was approached by McClure who had this intention. Gissing agreed to write an introduction to the novel, but his death caused the project to collapse. Eventually, C. A. Brewster, of Troy, New York, brought out the first American edition of *New Grub Street* in 1904.

Now that everybody is reading *The Whirlpool,* it may be hoped that interest in a book of George Gissing's which has never been fully appreciated will be speedily revived. *New Grub Street,* in fact, has not been published in this country at all, we believe, and while some of the author's books are well known in America, this production, which is one of great power and originality, is practically a dead letter. Mr Gissing has never written a better book than this. Dreary it is, to a heart-rending extent, and this may account for its never having achieved any popularity, but by this time the world has grown accustomed to the tragic note. If people can enjoy being harrowed by *Quo Vadis* we do not see why they cannot enjoy a book like *New Grub Street.* Suppose the glamour of the past is missing, and that the author shows no taste for the glamour of the present. At least he pierces to the core of human things, at least he reveals the keenest understanding of the griefs which shake commonplace souls, and somehow his sombre, even pessimistic book leaves the mind strengthened, for it paints right and wrong in their true relations, exposes the shabbiness of small souls and points out the chances offered to those who are capable of rising to better things. We have never found George Gissing a novelist of charm. He works with too hard and too gloomy a pen. But he is a writer of indubitable power, his sincerity is unquestionable, and, dreary though he may be, he nevertheless works out of a high-minded and stimulating enthusiasm. *New Grub Street* has the further attraction, we may add, of painting to the life those mediocre figures who have figured so conspicuously in the literary life of Victorian London, especially during the last twenty years or so. Mr Gissing has seen through his models with wonderful clearness. Their pettiness, their ignorance, their unspeakable pretence and vulgarity he has painted once and for all. Quite aside from its significance as a study of human nature pure and simple, this is a brilliant book. It gives an irresistible portrait of a class. The American publishers of *The Whirlpool* might do worse than reprint *New Grub Street* in a single-volume edition.

DENZIL QUARRIER

February 1892

Denzil Quarrier was published when Gissing was correcting the proofs of *Born in Exile*. He was, on the whole, pleased with the critical reception accorded the novel, remarking both to his sister Ellen (14 March) and to Bertz (17 March) that *Denzil Quarrier* was favourably reviewed. He regarded the book as 'in fact, a strong defence of conventionality' and thought most readers could perceive this intention (*Letters of George Gissing to Members of His Family*, p. 326).

63. Unsigned review, *Chicago Tribune*

13 February 1892, 13

Reprinted in the *Literary News*, March 1892, 74.

It was in the *Chicago Tribune* that Gissing made his literary debut in March 1877 with a short story entitled 'The Sins of the Fathers'. It was, therefore, natural that the staff of the newspaper should watch the development of his career with particular attention. *Denzil Quarrier* was granted more than a column and was headed 'To-Day's Literature—"Denzil Quarrier", Mr George Gissing's latest effort. It is a Strong and Impressive Though Not a Great Work—He Dispenses with Poetic Justice, Triumphant Virtue, and the Conventional Happy Ending—The Characters in the Book Analyzed.'

Whether or not Mr George Gissing is the 'coming man' among English novelists is perhaps too early to decide. *Denzil Quarrier*, his latest effort, is a strong and impressive, though not a great work. One swallow does not make a summer, and *Denzil Quarrier*, promising a story as it is, affords but a partial test of its author's capacity.

The omens, however, are decidedly favorable to Mr Gissing. The future historian of English fiction may possibly regard this novel as more truly significant and representative, more genuinely a product of the age than many a finer and more famous work. For Mr Gissing swims with the stream; consciously or unconsciously, he is animated by the Time-spirit and receives and transmits the influence that rules the hour. In matters intellectual the one dominant characteristic of the age is its naturalism. Not the naturalism of Zola, but the naturalism of Goethe and Arnold; the craving to get at the root of things, to 'see clear and think straight'; the demand that a term shall answer to some reality; the disposition to ignore the claims of authority, and to ask, 'But *is* it so? Is it so *for me*?' Realism in fiction is only one of the currents of this great stream, and—dare we say it?—it is not the main current. A writer may call himself a realist and yet be steeped in illusions. A 'sad sincerity' is the true note of the naturalism of our day; pessimists we are not; to the optimists we say with Montaigne 'Que sçais-je?' Optimism itself has been transformed; Browning we call an optimist, but Browning's Christian Stoicism, or Stoical Christianity—the latter is perhaps the better phrase—would have disgusted our grandfathers. Half-tones have succeeded for a while the strong lights and vivid colors of pre-scientific days.

This low key is characteristic of *Denzil Quarrier*. Poetic justice, triumphant virtue, the conventional 'happy ending'—with all of these the author dispenses. The story has tragic elements, but is not pure tragedy. The victims do not 'breast the pressure of life.' Rather they seek to evade it, and when at last the 'fell Sergeant', Nemesis, makes her 'strict arrest' his methods reflect scant credit on the Detective Bureau of Olympus. The gentle, girlish heroine, who bears the sweet and significant name of Lilian, pays the penalty of a false position. She is needlessly sacrificed in a conflict of love and ambition—needlessly, since, in spite of her misgivings, Quarrier loves her sincerely, and would at any time account 'the world well-lost' for her sake. Quarrier himself is admirably drawn. Honest, impulsive, sanguine, self-assertive, hopelessly deficient in tact and finesse, he is an excellent specimen of a kind-hearted, blundering Englishman.

Simply and directly told, the story is an excellent bit of work, regarded from a technical standpoint. The author has no hobby to ride, no mission to fulfil; our own remarks in reference to his *fin de siècle* attitude are not warranted by any superficial indications. Mr Gissing does not write for the tyrannical 'young person'; to mature and intelligent readers, however, his book may be heartily recommended.

64. Unsigned review, *Daily Chronicle*

20 February 1892, 3

In the newspaper the review was entitled 'A Political Novel'.

Reviewers ought to deal harshly by Mr Gissing, for he takes up much of their time. He makes them read him. One has to go right through with Mr Gissing, from cover to cover. Yet it is done without complaining, the truth being that one feels a little the better for the task. It is a grateful business, after all, praising a workmanlike novel; and one always accompanies Mr Gissing with the comfortable feeling that he is a fine and finished artist with a conscience, who will strive to entertain one with his best, from the beginning to the end of the journey. There is nothing trivial and nothing careless in him. He is serious, and on his mettle, from start to finish. He wastes no words, he is a precisian in style, never a decorative sentence disfigures his page. The worst that one can say of him is in the nature of a compliment, which is, that he is quite ready to present his characters unsympathetically in his unflinching resolve to present them faithfully.

The interest of *Denzil Quarrier* is to a certain extent political. That is to say, the hero develops a political ambition, and the main story concerns his election to Parliament. Most novel readers, we hope, detest the 'filthy dowlas' of party politics, in which, from the aesthetic point of view, there is no conceivable interest. But Mr Gissing makes a very live man out of a slightly blatant young politician, and the dirty little provincial scenes into which Quarrier is thrown when he decides to contest Polterham are life-like enough to make a good many bright pages out of a rather sordid theme. The raucous draper, the unwholesome parson, and the somnolent Tory member are good and impressive in their several ways, by reason of their uncompromising individuality. They are humorous—albeit in a rather painful way—by virtue of their grim reality. Quite subordinate creatures in the story, they make the political part of it tingle with an ugly, downright actuality.

But the serious and human interest of the story lies apart from the vulgar little politics of Polterham. It is a rather ordinary social problem, turned to imaginative and tragic account by a skilled and artistic hand. There is a delicate villain, whom Mr Gissing has rather subtly imagined, who makes an admirable contrast with the robustious political hero, and who contrives by a sad fatuity to wreck a life where he had proposed only to check a career. There is a rather novel type of widow, whose share in the plot ought not to be explained in a review, and who contrives to precipitate the tragedy by a tenderly malicious word. The scene between Mrs Wade and Lilian, in Mrs Wade's cottage, is one of the best in the book. The book ends drearily, but very exactly. It could not rightly have ended otherwise. Lilian disappears quite as her nature orders her. It would have been easy to save her by a ruse familiar to novel-wrights and novel readers, but she slips from the scene just in the way that she should do.

The book is written tersely and vividly, with never a word too much and never a word too little. There is no 'colour' in it. Every sentence achieves its end by containing not a syllable more than the author felt to be sufficient for his purpose. Other merits apart, Mr Gissing seems to understand a great deal better than any of his contemporaries the art of leaving out. Where George Meredith, wanting to drive one of his characters to a railway station, would call upon the gods to summon him a coach, Mr George Gissing would be content to whistle for a hansom.

65. Unsigned review, *Saturday Review*

5 March 1892, lxxiii, 276

In a letter to his sister Ellen who, like Margaret and their mother, disapproved of the audacities of *Denzil Quarrier*, Gissing quoted maliciously the reviewer's assertion 'A bolder theme may possibly suit this author better' (*Letters of George Gissing to Members of His Family*, p. 326). When writing to Eduard Bertz three days later on 17 March he added: 'They tell me that not a single paper has objected to the theme. Indeed, after Hardy's "Tess," one can scarcely see the limits of artistic freedom' (*The Letters of George Gissing to Eduard Bertz*, p. 149).

Denzil Quarrier is a story which is almost excellent. It has some well-drawn characters, which are quite within the author's power and grasp, and the main idea of the story is quite sufficient. The fault is one of certain minor disappointments. Denzil Quarrier is a man who has tried several vocations, including the navy and the Bar, but who is of a restless disposition, and is hard to satisfy. Before the story opens he has settled down in life with a young lady whose husband has been arrested for forgery as the bridal pair had left the church. This girl, Lilian, is a sweet creature with great possibilities; and the story is, indeed, a sad one which forces her from the retirement and wherein there is alone safety for her when her husband has been released from prison. The irregular union of Denzil and Lilian has all the elements of permanence, and throughout the story there is no question on either side of weakening the voluntary bond. Denzil Quarrier, partly through inclination and partly through force of circumstances, becomes a Parliamentary candidate for his native town, thereby secretly offending an old friend, Eustace Glazzard, a mean-souled dilettante, who has had intentions of a similar kind himself. Glazzard is the person who knows the secret history of Lilian, which has been confided to him by Denzil, and when the latter, having presumably been married in France, brings home his quasi-bride to Polterham the disappointed man finds revenge by seeking out Lilian's husband, Northway, and inducing him to come to Polterham, and openly claim her as his wife on the day of the election. How this is done, and the sad result of plotting, may best be read in the book, which is charmingly written, in a clear, simple style. Throughout the book there is nothing to violate possibility, or even probability, and everywhere there is evidence—though unobtrusive evidence—of scholarly research and of a mind well abreast of the time. A bolder theme may possibly suit this author better, and good honest work may be always expected from him.

66. Unsigned review, *The Times*

12 March 1892, 5

In letters to Ellen Gissing and Bertz, Gissing states his satisfaction with this review.

Fresh from exposing 'New Grub Street' and its obliquities, Mr George Gissing gives us, in *Denzil Quarrier*, an electioneering novel—a novel, at least, in which electioneering humours form the seasoning. Very effective is his little satire upon the working of representative institutions in the borough of Polterham twelve years ago. One is diverted in turn by the candidates, vehement in public and nonchalant in private, by the officious Tapers and Tadpoles who 'turn the machine,' and by the prattle of Mrs Taper and Miss Tadpole. But Polterham politics, after all, are only the accessory of a story of more than usual psychological interest—a story which leaves no solution of more than one of its problems to the imagination. The hero—let us say the principal character—is one of the candidates for the representation of Polterham. He reminds us now of Mr Boythorn in *Bleak House*, such is his strength in superlatives; now of Mr Victor Raynor in *One of Our Conquerors*, such his sanguine, all-subduing spirits. He resembles Mr Meredith's latest hero in another respect, that he is braving Society with a union not recognized by law, though morally not blameworthy. Only one man, and that one Denzil Quarrier's friend from boyhood, is in possession of Denzil's secret. The first question is whether any sufficient reason is shown why this familiar friend should have committed an act of deliberate perfidy. The traitor himself 'is not sure that he understands why he did it.' We are afraid it is becoming too common a trick among novelists to take refuge in the incalculable in human nature as a substitute for intelligible motive. Again, the author maliciously leaves us a legacy of perplexity in his concluding sentence. After Eustace Glazzard has confessed his perfidy, Denzil is made to walk away and ponder the matter. Presently his thoughts

> summed themselves in a sentence which involuntarily he spoke aloud: 'Now I understand the necessity for social law.'

But why 'now'? Is the possibility of treachery on the part of a bosom friend the only sanction of marriage?

67. Unsigned review, *Guardian* (London)

23 March 1892, xlvii (1), 439

Gissing does not seem to have seen this, but he remarked in his letter of 14 March 1892 (see headnote to No. 65) that he would be curious to see what the *Guardian* had to say about *Denzil Quarrier*, as it was always very complimentary to him.

Denzil Quarrier as a sketch of modern politics in a country town is excellent reading. All the politicians, male and female, of Polterham are eminently lively and life-like. The only fault we should venture to find with this part of the novel is that the stage is rather too crowded for its size, though we confess that we would not willingly lose any of the performers. But there is a painful story mixed up with the graphic sketches of rural Toryism and Radicalism. The Radical candidate, who is the hero of the story, is a man of generous impulses and no particular principles, as regards politics having an impartial contempt for all parties, and as regards morals holding, to quote the author's own words, that 'love was a sacred truth, cancelling verbal untruth.' This disregard of the common-sense view of honour leads him to pass off on the society of Polterham a young lady as his wife, who is in reality the wife of a scoundrel who was arrested at the church door after their marriage, and whom she has never seen since. Her nervous dread of discovery—the simplest reader must know, of course, that discovery is inevitable—is delicately contrasted with her lover's light-hearted carelessness and confidence, but not even the author's artistic handling can make the theme other than unpleasant, and the tragic ending makes one lay down the book with an increased feeling of dissatisfaction. We heartily wish that Mr Gissing had confined himself to politics.

BORN IN EXILE

May 1892

68. Unsigned review, *Speaker*

14 May 1892, v, 598–9

The *Speaker* was a liberal review of politics, letters, science and the arts. It devoted considerable space to book reviewing. Gissing had bought the first number in April 1890 and found it extremely dull.

It would not be necessary to remind anyone who had read *New Grub Street* that Mr Gissing is a pessimist. It seemed, indeed, hardly possible to conceive anything more gloomy than that novel, although the strength and fascination of it were remarkable. Yet *Born in Exile* is at least as sombre in its tone. Mr Gissing has looked out upon the world and seen that it is not all good: or, perhaps, in the course of his literary career he has grown contemptuous of writers who secure the happiness of their characters at the expense of the conviction of the story. At any rate even in the opening pages of *Born in Exile* we have the gloomy atmosphere; we are present at a prize-giving at Whitelaw College, and it is characteristic of Mr Gissing that we view this prize-giving chiefly from the point of view of the disappointed. The same depression is to be felt in the following chapters; the hero, Godwin Peak, is a boy at Whitelaw College, vexed by terrible poverty and more terrible pride. We read of miserable economies, wretched vulgarities, sordid struggles. When, at the close of the first part of the story, the hero decides to leave Whitelaw College for London, it is not because London holds out for him any bright hopes, any remarkable allurement; it is because he cannot face the humiliation which would attend him if he returned to the College. An insufferable Cockney uncle has taken a shop near the College which he proposes to open as 'Peak's

Refreshment and Dining Rooms.' He has proposed, moreover, that this clever, sensitive nephew of his shall help to advertise the place, on a mutual system, among the students at Whitelaw College. In his delineation of the character of the hero Mr Gissing has achieved by far the best thing in these three volumes. Peak is intellectually brilliant, emotionally sensuous, at one moment really noble and at another contemptibly weak. It is impossible to sum up his character in a few words; one must hear him speak in the pages of the story; one must follow his unhappy career to appreciate him properly. It is a clear and vivid picture of a difficult and paradoxical character. He falls in love, and, believing that his irreligion would be fatal to his chances, he boldly avows that he intends to take orders. He would have done so had he not been found out. His hypocrisy was futile, and he finds—there is irony in the situation—that it was also unnecessary. The girl Sidwell is speaking:—

'But here is the proof how much better it is to behave truthfully! . . . I understand the new thought, and how natural it is for you to accept it. If only I could have come to know you well, your opinions would not have stood between us.'

Peak made a slight gesture, and smiled incredulously.

'You think so now.'

'And I have such good reason for my thought,' rejoined Sidwell earnestly, 'that when you said you loved me my only regret in looking to the future was—that you had resolved to be a clergyman.'

He leaned back in the chair, and let a hand fall on his knee. The gesture seemed to signify a weary relinquishment of concern in what they were discussing.

'How could I have foreseen that?' he uttered, in a corresponding tone. (Chapter V)

The hero was, he himself felt, born in exile—born out of his sphere; by birth a plebeian, he had the tastes, the sensitiveness of the aristocrat. He dies in exile, alone in an hotel at Vienna. Mr Gissing makes some attempt to relieve the gloom of his story by the introduction of one character, Malkin, whose amusing follies he treats in a saturnine manner. But the relief is very slight; and sometimes it must inevitably occur to a reader that more contrast would have been more artistic. One does not appreciate gloom best by having three large, closely printed volumes of it; in this respect the book is like a large dinner composed entirely of very cold mutton with no alleviating pickles. Mr Gissing is perfectly free to be a pessimist; but he is not free, on the score of his previous work, to be anything else but an artist. The story which is made up to look quite happy is necessarily inartistic; but it does not follow that a prolonged record of sordid unhappiness is necessarily art. *Born in Exile* is not in many ways so strong a novel as *New Grub Street*, but it is the work of an original writer, one who has a distinct individuality. With all its faults, it contains analysis of character which is in some instances really masterly.

69. Unsigned review, *Morning Post*

19 May 1892, 2

The thoroughness and ability displayed in Mr George Gissing's study of his hero, Godwin Peak, are beyond doubt. Yet it may be questioned whether the end and aim of fiction resides in analysis, however minute and clever, which is accompanied by the careful avoidance of any kind of emotion. This aridity has hitherto been conspicuously absent from Mr Gissing's productions, or at least from those which have made his name. It dawned in *Denzil Quarrier*, and many of the writer's admirers will regret to find that it is still more apparent in his newer work, *Born in Exile*. There are hardly any but painful traits in the character of Peak, miserably sensitive on the subject of his obscure birth, devoured by ambition, tormented by religious doubt, savagely independent, and yet betrayed by love into the depths of baseness. The strongest scene in the book is that of his confession to Sidwell Warricombe, and their consequent separation. The girl's seeming nobility of soul appears to hold out a promise of better things in the midst of the moral gloom that envelopes the lovers. This hope, however, is disappointed when, after years of waiting, Sidwell answers by 'I cannot' Peak's last endeavour to turn the sad current of his life, henceforth abandoned to the bitter pessimism which leads to utter despair.

70. Unsigned review, *Daily Chronicle*

26 May 1892, 3

In its original form, this appreciation was entitled 'Our One English Realist'. Gissing had copies sent to his brother and to Bertz. To the latter he wrote: 'The writer at all events gives a very fair and full account of my book. I believe this is as yet the only favourable notice' (19 June 1892, *The Letters of George Gissing to Eduard Bertz*, p. 157).

Mr George Gissing's work has many of the notes which for a time gave to French Realism its vogue, and, at the last, have brought about the idealist reaction. Of course, no novel which dipped much beyond the surface of the murky stream of psycho-physiology would find a place in English circulating libraries, or in English middle-class drawing-rooms; but the sordidness, the squalor, the 'dismal anarchy of life,' these one may paint, and, if the hand which lays on the colour be skilful, it wins popularity. Mr Gissing has skill, and he is becoming popular. He long ago mastered the technique of the Realist's craft. He has gone on steadily from strength to strength, and this, his latest achievement, is also his best. As an arrangement in black and grey it would be hard to beat from the point of view of artistic presentation. If life were really made up of leaden tints and sombre shadows it would leave little to be desired on the score of truth either.

The plot is of the simplest, and of 'sub-plot' there is, happily, none. The motive is one which must be common enough already, and likely to become commoner as the old social order gradually fades into the new. The hero, Godwin Peak, was born in the lower strata of the English *bourgeoisie*—that small-trading class which is only one social remove from the proletariat itself. Temperamentally ambitious and of really first-rate intellectual capacity, his few years in a provincial college, among social superiors, developed tastes already inherent in his being, and finally produced in him a revulsion from all the surroundings and characteristics of the class to which he by birth belonged. That was the dreary tragedy of his life. He conceived ideals destined never to be realised, and nourished desires whose gratification his circumstances forbade. His was not the vaulting ambition of the snob; it was the piteous, pitiful yearning of the man born in exile for his native land.

In yet another respect, too, he is typical. A time like this, when 'we stand between two worlds, one dead, one waiting to be born,' is fertile of men whose tastes are at constant war with their convictions—the men to whom Mark Pattison gave the cynical advice, 'Vote with the Liberals and dine with the Tories.' Of these was Godwin Peak. The world into which Fate forced him was democratic, sceptical, advanced, unconventional—and his brains told him that it was right. The land where he desired to dwell was conservative, orthodox, hide-bound to convention—and he believed it wrong. But there grew there the fine flower of inherited culture and cultivated refinement, and its perfume maddened and bewitched him. There, too, dwelt a woman whom he loved. He deliberately decided to be a traitor to his convictions. He pretended a belief in the creeds he despised, and carried the fraud to the point of preparing to take orders in the Established Church, and be tracked down, and to suffer perpetual banishment in the end. He died in exile.

We don't like him, of course, nor does his creator, but so masterly is the characterisation that, in spite of ourselves, our dislike of him is softened down by more than a dash of genuine pity. At one moment of his career we almost hope that his treason will succeed, and that success will work for him a miracle of redemption. But Mr Gissing never loves his heroes. His analysis is the analysis of cold intellect, not of warm sympathy, and that is why we close his books a little sadder than we opened them.

By a certain school of critics Mr Gissing will be taken sharply to task, and accused of forcing art into the service of polemics. Just as his first book, *Demos*, was condemned by the Socialists on the grounds that it made a Socialist appear detestable, so will *Born in Exile* be censured by agnostics, for that it portrays an agnostic justifying his falsehood and flouting his conscience. His defence is revolting, but on its own ground it is difficult to defeat.

The minor characters are drawn with as firm a hand, and are painted with as convincing a realism, as the central figure of the tragedy itself. One sees but little, for instance, of the Broad Churchman, the Rev. Bruno Chilvers, but one would recognise him anywhere—say in the pulpit of Westminster Abbey or on the pavement of Piccadilly.

Could anything be truer than this brief sketch of the average educated woman's view of the relations of science and faith?

Mrs Warricombe settled at last into a comfortable private opinion that though the record of geology might be trustworthy, that of the Bible was more so. She would admit that there was no impiety in accepting the evidence of nature, but held to a secret conviction that it was safer to believe in Genesis.

Mr Gissing has still something to mend in the matter of style and method. 'Nigritude,' 'susurration,' 'improval,' 'intemerate,' strike us as vile phrases, and the stopping of the action of a dramatic scene in order to analyse, at several pages' lengths, the minds and motives of the actors might well be left to Bostonian 'fictionists.' But spite of these obvious blemishes, *Born in Exile* is one of the cleverest and best written books of the season. It will leave an impression on all who read it—an impression permanent, if troublous.

71. Unsigned review, *Saturday Review*

11 June 1892, lxxiii, 688

Gissing thought this review 'surpassed in abusive misrepresentation anything I have come across, concerning my own work, of late years' (19 June 1892, *The Letters of George Gissing to Eduard Bertz*, p. 157).

We have had enough, perhaps more than enough, of late of the religious novel, with its antagonisms founded on the conflict between orthodoxy and agnosticism; nor, if we are to be reconciled to a further dose of that with which we are already surfeited, will it be at the hands of Mr Gissing, whose Godwin Peak appears to us the most unlovable creation that ever appealed to the misdirected sympathies of a reader, seeing that his theological tergiversations are founded not on religious conviction, but simply and solely on the grounds of social advancement. This interesting hero justifies his right to the title of 'Born in Exile' in that fortune, in the author's words, 'had decreed his birth in a social sphere where he must ever be an alien'—being, that is to say, the son of a chemist's assistant, and having received a good education in the college of 'a money-making Midland town'—an education which, by the way, he brings to a summary close because a relation of his has the bad taste to open an eating-house in the immediate neighbourhood of the college—he systematically ignores his poor old widowed mother, who has pinched herself to pay for his schooling, and deserts the agnosticism which has inspired him to demolish Christianity in the pages of the *Critical Review* for a very half-hearted profession of orthodoxy and a determination to take holy orders—and all for what? To figure favourably in the eyes of a more or less agreeable girl, and above all to obtain an entrée to pleasant country-house society. Part prig, part snob, all egotist, Godwin Peak inspires us with feelings where disgust and boredom strive for the mastery; his talk, his thoughts are ever of himself. The speech wherein he declares his passion for his mistress positively bristles with 'I—I—I,' and he cannot be left alone in his bedroom without 'gazing deliberately at himself in the glass,' and asking himself unanswered, and perhaps unanswerable, conundrums as to his course of conduct. There is plenty about theology, geology, and all sorts of other 'ologies' and 'isms' in Mr Gissing's pages; for his characters, when gravelled for lack of matter, have a simple habit of asking each other, in the manner of the American interviewer, 'Well, what do you think of such an one,' or 'What is your opinion of this, that, and the other?' and away go their tongues at score, making free with the contents of Mr Gissing's commonplace book. It is all very well to quote, as does the author of *Born in Exile*. 'Oui, répondit Pococurante, il est beau d'écrire ce qu'on pense; c'est le privilège de l'homme,' but he should remember that what is 'beau' to the writer may be anything but 'beau' to the reader, and that if it be the privilege of one man to write, it may be, at least, equally within the rights of others to skip.

72. Unsigned review, *The Times*

1 July 1892, 18

Gissing found this notice very satisfactory, but he was disturbed by the remark that his work was 'somewhat provincial' (unpublished letter to his brother Algernon, Yale).

Born in Exile is, like all Mr George Gissing's recent works, a suggestive novel, full of close thought and carefully-drawn character. To skim it is impossible. Read attentively, as it deserves to be, it must leave the impression of a power and penetration not possessed by many modern novelists. On the other hand, in lighter and far commoner qualifications, such as humour, pathos, picturesqueness, or stirring narrative, Mr Gissing is deficient. His novels appeal neither to the heart, nor the senses, nor the imagination, but almost exclusively to the head; and they, moreover, are pervaded by a certain provincialism of tone and topic. The principal characters belong to a group of rather clever young men educated at the institute of a big Midland town; and the odour of this institute and its classes tends to cling to the story from beginning to end. Of the young men, Godwin Peak is the most conspicuous figure. Described flatteringly, he is a natural aristocrat clogged by plebeian connexions and plebeian breeding. Described unflatteringly, he is a snob. We should be doing an injustice, however, to Mr Gissing's subtlety of treatment if we adopted this latter description. Peak goes forth into the world a fierce, if undeclared, Radical and atheist. But blended with his Radicalism and atheism is an intellectual disdain of the populace, which ripens first into a feeling of social repugnance, and finally into a yearning to move in the circles with which his mental and social affinities ally him. So far, Godwin Peak is an interesting and genuine study in human nature, and we cannot lightly dismiss him as a snob. But we cannot find the same plausibility in the false step which he is led to take by his overmastering desire to scale the social heights above him. Having been seized with admiration for a young lady of some social station, it suddenly strikes him that he might recommend himself to her and to her father by entering the Church—the Church which, as his intimates know, he derides in private, and has even derided in point. On the spur of the moment he calmly announces his intention to take Holy Orders. Forthwith he casts science to the winds, and settles down in the neighbourhood of his friends the Warricombes, reading divinity and preparing defences of the faith in order to improve his position with Warricombe *père*. For a while all is well. Then his falsity is detected and he is humiliated in the eyes of the woman whom he loves and who has begun to return his love. It does not seem to us that there is any adequate motive for Peak's unpremeditated treachery to himself. To a strong, self-contained, and proud character—and Peak's had been so presented—such a sudden and violent deflection from ordinary straightforwardness appears well-nigh impossible. However, it could hardly have failed to occur to Peak that in the nineteenth century he was far more likely to attain the social position he coveted by persevering in his own work than by masquerading as a clergyman. Nor does society receive every clergyman with open arms. It may be said that this is human nature, to go hopelessly astray just when one would have least expected it. Perhaps; but, if novelists are to avail themselves freely of human fallibility as a spring of action, where will consistency of characterization—heretofore considered the prime merit of the novel writer—come in? The minor characters are all cleverly drawn. The Rev. Bruno Chilvers, in particular, is an excellent satire upon the broad, complaisant clergyman who is so tolerant that he would smile benignantly upon Apollyon, and welcome him as a disguised supporter of the Christian religion. The author of the *Pseudodoxia Epidemica*, we might add, was Sir Thomas Browne, not Sir Thomas Brown. But here, no doubt, it is the reviser who is at fault.

73. Unsigned review, *Guardian* (London)

20 July 1892, xlvii (2), 1098

A novel by the author of *New Grub-street* must always be of great interest, and *Born in Exile* is one that it is hard to lay down, though it is a pessimist book, as all from this school are bound to be. Godwin Peak is an intellect of boundless ambition, 'born in exile,' that is to say, an aristocrat of low birth, with a strong taste for social refinements, but without the sense of honour of a higher class. His struggles for a livelihood and distinction are long and painful, and he exhibits the arrogance of a character unsoftened by any gleam of spiritual faith, and without any principle except self-seeking. The crisis of his fate appears in the temptation to affect Christianity and take orders, to win the hand of a religious girl. The deception is exposed by those associated in the production of Godwin's savagely anti-Christian writings, and some touching scenes follow, in which the Christian girl condemns, only to excuse, the hypocrisy of her lover. These scenes mitigate the hardness of the book, in which dialogue and characters are always of the diamond cut diamond order. In the end Sidwell adopts Godwin's scepticism, but cannot resolve to offend her kindred and marry him; and the book ends badly. The hard, dusty highway of life, trodden by all these people without hope and without faith, is a more distressing spectacle than the author probably meant to make it, and the hero approaches a Napoleonic ideal of cynical self-seeking.

74. George Cotterell, *Academy*

23 July 1892, xlii, 67–8

George Cotterell was the author of two books of poems, *The Banquet, a Political Satire* (1892) and *Poems: Old and New* (1894).

Intellectual scepticism has had a fairly good turn in the novels of the present generation, and, whether the effect be for good or harm, fiction has done its best to justify the attitude of doubt. Hitherto, however, the religious sceptic has been presented in a suitably heroic guise. We have seen him throw off one by one, with firmness if with reluctance, the fetters of his early training, and emancipate himself from fond errors to which he was too brave and true still to cling. His courage has involved him in many difficulties, and in painful personal separations, but in no modern novel until now—so far as my observation goes—has the doubter paltered with his doubts or compromised matters with his conscience. Yet it is certain that there are many sceptics who outwardly conform to the beliefs of the multitude, and it is this side of the problem of intellectual doubt that Mr George Gissing gives us in *Born in Exile*. The case he describes is an extreme one. It is not that of a man who holds his doubts so lightly that he continues from force of habit to act as though he had none. Mr Gissing's Godwin Peak is a student, whose scepticism is well-reasoned and aggressive. The ungenial conditions of his life fostered, to begin with, a temperament naturally unsympathetic, and his intellect avenged itself upon easy-going humanity by upsetting its beliefs. But ambition was a strong element in Peak's character, and this in its turn was fostered by the passion of love. Far above him in the social scale, far removed from him, as he supposed, in intellectual sympathy, was the girl he wished to marry. It seemed to him that the only way to win her was to join the Church, and take holy orders. The reader will wonder how this was to be done without an absolute recantation of his heterodoxy; but that would have been too commonplace an expedient for a man of Peak's mental resource. He preferred to try instead the more hazardous expedient of a double life, intellectual and moral; indeed, the casuistical attractions of such a choice made it almost welcome to him. One must not disclose the lines of the story; but it goes without saying that honest human nature will rebel against intellectual deceit as much as against any other. The story is almost necessarily a melancholy one, but it is singularly able; and those readers who do not at an early stage give it up as dull will gratefully admit that it is brilliant. The cleverness of the book is attested by the fact that Godwin Peak neither forfeits the reader's sympathy nor wins his admiration. We take him for what he is; and though the whole result is unsatisfactory, it includes much that is worth having. There are many passages in the novel that would bear quotation. Here is one, which will serve the double purpose of indicating the intellectual quality of Peak's mind—for he is the speaker—and of Mr Gissing's style:

'I can't pretend to care for anything but individuals. The few whom I know and love are of more importance to me than all the blind multitude rushing to destruction. I hate the word *majority*; it is the few, the very few, that have always kept alive whatever of effectual good we see in the human race. There are individuals who outweigh, in every kind of value, generations of ordinary people.'

75. Morley Roberts on George Gissing, *Novel Review*

May 1892, i, 97–103

On the whole Gissing had a rather poor opinion of Roberts's first article on his works. In April 1892, after seeing a rough draft of it, he wrote to his brother that it was not worth much, though on seeing it in print he found it did not read so badly after all. He reverted to his original view in a letter to Bertz of 20 May 1892: 'To tell you the truth, I was disappointed with Roberts's article. I don't think he understands my work in the very least!'

The article appeared in the first number of the journal, which was edited by a friend of Roberts, H. H. Champion, a socialist leader. Gissing was slightly acquainted with him. See also Champion's review of *The Crown of Life*, No. 134.

At thirty-five or thereabouts Mr George Gissing, the author of *Demos*, *The Nether World*, *New Grub Street*, and half-a-dozen more or less known, more or less liked, and more or less abused, books, has managed by dint of steady perseverance in the paths of comparatively unpopular fiction to make himself a name which has nothing so ephemeral as the smell of blood about it. For if the tricks of the average wily novelist are various, the most facile way unto a throne of cheap and tinsel notoriety lies through the slaughter of his sawdusty puppets and all the probabilities. But Mr Gissing is not given to bloodshed. It is true that his characters are not notoriously immortal; they indeed die, but if they do their hearts are affected, or they get pneumonia, or pernicious anaemia from unhealthy surroundings into which no sun of hope brings a single ray of joy. But he is not particularly fond of despatching the miserable. He is, on the contrary, rather given to showing how much wretched mortals can endure and yet live. His heroes are apt to doggedly suffer what would make any ordinary hero cut his own throat or some one else's. For dying is not their forte, and they rarely kill any one. I cannot recollect a single murder or manslaughter by hero or heroine in the long list of his books. Moreover, the part of the villain is only played as a secondary cause by any human being, for the great original villain, the primary scoundrel of all his dramas, is called Circumstance, or, by a periphrasis, the native malignity of matter. The entire universe being callous and the starlight cold, in the night of pessimism the sun goes out; there is a glacial epoch of indifference among us, and we die slowly, being unregarded by those who see their own death near at hand. For destiny is neither sudden of release nor apt at poetical justice.

There can be no greater mistake made in the critical estimation of contemporary novelists than to regard this writer as a philanthropist in the ordinary meaning of the word. He is by no means such a fool of prophecy as to offer us immediate therapeutics. To be a lover of his race as a matter of business would not appear to commend itself to his downright sincerity of purpose. He would rather leave that to other writers and those professional organisers of hardened charity to whom a finger in the profitable pie is equivalent to a bird in the hand. Nor does he ever attempt to salt the birds in the bush represented by the gaudier socialistic schemes.

Yet as he is still young he was once even younger, and at that time, judging by his earliest book, which was promising and nothing more, he appears to have been himself salted by the priests of the cult of Positivism, whose archangel on earth is the prophet Harrison. But this was a disease he speedily recovered from, for Positivism is rarely fatal to the young.

In his second and severely-let-alone book, *The Unclassed*, he began to be more distinctly offensive to the Philistines than is possible by the most dogmatic denial of ancient religious sanctions. He taught the possibility of redemption by love; he conceived the notion, incredible in a Christian age, that purity might dwell in the nether pit. For his heroine was of the half-world; and if the whole world were only half as good as she ended by being, or, indeed, was all through her unhappier history, refuges for the fallen would be at a distinct discount, unless they were in request as seminaries. In this book the Positivists were nowhere. Dostoieffski had long since sent them packing. The worship of sorrow displaced their plaster deity, and their God-self gave way to an English Sonia of a more intellectual type; for real life was too much for Mr Gissing, and the defiled streets of London seem to have afforded him no trustworthy data with which to exalt the humanity glorified in the later and self-destructive Comtism.

Thereafter he fell under the subtler influence of Tourguénieff, and wrote a finely analytic study of feminine character in *Isabel Clarendon*. Henceforth, however, Mr Gissing seems to have owed little to any writer, though at times we may find what analysts call 'traces' of Balzac in some of his late work. He had achieved himself and his independence with *Thyrza*, than which no truer study of the best of the lower classes is to be found in English literature. But since then he has been consistently hopeless; consistently careless of criticism; consistently pathological. For he is of the order of realists whose work, whether they know it or not, is neither more nor less than the study of disease in one form or another. And just as the pure pathologist is the most despairing of physicians so the realist is almost always doubtful of cure. He sees that all disorders come from law and circumstance, without being able to suggest either the knife of the social surgeon, the scientific drug of the legislator, or the empirical panacea of the demagogue.

But he is not so greatly an apostle of despair as to be refused a hearing by those who believe somewhat in the world's possible salvation. The highest value of such work as Mr Gissing's lies in the fact that he is absolutely honest in his delineation of all he sees. He is blind to the faults of no man; he notes the vices of all classes. He does not clamour for democracy; perhaps he rather fears it; while deprecating the parasitic existence of a rich class, he would rather level up than down; the God-sent great man he knows to be a delusion born of misread history. But this denial of hope has not led him wholly into barrenness of suggestion. The full recognition of a malady is the first measure of cure. The truth of health is implicit in the knowledge of the disease.

Thus in a sense, perhaps a limited sense, he is to be regarded as a social teacher, and in all things he is to be taken seriously, if we understand his drift. Doubtless he is sufficiently the artist to be read for his story; sufficiently the writer to be carefully considered for his style; but the matter is the main thing, and hence the comparative smallness of his attentive audience and the character of that audience. He is one of the few authors read by other literary men. Other writers occasionally read him, and not for the usual purpose of scoffing. Those who have gone through the bitterness of New Grub Street and been ground exceedingly small in the diabolic mills of journalism read him and shiver. Those who are yet between the stones would rather be excused beholding themselves as in a glass. But for most of them he ranks among the half-dozen men whose work as novelists is worthy consideration, being obviously not written merely to catch the asses' ears of the duller public and make them bray applause.

Yet Mr Gissing has doubtless some serious faults. If he had none he would probably be beneath criticism, for invariable success is an infallible sign of mediocrity. He is at times rather like Paganini when that artist began to play tricks. A sonata on one string may be delightful as a surprise, but for our more continual music we prefer the whole four. With marvellous skill, or with luck not commonly afforded by the gods to the harassed tribe of story-tellers, he has hitherto avoided the reproach of repeating himself. Yet his men are too often singularly unanimous in their unconsciously proclaimed lack of real male strength. That immortal spark of devilry which makes a man a man is frequently wanting. At times when they should be violent and break things and go 'berserk' they restrain themselves to the reader's great disappointment. As there are no murders so there is hardly an assault in his books; there are infinite provocations to 'forty shillings or a month' in any one of them, and even the sternest magistrate on the London bench would feel that if Mr Quarrier were brought before him for wringing Eustace Glazzard's neck, 'five shillings' would be a whole half-crown too much to fine him.

Though Mr Gissing has this fault he makes up for it in a natural, though unexpected, manner by creating women whom women themselves actually regard as feminine. So does Thomas Hardy; so does George Meredith. But as a general rule the women of the male novelist are those he would like, or those he would dislike and consequently misunderstand. Those he would prefer are ridiculous ideals, which make women hopeless of ever teaching any man that they are human beings with souls of their own, while those he would hate are contemptible caricatures. In any case his feminine readers feel incredulous if they happen to have brains differing in any way from what men would desire them to have. Fortunately, however, the vogue of most novelists depends on the fact that no one reads them. Yet there are men capable of drawing women sufficiently like life to be recognisable even without millinery. If it is true, as Coleridge said, that all men of genius are more or less androgynous, the saying also holds good of those who possess a high order of talent. Hence the possibility of intuitive creation and unbiased judgment. Mr Gissing's women are not hateful to men, or at any rate not more hateful than the vast majority of their sex, who, for their part, do not regard the author with any of those feelings which lead the ignorant ruck of provincial readers to attempt primitive criticism on the pencilled margin of their library books.

As in real life so in novels. If it is invigorating to meet by some happy chance a real woman in a drawing-room or a milking shed, so it is absolutely inspiring to run across a rare one in the pages of a book. Both are so very scarce that their authors must be congratulated as upon particular achievements, even though the fathers of real life either turn such daughters out of doors or lock them up until a bid is made for them. Mr Gissing frequently makes them just as unhappy as they are; he is not given to glozing. The time will come when he will be bolder than he has been. But even thus he has introduced many of us to several women who are of flesh and blood rather than sawdust. Mrs Mutimer is a reality; her mother-in-law is even startling in life-like presentation. When Thyrza died those who can feel pathos and the great pity of it all mourned sincerely. When some of these poor women could not die, because their artistic creator had endowed them with constitutions which resisted the inroads of continual and hopeless grief, we have mourned even more, while at the same we felt that quickening spark of anger at the author's relentless severity of purpose which makes a man in real life rebel against Fate.

But, whether in the delineation of male or female character, the acute reader can hardly help feeling at times that only a sense of artistic fitness and proportion keeps Mr Gissing from treating some of his characters with positive injustice, for he is by no means widely sympathetic; he never attains God's point of view, and he cannot look down upon all his equal creatures with pitying kindness. This narrowness of sympathy arises most probably from his never having had a wide experience of the world's full life. That he will never attain this is too much to say, yet his violent antipathies seem to forbid the possibility of his ever ranking with those writers who view mankind with a large and healthy tolerance. He cannot treat his species scientifically, and he differs from scientific men in this—that while they hate each other they love their subject. Strictly speaking, but one thing really interests him—the phenomena of superior and slightly scornful intellect. He is, perhaps, the Robespierre of literature, Robespierre with more than a touch of Arthur Balfour in him. He is in many things distinctly cold; his truest passions are aversion and scorn. Of real sexual love, which is full-blooded and over-mastering, which thrills and conquers, there is but very little in his work. As he himself seems to suggest a possible type of the future, when the race shall have passed through the bloody gates of passion into the cold and loftier regions of the purged intellect, so his favourite men and chosen women are exceptional by reason of the predominance of brain over body. It is to such that he devotes his sympathetic care. To these characters the others act as foils, and in these portraits he is possibly at his best. At any rate, they draw out the best of himself, which is better than his scorn for everything which does not partake of some kind of culture.

This is why we rarely laugh with Mr Gissing. His humour is savage and not to be trusted; it is rather to be found in the totality of a character or in the general view of a situation than in phrases or passages; it may turn out to be irony of the cunningest description. He is often ironical through a whole book. It is sometimes possible for a belated intellect to assume complacently that he is on the side of convention, that he regards the troubles of the world as brought to pass by the abuse of free-will. But there is no free-will here: as we read on we hear above the weary footfalls of tired humanity the heavier step of inexorable Fate, for he is without mercy: the dew that drops from his heaven is as virulent as vitriol.

Yet there are some signs of his making for himself another creed, or, if not another, of his infusing his present one with a little hope. As men grow up and out of the turbulent storm and stress of youth into the more lucid atmosphere and drier light of life's middle period their eager anxiety for immediate construction or destruction begins to leave them. They become weary of their task first, and then by calling in their energies they commence to recover. They see they were acted on by the same influences which they had watched at work. Their first hope for others lies in curing themselves, for this is the artistic charity which begins at home. The healthier minds have been the first to see the truth, for Walt Whitman was and Ibsen is, essentially healthy. However the movement, having them for its prophets, may be looked upon, it is at any rate essentially modern, and seems at last to have influenced Mr Gissing. Yet he stands at present between the reactionary and revolutionary idealists, and though there are distinct traces in *Denzil Quarrier* of the feelings which underlie this revolt, the main teaching of his last book is that man having become unnatural in convention is by no means to be trusted in any existing circumstances whatsoever.

This is why he is neither Socialist nor Anarchist. This is why he stands alone. Even the most odiously comparative of the comparative critics would fail to class him, for he owes nothing, or almost nothing, to the work of any living writer; certainly nothing to that of any Englishman. But he is cosmopolitan in thought and feeling, and will probably range himself openly before long with those who work and hope, believing that the only way to teach mankind responsibility is to trust them, and the only hope of doing that is to bid them trust themselves. At present, he says, life is to be endured: it is a fight, and a fight without the mercy of gods or men, and his advice to all is summed up in the bitter concluding words of a chapter in *A Life's Morning:* 'Put money in thy purse, and, again, put money in thy purse. For as the world is ordered, to lack current coin is to lack the privileges of humanity, and indigence is the death of the soul.'

THE ODD WOMEN

April 1893

76. Unsigned review, *Glasgow Herald*

20 April 1893, 9

Mr Gissing is a very prolific writer, for it cannot be six weeks since we reviewed his *Born in Exile*,* but one cannot grumble at a novelist for writing too often who gives us such excellent work as the book under notice. It distinctly marks a great advance in his art, showing him among the 'arriving' novelists of the day, if, indeed, he may not now be said already to have 'arrived'. There is always thought in Mr Gissing's books; sometimes more thought than action, but he has arrived at a happy and artistic combination in the work under review. It is altogether a story of odd women, women who suffer in the dreadful whirl of English daily life, because the brutal truth is there are too many women to be married, and most of them are quite unfitted to realise for themselves that to be successful, to burst the bonds which encompass their narrow, sordid lives, they must be 'odd'. It is Rhoda Nunn's mission, and that of her friend Miss Barfoot (Mr Gissing's characters have invariably the strangest names and the ugliest), to work with and for the helpless women; the women who do not belong to the working classes, but are ten times weaker than the women of that class, and pitiably helpless. They help them to find occupations which the age readily admits women can adequately fill. And across Rhoda's almost stern life, so full is it of duty, comes a romance. She, like other women, has at last a proposal, and even though she determines to refuse it, yet the fact makes her stronger and happier in a way Mr Gissing has very delicately and beautifully shown. The other men and women of the story present various aspects of the marriage question,

* *Born in Exile* had been reviewed in the *Glasgow Herald* on 9 March 1893, 9, but a copy of the new one-volume edition, issued in February 1893, had been sent to the paper. There was no indication in the book that this was a new edition

ingeniously contrasted and unsparedly outlined. We only wish that in the end Mr Gissing would occasionally make his men and women happy, or some of them. We always feel at the opening pages of his books inclined to say of his characters 'Heedless of their doom, the little victims play', for the author luxuriates as he closes in a holocaust of the affections—death, madness, or misery. Still it is all very human, and *The Odd Women* is a genuine work of art, remarkable among the novels of the day.

77. Unsigned review, *Saturday Review*

29 April 1893, lxxv, 459–60

Many of us—perhaps even most of us—disagree with Mr Gissing in his views of life and his plans for improving it; but the mere fact that he has any views at all gives him a claim to our interest and to our careful consideration. The 'Odd Women' who form the subject of his latest work have nothing in common with lunatics, but are simply the million or so of surplus females who have to struggle through their span somehow, independently of men. To emphasize his point the better Mr Gissing has drawn a sharp contrast. On the one hand there is a shiftless family of doctor's daughters who have been taught nothing that is useful at home; on the other there is a friend of these girls who sets to work to remedy her own helplessness, and ends by making a comfortable livelihood in the type-writing line. Of course the story is not as bald as this. The types of character are each distinct, and are not exaggerated either for moral or artistic purposes. The well-meaning, ill-educated, unhealthy, conventional Alice Madden; her equally well-meaning, ill-educated, unhealthy sister Virginia, who out of sheer poverty and weariness takes to drink; their younger, prettier, and more practical sister Monica, who wrecks her life by an unsuitable marriage out of a pardonable desire to escape from the shop in the Walworth Road where she is an assistant—these women are in no way single specimens of their kind, nor are they meant to be. No more is the harder, more successful Rhoda Nunn, above alluded to. Curious to state, Mr Gissing's women are far truer to nature than his men. Their conduct is intelligible from their varied points of view, but the personality and the behaviour of Mr Everard Barfoot, for instance, would baffle the understanding of most people. He is meant to be a charming and aristocratic (though rather wild) person: in reality he is a very pronounced cad. It is not very easy to see how far the doctrines of terminable marriages, and 'marriage in the sight of God' (which always means no marriage in the sight of men) are really Mr Gissing's own, and how far they are merely attributed to his characters. Mr Barfoot decides, when he declares his affection to that advocate of celibacy Rhoda Nunn, that if she consents to forego the ceremony he will make her his legal wife; but that if in the first instance she insists on even the Registrar, she will lower herself for ever in his eyes. This, at least, is what we have understood; but Mr Gissing has not expressed himself very clearly. The best chapters in the book are those which describe the loving and zealous tyranny of the middle-aged Widdowson, who having become the husband of the young and pretty Monica Madden, wishes to shut her up exclusively with himself, and drives her into telling lies and offering to elope with a gentleman, who looks on her proposition as manifesting '*trop de zèle*,' and there the matter ends. Humour is never the 'crowning glory' of Mr Gissing's novels; but he shows some when he allows us to see that he thinks that boredom is an excellent reason for rending marriage; only in a book that sets forth the perfect equality of women it is rather strange that the acts of boring cited should all be on the one side. And, in spite of her somewhat blatant self-assertion, it is at once sad and comic and true to notice that all her dislike to matrimony does not prevent Miss Rhoda Nunn from rising in her own esteem when, at the age of thirty-three, she has an offer. This is the attitude many persons assume towards life in general. They do not care to *have*, but they wish to be able to *reject*.

78. Unsigned review, *Athenaeum*

27 May 1893, 667

Gissing commented on this piece: 'A good notice of *The Odd Women* in *Athenaeum*,—except that the fool charges me with writing "journalese" ' (Diary, 27 May 1893).

As might be expected, Mr Gissing's new novel *The Odd Women* is intensely modern, actual in theme as well as in treatment. Amidst the vexed social questions that surround us on all sides, and seem to defy solution, he has chosen one of real interest, and has turned it to clever and original purpose. The problem of the odd woman and what is to be done with her presents, in truth, a grim enough aspect. As treated by Mr Gissing the interest is of almost too painful a character, yet it is full of suggestion and significance. Those who know him best recognize that his manner and method are generally vivid and, to some extent, individual, though by no means enchanting. Here, as in former novels, we have pages of something more resembling the reporter's than the artist's touch. The story is anything but crude or unsympathetic, yet in the telling it is often a little inadequate. Journalese is conspicuous, not by its absence. In spite of this the book is better than merely readable, it is absorbing. One feels that the author is more than master of his subject; that he has turned it about and around, and thoroughly knows its capabilities. As a novel it is decidedly 'uncheering'; the outlook is, in some ways, even more depressing than in *New Grub Street*. Yet latent in it all is an element of hope, a something that encourages the idea that with time and effort the baffling problem of the odd women may be successfully solved. Many of the characters and episodes are extremely well drawn; the dialogue is of the right sort—natural and to the purpose. Mr Gissing has not, perhaps, on the whole, written anything stronger or more striking.

79. Unsigned review, *Pall Mall Gazette*

29 May 1893, 4

Gissing read this review of his book and thought it 'very good' (Diary).

It would have been a real calamity if Mr Gissing had tried to palm off upon us under the guise of a novel, a treatise, or even a dialogue, on the Woman question. To an active mind like his, profoundly interested in the phenomena of the civilization round him, the danger must have been great. None the less, he has kept his story very free from sociological dialectic. To make a novel pivot on a sociological rather than what unquestioning fetish-worship calls a 'purely human' motive, is not at all the same thing as to write a narrative tract, after the manner of Mrs Humphry Ward or Sarah Grand. As the threads of society are complicated more and more it is difficult to avoid this, and Zola and Ibsen have shown us that the widest and loosest ideas can be treated in a purely artistic way. Mr Gissing succeeds in doing this, though obviously not without a certain effort. His book represents the Woman question made flesh; his people live it instead of talking it. His method is to take types that represent the question, or rather the fact, in all its divagations—the old love marriage, the marriage of convenience, the womanly old-maid, the emancipated woman, and all the rest; then to make them in a purely natural way develop that side of themselves that bears on the position of women in the society of to-day. Obviously the danger of the method lies in the difficulty of keeping the story together. On this count Mr Gissing has not been blameless in the past, and it is a palpable fault in *The Odd Women* that it tends to part into two divergent channels. That is the danger of taking too large an idea; it is too lax to bind all its modifications into an organic whole. But in our judgment Mr Gissing has succeeded as far as was possible in suggesting the general idea that puts all his characters on the same plane, and yet has not obtruded it so much as to make them counters in the game of sociology instead of living human beings.

Certainly his people live. You might brush against any of them in the Strand from morning till morning again. And, better, they live transfigured by the artist, who shows you the exact significance of each life. *The Odd Women* is a great vindication of realism from the charge of dulness. At afternoon tea his women, odd and even, would be totally uninteresting to any but the most sympathetic; in the book you follow them breathless. Moreover Mr Gissing steers clear of another danger that besets the psychological treatment of motive and character. His work is, in the main, presentative; many pages of wiredrawn analysis are replaced by one of living conversation. That parts off good from bad realism. Mr Gissing's power of unravelling the tangled influences that draw one hither and thither is admirably shown in the figure of Rhoda Nunn, the strong, self-reliant, revolted woman, with the old womanly woman still restless underneath as she fights against the recognition of it. Monica, the girl who marries in haste, Virginia, the lady's companion who drinks gin while she is waiting for her next engagement, are drawn with masterly insight and pathos. In fine *The Odd Women* falls short of genius only through its author's characteristic limitations—the complete lack of dash, the strange occasional flatness of the writing, the curious blindness (effective too, in its way, and especially in this book) that refuses to see any colour in the world but grey. But to a modern mind it is, for all that, the most interesting novel of the year.

80. Unsigned review, *Nation* (New York)

13 July 1893, 30–1

One of the most encouraging signs of the times is the recognition of the virtues of the 'old maid'. Unless she is rich, she is not yet accorded any particular social status, but she is no longer an object for contumely and derision, and it is generally conceded that she is not necessarily either an old cat or an old fool. When she gets a novel written in her praise and honor (euphemistically called *The Odd Women*), she may be said to have cast off the last shred of disability. If half that Mr Gissing affirms and predicts about them is true, the hope of the future certainly lies in our old maids. Through the intemperance of partisanship he has perhaps put a scourge in the hands of the enemies of that class which he wishes to exalt, the self-supporting unmarried women. His examples of marriage go to show that that institution is a failure, and the drift of his conclusions on sexual relations is in favor of the *union libre*. 'We told you so', cry the conservators of morals; 'freedom for women means license and the sacred hearth gone to the dogs!' Far be it from them to read patiently—to learn that Mr Gissing points to the voluntary relation between men and women only as the far-off ideal consummation of human striving towards self-knowledge, self-reverence and self-control. But the time is not yet, and we go so far with the adorers of home and humdrum as to fail to see that its coming is in the line of social progress. The great thing is for society to give the odd women a fighting chance, and to consider with charity those who fall in the fray.

The story in which 'The Odd Women' are then ably championed is excellent both for construction and for characterization. The novel with a good purpose is too apt to be a very bad novel, and it is a pleasure to testify that Mr Gissing's is, in spite of and on account of its intensity of purpose, an uncommonly good one.

81. Clementina Black, *Illustrated London News*

5 August 1893, ciii, 155

Clementina Black was a novelist and journalist, who wrote on labour and feminist problems. She had published the year before a collection of short stories, *Miss Falkland and Other Stories*, under the imprint of Lawrence & Bullen. Gissing read her article but did not record his impressions.

The 'odd women'—the half million or so for whom there is 'no making a pair'—these are the theme of Mr Gissing's latest novel, a novel which is in many ways a distinct advance upon anything which he has done yet. Like most persons who contemplate the problem of the unmarried and untrained woman, he is inclined to think the problem due to a far greater extent than is really the case to mere difference in the numbers of the sexes. It is not so much because, as one of Miss Mary Wilkins's personages says, there are not husbands 'enough to go round,' as because of various social and economic conditions that women (and men, too) remain unmarried. The apparent surplus of women is largely due to the fact that they live longer. If a hundred men and a hundred women were to be born every year, and if all the men lived to fifty, while all the women lived to fifty-one, there would be a permanent surplus of a hundred women, and yet every one of these might have been married to one of the hundred men born in the same year as herself. Still, it remains true for practical purposes that a large group of women, especially in the poorer middle class, has no opportunity of suitable marriage. That these women should be trained to callings by which they can live—partly, among many other reasons, in the interests of the dignity of marriage—is the moral of Mr Gissing's book, and he develops it out of a variety of different situations, all of which rise in natural connection. He gives us a shop-girl of gentle breeding who accepts marriage as a mere escape from slavery, and finds that she has but forged herself a heavier chain; an out-of-work 'companion' led gradually, by semi-starvation and lack of mental interests, to drink; a well-meaning young man debarred from marriage by the necessity of supporting his unmarried sisters, and consoling himself by a disastrous flirtation with another man's wife; and glimpses of several varieties of married life, mostly unhappy. Finally, he shows us a little group of active, intelligent women, working for themselves and for their sisters, and regarding the world with a courage and a resolution that make the bright spot in a gloomy picture. In the conversations of these women is contained the argumentative kernel of the book; and Mr Gissing has succeeded in the feat, so often attempted in the modern novel, but so seldom achieved, of giving to discussions of social problems the twofold interest attaching to them in real life—an interest, namely, in the thing said, for its own sake, and an interest in it as a display of character on the part of the person saying it. This double interest is especially well marked when the speakers are Rhoda Nunn and Everard Barfoot. The growth of intimacy and regard between the enlightened independent spinster and the rather dilettante wandering bachelor is singularly well told, but it leads up to the weak point of the story. We feel, as we read, that between two persons so clear-sighted, so outspoken, and so fully aware of the pitfalls of married life, the natural end would be a real marriage—that is to say, an equal union, in which each would respect the freedom and individuality of the other, and in which each would find the completest development. Surely such a man and woman—both, be it remembered, over thirty years old—are not likely to spoil their own and each other's lives by a display of sheer perverse stubbornness. As long as they hover on the edge of a decisive avowal their conduct is natural and reasonable enough; but when they come to the crisis they show themselves as touchy, as unreasonable, and as eager 'not to give in' as a pair of lovers still in their teens. The conduct of Rhoda, in particular, is gravely out of character. On one day she receives from Everard the most solemn, deliberate, and repeated assurances that no woman has any moral claim upon him, and that he has not 'during the past three months made professions of love or even pretended love to any woman.' On the next, a story reaches her which seems at first sight seriously compromising to him. Of course, such a story told of the man to whom she has just engaged herself would distress any woman; and a quite young girl, inexperienced in pain, might not improbably visit hers on her lover, as a child beats the table against which it has knocked its head. But surely a mature woman of unusually sincere, just, and open-minded character would not, while those words of assurance were still ringing in her ears, take up an attitude of cold estrangement. And if by any chance, in any sudden gust of unreasonable jealousy, she had taken up such a position, is it credible that later, when a complete explanation reached her, which not only exonerated Everard, but showed him ignorant of the very facts, she should still have kept up her offended attitude, experiencing no remorse and making no sign? Surely to such a woman as Rhoda the perception that she had acted unjustly and ungenerously would involve immediate confession of her error. But, no; *she* will not take the first step and *he* will not take the first step—which really, under the circumstances, is more pardonable; and when, after all, he does make the first advance, she neither acknowledges nor apologises for the grave wrong she did him, but refuses—still with the manner of an injured person—to make up the quarrel, which was so clearly no fault of his. This is the conduct of an ungenerous, a selfish, and especially an undisciplined woman, and is out of keeping with all the previous history of Rhoda Nunn. It would almost seem as if hatred of the conventional 'happy ending' had led Mr Gissing to that same sacrifice of truthful portraiture into which so many of his predecessors have been betrayed by their love of it.

Happily, in a good novel it is the impression of the best part which remains, while the weaker pages fade away. Who remembers the loves of Madeline Bray (if, indeed, that was her name) and Nicholas Nickleby? but who forgets Mrs Nickleby or the Crummles family? The parts that remain of *The Odd Women* are the picture of the three sisters Madden, and that of Rhoda and Miss Barfoot, comrades in work, hope, and friendship. These parts of the book are better, truer, and, it may be fairly added, better written than anything which Mr Gissing had previously published; and to say that is not to say little.

82. 'N.O.B.', Survey of Gissing's Work, *Echo*

16 October 1893, 1

This general article, signed 'N.O.B.', was seventh in a series entitled 'Novels and Novelists'. Gissing had seen the previous article (2 October 1893, 1) which, devoted to Walter Besant, had compared that writer somewhat unfavourably with himself. Gissing sent copies of this general appraisal of his work to Bertz and his relatives at Wakefield.

This is an age of notoriety, and the private life of our public men has become the property of the nation. Our actors talk of their domestic troubles across the footlights, and novelists like Robert Louis Stevenson or Walter Besant are constantly taking us into their confidence in newspaper interviews or by newspaper confessions. But there is one writer of the first rank, in the person of Mr Gissing, about whom the outside world has never evinced any unusual curiosity. *Thyrza* and its fellows can count on but a limited, if enthusiastic, circle of admirers. It is but natural, for their author indulges neither in sensational claptrap nor in sentimental optimism. All his work has concerned itself with modern life, mainly with the social problems of the hour, and in no case has he preached smooth words. He has pitched his scenes in unromantic spots, such as the grimy manufacturing towns of the provinces, or the squalid outskirts of London of the pattern of Hoxton, Camden-town, or Islington. One might almost attribute to him a partiality for 'regions of malodorous market streets, of factories and timber-yards, of alleys swarming with small trades, of filthy courts and passages leading into pestilential gloom.' Certainly it is here that his vivid powers of description serve him best. His country landscapes are often blurred and bare, but the broad strokes with which he dashes in an impressionist picture of Manor Park Cemetery, 'the abode of chill desolation,' or of Kentishtown, with its dead-faced houses, which crush the heart, with an uniformity of decent squalor, are worthy of comparison with the bold colouring of a Turner or a Whistler. Neutral tints seem to have a perverse attraction for Mr Gissing—perverse because he is so ardent a champion of culture and purity, of love and high thoughts, as to merit the title of an idealist. His harshest indictment of the workmen whose lives he has studied with such deep attention and kindliness is founded upon their absolute indifference—nay, their hostility—to all refinement. Yet his choice has been a wise one. His excursions into Society do not indicate more than a nodding acquaintance with its manners and morals. Mr Gissing's mission appears to be bound up with two sections of our population. He seems intended, on the other hand, to expose with sympathetic insight, the failings of the artisan class, and, on the other, to champion the cause of poor professional families, who, in his eyes, suffer far more hardships than the noisier submerged tenth. All his most successful characters are confined to the middle and working classes. He has given us the average clerk of middle age and mediocre intelligence in Hood, the tale of whose temptation and suicide (in *A Life's Morning*) is one of the most pitiful things in modern fiction, and again a well-known Northern type in Hood's employer, a shrewd, hard, coarse-grained man, doggedly persistent in his ends, but quite unscrupulous about the means. Thyrza, model of sweet self-denial; Amy Reardon, the wife made for fair weather only; Adela Waltham, purity incarnate—all these are representative specimens of middle-class English womanhood. Quite as powerfully drawn is the artisan household of the Mutimers, which in *Demos* is raised to sudden affluence by the death of a rich relative. From the old mother, who will not change her mode of life, and prophesies ill from the accursed wealth, to 'Arry, a born loafer who drifts into crime, all its members are sketched with a master hand. Mr Gissing has written two novels dealing with the working-classes—*Demos* and *The Nether World*, but the former is more interesting, by reason not only of its more ambitious title (it claims to be a story of English Socialism), but also of its stronger characterisation. The Labour question and its leaders have grown in importance since *Demos* was published, and we think Dick Mutimer, with his unintelligent eloquence and his abnormal vanity a very unfair portrait of the modern Socialist, just as we laugh at the amateurish schemes attributed to him. Yet a recent utterance of Mr Ben Tillett's might have come straight from Mr Gissing's pages. 'I will beard the capitalists in Parliament some day,' practically said Mr Tillett, and such was the boast of Dick Mutimer. If we may judge the author by the characters which seem to express his convictions, Mr Gissing is, with all his hatred of oppression, not enamoured of Labour agitation. 'English Socialism,' says one of his creatures, 'is infused with the spirit of shop-keeping;' it 'appeals to the vulgarest minds, and keeps one eye on personal safety, and the other on the capitalist's strong box.' With his tendency to confine his attention to the dark side, he sees interested motives at the root of most social discontent. His spokesman in *Demos* has no belief in the social revolution, for he thinks (as we do not) that the proletarian Socialists are not sincere. The poor do not ceaselessly groan, says he, beneath the burden of existence; the struggle to support their bodies leaves them no time to reflect over their condition, and they are happily not blessed with a lively imagination. So that happiness is, in his opinion, very evenly distributed among all classes and conditions. On the English artisan the novelist speaks often and with authority. Of the hardship of his lot he is not oblivious. 'The working people,' says their representative, 'have no religion; they have no time to think of it.' Their employers 'calculate how long a man can be made to work in a day without making him incapable of beginning again on the day following.' The writer admits, too, the strong domestic affection of the artisan, although so undemonstrative. His fatal defect is 'an absence of imagination, which comes to mean a lack of kindly sympathy.' Mr Gissing has met with many sorts of labourers, but there is one mystery that baffles him, 'that expression insoluble into factors of common sense—the Conservative "working-man." ' Of his Radical brothers he knows a few. There is the short stout man, very seedily dressed, who tears passion to tatters over a Duke, his especial bugbear; or the lean-faced snarling creature with personal motives in the background. He can paint for us the good-natured fellow who cheers all abuse showered upon the rich, but takes care never to risk a penny on the cause, or the wailing old man who, with one foot in the grave, pours out bitter phrases in a terrible arraignment of his own order. Mr Gissing is too much in accord with the last, too distrustful of the people. But though his views are reactionary, they deserve attention because based on an intimate acquaintance with his subject. He awaits the future with the deepest concern, and condemns unmercifully the system of universal education which has produced a class endowed with intellectual needs, and refused the sustenance they are taught to crave. And here we touch one of our author's favourite theses—the miseries of the needy professional classes. His two last books have dealt with it from the side of man and woman respectively, but the earlier of the two—*New Grub*

Street—is a far grimmer presentment of life, and a much more perfect work of art. The story traces the parallel development of two literary men, one a success, and the other a failure; and telling, as it does, with directness and truth, experiences many of us have encountered, it leaves the reader hardly prepared to endorse Browning's audacious dictum, 'All's right with the world.' For while we are vexed at the weakness of Edwin Reardon, the victim of overpressure, who, with a slender gift of originality, was forced to produce work too rapidly, we almost despise selfish, good-natured Jasper Milvain, who deliberately casts ideals aside and devotes himself (with triumphant success) to unscrupulous search of money and fame. And characters like Alfred Yule, the hard-working journalist, with the heavy style, soured nature, and unpresentable wife, or Harold Biffen, the self-contained realist, who treats of 'the ignobly decent' in life, and finally commits suicide, only add to the general gloom. The loveable people all fail and the meaner nature[s] triumph. Yet this is too often an item in our own experience to make us reject books brimful of accurate observation, skilful analysis, and palpable vitality. And we can learn much from Mr Gissing. Hear him on these failures:—'Nothing is easier than to condemn a type of character which is unequal to the coarse demands of life as it suits the average citizen.' Yet usually such men are endowed in especial with the kindly and imaginative virtues. 'It is their nature and their merit to be passive. The sum of their faults is their inability to earn money; but that inability does not call for unmitigated disdain.' No, indeed.

IN THE YEAR OF JUBILEE

December 1894

83. Unsigned review, *Daily Telegraph*

21 December 1894, 6

Mr George Gissing's latest three-volume novel, *In the Year of Jubilee* deserves a no less cordial reception at the hands of that genial author's many admirers than that which has been at different times accorded to several of his previous works, and in particular to *The Odd Women*, signalised at the time of its production as one of the most thoughtful and introspective contributions to our latter-day fictional literature. The story now before us deals exclusively with persons of a social class for which our tongue lacks a term of accurate definition—that of 'la petite bourgeoisie' having no exact equivalent in English. All Mr Gissing's characters are people of no importance, for the most part connected with one or another branch of retail trade, ignorance and frivolity being the leading characteristics of the women, superficiality and narrow-mindedness those of the men. Two of the latter, Lionel Tarrant and Horace Lord, are selfish idlers, so cleverly differentiated that they have no defects in common save egotism and indolence; another, Luckworth Crewe, is an irrepressible advertising agent, deeply astute, brilliantly inventive, and appallingly vulgar; a fourth, Samuel Bennett Barmby, is an admirably designed and finished type of the well-to-do, absolutely commonplace, middle-class young man, crammed with useless statistics, a retailer of fourth-hand platitudes, perfectly dull, vain, self-confident and well-meaning. Into the 'inner selves' of such petty folk as these Mr Gissing possesses a clear and comprehensive insight that enables him to depict them with convincing verisimilitude. His puppets, as a matter of fact, are invariably 'true to nature', and those who play the leading parts 'In the Year of Jubilee' are among the most lifelike of which he has heretofore pulled the wires.

84. L. F. Austin, *Sketch*

9 January 1895, 517

Gissing was gratified to receive from C. K. Shorter, editor of the *Sketch*, this full-page review entitled 'A Study in Drab' which was published with an accompanying portrait of himself. He sent copies of the magazine to Bertz and his relatives at Wakefield.

For details about L. F. Austin see headnote to No. 55.

Mr Gissing is one of the few English novelists who take the trouble to have a view of life. In his case the view is not sanguine. A squalid street on a wet day does not disclose much buoyancy of aspect, and Mr Gissing seems to spend most of his time and observation, so to speak, in that street, watching dreary figures under dripping umbrellas. In the present work he has chosen Brixton, and the region there adjacent, as the background of his drama—and anybody who has even a superficial acquaintance with the social economy on that side of the river may suspect the infinity of sordid misery which unfolds itself to a remorseless eye. Personally, I am ready to believe anything of Brixton; but I have been staggered by Mr Gissing's revelations. Here is a typical family, named French. Ada is married to one Arthur Peachey. Her sisters, Beatrice and Fanny, live in disinterested contemplation of the Peachey household, which is racked by Ada's temper, and illuminated by side-lights of sisterly vulgarity. Peachey, a quiet man, leaves Ada, taking his child with him; and his wife proceeds to smash the furniture. Beatrice cannot tolerate 'wanton destruction of property,' and this is the cheerful scene that ensues—

> Now, indeed, the last trace of veneer was gone, the last rag of civilisation was rent off these young women: in physical conflict, vilifying each other like the female spawn of Whitechapel, they revealed themselves as born—raw material which the mill of education is supposed to convert into middle-class ladyhood.

Take another flower of Brixton—Jessica Morgan. She ruins her health by cramming for the examinations at Burlington House, and in her case the mill of education turns out a rancorous mass of blighted sexuality and spite. Then consider Samuel Barmby. He, I think, represents the genius of Camberwell. He has been brought up on paragraphs, and knows how many miles would be covered by all the cabs in London if they were arranged in a line, 'back to back.' He lectures at debating societies on national progress, and, in his capacity as executor of an estate, proposes to condone the evasion of the will by immoral relations with a married woman. How is that for Camberwell? Then there is Mr Luckworth Crewe, who began his career as a foundling on a doorstep. He has a keen sense of humour, which finds its highest gratification in a row at Lillie Bridge, where the mob stormed the refreshment-room, and the 'bobbies' were pelted with bottles, stones, and logs of wood. 'And the swearing that went on!' says Mr Crewe, describing this agreeable diversion to Miss French; 'it's a long time since I heard such downright, hearty, solid swearing. There was one chap I kept near, and he swore for a full hour without stopping, except when he had a bottle in his mouth; he only stopped when he was speechless with liquor.' 'I wish I'd been there,' said Miss French gaily; 'it must have been no end of fun.'

These specimens of Brixtonian culture are only incidental to the story, which concerns itself mainly with Nancy Lord, who is seduced; her lover, who marries her at once, and betakes himself to foreign parts; her father, who dies early in the book, after giving much excellent advice; her mother, who has been divorced; her brother, who kills himself by vicious courses; and the housekeeper of the family, who is the one entirely blameless person, and a mere shadow. Horace, the brother, is engaged to a shy young woman with money. I had a faint hope that she, at all events, would be redeemed from the general squalor, but no—she is a damaged lot in the marriage market. Horace throws her over and marries Fanny French, who, in the meantime, has been amusing herself in Paris. The divorced mother lavishes affection on the boy under the pretext of being his aunt, but is unable to save him from ruin; and the disclosure of her real relation to Nancy excites no affectionate impulse in that young woman's mind. Do not suppose, however, that the story is a mere monotony of vice and gloom. I have given the atmosphere because that is indispensable to a proper understanding of Mr Gissing's view of life. Unlike Mr Traill, he sees skeletons everywhere. He has a poor opinion of what is called progress, and much scepticism about the blessings of education—such education as is possible to the social conditions of Brixton. There may be a good deal of exaggeration in this pessimism, but it is the honest belief of a skilled observer, and it gives to Mr Gissing's novels an intellectual quality, an austere sincerity in the face of shallow optimism, a moral weight, entirely lacking in the mass of current fiction. More than that, the book before me is extremely good reading, with all its grimness, and the character of Nancy Lord is a study of which any novelist, whatever his eminence, might be proud. Brixton may take heart from the courage and independence of this girl, despite the sorry shifts to which she is driven to conceal her marriage. Old Lord has left her half his money, with the proviso that she shall forfeit it if she marries before the age of twenty-six, a condition inspired by not unreasonable distrust of both his children. Nancy, indeed, gives herself in a moment of passion to a man of whom she knows little, and who, though he has the manliness to marry her, is coward enough to leave her to struggle with her secret alone, to hide the birth of her child, while he, suddenly deprived of an income which he did not earn, goes on a wild-goose chase to the Bahamas. Certainly Lionel Tarrant is not an imposing figure, and yet he is not a scoundrel. To an observer like Mr Gissing there are infinite possibilities between those extremes, and Tarrant's flight for a time from his responsibilities is just the unheroic expedient to which the average sensual man, put into a sore strait by a stroke of ill-luck, would probably adopt. He is not at this juncture in love with his wife; he blames her with the usual logic of the male for having yielded to him; he blames himself for the quixotic haste of the special license; he is irritated by her impending motherhood. It is one of those cases in which a man of that type, a much more common type than the optimists will admit, can be won and held only by pride and strength of will in the woman. Nancy is weak enough at first; but the maturing of her mind is indicated with remarkable skill. The reader who wants in novels an exact compliance with moral maxims—above all, the decent veiling of that selfishness which is the ordinary mainspring of a man's actions, especially a man who is suddenly plunged from easy indulgence into rank poverty—will get no comfort from Mr Gissing. The matron who cultivates deliberate ignorance of life will see no merit in Nancy, and will be shocked by the terms on which Tarrant and his wife eventually make the stability of their happiness. She conquers him by 'rational acquiescence' in his defiance of the convention that husband and wife are not twain, but one flesh. 'Husband and wife should interfere with each other not a jot more than two friends of the same sex living together.' Tarrant lives in lodgings, Nancy under another roof. 'I am content,' she says. 'You are working hard, and I won't make it harder for you.' 'Speak always like that!' he cries. 'That's the kind of thing that binds man to woman, body and soul.' This is a hard saying for the multitude of citizens who have been taught that to chain a man and woman together hand and foot as if they were dangerous convicts is the only moral safeguard of marriage.

85. Unsigned review, *Athenaeum*

12 January 1895, 45

Gissing considered this notice 'excellent' (Diary, 12 January 1895).

The suburbs owe a debt to Mr George Gissing, who has vindicated them triumphantly in his latest novel from the cheap sneers of the superior modern journalist. For although the life which he describes in his usual uncompromising fashion is generally unlovely and often hideous, it is full of human interest, and rises at times to a genuinely tragic level. *In the Year of Jubilee*—the title is solely derived from the date at which the story begins—is a plain, unvarnished tale of middle-class life, in which the modern spirit of revolt is illustrated in half a dozen different types. Nothing, at first sight, could be more unpromising than the materials selected; none the less the book is of absorbing interest, and—with the exception of the sole personage who does not belong to the *bourgeois* stratum, Lionel Tarrant, whose preposterous views on the married state are developed with fatiguing iteration—singularly convincing in its presentment of human nature. Apart from the somewhat shadowy figure of the faithful domestic servant, the only character which makes any real or successful appeal to the sympathies of the reader is that of the heroine, whom, in spite of her hasty self-surrender, and of her acquiescence in a long course of systematic deception, it is impossible to help respecting for her unflinching courage amid her many trials. Much of the book is painful reading, notably that which deals with the squalid squabblings of the Peachey household, and the effects, as exemplified in the person of an hysterical governess, of 'charlatan education operating upon crude character.' Still here and there the reader encounters a gleam of wintry sunshine, and, in the issue, possibilities of repose and even of happiness are opened up to the sorely tried heroine. The impressiveness of this remarkable book is greatly enhanced by the admirable style in which it is written—always direct, forcible, and free from mannerism.

86. Unsigned review, *Manchester Guardian*

22 January 1895, 10

The singular severity shown by the strongest of our most recent novelists, Mr George Gissing, towards his own characters is not wholly undeserved. As if to revenge himself for some experience of an odious class of society, he impresses its dreadfulness on the reader's mind with the force of a rigid and penetrating style. If at the same time his picture is impressed the more deeply on his own, to the abuse of irony and the partial deadening of the senses of humour and beauty, this perhaps is the price to be paid for such success. The suburbs, London or provincial, will never recognise with what completeness their pretensions are stripped naked by this student. The text of Mr Matthew Arnold against the middle classes is driven home with a zeal that shows not only the satirical but the Protestant strain. For, though the writer shows no leaning to a Protestant formula, it is from this strain in our national character that he draws both the exposing zeal which guides his pen and also the element of relief which he allows to his pictures of the sordid—the moral relief, we mean, without which those pictures would be bad, insupportable art. A world of persons nominally of good consideration but living ravenous little reptilian lives, and a chosen few who make their way out of that world much the worse for wear and with little life left in them for enjoyment, but saved—such, or nearly such, is the formula of Mr Gissing. The tale called *In the Year of Jubilee* gathers about two households. The three sisters French, the best of them coarse and ambitious, the second a mere domestic hyaena, the third a predestined wanton, are examples, presented in harsh photography, of typical low life in 'respectable' society. The only relieving incident, happily told, is the escape of the husband of the second sister with their child. The other household is that of the Lords—Horace, the vapid, consumptive son, amorous of the appropriate Miss French; old Lord, gnarled, inhuman, and honest; the servant Mary, whom Mr Gissing attempts with great but scarcely successful pains to make attractive; and the heroine, Nancy. The mother appears in the course of the book under an *alias* which never deludes the reader and could scarcely delude the characters; she, again, is elaborately but wastefully drawn. The real story is the growth of Nancy from a pseudo-educated girl with perilous instincts into a woman of experience who understands her part in life. The instruments of this change are her seducer, who is her subsequent husband, Lionel Tarrant, and her child; besides the temptation (to which she long succumbs in order to inherit under her father's queer will) to deny her marriage, while being compelled to own her child. The husband, described as a journalist of a certain savage talent, is not ill presented. His desertion and recourtship of his wife are not conventional. The stages of their reconciliation, the embarrassed visits of husband and wife to one another, show a gleam of humanity at last, after the howling wilderness of recrimination, greed, and lies which the rest of the story portrays. Neither is the end commonplace, though it is not theatrical. The Tarrants, at the instance of the husband, agree to live separately, visiting occasionally, and remain on terms of real respect, Tarrant helping to maintain his wife and child. The weakness of this situation is that while Nancy emerges a fine and pure if too docile character, Tarrant, in his marital fireside philosophy, becomes self-complacent and priggish. The author does not observe that his assertion of his superior greatness, sense, and intellect is, after all his currish conduct, ludicrous. We speak thus particularly of Mr Gissing because he has more to say than anyone else of a certain kind of contemporary life, and because his unsparing utterance betokens a mind of unusual honesty. Misdirection of force is its chief defect, whether by way of over-emphasis or in laboured and doubtful character drawing; but force, the condition of most excellence, is there indubitably.

87. James Payn, *Illustrated London News*

26 January 1895, cvi, 98

James Payn (1830–98) was a well-known literary figure in the last forty years of the nineteenth century. Gissing came to know him in 1885 as manuscript reader for Smith, Elder and editor of the *Cornhill Magazine*, in which *A Life's Morning* appeared from January to December 1888. Gissing's difficulties with Payn during the period from 1885 to 1891 have been related by all Gissing's biographers. Payn, who was the author of many best-selling novels now completely forgotten, held the view that a novel must first of all be an entertainment, a view which Gissing strenuously opposed and fought. He read the following piece and disposed of it summarily in his diary: 'Meant as laudatory, but showing little understanding of my work' (25 January 1895). Further comments are to be found in No. 89.

Mr George Gissing is an author apart; he belongs to no school, and has founded none. He describes human life with the relentlessness of a Zola, but without his uncleanness. His characters do not lead happy lives, nor, it is fair to add, do they generally deserve to do so. No doubt he could draw gentlemen and ladies if he chose, but he does not choose. The subjects of his pen are, for the most part, at best genteel, and not so very genteel. So far as I remember, he never indulges in humour, nor permits his *dramatis personae* to do so. Their lives are not worth living, but thanks to the genius he unquestionably possesses they are well worth describing. He contrives to interest us in them in spite of ourselves. They are unhappy and frequently morose, their views are commonplace and sordid, they are often vicious in an unattractive fashion, yet we feel that they are real people, photographed from the life; indeed, they are themselves like photographs—cheap ones—ungainly, uncomely, and colourless. Their end, like their beginning, is almost always an unhappy one. The note from first to last is pessimist. Still, out of these unpromising materials it is seldom that Mr George Gissing fails to weave an attractive tale. He is obviously in earnest, and yet so disinclined to preach, so sympathetic, yet without a particle of gush; above all, he strikes one as being honest as the day, with entire freedom from affectation. He deals with the vulgar from their own standpoint—not humorously, as Dickens did, and far less *de haut en bas*; he describes them with pitiless accuracy, but without apology. *In the Year of Jubilee* is quite as good as anything he has written. It is, as usual, crowded with characters not one of whom can lay claim to be a hero, though none has a *valet de chambre* to question it. Mary Woodruff, a housekeeper worthily translated to the parlour, is the only one of the *dramatis personae* who is favourably presented to our notice. The principal personage, Lionel Tarrant, speaks of her as 'that most wonderful phenomenon in nature—an uneducated woman who was neither vulgar nor foolish.' And all the other women in the book are uneducated. Tarrant—though when he throws off the slough of dissipation he becomes a prig, and has views he believes to be philosophic, but which in fact are very silly, about marriage and other social matters—is an interesting study, full of contradictions, and yet singularly lifelike. This, indeed, is the charm of the novel: the people in it are all alive; there are no marionettes, which is fortunate, since there is no dance-music provided for them.

88. Unsigned review, *Spectator*

9 February 1895, lxxiv, 205–6

Gissing regarded this article as an attack on him for his 'perverse idealism'. The extent of his displeasure may be estimated by a reading of No. 89.

Fifteen or twenty years ago, there was a vacant place in English fiction, waiting for a competent writer to fill it. We had novels of high society, written sometimes with knowledge, frequently with more or less of startling ignorance; we had novels of low society, virtuous, vicious, and mixed; and we had a still greater number of novels dealing with members of the class for which the prayer of Agur has been answered,—people who have neither poverty nor riches, but who are fed with material and mental food convenient for them, and who, being emphatically well-to-do, have that measure of intelligence, grace, and culture which is the fitting accompaniment of well-to-do-ness. The class which waited for a delineator was a large and important one,—that vaguely outlined lower middle section of society which, in the matter of physical comfort, approximates to the caste above it, and in its lack of the delicate requirements of life has something in common with the caste below it, but which is, nevertheless, so recognisably differentiated from both, that confused classification is impossible even to the most superficial observer. The families of the imperfectly educated but fairly well-paid manager or clerk, of the tradesman who has 'got on' pecuniarily but hardly 'gone up' socially, and, to speak generally, of the typical ratepayers in an unfashionable London suburb, had not, perhaps, been entirely neglected, for Dickens and others had given them occasional attention; but they lacked a novelist of their own who should devote himself mainly or exclusively to them, and do for them what had been done by others for the classes and the masses.

They have at last found one in Mr George Gissing, who, for some years, and in various volumes, has delineated the members of this particular social grade—their manners and customs, their modes of thought and life, their relations to each other and to those who stand just above or just below them on the social ladder. And yet we think it very probable, indeed almost certain, that though the portrait-painter has come, the sitters (at any rate those of them who subscribe to a circulating library) will turn away from the finished work 'as if dissatisfied.' They will not be able to dispute its knowledge or deny its skill; they will find themselves all but powerless to lay a finger on a single detail and say, 'Here is a false or fumbling touch;' they will only feel in a vague, uncomfortable, resentful sort of way that the general effect is false, misleading, even libellous; that it is in essence caricature, though it has been produced without any of those obvious tricks of draughtsmanship which make ordinary caricature at once recognisable for what it is.

Of course, the general method of caricature is the method of exaggeration. If a man possesses a large nose it is made larger, if he wears a high collar it becomes higher, if he has an occasional trick of gesture it is represented as constant and obtrusive. But it is to be noted that a very similar effect can be produced by the converse method of suppression and exclusion; for if nothing is added but something is simply ignored and left out, the expression of what remains is as much altered as it can be by deliberate accentuation. This is the method of portraiture adopted consciously or unconsciously—possibly the latter—by Mr George Gissing. In many of his books, and especially in this his latest novel, *In the Year of Jubilee*, the characters have been subjected to a depressing process,—they are allowed just as much, and no more, of the common humanity as shall serve to give life to the selected type. The artist who sees life steadily and sees it whole, never allows us to forget that whatsoever be a man's caste, or calling, or condition, he is first of all a human being, and only secondarily a courtier, a rustic, a lawyer, a publican, a barbarian, or a Philistine. The humanity which unites him to his fellows is really more significant, and should, in any serious art, be made more emphatic than the idiosyncrasies which distinguish him from them; but it is Mr Gissing's way to give distinctness and force to his delineation of a species by emphasising its special isolating features, which are frequently, if not generally, the features that indicate weakness or limitation.

In the Year of Jubilee provides a striking example of this method. We cannot say that a single member of Mr Gissing's group of unpleasant characters is untrue to the facts of life, as those facts may be observed in any typical middle-class suburb, Camberwell or Peckham, Hackney or Holloway. The seniors live a dull, colourless vegetating life, unglorified by a single fine emotion or elevating instinct; the young throw the energies of youth either into sham culture, which leads only to unlovely priggishness, into degraded pleasures which land them in still more unlovely profligacy, or into a sordid money-worship which, in the young, is perhaps the unloveliest, because the most unnatural, of all. Among the not numerous prominent characters are a divorced woman; two girl-victims of seduction,—if indeed the phrase be not misapplied to lapses from virtue which have hardly waited for temptation; one young man, whose dissipation is of that vulgarest kind which comes not of strong passion, but of dull brain; a second young man, who is a mere accumulating machine which makes money and makes love with the same revolution of the wheels; and a third, a dull, sententious fool, who sprouts platitudes at suburban debating societies, and interlards his familiar talk with dry chips of trite didacticism or irrelevant general information.

Now, no one will deny that such characters as these represent existing types, or that such types (at least some of them) are most frequent in communities where the materials of comfort are in marked excess of the resources of culture; but to paraphrase Matthew Arnold, even in a cheap suburb life may be lived well,—certainly not less well in the main than in any other civilised human sphere. But in Mr Gissing's pages the brutish stupefaction of his men and women is obviously treated as the inevitable, unescapeable result of their social conditions and surroundings; therefore, in so far as fidelity to the fact is essential to art (and to realistic art such fidelity is the one thing needful), his treatment may be challenged on purely artistic grounds by critics who would treat its fatalistic pessimism as an indifferent thing for which they have neither approval nor condemnation.

There is no error more frequent in contemporary appraisements of art than the common assumption that any vivid presentation of the ugliness of life must needs be *realistic*. The difference between idealism and realism is not a difference of effects but of methods; the realist endeavours to present all the facts, and to preserve in his presentation their true proportionate values; while the idealist, consciously or instinctively, selects the facts, and confers upon them a value of his own for the sake of achieving a certain effect or impression. Generally, no doubt, the idealist will strive after an effect of beauty, simply because to the majority beauty is more admirable than ugliness; but this choice is not inevitable. A distinguished critic has shown that M. Zola, often spoken of as the most relentless of realists, is, as a matter of fact, a typical idealist. Just as that first of idealists, the Greek sculptor, selected from one model an arm, from another a foot, and from a third the set of the head upon the neck, in order to produce a type of perfect beauty, so in his most characteristic novels M. Zola deliberately selects social features that are specially ugly, in order to combine them in a picture of ideal ugliness. The ends of the two artists are opposite, but the means they employ are identical; and this identity of methods proclaims them members of one artistic family.

Mr George Gissing must therefore be regarded not as a realist, but as an idealist of the new school. What is supposed to be his realism inheres only in his rendering of detail, which is certainly characterised by remarkable knowledge and skill. His acquaintance with certain social features is hardly less intimate than that of the Greek sculptor with certain anatomical features; but just as we know that there never was a living man or woman so physically perfect as the Apollo Belvedere or the Venus of Milo, so do we know that there never was a civilised community in which human nature was so largely denuded of its attractive elements as is the human nature of the community depicted in Mr Gissing's latest story. He has lately been the recipient of enthusiastic praise, and though we think that some of it has been extravagantly expressed, we do not grudge it to him. But it is in the interests of art that praise should be awarded on the right grounds; and praise can be awarded to Mr Gissing only for the vigour and vividness with which he renders his own vision—a most distorted vision it seems to us—of the vulgarity, sordidness, and ugliness of life.

89. Gissing and his critics, letter to Morley Roberts

10 February 1895

On 9 February 1895 Gissing received a letter from his friend Morley Roberts asking permission to write a critical article on him for the *Fortnightly Review*. Gissing took advantage of the occasion to suggest a line of defence against the recent attack published in the *Spectator* (No. 88). The reviews in the *Sketch* and the *Illustrated London News* referred to in the letter are reproduced as Nos 84 and 87. Gissing's letter to Roberts was first published in the London *Bookman*, January 1915, 123–4.

My dear Roberts,—What objection could I possibly have—unless it were that I should not like to hear you reviled for log-rolling? But it seems to me that you might well write an article which would incur no such charge; and indeed, by so doing, you would render me a very great service. For I have in mind at present the careful and well-written attack in the current *Spectator*. Have you seen it? Now I will tell you what my feelings are about this frequent attitude in my critics.

'The general effect is false, misleading, even libellous, it is in essence caricature'—'the brutish stupification [*sic*] of his men and women'—'his realism inheres only in his rendering of detail'—etc. Now I maintain that the writer exhibits a twofold ignorance; first, of the life I depict, and again of the books in which I depict it. He speaks specially of *Jubilee*; so for the moment we'll stick to that. I have *selected* from the great mass of lower middle-class life a group of people who represent certain of its grossnesses, weaknesses, etc., peculiar to our day. Now, in the first place, this group of people, on its worst side, represents a degradation of which the critic has obviously no idea. In the second place, my book, if properly read, contains abundant evidence of good feeling and right thinking in those members of the book who are *not* hopelessly base.—Pass to instances. 'The seniors live a . . . life unglorified by a single fine emotion or elevating instinct.' Indeed?

What about Mr Lord, who is there precisely to show that there can be, and are, these emotions in individuals? Of the young people (to say not a word of Nancy, at heart an admirable woman), how is it possible to miss the notes of fine character in poor Peachey? Is not the passionate love of one's child an 'elevating instinct,' nor yet a 'fine emotion'? Why, even Nancy's brother shows at the end that favourable circumstances could bring out in him gentleness and goodness. And Samuel Barmby—but this is a crucial case, and of him I must speak at length.

'A dull, sententious fool, who spouts platitudes at suburban debating societies, and interlards his familiar talk with dry chips of trite didacticism or irrelevant general information.' Now if this gives the faintest idea of Samuel, I am strangely misled. To begin with, the man is distinctly amusing, with his comical and characteristic habit of quoting scraps from *Tit-Bits*. Then again, he is, morally, a very favourable specimen of the men of his class. But read the description lately given in the *Sketch*. 'In his capacity as executor of an estate, he proposes to condone the evasion of the will by immoral relations with a married woman.' Now this, if you like, is libellous. That whole scene of his with Nancy, one of the most important in the book, exhibits with the utmost care Barmby's essential *naïveté* and incapability of baseness. The whole point, the humour of the situation, lies in the fact that *all he wants from Nancy is a recognition of his moral excellence, of his superb generosity*. This, for him, is sufficient reward for his connivance at her dishonesty—a connivance in itself anything but gravely criminal. No, the man is anything but a 'dull, sententious fool.' He is not a bit of a caricature, but mere humanity through and through.

'The general effect is false,' etc. Why, yes; to a very rapid skimmer of the book. Precisely as the general effect upon a rapid observer of the people themselves would be false. I want to insist that if people think it worth while to write at length about my books, they must take the trouble to study them seriously. In this section of the lower middle class, the good is not on the surface, neither will it be found on the surface of my narrative. But there it lies, to be found and recognised by a competent reader. I can't allow that my 'vision' is 'distorted,' and assuredly my 'rendering of detail' is not my only 'realism.' If the man had instanced an individual; if he had said, 'There exists no woman so base as Fanny French'; he would have been on safer ground; for it is undeniable that the possibilities of goodness in Fanny are microscopic. Such women there are in plenty, but he knows not of them. To class the whole group of characters as he does is to show either carelessness or incompetence.

Thus much of this particular book. Now I want to say something of my books in general.

The other day James Payn had a paragraph about my work, as a whole, in the *Illustrated London News*. 'The subjects for his pen are, for the most part, at best genteel, and not so very genteel. Their lives are not worth living. He contrives to interest us in them in spite of ourselves. Their views are commonplace and sordid' etc., etc. Now, pray tell me, does this give a fair idea of my books, taken altogether? I don't think so, but the mischief of it is that this impression is getting fixed in people's minds.

My books deal with people of many social strata. There are the vile working class, the aspiring and capable working class, the vile lower-middle, the aspiring and capable lower-middle, and a few representatives of the upper-middle class. My characters range from the vileness of 'Arry Mutimer, to the genial and cultured respectability of Mr Warricombe (*Born in Exile*). There are books as disparate as *The Nether World*, and *The Emancipated*. But what I desire to insist upon is this: that the most characteristic, the most important part of my work is that which deals with a class of young men distinctive of our time—well educated, fairly bred, but *without money*. It is this fact (as I gather from reviews and conversation) of the *poverty* of my people which tells against their recognition as civilised beings. 'Oh,' said someone to Bullen, 'do ask Mr Gissing to make his people a little better off!' There you have it.

Now think of some of the young men, Reardon, Biffen, Milvain, Peak, Earwaker, Elgar, Mallard. Do you mean to say that books containing such a number of such men deal, first and foremost, with the commonplace and the sordid? Why these fellows are the very reverse of commonplace: most of them are martyred by the fact of possessing uncommon endowments. Is it not so? This side of my work, to me the most important, I have never yet seen recognised. I suppose Payn would class these men as 'at best genteel, and not so very genteel.' Why 'ods bodikins! there is nothing in the world so hateful to them as 'gentility!' But you know all this and cannot you write of it rather trenchantly?

I say nothing about my women. That is the moot point. But surely there are some of them who help to give colour to the groups I draw.

No, people are running off on a side issue. Do try to put the other view of the case.

I write with a numbed hand. I haven't been warm for weeks. This weather crushes me. Let me have a line about this letter.

Ever yours,
G.G.

90. Unsigned review, *Nation* (New York)

17 October 1895, 277

A cutting of this is to be found in Gissing's album of press clippings.

In *The Year of Jubilee*, Mr Gissing's dreadful subject is 'The New Woman', whom he handles without gloves. He does not pluck her from among the idle ladies of the aristocracy who live for notoriety, nor from the needy literary ladies who perhaps can't manage to live without it, but hales her forth from the obscurity of the middle class. Here he finds her diversely manifested, but always in active revolt against the respectable dulness proudly enjoyed by her mother. In the French family she assumes deplorable shape or shapes. There are three Frenches, each provided by a defunct father with an income sufficient for an old-fashioned girl, and by nature with a store of coarseness and vulgarity. Not one has an elementary notion of duty or regard for religious, moral, or social restrictions of personal liberty. Each pursues her own ends with an unflinching selfishness which excludes not only family affection, but the tribal instinct of union for defence. Flouting principles and propriety, and cynically frank of speech there is little to choose between the clever, commercial Beatrix, the frivolous Fanny, and the mendacious virago, Ada. The last-named lives earnestly up to the conception of matrimony as of a blessed state in which a woman may shed responsibility, do no work, dress gorgeously, and behave badly, all at the expense of her hapless deliverer from spinsterhood.

Scarcely less offensive than the Frenches, but not so devoid of virtue, is Jessica Morgan, the daughter of reduced circumstances and a vague tradition of gentility. She declares her right to belong to the new order by setting herself to achieve intellectual distinction so far as that may be advertised by matriculation at London University. Worsted in her struggle with 'exams', this feeble creature avenges herself for failure by vindicative betrayal of her friend Nancy Lord, and, that occupation gone, grasps a poor publicity as a fervent leader of the Salvation Army.

The several streams of the narrative merge in the story of Nancy Lord, and the romance interest is attached to her and a lover socially superior to Camberwell tradespeople—Mr Lionel Tarrant. Nancy is sown with the seeds of corruption, but, for various reasons, offers some resistance to their growth. She is as discontented as are the Frenches and Jessica, but saner; as keen for 'life', but more fastidious, less egotistical, more passionate, infinitely more difficult to see through and forecast. She alone of the group is capable of abandonment to feeling without calculation of cost; she alone has enough moral sense to know when she has transgressed and to be ashamed. The unpleasantness of the situation between her and Tarrant is seldom mitigated by its treatment in fiction, and it is not for Mr Gissing to gild facts; yet, alike without gilding or grossness, by a presentation which impresses our reason and feeling, he has stamped the episode with an inevitableness which lifts it beyond questions of taste, and relieves it from any need for justification. The delineation of Tarrant is quite appallingly cold and judicial. A faint suspicion of possible virtue always surrounds him, but the evidences are so scanty and intermittent that, almost to the end, one cannot determine whether such suspicion has not done him injustice. There is, however, no doubt that he is a common product of his time, that Mr Gissing knows all about him, and, in imparting that knowledge, shows fine technical skill, particularly in illustrating the principle of dramatic suspense.

Since we have and support a school of fiction that aims only at reproducing more or less shocking reality, to *The Year of Jubilee* let a high place be given. The reality here is perhaps of the most shocking kind, because the author's observation is radical, his courage to expose dauntless, and his criticism of wide application. Yet is he not apprehensive! A not unfair generalization from the novel would be that modern education and opportunity have demoralized women, that they have dropped religion, discarded duty, and, in pursuit of luxury and license, may be led into any immorality that seems to pay. This is, of course, not true, for it takes no account of the women who use freedom from narrow domesticity for intellectual and spiritual advancement. Nancy Lord, it may be remarked, escapes the worst results of her follies from causes quite independent of education or opportunity. Perhaps no novelist can escape his temperament, certainly not Mr Gissing, no matter how studiously he avoids the appearance of prejudicing the reader. His story is fashioned by his feeling as certainly as his method is devised by his strongly constructive mind. Technically his work is very admirable, and his cold, undecorated style is perfectly suited to concentrate attention on the narrative, and not on the narrator. He is as good a novelist as his school has produced, and for his not being a better one we may blame the pressure of the times.

EVE'S RANSOM

April 1895

91. Unsigned review, *Manchester Guardian*

30 April 1895, 10

Gissing pasted this review in his album of press cuttings but made no comment on it.

Eve's Ransom, Mr Gissing's last novel, is not only fully up to the intellectual level of Mr Gissing's former work, but it is for the first time, to our thinking, possessed of just that subtle power of arresting the attention and arousing the sympathies of the reader which such work as *In the Year of Jubilee* or *The Emancipated* lacked. The central figure, Maurice Hilliard, is a study of great and unusual interest. When the story opens he is a mechanical draughtsman on a salary of £100 a year, of which he gives £50 away to his brother's widow. His work is uncongenial to him; he has no prospect of ever being able to gratify the rather fastidious tastes with which he was born; life stretches before him like an arid waste; and in order to blind his eyes to the prospect and to dull his nerves he is beginning to drink. Just at this moment a former creditor of his father's, being seized with qualms of conscience, sends him a cheque for £400. In a moment everything is changed and he becomes a new man. 'And what are you going to do?' asks his friend. 'I'm going to live,' replies Hilliard; 'going to be a machine no longer. Can I call myself a man? There's precious little difference between a fellow like me and the damned grinding mechanism that I spend all my days in drawing. I'll put an end to that. Here's £400. It shall mean four hundred pounds worth of life. While this money lasts I'll feel that I'm a human being.' And so he does. The craving for drink, born of monotony and hopelessness, disappears, swallowed up in the satisfaction of long-repressed and rational desires. In the use to which Maurice Hilliard puts his freedom is to be found the story of the book, while the effect of freedom upon a nature so constituted forms its central and underlying idea. The first impression left by the book is one of acute depression. Is it really true, one asks oneself, that the average clerk leads the consciously repressed starved life of Maurice Hilliard before his emancipation? In other words, is the case selected by Mr Gissing for presentation typical? At first, so complete is the illusion produced, one feels inclined to believe that it is, following therein the natural inclination to argue from the particular to the general. And while this impression lasts depression is inevitable, for were it really so it would prove beyond doubt that this is the worst of all possible worlds. But in the end the conviction that Maurice Hilliard is and always will be an exception wins the day, though that he should exist at all is bad enough. The real *amor intellectualis* is as rare as the passionate desire for freedom. Most men hug their chains, and if you gave the average man £400 and his liberty the chances are that he would gamble it away on the nearest racecourse. As a rule man fits his environment, and it is only rarely that a square individual finds himself in a round hole, though when it has so happened the individual has generally had his angles remorselessly pared to make him fit like the rest. But we are coming to see that the helping of the square individuals out of round holes into square ones is one of our principal duties as human beings, even though it should involve the gradual reconstruction of human society.

92. Unsigned review, *Daily Chronicle*

9 May 1895, 3

This review, entitled 'In a Black Country', appears in Gissing's album without any comment.

Victor Hugo has said somewhere that perhaps the reason that inanimate objects do not speak is their taciturnity. There is dignity in this reticence, but if a concession may be made in favour of the morning stars Mr Gissing may claim mere wood and iron for his side. For him inanimate nature suffers like the rest, and the human drama is ushered in by the 'yell of brake-tortured wheels' in the sordid gloomy railway station of Dudley Port. It is a raw and grimy world to which this somewhat strained use of the pathetic fallacy introduces us—a dirty night, a third-class carriage, and a disagreeable colloquy between a coarse and vulgar rich man and the hero (using the word in its technical sense), Maurice Hilliard:—

'Excuse me, I think your name must be Hilliard.'
'What then?' was the brusque reply.
'You don't remember me?'
'Scoundrels are common enough,' returned the other, crossing his legs, 'but I remember you for all that.'

Now, it is disagreeable even for a self-made man to be called a scoundrel, especially by one whom he ranks, quite sincerely, as a 'blackguard.' Mr Dengate could not be wholly bad; he had at least sufficient virtue to appreciate a pose. Irony is a strong point with Mr Gissing, and this incident of the payment of a debt of honour is a good example of it. For from the most unpromising of skies, the comfortable sum of £436 brightens suddenly the world of the poor mechanical draughtsman, who earns £2 a week, and spends half of it to pension a poor relative. It has been his misfortune to have sufficient intelligence to appreciate the misery of his condition, and he has arrived at a state of mind that is described as 'desperation centred in self.' Now, with the sudden access of all the possibilities that money brings, he steadies himself for a careful choice. His wretched environment, his life of drudgery, his expanding instincts, all impel him to a course deliberately epicurean. He throws up his situation; he will taste life at last; not the stale make-believe of a mechanical routine, but the best that civilisation and art can offer to a man of his capacities. After that—the deluge. It is a bold and striking choice; it creates a situation of great and growing interest, and it carries our sympathies.

In this search for his true life he carries a clue; it is no more than a suggestion—faint, tentative—of no more power than the thousand motives, seemingly initial, which die away without result. It is the portrait of a woman.

[Here follows the description of Eve Madeley from ch. iv.]

This description is not merely admirable in its perfect economy of expression, it is the keynote of the woman's character, firmly struck and consistently maintained. What is more, it gives to Hilliard the dignity of a fine ideal. It is a detail of only general significance that in the first instance he 'yielded to London's grossest lures.' His capital was rapidly diminishing when he left temptation behind him in setting off for Paris. 'Arrived in Paris he felt himself secure and soon recovered sanity.' Here Mr Gissing has introduced a brilliant innovation. Paris for safety and morality, he seems to say, for Paris is the home of happiness, or at the least of pleasure, and sin is ever the close ally of misery. We trust that *Eve's Ransom* may soon be translated into French, if only as an international amenity, a counterblast to our Puritan judgments on the maligned city. Swayed by the motive of a possible meeting with the original of the portrait, Hilliard soon returns to London. He continues, with a fine discretion, the contraction of his 'Peau de Chagrin,' he buys a treatise on the cathedrals of France for five guineas—well-spent, for architecture is his special culture—and he meets Eve Madeley, who is at once less and more than his imagination had painted her. Her position is curiously like his own. By an accident she has come into possession of a small sum of money, and she, too, shares that insatiable craving for more choice sensations, which may be the curse or the mitigation of such lives as theirs. By this time Hilliard is able, at a restaurant, to 'sketch to the waiter a modest but carefully chosen repast,' and to distinguish with salient comment 'between the life of people who dine and of those who don't.' Their fortunes provoke a curious comparison:—

'Well, what do you aim at?' Hilliard asked, disinterestedly.

'Safety,' was the prompt reply.

'Safety! From what?'

'From years of struggle to keep myself alive, and a miserable old-age.'

Here, then, is the difference between them, a difference not insisted on too much, for Hilliard too knows well the life of drudgery and its common outcome. But here, stronger than every emotion of a young and beautiful woman, is the cold desire for material safety, a mere provision for old-age. Mr Gissing is too good an artist to labour his point, and this impression of the effect of sordid cares is intensely moving and appalling. We seem almost face to face with those great problems that loom before us, when every slave feels within him the possibilities of a richer life. The tragedy does not begin and end with Eve and Hilliard. They stand as types of the toilers emerging; they suggest untold depths of grim repression, and though their particular case results in a kind of compromise, which is, perhaps, as far as we can expect Mr Gissing to go in the direction of a 'happy ending,' the whole effect is profoundly depressing and, in a deep sense, pessimistic. Indeed, Mr Gissing's pessimism—we fear that he must be tired of a word that is used so frequently of his work—seems to be not merely the pressure of realities; it is a kind of idealism, arising from no shallow cynicism, but perhaps rather from the disappointment or the perversion of deep sympathies. The workmanship of this interesting book is strong and adequate. Hilliard and Eve are well imagined and presented with delicacy and force. We find in their relations a growing interest, an expanding curiosity, the touch of fantasy that makes life possible. Perhaps there are not many women like Eve Madeley, though in the time that is coming there may be, and if Mr Gissing's world is very far from being a place of flawless beauty, there may yet be extracted from it some grains of spiritual worth.

93. George Cotterell, *Academy*

18 May 1895, xlvii, 422

Mr George Gissing, in *Eve's Ransom*, writes of sad things without being pathetic, of mean circumstances without being sordid. Down in the Black Country, whose lurid nights and smoky days and barren wastes Mr Gissing knows so well, there lives a young man, Hilliard by name, fettered by poverty to an occupation he does not like, and by generosity to his poor and unsupported sister-in-law. A stroke of luck sets him free for a time, and he goes to London to 'live'—and to meet Eve Madeley, who alters his whole existence. Earlier in the book Hilliard rather loudly proclaims that he shall never love or marry. We are notified of no change in his sentiments until he suddenly surprises you by making violent love to Eve. The story is curiously rather the history of events and utterances than a record of feelings as they lead up to acts. Eve herself is absolutely objective. You see her through the eyes of the other persons: hardly at all do you look at the world or at herself through her own eyes. She is at once impalpable and life-like. Her actions are quite consistent with what you gather of her character, but the fascination she has for Hilliard rarely extends to you who know her so little. The book is extremely interesting, as being a love-story in the subdued tones of lower middle-class life, without any of the misleading glamour of romance, and as, in its own way, achieving realism without nastiness.

94. Unsigned review, *Bookman* (New York)

May 1895, 265

The American *Bookman* started publication in February 1895, sometimes printing the same reviews as the English *Bookman*, founded in 1891 by William (later Sir William) Robertson Nicoll, whom Gissing knew personally.

Mr Gissing's last volume is much slighter, both in conception and in execution, than *In the Year of Jubilee*, which we had occasion to notice two months ago. It is to be hoped that he is not going the way of so many writers, and producing too rapidly for his own reputation. Nevertheless, although inferior to his greatest work, *Eve's Ransom* is a strong and impressive story, and one that holds the attention of the reader to the end. The principal male character is a young mechanical draughtsman from the Black Country, who works from morning to night for a meagre salary of two pounds a week, and with nothing to relieve the monotony of existence. Becoming unexpectedly possessed of a few hundred pounds, he resolves, as he says, at any rate for a few months, to discover how it feels really to live, so that he may at least have something to remember in after years. He casts aside his work and rushes up to London, visits Paris, and plunges into various forms of distractions, but at first in utter loneliness. At this stage of his career, he makes the acquaintance of a more or less attractive young woman, who, like himself, has led a narrow, provincial life, and longs for a glimpse of the world of luxury. It is easy to see to what end one of the decadent school of fiction would have conducted this affair; but Mr Gissing, though pessimistic, is no decadent. His heroine is very unconventional, but nothing worse. The book deals largely with the development in the man of a perfectly unselfish affection, and with the conflict in the woman between unselfishness and motives that are mercenary. The latter are made to win. The psychology of Eve Madeley is a very curious study, and perhaps involves a certain amount of paradox; but the analysis is carried out very convincingly by Mr Gissing, and the book on the whole will detract nothing from his reputation.

95. Harold Frederic on Gissing, *New York Times*

8 December 1895, 16

Harold Frederic (1856–98) achieved fame in the history of the American novel with *The Damnation of Theron Ware* (1896) among many other works of fiction. He was the London correspondent of the *New York Times*. Gissing met him several times, at the Omar Khayyám Club in particular. A cutting of Frederic's article, entitled 'George Gissing's Works', had been sent him by C. W. Tinckam, his former Brixton landlord.

The fact that George Gissing seems at last to have attracted the attention of the novel-reading crowd is a very welcome sign. It comes, too, at a particularly opportune time, for people who used to take pleasure in the belief that the increasing spread of popular education must necessarily lift the popular taste in reading matter have been of late in a gloomy state of mind. The books which made the biggest running in 1894 were calculated to shake one's faith a little in this approach of the literary millennium. Those which have made the most money and achieved the loudest notoriety this year are so grossly inferior to the successes of 1894 that despair seemed fairly warranted. What could be hoped, men asked themselves, of a public which took Grant Allen's *Woman Who Did* as a serious performance, worthy of thought and discussion? And what was to be said of a public which snapped up huge editions of Marie Corelli's ill-written and vacuous twaddle? I hit upon these two names as typical—one of the popular passion for anything that was rumored to be dirty, the other of the popular willingness to accept assurance for ability and pretentious balderdash for good writing, if only the cheap-jack wares were pushed with sufficient vigor and persistency. There are plenty of other examples at hand. Perhaps the most valuable to the lot, when everything is considered, is furnished by the case of Mrs Humphry Ward. After all, the Grant Allen boom could be set aside as an ephemeral and more or less adventitious affair, and the Corelli taste of to-day is a legitimate representative of the Mrs Henry Wood fashion of a generation ago. The public can always be startled temporarily beyond self-control by some unexpected freak of sexual impudence, and the great mass of middle-class female devourers of novels are still only an inch or two above the servants in their kitchens in the matter of literary standards.

But Mrs Humphry Ward stands upon a different footing. Her personal position is dignity itself. She is, of course, incapable of advertising her works, either by such exhibitions of diseased egotism as the author of the 'Hilltop' idea imposes upon us, or by wrangling with her critics in the public highway. She offers her books in all seriousness as literature, and half the reviewers of England seem honestly to believe that they are literature. Her admirers speak of her as a second George Eliot, and by dint of their iteration the parallel has come to be taken for granted by the mass. You find at every turn the author of *Middlemarch* being weighed in the critical scales against the writer of *Marcella*, as if there were no longer any dispute whatever about the propriety of a comparison between the two. The fact that Mrs Ward has this year received the highest price for serial rights in her latest novel, *Sir George Tressady*, ever paid (up to that time) naturally confirms this impression in the general mind. It was thought a year ago that she was falling off in popularity here in England. So shrewd a judge as Mr Fisher Unwin so firmly believed this to be the case that he relinquished the British agency of the *Century Magazine* rather than commit himself to the exceptional sale of this new novel, which the price paid for it made it necessary to count upon. But I am not sure that the mere mention of the figures—$18,000—has not fully revived her waning hold upon the British reviewers' and novel-readers' imagination—if, indeed, it ever did suffer diminution.

This apotheosis of Mrs Ward has, as I have said, been felt to be a much graver matter than any mere momentary rattling of the multitude's wits by the Grant Allens of the hour. It has seemed to indicate an organic deterioration among the so-called cultured and educated classes of the community. That a generation should accept the idea that its *David Grieve* could honestly be compared with the *Daniel Deronda* of its predecessor, appeared inexplicable upon any theory other than that of a universal lowering of mental standards. The thought was profoundly depressing.

One's gloom was not lessened by the fact that George Meredith is nearing the seventies, and after his brilliant flash of *Lord Ormont and His*

Aminta, seems unlikely to lead us again anywhere near the top mark of his genius, and that Thomas Hardy has gone definitely down the wrong turning and wanders with each new work still further away into the unlovely marsh of prurient unhappiness. The space between *The Return of the Native* or *The Woodlanders* and this latest *Jude the Obscure* yawns like an unbridgeable gulf. To repeat, one saw Meredith passing into unproductive old age and Hardy willfully effacing himself, and the prospect darkened under the menace of Mrs Humphry Ward's recognition as the representative British novelist, rising like a cloud on the horizon.

So all the more eagerly does one clutch now at the sign of promise which seems to be involved in the advance of George Gissing. He has been known to the few for ten years. Suddenly, within the last six months or so, there have risen indications that the many have at last heard about him. A uniform edition of his earlier works, or of such as he was not compelled by poverty and the hopelessness of commanding copyright terms to sell outright, has appeared, and I am told is selling fairly well. You begin to hear his name mentioned in those conventional talks about books which pass for literary conversations at dinner tables of non-bookish people. Very often now it happens that, when the names of Meredith and Hardy are quoted, that of Gissing is bracketed with them.

Whether he is known in America, I have no means of guessing. Whether he will ever be greatly liked there, too, is a doubtful matter. It is, or rather was until recently, the habit to dismiss him with the remark that he was too 'pessimistic.' This overworked word was meant to convey, in his case, that his characters were chiefly poor people, who lived cheerlessly and whose annals approached, through a melancholy atmosphere, endings the reverse of joyous. For years even those who appreciated the man, and made a point of following his work, raised this objection to him. I think it likely that it was the success of George Moore's *Esther Waters* which turned the tide in Gissing's fortunes. Mr Moore had a considerable following of readers for anything he chose to write. He exploited a vein quite new to him in *Esther Waters,* with the result of not only producing the one great book he will ever write, but of stirring up a general public interest in that particular kind of subject. People suddenly realized that here was a whole mine of material, strikingly dramatic, terribly human, which their novelists had ignored. It was neither refined nor respectable, from Mrs Grundy's point of view, but it was tremendously real. If Mr

Moore had disclosed the desire or ability to go further into this novel field, the public would gladly have followed him. But he is a born trifler, who spends his best years in the half-way pursuit of one whim after another, and has never recovered from his amazement at his own performance in having seemed to be in earnest, throughout the construction of an entire big book.

Meanwhile the public, having discovered that after *Esther Waters* Mr Moore had nothing better to offer than the sickly rehash called *The Celibates*, began to hear vaguely that there was a man who for ten years had been doing work of the same sort as *Esther Waters*—who had indeed made that whole humble and squalid milieu of London's basements and cellars and reeking taprooms his own long before George Moore ever thought of taking it up. Gissing's longest and, perhaps most important work, *In the Year of Jubilee*, appeared at about the same time, and the reviewers fastened upon it. Four of his earlier tales—*New Grub Street*, *Thyrza*, *Demos*, and *The Nether World*—were lying about on the stalls in the familiar pictured boards of the two-shilling novel. They had been neglected before; people bought and read them now. Then came the 'boom' of which I have spoken—although in this case the word seems sadly out of place—and now we have a uniform edition of six novels not enumerated above. Of these *Denzil Quarrier* is the least worth while. *Eve's Ransom* and *The Emancipated* I do not as yet know. *The Odd Women*—a powerful study of the struggles and tragic failures of the orphaned daughters of a kind professional father who lived easily through his income and died suddenly, leaving them penniless—is about as painful a book as I have ever read, but it cries aloud for rereading none the less.

The Unclassed is, I should think, the first long story Mr Gissing wrote. It dates back to 1884, and is, as he says in the preface to the new edition, 'the work of a very young man, who dealt in a romantic spirit with the gloomier facts of life.' At the time it did worse than attract no attention. It was considered too vulgar and too frank about low topics to be reviewed by respectable papers. Nowadays, as the author grimly hints in this same preface, these qualities would be regarded as added claims to notice and popularity, but it was otherwise eleven years ago. But this book, while it discussed with great freedom a class of subjects which the polite fiction of the early eighties could not dream of mentioning, is in its essentials entirely sweet and wholesome. It has immaturity written large all over it, but none the less, I find it in many respects the most interesting of all Gissing's books. It reveals him as starting without the most rudimentary vestige of humor. There is not a witticism in the whole 300 pages, or the slightest indication of a frolicsome mood. There are two minor characters who seem to have been intended as comic, but it would occur to no one to smile at them. They are as sad as the rest. Most of the Gissing books which followed this were distinguished by this same grave, stern, yet not unkindly insistence upon the serious side of things. It was not, indeed, until *In The Year of Jubilee* that the author found himself able to jest about anything. Even in that latest work, his spirit of fun is by no mean obtrusive. In the early *The Unclassed* it is non-existent.

As he says, 'Male and female, all the prominent persons of the story dwell in a limbo external to society. They refuse the statistic badge—will not, like Bishop Blougram's respectabilities, be "classed and done with."' The queer thing is that the reader does not feel conscious anywhere that these people are specially different from other people. There are no livid flashes of stage lightning, no exaggerated shadows, no hysterical moanings of the orchestra to mark where one's feelings ought to be harrowed. The whole long book proceeds calmly, dispassionately, along an inexorable path. The entire absence of artifice in so young a writer as Mr Gissing must have been then, is, perhaps, the most noteworthy thing about this remarkable *The Unclassed*. It is hard to understand now what London critics were about eleven years ago in letting this piece of solid and honest work pass unnoticed to the dustbin. Fortunately it has been fished out again and given a place on the shelves along with maturer and more striking products of the same pen. I think people who read it will remember it.

SLEEPING FIRES

December 1895

96. H. G. Wells, *Saturday Review*

11 January 1896, lxxxi, 49

The authorship of this review, published anonymously, was established by Gordon N. Ray in *H. G. Wells's Contributions to the Saturday Review*, Bibliographical Society, London, 1961.

Mr Gissing's new book will astonish his admirers. It is totally unlike anything of his we have read before. Apparently, so far as method goes, he has been studying Mrs Hungerford, 'John Strange Winter,' Mr Norris and the 'Young Ladies' Journal.' The result is a grammatical novelette. Langley and the widow Lady Revill loved long ago, and did not marry because she was pure-minded, and Langley, albeit a bachelor, was a father. So she married an elderly baronet to mortify the flesh. Afterwards, unknown to Langley, she adopted the boy. Then, in the simple way of novelettes, the father and the son meet at Athens, and the reader is amazed at the stupidity of Langley and the world generally, in ignoring the glaring, the scandalous likeness upon which Mr Gissing insists. The son dies, and the widow and Langley rejuvenesce and marry. In addition to the story, there is a curious flavour of purpose in this book which is strange in Mr Gissing's work. Instead of being driven by the inevitabilities of character, these people move just as Mr Grant Allen's Hill Top populace moves, on the strings of principle. Lady Revill is respectable, religious, and given to making herself miserable, out of sheer righteousness, and the backbone of the book is her conversion to a belated joyousness. It would be a commonplace story from anyone but Mr Gissing. From him it is possibly something more than an artistic lapse; it may be the indication of a change of attitude. We must confess that the possibility of a gospel of Greek delight from this minute and melancholy observer of the lower middle-class fills us with anything but agreeable anticipations.

97. Unsigned review, *Athenaeum*

25 January 1896, 116

In *Sleeping Fires* Mr George Gissing has added to the 'Autonym Library' a story which, without his name on the titlepage, would scarcely have been fathered by any of his readers upon the author of *Eve's Ransom*. It is a brave venture in a new style, and seems to show that Mr Gissing might, if he chose, deal on a higher plane with loftier themes and more attractive characters than his earlier stories have accustomed us to look for from his pen. This impression is due, perhaps, more to the conception and first plotting of *Sleeping Fires* than to the whole execution of the design, which is of a somewhat variable strength. The drawing of the women is not quite equal to that of the men, though the action turns mainly upon the influence which they exert over a man of forty and a youth of eighteen. It is in the last-mentioned couple, in their relations to each other, in the charming features of their brief intercourse, under a Grecian sky and with a lightly touched background of Greek reminiscence, that Mr Gissing has secured his best effects, and justifies the impression already recorded. If we add that the author struggles with a problem in morals, and solves it by the methods of the present generation rather than by those of the generations that lived before us, it is not with any desire to warn off the reader who has had enough and to spare of latter-day morality problems. Mr Gissing is sane and delicate; he may have sacrificed some of the intensities that a keener spirit would have read into such a theme as he has chosen, but he has worked out his story on straight and sensible lines. He does not, however, commend his scholar to our good opinion by making him jump on the railway platform at Corinth with an articulate 'Non cuivis homini,' nor his archaeologist by making him speak of 'the Pagasaean Gulf (Gulf of Volo, they barbarously name it).' Yet these are slight flaws, and even the hypercritical will not find many such.

98. George Cotterell, *Academy*

22 February 1896, xlix, 154

Gissing was acquainted with this review, a clipping of which is in his album.

In the 'most pellucid air', and among the joyous gods of Greece, Mr Gissing has thrown off the pessimism and absorption in the more sordid side of life which one has learnt to associate with his name. Throughout this 'Autonym' volume there is a note of hope, of acquiescence in the higher destiny of man and man's power to attain it if he only will; and the end is a triumphant proclamation of the gospel of joy. 'Health and joy,' says Langley, the hero, 'it is what life demands of us.' He and Agnes Revill have sorrows and shame in their past; and this is the answer he makes to her faithfulness to them, and her shrinking from the happiness that offers itself. The three men who occupy the first half of the book are an admirable play of character—the pedant, out of touch with life already in his middle age; the boy, full of fine enthusiasm and chivalry; and Langley, the half-wearied but still young man of the world, to whom comes all unexpectedly a second youth. As always, Mr Gissing gives every thought its fitting mood, every motive its appropriate act, and every act its inevitable consequences.

99. Unsigned review, *Literary World* (Boston)

18 April 1896, 117

Mr George Gissing is being extravagantly praised and severely criticised. That he is a favorite contributor to the 'Yellow Book' perhaps does not add to his glory in the eyes of sensible readers, and yet no impartial critic can deny to the present vivid and original sketch, which he calls *Sleeping Fires*, unusual power. In the eyes of conservative readers, for a writer to take up a certain side of life relating to the sexes is enough for them to decry him as coarse; to the eyes of readers of the 'Yellow Book' a writer who treats these phases of life is, no matter how unskilfully he wields the pen, certain to be strong and 'virile'.

[Here follows a paragraph-length summary of the plot.]

In the drawing of Langley's character the writer shows great skill, and Lady Revill is a woman of a most unusual type. When we consider how short a sketch is *Sleeping Fires*, and yet how strongly differentiated are its four principal characters, we realize that Mr Gissing deserves much, if not all, of the commendation which he has received. We find his work original, artistic, and dramatic. We prophesy for him an increasing popularity, and we think it must be admitted that he handles disagreeable themes with unusual refinement. We should like to see him at work upon themes of a different character.

THE PAYING GUEST

January 1896

100. Unsigned review, *Daily News*

10 January 1896, 6

Mr George Gissing is the English Balzac of middle-class suburban life. The tragedy of its respectability, its genteel inanities, its dulness and vulgarities is depicted with convincing and unexaggerated truthfulness. The stamp of sincerity is on all that Mr Gissing writes. His last story, *The Paying Guest*, the new volume of Messrs Cassell's Pocket Library, contains in a minute compass many of his finest qualities. It is a faithful record of what is, after all, not much worth recording; its worth comes in that it is all so finely observed, so admirably well executed. The scene is a genteel suburban residence in Sutton. A young, not too well off, couple sufficiently refined are tempted to take a 'paying guest'. Louise Derrick, the guest in question, is the fatherless daughter of a grossly vulgar and violent-tempered mother, who has lately married again a rich City man. Between Louise and her stepsister there is no love lost. Miss Derrick herself has been fairly educated, she is lawless, self-willed. She has no distinction or delicacy of perceptions, but she is good-natured, has a certain rough sense of justice, and she recognises and is impressed by the superior manners and culture of her host and hostess. She takes a liking to them and to her new surroundings. The irruption of this young woman into the well-ordered domestic household is as that of the familiar bull in a china shop, and the consequences are as disastrous. Her unromantic love affairs are presented with touches of quiet humour that help somewhat to relieve the sombre sordidness of an ignoble comedy. Mr Thomas Cobb, the successful suitor, with his brutality of plain speech, his commonness and sturdy honesty, is not attractive, yet he interests us. Almost every figure in the book interests, only because it is so alive. Mr Gissing's style is admirable. There is not a bungling touch throughout marring the clearness of his execution.

101. Unsigned review, *New York Times*

25 January 1896, 10

Mr Gissing's studies of English middle-class life and character are models of veracity, and are always as interesting as any fiction of a sober and unromantic character can be. *The Paying Guest* is a mere sketch, not even a novelette, so far as the story is concerned, but it is as fine and true in its way as *In the Year of Jubilee*.

The central personage is a young woman of twenty-two years, who might well find a place in that dubious society pictured so graphically in the longer story. Louise Derrick is of very common origin, removed by one generation from the ordinary small-shop-keeping class, whose tastes have been perverted, rather than formed, by wealth. Her mother, scarcely over forty years, is a stout, vulgar, ill-tempered matron who already looks an old woman. She is married—a second time—to a prosperous man in her own station who has a daughter older than Louise by a former marriage, and his household is in a state of perpetual war.

Louise is pretty, and has a certain taste in dress which is a bad taste, but is, perhaps, better than none, and young men are generally attracted by her. Her schooling was ended abruptly because she wished to shine as a 'young lady'. Most of her girl friends belong to the self-supporting class, and are doubtless much happier in their lives than she, but they are not considered 'possible' in her vulgar, overfed, unattractive home circle.

As she cannot live comfortably at home, Louise looks for board and lodging with a respectable family, through whom she may come into touch with 'nice people,' and thus she becomes the 'paying guest' of the Mumfords in the suburb called Sutton. The graphic portrayal of Miss Derrick in all her moods and fits of temper is not, however, the main object of Mr Gissing's little book. The Mumfords, Clarence and Emmeline, are types themselves. They are representatives of the refined and reasonably well-educated middle-class folks, who are removed several generations from poverty and vulgarity, who have aspirations just a little above their means, and a few pretenses, perhaps, that are not quite justified. The influence of their 'paying guest' upon their characters makes the story, which is very entertaining and profitable reading for people who know human nature when they encounter it in a book.

102. Percy Addleshaw, *Academy*

29 February 1896, xlix, 173

William Percy Addleshaw was a minor poet and critic. He also wrote a booklet on Exeter Cathedral in Bell's Cathedral Series.

Mr Gissing's new story will surprise many of his admirers; I trust it will not alienate them. It is very short, and very amusing. As a rule, his novels are lengthy and lugubrious, the reader not objecting to these sombre qualities because of the gripping power and notable sincerity evident on every page. Strength and truth are again apparent; the lightness of touch, the 'fun' of the new story are the astonishing revelations. Yet there is pathos in the book for those who have eyes to see, pathos none the less real because only hinted at. Miss Derrick, the paying guest, is drawn by a master hand. No doubt the prosaically worthy couple at 'Runnymeade' found her a great nuisance while she stayed with them at their magnificently named suburban villa. One can feel a good deal of sympathy for them, but they who interpret the story acutely will think still more kindly of the unfortunate young woman. Even Mr Gissing will find it hard to equal *The Paying Guest*. It is a subtle study of human nature, an excellent bit of writing and composition.

103. H. G. Wells, *Saturday Review*

18 April 1896, lxxxi, 405–6

The authorship of this anonymously published review was established by Gordon N. Ray in *H. G. Wells's Contributions to the Saturday Review*, Bibliographical Society, London, 1961.

Here is Mr Gissing at his best, dealing with the middle-class material he knows so intimately, and in a form neither too brief for the development of character nor too lengthy for the subtle expression of his subtle insight to grow tedious. The paying guest is a young person, 'not quite the lady,' who has quarrelled with her stepfather and half-sister at home; and the genteel entertainers are the Mumfords of Sutton. They are thoroughly nice people are the Mumfords, and they know the Kirby Simpsons of West Kensington and Mrs Hollings of Highgate; and, indeed, quite a lot of good people. Then there are the Fentimans—'nice people; a trifle sober, perhaps, and not in conspicuously flourishing circumstances; but perfectly presentable.' The Mumfords live at Sutton, 'the remoteness of their friends favoured economy; they could easily decline invitations, and need not often issue them. They had a valid excuse for avoiding public entertainments—an expense so often imposed by mere fashion.' What a delightful analysis of the entire genteel spirit that last phrase implies! And they kept three servants to minister to their dignity, although entertainments were beyond their means. In the remote future, when Mr Gissing's apotheosis is accomplished, learned commentators will shake their heads over the text, well nigh incapable, in those more rational times, of understanding how these people with their one child could have been so extravagantly impecunious. Yet we, in this less happy age, know how true it is. In and about London there must be tens of thousands of Mumfords, living their stiff, little, isolated, pretentious, and exceedingly costly lives, without any more social relations with the people about them than if they were cave-dwellers, jealous, secluded, incapable of understanding the slightest departure from their own ritual, in all essentials savages still—save for a certain freedom from material brutality. Mrs Mumford's great dread was that this paying guest of hers would presently drop an aspirate; but that horror at least was spared her. But the story of the addition of the human Miss Derrick to the establishment, her reception, her troubles, and her ignominious departure, must be read to be believed. The grotesque incapacity of everyone concerned to realise for a moment her mental and moral superiority to the Mumfords is, perhaps, the finest thing in an exceedingly entertaining little volume. Why, one may ask, is it so much more entertaining than the larger novels of Mr Gissing? Mr Gissing has hitherto been the ablest, as Mr George Moore is perhaps the most prominent, exponent of what we may perhaps term the 'colourless' theory of fiction. Let your characters tell their own story, make no comment, write a novel as you would write a play. So we are robbed of the personality of the author, in order that we may get an enhanced impression of reality, and a novel merely extends the preview of the police-court reporter to the details of everyday life. The analogous theory in painting would, of course, rank a passable cyclorama above one of Raphael's cartoons. Yet so widely is this view accepted that the mere fact of a digression condemns a novel to many a respectable young critic. It is an antiquated device, say these stripling moderns, worthy only of the rude untutored minds of Sterne or Thackeray. By way of contrast and reaction, we have the new heresy of Mr Le Gallienne, who we conceive demands personality, a strutting obtrusive personality, as the sole test of literary value. Certainly the peculiar delight of this delightful little book is not in the truth of the portraiture—does not every advertising photographer exhibit your Mrs Mumford and her guest with equal fidelity at every railway station?—nor in the plausible quick sequences of events, but in the numerous faint flashes of ironical comment in the phrasing that Mr Gissing has allowed himself. We congratulate Mr Gissing unreservedly on this breaking with an entirely misleading, because entirely one-sided, view of the methods of fiction. Thus liberated, his possibilities widen. Mr Gissing has an enviable part as a novelist; a steady conquest of reviewers is to his credit. He has shown beyond all denial an amazing gift of restraint, a studious avoidance of perceptible wit, humour, or pathos that appealed irresistibly to their sympathies. Now if he will let himself go, which he may do with impunity, and laugh and talk and point with his finger and cough to hide a tear, and generally assert his humanity, he may even at last conquer the reading public.

104. Kate Woodbridge Michaelis, 'Who Is George Gissing?', *Boston Evening Transcript*

21 February 1896, 11

This article was sub-titled 'The Great English Novelist of the Cruelty of Life'. A copy of it was retained among Gissing's album of press cuttings.

A few weeks ago, when 'Gissing' was mentioned to me by a person whose esteem I greatly value, I dared not confess that the name suggested nothing (I have since found that I had, even at that time, read and enjoyed two of his books), lest I alone of the mass of interested readers of good modern fiction knew nothing of the writer in question. Since then, I have devoured such of George Gissing's books as can be procured in this country at short notice, have studied the English reviews of those unattainable, and am now ready to be catechised in all the writings of one of the strongest and most thoughtful of presentday novelists.

As to the man of whom I was but lately so ignorant, a recent number of a periodical much given to short and breezy notices of current writers, such, for example, as that 'Mrs Helen Gardener, author of "Is this your son, my lord?" is the gifted daughter of Mrs Julia Ward Howe, and has inherited much of her mother's talent,' says that 'George Gissing, a novelist now much praised in England, is a young and very accomplished man. He has travelled much, and speaks several languages. He lives at Epsom, and seldom visits London. He is described as "an extremely handsome man, with auburn hair and moustache, and large, intelligent eyes,"' which would be most interesting were we not somewhat shaken in our confidence as to the trustworthiness of the periodical in question, by the singular inaccuracy of the first quoted item.

More reliably, one of the most recent of the various biographical dictionaries gives George Robert Gissing (the middle name is now disused) as born in Wakefield, Yorkshire, in the year 1857, and educated at Owens College, Manchester, an institution of learning founded not long before the birth of this her gifted son.

Formulating the man from his books, I should describe him as unhappily married to an unappreciative wife, blessed with a large number of unpleasant women friends and relatives, I should add that children, either his own or other people's, were to him an unknown quantity, that he was absolutely destitute of the saving grace of humor, that he had never been instructed in the fundamental principles of the Christian religion, and that he had been most unfortunate in his choice of clergymen of the established Church with whom he had associated. It would also seem that he had been shut out from the companionship of any truly happy man or woman for the whole of his less than forty years of life. All of which would probably be as untrue as was the distinguished parentage of the author of 'Is This Your Son?'

But what books he writes—oh, what books he writes! What masterly pictures of life, couched in pure and simple English! How he hates sham, how he scorns seeming and not being, how much he has added to the literature of today!

Fifteen books in as many years, each one crimson with the heart-blood of its writer, each one a passionate protest against the cruelty of life, each one voicing a solemn problem of the hour.

His first novel was published before he was twenty-three years old, and caused quite a little flurry among the reviewers. Here was an absolutely unknown writer, who had never tried his 'prentice hand upon anything small, coming forward with a three-volume novel so earnest, thoughtful and intense that it absolutely forced recognition of its unheralded author. 'Even if Mr Gissing has not come to stay,' said one critic, 'even if he gives us no other book like *Workers in the Dawn*, he has in it contributed something permanent to modern literature.' This book presents several of his favorite problems, such as:

Is it worth while to have talent—nay, genius—and to be full of noble desires and ambitions, if you are cursed by nature with an irresolution and weakness which will stultify your efforts for mankind and ruin your own career?

Is it worth while to expend anything but brute force upon the redemption of an inherently vicious woman?

Can marriage be happy?

Is there any class of men outside the prison houses much worse than the clergymen of the English Church?

The hero of *Workers in the Dawn* is a man gifted in every way, fitted to succeed in life, but he has no 'moral backbone', so makes a general muddle of things. He marries a girl who has been ruined by her social superior, marries her to save her and seems to succeed, but not being willing to keep her in a dungeon, he helplessly watches her drift back into vice. He loves a beautiful, thoughtful girl, who is at twenty an earnest, devout atheist—up to that mature age she had been an earnest and devout Christian, but probably saw too much of clergymen, and so tried what was to her but a new form of religion. Not finding in it, or in life, the happiness for which she yearned, she dies at twenty-two. The carefully drawn pictures of the middle-class world in which these people live and move and have their being are so painful that they must be true, and we are thankful never to have met the unpleasant Pettindunds, who scrape and save all the year in order to out-do their neighbors at Christmas, which festival they turn into a selfish orgie from which they emerge more sullen, sordid and unlovable each year.

Shortly after this first venture, Gissing wrote a novel called *Demos* and published it anonymously. It then received but scant notice, but since the 'Gissing boom' it has appeared under his name and with more favorable results.

Then came *The Unclassed*,* saddest and grimmest of books, which treats of subjects up to that time quite unfashionable in English fiction. It is noteworthy of Gissing that he handles delicate matters in a manner peculiar to himself, as devoid of unction, embarrassment and self-consciousness as is the seventh commandment.

A lingering pleasure in writing of questionable things that characterizes George Moore, Hall Caine and—alas, that it should be so!—Thomas Hardy, is conspicuous by its absence in all the work of George Gissing. Sin exists, therefore he does not deny it; but he meets it gravely, sternly, almost solemnly, never gloating over it and never dragging it in by the heels for the delight of exhibiting it.

It is impossible within the limits of the present article to dwell, as one could, upon each of Gissing's books. Some must be left untouched and some passed with briefest mentions. Of *The Emancipated*, one that may be described in a word as repulsive, it is only possible to say that it contains a curious distinction between men and women. 'Men,' he practically says, 'do not have to be emancipated from religion, because they are born superior to it. For them it has no existence. For women its sufficient substitute is "a warm, strong, human affection." If a woman is not sure of being deeply, devotedly loved, she had best

* The reviewer's chronology is inaccurate.

cling—if she can—to certain curious old beliefs.' He rather strikingly makes one woman who has emancipated herself from the restraints of religion, and the restraints of society, suddenly arrested by the restraints of her sex, and brings home to her the conviction that her real tyrant is Nature, the inexorable mistress whose limits can never be overstepped.

It is hard to neglect *A Life's Morning*, for it contains so much silent, unusual tragedy, and also so much beauty. Curiously enough, the most carefully drawn character, Beatrice, is the least effective, and the sublimity of her self-sacrifice leaves the reader all unmoved. The book should, artistically, be a tragedy, but it ends happily.

In *Denzil Quarrier* a man and woman have each betrayed a trusting friend. After the gentle Lilian is driven by them to suicide, the man models a head of Judas Iscariot, and tortures himself vainly for the rest of his life, while the woman does not recognize that she has sinned until she finds that her crime has not secured for her the desired love of Lilian's husband. Then it occurs to her that she did not behave quite well, but one is certain that had Denzil turned to her for consolation, she would have gone joyfully on to the never-bitter end, without a single qualm of conscience. Most women are like that.

One does not generally remember the setting of Gissing's books, but in *Eve's Ransom*, there are two that so harmonize with the mental condition of the hero that they become part of the story. In the beginning, when he is on the verge of suicide, the oppression of the heavy, yellow fog, through which red lights gleam dully, the smoke of many chimneys settling down upon an already choked and gasping world, the numbing, violent sounds that penetrate to tortured brains, all correspond to the mist of misery and despair which surround the defeated man. At the end, when he knows that he has truly 'ransomed' the girl he once loved, and that though she is his friend's wife, and lost to him, she is greater than his fondest hopes, he realizes that his pain has been worth living through. Then, a free man, he looks gladly upon the world with unclouded eyes, and sees it sparkling in the clear, frosty air, the light flashing through myriads of ice-prisms, and though the warm glow of love is wanting, all is life, exhilaration and hope!

There are three of Gissing's books that group themselves in the front ranks, and of them, *The Odd Women*, is to me the most successful thing ever written with which to make one's self entirely miserable. To it might be applied a little girl's description of 'The Gladiator,' as played by Salvini. 'It was so beautiful, papa, and so awful! And, papa, at the end, when there wasn't anybody left that wasn't killed, 'cept the lions and tigers, the walls fell down and killed them!' The story opens with an innocent little family party of a father, his six daughters and their girl friend. The father drops out after two or three pages, and the book, skipping nearly twenty years, carries these girls and a few others to an end resembling the child's recital. The title is the keynote of the novel.

'In England,' says Rhoda to Miss Barfoot—the only endurable woman in the book—'or, rather, in the United Kingdom, there are half a million more women than men—"odd women"—without possible mates.' The riddle propounded but not answered by the author is, 'what are you going to do with them?' By the close of the tale the number is slightly reduced. One superfluous woman has died by accident, one by consumption, one by suicide, one, at the time of her child's birth, of a broken heart—she is the only one who marries—one is lost utterly, one is a drunkard, one lives on bruised and broken, and two have formed an absorbing and unnatural friendship that cuts them off from the rest of the world.

Rhoda Nunn is the irritating and objectionable heroine. She professes most advanced views on the marriage question, but when a charming man, Everard Barfoot, the only bright spot in the book, in order to test her affection and sincerity, offers her love, without marriage, she indignantly and inconsistently refuses it. Everard goes away, disappointed, not that he shared her views on the marriage question, but because he doubts her. While he is absent Rhoda thinks it over, and comes to believe what she before merely professed. Her lover then returns and tells her that he wishes to make her his wife, and that he was not sincere in wishing, on the previous occasion, to insult her. At this Miss Nunn is deeply incensed. This is an insult not to be forgiven—his first offer can be easily pardoned, but 'make game' of her! Never! So he departs, carrying with him the congratulations of the reader. In spite of all this, the book is a grave and earnest study of the existing lives of a certain class and set of women, and is inspired by a heartfelt desire to aid them in reaching a better plane of life.

A more powerful and heart-breaking book than *New Grub Street* it would be hard to find. Edwin Reardon is the most skilfully delineated of Gissing's pathetic geniuses who lack strength to conquer fate. So delicate and fine is his nature, so noble his struggle to be true to his art and to his best self, that he commands from a casual reader sympathy and tenderness that only his tragic death drew from his wife. One reads this pitifully and undeniably true book, puts it down with a sigh that is half a sob, takes it up for rereading, and even when the words become sadly familiar turns to it again and again with pain that is still pleasure. At one and the same time, it seems as if this book should never have been written, and that it demanded writing. No student of letters can afford to neglect it.

In all Gissing's work the tragedy of marriage is more or less exploited. Not the daily newspaper tragedy, but that everyday variety that may lurk unsuspected in the household of your next-door neighbors, 'the inner lives of the turtle doves' of which the world is happily ignorant. Especially does he treat this subject in *In the Year of Jubilee*, that strong and masterful book that a few months ago set the world at large to reading the previously neglected works of Gissing, and contrasting him, to his great advantage, with George Moore. Here he takes the bull by the horns, seeming to ask how married lives can be made happy, and in a measure answering his own question. Bliss long denied to man—and women—he seems to believe can be attained by guarding individuality to a greater degree than at present, by more mutual independence, more mutual tolerance, and by an attitude on the part of woman which can best be described in his own words.

He says of Nancy: 'She looked up, and commanded her features to the expression which makes whatever woman lovely—that of rational acquiescence. On the face of most women such a look is never seen.' Gissing does not mention what expression the face of man is to wear in order to be lovely, possibly he is always so to the rationally acquiescing wife, for on examining his various descriptions of lack of marital bliss, we are convinced that all that was needed in the several households was the cultivation of that lovely expression on the face of the wife. Had it been there, even in the house of the Peacheys, most revolting of middle-class homes, all would have been well.

But it seems more than presumptuous to speak thus lightly of so remarkable a creation as *In the Year of Jubilee*, with its vivid and clearly-drawn picture of life that is but a sham, of Brummagem polish and surface culture, the life that is a recent and repulsive development in sturdy England. Gissing honors learning and refinement, no man more sincerely; he honors and respects honest labor and honest poverty, no man more truly; but for pretences of all kinds he has no tolerance or forgiveness, and the people who live beyond their means mentally, he holds up to scorn as contemptuously as if they had committed a crime which the law could reach. As a study of a peculiar phase of the life of today, this novel must command interest and attention, even from those who, with an eminent critic, find Tarrant 'a lamentable hero,' and cannot forgive pretty Nancy.

The Paying Guest, just published, is the shortest book that Gissing has written. It is something after the manner of the potboilers that poor Edwin Reardon wrote with his heart's blood, though Gissing now can have no need to truckle to the public, which is his to command; but it is well written and meant to be amusing. It is not Gissing's fault that he takes a bludgeon to kill a fly, and it is his triumph that his intense earnestness makes us feel that no other weapon would so successfully do the fell deed.

We await with eagerness *Sleeping Fires*, which Appletons publish this month, and also a new novel, the title of which is not yet announced, on which Mr Gissing is at work, and which will take all his time for the coming year, and which he considers his greatest book.*

* This was to be *The Whirlpool*.

THE WHIRLPOOL

April 1897

105. Unsigned review, *Manchester Guardian*

13 April 1897, 4

Novel readers who are weary of the conventional love story turn with a certain satisfaction to the works of Mr George Gissing, where they are sure to find a thoughtful presentment in dramatic form of some of the wider and more complicated issues of modern society. If *The Whirlpool* offers a less vivid and compact picture than one or two of Mr Gissing's earlier books, it is partly because it covers a larger canvas. We are introduced to a large number of men and women of the upper middle-class, leading the ordinary life of their kind, and whom it is for some time difficult to distinguish and grasp. Only very gradually does the real unity shape itself before us in the relentless clutch of Mammon upon the lives of all. The curse works itself out in various ways—there is the frenzy of speculation ending in misery and ruin; the weak man going under altogether and leaving his children waifs upon the world, the man of physical energy doomed to waste his strength and vigour in London drawing-rooms, where they have no scope, the youth of strong passion condemned to an unnatural and fatal celibacy because he cannot provide for the woman who loves him luxuries she does not want, the burden of housekeeping where convention and not real comfort makes the law, the restlessness and ambition of women, resulting in sleeping draughts and the neglect of children, if not in worse. All this is put before us not didactically, but in the use and habit of everyday life, and only dimly does Mr Gissing allow us to catch the outline of two hopes, one in a country home, the other in Jingoism. It is easy, of course, to take exception to both of these. The first may be called impracticable or inadequate, and if the evils of over-civilisation can only be cured by a frank return to barbarism, some at least will continue to prefer the disease to the remedy. But as Mr Gissing is not a preacher, but an artist, there is no need to quarrel with him on that account, and the indictment he has drawn against modern life in certain classes in great towns is undoubtedly both accurate, as far as it goes, and impressive. The two chief figures, Harvey Rolfe and his wife Alma, are finished studies. Both endowed with very mixed qualities of good and evil, the development of each in opposite directions gives a subtle illustration of the different working out of a character which, with all its faults, has a germ within of honesty and self-criticism, and that of one which, however attractive and gifted, has the essential vulgarity of a continual pose before self as well as the world.

106. Unsigned review, *Pall Mall Gazette*

27 April 1897, 4

Mr Gissing's persistent pessimism is but the more annoying by reason of its obvious sincerity, and doubly dangerous because it is so convincing. In *The Whirlpool* his art almost convinces us that it does not much matter what you do, since everything is certain to turn out badly. If you marry your life will be wrecked, and if you do not marry that abstention will probably wreck your life as completely as the most reckless love-match of them all. That your life is going to be wrecked is a foregone conclusion, and not worth bothering about; it is the question of how the wreck is to be accomplished that lends to life its interest. This Mr Gissing implies, and this you, reading his book, accept as truth, and the more unwilling your acceptance the greater the victory of his art. It is not till you have laid aside his novel, and have again moved for awhile in the real world which his imagined world so closely resembles, that you realise how, after all, the mirror he holds up has in it so slight a flaw, perceiving that it does not reflect, exactly, things as they are, and that after all the world is not so crooked as he would have you to believe. There are indeed enough unhappy days in life; but there are good moments too, and these the bent of Mr Gissing's genius leads him to ignore. It is always a grey sky that he would choose to paint. When the sun shines Mr Gissing shuts his eyes.

The first thing that strikes one in *The Whirlpool* is the number of characters; the multitude of them bewilders and irritates, but not for long. Soon they cease to be 'characters'—they cease to seem too numerous. They grow distinct and definite, take their places on the stage, and move, living men and women, before one's eyes. As the story develops, the reader's interest, while not withheld from any person in the drama, yet concentrates itself on four figures—Harvey and Alma Rolfe, and Hugh Carnaby and Sibyl his wife. In the story of these the author's pessimism has full swing. Sibyl is bad through and through, at any rate as far as one of the Commandments is concerned. Yet, deceiving her husband to the end, she makes his home comfortable, and keeps intact his faith in her and in virtue. Alma never did anything really 'wrong', but she spoiled her husband's life by her follies. The moral seems to be that you may as well be thoroughly wicked while you are about it, and that it is better to be wicked than silly, and much less perilous. The character of Alma is one of those careful, accurate, and perfectly truthful studies which Mr Gissing alone among English novelists can produce. She literally 'lived for others'—not, however, in any sense implying altruism or the old-fashioned unselfish virtues: her author would never see such a character as that, or, seeing it, deem it worth analyzing. Mrs Rolfe lived for others, in that she lived for their praise, their admiration, their approval. Her many enthusiasms, her pursuits, her music, her painting, her longings for a simple life, her desires for social success, all sprang from this root passion of her life, the love of applause. This ruling motive in Alma's life is not roughly thrust upon you in the author's narrative. You watch its development in her words and actions, and perceive its growth before you are able to tell yourself clearly what manner of plant it is that is thus unfolding before you. Your gradual enlightenment keeps pace, but does not overpass the disillusionment of her husband—an effect somewhat rare in art. In all the mass of detail with which the pages are filled there is no detail irrelevant: each has some influence on the destinies of the men and women whose lives make up the story. All who know Mr Gissing's work will hasten to read *The Whirlpool.* And there should be no lover of the art of fiction to whom his work is unknown. For he has this great claim upon us. He is the only writer of fiction who has drawn for us the middle class as it is (or almost as it is; his insidious pessimism forced the reiterated reservation); without cheap satire as without cheap sentiment.

107. Review, *Bookman* (London)

May 1897, 38–9

This review is signed 'A.M.' Its author may have been Allan Monkhouse (1858–1936), a journalist working on the *Manchester Guardian* who also contributed to other newspapers and reviews. He later achieved some reputation as a playwright. Monkhouse wrote about Gissing on various occasions: see Nos 174 and 182 in particular.

The Whirlpool is a very serious book. It is an indictment of the way we live now written by a man who is profoundly perturbed as to the outcome of it all. Mr Gissing has a conscience of the next generation, to whom he thinks we are not playing fair. He would like to be an autocrat, and compel us to live reasonably; only he is far too honest to prescribe any remedy as infallible; and he is even divided in his mind as to where he would like the remedy to lie. The malady is restlessness, in money-getting, in pleasure-seeking. Change and notoriety, and meaningless show are constant needs; homes are growing obsolete, men unmanly, women learning to despise old duties without learning anything compensatory in their stead. Now he looks with hope to the surging up of the brutal fighting instincts, which will send the men, at least, ten ages back in refinement from this hot-bed day of ours. But at bottom he has no faith in salvation by fist and jingoism. Then he would fain lead a crusade to the country, to the country towns, to the places where pleasure still dwells, where settlement and calm can still make a home. 'If I followed my instincts', says Rolfe, in this book, often, I think, a spokesman of Mr Gissing, 'I should make the boy unfit for anything but the quietest, obscurest life. I should make him hate a street, and love the fields. I should teach him to despise every form of ambition; to shrink from every kind of pleasure, but the simplest and purest; to think of life as a long day's ramble, and death as the quiet sleep that comes at the end of it.' And then he adds: 'If I carried it out, the chances are that I should do him an intolerable wrong.' For he knows that the battle-fields of this generation are not in quiet homes with calm and leisure and reasonable content; and that he who chooses these may be not after all the virtuous philosopher, but only the shirker. True, he sends Rolfe back to his beloved sleepy old midland town; but then Rolfe was not a person of abounding energy.

In his exposure of vulgar restlessness he is right a thousand times, even if what he shows be only the underside of a phase of life of extraordinary energy, teeming with mental activity, prolific in experiments, heroic in effort. It is an underside dangerously influential. Mr Gissing makes no heroes and heroines, but second and third-rate people; and his themes are from the weak and the vicious, and the hysterical and the stupid are affected by the particular temptation of London to-day. Without being what is euphemistically called 'realistic', he contrives to make a very hideous picture of the possibilities of the very ordinary human being. His closest work is here in the portraiture of Alma. Now she appears as the artist, now as the dutiful wife, a disciple of the doctrine of simple living; again as the artist, then as the good mother, always straining herself to the utmost, yet having no self at all—save perhaps a skulking ignoble one, unseen in any of these personations—played on by every passing influence, but obstinate, even unprincipled and audacious in each role till it is played out. As wife to a weak, a watchful and an intensely critical husband, as mother to a sensitive little son, she is a sorry spectacle, but Mr Gissing, one feels, went out of the right way in making her hiss out a spiteful vengeance on Sibyl at the end. Her career would have been instructive enough without that, without even the incident that made her the indirect cause of a murder. While we acknowledge his fine care in the representation, we feel that we are reading a conscientious schoolmaster's report. Over and over again a more sympathetic interpretation occurs to one. For he is a pedant to human nature. Some temperaments when he touches them ring always false and sound flat. No novelist has taken more pains to understand the condition of the average woman's life to-day, to study her ambitions, to mete out to her an austere kind of justice. But the schoolmaster in him is ever deploring their methods, and even while he is holding the scales of justice, and donning the spectacles of understanding, he raps out an ungenerous or a querulous judgment. They hide from his elaborate examination. They refuse to be scheduled. And so the best of his women are not women at all, but illustrations out of a treatise on the times. His faith in education, in methods of upbringing is pathetic. 'It remains a doubt,' says Morton, a very sensible man in the book, 'whether education has any influence worth speaking of.'

And Rolfe answers, 'To me the doubt seems absurd.' The whole of Mr Gissing's dealing with human nature justifies us in thinking Rolfe utters his own views. Life is a black enough thing to him at best. In *The Whirlpool* he is only a little more dismal than usual with regard to marriage and all the other important human affairs. But a good part of his gloom comes from his annoyance that men and women, especially women, do not habitually follow his clear, sane system of development. In his consequent fatigue he writes his reports. But the other side of this elaborate interest in that solemnly fraudulent thing called education must be mentioned, too, a most tender and beautiful love of children, not merely as the anxious hope of the race, but for their own sweet selves. 'All pleasures, aims, hopes, that concerned himself alone, shrank to the idlest trifling when he realised the immense debt due from him to his son; no possible sacrifice could discharge it. He marvelled how people could insist upon the duty of children to parents.'

If, however, you take for granted Mr Gissing's points of view, there are few faults to be found with his newest book. Like all his best work, and this is his best since *New Grub Street*, it is impressive, suggestive and made out of his brain and his heart; ungracefully conscientious, uncharming because it reflects no joyful, but only dutiful labours; but a real book all the same, and the book of a real man.

108. Unsigned review, *Academy*

15 May 1897, li, 516–17

Before publishing this review the *Academy* had given copious extracts from notices of the novel in the *Saturday Review* (10 April 1897, 363), *Daily Chronicle* (10 April 1897, 3), *Scotsman* (12 April 1897, 3), *Manchester Guardian* (see No. 105) and *Weekly Sun* (18 April 1897, 2). See the *Academy*, 24 April 1897, 459.

A salutary and valuable investigation of grime and grayness in social life; a mournful, mocking, strong book. Penitents, from time to time, go through an 'examination of conscience': what most profoundly saddens most of them is no monstrous magnificence of sin, some exceptional audacity in wrongdoing, but the sordid average of petty faults, the mean level of ignobility, the general prevalence of littleness and insignificance, the dreary mass of cowardly concessions and drifting compromises. That is much the burden of Mr Gissing's dreadful and admirable story: we are all in 'the whirlpool' of modern life, society, culture; we give in, as Stevenson has it, to 'this stuffy business of living in houses,' with what it involves; we are polished and urbane Frankensteins, creating heartily the silliest and most oppressive monsters. And somewhere—there are free sky and air, the feeling of a joyous activity, a sense of rational existence, a possibility of 'plain living and high thinking'; but *we* are caught in 'the whirlpool,' and we suffer grotesque miseries all our lives. 'Appearances,' and the imperious duty of 'keeping them up,' are our chief realities; we struggle on in a perpetual gray sickness; we are dazed and dizzied round the whirlpool. Money, and the part it plays in modern life, are to Mr Gissing themes of fascination; he states his tragedies in terms of money. All London speaks to him in the language of money; streets, clubs, theatres, lodgings, restaurants, suggest to him the human fight and fret and fume over money, its conventional tyranny and exigence. In this book he does not treat of the poverty of the penniless, of anxiety about pence; not the brave penury of Johnson and Goldsmith, or the miseries of 'the sweated' and of 'casuals' and of 'submerged.' It is the harassing, haunting preoccupations of those who seem forced to make one thousand do the work of two, or to abstain from marriage, because marriage is 'out of the question' upon five hundred pounds; those who are coerced by social opinion in matters of service and establishment. He dwells upon the demoralising influence of the supposed need for costly superfluities of civilisation, upon the wretched and dishonouring crime that comes of it, the squalid frauds and ugly intrigues and paltry ambitions. All this, told with a curious, simple sincerity, with no forced or violent emphasis, leaves the reader with a kind of aching admiration or jaded enjoyment of Mr Gissing's very notable art. You have had a good walk; but you are splashed with mud, you are rather fagged, the day has been depressing: you want a warm bath, clean things, a cheering dinner, and then to lose yourself in *Elia* or the *Odyssey*. But the walk was a good walk, no doubt of it.

The story turns upon money, and upon money in main connexion with marriage and its problems. Harvey Rolfe and his wife Alma, Hugh Carnaby and his wife Sibyl, with all the minor characters, their relatives and acquaintances, illustrate the action of the 'whirlpool,' in which society, the middle classes, the rank and file of the professions and arts, the people of comparative leisure, the men of business, are engulfed. There is definite, straightforward tragedy in the book; suicide and homicide are among its important incidents. But the dominant tragic note is not struck in scenes of passionate action; it is heard in the obscurer colloquies and debates of the will, in the timorous hesitations of decision and choice, in the sense of life as a thing tangled, involved, perplexed. It seems dangerous to take any step in any direction; there is nowhere any simplicity; it is as though a rational human existence were no longer possible. Or, if possible it be, it is away from the whirl and clash of city life and interests: in some peaceful, ancient town, the home of your forefathers, where you have lived from childhood, where you pursue a life of decent business, keep your mind open and alert, and have wife and children as rational as yourself. That was the happy lot of Basil Morton, corn dealer and old-fashioned scholar; and, grimly enough, he and his are the only successful and contented folk in Mr Gissing's book. It had been more satisfactory had he planted them in Bloomsbury or West Kensington, and shown that, to alter a word of Arnold's sonnet, 'even in London life may be led well.' We cannot all, in Turgeneff's favourite phrase, 'simplify' ourselves by electing to live and prosper in Arcadia. But Mr Gissing has no relenting mercies: his other folk, with scarce an exception, succumb to the miasmatic influences of London and its ideals: most of them are well-meaning, but the fatality is heavy upon them all, and they drift or drive into unhappiness or dishonour. And the worst of it is, that Mr Gissing's method is terribly and disastrously strong unto conviction: subtly, quietly, imperceptibly he persuades us that these ghastly, marred, soiled broken lives are nothing uncommon. We have met so many of them: the futile weaklings, the just tolerable cads, the maddening toadies and artistic pretenders, the riff-raff of gentility and culture, the people of sinister success, and the people of pitiable failure, with the crowds of the entirely uninteresting, who do not enjoy the lives they lead, yet persist in living them. No one is to blame, nothing can be done: 'the whirlpool' or, in Aristophanes' phrase, 'whirligig is king.' Harvey Rolfe and Hugh Carnaby, each after his kind, were excellent fellows; but they and theirs are caught in the bewilderments of modern life, as it were by some pathetic necessity, some inevitable taint and infection in the air. One may seek peace and simpleness in Welsh valleys, the other chase adventure and prosperity at the Antipodes; but fatality, *plus* their wives, bring them back to malarious London, its rottenness and stifling ways. We are left with the consolation, of doubtful efficacy, that perhaps the robustious and shouting genius of Mr Kipling heralds an age of blood and iron, with the British Empire on the war-path—or the raid. The soliloquist of *Maud* spoke in that spirit; and he was mad.

This may not be Mr Gissing's masterpiece; but certainly no other of his books can show more brilliant characterisation. His creatures are marvellously living; here is realism of a real kind. Those men and women grip the memory; we have a perfect faith in every one of them. Yet the story, the plot, is not of itself arresting; it would lose all its excellence in a summary. But the play of forces, the collision of motives, the inner spring of action and passion, the spiritual pathology, these are felt and realised with rare strength and sureness. Mr Gissing is in love with ideas, and can illustrate them through flesh and blood: his work lives.

109. Unsigned review, *New York Tribune Illustrated Supplement*

27 June 1897, 13

This piece was reprinted in the *Literary News*, November 1897, 327.

The novel of sordid motives and prosaic characters has been made so revolting by Zola and his followers that the reader who gives a brief preliminary glance to Mr Gissing's *The Whirlpool* feels tempted to put the book down. But if he has remembered any of this author's other books he perseveres through the many pages of the present volume and relinquishes it unwillingly at the end. For Mr Gissing is one of those rare writers who, without professing to find romance or beauty in every-day life, nevertheless wrest from such unpromising material a certain human and spiritual significance which is in its way beautiful and romantic. *The Whirlpool* is persistently and superabundantly sordid. There are touches of such brilliancy as might be expected in a book dealing more or less with fashionable society in a great city, but a drab tone ultimately kills whatever color the novelist may have sought to secure. The fact is he does not seem to have been in search of any color at all. He is vivid, but it is with the vividness of a strong draughtsman in black and white. His aim is for subtleties of feeling and emotion, not for the external nuances of a social spectacle. It shows his power. A lesser man, desiring to touch the imagination with a sense of the evil at work in the lives of men and women in the world, would have thought it necessary to paint their world as well as their own characters. Mr Gissing leaves us to draw our own conclusions as to the environing causes of the deterioration which we see going on among the actors in his drama.

Yet he is not an obscure writer. On the contrary, he leaves an impression of great thoroughness and even minute realism. But he knows that the realism of surfaces is one thing, the realism of human nature another, and there are no wasted words in his long story. The shallow, ambiguous but fitfully brilliant woman who is the central figure in the book becomes a striking proof that out of an unattractive material a novelist of power may make an absorbing type. Mrs Rolfe is weak, false, malicious, and, on the whole, vulgar; but in the analysis of her traits Mr Gissing gets very near to universal passions and universal truths. He does not make his heroine heroic—that he would scorn to do—but he makes her profoundly interesting, and his skill has been hardly less sure or less fruitful in his portrayal of the remaining personages. They are all alive, each is individualized, and while one may begin by thinking it rather unprofitable to write a book about what everybody knows—that our modern social life makes sadly for pretence and insincerity—it is impossible to escape the conviction that Mr Gissing sheds new light on the well-worn subject. He sounds new and unexpected depths. In other words, Mr Gissing is a realist in the best sense, one who is a realist for life's sake, not a realist for the sake of 'art'. He has not written a better book than *The Whirlpool.*

110. Unsigned review, *Critic* (New York)

5 March 1898, 159

This review was headed 'A Good, Gray Novelist'. Gissing had a cutting of it in his album of press clippings.

Under a heavy leaden sky, a flat gray desolate expanse picked out with blurred unhappy spots of black—that is this world as Mr George Gissing sees and paints it. His work is like a picture by one color-blind. The drawing is accurate, painstaking, praiseworthy in every detail, but the whole impression is unnatural and distressing, for happily the consensus of the competent pronounce that grass is green and sky is blue. The one thing in literature comparable to his presentation of life is the starved, leprous-looking landscape Browning depicted in 'Childe Roland to the Dark Tower Came'. Naturally an artist with this vision does not make pretty pictures for the walls of home. From this fact follows the other, that Mr Gissing has been working long for the recognition of his merit which is at last grudgingly accorded. Why, indeed, should the world give cordial approval to a man who apparently doubts and disapproves *it*?

The Whirlpool is a novel of London. Underlying the evolution of plot and the careful delineation of character is a study of the influence of the great city on life and mind. Heretofore Mr Gissing has dealt chiefly with fortune's outcasts, the very poor or the very miserable, and his readers supposed his books unhappy reading because of this fact; but *The Whirlpool* definitely proves that the writer's point of view and not his subject matter is at fault. The people in this book have no legitimate excuse for being unhappy or uninteresting. They are intelligent, cultivated, well-to-do, and they have a social position good enough to give them a certain opportunity for selection in their choice of associates. But these good things profit them nothing for happiness. The leading characters, whose fortunes are interwoven throughout, are two married couples, Hugh Carnaby, who was designed by nature for a frontiersman or a fighter, and his wife Sibyl; Harvey Rolfe, whose ideal of happiness is a country life among his books, and his wife Alma. Had it not been for the women these men apparently would have had the strength to break away from what is to them the malign influence of London, but Sibyl is essentially a city-dweller to whom luxury and admiration are life, and Alma is restless without excitement and flattery. London calls to the one from the ends of the world, and she deliberately brings her husband back to a life for which he is unfitted. The affairs of Alma and Rolfe are more complicated. Alma has imagination, and is capable of seeing a cottage in the country with 'no show, extravagance, or pretence,' every comfort and the society of friends as the ideal life, but unfortunately her vision is not sustained. She tires a little of the kind of life best worth living, and her husband, although the choice is in his own hands, allows a touch of personal unrest and his pride in leaving his wife a free agent to decide the matter, and so they go back to the edge of London and the whirlpool life in which 'instead of conversing people just nod or shout to each other as they spin round and round the gulf.' After these returnings follow money troubles, sordidness, intrigue, shame, murder, death, in a not unnatural sequence. It is a little hard to imagine all these things coming to people of character simply through the chance of environment; and perhaps Mr Gissing's case against London, though strong enough in all conscience, is not so strong as his case against human nature, which, as he represents it, is a poor, hideous, hampered thing, for which he has much pity, some comprehension, but no least touch of admiration. In the lifeless air where the creations of his brain live and move, there is no oxygen nor hint of sunshine. Misled by their ambitions, betrayed by their passions, they stumble heavily along a miry road, their faces to the earth. They seem never to have heard any of the master-words of life. The ideal has no power over them, and it does not occur to any of them that there is blessing or glory or privilege in being a man or a woman. Some people are like this, perhaps, but certainly not all. There is nothing like a worldful of them.

Any criticism of Mr Gissing's art is bound to begin and end with a criticism of his point of view. He paints the world as he conceives it with conscience and ability, but the result is not comely. Why then hold the mirror up to it? There have been other and greater artists who have suffered from something of this vision. Evidence is not wanting that life gave Stevenson the horrors, but he did not waste his talent in recording the malarial impressions, but, deliberately ignoring them, set himself to the making of brave tales of romance and adventure that folk might be the happier for his living and writing. Some day the artist who takes the world into his jaundiced confidence and tells it all the oppressive things he thinks about life, will be deemed as anti-social as the man who poisons the source of the city water-supply or lets some fever-breeding pool lie undrained beneath his neighbor's windows.

But it must not be understood that Mr Gissing belongs to the pestilential type of novelist. He is earnest, sincere, accurate. He has definite, if limited, views of the good life and how it is to be obtained, and he inculcates these unobtrusively. His characters move in a world which is externally very like the world we know and he is at great pains to make it so. He has something of the immense patience of Balzac and his conscientiousness compels the reader's admiration. But when all is said and done, realistic as his people are, they are not real. The breath of life has not been breathed into their nostrils. Not one of them, virtuous or vicious, seems to have the indefinable thing we call a soul. And the secret of their creator's failure lies in the fact that he has not thought such an appendage a necessity. No picture of life is complete which takes no account of its finer aspects, and no man has a right to call himself a realist who ignores the existence of the spirit. No novelist can do great work without an apprehension that existence is as high as it is deep. Mr Gissing's qualities are those that ultimately tend to greatness rather than to popularity. It is regrettable that the final touch of insight has been denied him.

111. Herbert Paul, *Nineteenth Century*

May 1897, xli, 790–1

Herbert Woodfield Paul was a minor historian, biographer and critic. He wrote lives of Gladstone (1901), Froude (1905) and Queen Anne (1906) in addition to the volume on Matthew Arnold in the English Men of Letters Series. The following is a short extract from a somewhat simple-minded article grandiosely called 'The Apotheosis of the Novel under Queen Victoria', 769–92.

Mr Gissing's books are not altogether attractive. They are always rather cynical. They are often very gloomy. They do not enable the reader to feel at home in fashionable society. But their literary excellence is not far from the highest. They are complete in themselves. They are perfectly, sometimes forcibly, actual. There is an unvarnished truth about them which compels belief, and an original power which, once felt, cannot be resisted. A little more romance, a little more poetry, a little more humour, and Mr Gissing would be a very great writer indeed.

112. Henry James, *Harper's Weekly*

31 July 1897, 754

James's literary letter, headed 'London July 1, 1897' in the magazine publication, was reprinted in his *Notes on Novelists* under the title 'London Notes', Scribner's, New York, 1914, pp. 436–45.

Occupying the letter for June had been James's comments on the public Jubilee celebrations. The letter for July begins by stressing the need to retreat from the public world of national self-congratulation into the private world offered by writers of fiction. Thus James seeks, in his reading of Gissing and Pierre Loti, 'the great anodyne of art'.

I am afraid that, profiting by my license, I drag forward Mr George Gissing from an antiquity of several weeks. I blow the dust of oblivion from M. Pierre Loti and indeed from all the company—they have been published for days and days. I foresee, however, that I must neglect the company for the sake of the two members I have named, writers—I speak for myself—always in order, though not, I admit, on quite the same line. Mr Gissing would have been particularly in order had he only kept for the present period the work preceding his latest; all the more that *In the Year of Jubilee* has to my perception some points of superiority to *The Whirlpool*. For this author in general, at any rate, I profess, and have professed ever since reading *New Grub Street*, a persistent taste—a taste that triumphs even over the fact that he almost as persistently disappoints me. I fail as yet to make out why exactly it is that going so far he so sturdily refuses to go further. The whole business of distribution and composition he strikes me as having cast to the winds; but just this fact of a question about him is a part of the wonder—I use the word in the sense of enjoyment—that he excites. It is not every day in the year that we meet a novelist about whom there is a question. The circumstance alone is almost sufficient to beguile or to enthrall; and I seem to myself to have said almost everything in speaking of something that Mr Gissing 'goes far' enough to do. To go far enough to do anything is, in the conditions we live in, a lively achievement.

The Whirlpool, I crudely confess, was in a manner a grief to me, but the book has much substance, and there is no light privilege in an emotion so sustained. This emotion perhaps it is that most makes me, to the end, stick to Mr Gissing—makes me with an almost nervous clutch quite cling to him. I shall not know how to deal with him, however, if I withhold the last outrage of calling him an interesting case. He seems to me above all a case of saturation, and it is mainly his saturation that makes him interesting—I mean especially in the sense of making him singular. The interest would be greater were his art more complete; but we must take what we can get, and Mr Gissing has a way of his own. The great thing is that his saturation is with elements that, presented to us in contemporary English fiction, affect us as a product of extraordinary oddity and rarity: he reeks with the savour, he is bowed beneath the fruits, of contact with the lower, with the lowest middle-class, and that is sufficient to make him an authority—*the* authority in fact—on a region vast and unexplored.

The English novel has as a general thing kept so desperately, so nervously clear of it, whisking back compromised skirts and bumping frantically against obstacles to retreat, that we welcome as the boldest of adventurers a painter who has faced it and survived. We have had low life in plenty, for, with its sores and vices, its crimes and penalties, misery has colour enough to open the door to any quantity of artistic patronage. We have shuddered in the dens of thieves and the cells of murderers, and have dropped the inevitable tear over tortured childhood and purified sin. We have popped in at the damp cottage with my lady and heard the quaint rustic, bless his simple heart, commit himself for our amusement. We have fraternised on the other hand with the peerage and the county families, staying at fine old houses till exhausted nature has, for this source of intoxication, not a wink of sociability left. It has grown, the source in question, as stale as the sweet biscuit with pink enhancements in that familiar jar of the refreshment counter from which even the attendant young lady in black, with admirers and a social position, hesitates to extract it. We have recognised the humble, the wretched, even the wicked; also we have recognised the 'smart.' But save under the immense pressure of Dickens we have never done anything so dreadful as to recognise the vulgar. We have at the very most recognised it as the extravagant, the grotesque. The case of Dickens was absolutely special; he dealt intensely with 'lower middle,' with 'lowest' middle, elements, but he escaped the predicament of showing them as vulgar by showing them only as prodigiously droll. When his people are not funny who shall dare to say what they are? The critic may draw breath as from a responsibility averted when he reflects that they almost always *are* funny. They belong to a walk of life that we may be ridiculous but never at all serious about. We may be tragic, but that is often but a form of humour. I seem to hear Mr Gissing say: 'Well, dreariness for dreariness, let us try Brondesbury and Pinner; especially as in the first place I know them so well; as in the second they are the essence of England; and as in the third they are, artistically speaking, virgin soil. Behold them glitter in the morning dew.'

So he *is* serious—almost imperturbably—about them, and, as it turns out, even quite manfully and admirably sad. He has the great thing: his saturation (with the visible and audible common) can project itself, let him get outside of it and walk round it. I scarcely think he stays, as it were, outside quite as much as he might; and on the question of form he certainly strikes me as staying far too little. It is form above all that is talent, and if Mr Gissing's were proportionate to his knowledge, to what may be called his possession, we should have a larger force to reckon with. That—not to speak of the lack of intensity in his imagination—is the direction in which one would wish him to go further. Our Anglo-Saxon tradition of these matters remains surely in some respects the strangest. After the perusal of such a book as *The Whirlpool* I feel as if I had almost to explain that by 'these matters' I mean the whole question of composition, of foreshortening, of the proportion and relation of parts. Mr Gissing, to wind up my reserves, overdoes the ostensible report of spoken words: though I hasten to add that this abuse is so general a sign, in these days, of the English and the American novel as to deprive a challenge of every hope of credit. It is attended visibly—that is visibly to those who can see—with two or three woeful results. If it had none other it would still deserve arraignment on the simple ground of what it crowds out—the golden blocks themselves of the structure, the whole divine exercise and mystery of the exquisite art of presentation.

The ugliest trick it plays at any rate is its effect on that side of the novelist's effort—the side of most difficulty and thereby of most dignity—which consists in giving the sense of duration, of the lapse and accumulation of time. This is altogether to my view the stiffest problem that the artist in fiction has to tackle, and nothing is more striking at present than the blankness, for the most part, of his indifference to it. The mere multiplication of quoted remarks is the last thing to strengthen his hand. Such an expedient works exactly to the opposite end, absolutely minimising, in regard to time, our impression of lapse and passage. That is so much the case that I can think of no novel in which it prevails as giving at all the sense of the gradual and the retarded—the stretch of the years in which developments really take place. The picture is nothing unless it be a picture of the conditions, and the conditions are usually hereby quite omitted. Thanks to this perversity everything dealt with in fiction appears at present to occur simply on the occasion of a few conversations about it; there is no other constitution of it. A few hours, a few days seem to account for it. The process, the 'dark backward and abysm,' is really so little reproduced. We feel tempted to send many an author, to learn the rudiments of this secret, back to his Balzac again, the most accomplished master of it. He will learn also from Balzac while he is about it that nothing furthermore, as intrinsic effect, so much discounts itself as this abuse of the element of colloquy.

'Dialogue,' as it is commonly called, is singularly suicidal from the moment it is not directly illustrative of something given us by another method, something constituted and presented. It is impossible to read work even as interesting as Mr Gissing's without recognising the impossibility of making people both talk 'all the time' and talk with the needful differences. The thing, so far as we have got, is simply too hard. There is always at the best the author's voice to be kept out. It can be kept out for occasions, it can not be kept out always. The solution therefore is to leave it its function, for it has the supreme one. This function, properly exercised, averts the disaster of the blight of the colloquy really in place—illustrative and indispensable. Nothing is more inevitable than such a blight when antecedently the general effect of the process has been undermined. We then want the report of the spoken word—want that only. But, proportionately, it doesn't come, doesn't count. It has been fatally cheapened. There is no effect, no relief.

I am writing a treatise when I meant only to give a glance; and it may be asked if the best thing I find in Mr Gissing is after all then but an opportunity to denounce. The answer to that is that I find two other things—or should find them rather had I not deprived myself as usual of proper space. One of these is the pretext for speaking, by absolute rebound, as it were, and in the interest of vivid contrast, of Pierre Loti;

the other is a better occasion still, an occasion for the liveliest sympathy. It is impossible not to be affected by the frankness and straightness of Mr Gissing's feeling for his subject, a subject almost always distinctly remunerative to the ironic and even to the dramatic mind. He has the strongest deepest sense of common humanity, of the general struggle and the general grey grim comedy. He loves the real, he renders it, and though he has a tendency to drift too much with his tide, he gives us, in the great welter of the savourless, an individual manly strain. If he only had distinction he would make the suburbs 'hum.' I don't mean of course by his circulation there—the effect Ibsen is supposed to have on them; I mean objectively and as a rounded whole, as a great theme treated.

113. H. G. Wells, *Contemporary Review*

August 1897, lxxii, 192–201

Wells had intended to review *The Whirlpool* in the *Saturday Review* but had been anticipated by Harold Frederic, the American journalist, novelist and London correspondent of the *New York Times*. To remedy this situation, Wells wrote the following article on 'The Novels of Mr George Gissing'. Gissing's comments can be read in his letter to Wells of 7 August 1897, and Wells's reactions appear in an undated note doubtless written on 9 August, as it reached its recipient the next day (*George Gissing and H. G. Wells: Their Friendship and Correspondence*, ed. Royal A. Gettmann (1961), 46–52). Gissing corrected his friend's interpretation of Harvey Rolfe's character in *The Whirlpool*, pointing out in particular that Rolfe by no means tended to the 'barrack-room' view of life, but only watched the process of destruction around him with humorous resignation. In his letter, Gissing also refuted Wells's statement that *The Whirlpool* amounted 'very nearly to a flat contradiction of the ideals' expressed in *The Emancipated*.

Although he wrote to Wells with some geniality about the article, he was disappointed to encounter such serious misinterpretations of his fiction. However, Wells was not the only commentator to think that Rolfe endorsed Kipling's view of existence, whereas of course Gissing was satirizing such an attitude.

Dr Foerster of the University of Zurich similarly imagined that Rolfe glorified Kipling—another misinterpretation which infuriated Gissing. (See his letter to Bertz dated 11 December 1899 in *The Letters of George Gissing to Eduard Bertz*, p. 268.)

Israel Zangwill, an admirer of Gissing's work, made a comparable error when declaring that 'in *The Whirlpool*, Gissing went out of his way to pay a tribute to Kipling's imperial muse' ('Without Prejudice: George Gissing', *To-Day*, 3 February 1904, 433–4). See also the conclusion to No. 122.

In the general acceptation and in the spirit of most reviewing, a cheerful alacrity of story, together with certain grammatical observances, are apparently the end of the novelist's art. It is, no doubt, the most obvious function of the novel of commerce, that it should fill, if possible without resort to split infinitives, the gaps where the texture of unadventurous lives thins out to the blankly uneventful. But if the novel is to be treated as literature, it must rise unmistakably above this level of bogus gossip entertainingly told. Tried by the lower standard, it is doubtful if the novels of Mr Gissing would procure him a favourable verdict; it is said they are 'depressing'—a worse fault surely even than 'unreadableness.' But in the study, at any rate, they are not so lightly dismissed. Whatever their value as pastime, it is undeniable that so soon as Mr Gissing's novels are read with a view to their structural design and implications they become very significant literature indeed.

The earlier novelists seem to have shaped their stories almost invariably upon an illustrative moral intention, and to have made a typical individual, whose name was commonly the title of the novel, the structural skeleton, the sustaining interest of the book. He or she was presented in no personal spirit; Tom Jones came forward in the interests of domestic tolerance, and the admirable Pamela let the light of restraint shine before her sex. Beauty of form does not seem to have been sought by the earlier novelists—suffice it if the fabric cohered. About the central character a system of reacting personages and foils was arranged, and the whole was woven together by an ingenious and frequently complicated 'plot.' The grouping is at its simplest and best in the gracefully constructed novels of Jane Austen. As the novel developed in length under the influence of periodical publication, the need of some sustaining structure of ampler dimensions than the type individual led to the complications of 'plot' to hold the bulk together. Plot grew at last to be the curse of English fiction. One sees it in its most instructive aspect in the novels of Dickens, wherein personages, delightfully drawn, struggle like herrings in a net amidst the infinite reticulations of vapid intrigue. Who forgets Mr Smallweed, and who remembers what he had to do with Lady Dedlock's secret? And in the novels of Wilkie Collins the plot in its direst form tramples stark and terrible. But in the novels of Dickens there also appears another structural influence. As Poe admirably demonstrated, the 'plot' of *Barnaby Rudge* collapsed under its weight of characters, and the Gordon riots were swept across the complications of the story. The new structural conception was the grouping of characters and incidents, no longer about a lost will, a hidden murder, or a mislaid child, but about some social influence or some far-reaching movement of humanity. Its first great exponent was Victor Hugo, as Stevenson insists in one of his all too rare essays, and in the colossal series of Balzac each novel aims to render a facet in the complex figure of a modern social organisation. Zola's *Lourdes* and *Rome*, and Tolstoi's *War and Peace* are admirable examples of this impersonal type of structure. This new and broader conception of novel construction finds its most perfect expression in several of the works of Turgenev, in *Smoke*, for instance, and *Virgin Soil*, each displaying a group of typical individuals at the point of action of some great social force, the social force in question and not the 'hero' and 'heroine' being the real operative interest of the story.

No English novelists of the first rank have arisen to place beside the great Continental masters in this more spacious development of structural method. The unique work of Mr Meredith and the novels of Mr Hardy are essentially novels of persons, freed from the earlier incubus of plot. Diana and Ethelberta, Sir Willoughby Patterne and Jude, are strongly marked individuals and only casually representative. In the novels of Disraeli—in *Sybil*, for example—political forces appear, but scarcely as operative causes, and George Eliot and Mrs Humphry Ward veil a strongly didactic disposition under an appearance of social study rather than give us social studies. Within the last few years, however, three English novelists at least have arisen, who have set themselves to write novels which are neither studies of character essentially, nor essentially series of incidents, but deliberate attempts to present in typical groupings distinct phases of our social order. And of these the most important is certainly Mr George Gissing.

The Whirlpool, for instance, Mr Gissing's latest novel, has for its structural theme the fatal excitement and extravagance of the social life of London; Rolfe, Carnaby, Alma, Sibyl, Redgrave, and Mrs Strangeways are, in the first place, floats spinning in the eddy. The book opens with the flight of the insolvent Wager, leaving his children to the landlady's tender mercies, and broadens to the vivid contrast of the suicide of Frothingham in his office, while his home is crowded with a multitudinous gathering of the semi-fashionable. The interlacing threads of the story weave steadily about this theme. Rolfe marries Alma, and for a couple of years they live an ostentatiously simple life in Wales, only to feel the fatal attraction grow stronger, and come circling back at last towards the vortex. Carnaby and his wife wander abroad seeking phantasmal fortunes for a space, but the fortune does me not coand the exile becomes unendurable. Sooner or later the great eddy of strenuous vanity drags them all down (saving only Rolfe) to shame and futility, to dishonour and misery, or to absolute destruction. The design has none of the spare severity that makes the novels of Turgenev supreme, but the breadth and power of its conception are indisputable. It is, perhaps, the most vigorously designed of all the remarkable series of novels Mr Gissing has given us. But the scheme of his *The Emancipated* is scarcely less direct, presenting as it does, in an admirably contrived grouping, the more or less complete release from religious and moral restraints of a number of typical characters. *In the Year of Jubilee* is more subtly and less consistently planned. The picture of lower middle-class barbarism, relieved by the appreciative comments of Mr Samuel Barmby, voracious reader of a latter-day press, was conceived in a fine vein of satire, but the development of the really very unentertaining passions of the genteel Tarrant robs the book of its unity and it breaks up into a froth of intrigue about a foo lish will and ends mere novel of a very ordinary kind. But Samuel Barmby, with his delightful estimate of progress by statistics, the savage truthfulness in the treatment of the French sisters, the description of Nancy's art furnishing, the characters of Horace Lord and Crewe, atone for a dozen Tarrants.

So far as the structural scheme goes there is an increased conventionality of treatment as we pass to Mr Gissing's earlier novels, to *Thyrza*, *Demos*, and *The Nether World*, and from these the curious may descend still lower to the amiable renunciations in *A Life's Morning*. *The Unclassed* has its width of implication mainly in its name; it is a story of by no means typical persons, and with no evident sense of the larger issues. But *The Nether World*, for instance, albeit indisputably 'plottesque,' and with such violent story mechanisms in it as the incredible Clem Peckover and that impossible ancient, Snowdon, does in its title, and here and there in a fine passage, betray already an inkling of the spacious quality of design the late works more and more clearly display. Witness the broad handling of such a passage as this:

With the first breath of winter there passes a voice half-menacing, half-mournful, through all the barren ways and phantom-haunted refuges of the nether world. Too quickly has vanished the brief season when the sky is clement, when a little food suffices, and the chances of earning that little are more numerous than at other times; this wind that gives utterance to its familiar warning is the *avant-courier* of cold and hunger and solicitude that knows not sleep. Will the winter be a hard one? It is the question that concerns this world before all others, that occupies alike the patient work-folk who have yet their home unbroken, the strugglers foredoomed to loss of such scant needments as the summer gifted them withal, the hopeless and the self-abandoned and the lurking creatures of prey. To all of them the first chill breath from a lowering sky has its voice of admonition: they set their faces, they sigh, or whisper a prayer, or fling out a curse, each according to his nature.

The treatment of the work of Mr Gissing as a progress, an adolescence, is inevitable. In the case of no other important writer does one perceive quite so clearly the steady elimination of immaturities. As a matter of fact his first novels must have been published when he was ridiculously young. I cannot profess research in this matter, but a raid upon dates brings to light the fact that a novel—it is unnecessary to give the curious the title—was published before 1881. It was long, so long that a year, at least, must have gone in the writing of it. And a convenient compendium of literary details informs me that in this year of grace 1897 Mr Gissing is thirty-nine years old. This helps one to observe, what is still apparent without this chronological assistance, that he has been learning life and his art simultaneously. Very few novels indeed, of any literary value, have been written by men below thirty. Work essentially imaginative or essentially superficial a man of three and twenty may do as well as a man of forty; romance of all sorts, the fantastic story, the idealistic novel, even the novel of manners; all these are work for the young, perhaps even more than the old. But to see life clearly and whole, to see and represent it with absolute self-detachment, with absolute justice, above all with evenly balanced sympathy, is an ambition permitted only to a man full grown. It is the consequence of, it is the compensation for, the final strippings of disillusionment. 'There am I among the others,' the novelist must say, 'so little capable, a thing of flimsy will, undisciplined desires and fitful powers, shaped by these accidents and driving with the others to my appointed end.' And until that serene upland of despair, that wide and peaceful viewpoint is reached, men must needs be partisans, and whatever their resolves may be, the idealising touch, the partiality, the inevitable taint of justification, will mar their handiwork.

Through all the novels of Mr Gissing, fading with their progress, indeed, and yet still evident even in the latest, runs this quality of bias, that intervention. Very few of them are without a 'most favoured' character. In *The Whirlpool* Rolfe plays the chief sympathetic part.

Contrasted with the favoured characters of the earlier works he is singularly inert, he flickers into a temporary vitality to marry, and subsides; his character persists unchanging through a world of change. The whole design is an attraction, a disastrous vortex, but he survives without an effort; he remains motionless and implies fundamental doubts. He reflects, he does not react. He has, in fact, all the distinctive inhumanities of what one might call the 'exponent character,' the superior commentary. If he errs he errs with elaborate conscientiousness; in all the petty manifestations of humanity, irritability, glimpses of vanity, casual blunders and stupidities, such details as enrich even the most perfect of real human beings, he is sadly to seek. Beside such subtle, real and significant characters as the brilliantly analysed Alma, Hugh Carnaby and his wife, Buncombe, Felix Dymes and Morphew, he gives one something of the impression one would receive on getting into an omnibus and discovering a respectably dressed figure of wax among the passengers. But Rolfe is but the survivor of a primordial race in the Gissing universe; like the ornithorhyncus he represents a vanishing order. Personages of this kind grow more important, more commanding, more influential in their inhuman activities, as one passes towards the earlier works, and to compare Rolfe to Waymark (of *The Unclassed*) and that eloquent letter-writer, Egremont, in *Thyrza*, is to measure a long journey towards the impersonal in art. In *The Nether World* there are among such indubitable specimens of the kindly race of men as Pennyloaf and the Byasses, not only 'good characters' but 'bad' also. The steady emancipation is indisputable.

In one little book at least, *The Paying Guest*, published about a twelve-month ago, the exponent personage has no place; so that is, indeed, in spite of its purely episodical character, one of the most satisfactory of Mr Gissing's books. It presents in a vein of quiet satire, by no means unfeeling, and from a standpoint entirely external, the meagre pretentiousness of a small suburban villa, the amazing want of intelligence which cripples middle-class life. It is compact of admirable touches. The villa was at Sutton, so conveniently distant from London that 'they had a valid excuse for avoiding public entertainments—an expense so often imposed by mere fashion.' And while the negotiations for the Paying Guest were in progress, 'at this moment a servant entered with tea, and Emmeline, sorely flurried, talked rapidly of the advantages of Sutton as a residence. She did not allow her visitor to put in a word till the door closed again.' These are haphazard specimens of the texture. Their quality is the quality of Jane Austen, and whenever in the larger books the youthful intensity of exposition, the stress of deliberate implications relaxes, the same delicate subtlety of humour comes to the surface. Nearest to *The Paying Guest*, in this emancipation from the idealising stress, come that remarkable group of three figures, *Eve's Ransom*, and the long novel of *New Grub Street*.

Apart from their aspect as a diminishing series of blemishes, of artistic disfigurements, the 'exponent' characters of Mr Gissing deserve a careful consideration. If they are, in varying proportion, ideal personages, unstudied invention that is, they are, at any rate, unconventional ideal persons, created to satisfy the author rather than his readers. Taken collectively, they present an interesting and typical development, they display the personal problem with a quality of quite unpremeditated frankness. In that very early novel, *The Unclassed*, the exponent character is called Waymark, but, indeed, Egremont, Quarrier, Ross Mallard, Tarrant, and Rolfe are all, with a varying qualification of irony, successive Waymarks. At the outset we encounter an attitude of mind essentially idealistic, hedonistic, and polite, a mind coming from culture to the study of life, trying life, which is so terrible, so brutal, so sad and so tenderly beautiful, by the clear methodical measurements of an artificial refinement, and expressing even in its earliest utterance a note of disappointment. At first, indeed, the illusion dominates the disappointment. *The Unclassed* is still generous beyond the possibilities of truth. It deals with the 'daughters of joy,' the culinary garbage necessary, as Mr Lecky tells us, to the feast of English morality; and it is a pathetic endeavour to prove that these poor girls are—young ladies. Jane Snowdon, the rescued drudge in *The Nether World*, Mr Gissing's parallel to the immortal Marchioness, falls short of conviction from the same desire to square reality to the narrow perfections of a refined life. She is one of nature's young ladies, her taste is innate. She often laughs, but 'this instinct of gladness had a very different significance from the animal vitality which prompted the constant laughter of Bessie Byass; it was but one manifestation of a moral force which made itself nobly felt in many another way.' The implicit classification of this sentence is the essential fallacy of Mr Gissing's earlier attitude:—there are two orders of human beings. It is vividly apparent in *Thyrza*. It is evident in a curious frequency of that word 'noble' throughout all his works. The suburban streets are ignoble, great London altogether is ignoble, the continent of America also, considered as a whole. This nobility is a complex conception of dignity and space and leisure, of wide, detailed, and complete knowledge, of precision of speech and act without flaw or effort; it is, indeed, the hopeless ideal of a scholarly refinement.

As one passes to the later novels the clearness of vision increases, and the tone of disappointment deepens. *The Emancipated* is a flight to Italy to escape that steady disillusionment. People say that much of Mr Gissing's work is 'depressing,' and to a reader who accepts his postulates it is indisputable that it is so. The idealised 'noble' women drop out of these later works altogether, the exponent personages no longer marry and prosper, but suffer, and their nobility tarnishes. Yet he clings in the strangest way to his early standards of value, and merely widens his condemnation with a widening experience. In *Eve's Ransom* and *New Grub Street* the stress between an increasingly truthful vision of things and the odd, unaltered conception that life can only be endurable with leisure, with a variety of books, agreeable furniture, service, costume, and refined social functions, finds its acute expression. The exponent character—a very human one—in *New Grub Street*, Reardon, is killed by that conflict, and the book ends in irony.

[Here the conclusion of the novel is quoted.]

So ends *New Grub Street* with the ideal attained—at a price. But that price is still only a partial measure of the impracticability of the refined ideal. So far, children have played but a little part in Mr Gissing's novels. In *The Whirlpool*, on the other hand, the implication is always of the children, children being neglected, children dying untimely, children that are never born. *The Whirlpool* is full of the suggestion of a view greatly widened, and to many readers it will certainly convey the final condemnation of a 'noble' way of life which, as things are, must necessarily be built on ignoble expedients. Mrs Abbott's room, 'A very cosy room, where, amid books and pictures, and by a large fire, the lady of the house sat reading Ribot,' would surely have been the room of one of the most exemplary characters in the days before *New Grub Street*. But the new factor comes in with, 'She had had one child; it struggled through a few months of sickly life, and died of convulsions during its mother's absence at a garden party.' In the opening chapter, moreover, Rolfe speaks of children, putting the older teaching into brutal phrases:

'They're a burden, a hindrance, a perpetual source of worry and misery. Most wives are sacrificed to the next generation—an outrageous absurdity. People snivel over the death of babies; I see nothing to grieve about. If a child dies, why, the probabilities are it *ought* to die; if it lives, it lives, and you get the survival of the fittest.'

The fashionable, delightful, childless Sibyl 'hates housekeeping.' And Alma, pursuing the phantom of a career as a musical genius, leaves for the future one little lad, 'slight, and with little or no colour in his cheeks, a wistful, timid smile on his too-intelligent face.' In the early novels it would seem that the worst evil Mr Gissing could conceive was crudity, passion, sordidness and pain. But *The Whirlpool* is a novel of the civilised, and a countervailing evil is discovered—sterility. This brilliant refinement spins down to extinction, it is the way of death. London is a great dying-place, and the old stupidities of the homely family are, after all, the right way. That is *The Whirlpool*'s implication, amounting very nearly to a flat contradiction of the ideals of the immature *The Emancipated*. The widowed Mrs Abbott, desolate and penitent, gets to work at the teaching of children. And finally we come on this remarkable passage:

It was a little book called *Barrack-Room Ballads*. Harvey read it here and there, with no stinted expression of delight, occasionally shouting his appreciation. Morton, pipe in mouth, listened with a smile, and joined more moderately in the reader's bursts of enthusiasm.

'Here's the strong man made articulate,' cried Rolfe at length. 'It's no use; he stamps down one's prejudice. It's the voice of the reaction. Millions of men, natural men, revolting against the softness and sweetness of civilisation; men all over the world, hardly knowing what they want and what they don't want; and here comes one who speaks for them—speaks with a vengeance.'

'Undeniable.'

'*But*——'

'I was waiting for the *but*,' said Morton, with a smile and a nod.

'The brute savagery of it! The very lingo—how appropriate it is! The tongue of Whitechapel blaring lust of life in the track of English guns. He knows it; the man is a great artist; he smiles at the voice of his genius. It's a long time since the end of the Napoleonic wars. We must look to our physique, and make ourselves ready. Those Lancashire operatives, laming and killing each other at football, turning a game into a battle. Women turn to cricket—tennis is too soft—and to-morrow they'll be bicycling by the thousand; they must breed a stouter race. We may reasonably hope, old man, to see our boys blown into small bits by the explosive that hasn't got its name yet.'

'Perhaps,' replied Morton meditatively. 'And yet there are considerable forces on the other side.'

'Pooh! The philosopher sitting on the safety-valve. He has breadth of beam, good, sedentary man, but when the moment comes——The Empire; that's beginning to mean something. The average Englander has never grasped the fact that there was such a thing as a British Empire. By God! we are the British Empire, and we'll just show 'em what *that* means!'

'I'm reading the campaigns of Belisarius,' said Morton, after a pause.

'What has that to do with it?'

'Thank heaven, nothing whatever.'

'I bore you,' said Harvey, laughing. 'Morphew is going to New Zealand. I had a letter from him this morning. Here it is. "I heard yesterday that H.W. is dead. She died a fortnight ago, and a letter from her mother has only just reached me in a roundabout way. I know you don't care to hear from me, but I'll just say that I'm going out to New Zealand. I don't know what I shall do there, but a fellow has asked me to go with him, and it's better than rotting here. It may help me to escape the devil yet; if so, you shall hear. Good-bye!" '

He thrust the letter back into his pocket.

'I rather thought the end would be pyrogallic acid.'

'He had the good sense to prefer ozone,' said Morton.

Of course Rolfe here is not Mr Gissing, but quite evidently his speeches are not a genuinely objective study of opinions expressed. The passage is essentially a lapse into 'exposition.' The two speakers, Morton and Rolfe, become the vehicles of a personal doubt, taking sides between the old idea of refined withdrawal from the tumult and struggle for existence, and the new and growing sense of the eternity and universality of conflict; it is a discussion, in fact, between a conception of spacious culture and a conception of struggle and survival. In his previous books Mr Gissing has found nothing but tragedy and the condemnation of life in the incompatibility between the refined way of life and life as it is. But here, in the mouth of a largely sympathetic character, is a vigorous exposition of the acceptance, the vivid appreciation of things as they are.

Enough has been written to show that *The Whirlpool* is a very remarkable novel, not only in its artistic quality, but in its presentation of a personal attitude. The clear change in the way of thinking that Mr Gissing's Rolfe is formulating (while the Whirlpool should be devouring him) is no incidental change of one man's opinion, it is a change that is sweeping over the minds of thousands of educated men. It is the discovery of the insufficiency of the cultivated life and its necessary insincerities; it is a return to the essential, to honourable struggle as the epic factor in life, to children as the matter of morality and the sanction of the securities of civilisation.

To those who are familiar with Mr Gissing's work, the conviction that this character of Rolfe marks a distinct turning-point in his development will be inevitable. That his next work will be more impersonal than any that have gone before, that the characteristic insistence on what is really a personal discontent will be to some extent alleviated, seems to me, at any rate, a safe prophecy. Mr Gissing has written a series of extremely significant novels, perhaps the only series of novels in the last decade whose interest has been strictly contemporary. And even this last one, it seems to me, has still the quality of a beginning. It is by reason of his contemporary quality, by virtue of my belief that, admirable as his work has been, he is still barely ripening and that his best has still to come, that I have made this brief notice rather an analysis of his peculiarities and the tendencies of his development than the essay I could write with ease and sincerity in his praise.

114. Frederick Dolman, *National Review*

October 1897, xxx, 258–66

Frederick Dolman was a writer on social and political questions. He edited the *Junior Liberal Review* from 1884 onwards and published *Dr Nansen: the Man and his Work* (1897). In 1891 he had vainly sought to obtain an interview from Gissing (Diary, 2 April 1891, in *Letters of George Gissing to Members of His Family*, p. 317).

Three friends of the novelist—Miss Orme, A. H. Bullen and H. G. Wells—sent this article, entitled 'George Gissing's Novels', to him while he was in Italy. Gissing complained that the survey was several years old—*Eve's Ransom* (1895) was referred to as his last book—and that no one had troubled to bring the work up to date (Diary, 23 October 1897).

The slow growth of Mr Gissing's reputation as a novelist must be regarded as one of the literary problems of the time. It is eleven years since the publication of his first novel, *Unclassed*; it is seven years since the appearance of *Demos** convinced most of us who read the book that in him we had a writer of great, if not of supreme, power. In the meantime a dozen or more new men and women have won their way, carrying it by storm in some cases, to the heart of the great British public. To most households, on the other hand, Mr Gissing's books, with their rich qualities of dramatic force, realistic picturing, and trenchant style, are still strangers. He has steadily gained in favour, it is true, with a certain circle of readers, but on the great every-day world to which his novels, by virtue of their themes, must surely appeal, his hold would seem to have increased by almost imperceptible degrees.

Those who are well acquainted with Mr Gissing's work must surely ask, Why is this? The most obvious answer is to be found in the vein of pessimism which runs through all his novels. It has long been a truism that there is nothing in fiction which most people dislike more than the

* Gissing's second novel, *The Unclassed*, appeared in June 1884. *Demos* was published in March 1886.

failure of events to 'rhyme with each other,' to use Thomas Hardy's phrase, such as they witness in their own lives, and that the novelist who totally denies 'poetical justice' to his characters must be prepared to defy popular prejudice. But curiously enough, this note of pessimism is most predominant in the two books which at present are by far the best known, *Demos* and *The Nether World*.

In these two novels Mr Gissing deliberately sets himself to examine the existing condition of society and the prospect of its improvement. He finds it as bad as the Socialist represents it to be, and, on the other hand, has no mercy for the illusions with which the Socialist supports his bright hopes for the future. In *Demos* Mr Gissing takes a most favourable specimen of Socialistic human nature, an English artisan who has 'the best qualities his class can show,' and subjects it to a test in the altruism of the Fabian Society. Richard Mutimer, by a strange stroke of fortune, is enriched with money and estate. At first his resolves are all that altruism would demand; his fortune shall be devoted to the furtherance of the cause which, as a workman, he had preached at street corners and in East-End clubs. The mines and iron-works which he had suddenly inherited are still to make private profit, it is true, but that is because in the existing commercial system any other course is economically impossible. And, while practically the entire profit is to be used in the propaganda of Socialism, the miners and the ironworkers are to be as comfortable as it is possible for wage-earners to be in a competitive state of society.

Thus far, Theory. The practical fate of Mutimer's high resolves strikingly illustrates the novelist's little faith in the innate goodness of mankind. The London work-girl he had promised to marry is 'jilted' in favour of a wife of the social rank to which fortune has removed him. Workmen are summarily dismissed, and, in one case, he shows no mercy when Mrs Mutimer appeals on behalf of the wife and children. Such conduct can only be justified from the standpoint of the capitalist, and in many other ways Mutimer acts in accordance with the view that 'men with large aims cannot afford to be scrupulous about small details.' The climax comes with Mrs Mutimer's discovery of a will which bequeathed the property to another, when the erstwhile artisan proposes to destroy the document. The lady rejects the proposal with scorn, and insists on the surrender of their ease and comfort. In these circumstances it might be supposed that George Gissing wished to point a contrast between the ignoble instincts of common men and a lady's ingrained sense of honour, but for the further circumstance that the rightful heir happens to be a young man who was once her lover and whom she is already regretting not having made her husband. But before the end of the story is reached its readers are sufficiently impressed by the exaggerated importance Mr Gissing is prone to attach to the distinctions of class. And the end is melancholy enough for the most confirmed sceptic in social reform. Mutimer is killed by a mob on Clerkenwell Green whose wrath is excited by the collapse of an undertaking in which he had invested the pence of the poor, the agitator's last words being, 'Listen to them. That's the people, that is. I deserve killing, fool that I am, if only for the lying good I've said of them.'

At the same time, the cynicism of this conclusion does not do justice to the general trend of thought and feeling in Mr Gissing's novels. There are some parts of *Demos*, indeed, to which it is in flat contradiction, such as the story of Emma Vine, the forsaken sweetheart of Hoxton, and the ideal life of Westlake, the artist. In *The Nether World* these brighter rays are heightened by the gloom of the picture which, with wonderfully realistic touch if with greatly deficient humour, Mr Gissing draws of the daily life of what are called 'the lower classes.' The novelist in this book does not, as its name might suggest, penetrate to the lowest stratum of London life; had he done so there would assuredly have been more warrant for the sad hopelessness, the black despair, which pervades too many of its pages. The central figures in the book, Sidney Kirkwood and Jane, belong to the working-class, but are in their characters, if not in their circumstances, very far removed from the misery, vice, and crime of which Mr Gissing gives us several vivid glimpses. But the evil destiny which seemingly mocks the gods in this nether world lays its heavy hand upon their lives, and spoils them beyond redemption. At the same time the artistic fashion in which Mr Gissing turns their hopes awry and abandons them to the perversity of circumstances must be fully acknowledged. Underlying the reader's sense of disappointment, too, must be some recognition that, in part at any rate, the book has a pathetic truth, and in the novelist's closing words, 'the pity of it' is feelingly softened:—

In each life little for congratulation. He, with the ambitions of his youth frustrated; neither an artist, nor a leader of men in the battle for justice. She, no saviour of society by the force of a superb example; no daughter of the people, holding wealth in trust for the people's needs. Yet to both was their work given. Unmarked, unrecognized save by their love of righteousness and mercy, they stood by the side of those more hopeless, brought some comfort to hearts less courageous than their own. Where they abode it was not all dark. Sorrow certainly awaited them, perchance defeat in even the humbler aims that they had set themselves; but at least their lives would remain a protest against those brute forces of society which fill with wreck the abysses of the nether world.

That Socialism, the great social question, was the theme of *Demos* and *The Nether World* most probably explains the exceptional vogue, as compared with his other novels, which these two books of Mr Gissing's have obtained. With Socialism so much in the air, with the social question on everybody's lips, it would have been most surprising had two such novels, written with knowledge, earnestness, and literary verve, failed to make their mark. *Thyrza*, which was published a year sooner, *A Life's Morning*, which appeared a year later, than *Demos*,* and *New Grub Street*, which is a more recent work than either, touch at many points the condition-of-the-people problem, but their *motif* and interest are not bound up with it in the same way. *Thyrza* is the story of that rare figure in fiction—a heroine of the London working-class. A mere factory 'hand,' with little or no education, Thyrza Trent is nevertheless a girl whom Mr Gissing succeeds in making very real and interesting to us. With much natural refinement, uniting an imaginative temperament and a personal beauty of the spiritual rather than the sensual type, the development of her life and character amid the squalid surroundings of a back street in Lambeth becomes in Mr Gissing's hands a narrative in which the interest, though absorbing, is more psychological than dramatic. To this fine conception the other characters become more or less subordinate, although, as is nearly always the case in Mr Gissing's novels, each has a well-defined individuality—Gilbert Grail, the workman-student, who, given means and leisure, 'would have become at the least a man of noteworthy learning'; Walter Egremont, the young idealist who under the influence of Ruskin devotes himself to the promotion of literary culture among the Lambeth artisans; Luke Ackroyd, another type of the workman in mental revolt against religion and society of whom Mr Gissing has made so careful a study, and Totty Nancarrow, the work-girl whose normal qualities only serve to accentuate the abnormal of which Thyrza is a portrait.

A Life's Morning, likewise, has a strong feminine interest in the character of Emily Hood. But there is a sterner and sadder side to the story.

* *Demos* was published in March 1886, *Thyrza* in April 1887, *A Life's Morning* in November 1888.

Overshadowing Emily's romantic attachment to a young man much her social superior is the tragedy of her father's life. James Hood is one of several most pathetic figures in Mr Gissing's portrait gallery—men of good moral worth, of warm affections, with some artistic capacity, whose lives are wrecked by their inability to earn a living on the terms that society imposes. Such men, in Mr Gissing's eyes, are as tragic as any of Shakespeare's characters. James Hood ends his life by his own hand, and although his daughter's love prospers to the end, the book leaves in the reader's mind a strain of bitter sadness.

In *New Grub Street* Mr Gissing has endeavoured to depict the shady side of literary life in an age dominated by the commercial spirit. On the whole it is in its realism perhaps the least convincing of his novels, whilst being undeniably the most depressing. It is not that Mr Gissing's picture of poverty in the literary profession is wanting in the elements of truth, although, even in that profession, there is more eccentricity than the novelist leads us to suppose in the social position and evil plight of such men as Edwin Reardon and Harold Biffen. But the contrast between Edwin Reardon, the conscientious artist, loving his art and working for its sake, and Jasper Milvain, the man of letters who prospers simply because he is also a man of business, which is the main feature of the book and the principal support of its theme, strikes one throughout as strained to the point of unreality. In the first place, it seems almost impossible that a man of Milvain's mind and instinct should have deliberately chosen literature as the occupation of his life; with money and success as his only aim he would surely have become a stockbroker or a money-lender. In the second place, Edwin Reardon's dire failure, with his rapid descent into extreme poverty, is clearly traceable not so much to a truly artistic temperament in conflict with the commercial spirit as to mental and moral weakness which could not but have a baneful influence on his work. Such a man would have made a worse failure, we feel sure, in the old Grub Street when, instead of having to regard literature as a matter of marketable value as well as of intellectual effort, he would have had to seek for the crumbs which fell from rich patrons' tables. And in his treatment of this theme Mr Gissing's besetting sin as a novelist has full sway. The pessimism is almost morbid. In other hands, the scenes between the poverty-stricken literary men, Reardon and Biffen, would have been full of humour, grim, no doubt, but genuine for all that; as it is, only one or two poor gleams of wit relieve the gloom of their distresses. In none of Mr Gissing's books are we more conscious of that deficiency in the sense of humour which, with their pessimism, has hitherto made their other fine qualities so unacceptable to men in the street.

In each of these novels Mr Gissing gives evidence of an extraordinary knowledge of the social and moral condition of our great cities—more particularly of London. There cannot be a corner of the metropolis which, with observant eye and quick ear, he has not explored, not a phase of its varied existence that he has not studied. The shallow optimism that comes of shallow knowledge is with him utterly impossible; indeed, it is the hard substratum of fact which is seemingly behind his pessimism that makes it at times so awesome and terrible. Mr Gissing is not entirely free, I think, from the natural tendency of brilliant writing to paradox and cynicism, but it is seldom that he gives his reader this just cause of quarrel. Our own feeling and temperament may revolt against his gospel of despair, but the reason cannot easily cast it aside. We close the book with the conviction that, as a picture of present-day life among the poor and the ignorant, it is of too hopelessly dark a hue, but, on the other hand, we find it difficult to say where and how the artist has gone wrong in the use of his colours. That we cannot immediately rally our forces of hope in the coming of better things, our belief in the law of progress is possibly the best proof of Mr Gissing's realistic power.

Mr Gissing's later novels, notably, *In the Year of Jubilee*, *The Emancipated*, and *Eve's Ransom*, have concerned themselves much more with the problem of sex than the problem of society. It may be supposed that in these books he has thus merely set himself to fall in with the fashion of the time, to satisfy the mood of the moment. But those who have read *The Unclassed*, first published in 1884 and recently republished in one volume, will remember that in what was, I believe, Mr Gissing's first novel much was anticipated of that which has since been said in fiction respecting the relations of the sexes. These other novels, too, have been written with considerable independence of thought and originality of view. With a daring in idea which has hardly been equalled in any of the novels of 'sexual interest,' to use the phrase of their hostile critics, that have since become popular, and a delicacy of treatment which has certainly not been excelled, Mr Gissing made the heroine of *The Unclassed* a courtezan and the daughter of a courtezan, whilst at the same time claiming for her the fullest sympathy and admiration of his readers. Ida Starr, according to Mr Gissing's story, touches pitch without being defiled. Before he has done with her she becomes a devoted friend, a faithful lover, and an angel of light and goodness to a horde of slum children, the redemption being brought about by a course of events and a development of character seemingly as natural as those which led to the fall. The point of view from which Ida, a girl of education and refinement, is able to justify her way of life is put by the novelist in the following words:—

'Let me give evidence to you of a self-knowledge greater than your own knowledge of me, and you have no right to take for granted the moral iniquity of any course I choose to pursue. Only then are your instincts (which is the same as saying your powers of moral judgment) more valid for me than my own, when you prove that you have learnt me by heart, have got at my mystery, appreciate every step which has brought me to my present position, and miss no item of the circumstances, internal and external, which constitute my being.'

The Unclassed exhibits powers hardly less mature than those with which Mr Gissing now writes, while at the same time it has a freshness and spontaneity which, almost inevitably, his later work has partially lost. Among contemporary novelists who have written as much there is probably none whose work is so little stereotyped as George Gissing's. Mr Gissing never fails to provide us with a piquant variety of incident and character in the telling of his story, whether the story be of the degeneration of the middle class, as in *In the Year of Jubilee*, the unhappy lot of the superfluous female, as in *The Odd Women*, or of rebellion against the old traditional morality, as in *The Emancipated*.

It is difficult to speak with any certainty of George Gissing's views on the great sex-problem as set forth in these novels. They contain such cross-currents of thought, such contradictions in speech, as can be reconciled only by reference to the attitude of Osmond Waymark in *The Unclassed*, who 'felt neither the power nor the desire to formulate a moral creed, being quite satisfied to judge of each case as it arose, without prejudice or precedent.' The truly immoral man, according to Gissing, 'is still in the bondage of formulae, and his sin consists in the conscious violation of principles which in his heart he believes ought to guide him.' But although Mr Gissing's heresy is not altogether definable in set terms, of his heresy there can be no shadow of doubt. Thus, he protests against the dogma—none the less strongly because only by implication—that a woman's 'fall' is necessarily and inevitably fatal to her moral character, irreparable and all-important. Thus he more than once gives countenance to the view—notably in *The Odd Women*—that, given a certain cast of mind and soul, the ideal union between a man and a woman may be one of freedom. And Mr Gissing's cause of quarrel with the old order of novelists is put, one feels, with lucidity, if with some exaggeration, in the words of Rhoda Nunn, the young lady in *The Odd Women* who forswears marriage—in vain, as the event proves—and employs herself in training her sex for other vocations:—

'If every novelist could be strangled and thrown into the sea, we should have some chance of reforming women. The girl's nature was corrupted with sentimentality, like that of all but every woman who is intelligent enough to read what is called the best fiction, but not intelligent enough to understand its vice. Love—love—love; a sickening sameness of vulgarity. What is more vulgar than the ideal of novelists? They won't represent the actual world; it would be too dull for their readers. In real life how many men and women fall in love? Not one in every 10,000 I am convinced. Not one married pair in 10,000 have felt for each other as one or two couples do in every novel. There is the sexual instinct, of course, but that is quite a different thing; the novelists daren't talk about that. The paltry creatures daren't tell the one truth that would be profitable. The result is that women imagine themselves noble and glorious when they are most near the animals.'

It would doubtless be wrong to attribute to George Gissing this pessimistic view of love simply on the strength of a speech put into the mouth of one of his characters. But the same thought occurs again and again in these novels. 'As a rule,' we are told, 'marriage is the result of a mild preference, encouraged by circumstances and deliberately heightened into strong sexual feeling.' And again, 'The days of romantic love are gone by. The scientific spirit has put an end to that kind of self-deception.' On the other hand, even Mr Gissing puts off his pessimism and becomes the enthusiast in face of the principle of equality between husband and wife, 'that gospel,' to quote his own words, 'which in far-off days will refashion the world.'

In the three remaining books which, so far, complete the tale of Mr Gissing's published work, *Born in Exile*, *Denzil Quarrier*, and *Eve's Ransom*, there is the same strenuous insistence on the disillusion of most lives. In *Eve's Ransom*, which was the last book given by Mr Gissing to his readers, we find his powers of dramatic description and analysis of character fully matured, but it is little better endowed with what is popularly regarded as the redeeming grace of humour than his earliest work. Mr Gissing has a fine, clear eye for the tragedy of life—no paint nor powder, frippery nor pretence, ever deludes it—but too much of the comedy escapes his vigilance, and there is comedy sometimes even in tears. The serene philosophy of Browning's lines—

> God's in his heaven,
> All's right with the world—

is probably not that of at least the majority of novel-readers nowadays, but, on the other hand, they cannot in their philosophical moments—much less in their hours of recreative reading—reconcile themselves to the view that everything is all wrong with the world, and there is no rational hope of ever putting it right. It has been said that fictitious sorrows harden the heart to real ones; the sorrows which fill the novelist's soul are fictitious only in a sense, of course, but they would seem to have hardened his heart to real pleasures. In a word, Mr Gissing has denied himself any 'comic relief,' as it is called on the stage; and it remains to be seen how long this self-denial, in contest with the otherwise magnetic powers of his literary work, will cost him his popularity. For Mr Gissing leaves us in no doubt but that he is fully conscious of the restriction he has himself placed on the number of his readers. The passage I have just quoted from *The Odd Women* suggests that much, and more than one passage in the literary talk of *New Grub Street* fully proves it. This being so, we must concede to George Gissing the respect due to conscientious and self-sacrificing adherence to an artistic ideal, though we consider that ideal to be largely a mistaken one.

Because Mr Gissing is a pessimist in most things, it would be wrong to suppose that his books have not their points of sympathy for the most optimistic of reformers. Of these, the most important is succinctly expressed by one of the characters in *A Life's Morning*, who declares that 'men and women go down to their graves in wretchedness who might have done noble things with an extra pound a week to live upon.' This is a text from which George Gissing is never tired of preaching—if such a word can be used of a novelist who never forgets his art for a single page. It gives a distinctive strength and verisimilitude to all his work—this constant recognition of the limitations which are placed upon the conduct of life by the most sordid and seemingly most trivial of circumstances. Poverty, with all that it means, has been too much treated by the novelist as if it were as much a part of nature as death, heat, and cold, the power of the elements or the passage of the seasons, and therefore to be dealt with in the same way simply as a source of incident, an instrument in the dramatic or picturesque. With

Mr Gissing, on the other hand, it is something quite apart from and independent of nature, a condition of society as society is at present constituted, which nevertheless is more potent, on the whole, in shaping human lives than all the passions of mankind. This may or may not be an absolutely true view of the great interchange of cause and effect in the life of the masses, and in Mr Gissing's hands, as we have seen, it is too much bound up with the philosophy of pessimism. But there is health in the reaction from the old fallacy, and to most men, happily, this insistence on the undue importance which money now has in our life will produce a feeling by no means making for pessimism—will drive them to the conclusion, in fact, that after all there must be great material changes if there is to be continued moral progress. As for the rest of Mr Gissing's social philosophy—the philosophy which more or less gives form and colour to all his books—it may be briefly summed up as impatience with the present competitive phase of society, with its mad striving for wealth on the one side and its painful struggle for subsistence on the other. With this phase of the world's development John Stuart Mill, even in his masterpiece on political economy, was as discontented as George Gissing. But the artist, whilst rebelling with all his soul against the present, has not the scientist's calm faith in the future which evolution must bring forth, and this it is which does so much to neutralize the great qualities of his books.

HUMAN ODDS AND ENDS

November 1897

115. Unsigned review, *Academy* (Fiction Supplement)

18 December 1897, lii, 125–6

This is, we believe, Mr Gissing's first essay in a new art. He has been responsible, first and last, for over a dozen novels of the orthodox length; here he makes his appearance as a writer of short stories. Truth to say, some of the contents of this volume are not stories at all, they are the raw material of fiction, sketches, and studies, mere scraps and suggestions, without the unity and finish that in its way the *conte*, no less than the *roman*, demands. These should have been omitted; the *debris* of the workshop, they swell the bulk of the volume and blur the effect of the score of really fine *contes* with which they are associated. As a *conteur* Mr Gissing has developed certain qualities which have not been so noticeable in his more elaborate work, and will probably react upon that for good. He has learnt to trim away the unessential, to be immediate, vivid, to aim at the centre. He begins to show a feeling for style which hitherto has rather lain dormant. The material of his tragedies is sordid enough, but in the impersonal reticence of the telling they find an expression which is very far removed from the sordid. Such keenly observed, straightly put narrative as Mr Gissing gives us in 'The Day of Silence' is art of a very fine order. . . .

It need hardly be said that in these short stories Mr Gissing's interests remain the same as in his longer work. His themes belong to his habitual order of ideas, and his treatment of them is familiar. The dreariness and squalor of London middle-class life, or, more rarely, as in the story just quoted, of London slum life; the pressure, upon all but the coarsely fibred, of grinding social conditions; the pity of trivial broken ideals and peddling ambitions unsatisfied: these are the burdens of every story. Mr Gissing is as remorseless, as deliberate, as logical a pessimist as ever; his indictment of things is as grave and as comprehensive. Some relaxation, however, he permits himself, to handle the matter, by way of a change, in irony, or even in the levity of a grim humour. You find a smile in 'The Justice and the Vagabond,' when Mr Richard Rutland, after twenty-two years of respectable affluence, makes up his mind to travel with a disreputable old crony, and hurries his preparations to anticipate his wife's return; and you find it in 'Two Collectors,' when the bookseller's porter, Alfred Wormald, hears an order given after forty years for the poems he had himself published in youth. . . . Yes, there is humour; but in both stories the humour is inextricably mingled with tragedy or pathos, the momentary gleam of light dies away into gloom.

116. Unsigned review, *Bookman* (London)

December 1897, 106

How much more pitiful Mr Gissing has grown of the human beings he creates for us! He still shows them to us in hard, or sordid, or hopeless plights, and he reveals more and more his disbelief in hardship as a blessed influence. Poverty is mostly ugly, and to sensitive souls generally demoralising. But sometimes, of late, he goes further and shows he cannot bear the thought of help being withheld in so much curable human misfortune, and his hand is stretched out in rescue. The hopeless, harmless wretch in 'An Inspiration', gets vitality and an awakening to an old romance and a new future by a dinner. Mr Mayhew, the hero of 'In Honour Bound', is saved from paying the uttermost farthing of a debt that would have dragged him down. The poor, tired woman of 'A Day of Silence' dies before the bodies of her husband and child are brought home. There are other lighter, more amusing stories. But such as tell of the struggle with fate, of the shadow of poverty and of unsympathetic presences, are the stronger and give the colour to the book. As a writer of short stories, Mr Gissing is advancing with rapid strides to a high place. There is no waste, there are no preambles, in his straightforward, forcible narratives of the life of the less fortunate to-day.

117. Unsigned review, *The Times*

14 February 1898, 10

Mr George Gissing is the biographer of the Unfortunate. He looks at life through tinted spectacles from which every touch of rose-colour has been carefully excluded; all the world is drab to him, save for a black spot or two where wretchedness has led to crime. Being well acquainted with these facts we opened *Human Odds and Ends* with feelings the reverse of those one entertains in releasing the cork of a champagne bottle; and we were not what is called 'pleasurably disappointed.' At the same time we have known Mr Gissing in a more depressed condition. Three out of the thirty short stories of which the volume is composed end quite cheerfully; this must have cost him something, and we thank him for it. Nevertheless, most of them, as is usual with his writings, strike one as true to life, which is indeed a sad business with too many people. Some of the stories are concerned with vagabonds, and it is curious to mark the contrast between himself and Stevenson when treating of this class of persons. The latter author makes them almost always cheery; with Mr Gissing they are as gloomy as undertakers when business is slack. They do not, indeed, take their pleasure sadly, but that is because they have no pleasures. When he has a very melancholy story to tell, such as 'A Day of Silence', he seems to 'do his work in joy intense, as when an earthquake smacks its mumbling lips o'er some thick peopled city'; he thoroughly enjoys himself. In the present work he has developed a new system of aggravating the reader; instead of giving a bad end to his story, he gives us none at all. At the same time he proves himself a most diligent student of human nature; no detail escapes him concerning the unfortunate. In the excellent story called 'An Inspiration' he shows what an admirable effect upon the mind of one who has been used to privation has good physical refreshment; not mere food, but a dinner. We do not doubt that his view would be corroborated by medical science, but it is new in fiction.

CHARLES DICKENS, A CRITICAL STUDY

February 1898

118. William Archer, *Daily Chronicle*

23 February 1898, 3

William Archer (1856–1924) achieved distinction as a leading dramatic critic and as translator of Ibsen and Maeterlinck. He also wrote, among other works, a life of Macready (1890) and a study of Henry Irving (1883).

The following review is unsigned but the authorship is established by its inclusion in Archer's *Study and Stage. A Year Book of Criticism* (Grant Richards, London, 1899, 28–32), where it bears the same title as in the *Daily Chronicle*, 'Mr. Gissing on Dickens'. The novelist had a clipping of the article in his album of press cuttings.

A whole volume of the Victorian Era Series is devoted to Charles Dickens; very rightly, for he was beyond all question one of the great forces of the period. And Mr Gissing proves himself the very man to grapple with this complex and disconcerting subject. Disconcerting, I say, because of all writers that ever lived Dickens sets formal criticism, the criticism of rule and plummet, most audaciously at defiance. He is like Sam Weller in the witness-box—there is no cornering him. He flouts our sober judgment at every turn, and makes us ashamed of the merest artistic common sense, as of an impertinent pedantry. Of such a writer—so astonishing a genius, so unequal and in some ways misguided an artist—it is very hard to treat without falling into excess, whether of praise or blame. Mr Gissing avoids both dangers, and without swerving from his allegiance to an artistic ideal more serious and strenuous than Dickens ever conceived, shows that the keenest sense of a great man's limitations is not inconsistent with the most ardent appreciation of his unique and beneficent genius.

The critic sets about his task with a plodding conscientiousness which at first augurs rather ill for his success. Though it be not essential that 'who drives fat oxen should himself be fat', we somehow expect that who writes of a great humourist should himself show humour. But presently we recognise that this is a foolish demand. Mr Gissing keeps his own humour in abeyance throughout, yet leaves us in no doubt of his alert comprehension and enjoyment of the humour of his subject. His ultra-conscientiousness results in nothing worse than a slightly awkward division of his subject, under headings which imply a good deal of cross classification. He gives separate chapters to 'The Story-Teller', to 'Art, Veracity, and Moral Purpose', to 'Characterisation', 'Satiric Portraiture', 'Women and Children', 'Humour and Pathos', and 'Style'. Now it may almost be said that each of these topics—except, perhaps, the first and last—inseparably involves all the rest, and Mr Gissing complicates his task by attempting to adhere consistently to so artificial an analysis. A chronological exposition of the development of Dickens's mind and art from book to book would surely have been simpler and not less interesting. What one chiefly misses in Mr Gissing's criticism, indeed, is sustained psychological study. It is perhaps in order to bring his book more within the scope of the Victorian Era Series that he approaches his theme from the sociological rather than from the psychological point of view. He considers Dickens rather as an element in our social history than as a phenomenon in the spiritual history of the world. This merely means that he has not exhausted his subject, which was not, after all, what he set forth to do.

Though Mr Gissing's tone is measured and unemotional, I have read his book with real emotion. As he passed in leisurely review the figures of this 'human comedy', I could not but feel a novel realisation of all that England owes to the humanest of her master spirits. Mr Robert Buchanan long ago found the just word for Dickens, when he called him the Good Genie of modern fiction. Mr Gissing does not explicitly take this point of view, but surely it is the right one. A poet in the truest sense of the word, a man of incomparable vision and imagination, Dickens transmuted the ugliness of mid-century London into a fantastic fairyland, closely modelled on reality, yet quaintly differentiated—at once a searching commentary upon everyday life and a delightful refuge from it. This fairyland is still with us, and shows no sign of vanishing away. Those who despise Dickens little know how deeply they are in his debt. They do not realise how much duller this world would be if the Good Genie had not, at a thousand points, touched it with his wand. And it would be an appreciably worse world as well. Mr Gissing shows clearly that not only by preaching the gospel of human kindness in general, but in virtue of conscious efforts toward definite ends, Dickens was a true benefactor to his country. Surely, then it is an ungrateful impertinence to complain that a Good Genie does not obey the rules of art with which lesser men strive to supply the place of inspiration and magic. And the rules by which Dickens is condemned are generally the rules of a quite different art from his, identified with it by sheer confusion of thought. In his own art—the art of illumination by differentiation (or idealisation as Mr Gissing prefers to call it)—he was a master, not only great, but supreme. Make all possible deductions for his failures and mistakes—admit that he had not the knack of plausible construction, that his heroes, heroines and villains were apt to be lay figures, that he seldom made a character live without the aid of some touch of oddity, that at best his creations have scarcely any intellectual, spiritual, and passional life—admit all this, and what a glorious residue remains! He has peopled our imagination with a whole world of delightful creatures, more real than reality; he has unsealed our vision, he has stimulated our sympathies, in a hundred directions; and he has given unalloyed, unaffected, and harmless pleasure to incalculable multitudes of people all the world over. An English guest at a Viennese 'aesthetic tea', the other day, was surprised to find the company unanimous in singing the praises of a great English *Dichter*, whom they named 'Boats'. Even when he had divined this to be the Teutonic rendering of 'Boz', his surprise was scarcely diminished. But the Austrians were right—there is no greater name than that of 'Boats' in the literary record of the Victorian era.

Mr Gissing justly traces many of Dickens's limitations to the very source of his greatness—the fact that he was a typical incarnation of middle-class English character. He did not 'write down' to his audience—he felt with them in every particular, and had no effective impulse to write otherwise. He had no relish for the novel of passion, which he probably found it hard to distinguish from the novel of sheer lubricity. Therefore, as Mr Gissing subtly suggests, such an episode as that of Little Em'ly, like the central incident in *Adam Bede*, comes upon one, at the first reading, as a moral shock:

So determined are these novelists not to offend our precious delicacy, that in the upshot they offend it beyond endurance, springing upon us, so to speak, the results of uncontrollable passion, without ever allowing us to suspect that such a motive was in play. The effect of this is a sort of grossness, which dishonours our heroine. So far as we are permitted to judge, there is much reason in the insults hurled at Emily by the frantic Rosa Dartle—a pretty result, indeed, of all our author's delicate gliding over slippery places.

The Emperor Augustus, we are told, objected to the presence of women at the public games when athletes appeared unclad; but he saw nothing improper in their watching the death combats of gladiators. May we not find a parallel to this in the English censorship? To exhibit the actual course of things in a story of lawless (nay, or of lawful) love is utterly forbidden; on the other hand, a novelist may indulge in ghastly bloodshed to any extent of which his stomach is capable. Dickens, the great writer, even appears on a public platform and recites with terrible power the murder of a prostitute by a burglar, yet no voice is raised in protest. Gore is perfectly decent; but the secrets of an impassioned heart are too shameful to come before us even in a whisper.

Without defending 'the English censorship' in all its workings, one cannot but point out that the convention which accepts of gore while it discountenances passion is not quite the counter-sense which Mr Gissing would make of it. Homicide, though it may be grossly and brutally overdone, is a much less inflammatory topic than the instinct which 'makes the world go round'. If Mr Gissing will for a moment imagine one of our blood-bolstered African romancers left free to welter in 'passion', as he now wallows in carnage, he cannot fail to perceive that the line which society instinctively draws is not wholly irrational or arbitrary. None the less just is his suggestion that the over-delicacy of so much English fiction is apt to produce effects, now and then, which are no more edifying than artistic.

Surely the facts do not bear out Mr Gissing's statement that 'with female readers Dickens never was a prime favourite'. In my own circle of acquaintance he has been and is a prime favourite with many women, and I have no reason to think them exceptional. It is true that Dickens's gallery of 'foolish, ridiculous, and offensive women' is long and masterly; but just because it is masterly, and because it is redeemed by the irresistible grace of humour, women of sense do not resent this unflattering portraiture. It would be an irreconcilable 'feminist' indeed who should make haste to put on the cap, or champion the cause, of Mrs Nickleby or Flora Finching, Miss Pecksniff or Mrs Gargery.

119. W. E. Henley, *Outlook* (London)

5 March 1898, 134–5

William Ernest Henley (1849–1903) made himself a reputation as a poet, writing also plays in collaboration with R. L. Stevenson. To the general public he was above all the editor at various times of such journals as *Magazine of Art*, the *National Observer*, the *New Review* and *Outlook*. The latter had only reached its fifth number when it published the following review under the title 'Charles Dickens'. Wells brought the review to the attention of Gissing who found it 'excellent' (Diary, 9 March 1898).

Time was, and that not very long ago, when to write with enthusiasm of Charles Dickens was to incur the scorn of the Superior Person. That gifted creature, it is true, knew nothing, or next to it, of his author, and at most had only read him here and there—mostly to pick up a laugh; sometimes ('tis feared) to reflect that it was not thus that Thackeray wrote, and Scott, and the 'inimitable Jane.' Yet Dickens was none the less a master feature in the great aspect of English letters—was none the less, I like to think (as I have always thought), one of the three or four who may at their best be held to vie with the Shakespeare who expressed himself in prose: the Shakespeare of Falstaff and Lucio, of Sir Toby and Sir Andrew and the Nurse, of Malvolio and Shallow, and the group that clatters and drinks and swaggers round the wild Prince and Poins. 'Tis sixty years or so since he stepped forward—so said Thackeray: Thackeray, who knew what writing is, and could value a writer as he deserves—and took his place at the head of English literature; and, for all the works of all the Superior Persons that ever lived or will ever live, from that place he has never for a moment been, nor will ever for a moment be, in danger of deposition. There is no denying that certain people tired of him, or said they tired of him, or pretended to tire of him. But certain people went the same idiot way with Scott; and, as in Scott's case so in Dickens's, there was a kind of rush in the quest of strange gods. But, all the while, edition after edition was pouring from the press; and all the while Scott and

Dickens were enlarging the borders of their several empires abroad—were annexing new provinces, and exploring new territories, and subjugating new dominions—and at home were establishing their foundations deep and ever deeper in the regard of their countrymen. All the while, in fact, the whirligig of Time was bringing on his revenges.

Let me put the matter in a reminiscence. Somewhere in the 'sixties a Superior Person (he had had 'a college education,' he wore spectacles, he died young) saw little difference, or none, in essentials between Dickens and Hablot Browne. This trash was solemnly produced in a journal of mark—I believe it was the old *Saturday Review*—and still more solemnly reproduced in the posthumous volume which is all that remains of the Intellectual Young Man who (if I may say so) pulled it off. The change is heavy, indeed! Here, in '98, is Mr George Gissing: as ardent a seeker after Truth, as he sees it, as we have; as devout and as expert a student of character, as he sees it, as we have; as accomplished an artist in fiction, as he sees it, as we have; with a book about Dickens for which I, an old and hardened and unblushing Dickensite, have little or nothing but the warmest commendation.

Of course I do not agree with Mr Gissing all along the line. I do not, for instance, admit that Sidney Carton is 'easily forgotten'; for I read *The Tale of Two Cities* when I was a boy, as it appeared in *All the Year Round*, and Sidney Carton has been an influence—in some dim way, perhaps, an ideal—ever since. Again, I do not, and will not, for a moment entertain the idea that the American scenes in *Martin Chuzzlewit* are exaggerated; for (*a*) I've always believed in them; (*b*) they are immitigably consistent with each other and with their author's conception (this is one of Mr Gissing's best points in his estimate of Dickens, as a painter of character at least); and (*c*) I talked not long since with a distinguished novelist—the best distinguished, let me say, of all *les jeunes*—who assured me positively, out of the fulness of his own experience, that, take away lifts and telephones and the like, the U.S.A. of *Martin Chuzzlewit* is the U.S.A. of to-day, and that Pogram and Hannibal Chollup and the rest are as vocal as ever, if a little better civilised—on the surface. Here are two points of dissent; and there are others, naturally, on which I do not care to insist. For, an two men ride on a horse, one must ride behind; and an two men join in loving a man, as Mr Gissing and I in loving Dickens, there must certainly arise occasions when the two men differ, and each is more than willing to punch the other's head. I do not think, if I may say so, that Mr Gissing is just to Silas Wegg or to the book in which he appears; I do not think that he is sufficiently alive to the potentialities of Farce, or to the share of the Muse of Farce in such creations as Pecksniff and Micawber, and Gamp, and the Wellers, *père et fils*, and the Todgers group—to name but these; I think he has scarce realised that in Dickens, with the finest and broadest, yet the most searching and delicate, humour expressed in terms of English since Shakespeare, there coexisted what Mr Henry James (I think it is he) has very beautifully described as 'an immense and far-reaching instinct of the Picturesque.' I do not think that Mr Gissing has anywhere touched on the fact that the short story, as it existed through Balzac long before it existed through Maupassant, existed by virtue of Dickens long before it existed by virtue of Mr Kipling. I do not think that Mr Gissing shows his wonted grip of character and life when he takes Daudet's assertion—that he had never read Dickens—seriously and with respect. I do not think—but I am but stating differences after all! And if Mr Gissing and I were to talk these over, we should probably arise 'in a glow of mutual admiration,' and in the conviction that between us we had done almost as much for Dickens's fame as Dickens himself contrived to do in thirty years of vigilant, devout, unwearied effort and achievement.

I had meant to say much in detail in the praise of Mr Gissing's book. But I have talked at large on Dickens, and at large on my differences with Mr Gissing. And, as I haven't the heart to cut down what I've said already, so I haven't the room to note the striking excellences of which Mr Gissing's book is all compact. In truth, I have read nothing about Dickens which has pleased half so well as this bookling. The author is, I hear, a realist and a pessimist. It may be so: I hope for his own sake and the sake of English Literature it is *not*. For if he can read men and women, if he can take on the great book of Human Life, as intelligently, above all as cordially and as genially, as he here takes on his Dickens, then shall English Letters profit by him. He has most of the qualities that go to make a critic: sanity, clarity of thought and style, a point of view, the capacity for appreciation, that excellent sense (so woefully lacking in so many!) that, although the man he is writing about is bigger than himself, it is not therefore incumbent upon him to bring the man about whom he is writing down to his own level. Also, he has courage—intellectual courage; and it compels him to say true things. As when he more than hints that Flaubert, for all his moiling and toiling, for all his paining and straining, wrote not so well as Dickens in the end; and that, if we have to look for a literary parallel to the abounding richness and propriety of Mrs Gamp, we cannot choose but hark back (*mutatis mutandis*) to the greatest figure in comic literature. Which is only a roundabout and journalistic way of saying the three words 'Sir John Falstaff.'

In truth, an admirable little book. I should like to talk of Mr Gissing's theory of what I may call 'realisation by elimination.' But, as I said before, I haven't room. In any case, an admirable little book. I wish it no worse fortune than that to be read by a twentieth part of Dickens's public.

120. Unsigned review, *Literature*

19 March 1898, ii, 311

Gissing had a clipping of this review in his album of press cuttings.

Has the popularity of Dickens declined? The tendency of recent years has been to answer this question in the affirmative; but the appearance within the same publishing season of three volumes all concerned with him certainly points to the contrary conclusion. Of the three, Mr Gissing's *Charles Dickens: A Critical Study* is unquestionably the most important. We turned to it with interest, for the criticisms of a distinguished novelist upon a predecessor in his own art could not fail to command attention. Yet previous experience of similar essays did not conduce to confidence in its quality. Mr Black's *Goldsmith* is far from being the best of the English Men of Letters Series, and Anthony Trollope's *Thackeray* is not far from being the worst. But if any reader, recollecting these examples, opens Mr Gissing's volume with misgiving, he will soon have his fears dispelled. We do not hesitate to say that this is the best study of Dickens we have ever read. It is brightly and vigorously written, stimulating, sympathetic in tone, keen in judgment; and besides all this, not the least agreeable feature of the book is its perfect modesty and self-repression. The reader would hardly suspect from the volume before us that the author is himself a man of distinction, and has himself won a high reputation as a writer of fiction; but knowing this, he will perceive that the felicity of Mr Gissing's criticism is in no small measure due to his intimate knowledge of the conditions of the art, and to his familiarity with the life which Dickens depicts.

The value of Mr Gissing's book lies mainly in the fact that it produces a vivid and definite impression as a whole. The author has a clear conception of the art of Dickens, and writes in support of his view with force and earnestness. Dickens, according to him, was an idealist. 'He sought for wonders amid the dreary life of common streets.' 'Caricature proceeds by a broad and simple method. It is no more the name for Dickens' full fervour of creation than for Shakespeare's in his prose comedy. Each is a supreme idealist.' This is bold criticism. A hundred characters from Dickens' novels rise up in the mind against it. Where, we are tempted to ask, is the idealization in Bill Sykes, in Quilp, in Sampson Brass and his sister, in Bumble, in Squeers, in innumerable types of vulgarity, cruelty, and crime? But Mr Gissing is fertile in illustration, and even those who differ from him will find themselves forced to respect his opinion. He draws an excellent contrast between Dickens the idealist and Hogarth, who 'gives us life—and we cannot bear it.' He makes a still more excellent analysis of Mrs Gamp, who might perhaps have been adduced by the unwary as a specimen of realism:—

> The Mrs Gamp of our novel is a piece of the most delicate idealism. It is a sublimation of the essence of Gamp. No novelist (say what he will) ever gave us a picture of life which was not idealized; but there are degrees, degrees of purpose and of power. Juliet's Nurse is an idealized portrait, but it comes much nearer to the real thing than Mrs Gamp; in our middle-class England we cannot altogether away with the free-spoken dame of Verona; we Bowdlerize her, of course damaging her in the process. Mrs Berry in *Richard Feverel* is idealized, but she smacks too strongly of the truth for boudoir readers. Why, Moll Flanders herself is touched and softened, for all the author's illusive directness. In Mrs Gamp, Dickens has done his own Bowdlerizing, but with a dexterity which serves only to heighten his figure's effectiveness. Vulgarity he leaves; that is of the essence of the matter; vulgarity unsurpassable is the note of Mrs Gamp. Vileness, on the other hand, becomes grotesquerie, wonderfully converted into a subject of laughter. Her speech, the basest ever heard from human tongue, by a process of infinite subtlety, which leaves it the same yet not the same, is made an endless amusement, a source of quotation for laughing lips incapable of unclean utterance.

This is striking, and its force is greatly increased by the numerous other illustrations of the same contention which Mr Gissing's book contains. Yet we remain unconvinced. In the first place, Mr Gissing proves too much. If no novelist ever drew a picture which was not idealized, then the question is one of degree, and we may admit Mr Gissing's premises without drawing his conclusion. Moreover, those other figures of Dickens will not be banished from the mind. Neither can we forget his admiration of George Colman's description of Covent-garden. 'He remembered,' says Forster, 'snuffing up the flavour of the faded cabbage-leaves as if it were the very breath of comic fiction.' Does not this admiration throw light on Dickens' own art? and, if so, does it point towards idealism?

Space forbids us to dwell upon the many other admirable points in Mr Gissing's volume. We must content ourselves with recommending it heartily as a book to be read both for pleasure and for profit, and pass to the other volumes with which we have to deal.

121. Unsigned review, *New York Tribune Illustrated Supplement*

3 April 1898, 16

This review was entitled 'Dickens. A Valuable Study of His Works'.

There is but one biography of Charles Dickens, the solid monument which John Forster erected to the memory of his friend, but of such a volume as that which Mr Gissing has just produced there has been great need. Hitherto it has seemed impossible to write about the novels without deep prejudice either one way or the other. Those who love Dickens are disposed to show the faith that is in them with all the vehemence possible to their natures. Those who hate him—but, after all, it is of very little consequence what they say, or how they say it. Mr Gissing, at all events, maintains with ingratiating good temper the balance that the eulogists as well as the wrathful ones have made us anxious to see restored. He loves his author wisely, but not too well. He glories in his genius and deplores his defects, but he is neither maudlin on the one hand nor patronizing on the other. Equipped as perhaps no other writer of to-day is equipped for a thorough and sympathetic examination of the works of Charles Dickens, he has summarized them with tactful authority. We could not desire a better book.

It is a little strange, perhaps, to find so complex a world as that created and peopled by the novels dissected and described with scientific system, but if there is one thing more than another of which Mr Gissing convinces his reader it is the necessity for pursuing exactly such a method in the study of Dickens. Read him swiftly, broadly, and with an eye to the broad impression he has to convey, and, curiously, the result is no unit; on the contrary, the mind is then left full of those contradictions and qualifications which make the true appraisement of Dickens so hard. Consider him in cold blood, after the fashion of Mr Gissing, and under the dry light one element of the subject after another comes up to be judged, at last, at its true value. It is disconcerting to find that again and again the true value is not so impressive as we once thought. But the achievement of the truth carries its penalties with it, and in the end, as it happens, the pre-eminence of Dickens in his own field stands unchallenged. It is as if the rights of the case were only arrived at by a process of elimination, and the residuum found to be infinitely more precious than had at first been supposed. At the same time Mr Gissing's analysis starts off from no ambiguous point. He states boldly that Dickens worked, in the first place, for his own time, and that he brought to his art a tremendous moral force. Those two facts alone count heavily in the consideration of the novels, and that process of elimination to which we have alluded means more in the field of what might be called the technique of writing than it means in the sphere of pure genius. Mr Gissing, facing the charge of exaggeration which has so often been brought against Dickens, is at some pains to show us that the novels really reflect the life of an epoch long since passed away, and are not, on the whole, exaggerations in any essential points. This is a great step in the appreciation of the man. His latest critic, who surely ought to know, for his own works have been based on English middle-class life, is not only persuaded that Dickens drew from the life, but asserts that many a picture in that gallery of immortals is justified by types discoverable to-day. Thus the figures that a careless reader dismisses as exaggerations, or as being, at the best, eccentrics of the rarest kind, become for us the representatives of classes that have changed only in external aspects. We have said that Dickens wrote for his own time, but if the dress and habit have become modified, the social progress of England clothing the old types in new colors, we may be sure that the traits of these people endure. We accept Mrs Gamp—even Mrs Gamp—as a lasting member of the human race. Mrs Gamp, we may be told, is no longer encountered even in the houses of the very poor in London, but, aside from the fact that we cannot be sure of that, the kernel of her immortality remains; she is human; she is, in short, one of those personages, like Sancho or Falstaff, whom we may never meet in actual life, but whom we believe in as we believe in any captain in history. Here appears Mr Gissing's explanation, and, we believe, the gist of his book. He says: 'The Mrs Gamp of our novel is a piece of the most delicate idealism. It is a sublimation of the essence of Gamp.'

At more than one point Mr Gissing returns to this novel hypothesis of his; novel, it may be observed, only in that it is here applied to Dickens. Other accepted realists, notably Zola, have driven their critics to the same conclusion. That our critic should make his argument good to the satisfaction of all is improbable, for Dickens has been called a realist through many years, and Mr Gissing cannot hope for a wide-spread and immediate recantation. Yet it is hard to see how his points can be refuted. It is plain from his analysis, as it must be plain to every careful and impartial reader of the novels, that Dickens worked from something not unlike a definite literary plan, from one which led him into many mistakes—as, for example, the artificiality and melodramatic character of his plots, the staginess of many of his personages—but from which there sprang also the tremendous power of his books. He made up his mind, we will say, to choose a theme which would appeal to the sympathies of a particular audience—to the respectable, commonplace and yet tender-hearted Britons of his day. He wished to hold the mirror up to nature with a vengeance, to strike at abuses which the very people he addressed were supporting, to scourge the very types in which their homes abounded. He told his story in the manner he thought best adapted to this audience, not writing down to it, but expressing himself as was natural to him. His genius never detached him from the people among whom he was born and bred. Now, in the manner of his story he was misled by the plan we have mentioned. He thought melodrama would touch the hearts of his public. He proved that he was right. On the other hand, had he written otherwise he might have touched the imaginations of his later critics. That is a surmise, however, over which we need not linger. The main point is to recognize that while Dickens wrote to his contemporaries somewhat as he would have talked to them, he also wrought—and this is where his genius counted—with that breadth which is only possible to the artist who sees the larger issues in life, and deals with one man's traits as he would deal with the traits of a race. Such an artist, we say, has the quality of human nature in his work. Because he makes his individual a representative creature, because contemplation of one of his figures sends our imaginations drifting through the whole world of living, breathing beings, we call him an idealist. Hence Mr Gissing justly throws overboard the time-honored description of Dickens as a realist and tests all his characters in the light of an idealistic purpose. That such a purpose underlies the best work of Dickens we have not the smallest doubt.

In his apparently careless fashion, producing novels that seem more like improvisations than deeply pondered narratives, he was a consummate artist. That is to say, he preferred art, in his books, before nature. It was not his aim to paint Bill Sykes or Nancy exactly as he or she appeared to him in the slums he knew so well. He left that to the novelists who were to come after him, being disinclined, himself, to shock his reader before he had the opportunity to impress him. We cannot conceive of Dickens writing such a nightmare of a book as *A Child of the Jago*, which Mr Morrison wrote the other day, and which in some quarters at least was hailed as a miracle of veracity. Dickens sought a veracity less miraculous but more persuasive. He knew that the way to the heart does not always lie through striking terror there, or through arousing disgust. He even went so far as to make some of his worst rascals companionable, or, if not wholly that, comprehensible, human, kind with ourselves. The novelist of to-day carries the imagination forcibly to the brink of the infernal regions. Dickens gives us fearful glimpses, but he is always at our side, points out the connection between that world and our own, makes the lost souls comprehensible, puts us in a mood to think over these woes and to come from them with wiser and purer hearts. It is not that he preaches. Few novelists of his greatness preach so little. But with that alchemy of genius that makes an imaginary world real, he makes all the fantastic creatures of his books vivid, and part of our lives forever.

That they are often fantastic not even Mr Gissing can deny. But he points out that the fantastic in Dickens is something which we would call glamour in a writer of more romantic ideas, and we are not sure that we are pushing the uses of the word too far in employing it boldly as significant of the very thing that makes Dickens great. Mr Gissing comes home to it at the end of his book, though he does not set down the word in cold type; he is aware of it, in fact, all through his book, and if the Dickensite outraged by the candor of many of these pages turns upon the critic for an amend, it is honorably made; Mr Gissing admits that all along he has known that Dickens is too great for any of his blemishes to be held in much concern. Thus the book before us resolves itself into a measured, discreet but nevertheless generous appraisal of its subject. Mr Gissing shows us the spots on the sun, adding that it is the sun, after all. To know the blemishes is useful, and takes nothing from our admiration of Dickens. We do not cherish any the less such companions as Mr Pickwick, Dick Swiveller, Mrs Gamp and Joe Gargery. We only feel that our love of them is saner, and a little more creditable to ourselves as well as to them. We must not close without referring to the admirable manner in which Mr Gissing has done his work. His style has never been remarkable, and it is without much grace or color in this book; but it is always clear and forcible.

122. Unsigned, 'Is Pessimism Necessary?', *Critic* (London)

5 March 1898, 25

This sixpenny periodical, with which was incorporated the *African Critic*, was a weekly then in its third year of publication, edited by Henry Hess. The article was inspired by a mendacious interview with Gissing which had appeared in the *Book Buyer*, a New York monthly, under the title 'The Author of *The Whirlpool*' (February 1898, 40–2). It was signed by John Northern Hilliard, a journalist who had once been in epistolary contact with Gissing. The *Academy* quoted at length from it in its supplement of 5 March 1898, 258, in an article named 'Mr George Gissing at home'. Herbert Sturmer, a friend of the author's, sent him a cutting of the article, which roused Gissing's anger, as he had never pronounced the words attributed to him by Hilliard. From Rome, he sent a letter of protest to the editor of the *Academy* which was printed in this journal on 19 March 1898, 334. The anonymous writer in the *Critic* made in the last paragraph the same error as H. G. Wells in No. 113. See headnote to this item.

Gissing had a clipping of the article in the *Critic* in his album of press cuttings.

Though it is no news that Mr George Gissing inclines to pessimism, it is, none the less, something of a shock to find him upholding pessimism as an article of faith, which, except a man believe, he cannot be artistically saved. Yet that is what it comes to, if we may believe the interviewer. The latter, it appears, had remonstrated with Mr Gissing because 'cheerfulness' did not 'keep breaking in' upon the gloomy scenes of *New Grub Street*, and other works of genius; and Mr Gissing answered, sorrowfully:—

'Show me the great masterpieces of art, music, and literature, and I shall show you creations which absolutely palpitate with sadness.'

Under any circumstances the saying would have been a striking one; but it gains a further pleasing piquancy from the particular circumstances under which it happened to be uttered. For it has been announced that Mr Gissing has just written, and will shortly publish, a critical appreciation of the works of Dickens. Therefore, of two things, one. Either Mr Gissing has satisfied himself that Dickens did not write masterpieces; or else he is prepared to demonstrate to us that, in some subtle fashion, *The Pickwick Papers* palpitate with sadness. In the interest of the gaiety of nations, I sincerely hope that he has adopted the latter alternative; and in the meantime, I propose to respect Mr Gissing's character and examine his proposition concerning the relation of pessimism to art, partly because this is a literary column, and partly because that is the art with which I, like Mr Gissing, am best acquainted. Let us see, then, what the history of literature has to say about the matter.

If there had been no literature before the beginning of the present century, there would, no doubt, be something to be said for Mr Gissing's view. An exponent of that view would have to assume that history is not literature, so as to rule out the unruffled serenity of Lord Macaulay, whose diary is full of passages to the effect that his life had been a happy one; he would also have to 'posit', as the philosophers say, that *Pickwick* has no more to do with literature than *Three Men in a Boat*, that Kipling is a negligible quantity, that Alexandre Dumas and Victor Hugo do not count. If these large assumptions were allowed to him, he would have a case. He could refer to Flaubert, and quote the marvellous touch of pessimism on the last page of *L'Education Sentimentale*; to de Maupassant, whose mocking laughter is always full of bitterness; to Zola who once told the Paris students that life was only tolerable on condition that one was always busy; to Russians, like Turgueneff and Dostoieffsky, who boasted that they were consistent in their pessimism, and did not enjoy their dinners; to Mr Thomas Hardy, who views man as the mere plaything of malicious deities; to Mr Gissing himself; to Gabriele d'Annunzio, who lays himself out to prove that inward happiness is most impossible when outward circumstances are most favourable; and so forth. It would be easy to extend the list. So far as the nineteenth century is concerned, the process of counting noses results in favour of the pessimists. But how about the other centuries? What has Old Grub-street got to say about New Grub-street's attitude towards life?

The answer to this question is that, to Old Grub-street, pessimism was a temporary phase, and not a permanent point of view. Great men passed through pessimism and came out the other side very much as children get measles and recover from it. It is almost impossible to find a man among them who was pessimistic all the time, as Flaubert was, and as Mr Gissing is.

The thoroughgoing, unvarying kind of pessimism comes from France and Russia, and the process of its evolution can be pretty clearly traced. In France it is the inheritance of the anaemic generation, born at the epoch when all the vigorous potential ancestors had been killed off in the Napoleonic wars. In Russia it is the result of a combination of causes of which the most conspicuous are a depressing climate, monotonous landscapes, the exclusive use of bad spirits, and the natural disgust of intelligent men at the political institutions of their country. Modern English pessimism is more literary than real, and has principally been brought about by conscious, or unconscious, emulation of Flaubert and Turgueneff. But, as I have said, pessimism before Flaubert is seldom more than that transitory gloom which comes for a period, to most brilliant young men, making them sad as night only for wantonness. Looking at the career of these earlier writers, we almost invariably find that the pessimist of to-day is the optimist of yesterday and to-morrow.

Here, again, we have only to look up our literary history, and count the heads. It was thus with Byron, who was a pessimist when he wrote *Childe Harold*, but an optimist when he wrote *Don Juan*. It was so with Goethe. *The Sorrows of Werther* is of the very essence of pessimism; but the author said that he began to feel better as soon as he had finished writing it. It was so even with Shakespeare himself. He began in high spirits, and continued in high spirits for a long time. To this period belong, among other masterpieces, *As You Like It* and *The Merry Wives of Windsor*. Then followed a spell of great and ever-deepening gloom, which produced *Hamlet* and *Othello*, and found its supreme expression in *King Lear*; the personal reasons which accounted for it can be discovered by a diligent student of the Sonnets. But the gloom passed, and the clouds were scattered. Shakespeare once more learnt to perceive that life is beautiful; and *The Tempest* by no means 'palpitates with sadness'.

How is it going to be with Mr Gissing? I hesitate to prophesy; but in his later books I have noticed some indications. The British Empire passages towards the end of *The Whirlpool* distinctly suggested hopefulness, so that it may well be that presently even his work

May acquire, if not the calm
Of its early mountainous shore,
Yet a solemn peace of its own,

and leave professional misanthropy to the ripe experience of younger men.

THE TOWN TRAVELLER

August 1898

123. Unsigned review, *Pall Mall Gazette*

2 September 1898, 4

This review was printed under the title 'Missing Words and Husbands'.

The period of Mr Gissing's latest story might be computed from direct internal evidence. 'Come Where the Booze is Cheaper' was then a popular refrain, and the great missing-word competition is the divine gift from the wittily worked machine which enables the people to sort themselves out in pairs at the end. An antiquarian of the future might also, if he had lost the title-page, restore its date as 1898, on account of the leading fact of the story, the identity of the vanishing husband with a peer of the realm. But that might only be a lucky accident; at any rate, if a certain famous case gave Mr Gissing the idea, there is no further similarity between that case and the ingenious and delightfully funny story woven round 'Mr Clover.' Mr Gissing does not need to be topical to be actual; to say that a tale is by him is to say that its period is very much now, and its scene very much here, in the London where they sell cricket extras and pull up the Strand.

And yet not exactly here. When Mr Gissing takes Christopher Parish and the reader temporarily out West, the reader feels as uncomfortable as Mr Parish. Nor does he flee to the other extreme, 'Lizer's Lambeth, or the East of Sir Walter Besant's earnest young cranks. This London of his is those impossible places, Kennington-road, Battersea Park-road, and Shaftesbury-avenue, which the average reader has heard of or seen, but never even imagined as places to live in. Yet these commercial travellers and china-shop women and programme girls of Mr Gissing's do live there, and, what is more, they do *live* there. Their life, speech, and ways are the real thing, plainly; Mr Gissing has never got much more 'inside' London than here. What is even more, and not so invariable with Mr Gissing, the book leaves no kind of bad taste in the mouth, no sense of the unutterable possibilities of washed-out dulness that lie, say, west of Hampstead-road. It is a bright and witty book above all things; sad things happen to several more or less vulgar people, but life is quite worth living after all.

The story, thank goodness! seems to have absolutely no 'purpose.' It has also no hero, even the flawless Minnie is so seldom and sketchily glanced at that one doesn't mind her. Nor has it a villain; Greenacre, though suspicion of blackmail attaches to him, hardly counts, and poor 'Mr Clover,' reprehensible as he is, is rather the sort of man that one pities as a mistake of Nature's. But there are two good characters—Mr Gammon, the traveller, light-hearted, smart, and very London-like, and little Mr Parish, the sublimely commonplace, timid, 'igh-'atted clerk; and one brilliant one. The combination of virtue, 'high colour, finely-developed bust and freedom of pose,' bad temper, greediness, honesty, absence of false modesty, and utter Londonliness in Polly Sparkes is a splendid bit of work. A book which contains Polly, the glorious row in the lodging-house, and such a brisk plot, moving so smartly, lightly, and easily, will not detract from Mr Gissing's reputation.

124. Unsigned review, *Morning Post*

8 September 1898, 2

We are not accustomed to associate mirthfulness with Mr George Gissing, who has, indeed, made for himself a distinct position among English writers by the production of some of the most depressing novels ever penned. Firmly convinced, apparently, of the hopeless nature of the fight against adversity, he has painted for us, with close attention to details and a wealth of sombre colour, the struggles of wretched men and women caught in the widely-expanded net of poverty and despair. He has, however, had his brighter intervals, and never has he been less inclined to despondency than in the novel which he has published within the last few days. *The Town Traveller* is, it may fairly be assumed, the first fruits of the renewed study of the methods of Charles Dickens essential to the preparation of the excellent little book on that famous author which Mr Gissing brought out not long since. The present story of a certain phase of London life is in no sense an imitation. There is not a scene or a character that can be described as a copy, yet from the first incidents in the fourth-rate boarding-house to the last in the 'gleaming china shop' with its cosy back-parlour, we are in an environment that reminds us at every turn of the man who made the joys and sorrows of lower middle-class life familiar to our youth. Tom Smart himself, the genial bagman, has no unworthy representative in Gammon, the brisk and honest 'commercial' who gives a title to the book. Mrs Bubb, the landlady, who prides herself on being 'the widow of a police officer,' and her first-floor lodger, Mr Cheeseman, recall not a few familiar figures, while Mrs Clover, who has been so badly treated by her supposed husband, and who at last fills for Mr Gammon the place that the agreeable widow filled for Tom Smart, offers a type that Dickens always loved to depict. Such reminiscences, while in no way reflecting on Mr Gissing's originality, are on the other hand very creditable to his forerunner in the investigation of the particular 'spear' of life concerned. It is rather the fashion to speak of the people in Dickens's novels as caricatures, and many of them no doubt are greatly, even grossly, exaggerated. But when we find an undoubtedly conscientious and keen observer, after an interval of half a century, painting the same social strata and showing their components to be possessed of the same essential characteristics which the earlier artist noted and reproduced, we may regard it as proof positive that, while there have been changes in the boarding-houses of Kennington-road and the back-parlours of Battersea, as in the other dwelling-houses of London, the broad features of lower middle-class life have remained the same since Mr Raddle cowered before his wife, and Mrs Quilp before her husband. It is, however, not merely for these reasons that Dickens 'runs in our heads' while we read Mr Gissing's book. The names of the characters, and the very headings of the chapters, force reminiscences on us. Bubb and Quodling and Gammon, 'The Head Waiter at Chaffeys,' 'The Name of Gildersleeve,' 'The Husband's Return,' how familiar it all seems. Yet, as already suggested, not the least opportunity is afforded for the compiler of 'parallel columns' to exercise his skill, and *The Town Traveller* may fairly be described as an exceptionally original and convincing representation of the manners and customs of a vast section of the Metropolitan populace.

It is the people whose ill-cooked meals are laid on dirty table-cloths, whose favourite if not only reading is in penny novelettes and sensational newspapers, whose aesthetic taste delights in wax-flower ornaments and oleographs, that fill the pages of *The Town Traveller.* The most ordinary colloquialisms of the educated classes are so much Sanskrit to their ears, though their own fashions of speech are not as a rule difficult to comprehend, if the exact significance of a word may here and there be hard to appreciate. In some of them idiosyncrasies above their kind may be discovered. Mrs Clover, for example, the most refined of the women to whom we are introduced—unless we except her more attractive daughter—was impelled by habit 'to imply a weighty opinion by suddenly breaking off; a form of speech known to the grammarians by a name which would have astonished Mrs Clover.' Mr Gissing hastens to add for our instruction that 'few women of her class are prone to this kind of emphasis.'

It must, indeed, be held a fault in Mr Gissing's method that he so strongly insists on the fact that he is presenting a study of a particular social level. Polly, the dashing and obtrusively virtuous girl, who so enjoys her bad temper, and who possesses a gift of primitive sarcasm 'which few cared to face for more than a minute or two,' is always doing little things which betray her birth and upbringing, but we are not allowed to note them for ourselves. When, after bursting open Polly's bed-room door, with the best of motives and the worst possible manners, Gammon apologised to the girl, 'she answered in the formula of her class, "Oh, I'm sure it's granted." ' When the same offender declined to reveal a secret, even for a reward of kisses which had never been offered, 'Polly bridled—young women of her class still bridle—but looked rather pleased.' When the bagman took her to see his dogs, and she was shown a terrier 'whose latest exploit was the killing of a hundred rats in six minutes, she backed trembling, and even put out a hand to Gammon as if for protection. Polly's behaviour, indeed, was such as would have been proper in a fine lady forty years ago, the fashion having descended to her class just as fashions in costume are wont to do at a shorter interval.' This sort of 'aside' to the reader is a little aggravating. It is as though Mr Frith, in his 'Derby

Day,' that picture which far eclipses the works of Titian and Rembrandt in popularity with visitors to the National Gallery, had drawn attention at the bottom of the frame to the particular marks of 'class' to be observed in the occupants of the carriages, the acrobats, the thimble-riggers, and the country louts. Such things, in a written as well as in a painted picture, should speak for themselves. No doubt Mr Gissing could cite excellent authorities for the practice, but it is none the less a blemish in a book so generally well written. The mystery of Lord Polperro, the queer hobby of the impecunious Greenacre, and the internal economy of Mrs Bubb's establishment lend varied attractions to *The Town Traveller* and Polly Sparkes's one-sided love affair with the timid and innocent 'clurk' who marries her on the strength of his success in a missing word competition, is brightly introduced. Gammon, however, the light-hearted, the generous, the vulgar-minded, is the true hero of the story. A man who 'took what the heavens sent him, grumbling or rejoicing, but never reflecting upon his place in the sum of things,' and who 'had in perfection the art of living for the moment,' is drawn with a truly realistic pencil, and, in spite of his many resemblances to earlier men, he stands out as a fresh creation among the characters of the book. It is not a novel of any extraordinary merit, but it is a thoroughly sound and well-balanced piece of work, creditable alike to the author's powers of observation and of expression. Mr Gissing's works are not as a rule remarkable for humour, but mildly amusing passages are not wanting in the present instance. *The Town Traveller* is an excellent book for holiday reading, and as can be said of very few holiday novels—it is worth placing on the bookshelf when the time of renewed labour begins.

125. Unsigned review, *New York Tribune Illustrated Supplement*

2 October 1898, 15

Something has happened to change the color of life as Mr George Gissing sees it. For years he has looked at it in its drab phases, lingering over the doleful, sordid tragedies in which the dignity of the human soul rarely triumphs over its bourgeois surroundings, and over comedies with no gleam of the sunshine of humor in them. In fact we have been driven to conclude that humor was the one thing omitted from Mr Gissing's otherwise sound equipment as a novelist. It has been impossible to ignore his books—they are among the strongest things in contemporary fiction—but if one has admired them it has been in anything but a joyous spirit. Now comes *The Town Traveller*, and reveals Mr Gissing in a new light, with a laugh on his lips and with the liveliest relish for everything that is quaint and amiable and ingratiating in cockney life. What does it mean? Has it come from the author's recent writing of a book upon Dickens? That may have aroused a slumbering sense of the gayety [*sic*] in things. Perhaps Mr Gissing has realized that if Dickens could find laughter in the slums, he might find it there also. But he has known Dickens all his life. Why should he have waited all these years to emulate the great humorist? Question is piled upon question, but the pursuit is vain. If we follow it at all it is only because this volte-face of Mr Gissing's is such a surprising and tantalizing phenomenon.

The book is not tantalizing. On the contrary it is an unmixed pleasure. Gammon, the hero, is a bagman to love, and though Polly Sparkes, whom he almost marries, is a provoking young minx, she is also amusing, and the adventures of these two as they get themselves mixed up in the family affairs of Polly's aunt are as diverting as a play. It is not improbable, indeed, that *The Town Traveller* would make a rattling comedy of the slightly farcical sort. The ingenuities of the plot would be fruitful in a playwright's hands, and the characters are completely ready for him. But it must not be supposed that Mr Gissing himself has had any theatrical intentions. He tells a plain, straightforward tale, and if the astonishing nobleman who is the errant husband of Polly's aunt is not exactly the kind of creature one would expect to find in the private annals of Cockney life, he is at any rate plausible, besides being, merely as a curiosity, a figure for the memory to cherish. The narrative is happily ended, which must have cost the author a pang. He may console himself with the reflection that his readers will be rejoiced. We may commend the book, in passing, to the special attention of Mr Pett Ridge, whose painful efforts to make a novel out of Cockneydom we mentioned last week. Mr Gissing will show him how to do it. He will show him that the great thing is to know your characters through and through and to let constructive art follow upon observation, so that the things seen are welded together in a perfect whole. *The Town Traveller*, which is as a trifle compared to some of the author's previous books, is as consistent and homogeneous as any of those powerful books.

126. Unsigned review, *Guardian* (London)

12 October 1898, liii (2), 1594

It is very pleasant to find how much more cheerfully Mr Gissing writes now than in his earlier manner, and the bright picture of the middle classes of London, presented in *The Town Traveller*, is refreshingly free from sordid habits and disappointed lives. We positively have an unselfish 'traveller in fancy leathers,' Mr Gammon, who, while out of a job, devotes himself to helping all sorts of stragglers to a livelihood, and more particularly to tracing out a friend's lost husband. This leads him into such vagaries as forcing the door of a young lady lodger, two pair up, and carrying her down as an unwilling witness in the affair. The bold deed wins her heart, in spite of stair-rails wrenched out and scratches on the face given and received in the struggle. As we proceed we find that the lost husband is exactly like a Lord Polperro, and here the tale gets so mixed that we hardly know to the end whether

Mr Clover was really Lord Polperro himself, or if, rather, he was not a mysterious Quodling, of Quodling Brothers, who sometimes is the cousin, and sometimes the half-brother, of that erring lord. But it scarcely matters, for when Mr Clover is finally tracked down by Gammon, the plot entirely disappears in hurried journeys between Sloane-street, Streatham, and Ludgate-hill; and the reader, completely out of breath, feels relieved when Polperro (or Clover), still explaining nothing, dies quickly of exhaustion in a brawl outside St Paul's Cathedral. After this Gammon has a free hand to marry Mrs Clover, and a very nice woman she is, while Polly (the auburn-haired lodger of the fray) takes up with another lover, who has won £550 by guessing the word 'hygiene.' (The 'missing-word competition' craze is introduced here with capital effect.) Although the story matters little in *The Town Traveller*, there is briskness and vivacity, a good-humoured tolerance of weaknesses, and a rough-and-ready kind of reward dealt out to honesty, which keep the attention fixed, and are not unworthy treatment of the ground traversed half-a-century ago by Charles Dickens.

127. Unsigned review, *Critic* (New York)

December 1898, 509–10

This is a decidedly cheerful story of the lower middle-class English life, and the scene of it is laid in Dickens's London. That is to say, not only is it occupied with the classes of society with whom Dickens chiefly and most successfully dealt, but even with situations and individuals that might have been the elder novelist's own. Above all, the atmosphere is that of Dickens. About Mr Gammon and Mrs Bubb, and the Clovers, and poor inebriated Lord Polperro and the mysterious Greenacre is thrown a glamour which is very foreign to the customary atmosphere of Mr Gissing's novels.

It is not unfair to suppose that this effort is, to a certain degree, premeditated on the part of Mr Gissing and that it is part of a little experiment whereby the leopard endeavors to change his spots. Mr Gissing is well-known as a powerful but depressing novelist, who depicts with a strong and hopeless realism dreary and sordid people in dreary and sordid surroundings. At the same time he is a hearty and reverent admirer of Dickens, and his admiration seems to be largely based upon the sensations of good cheer and human comfort which it was the chief function of Dickens to diffuse. It may very well be that the younger writer proposed to himself an attempt to increase the pleasure of his readers, and to extend the field of his own usefulness, by reproducing, as far as possible, the atmosphere of comfort and hilarity which played a far greater part in Dickens's popularity than any other element.

This attempt, whether deliberate or accidental, is not wholly successful, and yet is so far from a failure as to make the critic wish that the writer would at least repeat the experiment before returning to his sombre natural manner. 'The Town-Traveller' himself is one Mr Gammon,

> a short, thick-set man with dark, wiry hair roughened into innumerable curls, and similar whiskers edging a clean razor-line half way down the cheek. His eyes were blue, and had a wonderful innocence which seemed partly the result of facetious affectation, as was also the peculiar curve of his lips, ever ready for joke or laughter, yet the broad, mobile countenance had lines of shrewdness and of strength, plain enough whenever it relapsed into gravity, and the rude shaping of the jaw and chin might have warned anyone disposed to take advantage of the man's good nature.

Given a hero of this wholesome type; a sharp-tongued, high-spirited and shrewish young woman to pit him against; and interwoven romance all about a peer married to a comely and estimable woman, who kept a china shop, and was unaware that her errant husband occupied an exalted station in life, and you have material which demands treatment quite the reverse of Mr Gissing's usual method. The cheerfulness of the story is, in fact, boisterous, and the mirth of the characters once or twice degenerates into horse-play.

As compared to most of Mr Gissing's other novels, the reader's gain in the present volume is preeminently a gain in comfort of so elemental a kind it is almost physical. The reader's loss, on the other hand, is psychical, and is due to the impressions of unreality which the book leaves upon the mind. When Mr Gissing is cheerless, he is convincing, but when he is cheerful, he is denied credence. It is to be hoped that this fact means, not that verisimilitude and cheerfulness are to be forever at war in this author's work, but merely that his first venture toward calculated jocundity is naturally less solid and symmetrical than the examples of his spontaneous gloom have been. He has clothed his imagination with a new garment whose fit is imperfect, but whose texture is more pleasing than that of the suit he has doffed. And, in general, the public may be relied upon to prefer optimism of any cut whatsoever to the most perfectly-fitting pessimism.

128. Unsigned leader, *Daily Chronicle*

29 September 1898, 4

Gissing recorded in his diary the publication of this leader and of the letter from a correspondent. He followed the course of the controversy but, apparently, did not see the last two letters in the debate or the article included as No. 129. Beneath the heading 'The Minor Clerk', the *Daily Chronicle* published four letters on 30 September, four on 1 October, two on 4 October, three on 5 October, one on 6 October and two on 8 October.

A correspondent, who signs himself 'A Minor Clerk', protests in our columns to-day against what he supposes to be Mr George Gissing's opinion of an estimable body of citizens. In *The Town Traveller*, Mr Gissing introduces us to Mr Christopher Parish, a clerk with two pounds a week, who is weak in his aspirates, Cockney in his dialect, and of such timorous inexperience that when he orders supper for Miss Polly Sparkes in a restaurant above his means, he does not know the dish he selects from the bill of fare, is overawed by the waiter, and eats 'large quantities of dry bread' to hide his nervousness. Our correspondent does not know anybody like Mr Parish in the 'great order of minor clerks', and offers to introduce Mr Gissing to a number of cultivated gentlemen who pay their guineas to Mudie's. We are quite sure that Mr Gissing has no desire to cast a slur upon the class of which our correspondent's letter reveals a vigorous and capable champion. Possibly the author of *The Town Traveller* has used in the character of Mr Parish some observation which antedates that spread of culture described by 'A Minor Clerk'. But Mr Gissing may say that Mr Parish is not meant to be the sum and content of the whole race of minor clerks. In another of this novelist's work, *In the Year of Jubilee*, there is a self-satisfied reader of *Tit-bits* whose entire education consists of reminiscences of the mileage which would be covered if all the cabs in London were placed in a line. Obviously this is not meant to represent the culture and refinement of the hundreds of thousands who read *Tit-Bits*. To take a higher illustration, Balzac's Cousin Pons is a collector of bric-a-brac, but Balzac did not mean that every collector of bric-a-brac is as insensible to the ways of the world as Cousin Pons. We know some collectors who are extremely wideawake. Moreover, our correspondent forgets that when he ordered the supper, Mr Parish was trembling before the charms of Miss Polly Sparkes. Is every minor clerk—even a subscriber to Mudie's—prepared to swear that he has never lost his presence of mind when entertaining the dashing young woman of his heart for the first time in a restaurant which is far beyond the capacity of two pounds a week?

129. Unsigned, 'Mr Gissing and the Minor Clerks', *Speaker*

8 October 1898, 429

This article both summarizes and concludes the controversy provoked by *The Town Traveller*. See No. 128.

Mr George Gissing has caused a serious commotion amongst the Minor Clerks. Sooner or later somebody in Brixton or Kennington was bound to turn upon the man who writes the small-beer chronicle of those districts. We thought the revolt would come when, in *In The Year of Jubilee*, Mr Gissing drew a Brixton scholar whose knowledge was entirely derived from the kind of journal which tells you how many sovereigns, all in a row, would make a girdle round the earth. How is it that Brixton did not protest against this reflection upon its culture? However, the worm has turned at last, and Kennington is angry with the portrait of a Minor Clerk in *The Town Traveller*. Mr Christopher Parish earns two pounds a week on a stool in the City. He succumbs to the charms of Miss Polly Sparkes, who sells programmes at one of the theatres, and he regales her with supper at a restaurant, where he is alarmed by the waiter, does not know the dish he orders at random, and sits munching dry bread in extreme nervousness. Moreover, his speech is not polished, and he hovers weakly on the brink of illiteracy. Mr Parish is a perfectly harmless young man with the most honourable intentions; but his very blamelessness seems to be a new offence in the eyes of Kennington. If he were a 'dog', his Cockney diction might be overlooked; but the spectacle of an abject milksop munching dry bread has prompted some Minor Clerks to vindicate the character of their Order. In Ouida's early novels it is enjoined upon our young nobility that, while they may disregard conventional morals, the dignity of their Order must never be compromised. It is this uplifting ideal which prompts one of them, in a famous passage, to fight his way through a riotous mob in a theatre. Every time his fist encounters the face of Demos he feels that he is victoriously asserting his Order. Now, had Mr Parish entered that restaurant with self-possession and his hat on one side, addressed the waiter like a tyrant, pooh-poohed the cookery, and ignored the dry bread, the Order of Minor Clerks might not have felt ashamed of him.

But this is not the issue they have raised. One of them indignantly pointed out in the *Chronicle* that Mr Gissing had traduced the Order, which, as he ought to have known, was composed of studious gentlemen who subscribe to Mudie's. The writer offered to introduce Mr Gissing to this cultivated circle, and convince him that the true Minor Clerks are not Parishes. Then followed a kind of correspondence which is full of pleasant divagations. A clerk with eighty pounds a year delivered himself on the uppishness of the clerk with a hundred, who lives in a thirty-pound house, calls the front passage the hall to distinguish it from the passage which communicates with the back-door, and that he gloried in the pink shade and even in oleographs. We regret these dissensions in the Order, when a united front ought to be offered to the enemy. Mr Gissing will note the pink shade as an emblem of social arrogance in Kennington, and he may devote a whole chapter to the topographical distinction between the hall and the back passage. What has all this to do with Mr Parish? Even if the front passage is unduly translated when it becomes a hall, how does that justify the picture of a hundred-pounder brainlessly devouring dry bread? Would a subscriber to Mudie's entertain Miss Polly Sparkes at supper? Is a subscription to Mudie's inseparable from the functions of the Minor Clerk—a sort of masonic rite through which he must pass before he is admitted to the Order?

On these points the correspondence in the *Chronicle* discloses some difference of opinion. There are Minor Clerks who boldly assert that Mr Parish does represent a good many gentlemen on stools in the City. One witness, who claims to have a comprehensive experience, says that Mr Gissing might have made Mr Parish much more despicable without violating the truth. This excites the suspicion that, after all, the Order is not entirely composed of subscribers to Mudie's, and that, like other Orders, it contains a great variety of human nature. Ouida's Order of young nobility is represented as frequently in the company promoter's prospectus as in the national scroll of fame; but nobody would say that a novelist who draws a noble 'guinea-pig' was traducing the whole aristocracy. It is quite sufficient for Mr Gissing's purpose that Christopher Parish is the type of a considerable class; and if he prefers to draw that type, why should the Minor Clerk, who drinks from the

Pierian spring of Mudie's, feel offended? With obstinate perversity Dickens was accused of attacking religion because he exposed a certain kind of hypocrisy in Stiggins and Chadband. Everybody knows that the religious hypocrite is one of the pests of society; but it was thought not honest to have it thus set down. Some critics gravely alleged that a novelist who painted hypocrisy was bound in honour to show the opposite in some character that testified to the sincerity of religious professions. By the same reasoning Mr Gissing might be required to supplement Mr Parish with a portrait drawing the Minor Clerk deep in the treasures of Mudie's under the pink shade. Even if he accepted this challenge, the result would offend somebody, for he might show that the wisdom of a circulating library does not always educate, that it may leave a man narrow, dogmatic, and incapable of drawing elementary distinctions. When a reader finds in a novel a character from the class to which he himself belongs, and exclaims, 'This must be a libel, because it is not in the least like me!' he merely shows that his educational process is incomplete. There is no obvious reason why the portrait should be like *him*, whether he be a Minor Clerk or a much more exalted member of society. Old Sir Pitt Crawley is unlike any other baronet in fiction, or any baronet familiar to many people in real life. His manners are atrocious, and his dialect occasionally less refined than Mr Parish's. To say that Thackeray intended Sir Pitt to represent the whole baronetage of England would be nonsense; but the portrait is none the less actual, for it is evidently drawn from life in every line. It is not the duty of a novelist when he lights upon a remarkably original piece of character, to say to himself: 'No, I must not reproduce this, for few people will recognise the truth of it, and many would say I was libelling a respectable and very distinguished body of citizens.' His duty is to be no respecter of persons, whether they belong to county families or to the Order of Minor Clerks.

THE CROWN OF LIFE

October 1899

130. Morley Roberts, *Review of the Week*

4 November 1899, 16–7

This was the first number of a short-lived penny weekly edited by Harold E. Gorst. In the same number appeared Gissing's anti-jingo article 'Tyrtaeus'. Roberts's contribution, entitled 'Mr Gissing's new novel and—Mr Gissing', is unsigned but its authorship is made clear by a postcard from Gissing to Roberts of 19 November 1899, held by the Berg Collection of the New York Public Library.

The history of *Review of the Week* is told by Gorst in his autobiography *Much of Life is Laughter* (Allen & Unwin, London, 1936).

'With bread and steel,' says the Eastern proverb, 'one may get to China,' and it is with bread and a steel obstinacy that Mr Gissing cuts his way towards the Celestial kingdom of a reasonable optimism. In *The Crown of Life* he has made a very notable advance; one may conclude from its final outcome that its author no longer sees all things darkly in the glass he holds to nature. Happiness is possible, he admits without any ironic intention, and of all happiness love is the greatest. It is characteristic of Mr Gissing that his story, though interesting, is of the very slightest: to tell it in a few words is to miss telling it at all: one may merely suggest that the lover pursues with a passionate heart (though without that mastering passion that compels), and circumstance no longer bars the way to fruition. Piers Otway, the chief character of the book, is well worked out: we not only see him 'in the round,' but we see all through him. Coming of a stock whose main characteristic is an enthusiastic futility, the reader follows his career with dread lest he, too, shall be futile, frustrate, and enthusiastic. By the narrowest he escapes such an end; but one perceives that fate rather than inborn force has preserved him. His sole real strength is an ideal love grafted upon strong passions. And this is the real point of the book; elsewhere Mr Gissing has suggested the theme, but here he develops it. Almost alone among modern writers he has dared to delineate the tortures of the undebauched celibate, and, delicate subject though this be, he has handled it truly, purely, and without offence. In one sense the book belongs to the class physiological, but the physiology is as discreet as the intention is plain. In becoming less gloomy Mr Gissing has not ceased to be a realist: he still postulates with firmness the unromantic fact that any hero must be a human being, who will probably bleed if cut, and certainly die if shot through the heart. And one may still be thankful for so much, even if the modern puppet, being better made than of old, only leaks sawdust on the greater provocation of a critical postmortem.

Nor are the women-folk of *The Crown of Life* any less lifelike than the men. It is perhaps true that one does not recognise why Irene Derwent possesses so overwhelming an attraction for Piers Otway, but that is probably evidence of the fact that she was his true mate by natural 'election.' It is common for men to wonder what their friends saw in their wives, and the trick of making the heroine in a novel loved by the public is proof positive of her actual unreality. Were the heroine real, they would compare her with some present reality, and conclude that a bird in the hand was worth any two in the bush of fiction. And it is very doubtful if Mr Gissing ever loved this heroine of his at all. For he is detached and aloof. He describes his world seriously and gravely, being obviously interested in a godlike manner. But he is not passionately devoted to his Greeks or Trojans, and rarely steps from Olympus into the plains of Ilium to overthrow any boasting warrior. It is this very aloofness of mind which is one of his chief attractions; in two senses, at least, he is a master.

Yet Mr Gissing, as he is himself a human being, and, as we picture him, a very reasonable human being, has some weaknesses. One of these is the weakness of logic. For the second underlying theme of the book is mainly Peace, in the sense of the Arbitration Societies. Of all objectionable things, we imagine that Mr Gissing finds physical force the most revolting. It is not only revolting to him: he esteems it absurd, ludicrous, provocative of sneers. He shows a certain passion (a passion reserved yet strong) in attacking it; and concludes that, as it is illogical, it cannot last. This is an optimism, indeed; but one that any student of his works must have been prepared for. For Mr Gissing's essence is reasonableness. He shows again and again that Hunger and Poverty and all the Unrighteousness of the Social Organism are not according to Cocker, are contradicted by Mill's Logic, and are unsupported by the Nature of Things as developed in the Kantian Categories. And if we say—therefore they exist, Mr Gissing says he is seriously displeased to observe it.

For, at the present day, in this writer alone, so far as we are aware, the true scholar's mind has been turned to the writing of novels. That Mr Gissing possesses the scholarly intellect is obvious; and if Mr John Morley had turned to fiction, Mr Gissing might not have sat alone upon his peak. It is not odd, then, to observe that the novelist has a curious dislike of the British Empire; or if not dislike, a certain feeling that the Empire is hardly fit to associate with. It is not a quiet, reasonable, and gentlemanly companion; it cannot be convinced by the plainest syllogism in Barbara; it says rude things in the bluntest way, and, rather than use indelicate finger nails, seizes its axe when axes appear to be indicated. And Mr Gissing (still logically) is of opinion that this unmannerly Empire is mistaken in its opinion of Russia and the Slav. The scholar's mind is ever individual, in that it is reserved and apart; and no amount of experience appears to be able to convince it that the conflicts and rivalries of nations are not yet a scientific branch of knowledge. Even if it perceives that the existence of social organisms on their present lines depends on the increase and perpetuation of trade, it does not draw the inevitable conclusion that a national organism will fight as hard to live as any individual.

We have endeavoured to indicate the underlying themes of this interesting book rather than the lines of the story, which everyone who is interested in English literature will read for himself. There is at any rate one overwhelming advantage in being really tinged with letters. Mr Gissing's work is always literature.

131. Unsigned review, *New York Tribune Illustrated Supplement*

5 November 1899, 13

This review was entitled 'An Unexpectedly Cheerful Book'.

It is very pleasant to read now and then a novel which is neither radiantly romantic nor grimly analytical, a novel in which the mature thought of a capable writer is temperately set forth. *The Crown of Life* is such a novel. We would be doing it a serious injustice if we questioned the fervor of its passion. Piers Otway, though an 'average' man, is capable of suffering, and does suffer. The heroine, though conventional in some ways, is a woman also fitted to inspire a great love. Mr Gissing is faithful, however, to the familiar truths of familiar strata of society, and the special value of his book resides in its strong treatment of a theme which would have sunk swiftly to a commonplace level in less skilful hands. The book is full of intelligence, full of insight into types and conditions characteristic of our modern life. Neither Otway nor the woman for whom he waits through eight hard years is idealized. Mr Gissing will not transfigure either of his characters by heroics any more than the man and woman themselves would have glorified their experiences. The story is of a friendship flaming instantly into love on the man's side, but controlling itself with manliness and patience, while with the woman it develops naturally and slowly under the pressure of circumstances which the author will never hasten or distort for the sake of dramatic effect. Restraint is the keynote of *The Crown of Life*, a restraint which we admire at once in the chief personages and in the novelist. The sobriety of the general scheme is visible in the execution of the details. The subordinate characters bear just the right relation to the principals, each one is portrayed freely, but with admirable finish, and flashes of humour illumine many of the pages. The author seems to have been deeply interested in his book; it reads as if it had been written with ease and spirit. The climax is surprising in the happy character, Mr Gissing having usually given a pessimistic turn to his last chapter, but like everything else in the book it seems true to life. He sees clearly and writes with the mastery that comes with truth. *The Crown of Life* is a novel that will increase his reputation.

132. Unsigned review, *St. James's Gazette*

7 November 1899, 12

This review was entitled 'A Good Novel.'

Mr George Gissing may be relied on to give us novels marked by an exceptionally observant knowledge of life, and his new story is full of all those fine qualities which have distinguished its predecessors, together with a somewhat happier tone than Mr Gissing always manages to introduce into his sphere of thought. *The Crown of Life* is no study of poverty or struggling gentility; its atmosphere has not that somewhat depressing effect which repels some readers from Mr Gissing's best former work; and it is satisfactory to those who have always admired this writer's work to find that he moves just as easily in these less drab surroundings. Mr Gissing is a realist, for whom every touch of the real, every faithful reproduction of life as it is really lived is invested with romance; and the result is that all those who are repelled more by staginess and convention than by the ease with which 'things go wrong,' find in his novels a peculiar and abiding interest. Where things therefore 'come right' there is an additional pleasure—at least, for everybody but the confirmed lovers of a painful ending. In the present case things come right. Piers Otway is by no means a conventional hero of fiction; he is a very human man, with conspicuous failings; yet he had the stuff in him of which fine acts come, and, while presenting his defects and his mistakes, Mr Gissing makes us like him, and retain our interest in him all the time. If our hero is only half a hero, our heroine is a charming girl and a ripe woman. Irene Derwent is one of Mr Gissing's most attractive creations; and the difficult task of representing her gradual recognition of her love for Piers—extending over several years, at the beginning of which the young girl's attitude towards him is rather that of a mother—is fulfilled with consummate skill and literary resource. In dealing with a novel of so much complexity in its details as this it is impossible to indicate the course of events. There is a largeness of conception in the progress of the story which cannot be summarised. You live with the characters through too many psychological changes for the plot to be reduced to a nutshell. But Mr Gissing traces these same psychological changes with a master hand. Alike in his grasp of the interchange between experience and character, and in his presentment of the turning-points which form the dramatic scenes in life, he is always original, and at the same time he avoids that ultra-modernity which is as far from truth as the old conventions. His dialogue is invariably dramatic and intrinsically interesting. The minor characters are all clever studies. In short, *The Crown of Life* is a novel of the first rank in the year's fiction. It will be considered by many to be Mr Gissing's best. At any rate it is well worthy of him.

133. Unsigned review, *Literature*

11 November 1899, v, 470–1

Mr George Gissing's new novel, *The Crown of Life*, was understood to be of an optimistic character. Different people have different ideas of optimism. The book certainly ends with a declaration of love and a promise of marriage, but as all, or nearly all, the people already married when the story begins are represented as disappointed with their experiences of that estate, the reader has his doubts whether he ought to rejoice with the couple who take leave of him on the altar steps. The plot is simple—not to say commonplace. A foolish, silly young man, after sundry lets and hindrances ultimately secures the affections of a beautiful but capricious young woman who took a long time making up her mind, and even engaged herself to another young man in the meanwhile. It is, in short, the sort of story one is accustomed to expect from lady novelists of the older school rather than from Mr Gissing. It is also the sort of story that the lady novelists used to make more convincing than Mr Gissing makes it. For he suffers from the defects of his qualities and exercises his great gifts of psychological insight to the point of destroying illusion. In a love story it is obviously desirable that we should know why the hero was attracted by the heroine, and why the heroine was attracted by the hero; but Mr Gissing, by his ruthless (though quiet and subtle) exposure of their imperfections, always prevents his readers from doing anything of the sort. When he wrote realistic novels about the sordid life of the lower middle classes this did not matter. We took a purely intellectual pleasure in the performance, and did not want to sympathize. In the case of a romance, the conditions are different. It may or may not make the reader think, it must make the reader feel. And Mr Gissing has this time given us a romance in which all sentiment is killed by too accurate observation, too careful description, and too acute analysis. The characters in *The Crown of Life* belong to a higher social stratum than that in which Mr Gissing usually delves with such success. They do not belong to the minor suburbs, but have good addresses at Queen's Gate, Bryanston Square, and so forth; they are not clerks and literary hacks, but prosperous professional men, empire builders, members of Parliament and the like. This social change of air will be pleasing to some of Mr Gissing's readers; but not to all of them. His descriptions have not the same deadly certainty of touch, as of old, nor do they evince the same intuitive perception of the things that may be taken for granted. On the contrary, there is a good deal of insistence upon unnecessary details—such details as that of a lady treated a visitor with 'courtesy,' that one young man washed, and that another kept his nails clean. Is it more necessary to say all this than it is to say that the member of Parliament did not eat his peas with a knife, or that the empire builder did not come down to dinner in carpet slippers? There is also a good deal of unpatriotic sentiment in the book, and much petulant protest against the expansion of England. *The Crown of Life* cannot be reckoned among Mr Gissing's successes.

134. H. H. Champion, *Book Lover* (Melbourne)

January 1900, ii, 2

Henry Hyde Champion (see headnote to No. 75) was editor of the *Book Lover* and maintained a desultory correspondence with Gissing at the turn of the century. In an undated letter to Miss Clara Collet, Gabrielle Fleury commented on the following article as 'excellent', 'intelligent and laudatory'. She doubtless reflected Gissing's opinion.

It is almost a platitude to remark that the majority of the most popular novels of the last two decades will be forgotten in a few years. Not many writers possess that convincing mastery which converts some flimsy sheets of paper into a monument more enduring than stone or bronze. Of how many living novelists, for instance, are the works likely to survive for a generation? You may count them on the fingers of one hand. I have been led into this train of thought by a perusal of George Gissing's *The Crown of Life*. I closed the book with my old conviction confirmed and strengthened, that Gissing will be read more by the next generation than he is by this.

George Gissing published his first novel fifteen years ago, and is very slowly working his way to the front rank, but he will arrive there, and stay there. The undisguised pessimism of his earlier works accounts for their lack of popularity. He seemed to have taken for his text that passage of Ruskin in *Fors Clavigera*—'The very light of the morning sky has become hateful to me, because of the misery I know of and see signs of where I know it not; and which no imagination can interpret too bitterly. Therefore I will endure it no longer quietly, but henceforward do my poor best to abate this misery.'

This 'saeva indignatio' Gissing put into his books, and it proved bitter reading. No better criticism of these earlier works has yet been made than Gissing himself puts into the mouth of Ida Starr in *The Unclassed*. She says of Osmond Waymark's book, 'It held me as nothing else ever did. It was horrible in many parts, but I was the better for reading it.' Gissing laid bare in merciless fashion the misery, squalor, and hideousness of the underside of modern life; he did it with remarkable insight into the more striking problems of the life of to-day, with a rare perception of the curious complexities of human nature, and a literary skill and honesty that is not surpassed, is not equalled save by one or two of his contemporaries.

As time went on Gissing came to recognise, as all sane genius must, that life is not all tears. And with this recognition came the maturing of his powers. The bitter pessimism of his earlier day became merged in a more hopeful outlook, a change which was naturally reflected in his work. And what is that work? *The Unclassed*, *The Emancipated*, and *The Whirlpool* have not attained the ephemeral popularity, the rush of editions, that can be claimed by the novels of a Corelli or a Boothby. But they will stand, their day of editions will come, for they are literature in its best sense, a reflex of their time produced by a master hand.

The Crown of Life is another step forward and will increase Gissing's reputation. Ostensibly it is a love story from cover to cover, but a love story of no ordinary kind. It is also much more than a love story, for we have discussed in it in a masterly and impartial manner, in a manner to interest the most frivolous, the questions of Imperialism, the destiny of Russia, and an indictment of the militarism of the age. Nor are these topics introduced in other than an artistic way; they are the natural outcome of the characters of the story. As in Gissing's other works, the historian of the future will find in *The Crown of Life* valuable materials and testimony, when he comes to write the social history of the nineteenth century.

The hero of the book is at the opening of the story a somewhat vacillating and impressionable young man of twenty-one. He is accidentally thrown for a few days into the society of a beautiful and highly gifted girl, with whom he falls violently in love—a love that for social and other reasons must be apparently hopeless. The love, however, dominates him, rules his life, and moulds his career and character, and we find him as he nears thirty a man of tenacity of purpose, determination of character, and with an assured position won by his own efforts. And love comes to him, 'the crown of life,' and brings after his passionate struggles 'such peace as follows upon the hallowing of a profound passion, justified of reason, and proof under the hand of time.'

Of the varied merits of this book, I may say something further on a future occasion: a single reading scarcely suffices to do it full justice. For much might be written of the author's rare insight into human weaknesses and human foibles, of his wide outlook on the tendencies of the time, of his sympathetic delineation of characters, good, bad and indifferent. The book should be widely read, and no one, not even the young person, will be the worse, but the better, for reading it.

135. Arnold Bennett, 'Mr George Gissing, an Inquiry', *Academy*

16 December 1899, lvii, 724–6

The article, signed 'E.A.B.' in the journal, was reprinted in Bennett's *Fame and Fiction* (Grant Richards, London, 1901, 197–208). Gissing thought that 'it was rather more intelligently done than usual, but like everybody's writing on this subject, showed an imperfect knowledge of my later work' (letter to Clara Collet, 29 December 1899).

[The opening paragraph, containing some general introductory remarks on the nature of criticism, has been omitted.]

The author of *Demos* enjoys a fame today which he certainly deserves, but which he owes to the critics exclusively. His novels contain less of potential popularity than those of almost any other living novelist of rank. They have neither the prettiness which pleases, nor the outward beauty which subdues, nor the wit which dazzles, nor the thematic bigness which overawes. And they are not soiled by any specious lower qualities which might have deceived an innocent public into admiration. There is nothing in them to attract, and much to repel, the general gaze. A West End bookseller and the proprietor of a circulating library said to me: 'My ordinary public will have none of Gissing. But I stock his novels. They have a steady, very slow sale. I can tell my "Gissing" customers at a glance. They may be divided into two classes, the literary and the earnest. By "earnest" I mean interested in social problems. As for other sorts of people—no, not at all. You see, his subjects are so unattractive. My ordinary public simply doesn't care to read about that kind of thing.' Thus the observant bookseller. Yet Mr Gissing is renowned. He stands for something. His words have authority, and his name carries respect even among 'my ordinary public' which will not buy him. He figures often in the magazines, and I have small doubt that he receives higher prices for serial rights than many authors whose editions far outnumber his own. The fact is, he has that peculiar moral significance and weight which exist apart from mere numerical popularity, and which yet have an assessable value in the commercial market. 'My ordinary public' may be conceived as saying to him: 'We often hear of you. We take you for a serious person of high motives. We are told you are rather fine, but we don't realise it ourselves; to us you are very grey and depressing. We prefer to be more cheerful. Still, we suppose there really is something in you, and since we have heard so much about you, we shall probably look at anything of yours that we may happen to see in the monthlies. In the meantime we leave your books to those who care for them.'

It is, of course, just this 'grey' quality of his subjects, so repellent to the public, which specially recommends Mr Gissing's work to the critics. The artists who have courage fully to exploit their own temperaments are always sufficiently infrequent to be peculiarly noticeable and welcome. Still more rare are they who, leaving it to others to sing and emphasise the ideal and obvious beauties which all can in some measure see, will exclusively exercise the artist's prerogative as an explorer of hidden and recondite beauty in unsuspected places. Beauty is strangely various. There is the beauty of light and joy and strength exulting; but there is also the beauty of shade, of sorrow and sadness, and of humility oppressed. The spirit of the sublime dwells not only in the high and remote; it shines unperceived amid all the usual meannesses of our daily existence. To take the common grey things which people know and despise, and, without tampering, to disclose their epic significance, their essential grandeur—that is realism, as distinguished from idealism or romanticism. It may scarcely be, it probably is not, the greatest art of all; but it is art, precious and indisputable. Such art has Mr Gissing accomplished. In *The Nether World*, his most characteristic book, the myriad squalid futilities of an industrial quarter of London are gathered up into a large coherent movement of which the sinister and pathetic beauty is but too stringently apparent. After *The Nether World* Clerkenwell is no longer negligible. It has import. You feel the sullen and terrible pulse of this universe which lies beneath your own. You may even envy the blessedness of the meek, and perceive in the lassitude of the heavy laden a secret grace that can never be yours. Sometimes, by a single sentence, Mr Gissing will evoke from the most obscure phenomena a large and ominous idea. The time is six o'clock, and the workshops are emptying. He says: 'It was the hour of the unyoking of men.' A simple enough phrase, but it lends colour to the aspect of a whole quarter, and fills the soul with a vague, beautiful sense of sympathetic trouble. This is a good example of Mr Gissing's faculty of poetical constructive observation—a faculty which in his case is at once a strength and a weakness. He sees the world not bit by bit—a series of isolations—but broadly, in vast wholes. He will not confine himself to a unit, whether of the individual or the family. He must have a plurality, working in and out, mutually influencing, as it were seething. So he obtains an elaborate and complicated reflection of the variety and confusion of life impossible to be got in any other way. So also by grouping similar facts he multiplies their significance into something which cannot be ignored. That is his strength. His weakness is that he seems never to be able to centralise the interest. His pictures have no cynosure for the eye. The defect is apparent in all his books, from *The Unclassed*, a youthful but remarkable work, wherein several separate narratives are connected by a chain of crude coincidences, down to the recently-published *Crown of Life*, of which the story loses itself periodically in a maze of episodes each interrupting the others. Out of the fine welter of *The Nether World* nothing emerges paramount. There are a dozen wistful tragedies in this one novel, of which the canvas is as large as that of *Anna Karenina*—a dozen exquisite and moving renunciations with their accompanying brutalities and horror; but the dark grandeur which ought to have resulted from such an accumulation of effects is weakened by a too impartial diffusion of the author's imaginative power.

I have said that *The Nether World* is Mr Gissing's most characteristic book. It is not, however, his best. In *Demos*, which preceded it by three years (appearing in 1886), the cardinal error of the latter work is avoided. *Demos* may be esteemed an unqualified success. The canvas is enormous, the characters a multitude, but as the narrative progresses it becomes, instead of a story of socialism as Mr Gissing intended, the story of one woman. The figure of Adela Mutimer—a girl of race married by the wish of her family to an artisan—monopolises more and more the reader's anxiety, until at length the question of her happiness or misery dwarfs all else. Adela is Mr Gissing's finest and loveliest creation, and the great scene in which she compels her husband to desist from a crime that could never have been discovered is unmatched in sheer force and conviction by any other in his work. It is, in truth, masterly. *Demos* has another point of particular interest in that the plot turns chiefly upon the differences which separate class from class. Many novelists have dealt with the consequences of a marriage between persons of unequal birth, but none has brought to the consideration of the matter that wide and exact documentary knowledge of caste and that broad outlook which mark Mr Gissing's conception. His philosophy seems to be that social distinctions have a profounder influence upon the general human destiny than is commonly thought. The tendency of men of wide sympathies among all grades is to insist on a fundamental similarity underlying the superficial dissimilarity of those grades; but Mr Gissing by no means accepts the idealistic theory that the rank is but the guinea stamp and a man's a man for a' that. He may almost be said to be obsessed by social distinctions; he is sensitive to the most delicate *nuances* of them; and it would seem that this man, so free from the slightest trace of snobbishness, would reply, if asked what life had taught him: 'The importance of social distinctions.' Listen to this about Adela Mutimer and her husband:

> He was not of her class, nor of her world; only by a violent wrenching *of the laws of nature* had they come together. She had spent years in trying to convince herself that . . . only an unworthy prejudice parted class from class. One moment of true insight was worth all her theorising on abstract principles. To be her equal this man must be born again.

Here is the spirit which informs the whole of Mr Gissing's work. It crops out again and again in unexpected places. It is always with him. Yet he shows no aristocratic bias whatever: he holds an even balance. If he has a weakness it is for the class 'created by the mania of education,' consisting 'of those unhappy men and women whom unspeakable cruelty endows with intellectual needs while refusing them the sustenance they are taught to crave.' The words are the words of the Rev. Mr Wyvern in *Demos*, but there are many indications that they express the thoughts of George Gissing. If his heart is hardened, it is against the commercial class . . . the supremely maleficent. They hold us at their mercy, and their mercy is nought. Monstrously hypocritical, they cry for progress when they mean increased opportunities of swelling their own purses at the expense of those they employ and of those they serve; vulgar to the core, they exalt a gross ideal of wellbeing, and stink in their prosperity. The very poor and the uncommercial wealthy alike suffer from them; the intellect of the country is poisoned by their influence.

Mr Gissing has often been called a pessimist: he is not one. He paints in dark tints, for he has looked on the sum of life, those few who have done this are well aware that life is dark; Clerkenwell is larger than Piccadilly, and Islington than Brixton. The average artist stays at home in life; Mr Gissing has travelled far, and brought back strange, troublous tales full of disturbing beauty; and he suffers for his originality. The audience is incredulous, and objects to anything which disturbs, even beauty. But Mr Gissing is not thereby constituted a pessimist; he is merely a man who can gaze without blinking; he is not soured; he has, I fancy, the marvellous belief that happiness is evenly distributed among the human race; he may sup on horrors, but he can digest them without a headache the next morning; he is neither gay nor melancholy, but just sober, calm, and proud against the gods; he has seen, he knows, he is unmoved; he defeats fate by accepting it. . . . This may be grievous, but is not pessimism. The thoughtless may say that it is scarcely diverting to read after dinner; but those who can bear to reflect upon the large issues of life will be grateful that an artist of Mr Gissing's calibre has used his art so finely for the inculcation of fortitude and serenity.

136. Jane H. Findlater, 'The Slum Movement in Fiction', *National Review*

May 1900, 447–54

Jane Helen Findlater (1866–1946) was a minor Scottish novelist who occupied the literary scene from the mid-1890s to the early 1920s. Her sister Mary (1865–?) also wrote novels and some stories were a co-production. The present article of which only a short extract is reproduced here was reprinted in *Stones from a Glass House*, by Jane Helen Findlater, (James Nisbet, London, 1904, 65–88). According to the author, the slum and the slum-dweller have been treated in at least five different ways: as a moral lesson, as a social problem, as an object of pity and terror, as a gladiatorial show or as an amusing study. Besides Gissing the article deals with Dickens, Richard Whiteing, Kipling, Arthur Morrison, Somerset Maugham and Pett Ridge.

It was in 1890 that Gissing brought out that extraordinary book *The Nether World*. This man would seem to have been in hell. Other men crawl to the edges of the pit and look over at the poor devils that writhe in its flames—he has come up out of it, and now, like the man of the parable, would testify to his brethren lest they too enter that place of torment! As no one else has ever done—I would almost venture to prophesy as no one else will ever do—Gissing writes the tragedy of Want. It is not written with brutality, and that is why it is so terrible and undeniable. This bald incisiveness beggars the vulgar exaggeration of other writers who by overstating their case deprive it of effect. As we know that every word is true—this is hunger, and heaven help the hungry!—this despair indeed—not the glib despair which the novelists deal in by the page, but that mortal disease of the mind which is past all cure. Gissing has no gospel of hope to offer his readers. 'Work as you will,' he says, 'there is no chance of a new and better world until the old be utterly destroyed.' The 'lower orders' are, to his seeing, one huge tragedy: '*A Great Review of the People. Since man came into being did the world ever exhibit a sadder spectacle?*' he enquires. There is no more awful fate by his showing than life in the East End. He writes of travelling 'across miles of a city of the damned, such as thought never conceived before this age of ours; stopping at stations which it crushes the heart to think should be the destination of any mortal,' and in this key of almost insane depression *The Nether World* continues from its first page to its last—a terrible book, but one that is deserving of more fame than it ever got.

This was in 1890. In 1892–3 Kipling published his first (and last) slum story, *Badalia Herodsfoot*, and the school of pity was fairly ushered in. Because, where Kipling goes it is safe to say that many follow. I do not mean to say that a man as clever as Arthur Morrison copies from anyone—it is only another instance of the provoking fact that where one clever mind strikes out an idea for itself another is almost certain to be striking out the same idea at the same moment—it is a sort of mental contagion which has to be reckoned with in literary matters. However that may be, Kipling published *Badalia* in 1893, and Arthur Morrison published *Tales of Mean Streets* in 1894, and the same spirit and temper ran through them both—humanity at its lowest social ebb, yet exhibiting brilliant, wandering lights of soul. We are well versed in the types now, after seven years' instruction in them—they came as a surprise to us in 1894. Henceforward Arthur Morrison became the most prominent exponent of the School of Pity. His *Child of the Jago* continued the tradition at its best, and exhibited the 'relentless' modern method very plainly. For here is the story of a boy of originally good, tender instincts, who, like Oliver Twist, is in training for a thief. Does innocence triumph here? Is there a measure of hope and comfort at the close? Impossible. Dicky Perrot—the 'Oliver' of our day—has never a chance from the cradle to the grave, and the grave has to swallow him up at the end, because it is probably the only way left for the author to take with his character. It is a book of searching interest and great power, of horrible detail, but withal of deepest pity. We all read the books of Arthur Morrison, and shuddered over them; some people were apparently reading them without the shudder, for in 1897 appeared yet another recruit to the ranks of slum literature, who, in slang phrase, seemed to be determined to 'go one better' than his predecessors. The brutal school had appeared. 'The vituperative vernacular of the nether world,' says Mr Gissing, 'has never yet been exhibited by typography, and *presumably never will be*'—but this prophecy was too sanguine; nine years later Mr Gissing would not have been so sure about what typography might be called upon to produce. There is practically now no limit to what may be done in this way—unless, indeed, we are forced to start a censor of novels as well as of plays. *Liza of Lambeth* saw the light in 1897. It is a story of brutal frankness and sickening import, and has, alas, too surely set a fashion for this sort of thing.

OUR FRIEND THE CHARLATAN

May 1901

137. Unsigned review, *Manchester Guardian*

5 June 1901, 3

Mr George Gissing's new book, *Our Friend the Charlatan*, is an interesting if not very cheering contribution to his studies in modern civilisation. The hero, if so he may be called, is no Colossus of the type of Quisante or Harry Richmond's father—a compound, in varying proportions but ever inseparable, of genius and vulgarity. From the very opening we can place Mr Dyce Lashmar among those intelligent weaklings, dupes of their own facile enthusiasm, who embark on the sea of life in the frail craft of borrowed opinions with the sail of a glib tongue and practically no ballast of humour or honest emotion. Mr Gissing's skill lies less in the creation of such a figure than in the fact that he has brought it within the range of our sympathies, has made of it, indeed, an embodiment of certain faculties which most honest people can recognise in embryo in their own breasts. The other characters, moreover, instead of being subordinated to the task of showing off Mr Lashmar by contrast or affinity, are worked out with equal care, and some, to our mind, even more successfully. Old Lady Ogram, for instance, the wealthy and childless despot on whom Lashmar depends for his political success, though hardly a very original or subtle character, is drawn with an incisiveness and precision of detail which make her figure a masterpiece in its way. Born of the people, she carries into her acquired sphere of wealth and influence the more primitive instincts of her class, unchastened by the influences of modern society. Of the three younger women, May Tomalin is a fainter copy of her grand-aunt's temper without the strength that comes of an assured position; Iris Woolstan, the young widow who believes in Lashmar to the end, belongs to the more commonplace feminine. Indeed it is not the least poignant of those ironies of destiny which await the 'Charlatan' that in his day of stress and humiliation he should find his last and only refuge in the unreasoning and hysterical side of womankind which he has always denounced. Constance Bride, Lady Ogram's secretary, though more interesting than her two rivals in Lashmar's regard, stands out less distinctly. We are not clear how long her early weakness for Lashmar survives or whether it dies an easy death. In the final scene Constance appears entirely sincere and self-reliant; her clear brain has pierced the shallow sophistries of the man and left him defenceless; but it would be interesting to know over what corpses of tenderness or passion the woman has reached this altitude. Two other figures deserve notice as illustrating those phases of thought which in the world of fiction Mr Gissing has made specially his own. Lord Dymchurch, an impecunious peer of thoughtful mind and honourable feeling, suffers from the conflict, so often seen, between generous popular sympathies and a hatred of those grosser aids to success frequently demanded in the working of even the best 'causes'. The quietism towards which this counterbalancing of forces tends would seem to represent not unfairly Mr Gissing's ideal in life. But it is spoilt in the case of Lord Dymchurch by an uneasy conscience telling him of his futility, until at last he finds satisfaction in the culture of the soil and the belief that to live as an honest man is work meet for the highest. More pathetic is the figure of Lashmar's father, the old Vicar, who also feels the world to be out of joint and himself unfitted to set it right. The Sermon on the Mount he holds to be 'the best' we have, but he cannot look forward to its triumph over the world in his own or indeed in any future day. The story, as such, is cleverly contrived up to the climax of Lady Ogram's death, which practically closes it, though some indications as to the actors' future lives prolong the volume for a few chapters. This sudden and awkward drop in the interest points to some fault of construction. But it is not as a drama that the book has its value. Of passion and action it contains singularly little, and the marvel rather is that Mr Gissing should hold us so long under the spell of what might be called a study of life from the intellectual standpoint, one-sided, not in the sense of a narrow exclusiveness, but of a mental preoccupation. Viewed thus the book is full of interest; full too—whether we like it or not—of suggestion, of warning, and surely also, in spite of its scepticism, of an unspoken protest for right and humanity.

138. Unsigned review, *Pall Mall Gazette*

6 June 1901, 4

This review was originally entitled 'Bio-Sociological'.

Although he is beyond question an original creation, Dyce Lashmar's main characteristics are so well known to us that Mr Gissing is justified in styling him 'Our Friend the Charlatan.' As a plagiarist, he is but a type of the all too common plagiarist, who habitually parades as his own the thoughts and theories he has stolen from others. Like many who are possessed of the fatal gift of fluency, he was charmed by his own eloquence into the belief that the matter of his conversation was even more valuable than the manner. Like many men of vast ambition and superficial cleverness, he hated work. In the readiness with which he persuades himself that he is acting from an unselfish and even noble motive, when his one desire is to win the praise and favourable opinion of others, he is but one of a crowd. Though his belief in himself was supreme, self-sufficiency and self-conceit equalling and excelling his, and with as little excuse for their existence, are too frequently met. It is in the deft combination of these qualities in one character, in their inter-play and in the resulting development of moral disease, that Mr Gissing is thoroughly original and even amazingly skilful.

When we first make Dyce's acquaintance, he has been taking a severe course of Izoulet, and has assimilated that brilliant and ingenious scientist's theory of sociology, that in this, as in biology, the ruling principle is that of association with the evolution of a directing power. Having assimilated Izoulet's views, he begins to propound them as his own, avoiding Fabian lecturers and economic zealots, and calculating correctly enough that the average man will know no more of Izoulet than he himself of Chinese. As he begins to practise his deception, he is not without qualms of conscience. For instance, it is with great difficulty that he is persuaded to accept a loan from his friend and admirer, Iris Woolstan, although he is in sore need of pecuniary help; but at the finish, notwithstanding that she is some years his senior and that he has for her no feeling akin, however remotely, to love, he eagerly marries her for the sake of the six hundred a year which she tells him is her own. His utter degradation is strikingly revealed by his brutality when he learns that the six hundred a year has dwindled to two, and although on recovering himself, he remarks, with his incorrigible optimism, 'Who knows? It may be the real beginning of my career', the reader sees him far on the road that leads to perdition.

However much it must be doubted whether any political charlatan or many statesmen of these latter days have half the knowledge of economics which Dyce possessed, the exaggeration is artistic and effective, and must therefore be pardoned; and it cannot lessen the pleasure with which we note that in depicting this character Mr Gissing has called all his forces to his aid, and has thus been able to give us a nearly perfect example of finished portraiture. Indeed, throughout the story the character drawing displays to us Mr Gissing at his best. It is true that the reader will wish that the people he is introduced to were not quite so unpleasant, and that the writer's satire was a whit less biting and poignant.

Mr Gissing has often pleased us more than in *Our Friend the Charlatan*, he has often moved us more, be it in the way of tears or laughter, but surely he has never written a book in which the psychology was truer or the purpose more manful and more honest.

139. Henry Harland, *Daily Chronicle*

10 June 1901, 3

Henry Harland (1861–1905) was an American novelist who became editor of the *Yellow Book* in 1894. He is best remembered for his romance *The Cardinal's Snuff-Box* (1900).

But he *wasn't* a charlatan, this Dyce Lashmar, whose character the four hundred and odd pages, the incidents and incidental personages, of Mr Gissing's book are intended to illustrate. Or, if he *was* a charlatan, then so are Tom, Dick and Harry, for the most part, charlatans; then so are all men charlatans, who would fain be taken at a higher valuation than their true one.

Not, for an instant, that we love Dyce Lashmar; on the contrary, we heartily share Mr Gissing's own dislike of him. With Mr Gissing we deplore his little triumphs, we rejoice in his humiliations, we gleefully watch his strugglings and his writhings. But Dyce is too frequent, one had almost said too cheap, a type to be distinguished by so exclusive and so suggestive a term as charlatan. He is, rather, the average man of a certain class. He is the average man of a certain class, subjected to the microscope and the scalpel of a terribly skilful and relentless demonstrator.

Dyce Lashmar is vain, and, in a small, vain way, ambitious. He craves notice, and admiration; he would make his way, he would have a career, he would rise, he would shine. But his opportunities are narrow, and his equipment—though, to do him justice, he no doubt genuinely deceives himself about it—is of the lightest. Anyhow, he tries to make Lady Ogram, Constance Bride, and the Liberal electors of Hollingford accept him as 'the coming man'. He is pretentious, and somewhat pompous. He pushes, and he poses. He poses as brilliant, profound, original; as disinterested; as a man of high aims. He is a glib talker; he has read a book or two, picked up an idea or two; and he retails these ideas in talk without announcing them as secondhand, without giving chapter and verse. Moreover, he is vaguely, feebly unscrupulous; he will tell little lies; he will do mean little things; he is paltry, vulgar, a bit of a sneak, a bit of a coward. He is willing to accept petticoat protection, and he grovels, by turns, before the petticoat whose protection for the time being seems to promise most—before Lady Ogram, that splendidly ogre-like old woman, before Constance, before May and Iris. All this is very contemptible. But—charlatan? Charlatans are made of sterner stuff. Dyce is merely an aspiring little humbug.

The deuce of it is—he fails, he comes to grief, he is found out. But say he had succeeded; say he had not been found out, had won his seat in Parliament, and married a lady with a fortune; then—charlatan, indeed? Dyce Lashmar, the rising young M.P.? *Allons donc*; it is malice that calls him so. If Dyce had succeeded, he would have loomed, in the world's eye, as a clever and enviable fellow, one who had known how to 'get on', one who would probably 'go far'. Mercy upon us, if we should eliminate from Parliament—nay (*chacun a son métier*) if we should eliminate from our own little Brotherhood of Scribblers all the Dyce Lashmars we could point at, would there not be a famous thinning of the ranks? But if we should contemn all our Dyces as charlatans, we should have to invent a new and stronger substantive to describe such really flagrant quacks as—alas, it is libellous to name names.

No, Dyce isn't a charlatan; he is merely rather a usual, half-conscious humbug, with an eager eye to the main chance. He is very much what average human nature is; very much what most of us can see, in some degree, potential if not actual, when we look honestly into—our neighbour's houses. Only Dyce happens to have fallen under the microscope and scalpel of a terribly able and relentless demonstrator. Of Mr Gissing's extraordinary ability there can be no question; of his ability, his sincerity, the authenticity of his aim and motive. Here is a book every movement of which is thought and felt and wrought. Of how many contemporary works of fiction could the same be said? And it is wrought in a manner that compels attention—you will hardly put the book down till you have finished it. And then—you will not send it to Booksellers' Row. You will place it on your shelves, above the shelf on which you have placed Zola, below the shelf on which you have placed Turgéneff—but near Turgéneff, in the same corner of your book-room.

140. Unsigned review, *Literature*

15 June 1901, viii, 519

It is almost impossible, in dealing with Mr George Gissing's last book, *Our Friend the Charlatan* to avoid a comparison with *The Egoist* of Mr Meredith. In many points Dyce Lashmar (who is the charlatan of Mr Gissing's novel) bears a strong resemblance to the great Sir Willoughby. True, he is not quite the gentleman, and the head of the house of Patterne, with all his faults, was always well-bred; he has no sense of chivalry whatsoever, whereas the baronet preserved some touch of the true feeling even in the most adverse circumstances. But both men laboured under a magnified sense of their own importance; both, curiously enough, found themselves engaged at different times—once at the same time—to three several ladies; and both ended by marrying, as a last resort, the woman whom they had at first ruthlessly sacrificed for the sake of greater attractions. These coincidences are sufficiently remarkable to make some comparison almost inevitable, and it is a comparison from which very few of our novelists could emerge unscathed. Mr Gissing's work is always interesting; he writes far better than the mob of novelists, and his psychology is wonderfully subtle and acute. Dyce Lashmar is drawn with great power and delicacy; as a character study he is hardly inferior to the Egoist himself, and, indeed, the characters, one and all, with the possible exception of Mrs Toplady, are unmistakably living men and women. But the story has not the breadth and spacious atmosphere of Mr Meredith's masterpiece—there is no Crossjay, and no Clara Middleton. This, of course, is to try the book by a lofty standard, but Mr Gissing invites comparison with the best. His work is very good indeed; his insight and observation very much above the ordinary. He has probed Dyce Lashmar relentlessly—perhaps almost too relentlessly—until we are all but forced to feel pity for a fellow mortal whose soul is so laid bare to the world. And, after all, was the conveyance of that 'bio-sociological' theory (from the French of M. Jean Izoulet) so very terrible a matter? Miss Constance Bride, to our thinking, was a little hard on the unhappy man about this business, in spite of the plausibility with which he argued his case. And Miss Bride herself, for some little time, seems to accept Lashmar at his own valuation. We confess that this very sensible young lady rather fails to carry conviction during her engagement. But the book is good enough to read without halting to examine flaws. The characterization is as strong as we get from any writer in these days, and the example of Dyce Lashmar may well be useful to young men with a tendency towards plagiarism and Parliamentary life.

141. Unsigned review, *Academy*

22 June 1901, lx, 535–6

This is the concluding part of a review article which was devoted to *By the Ionian Sea* and *Our Friend the Charlatan*. See No. 144.

It is pleasant to observe that this book indicates a kind of second spring in Mr Gissing's talent. We do not think that his recent novels, *The Whirlpool*, *The Town Traveller*, and *The Crown of Life* (especially the last) have approached the excellence of the best work. *Our Friend the Charlatan* does approach that excellence. On an elaborate background of social and political life, in the circles where money is less scarce than spirit, and busyness than philanthropy, he presents a disturbing portrait of a man who endeavoured to succeed by wit rather than honesty, and did not completely fail. We say 'disturbing,' because in Dyce Lashmar, Parliamentary candidate, every reader must see a partial portrait of himself—as in Sir Willoughby Patterne, egoist. One's resemblance to Dyce Lashmar, with his poses, his ingenious defences of lying and imposture, his rank selfishness, his miserable cowardice, is really annoying. There are other characters of equal veracity, notably those of Lady Ogram, the wealthy and venerable 'patroness,' and Constance Bride, her secretary. Miss Bride is indeed a child of her age: had she lived in London she would have belonged to the Fabian Society while scorning the members thereof. And Mr Gissing has included the woman of fashion and the tendril-woman. After the hero, the strength of the book issues from its women. The disposition of the plot is more satisfactory than anything that Mr Gissing has accomplished for some years. He has contrived to centralise the interest instead of diffusing it.

As one reads *Our Friend the Charlatan* one thinks constantly, somehow, of the author's nights at Cosenza. 'One goes to bed early at Cosenza; the night air is dangerous . . . darkness brings with it no sort of pastime. I did manage to read a little in my miserable room by an antique lamp, but the effort was dispiriting; better to lie in the dark and think of Goth and Roman.' (*By the Ionian Sea*) One thinks of him resignedly thinking, all alone in the dark. There is something 'jolly fine' about that, as William Morris used to say.

142. Unsigned review, *The Times*

29 June 1901, 5

Mr George Gissing's outlook has certainly changed since the days when he painted 'The Nether World' in such gloomy colours, and gave Demos so bad a character, and satirized with a bitter pen the methods that lead to success in New-Grub street. He is more inclined to smile now than to gnash his teeth at the pitiful ironies of life. In a recent book he even laughed outright—or, at any rate, constrained his readers to laughter. Therefore, although *Our Friend the Charlatan* is rather like Mr Gissing's earlier work in essence it is 'like, but oh! how different.' There is as much satire, but it is amused and not indignant satire. He still shoots folly as it flies, still holds up to ridicule the peculiar vices and absurdities of the hour; but he does it with the calm curiosity of a scientific investigator, and no longer in the 'woe! woe!' vein of a minor prophet. Mr Gissing is still, too, it may be noted, more interested in ideas than in men and women. Look back upon the many hours that have been profitably spent over his books and you will find that the characters you remember best are personifications of some idea rather than human beings drawn for their own sake. Take our friend the 'Charlatan', Dyce Lashmar, for example. He represents the idea of a man of shallow ability who would sacrifice everything to material success, and who makes his way (for a time) by adopting as his own an application of biological formulae to social problems which he has found in a little-read French author. Lashmar is so clever in his shallow way that now and then Mr Gissing almost wins sympathy for him. This is partly accounted for, however, by the unsympathetic nature of the people amongst whom Lashmar moves. They are all interesting, and some of them are amusing, but they all suggest that Mr Gissing divides natures into two classes—the likeable and weak, and the unsympathetic and strong. The character of Lady Ogram shows signs of the influence of Dickens, of whom Mr Gissing has been writing a good deal lately. Would it be unfair to say that she reminds us of Miss Havisham? Lady Ogram's secretary and niece, who embody respectively the ideas of independent strength and dependent weakness in woman, are both good specimens, if we may adopt an entomological idiom; and Lashmar's adventures towards a profitable marriage and his attempt to play several fish at once are very entertaining. One naturally thinks of Sir Willoughby Patterne and of Stensgard in *The League of Youth*, but Lashmar is a good third. The story is well told and very well worth reading; but we must wait longer yet, it seems, for the work of genius which Mr Gissing seems always to be just on the point of giving us.

143. Unsigned review, *New York Tribune Illustrated Supplement*

14 July 1901, 11–12

This review was called 'The Portrait of a Man "excelling in speciousness" '.

The title of a novel is seldom so well invented and so conclusively justified by the book it introduces as in the case of Mr Gissing's latest story. It is not simply that Dyce Lashmar is most accurately described by the word 'charlatan'. It is that he is emphatically 'our friend', a type so familiar in modern life that this book seems no less a work of portraiture than a work of fiction. It does not give us, we hasten to add, in the faintest sense a photographic portrait. Readers of Mr Gissing's sometimes depressing but always powerful studies of lower middle class society in England—and we like to believe that he has the wide public that he deserves—are well aware of the fact that with him realism means much more than the slavish reproduction of exactly what he sees before him. It has always meant—and never more thoroughly than in *Our Friend the Charlatan*—a remarkably clear vision of the things that lie below the surface of existing conditions, and a mercilessly truthful interpretation of them. No matter how much energy he may expend on the correct description of material facts, it is plain that what he is chiefly driving at is the discovery of the spiritual elements they symbolize or conceal. Dyce Lashmar has the touch of universality upon him. Probing into the innermost recesses of his character, and exposing all that they contain of dross and weakness with a skill that is all the more effective because it is exercised neither compassionately nor coldly, but with a kind of robust impartiality, Mr Gissing fulfills in the most wholesome manner the duty of the novelist to 'hold the mirror up to nature'. He knows how numerous are the men who, looking with sincerity into that mirror of his, could not help but recognise some at least of their own traits; but never for a moment does he take sides, never does he seem glad or sad, to grow mournful with regret or to chuckle with the amusement of the cynic. Simply the truth, because he loves it, is, we imagine, his goal.

His way of exhibiting it in this book is to take his hero through a series of experiences, covering but a short period of time, yet amply sufficient to test the man's character at every point and to disclose its very ingredient. Dyce Lashmar is a young Englishman, the son of a country clergyman, whose egotism, joined to a light-headed enthusiasm for the shallower political nostrums of his time, leads him far from his father's straight and narrow path into the facile highway of a glib materialism. Mr Gissing, who is well abreast of contemporary thought, is not indifferent to the weight of heredity. He indicates in those comparatively few pages which he devotes to the elder Lashmar and his wife a morbidly critical disposition on the part of the vicar, and an almost vulgar triviality in his helpmeet, that may fairly be taken to explain some of the defects in their son. But this acute student of human nature knows better than to seek in the sins of the forefathers for a mawkishly charitable absolution of the sins of the living generation. The vicar and his wife, after all, abide by the better rule. Dyce lets things go. 'His ideal was honesty, even as he had a strong prejudice in favor of personal cleanliness. But occasionally he shirked the cold tub; and, in the same way, he found it difficult at times to tell the truth.' He had glimpses of the light, but it is always easier to gaze toward it, talk about it, make plans for reaching it, than to gird up one's loins and get into close relations with it at all hazards.

Dyce had his ideal of manly independence; it annoyed him that circumstances made the noble line of conduct so difficult. He believed himself strong, virile, yet so often it happened that he was constrained to act in what seemed rather a feeble and undignified way. But, after all, it was temporary; the day of his emancipation from paltry necessities would surely come, and all the great qualities latent in him would have ample scope.

The explanation of his willingness to wait for his emancipation as though for a gift of the gods, instead of achieving it for himself, resides not alone in his laziness, but in the very essence of his own character.

Among the many possibilities of life which lie before a young and intelligent man, one never presented itself to Dyce Lashmar's meditation. The thought of simply earning his living by conscientious and useful work, satisfied with whatever distinction might come to him in the natural order of things, had never entered his mind. Every project he formed took for granted his unlaborious pre-eminence in a toiling world. His natural superiority to mankind at large was, with Dyce, axiomatic. If he used any other tone about himself, he affected it merely to elicit contradiction; if in a depressed mood he thought otherwise, the reflection was so at conflict with his nature that it served only to strengthen his self-esteem when the shadow had passed.

The function of such a man is necessarily parasitical and there is nothing surprising about the spectacle Dyce Lashmar presents when, with the true instinct of his breed, he discourses of the political ideas on which he means to base his career without hinting of the source from which he has derived them.

He did not care to dwell upon the fact that the views he had been summarizing were all taken straight from a book which he had just read. He had thoroughly adopted them; they exactly suited his temper and his mind—always premising that he spoke as one of those called by his author *l'Elite*, and by no means as one of *la Foule*. Indeed, he was beginning to forget that he was not himself the originator of the bio-sociological theory of civilization.

From sponging on the brains of others to sponging on their pockets or their influence in the world is only a very short step. Naturally, Dyce takes it, and, just as naturally, the friends to whom he turns for encouragement and help—always disguising the ultimate selfishness of his aims by high sounding periods on his ambition to serve mankind—are practically all women. We would like to dwell upon his adventures. Miss Constance Bride, the friend of his youth, is a woman with much strength of character, very interestingly displayed by Mr Gissing, and the part she plays in Lashmar's life is full of amusement and thought for the reader. Lady Ogram, the eccentric old philanthropist whose secretary she is, takes up 'our friend', and wonderful indeed are the results. May Tomalin, a young relative of Lady Ogram's, is decidedly a type, inviting more than a line of commemoration, and it is hard to pass over Mrs Iris Woolstan and Mrs Toplady with the same brevity. All these women have a hand in the career of the charlatan, and every one of them, like the ingenious Dyce, is alive. That is our reason for leaving the reader to make acquaintance with them for himself. *Our Friend the Charlatan* is scarcely to be called a narrative. It is life itself, life so truthfully and vividly presented on the printed page, with such completeness, such a rounded perfection that to detach any of its episodes from the whole is to be unjust to the author and to spoil the reader's pleasure. The latter may wonder if there is much pleasure to be found, really, in the portrait of a charlatan. He may not like charlatans. Neither do we. But we advise the reader to buy this book, and, as the reader knows, we always wish him well.

BY THE IONIAN SEA

June 1901

144. Unsigned review, *Academy*

22 June 1901, lx, 535–6

See headnote to No. 141.

[The omitted opening paragraph laments, in a period of abundant travel literature, the failure of novelists to write about their travels. Henry James and Paul Bourget are regarded as 'exceptions of the first class' to this general contemporary phenomenon.]

By the Ionian Sea is a little book of high and modest merit. Not the least part of its merit is that it illuminates the personality of its author. In writing a record of travel the author very literally gives himself away. He may produce many novels, and still withhold much of himself; but let him narrate his experience of a bad hotel, and you have him; let him fall ill in that hotel, and he is revealed like an intimate acquaintance. It is a common saying among lion hunters that novelists seldom correspond with their novels. 'Well, I expected quite a different sort of man!' That is the phrase. But novelists must of necessity correspond with their travel books; it could not be otherwise. *By the Ionian Sea* is really a valuable aid to the appreciation of the author of *The Nether World*. It increases one's respect for him. Mr Gissing went by steamer from Naples to Paola, thence over the mountains to Cosenza, thence by train to Taranto. At Taranto began the journey proper—southward along the length of the coastwise line from Taranto to Reggio, by the malarial Ionian shore. Mr Gissing selected Apulia, Basilicata, and Calabria, not because they are perhaps the least inviting and least known districts of Italy, but because they are Graecia Magna, and saturated with classical tradition. He wandered by the banks of the Crathis; he 'lunched at Sybaris'; he was very ill at Croton. This student of industrial and suburban London is steeped in classic and post-classic literature. We learn that on a Devonshire holiday he took with him two folios of Cassiodorus—and read them.

[An extract from ch. i, 'From Naples', follows.]

The civilisation whose middle strata he has so faithfully, with such fine, sympathetic melancholy, portrayed—that civilisation Mr Gissing contemns. As a traveller he loses no opportunity of exposing its pretensions. Praising the Calabrian pottery, he says:

> There must be great good in a people which has preserved this need of beauty through ages of servitude and suffering. Compare such domestic utensils—these oil-jugs and water-jars—with those in the house of an English labourer. Is it really so certain that all virtues of race dwell with those who can rest amid the ugly and know it not for ugliness? ['The Grave of Alaric', ch. iii.]

Again: 'It is better to die in a hovel by the Ionian Sea than in a cellar at Shoreditch.' (But, after all, O author of *Demos*, is it?) Sometimes his bias against modern England seems to amount to a rancour, and certainly tempts him to be inconsistent. For example, in describing the general talk at the café at Catanzaro, he says:

> They did, in fact, converse—a word rarely applicable to English talk under such conditions; . . . they exchanged genuine thoughts, reasoned lucidly on the surface of abstract subjects; . . . the choice of topics, and the mode of viewing them, was distinctly intellectual. Phrases often occurred such as have no equivalent on the lips of everyday people in our own country. ['The Breezy Height,' ch. xiii.]

Yet, he asserts: 'In all the South of Italy money is the one subject of men's thoughts; intellectual life does not exist.' ['Cotrone', ch. vii.] But it has been proved that one may love and hate the same object, and Mr Gissing is doubtless equally sincere in his love and his hatred of England. He has the rare faculty of loving without illusions. This faculty governs also his attitude towards Italy, a country which he sees steadily, and sees it whole. He never idealises, and seldom generalises. He has the virtues of the true traveller. His sensibility is so mature. He knows so much, and is so willing to learn. He has seen so much, and so broadly, that he is now a seer. He has an instinct for picking the one suggestive detail out of a mass of trivialities. He can be Roman in

Rome, and take what comes. He can 'put yourself in his place.' He is, above all, human. In his journeying, what occupies him first is man, not art nor relics. His sketch of the female drudge at the hotel at Cotrone is characteristic.

[An extract from 'Children of the Soil', ch. x, follows.]

Here is no rushing from the station to the cathedral and museum. An exquisite book like Bourget's *Sensations d'Italie* seems curiously lackadaisical, aloof, artificial, and 'precious' after *By the Ionian Sea*, which is quite equal to it in elegance, refinement, and learning. Bourget sees little in Taranto save the deathbed of Choderlos de Laclos, author of *Les Liaisons Dangereuses*, and is moved to a wonderful analysis of de Laclos' genius. But how remote! Contrast Bourget's disdainful and abrupt verdict on Catanzaro—'*Les brutes à face humaine . . . ville boueuse . . .*,' &c.—with Mr Gissing's intimate and charming picture of Catanzaro's social life. And when it comes to connecting humanity with art and history, Mr Gissing is magnificently equal to the occasion. The delicate and fine musings of Bourget show nothing comparable to this passage on the fishermen of Taranto.

[An extract from 'Taranto', ch. iv, follows.]

A book of this quality, a frank revelation of a strong and sensitive soul, cannot but increase the sanction of Mr Gissing's novels. The picture of the painter completes the picture itself. His novels give little overt sign, beyond the pervading classical severity of their art, that their author had not devoted a full life to the contemplation of a single epoch and the sordid, insular aspects of that epoch. We know now that his aesthetic and moral pre-occupations are of the widest. We know that the painter of modern squalor, sadness, gloom, and heroic futility, has had eyes continually on other scenes and other ages. We know that if he has chosen to deal artistically with much that is ugly and repulsive, it was from no morbid inability to discern a more obvious and a more sublime beauty than dwells in the domesticity of London. Mr Gissing has painted what he could. He did not choose, but the Fate which chose for him chose well. Who that admires his books could wish that they had been different from what they are? Who would stoop to defend them against the foolish charge of 'depressing'? If these novels depress, we like to be depressed; we are happy when depressed. Mr Gissing might put on his title-pages three lines from Wordsworth's 'Michael'—an excessively 'depressing' poem, but also one of the greatest in the English tongue:—

> Therefore, although it be a history
> Homely and rude, I will relate the same
> For the delight of a few natural hearts.

145. Unsigned review, *Literature*

29 June 1901, viii, 557

A perusal of Mr George Gissing's volume *By the Ionian Sea* naturally suggests a comparison thereof with the chapters of *Sensations d'Italie*, which deal with Magna Graecia. Bourget's wanderings were considerably more widely extended and led him over more unfrequented and inaccessible ways than those attempted by Mr Gissing, whose travels, indeed, amounted to nothing more ambitious than a steamboat voyage from Naples to Paola, a rough drive to Cosenza, a pilgrimage to the legendary tomb of Alaric, a railway journey along the coast as far as Taranto and then back to Reggio, at the 'toe of the boot.' But, in spite of the more ambitious scale of M. Bourget's work—of the extraordinary interest clinging to places like Oria and Lucera (unvisited by Mr Gissing) with their memories of the splendid State maintained by Frederic II and of his Saracen hordes, of the opportunity thus given for copious and apposite literary illustration—it certainly does not surpass in charm the volume before us. We doubt, indeed, whether M. Bourget equals Mr Gissing in just appreciation of the episodes of travel, in comprehensive insight as to their attractions and in sympathetic delineation. Mr Gissing possesses that happily constituted nature which is stirred by impetuous desire to visit in the flesh those famous spots whose names are linked with romantic and momentous events in the world's history. Perhaps the wisest are those who carefully plan their voyage to this and that renowned city, and wait and wait till Anno Domini tells them their day for such expeditions is past. Whether the more adventurous spirits who put their wishes into action choose the better part is a question which each one must answer according to his own temperament. In the final sentence of his book Mr Gissing sighs for a life in which he might 'wander endlessly amid the silence of the ancient world, to-day and all its sounds forgotten.' These words were written when his Calabrian wanderings were over, when he was once more in comparative comfort and civilization at Reggio, and they are almost certainly infected with the spirit of forgiveness of past discomforts which possesses us when we are happy in the consciousness that we have done with them for good and all, and shall behold their ugly faces no more. This, however, is a matter which concerns Mr Gissing himself; it was certainly a stroke of good luck for his readers that he did not listen to the gloomy vaticinations of his friends in Naples when he spoke of his journey to Calabria, or allow himself to be dissuaded therefrom. Every appreciative reader knows how to suffer with his author, to weep sympathetic tears over the troubles which beset travellers in the few by-ways now left in the world; and we, as we acknowledge Mr Gissing's vicarious sacrifice on behalf of arm-chair explorers, can assure him that the result achieved by him has not been purchased too dearly, even though the price paid included the horrors of the inn at Squillace and the attack of fever at Cotrone.

Mr Gissing has been known as a novel writer and a critic. We are not sure that he has not equal claims to distinction as a classical scholar. Certainly we doubt whether he has ever been so completely successful as in the issue of *By the Ionian Sea*. He possesses to perfection the gift of being able to bring before the reader graphic and living pictures of the scenes he views and the people he meets, and to tint these pictures with exactly the due amount of subjective emotion, so that we find ourselves affected by the spell of stony wilderness, of gloomy forest, of mouldering walls, or of glittering sea, just as he himself was affected. Over Mr Gissing's pages the reader can never forget that he is in the presence of a writer of subtle perception and exquisite literary gift. The book is full of masterpieces of prose writing—the dream which haunted his fevered brain at Cotrone, the discourse of the young men at the *caffè* at Catanzaro, and the miraculous story of the friar bound for Loreto, though, perhaps, the choicest of all is the apologia of his volume in the opening chapter. It is a legitimate cause of congratulation that Mr Gissing has demonstrated the ability of Englishmen to hold their own with the best of other lands in this particular field of literature; all the more because of the facile assent given by some of us to the claims of certain talented foreign writers to a foremost place. We hope that those who have been so generously appreciative of Bourget and Loti will condescend to read Mr Gissing. We have said enough of the book itself; it is simply a delight, and with its beautiful illustrations and its excellent print and paper it is as well set as such a gem deserves.

146. Unsigned review, *Guardian* (London)

31 July 1901, lvi (2), 1056

Mr Gissing's new book comes as a most delightful surprise to his friends. We knew him as a student of the dreary streets of outer London, and we realised that in him we had a charming writer of stories, an expert novelist, whose latest book was sure of a ready welcome; but there was hardly one of us who was able to appreciate Mr Gissing that had anticipated a book of travel such as this one from his pen.

To those of us who delight when reading the speeches in Parliament to come across in the weary waste of words a classical allusion, or, better still, a phrase in a classical tongue that takes up the whole question in its own epigrammatic manner, and who regret that the time is so fast passing away when such delights occur, it is a peculiar pleasure to take up this book and find oneself once more back again upon old familiar classical ground.

There are few travellers who visit the more southern parts of Italy, very few who go beyond Naples at all, and of those fewer still who wander off into the districts of the Basilicata and of Calabria, in search of the places mentioned in ancient Greek history, and who carry with them much of the student's love and of the classical reader's enthusiasm.

Here in this volume we find Mr Gissing going off to Southern Italy full of classic lore, visiting places that the tourist never sees, but that to him have all delight mainly because they formed part of Magna

Graecia and are replete with classical tradition. He journeys to Sybaris, to Tarentum, to Metapontum; his search is for the river Galaesus, for the ruins of Croton, for the city of Siris; and it is all done with a most contagious enthusiasm, refreshingly delightful in the present day. He has painted a fascinating picture of the towns and villages of that out-of-the-way part of the country; he has described their people with dainty and appreciative language; and the vivid life of the book, its tender sympathy with the people of the district, its clear analysis of their characters, and its glowing descriptions of the country side, have impressed us greatly.

One of the special features of this book is the evidence it gives us of the author himself, the way in which he lays himself bare for our enjoyment, and allows us to come into close contact with his own sympathies, and to travel with him in intimate friendship. His illness is described to us in words of such deep feeling that we eagerly wait around his bed and watch in his deserted room, waiting till he should gain strength and journey to Catanzaro, and then we rejoice with him in the glorious mountain air, and delight in the new vigour that comes to refresh his fever-stricken frame. He takes us up to the dreary town of Squillace, and we search with him for the home of Cassiodorus, where he rested in his old age and lived his monastic life; and then we visit together the caves which the old writer used as his fish preserves, and so we go on till we reach Reggio, and our only complaint is that our friend does not take us over to Sicily there to continue the wanderings so happily begun.

It is very seldom that a writer is found who is so strangely and deeply moved by the sonorous words of Latin and Greek that so move Mr Gissing. The words at Reggio that are so often hardly noticed—'Circumlegentes devenimus Rhegium'—that are to be found over the portal of the cathedral, stir his deepest feelings and he dwells pleasantly upon the words, the vivid fact, as he calls it, recorded in the music of the ancient tongue. He has murmured the words 'Tu es petrus, et super hanc petram aedificabo ecclesiam meam' in Rome even as we have often done, and he finds a noble solemnity and an historic significance in them such as no other tongue has the power to supply. Would that with him we could visit the Argiletum, could stroll along the Via Appia, or could rest at Paestum, or see the ruins of Selinus or Segesta, as no more fascinating guide could be desired!

Has he also been the artist to his own pages? We are told on the title-page that the coloured illustrations, which are admirable, are the work of Leo de Littrow, but nothing is said as to who did the equally charming ones in black and white, and in default of other evidence we are fain to ascribe them to the author, and to find in them fresh cause for praise. The printers and the publishers have united to produce this work in charming form, and altogether the book is one of the finest poetic feeling, the truest sympathy, and the clearest analysis that have ever been combined by the scholarly student with the description of travel in southern climes.

147. Morley Roberts, 'George Gissing', *Literature*

20 July 1901, ix, 52

On 11 May 1901, this journal had begun to publish a series of 'Literature Portraits'. Gissing was No. 11, following Hardy and Pierre Loti, preceding Stevenson and Hugo. He read the article in manuscript and in proof, and thanked Roberts heartily; he suggested a few stylistic alterations, and the substitution, at the end of the fourth paragraph, of the phrase 'the Renaissance scholar' for 'Cassiodorus'. However, despite his assertions of expansive gratitude, Gissing had small faith in Roberts's capacity to appreciate his work.

The literary descent of the second-rate is rarely in doubt. There can be no obscurity as to the parentage of the imitators or school fictionists who flood the markets with tolerable reading matter at six shillings per volume. But their individual descent, whether it be legitimate or illegitimate, has no interest for the critic. He is content to view them as he weighs them, in the mass, when he estimates common tendencies only. It is a different thing when a new development or a striking personality compels his attention and individual interest. Among those who have by slow, by very slow, degrees compelled this particular interest Mr George Gissing stands in a high and solitary place. Mr Gissing belongs to no school, certainly not to any English school. The sincerest form of flattery in any admirer cannot imitate and cannot even caricature him. There is truly nothing visible to copy. His essence lies in a bent, in a mood of mind, not by any means in any subject, even though his satiric dissection of what he has called 'the ignobly decent' showed his strength, and, indirectly, his inner character. His very repugnance to his early subjects led him to choose them. He declared what he wished the world to be by showing that it possessed every conceivable opposite to his desire.

Those who have read all his work and are interested in origins may have noted with particular pleasure that in *Isabel Clarendon* he showed an instinctive affinity for the lucid and subtle Tourgeneff. There is perhaps no more intensely depressing book in the entire English language than this short novel. Its last three chapters are of unsurpassable gloom, not because of any outward tragedy, but because of the utter futility of the man depicted. The hero's desire reached to the stars. But he was not able to steal or take so much as a farthing rushlight. Not even Demetri Roudine, that futile essence of futility, equals this, his literary child of bitter unable ambitions.

So much is certain, Tourgeneff moved what Zola had really failed to stir in Mr Gissing. For he was never a Zolaist even at his worst. No man without a style could have influenced him for more than a time. Even Balzac, fecund and insatiable, had, it is possible, no more true power over him. For Balzac, though his constructions were often imaginary and his perspectives a gigantic imposture, was truly a constructor and architectonic, even if barbarous. And construction is obviously alien from Mr Gissing's mind. He needs no elaborate architecture to do his thinking in. He would have been contented with the Porch.

Now, and at last, the critic has been given an opportunity of understanding the bent and nature of this author. In *By the Ionian Sea* Mr Gissing has not only put the coping stone to his reputation, but he has also declared himself. Able novelist as he is—and Tourgeneff, Flaubert, and Dostoieffsky would not have disdained his companionship—he is by nature a scholar, a man of the cloister, though not conventual. His pessimism is the natural pessimism of misplacement. Nowadays scholars, as he would understand them, do not properly exist. The learned have beome specialists; there is no broad culture possible to them. His ideal is the Renaissance scholar. Without any doubt he must be an admirer of Rabelais.

Perhaps his greatest book is *Born in Exile*. To say it is a masterpiece is for once not to misuse the word. It is intense, deeply psychological, moving, true. 'L'anatomia presuppone il cadavere,' says Gabriele D'Annunzio, but *Born in Exile* is intolerable and wonderful vivisection. Yet men do bleed and live, and Godwin Peak, the chief character of this book, bleeds but will not die. He is born out of the leisured class, and resents it with incredible bitterness, with a bitterness unparalleled in literature, but not unparalleled in life. This bitterness leads to a life of falsehood; he denies all his intellectual convictions for the sake of all his senses. The conflict with circumstances becomes a mental conflict. He is inevitably discovered; he returns into exile and dies. The story is simple and, without detail, unmoving. Yet Godwin Peak is an idealist. No greater idealist lives amongst those who look at once to Socialism or to Anarchism to cure all human social diseases. The warm human nature that loves all beautiful things is his, and he is given nothing. Unlike Kingcote in *Isabel Clarendon*, he attempts to take them. But the end is the same. By his very essence Mr Gissing is no revolutionist. Like many who are not, his nature gives the keenest incitement to revolution in those who are of kindred mind, yet given more to action, more to hope. There are two ways of hating modern civilization. Mr Gissing is an inverted idealist. He looks back. It is the more hopeless, the more impossibly vain.

In such a nature, displayed as it must be in all true literature, for men to read who can read, it would be idle to seek for that form of humour which inevitably compels laughter. It has been said untruly enough that Mr Gissing has no humour. It is quite possible that those who say it are even capable of missing his irony. His humour is of the subtler kind, it delights in the less sudden contrasts. He does not blow the tin horn of farce. It is utterly alien from his nature.

Nevertheless it remains true that the general effect of his writings is distinctly not merely amusing. But since the most characteristic and the most important part of his work done hitherto has dealt with those young men who, while fairly bred and well-educated, are without money, the themes themselves cannot be comic. The martyrdom of capable minds by their environment in the Devil's Twilight between the Dan of Camberwell and the Beersheba of Camden Town is for ever tragic. It was reserved for Mr Gissing to treat the middle class as a subject of serious study. And he has treated it as a pathologist whose business is not cure, and not even hope. If he has gone beyond this scientific method it is when he becomes a satirist of no mean order.

To such a literary intelligence, informed with all the learning of the past to which he leans, his style is essentially the man and his own. For the greater part it is lucid rather than sparkling; clear if not cold; with a subdued rhythm the result of much Latin and more Greek. For the metres of the Greek tragedies have always inspired him with their noble rhythms. Though he is often cold, especially in sustained irony, he can rise to heights of passionate description; he has a sense of luxury that here and there tinges his words with Tyrian purple—in spite of all his sense of restraint, which is more marked than in any living writer.

It is perhaps only those who, perceiving the essential evanescence of fiction, regard it as literary work almost certainly wasted who will wonder that a writer of this stamp gives himself to it at all. But while that commercialism exists which Mr Gissing obviously abhors, as much as he abhors the smoky skies beneath which it flourishes, there is no other practicable method for the man of letters to attain to speech. Perhaps few novelists see so clearly that fiction as a form of art is truly diagnostic of a disordered, if not necessarily dissatisfied, form of civilization. To him the idylls of Theocritus, of Moschus; the simpler tragedy; the natural woes or joys of him who ploughs the soil or works at the wine press, are the fitting themes of art.

It is, it must be, alien from the nature of the man who was so delighted by the wasted and solitary borders of the Ionian Sea to supply the market with novels, which, to be sold at all, have more or less to comply with the rigid formulae which take no note of the artist's mind, and deny him, especially in England, true liberty of subject or true spontaneity. But even so, Mr Gissing has done something, and not a little, to maintain a high standard in workmanship and in sincerity of purpose. He has dared to show his dissatisfaction with things as they are; he has declared that the writer is not necessarily on a level with the music-hall singer; of malice aforethought he has denied that the purposes of art are those of amusement only. He has appealed, not to the idle and to the foolish, not to the fashionable mob, but to a more august tribunal.

148. Unsigned, 'The Nobodies', *Academy*

8 March 1902, lxii, 247–8

The nobodies have come greatly to the front in literature of late years. In life they remain nobodies, in literature they are somebodies with a following. By the nobodies we mean the people who are nobody in the ordinary sense of the word: the crowd, the suburbs—or, say, nine-tenths of the population of London. Of course there are as many ranks among the nobodies as among the somebodies, and there is no need to seek close distinctions. Nor need a man be a nobody because he lives among and after the manner of nobodies. Whatever definition you adopt, whatever degrees of insignificance you recognise, the fact remains that the world is mainly peopled by nobodies—by men and women who can be lumped together by the hundred thousand. It cannot be otherwise. It is the nobodies who make the world and whose condition is the real condition of society. They bear that relation to the somebodies which the soil bears to the trees. The men who have moved the world have done it by applying themselves to this central estate of humanity. Below it the volcanic fires sleep. Narrow this to our own day and its literature, and what do we find? Ibsen, Zola, Sudermann, Gorki, and to a large extent Tolstoy, have applied themselves to the study of the common person. Their characters are chiefly, nay almost wholly, drawn from the nobodies. This is because no other ranks would have served their purpose. Their whole business was with the common clay of humanity, not with its infrequent gems. But the restriction is a testimony.

Outside the ring of giants there has been a growing tendency among novelists to enter this curiously neglected field. The good novel of Parliament, Diplomacy, and Mayfair can never be anything but important and entertaining; its existence is not for a moment threatened. But the novel of the Suburbs, the Train to the City, and the Mean Street has taken lasting root. Dickens did enormous service by introducing it with a cuisine and condiments which made it palatable. By discovering the grotesque elements in the characters and ways of nobodies he awakened the attention to the normal and, in the end, far more significant psychology of the ordinary person. Nothing but a real and fairly wide awakening of such an interest can account for the existence of Mr George Gissing's interpretations of the lower middle classes. By their patience and volume, and by their whole fibre, they require such an explanation. Mr Gissing's least sympathetic critics admit that he stands apart and that he stands for something. His case is this: that with widely different feelings and talents, he has followed Dickens into the study of every-day London. His method, if you can call that a method which is essentially individual, is so different from Dickens's as to seem its reaction. Dickens went into the crowd a great emotional interpreter of its surface oddities, pathos, and variety; whereas Mr Gissing has gone into it as a keenly interested but merciless searcher into its mind, habits, and tastes. Harold Biffen's enthusiasm for the 'ignobly decent' as material for literature (in *New Grub Street*) is really a sort of *locus classicus*, and we have always thought that it is Mr Gissing's clearest indication of his own task. 'What I really aim at,' says Biffen to Edwin Reardon, in his garret off the Tottenham Court Road,

'is an absolute realism in the sphere of the ignobly decent. The field, as I understand it, is a new one; I don't know any writer who has treated ordinary vulgar life with fidelity and seriousness. Zola writes deliberate tragedies; his vilest figures become heroic from the place they fill in a strongly imagined drama. I want to deal with the essentially unheroic, with the day-to-day life of that vast majority of people who are at the mercy of paltry circumstance. Dickens understood the possibility of such work, but his tendency to melodrama on the one hand, and his humour on the other, prevented him from thinking of it . . . The result will be something unutterably tedious. Precisely. That is the stamp of the ignobly decent life. If it were anything *but* tedious it would be untrue. I speak, of course, of its effect upon the ordinary reader.'

The ordinary reader has, we fear, endorsed Biffen's prediction. Mr Gissing's novels divide critics and almost separate friends. Of two men who commonly agree fairly well in literary judgments, one finds him depressing, almost insufferable, the other is keenly expectant of everything he writes. The controversy must be postponed. But Harold Biffen goes on to give an example of the 'ignobly decent' which, apart from controversy, it will be useful to quote:—

'As I came along by Regent's Park half an hour ago a man and a girl were walking close in front of me, love-making; I passed them slowly and heard a good deal of their talk—it was part of the situation that they should pay no heed to a stranger's proximity. Now, such a love-scene as that has absolutely never been written down; it was entirely decent, yet vulgar to the *n*th power. Dickens would have made it ludicrous—a gross injustice. Other men who deal with low-class life would perhaps have preferred idealising it—an absurdity. For my own part, I am going to reproduce it verbatim, without one single impertinent suggestion of any point of view save that of honest reporting.'

Here Mr Gissing allows Biffen to put his idea of the Novel of the Nobodies more crudely than he would put it in his own person. 'Honest reporting' is assuredly not one-fourth of Mr Gissing's art.

[Here follows a discussion of Lucas Galen's *Hospital Sketches* to demonstrate the greater degree of 'absolute realism in the sphere of the ignobly decent' and 'honest reporting' in this writer's work.]

Harold Biffen's phrase 'ignobly decent' is, of course, a narrow one. It would be boorish to use it in connection with many ranks of the great world of nobodies. Above the ignobly decent section of society is a population which might be described as the undistinguished decent, and above these a vast stratum which no one would think of eulogising in terms of decency. Higher still there is a section which Samuel Richardson would have described as 'not ungenteel.' And so on. Each stratum has in recent years obtained recognition in literature. . . .

Is it the destiny of the Novel, which has concerned itself with the Jews first, to deal also with the Gentiles; to gather in sphere after sphere of life, counting nothing common, following in the wake of the dusty, evolutionary pageant in which all Nobodies tend to become Somebodies?

149. Unsigned article, 'The Novel of Misery', *Quarterly Review*

October 1902, 391–414

The article, of which only an extract dealing with Gissing's work is reproduced, dealt with the following novels:

1. *Nell Horn, Le Termite, L'Impérieuse Bonté, La Charpente*: J.-H. Rosny, 1886–1900.
2. *Workers in the Dawn, The Unclassed, Demos, The Nether World*: George Gissing, 1880–9.
3. 'The Record of Badalia Herodsfoot' (in *Many Inventions*): Rudyard Kipling, 1893.
4. *Tales of Mean Streets, A Child of the Jago*: Arthur Morrison, 1894–6.
5. *Liza of Lambeth:* Somerset Maugham, 1897.
6. *East-End Idylls:* A. St John Adcock, 1897.
7. *Mord Em'ly:* W. Pett Ridge, 1898.
8. *Maggie:* Stephen Crane, 1896.
9. *Out of Mulberry Street*: Jacob August Riis, 1898.

Of all our novelists, Mr George Gissing has shown himself the most open to the influences of continental literature; but we doubt if even he, at the beginning of his career, set himself docilely to translate into English the last achievements of the realistic school of France. That they served as a slight impetus to his work is unquestionable, but he was too true an artist to be a mere imitator; and, even though he had in his youthful days a wish to equal their 'glorious effects of filth and outrage,' he had not the heart to do so. Some of the 'efflorescences' of his very early works no doubt hindered the appreciation of the original qualities which he exhibited, but they were merely passages of youthful braggadocio, and most of them have been omitted from later editions. His first novel, *Workers in the Dawn*, published in 1880, it would be unkind to criticise minutely. It was promising, but very immature. It shows what books influenced Mr Gissing when he was twenty-one years of age, more than what powers of observation he was to develop; for his characters are distinguished chiefly by the opinions which they are given to express concerning humanitarian matters and the conflicting theories of Comte and Schopenhauer.

In *The Unclassed*, published four years later, Mr Gissing made a great advance in the foundation of the novelist's art, in insight into human nature and experience of life. In spite of this, however, Mr Gissing still showed that he had yet to learn that the first quality of art was sincerity, and the second, in regard to his talent, moderation. Unfortunately he chose a very difficult and unpleasant subject, in the exposition of which all signs of his defects of insincerity and extravagance were intensified by the nature of the theme—a theme which only a man of genius, of the highest sincerity and self-restraint, had the right to attempt. The hero of the tale, Osmond Waymark, was, like Mr Gissing, a young novelist, whose first novel concerning the lower classes was not a success. To him are allotted the passages of braggadocio to which we have referred.

[A quotation from Bk III, ch. ix, follows.]

It is, in fact, this difficult and unpleasant subject [prostitution] that is dealt with in *The Unclassed*; but Mr Gissing's work is far from ranking with De Goncourt's *La Fille Elisa*. Instead of taking a low view of human nature, Mr Gissing, it seems to us, rated it too high. The story, in brief, is that of an unfortunate girl of strong and original disposition, who inherits, partly through her own obstinacy, her mother's calling, but who is redeemed by her love for the literary hero, Waymark. Their marriage, in circumstances of prosperity, ends the romance. In effect, the book is not unlike the *New Arabian Nights*. The figures resemble those in the late Mr R. L. Stevenson's tales by the manner in which they become acquainted with one another; but what in Stevenson was art was in Mr Gissing artlessness. Some of the characters are not realised, and in other cases their characterisation does not justify their actions. Abraham Woodcock, for example, is laboriously endowed with all the qualities of the general type of petty usurer—the analysis occupies six pages—and yet, towards the close of the book, he becomes a repentant and generous grandfather, who might have brought to a happy ending some Christmas story by Dickens.

As a matter of derivation, Mr Gissing, in his earlier essays in fiction, owed more to Dickens than to any realistic novelist. We say this in spite of the fact that many of the observations made by his hero might have appeared in the declaration of faith of some very young disciple of realism; for these passages, we think, represented not the result of Mr Gissing's own reflections, but the course of his 'reading.' Nevertheless, Mr Gissing did not imitate Dickens with the obsequiousness with which Mr George Moore, who began to write novels about the same time, imitated the French realists. The inspiration was indirect. Mr Gissing had not the master-faculty of the author of *Martin Chuzzlewit*, and he did not counterfeit it. But in studying the works of Dickens, he appears to have seen how much of the real gloom had been left out of the picture of the London populace; how much what was eccentric and humorous had been insisted upon, and how much what was joyless, and yet equally representative, had been omitted; and this darker and more unrelieved side of lower London life Mr Gissing determined to describe.

The result was seen in *The Nether World*, which appeared in 1889, and it justified the attempt, for the novel was impressive and original. Dealing mainly with the working-classes, however, the work contained neither any 'glorious effects of filth and outrage,' nor any realisation of a character of great nobility of soul, which, to paraphrase the saying of Renan quoted on the title-page, would vindicate the use by an artist of such effects. *The Nether World*, in fact, is hardly a correct title, as it is not a description of the lowest depths of London life. The hero, Sidney Kirkwood, is a working jeweller in a good position; Clara Hewett, whom he marries, is a girl of intellect and personality; and Jane Snowdon, whom he should have married, grows up into a kind, sensible, capable woman.

Yet for all this, *The Nether World* is one of the most depressing and powerful of the novels of misery. It is written in a spirit of despondency which affects one more keenly than all the outrageousness of the realistic school. The exceptional natures of the principal actors are fairly and sympathetically portrayed, only to intensify the hopelessness of their struggle to escape from the dull, mean, and yet respectable, condition of the working-classes. And it is also implied, unfairly, but skilfully, by means of secondary figures, that the picture is a representative one. Some of the characters are described as patient and tender-hearted; but this, it seems to us, is only done in order to show how useless their virtues are, how cunning, avarice, and cruelty, as personified in other characters, make all their efforts unavailing. Mr Gissing even went out of his way to make the creatures of his fancy unhappy. He was very unkind to Clara Hewett. She had obtained the part of the leading-lady in a touring company. A capable actress, waiting for an opportunity to reveal her power, her position was well assured; but, as she entered the theatre, an angry rival, by means of vitriol, disfigured her for life. Returning home, she renewed her acquaintance with Kirkwood, and covering her horrible face with a thick veil, she induced him to marry her, despite the fact that he was deeply in love with another woman. These incidents are as 'romantic,' to use Mr Gissing's word, as the idealism of *The Unclassed*. They are, however, of a piece with the misfortunes that overtake most of the other characters; and if these occurrences do not strike the reader as too improbable for belief, it is because of the skill by which Mr Gissing, in the story, sustains the atmosphere of wretchedness which they serve to intensify.

Yet the general sentiment of the novel is not so much pessimism as idealism in revolt. The author, with the intolerance of youth, was dissatisfied with the world as he found it, not because it was the worst of all possible worlds, but because it was not the best. His standpoint, we think, had become a purely personal one; and it was only by depicting in his hero and in the woman he marries two exceptional natures, discontented with their condition, that he was able to write so sincere and impressive a novel. Like Turgeniev's *Virgin Soil*, *The Nether World* has, in addition to the contexture of incident and characterisation, a social interest. As a picture of the lower classes we do not think it a fair one. Judging the proletariat from the standpoint of his own culture, Mr Gissing saw clearly all their defects, but overlooked many of their good qualities because he did not then share them. Most artists are able to endow the creatures of their imagination only with the powers which they possess or sympathise with; and the power which Mr Gissing lacked and did not appear to appreciate justly in others, was that exuberance of animal spirits of which, in literature, Dickens was the incarnation. A man of sensitive and refined nature, with little spontaneous gaiety, whose temperament is moulded as much by a reaction from mean and vulgar surroundings as by the direct stimulus of culture, is apt to foster a feeling of pitying contempt as a protection against the coarse, vigorous animal life around him. And although Mr Gissing, even in his earlier days, was too strong to give way wholly to this feeling, there still remained a mixture of pity and disgust in his descriptions of the populace. To picture with sympathy or gusto the diversions of a Bank-holiday crowd at the Crystal Palace, one must needs have the merry, kindly eye of a Dickens in selecting the picturesque details and overlooking the unseemly; or else that fierce delight of a Mérimée or a Rudyard Kipling in all the manifestations of the rude energy of life, which would enable one to forgive the accompanying vulgarity. With Mr Gissing a feeling of abhorrence and distant compassion effaced all other sensations, and his ironical description ends in an attack of the nerves. 'A great review of the people. Since man came into being did the world ever exhibit a sadder spectacle?'

It is not as a study of the lower classes that *The Nether World* resembles Turgeniev's novels. The Bank-holiday scenes, and the Peckovers, the Snowdons, and other subsidiary figures are not the essential part of the book. The real interest lies in Clara Hewett, and, more especially, in Sidney Kirkwood. Kirkwood, like Turgeniev's Bazaroff, is the study of a type. A good workman, but without the force of character or the power of mind which would enable him to rise far above his fellows, he had been made unhappy through being educated above his position. All the highest refinements of life, its social charm as well as its intellectual tastes, he had sufficient receptive capacity to esteem and hunger after, but not sufficient ability to acquire. He represents not an inconsiderable class of men, and a class that is increasing in number and in discontent. He is a product of a system of universal education which, instead of making technical instruction more thorough and more general, and thus replacing the obsolescent custom of apprenticeship, gives the more sensitive, and often the least powerful minds, intellectual needs that they will, for the most part, be unable to gratify.

In *Thyrza* and *Demos*, two earlier novels of Mr Gissing, there is the same forcible representation and gloom in dealing with the lower orders as in *The Nether World*; while the better classes, shown by way of contrast with their culture of mind and character, are described with an admiration so general that one can understand how it was that Mr Gissing, some years ago, saw more clearly the demerits than the merits of the rougher people. Mr Gissing's novels are in one respect a history of his opinions; and it is only fair to say that this merely reactionary admiration was soon replaced by a more critical view. In *The Whirlpool* and other later works the deficiencies of the cultivated world are observed with a maturity of power much in advance of the impressive but narrow conception underlying the earlier novels, which alone come within the scope of this article. Even *Thyrza*, the story of a disastrous attempt to introduce the faint sweetness and feeble light of culture, as a means of salvation, into a district of working people, must be passed over here.

Demos, on the other hand, is, like *The Nether World*, a striking study in what MM. Rosny would call the psychology of the English proletariat. In *Marc Fane*, MM. Rosny exposed the meaner side of French socialism, with the leaders intriguing against each other and against any recruit of ability who threatens their pre-eminence. In a work far superior in point of art, Mr Gissing gives us a subtle and interesting analysis of the vulgar and selfish side of British socialism. The defect of MM. Rosny's figures is that they are symbols, and, at times, merely speeches with a name; they represent ideas more than individuals. Mr Gissing, without the eloquent fervour and enthusiastic faith of the authors of *L'Impérieuse Bonté*, is a better novelist. His characters are, first of all, portraits of living beings, and only in a secondary way types; and this only because they have been selected as embodying typical qualities. For instance, Richard Mutimer, in *Demos*, is mainly interesting because of his energy and ambition, although, as a socialistic agitator, personifying some of the best attributes of the working-classes, he has also a representative value. Possessing a force of will that Mr Gissing's heroes often lack, he is analysed very clearly, and not always unsympathetically; and the manner in which his characterisation justifies his actions is a skilful piece of work. Our only regret is that Mr Gissing did not make the novel an equally convincing sociological study. He might have shown how a sincere and upright working-man, who held extremely one-sided ideas of socialism, was forced by his experiences as an employer of labour to see the other side of the question and relinquish the childish theory of the equality of men. Richard Mutimer is not sincere and upright. He is an ambitious egotist, wholly without natural refinement, who subtly changes his political creed when, by the death of a relative, he becomes himself an employer of labour. He is not a type of the man who rises by his own ability: he never would have risen; and the position of wealth and power which he by chance inherits is designed by Mr Gissing to show on a larger scale the essential vulgarity and selfishness of the agitator's nature.

All the characters of the novel are well realised, and one of them, Emma Vine, is a nobly-pathetic figure. In Mr Gissing's portraits of humble and patient sufferers there is never any excess of sensibility; in fact, he often seems to describe, in comparison with Coppée and Daudet, more the squalor than the pathos of their lot. In this instance, however, his restraint is more affecting than the tearfulness of the French writers. Emma Vine was a working-girl, whom Mutimer had engaged to marry, but whom, when he became rich, he cast off, leaving her not only in extreme anguish of mind, but in circumstances of increasing poverty and with increasing responsibilities towards the children of her drunken sister. Through all her troubles the girl remains silent, forbearing, and—this is art—natural. The reader of her story experiences that cleansing and ennobling emotion which is the effect of real tragedy. . . .

Mr Gissing, since his knowledge of life has increased, since his art has grown more objective, has written better novels than the earlier works which we have mentioned. He is the representative in English fiction of the development of the novel into a kind of criticism of some social movement, and he excels most of the living continental writers of this school by the greater complexity and individuality of his characterisation; but he has never described a more noble creature than Emma Vine.

It is one of the paradoxes of art that the sufferings of those born into misery are the least fit matter of a tragedy. It is easy to make them melodramatic, either in the sentimental or in the realistic manner; the reality of Mr Gissing's genius is shown by the fact that even in his earlier tales he did not often resort for effect to what R. L. Stevenson, in his essay on Victor Hugo, calls

> that sort of brutality, that useless insufferable violence to the feelings which is the last distinction between melodrama and tragedy.

FORSTER'S LIFE OF DICKENS

Abridged and revised by George Gissing
October 1902

---

150. Unsigned review, *Spectator*

18 October 1902, lxxxix, 576

Gissing disliked the reviewer's assertion that the book's interest would have been increased had an accounting been given of Dickens's total literary profits. He considered this 'an unworthy remark from such a paper' (letter to Bertz, 16 November 1902, *The Letters of George Gissing to Eduard Bertz*, p. 313).

Gissing's opinion was that there was far too much talk of money in relation to contemporary literature.

This abridgment is a good idea well carried out. Mr Gissing well says of Forster that 'he brought to the performance of this biography a sympathy which animates every page, and a judgment which never allowed his admiration of the man or of the writer to become excessive or uncritical.' It is impossible, indeed, to accept all Forster's critical judgments. Dickens's characters interest us, sometimes very greatly indeed; but it cannot be said that they are real people. 'Perfectly natural and intensely original' is the description of Sam Weller. That he is a great creation no one can doubt. The literature of humour has nothing finer; Sancho Panza himself, though more subtle, is not greater. But who can say that he is a real human type? However, this is not the place to criticise Dickens or Dickens's critics. It is enough to say that we are greatly obliged for this book. It is as readable a volume of its kind as we have seen for a long time. One thing would have added no little to its interest; that is an account, so far as it might have been possible to give it, of the total circulation of Dickens's works, and of his literary profits. He fared as have done other great writers, not receiving his due for his best work; but the balance must have been redressed. For *Edwin Drood* he received £7,500. The story of the circumstances under which he went through his last readings is very painful. No man ever disregarded plainer warnings of danger.

151. Unsigned review, *Daily Chronicle*

20 October 1902, 3

Gissing made the following comment in a letter to Henry Hick who sent him the paper containing this review: 'I fear you missed an amusing point in it. The reviewer greatly censures me for "dotting the i's" in my remarks on Dickens's failings, saying that Forster himself would not have spoken so plainly as I do in a certain passage—which he quotes. Now this passage is by Forster himself! See how reviewing is done' (letter of 26 October 1902).

Mr Gissing has done a heroic and probably a useful thing in making this abridgment of Forster's *Life of Dickens*. Useful, because all helps and incitements towards a knowledge of Dickens are to be welcomed; heroic, because the very act of abridgment must have cost the abridger incessant pangs. Nothing but a stoical sense of duty could have sustained Mr Gissing through his task of rejection and compression. He has reduced by two-thirds the bulk of Forster's work, and for all true lovers of Dickens he has reduced its delightfulness in very much the same proportion. Yet it was doubtless well that the thing should be done. 'In our days of little leisure,' says Mr Gissing in his preface, 'great biographies are too commonly "taken as read." Many who would like to make acquaintance with Forster's work are deterred by its length.' This is true; and it is better that such people should learn to know Dickens's personality in Mr Gissing's judicious pages than that they should remain unacquainted with it. But one chief use of the book, we hope and believe, will be to send readers on to the unabridged Forster. Mr Gissing has very wisely 'made it his guiding principle to preserve as much as possible of that autobiographic matter which Forster so largely drew upon.' Yet it is precisely here that he has had to make enormous sacrifices. He was bound, of course, to give the facts and dates, the skeleton, of Dickens's career; and so much space is occupied by these dry bones that the flesh of living utterance in which Forster had clothed them is sadly reduced. This process of maceration, however inevitable, must, we repeat, have been very distressing to so true a Dickens-lover as Mr Gissing has proved himself.

For example: Mr Gissing quotes a portion of Dickens's letter to Maclise announcing the death of his raven, the 'Grip' of *Barnaby Rudge*:—

Yesterday afternoon he was taken so much worse that I sent an express for the medical gentleman, who promptly attended, and administered a powerful dose of castor oil. Under the influence of this medicine he recovered so far that he was able at eight o'clock p.m. to bite Topping. His night was peaceful. This morning at daybreak he appeared better; received (agreeably to the doctor's directions) another dose of castor oil; and partook plentifully of some warm gruel, the flavour of which he appeared to relish. Towards eleven o'clock he was so much worse that it was found necessary to muffle the stable-knocker. At half-past, or thereabouts, he was heard talking to himself about the horse and Topping's family, and to add some incoherent expressions which are supposed to have been either a foreboding of his approaching dissolution or some wishes relative to the disposal of his little property—consisting chiefly of halfpence which he had buried in different parts of the garden. On the clock striking twelve he appeared slightly agitated; but he soon recovered, walked twice or thrice along the coach-house, stopped to bark, staggered, exclaimed *'Halloa, old girl!'* (his favourite expression), and died.

So far Mr Gissing reproduces this melancholy document; but here his sense of proportion bids him hold his hand. No doubt he is right; but what agony it must have cost him to suppress the sequel, which is in some ways (as Tony Lumpkin phrases it) 'the cream of the correspondence.' Dickens proceeds:—

He behaved throughout with a decent fortitude, equanimity, and self-possession, which cannot be too much admired. I deeply regret that being in ignorance of his danger I did not attend to receive his last instructions. Something remarkable about his eyes occasioned Topping to run for the doctor at twelve. When they returned together our friend was gone. It was the medical gentleman who informed me of his decease. He did it with great caution and delicacy, preparing me by the remark that 'a jolly queer start had taken place'; but the shock was very great notwithstanding.

Here our sense of proportion, in turns, bids us stop, though the remainder is equally affecting. And the case is typical. What Mr Gissing is forced, by his limits, to omit is often—one may say always—at least as delightful and significant as the passages he reprints. 'There's scarce a joy that he can give like those he takes away.' To choose a graver example, here is an invaluable glimpse into the psychology of character-creation, the omission of which Mr Gissing no doubt laments as much as we do. In discussing *Martin Chuzzlewit* Forster says:—

'As to the way,' he wrote to me of its two most prominent figures, as soon as all their capabilities were revealed to him, 'as to the way in which these characters have opened out, that is to me one of the most surprising processes of the mind in this sort of invention. Given what one knows, what one does not know springs up; and I am as absolutely certain of its being true as I am of the law of gravitation—if such a thing be possible, more so.'

Is not Dickens here describing the characteristic phenomenon which renders possible what we call realism in fiction? The widest observation must be fractional; but from the segments, of curves it presents, the man of genius knows how to complete the figure, accurately and convincingly.

Mr Gissing has further 'permitted himself to substitute here and there (by no means always) remarks of his own for Forster's critical comments on each of the novels.' This is on the face of it a very high-handed proceeding; but so fine is Mr Gissing's sympathy with Dickens that Forster himself, perhaps, would scarcely have resented it. One feels that what Mr Gissing says is probably very much what Forster might have said had he lived till to-day.

In treating of Dickens's character, Mr Gissing now and then 'dots i's' which Forster's piety had left undotted. We remember nothing in Forster quite so outspoken as these phrases, suggested by Dickens's complaints of 'the skeleton in his domestic closet': 'He became master of everything that might seem to be attainable in life before he had mastered what a man must undergo to be equal to its hardest trials'; and again, 'All this was characteristic of a man who never, since childhood, had known real hardship or misery, and who (to tell the blunt truth) had been a little spoilt by unprecedented success and praise.' Forster, probably, would not have demurred to the letter of these statements. They are literally true; but they are true only in so far as they are truisms, implying no more than that Dickens was not a faultless character. The far more essential truth, surely, is the opposite side of the medal. When we consider Dickens's origin and up-bringing; when we consider the miraculous suddenness and completeness of his success; and when we consider the high-strung and almost febrile sensitiveness which was the fundamental condition of his genius—the wonder surely is that he was so little spoilt, that his life, on the whole, was one of such eminent sanity and dignity. A struggling reporter at twenty-four, he was at twenty-nine the wonder and delight of two nations, receiving the freedoms of cities, and acclaimed like a royal prince or a victorious general. As Johnson said, speaking of Garrick's success: 'If all this had happened to me, I should have had a couple of fellows with long poles walking before me to knock down everybody that stood in the way. Consider, if all this had happened to Cibber or Quin, they'd have jumped over the moon.' The reader may substitute what names he pleases for Cibber and Quin, and apply the fable. Dickens *lived* so much more than other men, we could scarcely have marvelled if he had also erred more. But this his harshest critic cannot say of him. His character was not flawless, but it stood far above, rather than below, the average of human merit. Take it all round, his life is nothing less than another beneficent romance added to the incomparable benefaction of his works. If you have no time to read it in Forster, read it in Gissing.

152. Unsigned review, *Publishers' Circular*

27 December 1902, 690

It should be noted that the wording 'The Life of Dickens. Forster and Gissing' appearing on the spine and jacket of the book, and referred to by the reviewer, had not been devised, or desired, by Gissing.

Candidly, we do not like this unhallowed interference with our old favourites. If Mr Gissing, in whom we recognise an intelligent student of the novelist, wishes to write a life of Dickens, well and good, let him do so—we are certain we shall find much that is thoughtful and interesting in his work. But that he should graft himself, so to speak, on Forster, calmly taking all that was best in the work, and associating his own name with it, raises our wrath. On the front of the book now appear the words, 'The Life of Dickens. Forster and Gissing.' After this we may expect to see Boswell violently laid hold of and utilised to expound the views of some other writer. Our protest made, however, we are willing to admit that Mr Gissing has carried out his work of abridgment and revision with excellent judgment. This book is interesting, but it is no longer unadulterated Forster—that is our cause of complaint.

THE PRIVATE PAPERS OF HENRY RYECROFT

January 1903

153. W. L. Courtney, *Daily Telegraph*

4 February 1903, 12

William Leonard Courtney (1850–1928) was a well-known figure in the literary and journalistic world, a writer on philosophical, religious and literary questions. He edited the works of Captain Marryat and wrote a life of John Stuart Mill. When *The Private Papers of Henry Ryecroft* appeared he was the editor of the *Fortnightly Review*.

'Oh, golden book of spirit and of sense'—we know by whom that was said, and of what Théophile Gautier wrote his very clever and rather shocking romance, *Mademoiselle de Maupin*, half, it may be imagined, in youthful petulance and fun. Mr Swinburne gave him his generous praise in deadly earnest, and with no suggestion of humorous extravagance. However little it may be applicable to *Mademoiselle de Maupin*—which has both spirit and sense, but is hardly 'golden'—it is a pity that so good a phrase should be wasted. There is little enough of spirit, in the French meaning of 'esprit', in our literature, while as to 'sense'—the sphere which begins with our feelings, sensations, and emotions, and ends with passion and sensualism—we may be well content to leave both its more refined and its grosser forms to our neighbours. Yet I know not how better we can describe such a book as that which Mr George Gissing has just given us than by some adaptation to saner uses of Mr Swinburne's enthusiastic eulogy. There is a spirit pervading some books which lifts us into a clearer, purer air, not so much because of the subjects with which they deal as by reason of their manner, their style, their peculiar grace and inspiration. And if it be sense by which we see all the beauties of our world, and feel the serene influences of Nature acting upon us through a thousand channels—then let a book which can thus uplift us be given its full meed of praise as a 'golden book of spirit and of sense.' Often enough a work has to be noticed for the importance of its subject, or for the popular notoriety of its author. But Mr Gissing has never sought the bubble reputation, nor does he care for aught save what his literary art suggests to him—the art which he himself defines as 'an expression, satisfying and abiding, of the zest of life.' It is not, of course, life in its more gaudy aspects, in its resonant echoes, that we find in *The Private Papers of Henry Ryecroft.* The world, as most of us understand it, may go hang for all Mr Gissing cares. It is a subtler, more secret, more intimate life with which we are here concerned, the life of the seeing eye and the gently meditative mind, the reflection on a sensitive, cultivated consciousness of all that existence means and amounts to, in final philosophic estimate. The book is not interesting, in the stupid, commonplace way. Yet can there be anything of greater interest than the revelation of a distinct personality, when the man who thus pours forth his mind has something to say, and says it well?

We must accept 'Mr Henry Ryecroft' with the defects of his qualities; and it is certain that his idiosyncrasies will not be universally popular. He does not believe in a good deal of what we call modern progress; democracy, as such, he mistrusts; science he hates and fears with a mortal dread. The people of England were, in his opinion, much better and happier when they really lived in the country, and attended to their gardens, their cheeses, and their butter-makings, instead of crowding to towns and populating dreary and ugly flats. Nothing is quite so secure as to live under a benevolent despotism; nothing is more foolish than to attempt to get rid of Nature's marked distinctions of men into higher and lower. It is right for us to keep up our Constitutional monarchy; it is wrong for us to take turbid examples of Republicanism from our Colonies and the States. London is a great corrupter of men and things; the simple graces of innocence and honesty can only thrive in country lanes and old-fashioned farms, and close to sweet-smelling and flower-sprinkled hedgerows. In these respects, to which many others might be added, Mr Ryecroft is reactionary, for he is a born recluse, and when he at last, through a sudden gift of fortune, became independent, he shook from his feet the dust of metropolitan thoroughfares and hid himself in Devonshire.

But he is a hundred miles from priggishness and pedantry. He is a lover of good English beer, he knows the taste of the vintages of France and Italy, he thinks vegetarianism a forlorn and pathetic creed. Moreover, he likes English cooking, and laments the gradual extinction of the old round of beef. He defends his nation through thick and thin, and he will not hear our men called hypocrites and our women prudes. On hypocrisy, indeed, he has some very characteristic paragraphs. The real hypocrite is Tartuffe, by conviction an Atheist and a sensualist; your ordinary Englishman is very far removed from that frame of mind, or else Mr Pecksniff would not be so English. Our vice is rather pharisaism, self-righteousness.

'We are essentially an Old Testament people; Christianity has never entered into our soul; we see ourselves as the Chosen, and by no effort of spiritual aspiration can attain unto humility. In this there is nothing hypocritic. The blatant upstart who builds a church, lays out his money in that way not merely to win social consideration; in his curious little soul he believes (so far as he can believe in anything) that what he has done is pleasing to God and beneficial to mankind. . . . His religion, strictly defined, is an ineradicable belief in his own religiousness.'

Or, again, as to the charge levelled by foreigners against our women that they are prudes:

'It is said by observers among ourselves that the prudish habit of mind is dying out, and this is looked upon as a satisfactory thing, as a sign of healthy emancipation. If by prude be meant a secretly vicious person who affects an excessive decorum, by all means let the prude disappear, even at the cost of some shamelessness. If, on the other hand, a prude is one who, living a decent life, cultivates, either by bent or principle, a somewhat extreme delicacy of thought and speech with regard to elementary facts of human nature, then I say that this is most emphatically a fault in the right direction, and I have no desire to see its prevalence diminish. . . . We who know Englishwomen by the experience of a lifetime are well aware that their careful choice of language betokens, far more often than not, a corresponding delicacy of mind.'

Bravo, Mr Ryecroft! We have not many people nowadays who care so little whether they are called Puritans or not as you in your defence of English delicacy. Our author is what we complimentarily style an individualist, or, speaking more roughly, a selfish man. He likes living by himself, and loves to surround himself with his own modest household gods. All the fretful fever of politics and of national expansion, the tyranny of a scientific age, the slowly-evolving forces which make for democracy, or possibly Socialism, are for him as though they had no existence. He has his little garden and his cottage, his little corner of existence which smiles at him. The heathen may rage, and the nations devise a vain thing, but it concerns him not. The hot breath of the world passes him by and never scorches his cheek. He is happy in his independence and solitude, free from ambition and care. But, because he is entirely amiable and tender-hearted, I think he is a little sorry for those who have to bear the labour and heat of the day; and his pity is fortunately devoid of condescension. He probably knows in his heart that if everyone adopted his gospel the world would incontinently stop, and Galileo's great discovery be reversed. Meanwhile, he is pleasant and soothing to read, and when he talks about literature he is quite irresistible. Out of many passages I will choose but one, which I cannot deny myself the pleasure of quoting, especially as it proves in another way the author's immense pride and glory in being an Englishman.

[An extract concluding Summer XXVII follows.]

There is Mr Ryecroft at his best and most lovable, a literary student without a trace of pedantry, a man whose style shows no sign of the precious or the affected.

154. Unsigned review, *The Times Literary Supplement*

6 February 1903, 38–9

Mr George Gissing is a realist, although he does not belong to that popular school of realists in fiction of whom it may be said that their books would be merely dull but for their truth—and it is their truth which makes them dreadful. Mr Gissing's work is at once too sincere and too personal ever to be dull. The theory of life which he expresses is a sombre theory—it is reasonable, and painful, and hopeless. He is the champion, or rather he is the spokesman, of the dumb and the disinherited. His characters move in an atmosphere of care, and cruel effort, and perplexity. The lack of money, the lack of ease and security, the tragedy of sacrificed forces, the more sordid tragedy of daily want forever dog the footsteps of these unoffending and doomed modern men and women. We see them born to undergo every cramping and degrading condition of those who work for their bread in the crowded loneliness of great cities. And if, for a little, Mr Gissing's personages are allowed to escape from that mean Hell of mean houses which represents 'London' to the very poor—if their author introduces us to suburban life, or even to the life of country towns, it is only to show us the members of a more educated class starving for a more intellectual form of nourishment and suffering from a keener sense of deprivation. Joylessness and Labour possess in turn the world of Mr Gissing's imagination; but for all that it is a world which belongs to himself; which he grasps and understands and often sets before us with truly admirable and sober virility. Soberness, strength, an impeccable honesty; the unswerving, almost fatalistic, acceptance of the hardest facts, a deep, painful, vital sense of the brotherhood of our bewildered humanity; and the most masculine expression of pathos to be found in any contemporary English novelist—that brief, inexpressive, poignant pity for the individual, which can yet accept his pain as a necessary part of life—these are all characteristics of Mr Gissing. His style is plain, and clear, and forcible—unillumined by any sense of plastic beauty or any liberating throb of romance. He is curiously undramatic. He never appears to see situations as a whole, or in a series of pictures. His climaxes are all reached—and they are reached—by the accumulation of scores upon scores of direct, patient, and honest observations. Mr Gissing reminds us of Balzac in his methods of cumulative power; he is like Balzac in his disregard of the charm of words—the use of language as a fine art. Yet, take Mr Gissing at his best, and Balzac, with a hundred times more vitality, a hundred thousand times more imagination and genius, has never built more solidly.

Mr Gissing does not love London, but he knows it. In a dozen volumes he has given us a picture of the great stony-hearted city of unremitting toil, which is neither splendid nor complete, but which presents the thwarted average life of the average thwarted man with a force and a precision which cannot fail to command recognition. For Mr Gissing is never common, never glib, and never conventional.

What is stranger than this, he writes of the most painful facts and he is never brutal. His very sobriety and plainness of speech save him from cynicism. Possibly his style is not brilliant enough to be cruel; but the serious, sober respect for the exact limits of the fact, carried to this degree, is a literary quality rare enough to atone for much missing brilliancy. Mr Gissing may not amuse or excite his reader; he will always convince him. In this man's work we are never aware of that love of the phrase which underlines the hideous and dramatic side of life; we are not shown these men and women of the East-end silhouetted against a red background of savagery and horror, as in some of Mr Morrison's books, and notably in Rudyard Kipling's *Badalia.* Mr Gissing's treatment of these themes is more like the work of some old Dutch painter; it is to conscientiousness, to effort, and to truth that he owes his sober successes.

But as Sainte Beuve has written (and Alfred de Musset has repeated it in a noble set of verses) there exists in each man's heart 'un poète mort jeune et dont il se souvient.' In Mr Gissing's latest volume, *The Private Papers of Henry Ryecroft*, it would seem as if, at last, we had come upon traces of this dead and unforgotten poet. This book professes to be a collection of reflections and personal reminiscences, written in the Devonshire country, by a man of fifty-four. 'Like other mortals he had lived and laboured; like other mortals he has entered into his rest,' says Mr Gissing in the preface which contains his biographical sketch of the man he prefers to describe as his dead friend. Ryecroft, we are told, began life under the sternest conditions. Miserably poor, in failing health, he earned an insufficient pittance by long and strenuous effort:—

> Naturally a man of independent and rather scornful outlook, he had suffered much from defeated ambition, from disillusions of many kinds, from subjection to grim necessity. . . . He did a great deal of mere hack work; he reviewed, he translated, he wrote articles; at long intervals a volume appeared under his name. There were times, I have no doubt, when bitterness took hold upon him . . . but on the whole he earned his living very much as other men do, taking the day's toil as a matter of course, rarely grumbling over it. . . . It was a bitter thought that after so long and hard a struggle with unkindly circumstance he might end his life as one of the defeated. . . .

But, in this instance, at least, Mr Gissing did relent. After fifty years of London, Henry Ryecroft becomes the possessor of an unexpected life legacy of three hundred pounds a year. That he does not die in the very hour of this dazzling release from slavery, that Mr Gissing allows him four more years in which to taste the exquisite peace of rest, and cessation from toil, and security, is indeed something to be grateful for.

For Ryecroft loves the country with the passionate, the minute, the allusive, the sophisticated love which is only possible in the exile, the weary dweller in great cities, the man whose jaded feet have known too long

each chartered street,
Near where the chartered Thames doth flow.

This little book is the record of the Emancipation of the Literary Slave. . . .

[Various extracts, contrasting the passionate awareness of nature with 'the ink-stained world', follow.]

This book, we have said, may well stand for Mr Gissing's fullest expression of the poetry within him; the confessions of that mysterious poet who dies young and who is unforgotten. And how melancholy it all is!—how well written, how well felt, how well realized, and how infinitely joyless. Not even in Devon lanes and in high summer, can Henry Ryecroft forget that world where it is ever the man's bitter daily need—his poverty and not his will—that consents. The effect of this book upon any sympathetic reader holds the most vivid compliment to Mr Gissing's careful art and skill. It is undoubtedly a book destined to command a small, but very ardent, following. In its way, Mr Gissing has never written anything more remarkable. His cumulative method to which we alluded has never been used to better purpose. Yet, in the end, Henry Ryecroft is a character study rather than a character. Negation and self-suppression are undoubtedly necessary elements of life under modern conditions. But great art has never yet sprung from negation or suppression. Here we have the image of a man released from average and oppressive conditions, but we have not in Henry Ryecroft the final and authoritative type of such a man. Every detail carries conviction; the figure of Mr Gissing's hero is *documenté*; it is solid; it is sincere; only never for one moment is it alive and independent of all documents. Compare this conception of a scholar, a philosopher, a calm and melancholy contemplator of other men's action to that other contemplator and scholar and philosopher, M. Emile Bergeret. It has become the fashion, within the last two or three years, to speak of Mr Gissing as of a master; but this, which in many ways is his best work, strikes us as a *tour de force* of authenticity, never of revelation.

155. Unsigned review, *Athenaeum*

21 February 1903, 234

According to Gabrielle Fleury, Gissing was incensed by this dishonest review in which the critic applied to him what he had written of Ryecroft: 'It is the most treacherous and malicious way I have ever known of attacking an author, to seize the opportunity of running down his books in praising one, and to make him say that he ought not to have written them' (unpublished letter to Morley Roberts, 21 September 1904, Berg Collection).

The interest in Mr Gissing's latest work will largely be due to the natural assumption that a good deal of it is autobiography. *The Private Papers of Henry Ryecroft* appeared serially, if we mistake not, under the title 'An Author at Grass,' which very pleasantly describes the book. Henry Ryecroft, according to the author's preface, was a struggling literary man who had lived in Grub Street for thirty years; but at the age of fifty a small legacy enabled him to retire, and spend his declining years in Devon. Freed from the necessity of hack work, Ryecroft turned to record his impressions in a journal, and these papers are divided into the four seasons by his supposititious editor. Any one who is acquainted with Mr Gissing's novels will not be surprised to find that the life of London and the struggle for existence there are regarded by him with the distaste and horror due to the drabness of the one and the hopelessness of the other. Mr Gissing has always been an authority not only on Grub Street, but also on sundry phases of lower life in the metropolis. He has faithfully represented these in many volumes, but always from one point of view. What lends the special value to these 'Private Papers' is that we are enabled to identify that point of view, and see the reason of it. They betray a man who is at heart a recluse and a student, and who would have been probably more at home as a don than as a writer of realistic fiction. The sincerity of Mr Gissing's work is merely corresponsive to his nature. He could have been sincere over mathematics or over science, though he expressly informs us that he has no interest in the latter. No; it is quite clear that the man who treasures rare volumes of the classics, who remembers with a thrill, after twenty years, the purchase of Heyne's Tibullus, and who spends his leisure in versifying the Odyssey, was by nature intended for something else than a novelist. A man of letters, yes, but not a novelist. One who is blessed and handicapped with such tastes and purposes does not go to the tourney of this rough world very adequately equipped. And Henry Ryecroft, confesses that he was not fit for the struggle. He resigns without an effort, without the least remorse or regret. Indeed, he exhibits even a morbid dislike for the memory of what he has gone through in London.

It is also interesting to note that Mr Gissing (if we are right in identifying Ryecroft's opinions with his) is the reverse of democratic in temperament. His study of the lower-middle and upper-lower classes has not converted him to sympathy. He was emphatically not the man for the task, despite his gifts. This book discovers him in a mood which will be strange to those who know him by his novels alone. It is a miscellany of rambling reflections and arguments, dictated entirely by chance and circumstance. There are in it wit, philosophy, a feeling for learning, shrewd commonsense, and literary style, tempered by a long experience and quickened by an emotional nature. On the other hand, there is no humour visible. The defect of his novels is also the defect of this more personal and intimate revelation. Mr Gissing has been content, to all seeming, to tread pedestrian streets, grey roads, dull alleys, and to breathe the poisonous air of the great city without a murmur. In this book he astonishes by flinging up his arms and inhaling the country breezes. He can think of nothing but of his release. He is profoundly and gratefully content with his new fate. He is a failure, but he is happy. So life is more than art, and to enjoy is better than to achieve. He looks back with a shudder on the days when he received a circular from a typewriter:—

'If you should be in need of any extra assistance in the pressure of your Xmas work, I hope,' &c. How otherwise could one write if addressing a shopkeeper? 'The pressure of your Xmas work.' Nay, I am too sick to laugh.

There is a point of view here, and it is the point of view of one who is tired and glad to leave the arena. It is not quite wholesome, perhaps, but it is natural. Grub Street offers no rewards, and the difference between fifty and twenty is of the vastest. Ryecroft is no coward, but a sensitive man who has at last got out of the crowd and breathes freely. His work in Devon fascinates him, and he repeats again and again one note, the love of country and of nature. He thanks Heaven that the appreciation of these things grows keener with advancing years, and he laments the wasted years of town life when he might have been enjoying them. Such reflection he enjoys 'with something of sadness, remembering that this melodious silence is but the prelude of that deeper stillness which waits to enfold us all.' Ryecroft's mind, nevertheless, betrays its own feverish activity. Possibly it is because of the fever that he is able to appreciate the quiet. Mr Gissing has supplied us with an index of the subjects treated in the course of these rambling remarks, from which we gather that he wishes them to be seriously considered. In quality and variety they certainly exhibit a mind that knows men as well as books. One illuminating point is that Henry Ryecroft does not like knowing men. He is content with his work in Devon. Yet one doubts if he could be induced to keep silence. The silence that he loves is about him, yet must he talk. Hence these *Papers*. Well, if he talks so pleasantly, and so variously, and so well, no reader will grudge him his confidences. He is, above all, a simple-minded, cultured gentleman; he has faith in his country, and he embodies the national virtues. But he has also that enlivening kind of imagination which is not commonly national. He has insight also and delicacy, and it seems a pity that he does not live to be properly appreciated.

156. Unsigned review, *Pall Mall Gazette*

4 March 1903, 4

This review was entitled 'The Solitary Life'.

Mr Gissing's new book, while it has many possible aspects, is, in the main, an essay in defence of solitude—solitude, physical, emotional, intellectual. His hero, of whose latter life the book is an imaginary diary, praises many things, and denounces many things from one point of view—the supreme beauty of solitude. This ideal is presented before us in a singularly effective manner. Before we have read fifty pages of the book, we are sharing Ryecroft's gentle quietism, we are regarding his position as the only possible and the only right one in a complex and tiring world; we are ready to go into the wilderness with the eremites of old, and possess our soul in an ecstasy of patience. This, then, is certainly the most striking thing about Mr Gissing's book—the success he has in capturing his reader, in forcing him to accept an ideal which may differ widely from his own. Not a little of the achievement of the author's may be attributed to the amazing reality which he gives the impression produced by the scenery of that most wonderful part of England, the West Country. Ryecroft, who has been a struggling author for his whole life, suddenly comes into a legacy which enables him to live comfortably in a small cottage in the country. Then the old problems no longer worry, the poor are still poor, the rich are still rich; but what are they to him? The best he can do for himself and for the world is to attempt to realize his own nature in the way which he believes to be the only way for him. For him altruism must find its end and its beginning in himself, for one cannot do more than one's best; and Ryecroft is sure that his best is done by a calm, serene, and confident self-development. And so, in this diary which Mr Gissing gives to the world, Henry Ryecroft has jotted down the stages of his development, and the result is a book of great power and frankness. It is stupid to argue whether the manner of man which Mr Gissing has drawn has any justification in a busy, material world. For ourselves we think he has. At any rate, it is sufficient that the type exists, and that it never has been displayed with such truth, such sympathy, and such insight. This book is Mr Gissing's masterpiece.

157. Unsigned review, *Academy*

7 March 1903, lxiv, 228

This review was entitled 'An Author at Grass', which was the name Gissing had originally given to *The Private Papers of Henry Ryecroft* for serial publication in the *Fortnightly Review*.

The critic is probably never so true to his office as when he wishes to resign it under an impulse to accept and enjoy a book that touches him intimately. Speaking, no longer as a judge, but as a man overcome, he would say: 'This book interests, nourishes, calms me; it is a permanent addition to my pleasures; I shall read it often.'

We think that not a few critics would be content to offer only this personal witness in regard to Mr George Gissing's book, *The Private Papers of Henry Ryecroft*. Under a veil of biography Mr Gissing has given us a more compact and direct revelation of himself than can be captured in his novels. That such a revelation was worth having will not be questioned. To have read *New Grub Street*, *The Whirlpool*, *Born in Exile*, *Demos*, *In the Year of Jubilee*, *A Life's Morning*, *Our Friend the Charlatan*, *The Town Traveller*, is at least to have learned that Mr Gissing has an interesting mind. These twenty years he has been known for an intellectual novelist who unites observation made keen by experience with a literary power fed by scholarship. Mr Gissing's 'public' may not be large, but each one of his adherents had been individually won, not hustled into the ranks by a craze or a coterie. The career of no living novelist has been more individual. Year by year there has grown up a band of readers who, though they have never used the name (or invented a hymnology of discipleship), are sworn Gissingites. Some one said of a book, 'If Daudet wrote it, I want it,' and to-day there are those who say, 'I will read anything of Gissing's.' This is literary success: terms like fame and genius may wait.

Many may differ on Mr Gissing's achievement; but few will demur to any praise, however warm, of his native ability, his acquired skill, and his singleness of mind in an age of literary opportunism. Unlog-rolled, unboomed—alas! that we should use such words—he has fared on through periods and popularities, winning nothing more showy than the hearty respect of everyone who can recognise a true man of letters. Averse from pyrotechny of thought or phrase, he has produced books which the panting fuglemen of reputations could not read while they ran. Excellent error! Yet he has that to offer which grows rarer every year, a low, cultured, and sagacious grasp of reality. He has plunged into life with the crowd, then written of it with the grave solicitude of a thinker who knows that art is long and the world very old. It is inevitable that such work will engage men's minds afresh, will have a new and enlightened welcome.

And now, before his readers are really mustered, Mr Gissing writes a book which, in a manner, is the coping-stone of his literary life. 'Hoc erat in votis' are the simple Horatian words on the title page, and we are told of the suppositious Ryecroft: 'I suspect that, in his happy leisure, there grew upon him a desire to write one more book, a book which should be written merely for his own satisfaction.' The whole note of this, his imputed book, is heard in its personal testimonies of joy and regret. It is the man who is served by the author; the last touch of professional writing is gone; the things which had been said in character, or with circumstances of indirectness, are said with testamentary dignity—the gold of a life, hoarded and minted and rendered to Caesar. Perhaps every novelist of worth ought to write such a book, though to demand it would be presumption. Still, it would be good, if at the last, or earlier, a novelist would emerge from his world of creations and open his meaning in direct communications like these. That Mr Gissing has written such a book is matter for gratitude; that, being written, it makes such correspondence with all his work is a proof of intellectual consistency.

We have no mind to describe the book in detail, nor shall we ask the reader to see in many quoted fragments the charm of the whole. We might dwell on its long sigh of relief at escape from the London literary scramble; its long sigh of contentment with unlooked-for leisure to taste the earth, the simple realities, and the inner spirits of books. We might bring in the intimacies and repulsions of place from a memory which has stored the dreariness of the City Road in fog, and the whiteness of a little town on the Acroceraunian promontory. We might pass from Dickens to Tibullus, from Gibbon to Xenophon. We might seek the personal equation in many an arresting proposition. For the book remains the 'incondite miscellany' to which its four chapters, named after the four seasons, lend a semblance of order sufficient for the eye and the approach: a revelation of self must needs be broken and diverse to have the unity of truth.

With unusual feelings we leave these delectable pages. It is seldom that a new book seems fit to be wedged between old. As we close it the winds of March are already sweeping through the night; the rain flings cold on the window; in the blackness the poplars sway and despair; and, when these voices are still, the immeasurable soft tumult of the distant forest rises like some vaster synthesis of all that men feel and would fain utter in books. How great a gift is any book of which one is quietly aware that one will read it when twenty Marches have stormed over roof and field.

158. Unsigned review, *Pilot*

7 March 1903, 238

The *Pilot* was a threepenny 'weekly review of politics, literature and learning', edited by D. C. Lathbury. The following copious review was entitled 'The Personal Note'.

Mr Gissing has adopted the approved device of editing the diaries of a dead friend as an eminently convenient and graceful form in which to speak his mind on many matters. So long as such a convention does not stale by repetition, it is as welcome to the reader as to the author. It imposes a certain form within the limits of which discursiveness may have free play. Whatever of actual experience may add persuasiveness to the narrative or opinions of the supposed writer can be incorporated, and where autobiography no longer serves any useful end the author may at pleasure resume his disguise and speak through the mask he has chosen. And indeed to the novelist part born and part made it is the most natural way of addressing the public. For the artist's own personality is a thing of uncertain boundaries. In such a scheme, too, the form of the set essay, which may not be congenial, is avoided, and a subject dwelt upon at some length may be closed abruptly by an easy artifice of circumstance, while if the mood recur something may be added to the argument on a later page with no awkwardness in the introduction. An arrow may be aimed in a certain direction with no undertaking to empty the quiver in a determined effort to hit the gold.

Mr Ryecroft then, is a happily chosen figure for Mr Gissing's purposes. He is pictured as a man old before his time, by unexpected good fortune retired from the battle of life where he has fared hardly; worn, however, more by anxiety than work, and glad beyond measure to be quit of a struggle in which neither his temperament nor his powers fitted him for victory. Oftener in those who in their own sight at least seem to have failed than in those who have prospered will wisdom be found and understanding, though it has availed them little. Their experience is wider, their warnings carry a deeper sense of conviction. So at least it seems reasonable to suppose, and for our author's ends a man of this stamp and with such a history is the fittest to speak freely what it is well worth while to hear. A note of deep indignation sounds in Ryecroft's outcry against the waste of youth which the conditions of life compel, of its instincts, its energies, its opportunities. But if the hindrance that poverty opposes to so many were removed to-morrow, there would still remain the stumbling-block of defective health, of in-born perversity of heart recognised too late, and repented of in vain, between the things that might be and that are. 'With a lifetime of dread experience behind me, I say,' exclaims Mr Ryecroft, 'that he who encourages any young man or woman to look for his living to "literature," commits no less than a crime. If my voice had any authority I would cry this truth aloud wherever men could hear.' And except for those few whose daemon assures them of the highest prize, this is to a great extent true, principally, because the very gains of which they believed themselves to be certain, freedom and occupation with the things they love prove to be but wandering fires, and the monotony and dependence they trusted to have escaped overtake and keep them prisoners all their days. Still it would not be fair to ignore the compensations that even the unsuccessful may enjoy, the sense of having made their choice, companionship with kindred spirits and some commerce with the invisible that has kept their souls alive. The book deals largely with the delights of country life, and with national characteristics, treated by turns, in a lighter or a graver mood, but with a rightness of judgment and a sureness of vision that are admirable. The writer analyses with great skill the phenomena of what is usually called the Englishman's hypocrisy, and as English of the English is able to show exactly what it is of faith and of delusion that produces the familiar manifestation. On other pages he affirms, and with truth, the essential aristocratic bent of the national mind and believes that no people were ever so unsuited to democracy, dreading the future of his country if the old instinct is to perish. He himself has dwelt among the people, living their life by force of necessity, but was never of them. The Englishman, he says, must be profuse and large in his way of living; in mean circumstances all his virtue leaves him. A very personal note is struck in his passionate protest against conscription, but whatever may be the relative value of the pros and cons such a method of treating the subject is eccentric to the point of hysteria, and is the expression of opinion which is well-nigh insane.

Among the most charming passages, in a volume that is full of such things, is that in which Mr Gissing speaks of the change that the years have wrought in his judgment and his sympathies; how he whose choice was always for the wisdom of the head, has come now to see how much more beautiful is the wisdom of the heart, and to hold it far more precious. But the dominant notes that sound all through the book are the love of Nature and the love of country that merge into the one word home. Exquisite is the reminiscence he gives of going to the seaside as a boy and all it meant for him, and very touching is his account of his treasury of county guide-books which inspire him with the dream never, as he knows well, to be realised, of wandering at will over this beloved land. He has seen and admired the splendours of the South, but now he has no desire to set foot again outside this dear, dear country of which he can never have his fill. That is the refrain that recurs again and again, 'this beloved land.' A fervour and a tenderness of patriotism that is an instinct, a motion of the blood, the cry of the inmost man. *The Private Papers of Henry Ryecroft* is a book that moves the heart as it delights the ear with the haunting cadence of its language.

159. Unsigned review, *New York Daily Tribune*

4 April 1903, 8

The Private Papers of Henry Ryecroft is one of the most melancholy books that even Mr Gissing has written. Only this is intensely interesting, a fact inclining one to forgive much. Why it should be sorrowful we are at a loss to understand. The chapters of which the book consists are represented as containing the reflections of a man of letters who for thirty years has lived by his pen, doing the work of a hack. 'He was a struggling man, beset by poverty and other circumstances very unpropitious to mental work.' But better times came.

At the age of fifty, just when his health had begun to fail and his energies to show abatement, Ryecroft had the rare good fortune to find himself suddenly released from toil, and to enter upon a period of such tranquillity of mind and condition as he had never dared to hope. . . . In a few weeks he quitted the London suburb where of late he had been living, and, turning to the part of England which he loved best, he presently established himself in a cottage near Exeter, where, with a rustic housekeeper to look after him, he was soon thoroughly at home.

Was he happy there? Unspeakably happy, and during the too short period that was left to him before his death he gave himself up to the peaceful hours among his books and in the fields for which all his life he had deeply longed. But the diary from which this book is supposed to be derived is colored throughout by an incurable melancholy. The poor hack has been too long in harness. The galled shoulders feel their wounds, for all that the latter seemed to have been healed, and, though there are moments in which Ryecroft's delight in some passage in literature or some lovely scene passes into his prose, there is a note almost painful in everything he says. He is interesting, however, always interesting, and for that let us be grateful. Mr Gissing cannot blame us if we read an autobiographical significance into this volume. It echoes again and again the tastes, especially the classical tastes, which were unsuspected while he was known as a novelist alone, but which he freely disclosed in his fascinating book of travel, *By the Ionian Sea*. We have quoted from *The Private Papers* before, when the book was running serially through the pages of the *Fortnightly Review*, but we cannot better show its quality than by quoting from it again. Melancholy it is, but the reader will understand why we commend it to him with the utmost cordiality if he will but recognize the appeal in a fragment like the following:

[Here is quoted the whole of Autumn XX.]

160. Unsigned review, *Week's Survey*

4 July 1903, 619

The *Week's Survey* was a liberal journal then in its second year of publication. This review of Gissing's volume was entitled 'A Wise Book'.

When it comes to the matter of pure literature, a book is generally valuable for the amount of himself a man has put into it. Mr George Gissing's is a distinguished personality; it finds a sincere and spontaneous expression on every page of his book; and consequently *The Private Papers of Henry Ryecroft* is one of the most distinguished books that has been written in the last ten dull years, years of an astounding intellectual stagnation, brought about to all seeming by the commercialisation—an ugly name for an ugly thing—of literature. It is that rare book, the book which one buys and keeps for itself, not for a book of reference, for the information it contains, but for the pleasure of reading it again and again for its charm, its sanity, and the wholesome wisdom with which it is filled.

[Details of Ryecroft's life and reflections are paraphrased by the reviewer.]

This is the genuine wisdom of which this age is so barren, the wisdom of the man who has lived and suffered, and then given himself time to think, and thought slowly, trusting rather to the spirit than to the intelligence. It is the wisdom on which our age, in its fever to acquire knowledge and again knowledge, is losing its hold. Yet it is by wisdom rather than by knowledge that the human race advances.

Some readers will like best the account of Henry Ryecroft's early years, of his struggle when he was battling for dear life, when 'his health began to suffer from excess of toil, from bad air, bad food and many miseries,' his rare escapes from its hardness and squalor, his hunger, his loneliness, his sacrifices to buy books—'dozens of my books were purchased with money which ought to have been spent upon what are called the necessities of life.' All will rejoice at his escape to Devonshire. Others again he will delight when he writes of nature; and most he will delight by his simpler practical wisdom. Hear him on the much-abused English cookery.

[Several quotations from Winter VII follow.]

But whether Mr Gissing be writing of the mysteries, of nature, of the great issues, or the less impressive things of life, his book is the book of a wise man. Moreover, the book is the book of an English wise man; the admirations are always for the sound things of life, for the things that matter. Success, material success, even though it runs to millions, leaves him unmoved, so do the showy, meretricious brilliance, and the pretentious powerfulness which appeal alike to the vulgar, to France, and to America. And after all the great lack of this age is wisdom: of knowledge and information, worthless, windy stuff, it has enough.

161. Grace E. Martin, *Critic* (New York)

July 1903, 87

'You must consider your emotions very precious,' says Henri Taine in writing of Wordsworth, 'that you put them all under glass! There are only three or four events in each of our lives worthy of being related; our powerful sensations deserve to be exhibited, because they recapitulate our whole existence; but not the little effects of the little agitations which pass through us, and the imperceptible oscillations of our every-day condition.'

At this rate, M. Taine would hardly have had patience with the confidences of Henry Ryecroft in Mr Gissing's new book; and Henry Ryecroft was not, by his own statement, and on the face of it, a Wordsworth. His diary, a collection of short unconnected essays, is hardly, as the author describes it, written gossip. It is nowhere sufficiently personal nor sufficiently human for good gossip (for there is such a thing as good gossip). Nor does it carry conviction as an honest diary, except, of course, the diary of a literary man who hopes some day to sell his meditations. The suppositious author, while he was in a sense an individualist, had not the winning kind of egotism which makes a fascinating diarist.

As 'papers' of a scholarly and cultured Englishman the essays are interesting. . . . [They] chat of books, of gardens, of poverty, of art, of philosophy. He quotes Goethe's words, 'Was man in der Jugend begehrt, hat man im Alter die Fülle,' and says, 'I smile to thin khow true they have been in my own case! But what, exactly, do they mean? Are they merely an expression of the optimistic spirit? If so, optimism has to content itself with rather doubtful generalities. Can it truly be said that most men find the wishes of their youth satisfied in later life?' This is a question everybody asks, and Mr Ryecroft, or Mr Gissing, after talking about it, like a wise philosopher leaves it unanswered, except to state that the diarist himself had longed for 'bookish leisure,' and had attained it in abundance.

The *Papers* glow with real enthusiasm only when the subject of English cooking is touched upon. Henry Ryecroft, unlike many of us who are not philosophers, is satisfied that English cooking is the best in the world, and declares that he would far rather see England covered with schools of cookery than with schools of the ordinary kind. 'Think of the glorious revolution that could be wrought in our troubled England if it could be ordained that no maid of whatever rank might become a wife unless she had proved her ability to make and bake a perfect loaf of bread.' And let us hope that when the 'maid' had passed the required examination she would fall upon some cheerfuller fate than a life shared with Henry Ryecroft. 'My house is perfect,' he writes in his peaceful selfishness; 'very rarely do I hear even a chink of crockery; never the closing of a door or window. Oh, blessed silence!'

Enough perhaps has been quoted to show the scope and style of the *Papers*. Dignified even when the author is deliberately playful, written in excellent English and in Mr Gissing's scholarly style, the book has a genuine literary flavor which will commend it to those who watch and wait for the books—few each year—which are literature. It is a book for the thoughtful, and for those who, like the hero, have attained bookish leisure in abundance.

162. Nathaniel Wedd, 'George Gissing', *Independent Review*

February 1904, 280–2

Nathaniel Wedd was a journalist who had edited the *Orestes* of Euripides in 1895. The following extract contains his central arguments on Gissing's work.

The two things that Gissing saw most clearly and emphasised with the greatest wealth of illustration are, the vital importance of culture, and the degrading effects of poverty on all above a certain low level of spiritual development. Both these items of his creed are, as treated by him, something new in social criticism. In theory, of course, we have long learned of Matthew Arnold to pay at least lip-service to culture: and, as for education, is it not the favourite theme of every political platform? Are not Lord Rosebery and Mr Chamberlain at one, at least on the need of fighting the foreigner with increased efficiency in instruction? But we realise what culture and its absence mean in practice far more vividly from Gissing's pictures, alive as they are with the very breath of reality, than from any essays of the moralist, writing in the study and dealing with abstractions; while the education for which politicians clamour has little in its nature, and nothing in its aims, in common with education as Gissing understood it. What Gissing meant by education was the development of the feeling for the beautiful, the cultivation of interest in the things of the mind for their own sake. For this culture he found the readiest instrument in the study of Greek, and of the great civilisation which Hellenised Rome imposed on the world. The Graeco-Roman age, he tells us, was his Land of Romance; and visions of that gorgeous past were ever with him as a refuge from the squalid present which conscience, characters, and circumstance compelled him to study. That study taught him, that modern life is on wrong lines, because its endeavour is not towards spiritual things. Progress, so-called, aims at merely material goods; education, as at present understood, aims at fitting men to make merely material acquisitions. The result is, that progress does not bring happiness, education does but intensify our power of causing misery, civilisation is simply the process of putting more and more deadly weapons into the hands of 'ravening and reckless barbarians.'

What is wanted is to Hellenise the barbarians. Seek first the things of the mind, and the evils of society will disappear. The social order is the outward expression of the character of the people; as long as that character is savage, society will remain as we see it, a pandemonium of triumphant commercialism. This is the Anglo-Saxon's great defect: indifference to the beautiful, hatred of ideas that cannot be turned to immediate profit, contempt for intellectual things, stamp our civilisation as at least undeserving to survive in its present form.

[There follow several references to Gissing's view of Southern Italy, contrasting a people who have 'an innate respect for the things of the mind' with the 'Anglo-Saxon's great defect.']

That is one side of Gissing's teaching: it is to the spread of culture we must look for the reformation of society. The second lesson which experience taught him is, that, as things are, culture, and indeed all that goes to form a noble life, are incompatible with poverty. At first sight the two doctrines might seem to conflict. On the one hand, wealth is not to be the aim; on the other hand, without wealth we cannot attain the possibility of a decent life. There is an element of paradox in such a doctrine; and it is just this contradiction that produces some of the most poignant tragedies.

163. Unsigned, 'An Idealistic Realist', *Atlantic Monthly*

February 1904, xliii, 280–2

In the vocabulary of criticism the word 'realism' has been soiled with all ignoble use, and one would hate to apply it unconditionally to the work of a writer whom one admired. George Gissing, whose death is a loss to English literature none the less actual because he never won a wide circle of readers, would no doubt be called a realist by those who fancy that when once they have attached a label to a man there is nothing more to be said about him; but such a characterization cannot be accepted if it is meant to put him in the same category with Emile Zola, Flaubert, Mr George Moore, and Mr Howells, who are all realists in their different ways. With them it is the fact, and the fact only, which seems to count. But it is the fact transfigured by the imagination that one seeks in a work of art; and the finest realism is not found in the record, but in the interpretation of the record. Gissing was a realist controlled by an ideal. He might seem to insist upon the sordid side of life, but he had a passionate love of beauty. Consequently, in his analysis of the ugly there was always an implied contrast with the beautiful. This idealizing tendency grew upon him as he wrote. *The Crown of Life*, one of his last books, is far richer in spiritual nourishment than *The Unclassed*, one of his first.

Yet even in *The Unclassed*, and in *Demos*, and *Workers in the Dawn*, the difference between his method and that of others who have dealt with the under side of human existence was sufficiently marked. It was no doubt a fault in his art that he emphasized things evil unduly; but he did not fail to see the soul of goodness in them. He was not morbid and he was not indecent. He did not spare the dark touches necessary to complete the picture, but he did not put them there simply because they were dark. One feels that Zola gloated over his repulsive details, that Flaubert depicted vice with cold contempt, that Mr Moore attempts to discover in a spirit of bravado how much the public will stand, that Mr Howells more genially expounds the significance of the unessential. But George Gissing was obviously moved by the 'daily spectacles of mortality' he contemplated. His was not the detached attitude of the scientist; it was the keen sympathy of the artist. He did not let his sensibilities run away with him; he was never morbid or mawkish; he disdained the devices of a melodramatic sentimentalism; he was incapable of 'working up' pathos. He could put the situation before us as vividly as any realist of them all. But the deep and poignant emotion was there, even if the superficial reader did not discover it. No cold observation could have accomplished this. No novelist by a little intellectual slumming can really tell us how the other half lives.

In the second period of his career that *saeva indignatio* in him turned more to grim satire. He dealt, not with those whom all classes had cast out, but with a class least likely to have comprehensive sympathies, the class which one must still call, despite the objections of many persons to the term, the 'lower middle.' Perhaps *In the Year of Jubilee* is his most remarkable achievement in this respect. The dull monotony of the daily round, the sordid aims, the laxity of moral fibre, the incapacity to comprehend, much less to experience, the nobler emotions,—these things are portrayed with a distinctness which one may fairly call appalling. *Eve's Ransom* is a study of human selfishness. The man sacrifices himself for the girl, and she receives the sacrifice gayly, and goes her way, leaving him to cherish his hurt in silence. Yet even here Gissing's idealism has the last word. The man realizes that his pain has been worth living through. '*Entbehren sollst du, sollst entbehren,*'—that is the law of life. The lesson is taught with bitterer emphasis to the hero of *New Grub Street,* for whom '*la lutte pour la vie*' proves too much, and whose genius cannot survive the hardest blows of fate. In the struggle of Reardon to be true to his art against the most adverse conditions there is possibly some flavor of autobiography,—though for that matter every novel that is worth anything must have a glimpse of the writer's own soul. But Gissing was not the man to exploit his personality; he was not up to the tricks of the trade as practised by the commercial novelist; and it does not require for the appreciation of his art any impertinent intrusion into his life. *New Grub Street* is a book to be read. Those who choose to do so may take it as an argument against the marriage of men of genius to commonplace and selfish women. Indeed, the unequal bond of wedlock was often a theme with Gissing. But if so many marriages are unhappy, if a union brought about by anything less than perfect love and trust is certain to be unhappy, what place in the world shall the women who do not marry take? Such a question is hardly answered by *The Odd Women,* another novel far superior to most contemporary fiction. The heroine of that tale does not have, after all, the courage of her convictions. But then so few of us do!

The Odd Women manifested conspicuously Gissing's growing interest in wider and higher themes; it also marked a further growth of his idealistic temper; and therefore his later books may appeal to readers whom his earlier did not interest. *The Crown of Life* is, on the whole, the most remarkable of these; it reveals the passionate tenderness which is the root of all the author's convictions. Love is the crown of life, and the right woman is worth any man's while to wait for. And there are large public questions involved in the story,—imperialism, for example. *Our Friend the Charlatan* is a still closer study of political conditions, though what gives it its value is the unsparing analysis of the man who deludes himself no less than he deludes others. It is upon his skill in the delineation of character that the fame of the novelist is most likely to rest; plots are easily forgotten, but the Becky Sharps and Colonel Newcomes remain more real than the figures of authentic history. One cannot help feeling that Gissing would have done, had he lived, better work in the future than in the past. But he did enough to make his fame secure.

VERANILDA

September 1904

164. Frederic Harrison, Preface to *Veranilda*

1904

When Gissing died he left incomplete the manuscript of *Veranilda*, his novel set in sixth-century Italy. H. G. Wells was requested to write an introduction which, when circulated among the deceased author's relatives and friends, was found so offensive that it was rejected. Frederic Harrison, who had done much to help Gissing in his days of extreme poverty in the early 1880s, was then asked to contribute a short preface.

Wells's rejected piece was published under the title 'George Gissing: An Impression' in the *Monthly Review* for August 1904, 160–72, and in the *Eclectic Magazine* for November 1904, 580–7. It is more readily available as Appendix D in *George Gissing and H. G. Wells*, ed. Gettmann (1961).

The literary quarrel in which Wells and Harrison were involved has been related in detail in 'The Stormy Publication of Gissing's *Veranilda*', Pierre Coustillas, *Bulletin of the New York Public Library*, November 1968, 588–610.

This book appears under circumstances even more pathetic than those which must always attend a posthumous work. Not only was the writer cut off at the age of forty-six before this romance was in type, but he did not live to bring it quite to its natural close. It is printed by those he left behind him from his papers in the state in which they were found. There were no adequate materials to show how he had designed it to end. And it was out of the question to attempt to supply what he was not permitted to complete.

Yet it is not in any sense a fragment; nor is it at all a rough preliminary sketch. It is finished with that spirit of loving care and delicacy of touch which George Gissing gave to his best work. And the two or three missing chapters are not indispensable for us to judge the piece as a work of art. It is not at all a torso—a trunk without limbs or head. It is a finished piece of sculpture, from which some portions have been broken off and lost. To the thoughtful reader this *lacuna* will but add to the pathos and the charm of this singularly original book.

Veranilda, 'a story of Roman and Goth', is an historical romance constructed on a plan most unusual in the conventional historical novel. It deals with real historical personages and actual historical events; and it is composed after long and minute study of the best contemporary sources and what remains of the literature of the time. The epoch of the tale, the sixth century, the age of Justinian and Belisarius, is a time of which the general reader knows almost nothing, except for a few crowded pages of Gibbon, and indeed very few scholars know much at first hand. The scene is Rome, Central and Southern Italy, a country which was carefully studied by the author in his Italian travels. The period and the events are covered by the fourth volume of Dr Hodgkin's great work, *Italy and her Invaders*, to which many a reader of *Veranilda* will be glad to turn to refresh his memory. But the setting of the tale itself was drawn, not from any modern compilations, but from local observation of the scenes depicted in the story and elaborate study of the extant documents.

Fascinated as I have always been myself with the history, antiquities, and topography of Rome and its surroundings, I have read the proofs of *Veranilda* with keen pleasure; and I judge it to be far the most important book which George Gissing ever produced: that one of his writings which will have the most continuing life. It is, in my opinion, composed in a new vein of his genius: with a wider and higher scope, and more mellow tone than the studies of contemporary life which first made his fame. I do not pretend to have read all of these, nor indeed did I always feel in touch with everything of his that I did read. But in *Veranilda*, I think, his poetical gift for local colour, his subtle insight into spiritual mysticism, and, above all, his really fine scholarship and classical learning, had ample field.

If I was invited to read the sheets as they were printed and to write a prefatory note, it was as being one who had known the whole literary career of George Gissing from the first to the last. It was in 1880 (he was then but twenty-two), when he sent me his first book in three volumes: a book that very few have ever seen and which he subsequently declined to claim. Crude as it was, I recognised his power and did what I could to help him with work and introductions. Mr John Morley, then editor of the *Pall Mall Gazette*, was willing to employ his pen. Gissing, however, though sorely pressed at the time, resolutely declined to engage in any miscellaneous work of journalism or criticism, but devoted himself with fervour and self-reliance to imaginative composition. A really brilliant scholar, and a writer of most graceful verse, for many years he accepted day pupils preparing for school, whilst he laboured at night at his ideal creations.

This is not the place to offer any appreciation of his success, nor can I pretend to undertake such a task. It is not the place, nor is it yet the time, to make any record of his career:—of his sorrows, his sufferings, his dreams, and his hopes. I will add only that I think these pages contain his best and most original work.

165. Unsigned review, *Daily Chronicle*

28 September 1904, 3

This review was entitled 'Our English Realist'.

There is something peculiarly pathetic, as Mr Frederic Harrison suggests, in the publication of this posthumous novel—the last, unfinished work of George Gissing. For years Gissing had worked against the grain, picturing in his novels the world that surrounded him—a world which constrained his attention, while it repelled his sympathy. The circumstances of his life forced him, in spite of himself, to become a realist; but all the while his fancy would take wing to a very different world of the imagination, and he continually looked forward to the time when he should be able to indulge his leisure in a more congenial atmosphere.

Quite lately that leisure and that atmosphere were vouchsafed to him. His work began to be recognised; a measure of competency was secured; he had time at last to indulge his taste for study. Always a student by temperament, he was now able to follow his favourite pursuit to fuller issues, and he determined to crown them with a literary achievement that should be not unworthy of his long desire. All things seemed favourable, when, in the moment of consummation, death struck the pen from his hand. There is left to bear record of his hopes just this mutilated and unfinished book, which clearly lacked his final touches—the last evidences of his loving care. If such a story does not contain the pathos of the literary life, we are at a loss where to look for a sadder one.

Veranilda, it may be supposed, bears so little relation to Gissing's other novels that it is impossible to consider it from the same standpoint at all. Its praise has already been sounded in advance, and more than one of Gissing's friends have assured us that it is to be reckoned as the coping-stone of his career. Mr Frederic Harrison, for example, is quite emphatic upon this point:—

> I judge it to be far the most important book that George Gissing ever produced; that one of his writings which will have the most continuing life. It is, in my opinion, composed in a new vein of his genius, with a wider and higher scope, a more mellow tone, than the studies of contemporary life which first made his fame.

Mr Harrison is a critic from whom one naturally differs with hesitation, and some of his remarks are indisputable. That *Veranilda* is composed in a new vein of Gissing's genius, for example, is self-evident, and it may also be conceded that a certain mellowness of tone does, in this picturesque and highly-decorated narrative, supplant the familiar grey monotone of his earlier studies from the world of Pentonville and Clerkenwell. But that *Veranilda* is the story of Gissing's that will enjoy 'the most continuing life' we find ourselves reluctantly unable to admit. Indeed, for depth and sincerity of effect it does not seem to us to compare even remotely with *New Grub Street* or *In the Year of Jubilee*.

Let us consider the matter a little more closely. Gissing was immensely interested in classic study, and in this story besought to crystallise the result of much elaborate research. It is a tale of the conflict between Roman and Goth in the sixth century; and, as Mr Harrison says—

> It is composed after long and minute study of the best contemporary sources and what remains of the literature of the time.

Moreover—

The setting of the tale itself was drawn, not from any modern compilations, but from local observation of the scenes depicted in the story and elaborate study of the extant documents.

All this will be readily believed by anyone who is familiar with Gissing's literary methods. Just as in the old days of the Gray's-inn-road he was careful to gather each insignificant detail from close observation, so it was only to be expected that, when he turned to historical romance, the same sincere and accurate fidelity to fact would inspire all his workmanship. The misfortune is, however, that the two fields of literature demand two entirely different methods.

In the realistic treatment of contemporary life, where the appeal is directly to the reader's own knowledge and experience, the accumulation of detail is of the essence of the effect; the effect indeed is dependent upon its fidelity. But when the reader is transported into an unfamiliar field, and the appeal is no longer to his experience, but to his imagination, then an almost opposite gift is demanded in the author—the gift of wise and artistic selection; and this was precisely the gift that Gissing most conspicuously lacked. His effects were scarcely ever obtained by suggestion, and it is only by suggestion, and selection working with suggestion, that an unfamiliar age can be reasonably presented to the imagination.

Those, therefore, who most prized the real individuality of Gissing's earlier work could not have expected that he would make a great success of historical fiction, and we can hardly believe that *Veranilda* will prove these apprehensions baseless. It is a finely constrained and elaborately poised piece of work; the details of description and of historic perspective are most carefully worked out, the whole tale is full of dignity, and rich workmanship. But it lacks the one thing needful: it lacks the breath of life. There are force and opulence of treatment such as one might hardly have expected to find, but there is scarcely any charm.

And perhaps it is now for the first time that one has it borne in upon one that, after all, Gissing's work, with all its sympathy and true feeling, was always lacking in charm, though this lack was apt to be overlooked when the aim of the writer was to impress rather than to beguile. But imaginative fiction—romance of whatever order—must beguile, and to do so it must have charm.

Veranilda will be respected, and indeed admired, for many sound literary qualities, but it cannot possibly stand by the side of its author's sincere and poignant picture of a life of which he was compelled to write, whether he would or no.

166. W. L. Courtney, *Daily Telegraph*

28 September 1904, 6

For details of W. L. Courtney, see No. 153.

Unfortunate alike in his life and in his death, Mr George Gissing, even in his posthumous volume, appears to be an occasion for controversy. *Veranilda* was to have appeared with an introduction written by Mr H. G. Wells. For reasons with which the public is not concerned, it is published to-day with a preface by Mr Frederic Harrison. Both Mr Wells and Mr Harrison knew George Gissing well, and both are therefore eminently qualified to write about him. It is at least singular, however, that the book on which the author was occupied during the last years of his short and troubled career and which he seems to have recognised as his capital achievement, should have been the corpus vile for experiment or misunderstanding. Mr Wells published his introduction in the August number of the *Monthly Review*; a generous and sympathetic preface by Mr Harrison is prefixed to *Veranilda*, as it is now issued by Messrs Constable. The point would be of no public importance if it were not emblematic of much of the curious irony which surrounds George Gissing's life. He was a brilliant boy, a young man full of promise, above all, an obstinate and faithful lover of the classics. But the main part of the work by which we know him is exactly that in which his own classical tastes could find no room or opportunity. Such pieces of work as *Demos, New Grub Street, The Crown of Life, The Unclassed, The Nether World*, and *The Whirlpool* gave the impression of a man who desired to paint the tragi-comedy of an artist's career in the present age, an author who deliberately painted a dull and squalid canvas in the spirit of those melancholy realists that were once, both in France and in England, a transitory and melancholy fashion. His soul was not in books like these; the real nature of the man escaped into an atmosphere of its own, of which only his friends were aware. In two books—*By the Ionian Sea* and *The Private Papers of Henry Ryecroft*—we obtained some inkling of the real George Gissing, a meditative solitary traveller, a scholar whose mental home was in Italy and the neighbourhood of Rome. To the vast majority of his readers the man himself was practically unknown.

His life was a conflict because, through some curious failure of practical instincts, he never could express his real essence. He did task-work, and did it magnificently, but it was still task-work. He wrote novels, some of which will probably have a greater reputation hereafter than they have at present—*Eve's Ransom*, perhaps, *In The Year of Jubilee*, and *The Whirlpool*. And then suddenly he came by his own in the preparation of a work for which he was eminently fitted by his tastes and predilections; but which, with the accustomed irony which appeared to mock all his best efforts, he began too late. This is *Veranilda*, an unfinished romance, worked at feverishly in the Pyrenees, spoken of a month or two before he died 'with trembling,' and anxiously recognised by the author as 'possibly' a good thing. Only in one or two points is it unfinished; it is practically complete, although devoid of the final touches and truncated of its concluding chapters. It is obviously wrong artistically that one of the main characters, the Lady Aurelia, should disappear so early in the narrative and never be heard of again. That is one of the things, probably, which George Gissing would have set right. And the final end of the tragedy would have been described with all his customary incisiveness and power. We want to hear of the sack of Rome by the Goths; we miss the final scene, as Mr Wells suggests it would have been, a sunlit silence upon the empty Forum in Rome, shattered but unruined, and the hero, Basil, and the heroine, Veranilda, at last joined in happy union.

We must begin by recognising that this historical novel has to contend with the difficulty of its milieu and its time. Its plot is laid in the sixth century, and we are not particularly interested in such a period. Some of us know a chapter in Gibbon, chapter 43, one of the few hurried and confused narratives which the historian of the later Roman Empire composed, telling us about the struggle between Justinian and Belisarius on the one hand, and Totila and the Goths on the other. Justinian, of course, was far away in Bysantium; Belisarius, great military captain as he was, was for ever hampered by shortage of supplies, by the fitful and vacillating commands of his Emperor. In Italy, meanwhile, the Goths, under the leadership of Totila, were making great strides, and, indeed, deserved to do so, because within their ranks there were manhood and vigour, morality and discipline, the unspoiled spirit of a primitive race destined for empire. Bessas, luxurious and venal, although once he, too, had been a gallant soldier, held Rome for Justinian. Greek astuteness, Greek perfidy, were everywhere in the ascendant. The Roman Senators, the Roman youth, were weak, decadent, untrained in arms. There was a perpetual oscillation going on between those patriots who desired the victory of the Goths and those who dreamed blindly of a possible revival of antique virtue. It is a difficult period of history to understand and sympathise with. Yet it was this which fascinated the intelligence of George Gissing. He was not a man like Maurice Hewlett, interested in the Renaissance; he loved everything that would bring him back nearer to the Rome of Cicero and Virgil. 'I am delighted,' he writes in an enthusiastic letter, 'with the magnificent white oxen with huge horns which draw carts about the streets; oxen and carts are precisely those of Virgil.'*

It requires an effort certainly to breathe the sixth-century air, but it is worth while trying, for *Veranilda* is an historical romance such as we rarely see in our modern time. The author is no pedant, dragging his learning with him like a cumbrous cloak wherever he moves; he is a scholar who has a dramatic joy in life, a man who can describe character, who can make us feel the influence of the personages about whom he talks, live their life with them, understand their impulses and their ways. There is a young Roman noble, Basil, a keen, ardent, enthusiastic lover; no hero, because the times did not make for heroism, but just a young man of eager nature and inconsistent motives. He has by his side an infinitely more complex friend, Marcian, a traitor in heart, yet drawn after a fashion which makes him entirely human. There is also Veranilda, the heroine, a beautiful Gothic maiden, simple, sincere, the victim of many stratagems and plots. For her sake Basil joins himself with the Gothic forces and their king, Totila; for her sake, also, Marcian turns and twists in wily intrigues—a curious amalgam of opposite characteristics, at one time trembling with super-

* George Gissing to Edward Clodd, 6 November 1897. See *The Letters of George Gissing to Edward Clodd*, edited by Pierre Coustillas, Enitharmon Press, London, 1972.

stitious fear at the new hell with which Christianity daunted men's spirits, at another time thrilling with mere ordinary desires of the flesh. These figures are in the first plane of interest, but there are many besides. Bessas is described in a few graphic touches; so, too, is Totila; so, above all, is the magnificent courtesan, Heliodora. Then there is the scholar Decius, with head bowed over manuscripts, wondering whether, after all, Virgil's Fourth Eclogue was really a prophecy of Christ; Petronilla, a brave, ambitious lady, full of religious ambition, determined to prevent by all means, fair and foul, the union of Basil and his Gothic heroine; Leander the deacon, a bland, intriguing divine, whose aim was to secure the triumph of the Mediaeval Church amid all the welter of old institutions; to say nothing of a brilliant sketch of a manly senator, Venantius, fortifying himself in his country villa like a sort of feudal lord. I should like, also, to add the old man, Maximus, uncle of Basil, who dies early in the narrative; and the evasive personality of Aurelia, Maximus's daughter, who begins by being so important and disappears so unaccountably from the main course of events. It is a moving panorama of living personalities, who are not merely ghosts of forgotten classicism, but vivid agencies, potent for good and mischief.

The general course of the narrative is clear, for with the background of warring interests between Goth, Greek, and Roman, the life history and love interest of Basil and Veranilda are evidently designed, despite all the obstacles of unkind Fate, to win their appropriate haven. One or two powerful scenes are introduced. The chapters wherein Marcian kidnaps Veranilda and Basil discovers his treachery, killing him at the last with vindictive fury, are traced with a master hand; while the passages in Rome itself, especially those dealing with Heliodora, are full of picturesque and convincing power. Indeed, George Gissing makes us live in the time, if only we can succeed in abstracting ourselves from that modern world to which the author could never reconcile himself. The Imperial City crumbling to its ruin is menaced by war without and sedition within. The forces of Nature herself are leagued against Rome. The pestilence desolates her streets. And, with that love of illuminating detail which is over and over again exemplified in these pages, the author shows us how inevitable was the scourge of plague. The Roman baths used to be the chief glory and occupation of the Roman youth. Then, when the aqueducts were destroyed, the city became dependent upon wells and the Tiber; the conduits, great or small, were in ruins. Nobles and populace alike lived without the bath, grew accustomed to more or less uncleanliness, and thus became natural victims for the plague. This is only one of the innumerable touches by which George Gissing makes us understand the slow tragedy of the ruin of Rome. *Veranilda* can never, of course, be a popular book, but it is a fine piece of romantic work, the best monument to Gissing's abortive and unfortunate life.

167. Unsigned review, *Manchester Guardian*

5 October 1904, 3

George Gissing's posthumous novel, which has just been published under the title of *Veranilda* by Messrs Constable, will be read with more than a casual interest. The publishers are not quite correct in describing it as a complete story, but it is not, as Mr Frederic Harrison says in his preface, in any sense a fragment. Though it was printed 'from his papers in the state in which they were found', there is no sign of haste or carelessness in writing or design. We may suppose that it was actually within a few pages of conclusion when Gissing died, and though 'there were no adequate materials to show how he had designed it to end', it leaves no sense of incompletion.

The story is of Romans and Goths, and it deals with historical personages and events of the sixth century, the age of Justinian and Belisarius. Above all, Mr Harrison praises Gissing's fine scholarship and classical learning, and we can believe that this is a faithful and careful piece of work. The characters are generally conventional and perhaps, by Gissing's standard in his novels of contemporary life, rather elementary, but character seems in this case to have been a secondary interest. There is a plot of elaborate intrigue of which Veranilda, the Gothic princess, is the passive centre. Basil, her lover, is a Roman noble of divided sympathies, and his treacherous friend Marcian shares what there is of moral interest. Several of the minor figures are impressive, but it is evidently the period—the social state and even the political state—that prompted Gissing's historical investigations. The style is graceful and lucid, admirably fitted for its purpose, and radically different from his earlier style and temper. We may add, in all seriousness, that there is a great deal of information in the narrative. It strikes us as a respectable and even a remarkable accomplishment, but it is the cold performance of a writer who was capable of passion and penetration. Mr Frederic Harrison, who confesses that he did not feel in touch with everything he read of Gissing's, considers that *Veranilda* contains his best and most original work and is 'by far the most important book which George Gissing ever produced'. We should find it difficult to emphasise sufficiently our dissent from such a judgment.

Gissing, as those who followed something of his fortunes with interest and sympathy know, had a hard life and wrote books that reflected something of it. In such novels as *The Nether World* and *New Grub Street* he penetrated to an expression of fortitude in poverty and privation the force and truth of which have given him a place in English literature. This expression, it has been said, is 'full of ethical passion', and it is full, too, of the passion of revolt. From a squalor of physical circumstances and from mental suffering he emerged to something of peace and leisure that one shall not begrudge him; but his vital work was done. He entered upon an experimental phase, and several of his later works were conspicuously below his best standard. *The Town Traveller*, however, in which he returned with humorous intent to a vulgar social environment, was a brilliant success in a new vein giving promise of great things. He had not passed what we regard as this experimental period when he died, at the age of forty-six. The philosophic amiabilities of *The Private Papers of Henry Ryecroft*, the last book published in his lifetime, qualified as they were with something of the deeper experience, were hailed as his masterpiece, and now again we are asked to accept the further experiment of a scholarly historical romance as surpassing the novels of modern life that made his fame. Gissing did indeed write books of a real historical value in *New Grub Street* and *In the Year of Jubilee*, and the latter expressions of his taste or judgment may derive something like immortality from their association with these nobler works.

168. Unsigned review, *The Times Literary Supplement*

7 October 1904, 303

Veranilda was not quite finished when George Gissing was seized by his fatal illness. It was decided, however, to print the manuscript as it was left, and not, as was done in the case of Stevenson's *Saint Ives*, to invite another author to complete the work. The decision was, we think, a wise one. The interest of the story in no way depends upon the plot; and one's pleasure in reading it is not marred by the fact that it leaves off, like an epic, instead of ending, like a drama. Gissing's admirers, therefore, will welcome it; though it remains to be seen whether it will appeal to quite the same public as his realistic studies of the lower Bohemianism and the world of the shabby genteel. He had just achieved a success which, though not dazzling or overwhelming, justified him in making experiments, attempting a new *genre*, and writing to please himself without considering too closely what readers desired or expected from him. Very possibly, if he had been able from the first to write solely for his own satisfaction, the novel, in which he so unmistakably excelled, would never have been his medium. By taste and temperament he was a scholar. In spite of restricted opportunities, he made himself a scholar; not, perhaps, such a scholar as Shilleto and Mr Robinson Ellis, but rather such a scholar as Gibbon and Grote. He had, we have heard, made an elaborate study, and acquired a wonderful knowledge, of the Greek choric metres; and there are reasons for supposing that he would have preferred to devote himself to researches into these and kindred matters and to the leisurely writing of such cultivated books of travel as he achieved in his relation of his journey through Magna Graecia. But that could not be. The man who writes books for a living—if he be an artist and not a mere bookmaker or publisher's hack—must write novels; and it is right and proper, if not inevitable, that he should write of the life he knows. This Gissing did for rather more than twenty years. The life which he knew happened to be hideous, and he did not try to represent that it was beautiful. It was the life of those who dwell on the edge of the abyss, in continual danger of falling into it, deteriorating mentally and morally in the endeavour to keep out of it, cut off from the saving grace of culture by carking material cares: a world in which the battle is to the strong, and the delicately and sensitively organized go under in the struggle with those of coarser fibre. That is the environment, and the story is always of the organism at war with it. It is a note first definitely struck in literature, so far as we can recall, in *Madame Bovary*. Just as the tragedy of the heroine of that romance was that her surroundings were unfavourable to the life of sentiment, so the tragedy of Gissing's heroes and heroines is that their circumstances are unfavourable to the life of refinement and leisure and culture for which their gifts qualify them, and for which they long. The difference is that Flaubert wrote in irony, whereas George Gissing wrote in earnest. He resembled Flaubert in describing the life of which he wrote as if it would be a degradation to touch it with a pair of tongs. He resembled Flaubert also in employing minute description as the instrument of his disdain. But there the likeness ends. Gissing had not Flaubert's aloofness. He wrote as if he himself suffered from the coarse banality which it was his mission to depict. Book after book, exposing some aspect of that banality, reads like the protest and the bitter cry of the weak man who is hurt by the hustling in spite of his contempt for it—who feels that he is prevented by it from entering into his kingdom.

It seemed that he was just entering into that kingdom when death prematurely overtook him. His eyes, as we can see from any one of his novels, were always fixed upon some promised land; his hopes always running forward to the time when, having ceased alike to serve in Egypt and to wander in the wilderness, he would cross into the country that flowed with the milk and honey of scholarship and culture. During his latter years he felt himself drawing near to it. That is clear from *By the Ionian Sea* and *The Private Papers of Henry Ryecroft*; though he was still oppressed at that stage by bitter memories of the house of bondage. Even those memories seem to have been wiped out in the joy of living without interruption in the classic past at the time when he sat down to write *Veranilda*, a romance of Rome in the days of Justinian and Belisarius, when Greek and Goth were contending for dominion in Italy. Mr Frederic Harrison, in his brief introduction to the novel, pronounces it to be 'far the most important book which George Gissing ever produced: that one of his writings which will have the most continuing life.' If we decline to endorse that view, it is partly because of our great respect for George Gissing's other writings, and partly because of our strong feeling that a great writer must always be at his best in writing not of what he has imagined and studied, however lovingly, but of what he has felt and known. But we agree with Mr Frederic Harrison that the romance strikes a new note, and a note that one is glad that the author was able to sound before he died. There is no trace of bitterness in it from first to last. It is the work of a scholar—mellow and serene.

It is, indeed, as the work of a scholar who writes in the temper of a scholar (though by no means of a pedagogue) that *Veranilda* is chiefly distinguished from other notable novels about Rome. The popular novelists who feel impelled to write about Rome have, as a rule, very little claim to scholarship. The scholarship of Mr Hall Caine, for instance, is only to be compared with that of Zola; and the scholarship of Zola is only to be compared with that of Mr Hall Caine. Quite other matters than points of scholarship absorb their minds. The theme invites them to 'faire grand,' as the French say—to parade their private views on all subjects, political, social, and religious—to open the flood-gates of rhetoric and deliver allocutions—to see what they can do to keep the Pope up to the mark. Some of them have even gone so far as to express belief in his infallibility in one sentence and to offer him advice in the next. There is no pompous extravagance of that sort in Gissing's work. To a great extent, indeed, he precluded himself from indulgence in it by his choice of a period in which the populace used to pelt the Supreme Pontiff with brickbats for neglecting his duties in the matter of the gratuitous distribution of corn; but he really had no desire to preach either to the Pontiff or to the public; and it might be said of *Veranilda* much more reasonably than of *Paradise Lost* that it does not 'prove anything.' What it does is to depict a period that had first to be reconstructed at the cost of deep research—a period about which even scholars as a rule know next to nothing unless they are fresh from the perusal of Dr Hodgkin's *Italy and her Invaders* or Lord Curzon's prize essay on Justinian. Gissing seems to know it as well as if he had lived in it in a previous incarnation. At any rate he must have lived long in it in happy imagination before he sat down to write. His actual story, it is true, is of no very absorbing interest to the modern reader; but it could hardly be otherwise with a story of ancient Rome. Just as it is impossible to make any one really care for what purpose Balbus built his wall or what were the consequences of Caius's irritation of the wasp, so the love of Basil for Veranilda leaves us cold, and the perplexities of Marcian when the flesh lusts contrary to the spirit leave us indifferent. But the period lives if the characters do not. The archaeological details are as exact as in that companion of our school days, Becker's *Gallus*, though they are not thrust under our noses in the same obnoxious way. The picture, in short, is complete, drawn with the art which conceals art, and, though never exciting to the emotions, chastely beautiful throughout—rising even to eloquence in the chapter which describes the humble beginnings of the Benedictine Order, founded to keep alight the torch of pagan as well as Christian learning at the time of its threatened extinction by the barbarian invaders from the north. Save for the vows—and we do not pretend to know what view he would have taken of these—George Gissing would rather, we feel sure, have been a Benedictine brother than anything else, had his own lot fallen in those troubled times.

169. Unsigned review, *Outlook* (London)

22 October 1904, 352

This review was entitled 'Misdirected Patronage'.

The late Mr George Gissing's posthumous romance of the age of Justinian is prefaced by an introduction from Mr Frederic Harrison, in which he expresses a judgment of the book from which we cannot too emphatically dissent:—

I judge it to be by far the most important book which George Gissing ever produced: that one of his writings which will have the most continuing life. It is in my opinion composed in a new vein of his genius, with a wider and higher scope, a more mellow tone than the studies of contemporary life which first made his fame. I do not pretend to have read all of these, nor did I always feel in touch with everything of his that I did read. But in *Veranilda*, I think, his poetical gift for local colour, his subtle insight, his spiritual mysticism, and above all his really fine scholarship and classical learning, find ample field.

This is the sort of thing that makes us despair of serious English criticism. Mr Harrison is the only survivor of our veteran leaders in that branch of literature, now that Sir Leslie Stephen has gone; and for him to set this judgment on record about a novelist like Gissing, whose principal works he admits that he has either not read or cannot appreciate, is to put himself on a level no higher than that of the professional writer of advertisements. To say of Gissing that *Veranilda* is his 'best and most original work', is about as true as that Mr Harrison's own masterpiece is *Theophano*. Either statement misses the whole point of the talent of the writer in each case. It was bad enough that the leaders of criticism should have neglected Gissing in his lifetime; but this effusive misrepresentation of his genius now that he is dead is a still more deplorable demonstration of their inability to appreciate his real place in the imaginative literature of the last quarter of nineteenth-century England.

There is something peculiarly exasperating in the way in which these belated literary patrons of a man whose years of fruition were dismally spent in Grub Street now flatter his ghost with eulogies of 'the really brilliant scholar', and 'writer of most graceful verse', 'his really fine scholarship and classical learning'. George Gissing had very few friends in the days when he made what Mr Harrison now describes as his 'fame'—a word of irony, indeed, to those who remember; and Mr Harrison's statement that he himself was acquainted with him from the first, coupled with the further revelation that he did not read all Gissing's books, or like them when he did (for that is what it appears to come to), and with the fact that *Veranilda* now (alas! too late) rivets the attention of this magnate of English criticism, on account of its 'new vein of genius'—all this casts a flood of light upon the question of how much really helpful direction young talent is apt to receive from the great, wise, and eminent, who, with supreme seriousness, but precariously little insight, sit in judgment on originality, and put their influence, positively or negatively, between it and the public. That Gissing himself should in those last years have delighted in writing an historical romance of the sixth century, and devoting all his 'scholarship' to it, is comprehensible enough, but nothing to the point. What is really relevant is that he should not have been adequately encouraged to realise that, while there are plenty of scholars to write 'graceful verse', and rake up musty details about quite the least instructive period of Byzantine Rome, there was no other living writer qualified as he was to depict certain phases of the real life of his own time. Men with their heads in the clouds of 'historical scholarship' have valuable functions to perform; let us praise them unreservedly for their contributions to knowledge, and to the spreading of sweetness and light. Gissing himself could never have seen what he saw in the life of his own times unless he had been an accomplished student of other days and civilisations. But the really valuable function of the novel, in the hands of a master, is its power to illuminate contemporary life; and when a man who can do that, as Gissing could, is misdirected by criticism in the fashion which is suggested by reading between the lines of Mr Harrison's introduction to *Veranilda*, the only possible reflection is, what a lamentable effect of 'scholarly' ideals on the production of the living literature which to some future age may depict the realities of to-day!

The only thing to be hoped is that the earlier novels of contemporary life, on which George Gissing's 'fame' will certainly rest, if it survives at all, may come to be rather better appreciated, now that his charming autobiographical fragments, *The Private Papers of Henry Ryecroft*, and finally this posthumous historical romance, have compelled an authoritative recognition of his powers. *Veranilda* on its own account may be left to take its place with our old friends *Gallus* and *Charicles*, the classical masterpieces of that eminent archaeologist, Wilhelm Adolf Becker, of schoolday memory. Like those useful aids to Roman and Greek scholarship, it, no doubt, 'makes dry bones live', but the process of digesting revivified dry bones is not very exhilarating. We are totally unable to assent to the dictum that to be an auxiliary in that field is a modern novelist's best chance of immortality: we would willingly leave Belisarius and Totila, and the rest of them, to the historian. *Veranilda* may well be a monument of archaeological research, but as a story it is decidedly feeble and uninteresting. It is the business of fiction to deal with human beings, and here, for the first time in Gissing's writings, we find puppets. The dust of the property-room is upon them. The inspiration which he received fresh from life itself is gone. Those who want to know what sort of living, breathing, human creatures, torn and rent by actual passions, he could create, must go to *Demos*, *Thyrza*, *The Nether World*, *A Life's Morning*, *New Grub Street*, and others, where he was writing of the people he knew, and not of an environment which he had to 'get up'. They are personally inarticulate, these lower-middle-class and working-class characters, who form the staple of his work, and it is only by the accident of fate that a man of George Gissing's capacity is put into a position—dismal and painful enough to him—to interpret them. What if it led him to hate the modern conditions that produce the types he drew? It was life, nevertheless, drab, and dismal, and depressing, but real, and depicted with the hand of a true artist. You don't like these things? You want to read happy stories about jolly people? Then you must go elsewhere; the professional entertainers are legion. But for those who look for something higher in the novel, such intimate contact with life alone can keep the Art of Fiction on a level of dignity with the Art of History.

To win a high place among the few writers of fiction who have importance as critics of life, was within this writer's power. It is very doubtful whether he was given the opportunity to realise his powers, and whether his alleged 'fame' will last at all. If that be true, it will be because the criticism of his time did not know how to foster a unique and unpopular talent.

170. Frederic Harrison, *Positivist Review*

1 November 1904, 261–2

See headnote to No. 164.

If I may say a few words about a book by an old friend of my own, which I was requested to read in proof, and to introduce with a prefatory note, I will explain what I take to be its merits. It is a most conscientious study of a time very little understood, by a scholar of rare and curious learning, something of a poet, and something of a philosopher. He has made an elaborate picture of old Imperial Rome in its decay, as it was passing into medieval and papal Rome, of the unequal struggle of the Latin descendants of Scipios and Caesars with the Gothic conquerors from the North, of the long battle waged by early Christianity with the remnants of polytheist civilisation and manners, of Arian with Trinitarian fanaticism, of ascetic Catholicism against a humane Christian culture. It is a book to compare with *Hypatia*, though entirely without the fire and pomp, the polemics and the moralising of that brilliant romance. Gissing writes more as a historian, as a sympathetic student of religious phenomena, old or new, gentle or fierce, fanatical or tolerant. It was the age of the successors of Theodoric the great Goth, of St Benedict and the rise of Western Monasticism, of the sieges, captures, and desolation of old Rome—an age of upheavals and new birth in habits, beliefs, and government. I know no book in which all the elements in this vast cataclysm, the contrasts of race, of creed, of ideals of life, are painted with more profound insight and more impartial sympathy.

The story—for all this is put in the form of a romance—is meditative rather than exciting. The personages live with a kind of dreamy otherworldliness highly characteristic of times remote and out of joint, of ages of decadence, ruined efforts, and pathetic failures. Whether all this is precisely the material of a popular novel, I will not say. But it is entirely in the tone of the *fin-de-siècle* chaos of that epoch of false hopes and transient ambitions. I see with regret that this is not to the taste of some of the 'lightning critics' of our time. A silly Yankee 'notion' has captured our smart Press to issue reviews of books 'on the day of their publication.' Nobody wants four dozen notices of a book on the same day; but it is thought to be 'up-to-date' and to show smartness. Clever young women and handy youths who have attended 'Extension Lectures' will turn out a 'review' in 24 hours or less. The one thing necessary is to be smart, up-to-date, to show the 'note of modernity,' to be 'convincing,' to be 'realistic.' Realism too often means to copy the language and the fun of shop-men and shop-girls out for a bank-holiday. To *convince*, slang and practical jokes, the ways of the man in the street or of popular farces are essential. And the 'note of modernity' is to be studied in the Court presided over by Sir Francis Jeune. The language of Scott or Fielding was 'stilted,' 'conventional,' 'theatrical,' and hopelessly 'old-fashioned.' The up-to-date Shakespeare will read in the great murder scene—'Buck up, Mac, give the old boy beans, or else leave me to go for him!' And in the famous grave-yard scene, Hamlet 'up-to-date' will say: 'Is life worth living, Horry? you bet your bottom dollar it isn't.' We must all 'speak by the card' (of Fleet Street in 1904) or Equivocation (i.e., anything ideal) will undo us.

171. Unsigned review, *Outlook* (New York)

4 March 1905, 606

As Mr Gissing's remarkable book *The Private Papers of Henry Ryecroft* gave us a totally different side of his art and mind from that underlying his London social studies in fiction like *The Unclassed* and *The Whirlpool*, so the present posthumous romance of the sixth century gives us still another view of this versatile man—as a scholar and a student of history. The tale is unfinished but it was so nearly completed when the author died that the loss of the final two or three chapters does not seriously mar the reader's pleasure. In manner the narrative is dignified and careful. The human and story interests are strong and well maintained. The era is that when Roman civilization was being torn apart, one may say, by the alterning rule of the Eastern Empire at Byzantium and the Goths, and when, theologically, Arianism and the Athanasian Creed were dividing Christianity into two camps. Through the study of Roman life and customs in this era runs a very charming love story, and incidents of courage and danger enliven the tale. The book is easily one of the best of modern attempts at classical romance. Mr Frederic Harrison in an introduction speaks with warmth and truth of Mr Gissing's poetical gift for local color, subtle insight into spiritual mysticism, and really fine scholarship and classical knowledge.

172. Unsigned review, *Critic* (New York)

May 1905, 478

More than a literary interest is aroused by the posthumous publication of an unfinished work by so conspicuously able a writer as George Gissing. But the most indulgent and sympathetic critic will perhaps be able to find no other estimate of *Veranilda* than that it is a falling behind Mr Gissing's other work, a mistaken undertaking altogether. In his studies of contemporary life Gissing showed great strength, penetration, sympathy, humor. Curiously, none of these qualities is discoverable in *Veranilda*, and for the reason, undoubtedly, that the motive was wrong. In his most ambitious book he was urged, most unfortunately, by the historian's, not the novelist's impulse, and the result fairly reeks of the library and the note-book. However faithful it may be, therefore, to sixth-century Rome, it is not vital, which is a far more important thing. The Gothic heroine is a mere conventional suggestion not a definitely realized character. Throughout the style is stilted, the conversations absurd, the action tiresomely slow, and the story destitute of a single throb of real humanity. Fortunately, Mr Gissing will be remembered by his earlier substantial, even brilliant, achievements.

173. Jane H. Findlater, 'The Spokesman of Despair', *National Review*

November 1904, 511–22

This article may be seen as an extension to Jane H. Findlater's earlier thinking. See No. 136.

'Art nowadays must be the mouthpiece of misery,' says George Gissing in *The Unclassed*; and in these woeful words he sets forth the whole gospel of his Art, adding in the next sentence his view of life: 'For misery is the keynote of modern life.' Never writer wrote with deeper conviction than George Gissing; every sentence has come straight from the heart, and this fact alone, apart from its artistic merit, gives a poignancy and strength to his work which separates it at once from the common ruck of novel-writing. These books are terrible arraignments of life—their peculiar characteristic is this poignancy, this painting of life at its moments of unbearable crisis. Between misery and despair lies a whole world of difference: misery is what can be endured—despair is the unbearable, and George Gissing is the spokesman of Despair.

A great many people ask what is the use of writing books of this kind, which only add to the misery of the world? And in one sense there is truth in the objection. So forcible, so appallingly real are these books that they do sensibly add to the sum total of misery, but looked at in another light they have their uses. There is a callousness, a grossness of fat living among the men and women of our day that calls aloud for cure: 'For me,' said a very rich man not long ago in the writer's hearing, 'For me cold and poverty and hunger do not exist; I choose to forget that they are in the world.' He glanced as he spoke over his own richly furnished table, and continued his dinner. The food, strange to say, did not choke him, as it should have done. He was a not uncommon specimen of his class—a class which is increasing in our midst—it toils not, neither does it spin, and 'chooses to forget' that the overwhelming majority of its fellows have to do both these things, and even with that have to want. The only way in which persons of this callous, mundane type can be influenced is by the gradual pressure of public opinion—and (lest authors despair) public opinion is largely and strongly influenced by books. Since novels of 'purpose' came into being, for instance, it cannot be denied that philanthrophy has become more fashionable; and although this may be a silliness, it is a useful folly which leads to a certain amount of sympathy with the suffering poor.

Now, though George Gissing was a true artist he sometimes allowed purpose to appear quite openly in his books—as we shall see when we examine them in detail. But side by side with the special purpose of each book, you will notice that he always takes a wider view. He is not content with pleading for one specially miserable class, or exhibiting the grievances of one trade or profession, for he wishes in short to be 'the mouthpiece of misery,' and that necessitates more general views. The struggle for existence—the trampling of the weak by the strong, the pitiless pressure of circumstance, these are his continual themes. '*Il y a du sentiment, mais il n'y a pas de parti-pris,*' says Dick in *The Light that Failed*, as he criticises Maisy's picture: and this 'parti-pris,' the lack of which spoils so much art, is the strong point of Gissing's books; whether we agree with it or no, it gives distinction to his work. He has a certain view of life, knows what he wishes to describe, and does so, with the result that we get a definite mental picture from his words. The special problem which Gissing sets forth in his books is that of poverty as it affects morality. On this theme he plays endless variations, which all lead up to the same conclusion: Poverty is the root of all evil. *Want, want, want*, the word has stamped itself on to this man's brain, he never escapes from it. Sombre, almost uninteresting men and women fill these books, just such people as we meet every day and wonder why the Creator created them. This human creator of puppets has chosen these drab-coloured types on purpose, and we wonder at his choice till we begin to perceive that this is the very essence of his art. The romance-writer selects striking figures for presentation, unusual types, daring and dramatic; but Gissing will have none of these. The world he describes is that of ordinary men and women, incapable of brilliant destinies, unoccupied by brave projects, just all striving, with pitiful and infinite struggles, to maintain a foothold on the earth they find themselves born into. Oh callous rich man, read these books, and think, and repent and give of your goods to feed the hungry! For here you will read strange *new* descriptions of want: this is not the ordinary view that we all know so well, which is bad enough and heartrending enough in its own way, but something far worse. Here you will read the effects of want on character instead of its effects on flesh. In considering this problem, a distinction must be made between Poverty which may be defined as a lack of luxuries, and Want which means a lack of necessaries. The one is a bearable evil; in certain cases not an evil at all, while the other is an unbearable and unmitigated curse. This distinction has not been enough kept in sight by George Gissing in his impassioned tirades against our social system:

'The power of money,' he avers, 'is hard to realise; one who has never had it, marvels at the completeness with which it transforms every detail of life . . . *between wealth and poverty is just the difference between the whole and the maimed*.' Again he asserts:

> Poverty is the root of all social ills, its existence accounts even for the ills that are from wealth. The poor man is a man labouring in fetters. I declare there is no word in our language which sounds so hideous to me as poverty . . . poverty will make the best people bad if it gets hard enough. . . . Some great and noble sorrow may have the effect of drawing hearts together; but to struggle against destitution, to be crushed by care about shillings and six-pences, *that must always degrade*.

This is not the truth: care about shillings and sixpences has drawn many hearts together; as every genuine necessary human interest will: there is nothing degrading in the struggle against destitution, it implies a desire for independence, and an effort towards a higher level of existence. It is only when the destitute man ceases to struggle that his degradation begins.

But this view of the case seems to have been curiously overlooked by George Gissing. He assures us over and over again that poverty is entirely degrading, and quotes the delicious cleverness of Johnson to defend his position: 'Sir,' said Johnson, 'all the arguments which are brought to represent poverty as no evil show it to be evidently a great evil. You never find people labouring to convince you that you may live very happily upon a plentiful fortune.' The quotation, however, does not quite help out Gissing's theory. For, although Johnson speaks of poverty as an evil, he does not say that men must be degraded in character by it—any more than they must be by the physical evil of disease; that both are evils no one will deny; the question is, whether by a heroic attitude towards them character may not be strengthened instead of weakened? It would be difficult, I fancy, to produce evidence to prove that any character has ever been spoilt by an honest struggle against any evil—be it poverty, disease, or sin. Even if the struggle ends in failure something remains, were it nothing but the having attempted. Gissing cannot take this comforting view; the lost battle is to him lost indeed; he thinks it worse to struggle and fail than never to struggle at all. A peculiar bitterness belongs to his view of poverty.

[A quotation from Spring V in *The Private Papers of Henry Ryecroft* follows.]

This astonishing statement sums up Gissing's view of life. Here again he seems to us to confuse between poverty and want. The man who suffers dire and abject want must indeed necessarily find himself in a position where it is difficult to maintain friendships; but to say that a mere lack of luxuries, or even comforts of living, must separate friends is an absurdity. This morbid stress which he lays upon the decorums and conventions of existence is very characteristic of Gissing. He mentions, for instance, as a great hardship the fact that a hardworking journalistic family have no servant, and therefore the mistress of the house 'had herself to carry in the joint.' This humiliating incident seems to Gissing to cut off this poor family from all reasonable intercourse with their class. The same morbid pride is described constantly in Gissing's books as being felt by all self-respecting and poor men—if they cannot entertain their friends as they would like to, they will not entertain them at all. Gissing seems to forget how often the stalled ox has dulness therewith; and that the dinner of herbs where love is may be the finest feast in the world.

But, having cavilled so much to begin with at Gissing's theories, let us see how he works them out. A long list of novels stands against George Gissing's name. *The Unclassed*, *Demos*, *Thyrza*, *New Grub Street*, *The Odd Women*, *The Nether World*, *The Crown of Life*, and *The Private Papers of Henry Ryecroft*, are the best known among them. As I have said above, all these books are more or less an elaborate analysis of character as it is affected by poverty; and to explain his theories Gissing has worked out the problem as it affects widely differing groups of characters.

It is difficult for a writer to speak dispassionately of *New Grub Street*, for this terrible book describes the author's nightmare—the slow murder, by care and overwork, of the priceless gift of artistic imagination. Worse far than any realistic description of physical disease and suffering is this pitiless, unvarnished account of the death of Edwin

Reardon's powers. The only thing I know in literature at all analogous to it is Tolstoi's *Death of Ivan Illych*. With much the same professional calm which Tolstoi employs in describing the slow on-coming of physical death, Gissing analyses the steady decay of Reardon's powers.

Let every aspirant to literature read *New Grub Street* and be warned—the book, rightly considered, might avert many a tragedy. The story is worked out with pitiless sincerity. Reardon, at first, has high ideals of his art, and refuses to lower them; then the screw of poverty is turned on harder and harder; his wife urges him to write more 'popular' books, and reproaches him cruelly because he hesitates to do so. At last Reardon dies of misery and overwork. The moral is obvious: high ideals of artistic work *will not buy bread*; and if you want that you must sell your soul to buy it.

Now, in all this there is much that is sadly and indisputably true; but Gissing does not, perhaps, quite enough realise another truth about art—as surely as art will not buy bread, so fulness of bread will not buy art. For this is indeed a flower that blossoms in the dust; ease and luxury and the joys of living—the proverbial 'sunshine of prosperity' —is not needed to forward its growth. It would be interesting to collect statistics as to how many genuine works of literary art have been produced in easy circumstances; I venture to say that an overwhelming majority have sprung from the reverse of comfort, and a goodly number came into being while the wolf was scraping at the door. But this is a view of the case which Gissing never takes. He seems, indeed, to think that affluence, or at least entire freedom from sordid cares, would create artistic work. The mistake he makes here is, I think, in not quite enough taking into account the average artistic temperament. Reardon, his type of the literary artist, is a man of painfully morbid sensitivities, entirely without that *joie de vivre* which is part of the artistic nature. He is incapable of enjoying the passing moment, because he is living in fear of future want—every little discomfort of poverty tortures him, and he exaggerates the fancied humiliations of lack of money in a ridiculous manner. The average man of letters has more of the Bohemian in him, living happily in the present, not looking apprehensively to the future, and not minding the 'degradations' of poverty one whit. These very solid compensations of the artistic nature are entirely left out of court by Gissing in his study of the literary artist, with the result that the study is one-sided. That there are sensitive natures of the Reardon type is, of course, only too true, and, in selecting such a man as his type of the literary artist, Gissing has stated the case as extremely as it is possible to state it; but even here the picture is one-sided. For if the artist suffers, he also enjoys certain pleasures which the ordinary man can never experience: to him belong moments of creative ecstasy compared with which every common pleasure must appear cheap and worthless. This bliss of creation is never mentioned in Gissing's sombre picture of the artist's life; the pride and glory of attainment, too, are overlooked: 'If I had to choose between a glorious reputation with poverty, and a contemptible popularity with wealth, I should choose the latter,' says Reardon. It is strange that a man like Gissing, who so evidently possessed the artist nature, should take these sordid views of his calling. But so it is. Again and again we meet the same old complaint. Moreover, the joys of creation are lightly esteemed by him, and the toil of the craft seems to oppress him constantly. Would many authors write thus of their pen? 'Old companion —yet old enemy! How many times have I taken it up, loathing the necessity, heavy in head and heart, my hand shaking, my eyes sick-dazzled?' And once again he writes of the dark side of the writing life:—

> Hateful as is the struggle for life in every form, this rough and tumble of the literary arena seems to me sordid and degrading beyond all others.

This is true, every word of it, granting two conditions—firstly that unsuitable people try to pursue the calling of letters, and secondly if they are fools enough to suppose they can support themselves by it. There is drudgery in every profession—but not more in literature than in any other—always providing that it is followed by suitable persons. The element of drudgery comes in when books have to be *made* instead of being created, or rather coming into being by themselves. *New Grub Street* is a much-needed protest against this increasing evil of book manufacture. Eloquent, powerful, sincere, it stands high among Gissing's many and clever books; but in it the half only is told, and that the dark half. Many a heavy hour has been lightened, many a care forgotten, when the author, turning away from the painful present, enters the happy world of imagination.

The Odd Women—one of Gissing's best books—deals with the question of poverty as it affects women. No one who has read this book will ever forget it—no woman at least. Some men may call the picture exaggerated; but if they do, it is ignorance that makes them say so. For the pen cannot well exaggerate the sufferings of a certain helpless class of woman when she is left in poverty. This is the class that Gissing, with admirable feeling for truth, has chosen as his subject. The odd women are the *unnecessary* women of the world: those for whom there seems no niche prepared in life—no work, no husbands, no hope or help. Created we know not why, and living on we know not wherefore, they present one of the sorriest problems of the universe.

Gissing chooses a typical family of daughters for the subject of his book. They are ill-educated, delicate and unenterprising—and they are thrown upon the world, poor and helpless, to make their living in it. How do they do this? They starve and pinch and struggle—their sufferings degrade them body and soul; the youngest and best looking contracts a sordid marriage that is the merest selling of her person to escape from the poverty that is killing her; the second sister in her despair begins to drink, and the eldest struggles on as a barely paid nursery governess. The whole picture is appallingly true and unexaggerated: there are thousands of such women to-day living out life-stories quite as hopeless.

Now Gissing's object in writing this book was to prove that this 'ragged regiment' (as he calls it) is a social ill which may be combated by certain measures. He is a vehement advocate for careers, professions or trades for women. All women cannot marry, few have money, but each may, he asserts, have some well-paid calling. There are two female reformers in the book, who found a technical school of a sort, and there try to educate their sex for useful professions: the two reformers discuss the luckless heroines of the book in the following terms:

> 'The family is branded. They belong to the class we know so well—with no social position, and unable to win an individual one. I must find a name for that ragged regiment.'
>
> Miss Barfoot regarded her friend thoughtfully.
>
> 'Rhoda, what comfort have you for the poor in spirit?' she asked.
>
> '*None whatever, I'm afraid*—my mission is not to them—I'm glad it's not my task to release them.'

This quotation exactly shows the fault of the book: it is written to suggest a solution of a certain problem, and never faces it. For it is the 'ragged regiment' that need help—and exactly this class that it is all but impossible to reach by the means which Gissing suggests. The ineffectuality that characterises the type foredooms it to continuance. This Gissing does not sufficiently admit. He seems to think that training in business habit and general education will eliminate the ineffectuality and helplessness from women of this kind. Now it may do something, but no amount of training will convert the typical odd woman into a capable responsible being—she cannot escape from herself. Character, not circumstance, creates the odd woman. Moreover, Gissing's suggestions for careers are not very good. He has a great belief in typewriting for women, also in office work and clerkships. In suggesting these occupations he either did not realise, or else ignored, all the objections that exist to them as callings for women; as, for instance, the crowding out of men from their natural employments, thus making it less possible for them to support wives; or the lowering of wages that comes in with women workers; or the unwholesomeness of long office hours, so trying to the health of women. All these evils Gissing passes over.

As a solution of the problem it attempts to grapple with then, *The Odd Women* is not successful; but as a bit of literature the book stands by itself. The opening chapters, which describe the life of the sisters in their London garret, are unforgettable. Notice the Balzac-like touches: the 'vegetarian' diet 'advised by the doctor'; their early hours because 'lamp oil was costly, and indeed they felt pleased to say as early as possible that another day was done'; their calculations of ways and means where the margin was so narrow that every possible contingency was terrible to them. The whole picture of these luckless women is etched in which hundreds of fine unerring strokes. That a man should have been able to write all these pitiful secrets of woman's life is a remarkable instance of artistic intuition: the true artist does not need to have himself experienced all that he writes about—something in him (some sixth sense) makes known to him the secrets of other hearts. No underfed, anxious woman could have written with more convincing accuracy than Gissing the history of these sisters' struggles—he might have been an Odd Woman to judge by his knowledge of her ways.

Now perhaps some readers will object that this is not art—this painful depiction of pitiful lives and characters. And it must be at once admitted that it is not the greatest art; but, by reason of its truthfulness and power, it is unquestionably art. For you can make a picture out of anything if you are a sufficiently clever painter; but you may produce a mere daub of the grandest subject if you are an amateur. Art, in fact, is treatment far more than subject; though both must be combined to achieve great results.

Gissing has chosen, in all his books, to paint low, sad types of humanity. But so excellent is his treatment of these types that they only exhibit his cleverness in handling them as he does. It is not every one who could have made the story of three futile, characterless, unimportant women absorbingly interesting. To have done so is an achievement. Farther, though the book may not have solved the 'odd woman' problem, it must have done much towards rousing attention on their behalf.

Next in rank to *New Grub Street* and *The Odd Women* is *The Nether World*—that nightmare book. As its name signifies, it concerns slum-life. There is scarcely a ray of light in it from beginning to end; but you will find, if your heart does not fail before the task of reading such painful scenes, very wonderful descriptions in these dark pages. One chapter descriptive of a London Bank Holiday is a marvellous bit of writing. Here you get Gissing's true view of modern life—than which nothing can be more despairing. He does not think that there is any cure for the evils of our social system, unless, indeed, it is the drastic remedy of leaving things alone till, by their own weight of evil, they exterminate themselves. This hideous welter of low, worn-out creatures which is collectively known as the slums, cannot be of long continuance by its very nature. Another two generations unrecruited from country blood, and the breed will be too exhausted to continue itself. Better perhaps to attempt no amelioration of these hideous conditions. But yet Gissing will have his readers hear of these shameful evils. To read *The Nether World* is like gazing at a mass of corruption—often you will turn away from the printed page, almost ashamed to read. Has poor human nature really fallen as low as this? you ask, and blush for it if it has. Poverty is again the keynote here—or rather want of the direst kind. Every one in the book is struggling for bread, few can get even a crust. Respectability cannot earn a living wage; you must not blame men who try to earn it less honestly—and for the women, those of them that would keep their good name must starve and starve, and work their poor fingers raw even for the food to starve upon. Why write about these horrors is a question always asked when such a book as *The Nether World* is published? That such things are, is quite a sufficient justification for writing about them. Gissing was gifted with the insight necessary for such a task, and with a power of description that could make the most lurid scenes real to his readers. His sympathy with want is quite terrible in its intensity. Have you ever been hungry?—if not, and if you wish to know what it feels like, read *The Nether World*. There you will come to know the long-drawn out, pitiful, animal conditions of semi-starvation that has gone on for years. You will almost understand how a man would sell his soul for a morsel of bread; you will see how the spiritual side of things may disappear altogether before this struggle for the earthly necessaries. Perhaps, after reading *The Nether World* you will even think once or twice about your poor neighbours: if so, the book was not written in vain.

I cannot here speak particularly of Gissing's less noteworthy novels—such as *Demos*, *The Unclassed*, *Thyrza*, *The Whirlpool*, or *The Crown of Life*; nor can I find space to do justice to his study of Charles Dickens, a remarkable bit of criticism that makes us regret we have not more like it.

But two last efforts of Gissing's genius remain to be considered. *The Private Papers of Henry Ryecroft*, published shortly before his death, seems to sum up the whole of his life work. It is his most artistic book: there are passages of exquisite beauty in it, and yet sad as his other books were this last seems saddest of all. With only a thin disguise of fiction, we read here all the sorrowful secrets of the writer's life—his long struggles with poverty and unsuccess—his ill-health, his loneliness, and above all, the profound melancholy of his temperament.

'My life,' he says here, 'has been merely tentative, a broken series of false starts and hopeless new beginnings.'

We, the grateful readers of Gissing's many and valuable books, cannot think this a true estimate; it seems to us that he accomplished much. But a very curious experiment in art was to be Gissing's last attempt.

Veranilda, his posthumous novel which has just now appeared, breaks away completely from all his previous work into the domain of historical romance.

Is this a successful attempt?

It seems, to the writer, that *Veranilda* might have been the forerunner of other and more successful work of the same kind if Gissing had lived. It is manifestly an experiment. The artist is working in unknown material, he has not quite got over the technical difficulties of it. These must have been grave, and almost impossible hampering. For if you have written for twenty-five years about modern men and women it would seem terribly unnatural to begin to write about Romans and Goths of the year A.D. 600! Too manifestly the imagination has been strained to accomplish this feat; too plainly the writer is translating the talk of modern men and women back into the more dignified speech of the Roman world. Yet when this is allowed, we catch a curious glimpse of Gissing the man behind it all—the lover of the world beautiful, the passionate admirer of heroism, the seeker after peace. These qualities were all revealed in quite another manner in the old books, by his loathing of the squalid, and his horror of the conditions under which half the world has now to live. Only the lover of beauty could have shown up as he did the ugliness and degradation of modern life. It is, therefore, no surprise to attentive readers of Gissing's earlier work, that *Veranilda* should exhibit these qualities. The former books were not a gloating upon the hideous aspects of life, but a revolt from them—the bitter protest of a man who saw only too clearly what life should be under happier conditions.

Veranilda reproduces with careful anxiety (too careful) all the picturesque exterior of the ancient world: no detail is spared, as with loving admiration Gissing dwells on the splendid past and all its gorgeous trappings. But in spite of this wealth of detail, the picture remains unconvincing; or perhaps it is because the letter of the ancient world has been more insisted upon than the spirit of it. That, somehow, seems to have eluded the labouring pen that strove so hard to fix it to the page. We do not find here the bite of reality: something is awanting—reality—or else higher imaginative powers than Gissing possessed. As we have seen, his imagination could interpret for him all the secrets of worn-out, miserable womanhood; but to enter into the feelings of an ancient Roman citizen and a Gothic maiden is a more difficult task. Frankly, the writer cannot think that *Veranilda* has the same excellences that distinguish Gissing's earlier work. It is an interesting experiment, a careful attempt; but it lacks vitality.

The inherent justice of things makes it perhaps better that Gissing's first books should remain his most lasting memorial.

These children of the soul, conceived in bitterness and brought forth with anguish, should by rights rank before this later-born, the fruit, we are told, of leisure and greater prosperity.

174. Allan Monkhouse, 'George Gissing', *Manchester Quarterly*

April 1905, 106–23

For details about Allan Monkhouse see headnote to No. 107. The following article had been delivered originally as a lecture to the Manchester Literary Club on 12 December 1904.

The abundance of records will make the writing of history an afflicting labour presently, and yet the historian must consent to the co-existence of the novelist and may even presume to classify him. The novel cannot be summarised, and if it be written in good faith it gives something of the form and pressure of the time. Its historical intention is at most secondary, and it may be that the work of the greatest may have less historical significance—less, at least, of literal truth—than that of smaller men. Gissing is not a small man; he is in our time a figure of singular interest, compelling in a high degree sympathy and admiration, but even his most memorable work has neither the form nor the imagination of his greatest contemporaries. It has peculiar force and truth and a remarkable personal interest. Gissing, as those who followed something of his fortunes know, had a hard life, and wrote works that reflected something of it. In such novels as *The Nether World* and *New Grub Street*, he penetrated to an expression of fortitude in poverty and privation, the force and truth of which have given him a place in English literature. Such books are representative; they make a part of the essential record of our generation.

Gissing's literary adventure was of somewhat narrow range. He was of the unclassed, intellectually isolated, an uncompromising observer of several phases of society; hindered by physical ills, often falling below his best standard of work, yet pressing always to do the best that was in him. A life of continual struggle is reflected in his books. It is not necessary to determine how much of the experiences of Reardon or Peak is his own, nor whether Ryecroft's philosophic amiabilities represent a specific change. Gissing permeates his work; he is no artificer aloof but lives intensely in his books. They represent, in one form or another, the ordeal; they tell of the struggle in the depths and not of the adventure in the sunlight. We can believe that a life of bitter experiences was exalted by this great artistic effort. Gissing would be the last man to ask for our pity and yet his books show, very remarkably, the force and persistence of the social aspiration which may be scorned even when it cannot be disregarded. Several of his characters struggle upward, not only towards the spiritual heights, but pathetically, to social refinements. Yet, where Gissing sojourned he lived. At once he accepted and rebelled, and his books are a perpetual revolt from what he interpreted with profound sympathy.

A French critic, Dr Bonnier, of Liverpool University, has suggested a luminous comparison between Gissing and Zola. The English writer has not all the calmness of the scientific observer; he knows a bitter pleasure, an exquisite pain of revulsion. Zola observes but Gissing lives, and Gissing, says Dr Bonnier, in his pictures of brutal squalor, is Zola's superior in force. And it is not only himself that Gissing hurts; he has no mercy on his readers. He has that fine ruthlessness that, in the pursuit of an ideal, disregards the tenderness of shrinking nerves; he is not afraid to turn the screw. His acquaintance with sad misery is not that of the tanned galley slave with his oar. He is not lulled to the dulness of acquiescence; he endures his privations to the full. Dr Bonnier has a suggestive theory of Gissing. It is that his misery had made him, that his talent was to express the agony of this nether world, and that the personal escape was the intellectual extinction. These squalid and brutal surroundings had made him suffer but it was in suffering that his vital work must be done. He abandoned them, gained peace and leisure, and turned to a mere expression of ideals and opinions.

The Nether World is not throughout of Gissing's best quality. There is some lack of vitality in the story and a good deal of matter-of-fact narrative. But its tragic squalor is magnificent. The workman Hewett's marriage with 'Miss Barnes,' a woman convicted and punished for theft, has the generous idealism of revolt, and in the fortunes of their unhappy family the physical and the moral struggles go on side by side. Their daughter Clara, stimulated by the instinct of youth, has yet all the family capacity for wretchedness. A way of honour and happiness lies before her, and she rejects it in the frightful exercise of those incredible, meaningless antipathies that dog human happiness. With all his sympathy and idealism Gissing is continually preoccupied with these arbitrary and disastrous antipathies that come between husband and wife or between friends and lovers. Clara Hewett rebels against the misery of her home and work, and chooses the alternative of an insidious, dangerous position of the barmaid kind. Her lover, Kirkwood, a character very nobly conceived, sympathises with her, and without officious iterations, warns her. But life seems to her profoundly unjust, and the man's appeal for an ordered life,—a devotion to the principles of injustice,—involves him in her angry condemnation. Yet she cannot escape from the promptings of a nature that has its noble chances. Exhausted with a long walk and the waste of emotion in an interview with her lover, she accidentally breaks a pane of glass in the window of her room and cuts her finger.

The acme of self-pity was followed as always by a persistent sense of intolerable wrong, and that again by a fierce desire to plunge herself into ruin, as though by such act she could satiate her instincts of defiance. It is a phase of exasperated egotism common enough in original natures frustrated by circumstances—never so pronounced as in them who suffer from the social disease. The very force of sincerity, which Clara could not but recognise in Kirkwood's appeal, inflamed the resentment she nourished against him.

She is in the wrong, of course, but such truth of character and mood engages our anxious sympathy. The spiritual waste in such a woman is excessive. She marries Kirkwood, but it is too late for happiness. His generous affection, subdued by time and circumstance to the point of honour and the instinct of pity, has overcome the claims of a more suitable attachment, her own disgrace and, worst of all in this world of physical limitations, her disfigurement. Her vapours, her caprices, her desperate revolts against the inevitable,—the tragic likeness of a naughty child,—are met with all graciousness of concession and appeal. Kirkwood persists, in dreadful circumstances, sustained by a kind of moral consciousness; and we, too, are sustained in these depressing regions by the moral interest of the struggle. Without this interest the nether world would become too terrible; art could hardly sustain the burden. The exaltation of approval for these obscure, heroic struggles overcomes both pity and disgust. Yet Kirkwood must have his artifices, his stimulants; the simplicities of heroism are not sufficient. The toiler in the abyss may find his salvation in an attitude, a pose. Any device, any exhilaration of egotism may serve, as well as a great supporting principle, to avert catastrophe. At the depth of their privations and estrangement Kirkwood says: 'Mustn't all of us who are poor stand together and help one another; we have to fight against the rich world that's always crushing us down, down—whether it means to or not. Those people enjoy their lives. Well I shall find *my* enjoyment in defying them to make me despair! But I can't do without your help.' This is not the language of philosophy, but its appeal has the profound instinctive calculation of a necessity that is near to despair. Reason is left behind. In this strait the appeal—addressed to himself as much as to her—is to the primal instinct for battle, but the aim is self-respect, the safety of the soul. The woman is on another moral plane. 'Her desire to escape was due to a fear of yielding, of suffering her egotism to fail before a stronger will.' Yet Kirkwood gains some small, constrained victory; his tough, indomitable spirit does prevail, and the poor compromise continues a little further. We do not see the end, but such victories are recorded and cannot be effaced. It is the martyrdom of such men as Kirkwood that reconcile us to this world. 'Where they abode it was not all dark. Sorrow certainly awaited them, perchance defeat in even the humble aims that they had set themselves, but at the least their lives would remain a protest against these brute forces of society which fill with wreck the abysses of the nether world.'

A prime interest of Gissing's is the instinct of escape from this nether world. It is an instinct that may be thwarted, and there are many in that foul region that have no moral existence, no desires beyond the grossly material nor aspirations except for the social elevation that would be measured by the humiliation of their fellows. Gissing speaks from experience, and he shatters the shallow generalisation that no one is wholly bad—a middle-class fiction merely scientific, plausible in its limited application to those comfortable people who run on the lines. Such a woman as Clem in *The Nether World* is, in any moral assay, entirely evil. Her cruelty and rapacity cannot be overlaid by any convenient virtues. Perhaps Gissing is too good a hater to be an unbiassed novelist. He has not only the interest but the bitterness of experience. *In the Year of Jubilee*, the ironical title of which is a kind of counterblast to complacency over National Progress, he gives a picture of what is perhaps the most unlovely household in literature. The three sisters who embitter the life of an unfortunate householder at De Crespigny Park, Camberwell, are among Gissing's most brilliant accomplishments. To one of them, in the course of the story, is attributed some slight stirrings of *camaraderie* and a very respectable tenacity of purpose, though in the graces and decencies of life she is almost as deficient as her sisters. These women are drawn with detailed truth; they are a disquieting instance of suburban leisure, decent men find themselves incredibly involved with people like these. These women are the products of our Year of Jubilee, our National possessions. The Crystal Palace excursion, too, in *The Nether World*, is written, not with sociological intention nor even with human interest, but in the bitterest vein of irony. In such places the artist must be fortified by some kind of emotion, and Gissing nurses his rage against a world that can hold these things.

A phase of his satire is illustrated by the egregious Barmby, in *In the Year of Jubilee*, and perhaps Barmby is out of place in a work of serious human relation. He is as incredible as a Dickens villain or fool. This representative of the virtuous youth of the lower middle-class is full of such inspiring facts as that the cabs of London placed end to end would reach for forty miles, and he supports his statements with the formula: 'I saw it stated in a paper.' Pretences of high morality and intellectual distinction have nothing of the pathos of futility. His exclusion from sympathy is absolute.

Of another kind is the family of the Lords. The father is an intelligent, hard-working man, estranged from his children and from the world. Deep natural affections are obscured and overlaid, and his life has become an arid routine with concessions only to the lacerating passions of resentment and to a frightful, degrading appetite for grossly-seasoned food. Yet from this moral squalor Gissing rescues noble traits and fine relations. The great incitement, the chief stimulant and support of this so-called pessimistic novelist is this moral interest. It is a mere excursion to De Crespigny Park with its three furies; they are tremendous but they are not the point; they are only part of the furniture of the story.

There is no moral interest in the adventure of the righteous, and Gissing's themes are in the struggle upward from the base, or sensual, or in the lapse through self-betrayal or pressure of circumstance. Tarrant, in *In the Year of Jubilee*, is a man of some kindliness supported by the gentleman tradition, that queer, fitful tradition, the pale reflex of morality, with its compelling points of honour, its frigid half-recognition of the humanities. Nancy Lord is a woman of untrained sympathies and unruled passions, stimulated by instincts of devotion and enfranchisement. It is an unequal match for her temperament is the finer, but we accept a compromise that is little idealised. Tarrant had married her, so much his superior, 'to make an honest woman of her,' and he shrinks from the idea of her approaching maternity.

The education of Tarrant by the application of his cultivated intelligence to a woman of deep sensibilities is one of Gissing's remarkable accomplishments, and many of its passages give the exhilaration of something fine and right. A very different relation is that between Amy and her husband in his most famous novel, *New Grub Street*. This has some valuable pictures of the modern literary world—a dreadful portrait of the embittered critical journalist Yule; the antithesis of Milvain, the literary tradesman, Whelpdale, the originator of 'Chit-Chat,' and the men of letters, who are also men of consciences and mind, Reardon and Biffen. With all its professions of composure, its philosophical acquiescence, the book is a very bitter one. The suicide of Biffen, perhaps an obvious device of irony, is yet a piece of reassuring, almost of comforting idealism. It is well to be reminded that for Reardon, too, there is a way from his domestic troubles. After all our pretences and renouncements of the animal nature, physical ills are yet the hardest burden of life, but the narration of physical ills cannot be as poignant as the tale of mental anguish. Mind appeals to mind; and this ill-mated pair—Amy, formed for a prosperous affection, and Reardon, incapable of gracious concession to her poor ideals—make one of the sharpest pieces of misery in Gissing's books. Amy is more humane than her famous prototype, Rosamond Vincy, and by the suburban standards she acts generously enough to her incomprehensible husband. He is supported by a fantastic self-pity. He is one of those 'whom the vehemence of their revolt against fate strengthens to endure in suffering. . . . The stages of their woe impress them as the acts of a drama which they cannot bring themselves to cut short, so various are the possibilities of its dark motive.' Reardon is still the artist, though the pressure of his drudgery of toil has thwarted his nature, and he remains capable of the great expansions of humane emotion. Few things in Gissing are more illuminating or affecting than the passage in which Reardon, sunk to some humble work of clerkship for a charitable undertaking, enquires of some applicant, in the dull routine of his work, her occupation. Her simple, unstrained reply: 'I'm an unfortunate, sir,' rouses him to strange, rebellious sympathies. 'Why, so am I, my girl,' he would have said, and he feels that precious sense of a common lot with the weary and degraded that the person of culture and sensibility can rarely attain.

Gissing is a writer of revolt, and yet there is in his books a remarkable expression of the yearning to conform, to live in mental luxury, even the mere desire for polite society. Godwin Peak, in *Born in Exile*, is an ungracious, intellectual, unclassed young man. He is ashamed of his origin and relations, and though there are fine possibilities in his nature he is possessed by a desire for the kind of comfort that is called culture, and he meets the woman who is temptation in the guise of inspiration. We see him at the parting of the ways; he is placed for the struggle, and declines it. The central fact of his hypocrisy is hardly credible, and it is not obscured by any pretence of mystical psychology. His social chance comes in the profession of Christianity. It is a startling grossness of temptation strangely possible to an imaginative and contemptuous man. Salvation was possible if opportunity had not betrayed him. He did not deceive himself, and his intellectual honesty prevented the acceptance of Christian Dogma in some form of convenient symbolism. He lacked the hard, irreducible, final deposit of conscience, and the mere promptings of a moral tradition could not control him. Of course he hurts himself in these crooked ways, and his sacrifice is vain. He says to his friend Earwaker, an honourable man who knows the history and does not fall away from him:—'In England I have one friend only—that is you. The result, you see, of all these years' savage striving to knit myself into the social fabric.' Peak fails in his paltry venture. He cannot penetrate to the social life that he desires, and the woman that he loves, though the subjugation of her emotions is complete, cannot emerge from it. Gissing's insight shows us the manner of the revelation to her of this bondage. It is her effort for enfranchisement that reveals the indolence and timidity of her spirit. She tries to explain her case in writing to her father and it is impossible.

Lashmar, the hero of *Our Friend the Charlatan*, is another kind of study. He has not a moral kick in him. He is damned from the beginning and the damnation of such a soul is no very serious matter. The title promises comedy but Gissing seems here to miss the comic note. The book is clever, eloquent and ingenious, but it is not comic in the sense that *The Egoist* is comic. It is an over-weighted fancy or a study fancifully qualified; a novel of intrigue, the adventures of an opportunist and a lady 'who saw herself as the heroine of a psychological drama.' Gissing had shown his great comic gifts in *The Town Traveller*. In this later book he attempts comedy on another plane, and he had not the heart for it. Hardly better suited to his talent is the subject of *The Whirlpool*, a story which presents something of the ennui and degradation of the London racket. The society is only materially less squalid than in other books of Gissing's, the intrigues are sometimes tedious, occasionally harrowing. It is only small fry that are caught in this whirlpool, and all the forces of vanity, jealousy and dissipation, cannot raise the heroine to first-rate interest. It is an essay outside Gissing's scope; the true Gissing is not a clever society novelist.

It must be said that Gissing's novels are not all of the quality of his best. He wrote for bread; in a short life he must produce his twenty books and he had not the material for twenty masterpieces. The comparatively youthful and conventional *A Life's Morning*, has its place in his development. Dagworthy has not the right strain of passion, but this novel of situation and of ingenious, eloquent talk is remarkable for the dreadful pathos of Hood, the poor old clerk who yields in his distress to the simple temptation to steal. *Denzil Quarrier*, however, published the year after *New Grub Street*, seems to be out of its natural order. It is a melodrama in morals depending for its limited interest on two crimes committed by persons of culture and sensibility, and it is without passion or vivacity. *The Crown of Life*, too, almost the last of his published novels is hardly the work of a memorable writer. The average man may find in it many of his own thoughts, even, it might seem, of his intimate thoughts, but the trumpery misunderstanding and emotional crises of the story do not touch us.

Gissing's last book (with the exception of the posthumous *Veranilda*) *The Private Papers of Henry Ryecroft*, has a particular personal interest. It is not necessary to make any precise identification of this product of leisure and opportunity with the positive opinions of its author. Gissing had achieved something near to fame in a life of strenuous labour, and desiring rest, he devised 'one more book, a book which should be written merely for his own satisfaction.' Again he says, or Ryecroft says—and the mood must have been a familiar one to Gissing,—'I am made for the life of tranquillity and meditation.' We all say so; we all think so until we are condemned to it. Gissing, we may wel believe, sincerely craved rest and, we may hope, sincerely enjoyed it. Yet he has attempted in this book to define art as 'an expression, satisfying and abiding, of the zest of life.' *The Private Papers of Henry Ryecroft* is not an expression of the zest of life. It expresses rather, in many admirable passages, Gissing's taste or his judgment. It is a better piece of writing than most of his books; it is distinctly, in the limited sense, the most literary of them, and it has, with something deeper, a pleasant and variable succession of moods. There is even a mood in which he can write thus of boiled beef: 'But what exquisite memories does my mind preserve! The very colouring of a round, how rich it is. Yet how delicate, and how subtly varied! The odour is totally distinct from that of roast beef, and yet it is beef incontestable. Hot, of course with carrots, it is a dish for a king; but cold it is nobler. Oh, the thin broad slice, with just its fringe of consistent fat.' This is capital; it is excellent; it is in the literary tradition. It is like Stevenson or it is like Charles Lamb; it is like anyone but Gissing. This book of tastes and judgments in which, it may be, he has striven to give something intimate, is perhaps the least sincere of all. It has its beauties and its passages of unstressed truth, but on the whole it is the literature of deliberation and exhaustion. This exchange of 'Cares, miseries, endurance multiform,' for amiabilities about Church Bells and the English Sunday is not a real access of charity and liberality. We shall not grudge this phase to Gissing for at the end of his hard, noble life, it gave him, one may believe and hope, some rare solace and refreshment. But it was a phase even if it happened that he died in it. Dr Bonnier seems to believe that with the end of his material wretchedness the needful stimulus for his talent was lost. We may not know what powers were thwarted by death, but we would not readily believe that Gissing had worked his way to impotence.

Rather, a sympathy with this much enduring spirit would project itself into the possibilities of his future. In *The Town Traveller* we may see, perhaps, the beginning of new and great things. Gissing died young, but if he had had life and health his talent would have risen to fresh developments. It would be difficult to overpraise parts of *The Town Traveller*; it is a masterpiece of genial humour, splendidly fresh and spirited, and Gissing has never been more completely successful than with the admirable Gammon. The book was published in the same year as the critical essay on Dickens and it has something of the spirit of Dickens. In essence these two Londoners are very different; Dickens, too, had tasted something of the misery of the great city, and those autobiographical passages incorporated with *David Copperfield*, attest their kinship. Yet Dickens escaped in time and 'fate had blessed him with the spirit of boundless mirth.' He found in London a stimulus to a prolific imagination; he abounds in moral purpose and is almost without moral interest. Gissing, with no specific purposes, but intensely concerned with the moral interest, gave little practice to his faculty for humour. There are many promising touches. Malkin, in *Born in Exile*, is rather too much concentrated, but he is a comic conception; and Luckworth Crewe, in *In the Year of Jubilee*, is typical of a range of characters well within Gissing's power. Of the excellence of his ironic humour a single instance from *Born in Exile* is a sufficient witness. It is

Mrs Lilywhite, the clergyman's wife, who saw in Godwin Peak 'a great deal of quiet moral force.'

It may be said that *Our Friend the Charlatan* was published three years after *The Town Traveller*, and represents his mature conception of comedy. It is a disappointment, but Gissing, like Reardon, did a great deal of work when he was not in the vein. There is sometimes to be discerned in his books a kind of doggedness; there are traces of weariness. He writes occasionally with the merely formal intelligence of one who has lost touch with his characters. The order of his books is a doubtful guide to his development. The recently published *Veranilda*, printed 'from his papers in the state in which they were found,' might be called Gissing's *Romola*. Mr Frederic Harrison, who is perhaps unfitted by temperament to appreciate much of Gissing's work, says that it is 'by far the most important book which George Gissing ever produced.' Some of us can hardly emphasise sufficiently our dissent from such a judgment. It is a fine and careful piece of work—the cold performance of a writer capable of passion and penetration,—but Gissing's great historical works are *New Grub Street* and *In the Year of Jubilee*.

Ryecroft says: 'I am no friend of the people; I never was, and never shall be, capable of democratic fervour, and,' even more significantly, 'I could never feel myself at one with the native poor among whom I dwelt. And for the simplest reason—I came to know them too well.' It is a depressing confession, but it is not irreconcilable with the Gissing who gave voice to the desolate and oppressed. Certainly he is not capable of aristocratic fervour nor of a confident faith in the middle-class. He had no smug belief in humanity but a strong, tenacious sense of truth and a sympathy with those who fight for truth in the world and in their own hearts. To one capable of ideals and compelled by some accident of circumstance or temper to write realistic novels, the close pressure of man, material of long and dreadful labours, poor deposit of eternal possibilities, may become intolerable. Gissing had his vein of misanthropy. He may believe in salvation, but hardly in success. When Mutimer, the despicable protagonist of *Demos* is at the depth of moral and social failure, Gissing's sympathies veer round to him; he begins the process of rehabilitation. His sympathies with broken and degraded pieces of humanity are profound, but their clumsy attempts to cohere bring him into opposition with the mob that is a type of the world. He was not a politician, and his books can hardly be strained to the service of politics. Like most of our notable English novelists, he has been called didactic, and doubtless he does occasionally permit his characters to speak for him. His books are sometimes overweighted with intelligent talk, but *Demos* is almost without political interest, and it is only the mechanism of the story that requires Mutimer to profess socialism. Gissing is essentially a novelist, and in manner he belonged rather to the elder generation of his contemporaries than to the younger. He wrote for bread, and though his literary conscience was refined he could not afford any flimsy experiments. Sometimes it appears that he has a kind of even interest in everything and everybody, and his style corresponds to it in its undistinguished sobriety. Yet, as one of his critics has said, 'it rises to clear intensity and softens into delicacy upon occasion.' The occasion is often in the expression of his sympathy with the great class of the unclassed—those who must work out their own salvation unsupported by manners and tradition or the securities of regular labour.

Gissing's particular phase of historical realism extends not merely to manners, but to contemporary modes of feeling. In Amy and Reardon, Nancy and Tarrant there is something of the common and eternal, but something, too, of the nineteenth century; they are typical of degrees in the development of sexual relations which have passed beyond the extremes of sordid sensuality and stupid idealism. It is a great distinction of Gissing's work that he has not feared to suggest personal vulgarities or defects in those who may yet inspire fine passions. He has lovers who blurt out their declarations and realise with apprehensions that these must be justified conventionally. His sensual man is sadly confounded by the point of honour or the moral tradition. And this point of honour, the mere tenacity of grasp upon some shred of hope in a swirling world, may save us for better things. The married relation is more interesting to Gissing than the preliminary adventure, and if it brings compromise, satiety and disaster, idealism comes too, and sympathy in the struggle from the sensual abyss. This tragic struggle is made real to us by the pressure of hard, material circumstance. Passages in the Ryecroft papers recall a time of extreme physical stress without bitterness, with regret that this great exercise of living is past. It is not merely the acquiescence which says: 'Since there my past life lies, why alter it?' but the return of the spirit to its circumstance. In this last book Gissing sounded his moods and he found many regrets. 'Think what a man's youth might be,' he says; 'the possibilities of natural joy and delightful effort which lie in those years between seventeen and seven-and-twenty.' These compunctious visitings might obscure the time when the life of privation was the privilege of youth—

of youth which in Mr Conrad's austere conception is 'the test, the trial of life.' In such a youth there comes the precious moment, the exultation of endeavour, the joy in a strength to be broken on the wheel. Gissing, too, was upborne by 'something solid like a principle, and masterful like an instinct—a disclosure of something secret, of that hidden something, that gift of good or evil that makes racial difference, that shapes the fate of nations.' He wrote, often bitterly, of failures and compromises; perhaps he thought his own life a failure or a compromise. We shall not think so, and his work will be our enduring possession.

WILL WARBURTON

June 1905

175. Unsigned review, *Morning Leader*

23 June 1905, 3

If the author's lack of self-knowledge were not proverbial, it would be hard to believe that George Gissing imagined that the icy splendours of *Veranilda* represented his true bent and highest achievement, while he had a book like *Will Warburton* conceived, if not written. *Will Warburton* is in the old manner—the manner of *Demos* and all the books on submerged, half-conscious London. But it is more mature, more generous, more human than anything else Gissing wrote. Sombre it may be, as the earlier novels were, but it ends on a happy note, and the happiness is not the conventional kind derived from events, but the artistic happiness which springs from the development of character. In a word, *Will Warburton* shows Gissing near the heights to which he would inevitably have risen, had he lived; he is revealed as a great literary artist, master of his medium, but never playing tricks for the sake of effect. Every incident in the book is spontaneous and natural. Yet every page shows the deliberate consciousness of strength.

'Is it possible', says one of the chief characters, 'to get into such entanglements of reasoning about what one thinks and feels?' Temperament is an introspective thing: but Gissing knew better than to make his story merely a collection of self-revelations. Warburton is a thoughtful, even dreamy business man, who is ruined by a friend, and turns grocer. For half the book he thinks, interminably about himself and his friends; but towards the end circumstances—the grocery business, in effect—drive him from meditation into plain, straightforward sense, and he marries Bertha, the young woman who could not understand 'entanglements'. Then, again, Norbert Franks is self-conscious but his character is on the surface: he deliberately becomes, and so inevitably remains, a painter who vulgarises his art for the sake of popularity. His wife, the best drawn character in this remarkable book, is full of a thin emotion which at length finds itself in a sort of calculating sentimentalism. Outside these four, the minor characters all live; but the chief four are masterpieces. *Will Warburton* leaves the reader with a deep sense of the abiding loss English literature sustained in the death of George Gissing.

176. Unsigned review, *The Times Literary Supplement*

30 June 1905, 209

Not exactly optimism, but a certain colourable imitation of optimism gradually found its way into George Gissing's later novels, which were written far away from London, in the sunshine, and in comparative prosperity. It is, however, the irony of his career that his work, though always good, was only great when it was gloomy. The final word of criticism will surely be that his best books were those which he wrote 'in exile'—the books, that is to say, in which he expressed the hopeless yearnings after the life of leisure, culture, and ideals of some weak but high-minded hedonist, detained in the prison of sordid and banal circumstances. He wrote as a man who had rung all the changes on that joyless experience. It was his one great emotional discovery—his one new and original contribution to the common stock of fiction. It would be hard to name any one of his novels except *Veranilda* in which the note is not sounded, more or less loudly; but those of them which leave the most ineradicable impression on the reader's mind are those like *New Grub Street*, in which the ironies of the situation are most elaborately worked out. One remembers such books as one remembers some hideous nightmare. They depend for their effect altogether upon the theme, and the point of view, and the bitter perception of the ironies, and not in the least upon the drama, or the dialogue, or the drawing of character. The same helpless hedonist reappears in book after book, and goes under in the struggle, much as do the helpless idealists in Tchekoff's short stories. The secret of their power lay in the author's proximity to his subject; he not only had been, but actually was, at the time of writing, a part of what he told. In the end, more successful than his own heroes, he found his way back from exile, and was able to live, if not exactly as he would have liked to live, at least in a manner approximately in consonance with his aspirations; but, from the point of view of his art, he had escaped too late. He was tired, and had lost his receptivity. His first generalization about life had lost the poignant actuality which gave the earlier books the painfully true ring. No second generalization of equal force and value came to take its place. The technical skill remained. The stories were always well written and well constructed; the life, when it was within the range of the writer's observation, was always well observed. He tended, however, more and more, to write of things and persons beyond the reach of his experience, with a certain forced cheerfulness which seemed clumsy, like a man who was weary and had no longer anything particular to say. We should praise *Will Warburton* highly if any one but Gissing had written it; but he himself set the standard by which he must be judged. Estimated by that criterion, it must take a lower place among his novels; for he only says in it feebly what, in other books, he has said forcibly. The best thing in it is the study of the girl—we must not call her the heroine—Rosamund Elvan, drawn to illustrate Gissing's favourite theory about women—to wit, that those of them whom successful men find most charming are in reality self-seeking creatures, blind to ideals, and incapable of sacrifice. It is a theory, like another, easy to support by generalizing from a single instance. The weakness of Gissing's exposition of it is always the same; he makes such a woman's selfishness so much more apparent than her charm that we are left wondering what on earth was the secret of her fascination. That is certainly the case with Rosamund; and Rosamund, after all, is only an inferior replica of another similar character, studied with much more care, in *New Grub Street*. This last reflection, in fact, might be passed on the book as a whole. It is characteristic Gissing, but not good Gissing. His familiar effects are reproduced in a fainter form than of old, and there are no new effects indicating how, with further experience of life, his talents would have developed.

177. Unsigned review, *Athenaeum*

8 July 1905, 41

Obviously *Will Warburton* was written before *Veranilda*, but how long before does not appear. There is no word of preface or explanation in this book, which, in the circumstances, would have been welcome, if not desirable. It is clear, however, that this is a late work, and that Gissing had advanced in the knowledge of his art and of life considerably further than when he wrote *Demos* or *New Grub Street*. There is some resemblance between the latter and *Will Warburton*; but there is a vast difference in treatment and in spirit. A more genial temper characterizes this novel, which is described as 'a romance of real life.' It is, indeed, a realistic romance, which is not a contradiction in terms, and it is importantly different from Gissing's characteristic work. There is a positive sense of humour presiding over these chapters, and only occasionally does that humour become grim. As a rule it is amiable and friendly. Gissing seems to have been on his way to discovering a further interpretation of life when he wrote this, which makes our regret at his premature death all the sharper. He so persistently and for years painted in grey and drab that it is a relief to read a story by him with lighter effects. The sunshine here is not bright, but it is light—it is not all the winter of our discontent. And Gissing seems also to have developed a sense of irony. Take, for example, the two portraits, Amy Reardon from *New Grub Street* and Rosamund Elvan from the last novel. There is a good deal in common between them; they are both temperamentally selfish. But one feels that Gissing has conceived his later character with more kindliness, has used her with more toleration, and dismisses her with a cynical smile of which he was not capable in his more zealous days. All this marks a gain in power, in grasp, and in sympathy. But apart from this important development there is no change observable in style. It is open to the same objections as before; it has the same virtues. It is undistinguished, but it is clear and efficient. It lacks colour, but it has balance. Its matter-of-factness makes it easy for the reader, while at times chafing him when he feels it might rise to the occasion. It never does; it plods along like a devoted pedestrian. But it is making for the proper goal all the same; and there are evolved slowly before the reader's eyes real characters, firmly endued with flesh and blood, not painted shadows. That is the first essential of good fiction, and Gissing's was always good. It is sad to think that what is in some respects his best work should also be his last.

178. Edward Garnett, *Speaker*

8 July 1905, 352–3

Edward Garnett (1868–1937) was critic, biographer and playwright, the friend of W. H. Hudson, Conrad and Galsworthy. As he was writing this review, he remarked to John Galsworthy in a letter of 5 July 1905: 'There is not much doing in the book world. Gissing's last novel about a middle-class man who loses his capital and turns grocer is a *very clever* satire on English ideals. The papers are all decrying it—but E[dward] G[arnett] is pointing the moral!' (*Letters from John Galsworthy 1900–1932*, edited with an introduction by Edward Garnett, Cape, London, 1934).

Far better than the frigid *Veranilda*, which we note many literary pundits, seduced by the classical dignity of the theme, hailed as 'belonging emphatically to literature . . . the higher scope . . . his most original work,' etc., is *Will Warburton*, a novel which Gissing aims straight at the breast of our British commercial gentility. The story, which is double-edged, will probably arouse uneasy suspicions in the mind of the British public that Gissing is satirising the system by which the bulk of our middle-class draw their profits from trade of some kind or other while despising and eyeing uneasily the tradesman's life. Will Warburton, Gissing's refined and sensitive middle-class hero, a partner in a wholesale West India sugar house, having lost his invested capital by his partner's speculations, is forced to turn grocer to support himself and his mother and sister. Here are no learned archaeological researches amid the dust and ashes of Belisarius's and Totila's tombs, no pictures of problematical Roman nobles and imaginary Christian priests, but an atmosphere of shabby-genteel trouble in a London lodging and in a vulgar London shop, with the depressing dulness of the dingy Fulham streets to nerve the hero—another Gissing—to fight against the wearisome routine of his struggle with the indifferent world. Decidedly unpopular this novel should be with the majority of people, for the whole effort of suburban idealism is directed towards keeping the vulgar facts of commercial life in the background and losing all memory of the shop—if shop there be—in the tasteful refinements of villa culture. The novel, *Will Warburton*, is not the most powerful of Gissing's works, but it is saner, riper, and less pessimistic than the majority, and withal it is characteristic of the talent which doggedly set itself to paint the harsh, mean outlines of lower-middle class life in *Demos*, *New Grub Street*, and a dozen other works drab as the great town's smoke. Moreover, the paradox of Gissing's career is in the book: that he has taken his place in literature, that 'his work emphatically belongs to literature,' because he was unlucky and out of place in his environment. Had he not deliberately chronicled all the vulgar unloveliness, all the harsh, sordid cares and commonplace drudgery of 'this wilderness of brick and mortar,' had he been able to follow the tranquil scholarly life of a University professor, and 'the higher scope' of the classical studies that attracted him he would probably have won no more recognition than falls to the majority of talented scholars who lecture and coach and edit classical texts from year's end to year's end. But the mean, monotonous life led by hundreds of thousands of dispirited, anxious, toiling Londoners it was his distinction as an artist to stamp in literature with an insistence and a scrupulous patience that have left their mark. Beauty of style and beauty of feeling are alike too far lacking from his work for it to endure permanently as imaginative literature, but it will endure as a series of grim documents simply because Gissing alone had the courage to set down what he saw. All the others shrank from recognising that life. All the interested tribe of journalists and storywriters hastened to ignore it, all the great horde of readers naturally avert their gaze from it, hurrying along the wan London streets, journeying by 'bus or tram or rail from dreary London lodgings to dingy desks and offices. Gissing alone faced insistently the drabness and the vulgar tonelessness of that anaemic, joyless growth of London lower-middle class existence, a life so often drained of its ideals, depressed in its environment, and broken in, like the tired London cab-horse, to its lot.

It is a happy stroke of Gissing's rare and sardonic humour that this apparent tragedy of Will Warburton's life is actually the change from buying and selling sugar in bulk to retailing it over the counter! The gain and loss to Warburton by turning grocer is very neatly contrasted with the gain and loss to his friend, Norbert Franks, the artist, by becoming successful, sinking his ideals, and painting sentimental trashy work. The novel opens with the promising young artist, Franks, groaning over his lack of success, by which his *fiancée*, the charming Rosamund Elvan, is led to break off her engagement. Franks almost goes off his head, but, sustained by Warburton, sets to work and finishes two blatantly sentimental pictures, 'Sanctuary' and 'The Slummer.' When Warburton's financial crash comes, and he is forced to take to grocery for a living, concealing the fact from his friends, Franks is already on the road to attaining all that poor Warburton has lost—money, refined surroundings, and the esteem and applause of the world. The beautiful Rosamund, ignorant of Warburton's change of fortune, was prepared to love him as a prosperous West India sugar merchant, but when she discovers that he is actually shop-keeping in the Brompton-road she promptly makes up her mind to marry the rising artist. And very lucky for Warburton it is that she does so. For Rosamund, under the veil of her 'soft and subtle refinement of bearing,' is an odious young person, and it is an immense tribute to Gissing's cleverness that when we take leave of her and the successful Franks we seem to feel the artist struggling in the suffocating embraces of a prosperous Mrs Grundy. Franks will have a position, a nice house, a handsome wife, heaps of friends, etc., but he has prostituted his soul, and with Mrs Grundy by day and night at his elbow he will feel no spiritual impulse in his life to strive after. Warburton, on the other hand, by his courage in defying genteel prejudices, has won a splendid woman in Bertha Cross, and the reader who honestly asks himself which existence will be the most endurable—grocering with Bertha, or being incessantly kept up to the mark of worldly success by Rosamund—must plump for the Brompton-road household.

It is impossible to say whether Gissing would have developed greatly in his art, had he lived. But we certainly hold that *Will Warburton* gives ample evidence that his art had entered into a riper and maturer phase. As we have said, *Will Warburton* is itself the antidote to the faint snobbery that pervades *The Crown of Life*, with its ideal of villa culture as the *summum bonum*. If Gissing's work 'belongs emphatically to literature' it is because Gissing himself was marvellously representative of the English middle-class with all its thin-blooded idealism, its nervous susceptibility to class distinctions, its self-consciousness, reserve, conscientiousness of purpose, and lack of breadth of human passion. Will Warburton is a character, we should judge, much akin to Gissing's own, and this type of Englishman, modest, but timidly self-conscious, high-principled, generously self-sacrificing, but morbidly reserved and full of self-distrust, is a type so purely insular that we doubt if the continental reader would understand its intricacies of nature, or, indeed, be able to view it sympathetically. Gissing was extremely well-equipped by temperament to penetrate into both the weakness and the strength of middle-class English society, and we believe that his power of quiet satire might have been developed in a series of later novels which would have revealed the forces of latter-day Philistinism in a rather novel light.

179. Unsigned review, *Saturday Review*

19 August 1905, c, 251

This, the second book of George Gissing published since his death, exhibits the writer in a new phase. His earlier novels without exception are marked by a bitterness of conception, a hopelessness of outlook that are distinctly traceable to the author's own experience. Life did not deal too kindly with George Gissing. His apprenticeship to literature was hard and cruel. In spite of a long and bitter struggle with poverty he upheld his standard and never consented to pander to the public taste by ephemeral work or meretricious effects. Strength and sincerity characterised all he did. But it was impossible for a man of his temperament, placed as he was for the greater part of his life, to escape the taint of pessimism, and he would seem to have taken a sort of sombre delight in relentless delineation of failure. It was impossible for him to accept life at other people's valuation, nor could he consent to bow down and worship commonplace ideals. When at last worldly success came it arrived, as it generally does, almost too late. He was only to enjoy it for so short a time. And yet that brief time of prosperity stamped itself upon his work. His nature unfolded. His outlook upon life became more genial, better proportioned. *Will Warburton*, although not by any means the best of his books, shows no failure in power. It does not rank with such books as *The Nether World* and *Demos*. It has not their biting cynicism and remorseless analysis. It does not exhibit the same sense of struggle, but it is mellower, more hopeful, more amiable in tone and conception. The story is not unkindly satire on middle-class snobbery. Will Warburton is a sugar merchant who through the extravagance and mismanagement of his partner is obliged to turn grocer in order to save his mother and sister from want. There is no reason, of course, why a grocer serving in his shop in a white apron should not be a hero of romance, and the causes that impelled Warburton to the course are wholly admirable. The author is a little over-insistent perhaps on the pettiness and meanness of the calling to one of Warburton's temperament. It cannot be an exciting occupation to dole out pounds of sugar. But Mr Gissing made, we consider, an artistic as well as a psychological mistake in causing Warburton to carry on his business under an assumed name and lie about it to his friends. Of course the secret of his double life is discovered, and discovered in the most humiliating way by the girl whom he had met and loved in more prosperous days walking suddenly into his shop and finding him behind the counter. It is not difficult to understand that the girl experienced something of a shock, nor is she perhaps to be blamed as much as Mr Gissing seems inclined to think. After all she knew nothing of the heroism that lay behind his assumption of the white apron. She only saw a petty tradesman who, she supposed, had masqueraded as a gentleman. As will be seen, Mr Gissing's story is made out of commonplace materials and commonplace people. His art lies in the elements of distinction with which he endows them. His personages are all clean cut, well defined. They are endowed with life and individuality. Several of them are possessed of engaging qualities which awaken affection in the reader, and throughout the book there is an atmosphere of cheerfulness, of optimism, a recognition that things are not perhaps so bad after all.

180. C. F. G. Masterman, 'George Gissing', *In Peril of Change*

1905, 68–73

Charles Frederick Gurney Masterman was a liberal politician representing a Manchester constituency and author of works on social, religious and literary questions. One of his best-known books is *The Condition of England* (1909).

Of all the losses which literature has lately endured, the death of Gissing stands out as most exhibiting the ragged edge of tragedy. That Death should come just at the wrong moment was indeed entirely congruous with a life which seemed all through the sport of the gods. The irony of some malign or malicious power seemed to be laid upon the course of this troubled existence. It was almost with a clutch of some frantic laughter—a laughter more desolate than tears—that there came to his friends, at the moment when life at last seemed beginning, the news that life was at an end.

One's whole being revolted against such a bitter bludgeoning of fate. Readers of 'Mark Rutherford' will remember the restrained but passionate irony of the close. After the unendurable years are over, when life has emerged into afternoon, with a prospect of light at eventide, a few dispassionate sentences tell of a sudden chance chill, a few days' struggle, and then—another of earth's unimportant millions lies quiet for ever. So it was with George Gissing. A long struggle against heavy odds, the experience of the worst, public neglect and private tragedies, had at last given place to something like hopefulness and fame. Recognition, long deserved, had arrived. The crudest of life's cruelties had vanished. A benigner outlook, a softer, kindlier vision of the 'farcical melodrama' of man's existence had been apparent in these later months. The words of the last of his books he saw published sound strangely prophetic. 'We hoped'—so he wrote of 'Henry Ryecroft'—'we hoped it would all last for many a year; it seemed, indeed, as though Ryecroft had only need of rest and calm to become a hale man.' 'It had always been his wish to die suddenly. . . . He lay down upon the sofa in his study, and there—as his calm face declared—passed from slumber into the great silence.'

This is not the time to tell the details of that troubled life, of the tragedy which lay behind that arduous literary toil and coloured all the outlook with indignation and pain. Some day, for the edification or the warning of the children of the future, the full story will be told. All that it is necessary to know at the present is contained in those books in which the author, under the thin veil of fiction, is protesting out of his heart's bitterness against the existence to which he has been committed. 'For twenty years he had lived by the pen. He was a struggling man beset by poverty and other circumstances very unpropitious to work.' 'He did a great deal of mere hack-work: he reviewed, he translated, he wrote articles. There were times, I have no doubt, when bitterness took hold upon him; not seldom he suffered in health, and probably as much from moral as from physical overstrain.' The tyranny of this nineteenth-century Grub Street drove his genius into a hard and narrow groove. He might have developed into a great critic—witness the promise of his essay on Dickens. There was humour in him all unsuspected by the public till the appearance of *The Town Traveller*. And a keen eye for natural beauty, and a power of description of the charm and fascination of places, and a passionate love of nature and of home were only made manifest in *By the Ionian Sea*, and the last and most kindly volume.

All this was sacrificed: in part to a perverted sense of 'Mission,' the burden, as he thought, laid upon him to proclaim the desolation of modern life: partly to a determination to make manifest to all the world his repugnance and disgust. He remains, and will remain, in literature as the creator of one particular picture. Gissing is the painter, with a cold and mordant accuracy, of certain phases of city life, especially of the life of London, in its cheerlessness and bleakness and futility, during the years of rejoicing at the end of the nineteenth century. If ever in the future the long promise of the Ages be fulfilled, and life becomes beautiful and passionate once again, it is to his dolorous pictures that men will turn for a vision of the ancient tragedies in a City of Dreadful Night.

Gissing rarely if ever described the actual life of the slum. He left to others the natural history of the denizens of 'John Street' and the 'Jago.' The enterprise, variety, and adventurous energy of those who led the existence of the beast would have disturbed with a human vitality the picture of his dead world. It was the classes above these enemies of society, in their ambitions and pitiful successes, which he made the subject of his genius. He analyses into its constituent atoms the matrix of which is composed the characteristic city population. With artistic power and detachment he constructs his sombre picture, till a sense of almost physical oppression comes upon the reader, as in some strange and disordered dream.

There are but occasional vivid incidents; the vitriol-throwing in *The Nether World*; the struggle of the Socialists in *Demos*, as if against the tentacles of some slimy and unclean monster; the particular note of revolt sounded in *New Grub Street*, when the fog descends not merely upon the multitude who acquiesce, but upon the few who resist. But in general the picture is merely of the changes of time hurrying the individuals through birth, marriage, and death, but leaving the general resultant impression unchanged. *Vanitas vanitatum* is written large over an existence which has 'never known the sunshine nor the glory that is brighter than the sun.' Human life apprehends nothing of its possibilities of sweetness and gentleness and high passion. The energies, rude or tired, flaming into pitiful revolt or accepting from the beginning the lesson of inevitable defeat, end all alike in dust and ashes.

The Islington of *Demos*, the Camberwell of *In the Year of Jubilee*, the Lambeth of *Thyrza*: how the whole violent soul of the man revolted against existence set in these! The outward obsession of the grey labyrinth seemed to reflect the spirit of a race of tragic ineptitude. Comfort has been attained, and some security. But beauty has fled from the heart, and the hunger for it passed into a vague discontent. Religion has lost its high aspiration. Passion has become choked in that heavy air. The men toil—the decent and the ignobly decent—without ever a sense of illumination in the dusty ways, or the light of a large purpose in it all. The women—what an awful picture-gallery of women appears in Gissing's tales of suburban existence!—nag and hate, are restless with boredom and weariness, pursue ignoble, unattainable social aspirations, desire without being satisfied. The whole offers a vision more disquieting and raucous than any vision of the squalor of material failure. Here, the Showman seems to announce at intervals, always with an ironic smile, here is the meaning of culture, civilisation, religion—in the forefront of your noisy 'progress,' in the city of your heart's desire.

'Her object,' said Mr Hutton, of George Eliot's *Middlemarch*, 'is to paint not the grand defeat, but the helpless entanglement and miscarriage of noble aims, to make us see the eager stream of high purpose, not leaping destructively from the rock, but more or less silted up in the dreary sands of modern life.' I have often thought this might serve for a verdict upon all Gissing's characteristic work. To produce this result he had, indeed, to cut out great sections of human activity. The physical satisfaction in food and the greater physical satisfaction in drink; the delight in the excitement of betting, an election, an occasional holiday; the illumination which comes to a few, at least, from a spiritual faith or an ideal cause; even the commonest joy of all, 'the only wage,' according to the poet, which 'love ever asked':

> A child's white face to kiss at night,
> A woman's smile by candlelight:

—all these, if introduced at all, appear merely to relieve for a moment the picture of the desolation of London's incalculable, bewildered millions. Gissing set himself a legitimate artistic effort: the representation of modern life in a certain aspect, seen under a certain mood. It is London, not in the glories of starlight or sunset, but under the leaden sky of a cold November afternoon. The third of Henley's 'London Voluntaries' is the characteristic outward scene of Mr Gissing's gaunt picture; in which the 'afflicted city'

> seems
> A nightmare labyrinthine, dim and drifting,
> With wavering gulfs and antic heights, and shifting,
> Rent in the stuff of a material dark,
> Wherein the lamplight, scattered and sick and pale,
> Shows like the leper's living blotch of bale.

The vision does not even possess the sense of magic and mystery of twilight and gathering night. The universe is simply raw and wretched, with a wind scattering the refuse of the gutter, and, too hideous and grotesque even to evoke compassion, a few old tramps and forlorn children shivering in the cold.

It was because we saw in Gissing's later works an escape from this insistent and hideous dream, a promise of a warmer, saner outlook upon human development and desire, that we felt as a kind of personal outrage the news of his early death. For skilled, artistic craftsmanship he held the first place in the ranks of the younger authors of to-day. He was only forty-six years old. The later books seemed to open possibilities of brilliant promise. The bitterness had become softened. The general protest against the sorry scheme of human things seemed to be passing into a kind of pity for all that suffers, and an acceptance with thankfulness of life's little pleasures. The older indignation had yielded to perplexity as of a suffering child. With something of that perplexity —with a new note of wistfulness, the sudden breaking of the springs of compassion—George Gissing passes from a world of shadows which he found full of uncertainty and pain.

THE HOUSE OF COBWEBS

May 1906

181. R. A. Scott-James, *Daily News*

17 May 1906, 4

Rolfe Arnold Scott-James, journalist and critic, became editor of the *Daily News* in 1906. In the course of the first half of this century he wrote for such papers and reviews as *New Weekly*, *Daily Chronicle*, *Spectator*, *London Mercury* and *Britain To-Day*. Among his books are *The Making of Literature* (1928) and *Fifty Years of English Literature, 1900–1950* (1951).

Veranilda, *Will Warburton*, and now *The House of Cobwebs*—each in their turn these posthumous volumes—will have been eagerly welcomed in the hope of adding to Gissing's chance of a permanent place in literature. The sad, stunted years of his first literary activity gave scant opportunity for the full development of his genius, and if his earlier works were necessarily one-sided, full of the sense of monotonous misery illumined by ideals which were always set forth as unrealised ideals, at the end he seemed to be passing into a new phase of his art which had not time to be fully matured. The critics pronounced that *Veranilda* and *Will Warburton*, his latest books, fell short of complete success, that they were, as Mr Seccombe hints in his introduction, 'magnificent failures.' In the present collection of short stories, tardily issued, Gissing is returning to the dismal scenes of his own life and thought; but a little less dismally, perhaps, in his manner, sounding the note of tragi-comedy rather than that of unalterable gloom.

In an admirable and thoroughly appreciative introduction, Mr Seccombe surveys the literary history of George Gissing. He does not make it quite clear when the stories now collected were written, but I gather that they belong at any rate to the last ten years of his life.

'Gissing', he remarks in one place, 'understood the theory of compensation, but was unable to exhibit it in action. He elevates the cult of refinement to such a pitch that the consolations of temperament, of habit, and of humdrum ideals which are common to the coarsest of mankind, appear to elude his observation. . . . There is usually a streak of illusion or a flash of hope somewhere on the horizon.' Though this is a just criticism of much of Gissing's work, it is strangely untrue of many stories in the present volume. That is a good phrase, 'consolations of temperament,' and it very happily serves to suggest the state of mind of Mr Spicer in *The House of Cobwebs*. Here we have the disheartening picture of a man who had dragged out most of his life with few ambitions beyond that of being a chemist's assistant. Suddenly he heard that he had come into some leasehold property, and tasted for the first time the joys of possession. But the lease has nearly run its course. The old, unkempt, cobwebby house into which we are introduced will in a year's time revert to the ground landlord. Lawyer's fees had swamped his savings; he had no mind to put it in repair, but nevertheless he went to his top room, put therein his bed and his cooking stove, and his score or so of treasured books, and eked out his scanty annuity. But surely there are the 'consolations.' Though his 'mental development had ceased more than twenty years ago,' and he was commonplace in his qualities, he had his library.

[A quotation, detailing the library, follows.]

And then, the property is his until midsummer day of next year. The garden is a tangled wilderness, but there are some remnants of vegetables and flowers, and particularly Jerusalem artichokes. 'I've been making enquiry about the artichokes, and I'm told they are not ready to eat till the autumn. The first frost is said to improve them. They're fine plants—very fine plants.' And though it is true that the chimney blew down in a gale, and it was only by a miracle that he escaped destruction, and had to be removed from his house, nevertheless he had tasted the artichokes—'just at the time when they were touched by the first frost.'

[A paraphrase of 'The Pig and Whistle' follows.]

The idea of lost caste and cherished respectability appears in the majority of these stories. The atmosphere is generally that of the lower middle classes of suburban London, or people of a higher class who have sunk in fortune. Amid the endless round of routine, amid the intolerable pressure of pettiness and poverty, with its degradation and its meanness, the pathos is always that of something lost, of a fineness dreamt of and desired, but never realised. Comfort, conventional culture, and leisured respectability, things which those stronger people who possess them are wont to deride, are here elevated into things good and desirable in themselves. How often we hear that every class of people in England envies and emulates the social status of the class immediately above it! Gissing tells us how intense and pathetic a passion this may be, and shows the reverse picture—that of men and women who have been driven down to the class below them, in whom, perhaps, the only idealising element left is the desire for the insignificant things which they have ceased to possess. The sense of deprivation is worse than mere poverty; and we see 'a poor gentleman' cherishing his dress suit, though he works with his hands and has no decent boots; and 'the scrupulous father,' whose now aging daughter is always shut up in her remote suburb, dragging out monotonous days, pining for want of sociable company, but not allowed to talk to a man who is 'not quite a gentleman.'

[Here follows a paraphrase of the story 'Christopherson'.]

These stories are profound, searching, movingly realistic pictures of mean and petty life, but of a meanness and a pettiness which is lighted by the suggestion of other things infused into them by the genius of Gissing. They are short, sharp, trenchant, and will bear comparison with the best work of the author.

182. Allan Monkhouse, *Manchester Guardian*

23 May 1906, 5

See headnotes to Nos 107 and 174. This review is signed 'A.N.M.'.

The interest of a new volume by George Gissing, *The House of Cobwebs and Other Stories*, is enhanced by an 'introductory survey' by Mr Thomas Seccombe, who writes with judgment and moderation and yet in a cordially appreciative spirit. Of course one finds material for disagreement, as in a passage which seems to indicate that Mr Seccombe regards *The Private Papers of Henry Ryecroft* and the book on Dickens comparable in merit or importance, or whatever may be possible as a common denominator, with the novels of his most strenuous period. Again, it may be that neither Mr Seccombe nor Gissing himself has done justice to *The Town Traveller*, which is surely far better work than *Our Friend the Charlatan* or *Denzil Quarrier*, but we may all agree that as a novelist Gissing should be judged by certain selected works, of which *The Nether World*, *New Grub Street*, and *In the Year of Jubilee* are among the most notable. The stories in the present volume are hardly of the quality of these novels, but several of them may recall the lower and yet admirable kind of *Will Warburton*. Probably most of them were written in Gissing's later years, but some of them have a 'backward reach' which connects them with earlier work. They are very well written, with a fulness and simplicity of style that is characteristic of Gissing's maturity.

All the stories are interesting, though several of them, such as 'Miss Rodney's Leisure' and 'Humplebee,' are relatively insignificant. 'A Charming Family' and 'The Salt of the Earth' have a good deal in common. The one tells of a woman and the other of a man who are submissive victims to the extortion of social impostors. They suggest moral problems, but they are deficient in moral interest, and Gissing is hardly at his best in such studies of conventional humility. His best work is surprising in its truth, but here there is less than usual of the broken, irregular movements of life that save the art from becoming a mere pattern. Several of these stories seem the truthfully sober statement of the case rather than the vivid life behind it. Certainly some of the people are not very vivid personages; most of them are poor, diffident creatures who, hard pressed, keep yet some kind of hold on the humanities. In some of Gissing's finest characters his own strong personality speaks. These people seem rather to be observed; they are not fortified by his spirit of revolt, though they are derived from his experience and subject to his acquiescence. Gissing's tragic quality is in 'A Lodger in Maze Pond,' with its very strange and convincing catastrophe, and there is something of his peculiar, lurid illumination in the unhappy man's confession: 'I have told you before that I stand in awe of refined women. I am their equal, I know; I can talk with them; their society is an exquisite delight to me; but when it comes to thinking of intimacy with one of them——! Perhaps it is my long years of squalid existence.' Nothing else in the volume holds us like this, though 'The Scrupulous Father,' with its 'wholly reasonable and half-passionate revolt,' is a fine piece of a more impersonal kind, and 'A Daughter of the Lodge' is a very notable instance of Gissing's power to compel our anxious sympathy with a person who, in the preliminaries of his artful presentation, had merely stirred cold criticism. Altogether the book is a very valuable addition to what we know of Gissing's work.

183. Edward Garnett, *Speaker*

26 May 1906, 190–1

See headnote to No. 178.

It is always hazardous work to 'place' a contemporary writer, and the problem is a very puzzling one in the case of George Gissing, for modern literature owes him a debt which posterity, so to say, may repudiate.

[Extracts from Thomas Seccombe's Introductory Survey, pp. vii–ix, p. xlix, follow. These are reproduced in the context of No. 188.]

The complacent optimism of the great majority of Victorian novelists, as Mr Seccombe well says, 'was founded upon a conviction that the evil in the world was steadily diminishing.' A pathetic illusion, germinating in the comfortable middle-class mind, which steadfastly refused to look at, touch, or hear of the squalid misery and the grey leaden horizons of the seas of human life stretching at its doors. Gissing, 'living in garrets and dogged by hunger,' owes his place in literature to the fact that alone among our novelists he portrayed the grayness, the sordid ugliness, the petty, mean vulgarity of the life of the London crowd. It was by the accident of certain unfortunate occurrences that as a young man he was transplanted from the ordinary middle-class environment and found himself an exile, face to face for ten years with the sternest and bitterest poverty. Nothing could prove to us more clearly than Gissing's literary career how indirectly and partially our literature reflects the environment and outlook of the mass of towns-people. It simply is not recorded, people do not wish it to be recorded by the artist, the character of this everyday life, but now and again a Balzac or a Gissing shows us that the very meanness and drabness and sordidness of the life around us is interesting, because it is so inevitably human, so stupidly human, because its dull reality is so essentially the grey background against which the light shows. But how far is Gissing a truthful observer of life and what is the literary quality of the style of this 'detached remorseless photographic artist'? It is by the answers to these two questions that Gissing's place in literature will be determined. Mr Seccombe does not give us a direct answer, but in his sympathetic Survey he suggests again and again that Gissing will live in literature, if only for the picturesque spectacle of this refined, sensitive, and delicate mind, tortured by daily contact with the coarse and brutal facts of a sordid environment.

Mr Seccombe lays stress also, perhaps a little too much stress, on the subjectivity of Gissing's work. A more serious point is the charge brought against Gissing's style, that it is too lacking in distinction and beauty, and Mr Seccombe seeks to disarm us by quoting some fine passages from *Thyrza*, *New Grub Street*, *The Nether World*, and *Ryecroft*, and by asserting that in three books, *By the Ionian Sea*, *Dickens*, and *Ryecroft*, Gissing's style is 'a charmed instrument.' We cannot, however, go quite all the way with Mr Seccombe. We should, indeed, prefer to trace Gissing's comparative failure to take a high place as a literary artist to his failure to fuse and harmonise aesthetically the two men within him—the realist and the idealist. Take *Ryecroft*, for example, and note how thin and unsubstantial and, indeed, lacking in all illusion is the figure of Ryecroft himself. If we cannot believe in the channel, we cannot help discounting what is conveyed to us through the channel. Gissing the idealist has his fling in *Ryecroft*, just as Gissing the realist, in *New Grub Street*, has his nose too near to the grindstone. We say with conviction that these two men in Gissing are most happily harmonised in *By the Ionian Sea*, which must stand forth as his most perfect artistic achievement, far, far above the cold and frigid *Veranilda*, which the English critics, struck by the solemn classical subject, all elected to praise.

The fifteen short stories contained in *The House of Cobwebs* are full of Gissing's characteristic flavour. They are all carefully wrought, chiselled with a precise economy of touch, but a little meagre and niggardly in outline. What Mr Seccombe styles 'a shortcoming in emotional power,' or what might perhaps be termed a lack of freedom in emotional expression, is marked in all the tales and stamps them as genuine work of the English school. The cautiousness and reserve of the Englishman, the restrictions that his precise and careful temperament exercises upon his mental outlook, the sterilising effect of uncongenial conditions, a certain pettiness of social horizon—all this Gissing understands admirably, and details with a quiet fatalistic acceptation that enforces on the reader the sense of sharing in the spiritual imprisonment from which so many of his characters suffer. Perhaps the cleverest piece in the book is 'The Scrupulous Father,' a sketch of a highly respectable man 'profoundly conscious of social limits,' who keeps up the traditions of 'gentlefolk,' leading, with his daughter, the dullest and most monotonous of lives in a London suburb on the narrowest means. On their annual visit to a watering-place a manly and cheerful young man, who looks like a small clerk, tries to get into touch with the daughter, Rose, who surreptitiously encourages him and actually permits herself to exchange names and addresses with the stranger when her father's back is turned! The father behaves with a sense of frigid superiority to the intruder, and Gissing analyses very neatly the surprising conflict in the girl's bosom between the habits of a lifetime and natural inclination. The intricacies of the shades of class-feeling are well indicated in 'A Capitalist,' a study of a man who fiercely desires to be 'a gentleman,' with all the advantages that 'position' can buy; and the fine shades of social intercourse between an artisan's family and young Mr Rawcliffe, who, belonging to a 'very high-connected family,' is at liberty to take tipsy liberties with the daughters of the house, are also neatly painted. 'A Lodger in Maze Pond' is a very convincing psychological study of a man of weak temperament who twice, out of sheer sentimentality, makes 'a hideous mistake' in marrying women of a low class. On the second occasion, Munden knows how perfectly fatal is his action, but he cannot prevent his tongue from uttering the 'imbecile words, in spite of his brain.' It is significant that Munden, 'after long years of squalid existence,' stands in awe of refined women, and finds it an 'impossible thing to imagine himself making love to them.' This story goes deeper into the contradictions of human nature than any of the others, though 'A Charming Family' runs it close. The charming family of the Rhymers owes a year's rent to Miss Shepperson, a struggling woman who owns the house and forty pounds a year, and the story sketches for us the clever way in which Mr and Mrs Rhymer capture Miss Shepperson and, under the plea of giving her board and lodging, turn her into a domestic servant, finally walking off with the thirty pounds rent eventually paid her, which Miss Shepperson, in an access of soft-heartedness, presses into little Dora's hands. Gissing does her, with a restrained and delicate brush, what Dickens essayed in his telling, humorous caricatures from life. The stories, as Mr Seccombe hints, are too quiet and too delicate to appeal to 'the larger external rings of the book-reading public,' and for that reason we commend them to the attention of the *Speaker*'s readers.

184. Arthur Waugh, *Daily Chronicle*

26 May 1906, 3

Arthur Waugh, the father of Evelyn and Alec Waugh, was a member of the firm of Chapman & Hall for many years and as such published *A Hundred Years of Publishing, Chapman and Hall 1830–1930*. He was in touch with Gissing when his firm brought out *Our Friend the Charlatan* and *By the Ionian Sea* (1901). In addition to his biographies of Tennyson and Browning, Waugh wrote an amount of criticism for newspapers and reviews. His article 'George Gissing' (*Fortnightly Review*, February 1904, 244–56) was reprinted in *Reticence in Literature and Other Papers* (J. G. Wilson, London, 1915), 161–82.

The work which George Gissing left unpublished is being steadily brought to light, and this volume of short stories is the third of his books to make its appearance since his death. Short stories are now not much in vogue, and it is possible that some readers, who have faithfully followed him through *Veranilda* and *Will Warburton* will be disposed to overlook *The House of Cobwebs*; but everyone who does so will miss a thoroughly characteristic volume, full of the ripest and most impressive of his work. It is natural and commendable when a man is dead to speak gently of work which he is known to have valued himself; and, because Gissing set great store on his excursion into the field of historical romance, his critics have, many of them, with the most admirable sentiment, endeavoured to persuade themselves that *Veranilda* was a fine and living piece of literature. Well, it is scarcely taking a difference of opinion too seriously to affirm one's confidence that time will not bear out that judgment.

Gissing's most significant work was always that which he had seen with his own eyes and lived with his own heart, and this volume of odds and ends—chips, so to speak, from his workshop—comes far nearer to the true Gissing than the rather overladen pastiche into which he poured so much of his enthusiasm for the world of his fancy and his consolation. For in imagination Gissing was almost entirely lacking, but in observation and 'actuality' he excelled. And these collected stories are full of his abundant quality; they register, with unfailing keenness, a multiplicity of moods and temperaments. Moreover, they are almost all veiled in his inevitable atmosphere of drab; they picture the unideal aspects of life, illumined by fitful flashes of a hope which generally proves illusory. They are scarcely stimulating food, but they are at least the real thing—life, as it shows itself to the majority of its tired wayfarers in our complicated city struggle of to-day.

The stories are preceded by a critical essay by Mr Thomas Seccombe, which will probably rank as the best and most sympathetic study of Gissing's work yet printed in this country. The austerity of the subject has diverted Mr Seccombe from some of his characteristic charm; we have read criticism of his that 'lit up the candelabra in the brain' with a fresher air of communicativeness. But we should not be prepared to say that we have ever found him going straighter to the heart of his subject, or creating a firmer fabric of judgment with fewer or more definite strokes. So careful and sincere an 'essay in criticism' cheers one up in the cause of one's own generation; it is clear that, despite all the present temptations towards showy and meretricious writing, the mantle of criticism has not yet fallen in the river amid the perpetual scurry upon the bank!

As for the stories themselves, it would serve no good purpose to enumerate their emotions; and, indeed, where the whole art of the story-teller depends upon a temperamental impression, often of a very sensitive order, comment and description are apt merely to confuse the issues. The tales which strike us as being the most masterly of an entirely masterly collection are 'The Scrupulous Father', 'Christopherson', 'Topham's Chance', and 'Fate and the Apothecary'. The last-named is, perhaps, almost intolerable in its unflinching acceptance of the old Greek theory of Atè, but all the others have little wandering airs of humour, traversing their grey ways; and if, as Mr Seccombe seems to suggest, they belong to a wide field in the career of Gissing's activity, they certainly give one the impression that the larger canvases were apt to destroy the effect of some of those lighter touches which may still be traced by the careful reader in even so sombre a picture as that of *New Grub Street*.

Mr A. H. Bullen, one of Gissing's most discriminating admirers, has always maintained that his genius was seen to peculiar advantage in the short story, and a further study of *Human Odds and Ends*, combined with the recent reading of *The House of Cobwebs*, confirms me in the conviction that Mr Bullen's judgment is here, as so often elsewhere, infallibly sound.*

185. Unsigned review, *Glasgow Herald*

31 May 1906, 11

The fifteen short stories included in this volume constitute the final posthumous contribution to literature of one of the greatest and, within his strictly defined limits, most perfect of English stylists. Mr Seccombe's well-written and sympathetic prefatory monograph makes no mention of the previous appearance of these stories, one at least of which we remember having read before. The subject matter of most of them relates to personal experiences far back in the author's career, and, in common with all save one or two of his other works, they bear the searing impress of those unhappy early struggles which darkened his whole outlook upon life, and whose deferred consequences cheated him out of that crepuscular calm of lettered ease, so pathetically anticipated in the choice pages of his semi-autobiographical masterpiece. The reading-world is already sufficiently acquainted with the peculiar defects, though it is slow to recognise the very rare and special excellences of Gissing as a story-writer. Both of these are present to a very characteristic extent in the volume before us, which we may sum up by saying that there is not a page which is not pure Gissing, and not a story but would have been utterly spoiled by another hand. The more than Maupassant-like disdain of mere plot of the conventional 'story' is here unfettered by the prudential considerations which account for the happy endings of one or two of the longer novels; the occasional touches of romance are only the spasmodic revolts of a sensitive nature against the dingy horrors of scenes which he had trained

* Arthur Henry Bullen, the Elizabethan scholar and partner of Lawrence & Bullen, published eight books by Gissing in the 1890s.

himself to regard with the microscopic curiosity of a Hogarth; each tale but raises the curtain, as if by accident, upon the downward career of some picturesque dead-beat or under dog, some hapless round peg in a square hole, and lets it fall again with full regard to pictorial, but with scarcely any to dramatic, effectiveness; while the dignity of human nature is vindicated by the affectionate delineation in such stories as 'The Salt of the Earth' or 'A Charming Family', of people whose blind trustfulness and calamitous unselfishness would have earned the withering contempt of a Dr Smiles or a Dr Carnegie. A terse, mature, yet exquisitely unusual style, a descriptive accuracy which might be called photographic if it could be attained by any but a very great artist, and a psychological insight which, while it may be only the outcome of brooding self-analysis, is so admirably apportioned as to endow every one of his personages with an absolutely self-consistent individuality—such are the distinguishing features of this, as of all the best work, of a writer who hewing at the sodden dough of London proletarian existence with the chisel of a great craftsman, raised English fiction higher into the region of pure literature than any writer since Thackeray.

186. Unsigned review, *The Times Literary Supplement*

8 June 1906, 208–9

Mr Seccombe has prefaced this volume of remains, containing fifteen short stories by the late George Gissing (1857–1903), with a discriminating essay of considerable biographical and critical interest. In his lifetime George Gissing's work as a novelist received but scanty encouragement, and Mr Seccombe admits that 'upon the larger external rings of the book-reading multitude it is not probable that Gissing will ever succeed in impressing himself.' The pathetic details of his life, in so far as they can well be narrated at present—'hampered for ten years by the sternest poverty, and for nearly ten more by the sad, illusive optimism of the *poitrinaire*'—are sympathetically touched upon by Mr Seccombe. The £50 he got for *Demos* (1886) was then riches. The £250 he got for *New Grub Street* (1891) was his high-water mark for pecuniary profit from his books. His publishers paid him £200 for *The Nether World* (1889), and lost by it.* A man of fine scholarship, remarkable literary gift, and, by compulsion of the 'twin monsters Bread and Cheese,' cast amid the shabbiest genteel or lower life of modern London, he followed the call of his genius by portraying what he knew, and all but starved. The public and the literary magnates found his stories drab and dreary and depressing. At the end of his life, when he published *The Private Papers of Henry Ryecroft* (1903)—a volume of meditative self-revelation, of a quality rare in English literature—the average reviewer began to rub his eyes. The posthumous *Veranilda* (1904)—a Byzantine romance full of archaeological learning, and dead as a doornail—was eulogistically prefaced by an eminent writer who had employed Gissing as a classical tutor in earlier life, but confessed that he could not enjoy his social novels. Yet if publishers, who after all are men of business, and literary magnates, who sometimes prefer their own tastes to the encouragement of an uncomfortable originality, did little for Gissing in his lifetime, and reviewers who can find you a 'modern Thackeray' in a successful serial-writer never gave him a niche in their English Pantheon, Mr Seccombe (who is indeed no tiro in the estimation of biographical and literary merit) contends that 'he will *sup late*, our Gissing,' and that a 'place is reserved for him' among the immortals, though not of the highest rank. Mr Seccombe's careful and judicious essay must speak for itself on this point, and prophecy is a dangerous thing. He is at all events echoing a judgment which has been that of an honourable minority since *Demos* impressed itself on them in 1886. And this new batch of posthumous short stories, though they can add nothing to Gissing's reputation, are all alive with his characteristic touch.

No critic of any literary or human sympathy will question the charm or power of *The Private Papers of Henry Ryecroft*. But, after all, the place of George Gissing in our literature depends on his novels. Nobody is concerned to deny his literary capacity. He was a man of rare educational refinement, well equipped in the studious arts, a critic him-

* Actually the sums paid to Gissing were £100 for *Demos*, £150 for *The Nether World* and again £150 for *New Grub Street*.

self of letters in the best sense; his book on Dickens (1898) is the finest appreciation ever written on the subject. It was, no doubt, partly the mere writing, the style of the man—clear, restrained, modern, full of observation, yet (as the Americans say) 'without frills'—that attracted some of us from the first. But no amount of excellent style, that is yet not an art-form *per se*, will save a *Veranilda* from oblivion. Nothing is more difficult than to pick out from the mass of English fiction of the later nineteenth century (outside the acknowledged masters) the select library of the future, which has permanent value as creative literature. Such books must have in some way a centre of force in themselves as contributions to a knowledge of life and manners, if, indeed, they are true 'novels' at all, and not merely the easy amusement of a lighter moment—a *genre* which has its own justification. In suggesting, quite rightly, a comparison with Mr Hale White ('Mark Rutherford'), Mr Seccombe hardly makes Gissing's permanent place among writers of English fiction any more easy to define. But Gissing's really representative books—*Demos, Thyrza, A Life's Morning, The Nether World, New Grub Street, Born in Exile, The Odd Women, In the Year of Jubilee, The Whirlpool*—form a body of work which has a value more calculable historically than that of 'Mark Rutherford's' *Revolution in Tanner's Lane*. In these novels Gissing filled in the half-lights and shadow of a phase of life, psychologically obscure, yet full of social meaning, as he knew it from actual contact. It is not every day that you will get a gentleman and a scholar, with the gift for expression in fiction, knowing the germinating 'nether world' of London—the lower middle class, the artisan class, the latter-day medley of 'half-baked' humanity which is gradually creating the 'labour movement,' men and girls—as Gissing knew them, from the inside. Nor has any one else given dramatic reality to precisely that *couche sociale*, in spite of all the serious and comic representations by others of companion types intellectually and emotionally simpler. Certainly the picture is predominantly drab in colour to the eyes of those who can afford to subscribe to circulating libraries. So was Gissing's own life. These things are life; yet they are not unrelieved by the finer emotions, as *Thyrza* shows. Mr Seccombe, who is inclined to over-accentuate Gissing's purely literary genius, whereas it is his vivifying power in dealing with a fundamental phase of contemporary society that isolates him among other competent *littérateurs*, hardly does justice to the early insight shown in *Demos* into the workings of the lower class mind in relation to socialist economics and politics. Gissing's grasp of the problem of the rising proletarian and the 'educated' degenerate of both sexes, together with his rather cold-blooded sincerity, combine to create an artistic pleasure proper to the novel in readers who want reality and not romance, and who do not confuse the mere reporter of facts with the author who welds them into a criticism of life and an illumination of character. If Gissing has any permanent fame, it must be by reason of his unique embodiment of this aspect of the new social England in these—his peculiarly characteristic—novels.

187. Unsigned review, *Nation* (New York)

20 September 1906, 246

The fifteen brief sketches that make up this posthumous work by George Gissing have a very uniform quality which readers unused to the finer literary discriminations will perhaps find monotonous. In fact the effect of the book is cumulative, and one must have read far before he realizes how remarkable a survey it is of the narrow world in which Gissing lived most of his life—the grey limbo of shabby gentility, with its meticulous scruples maintained in the face of penury, its obscure tragedies and comedies, its furtive generosities, its lonely intransigencies. And Gissing has invested this chronicle of those who fail with a curious dignity. His heroes may have failed, but at least they have not consciously surrendered. Rebuffs are their daily bread, which they eat with patient stoicism. They one and all retain the respect due to those who, perforce, live alone or in alien companionship, yet indulge no bitterness toward the prosperous world. Indeed, this group of reduced gentlemen, impoverished bibliophiles, penniless authors, and the like stands in tacit, but damning contrast with the children of worldly success who occasionally intervene—the money lenders, the prosperous friends who lightly promise but as quickly forget, the whole lucky rabble that has no time to indulge delicate feelings.

Nobody has traced the hidden lives that rim and permeate London with quite the tact and knowledge of Gissing. He has written better books than this perhaps, but here is the quintessence of his art. It would be interesting to trace the double strand that runs through these stories and all his works—the eager humanitarian curiosity that he learned from Dickens, and the austere restraint of phrase and feeling imposed by his life-long classical studies. One may note a somewhat analogous case in that other Dickens disciple, Alphonse Daudet. But these considerations lie aside from a brief notice, and it is enough to say that the observation in these sketches is originally fine, and then highly selective; the English of great purity and incisiveness; and that a certain thinness of tone and lack of humor are necessary results of gruelling personal experience with the matter in hand. It is a book for those who love impeccable workmanship. In a period where slapdash and over-emphasis are in favor, it may not win the general ear, but it will, we are confident, find the kind of audience that conveys a volume to posterity.

Space fails to do more than mention Mr Seccombe's sympathetic study of Gissing which raises issues of life and letters beyond the scope of a mere book review.

188. Thomas Seccombe, Introductory Survey to *The House of Cobwebs*

1906, vii–liv

Thomas Seccombe (1866–1923) was a critic and journalist whose publications dealt mainly with the eighteenth century. He had watched the development of Gissing's career very closely and for this reason was requested by Constable to write an introduction to *The House of Cobwebs*, of which two extracts are reprinted here.

In England during the sixties and seventies of last century the world of books was dominated by one Gargantuan type of fiction. The terms book and novel became almost synonymous in houses which were not Puritan, yet where books and reading, in the era of few and unfree libraries, were strictly circumscribed. George Gissing was no exception to this rule. The English novel was at the summit of its reputation during his boyish days. As a lad of eight or nine he remembered the parts of *Our Mutual Friend* coming to the house, and could recall the smile of welcome with which they were infallibly received. In the dining-room at home was a handsomely framed picture which he regarded with an almost idolatrous veneration. It was an engraved portrait of Charles Dickens. Some of the best work of George Eliot, Reade, and Trollope was yet to make its appearance; Meredith and Hardy were still the treasured possession of the few; the reigning models during the period of Gissing's adolescence were probably Dickens and Trollope, and the numerous satellites of these great stars, prominent among them Wilkie Collins, William Black, and Besant and Rice.

Of the cluster of novelists who emerged from this school of ideas, the two who will attract most attention in the future were clouded and obscured for the greater period of their working lives. Unobserved, they received, and made their own preparations for utilising, the legacy of the mid-Victorian novel—moral thesis, plot, underplot, set characters, descriptive machinery, landscape colouring, copious phraseology, Herculean proportions, and the rest of the cumbrous and grandiose paraphernalia of *Chuzzlewit*, *Pendennis*, and *Middlemarch*. But they received the legacy in a totally different spirit. Mark Rutherford, after a very brief experiment, put all these elaborate properties and conventions reverently aside. Cleverer and more docile, George Gissing for the most part accepted them; he put his slender frame into the ponderous collar of the author of the *Mill on the Floss*, and nearly collapsed in wind and limb in the heart-breaking attempt to adjust himself to such an heroic type of harness.

The distinctive qualities of Gissing at the time of his setting forth were a scholarly style, rather fastidious and academic in its restraint, and the personal discontent, slightly morbid, of a self-conscious student who finds himself in the position of a sensitive woman in a crowd. His attitude through life was that of a man who, having set out on his career with the understanding that a second-class ticket is to be provided, allows himself to be unceremoniously hustled into the rough and tumble of a noisy third. Circumstances made him revolt against an anonymous start in life for a refined and educated man under such conditions. They also made him prolific. He shrank from the restraints and humiliations to which the poor and shabbily dressed private tutor is exposed—revealed to us with a persuasive terseness in the pages of *The Unclassed*, *New Grub Street*, *Ryecroft*, and the story of 'Topham's Chance.' Writing fiction in a garret for a sum sufficient to keep body and soul together for the six months following payment was at any rate better than this. The result was a long series of highly finished novels, written in a style and from a point of view which will always render them dear to the studious and the book-centred. Upon the larger external rings of the book-reading multitude it is not probable that Gissing will ever succeed in impressing himself. There is an absence of transcendental quality about his work, a failure in humour, a remoteness from actual life, a deficiency in awe and mystery, a shortcoming in emotional power, finally, a lack of the dramatic faculty, not indeed indispensable to a novelist, but almost indispensable as an ingredient in great novels of this particular genre. In temperament and vitality he is palpably inferior to the masters (Dickens, Thackeray, Hugo, Balzac) whom he reverenced with such a cordial admiration and envy. A 'low vitality' may account for what has been referred to as the 'nervous exhaustion' of his style. It were useless to pretend that Gissing belongs of right to the 'first series' of English Men of Letters.

But if debarred by his limitations from a resounding or popular success, he will remain exceptionally dear to the heart of the recluse, who thinks that the scholar does well to cherish a grievance against the vulgar world beyond the cloister; and dearer still, perhaps, to a certain number of enthusiasts who began reading George Gissing as a college night-course; who closed *Thyrza* and *Demos* as dawn was breaking through the elms in some Oxford quadrangle, and who have pursued his work patiently ever since in a somewhat toilsome and broken ascent, secure always of suave writing and conscientious workmanship, of an individual prose cadence and a genuine vein of Penseroso:—

> Thus, Night, oft see me in thy pale career . . .
> Where brooding Darkness spreads his jealous wings,
> And the night-raven sings.

Yet by the larger, or, at any rate, the intermediate public, it is a fact that Gissing has never been quite fairly estimated. He loses immensely if you estimate him either by a single book, as is commonly done, or by his work as a whole, in the perspective of which, owing to the lack of critical instruction, one or two books of rather inferior quality have obtruded themselves unduly.

[In later years] Gissing spent an increasing portion of his time abroad, and it was from St Honoré en Morvan, for instance, that he dated the preface of *Our Friend the Charlatan* in 1901. As with *Denzil Quarrier* (1892) and *The Town Traveller* (1898) this was one of the books which Gissing sometimes went the length of asking the admirers of his earlier romances 'not to read.' With its prefatory note, indeed, its cheap illustrations, and its rather mechanical intrigue, it seems as far removed from such a book as *A Life's Morning* as it is possible for a novel by the same author to be. It was in the South of France, in the neighbourhood of Biarritz, amid scenes such as that described in the thirty-seventh chapter of *Will Warburton*, or still further south, that he wrote the greater part of his last three books, the novel just mentioned, which is probably his best essay in the lighter ironical vein to which his later years inclined, *Veranilda*, a romance of the time of Theodoric the Goth, written in solemn fulfilment of a vow of his youth, and *The Private Papers of Henry Ryecroft*, which to my mind remains a legacy for Time to take account of as the faithful tribute of one of the truest artists of the generation he served.

In *Veranilda* (1904) are combined conscientious workmanship, a pure style of finest quality, and archaeology, for all I know to the contrary, worthy of Becker or Boni. Sir Walter himself could never in reason have dared to aspire to such a fortunate conjuncture of talent, grace, and historic accuracy. He possessed only that profound knowledge of human nature, that moulding humour and quick sense of dialogue, that live, human, and local interest in matters antiquarian, that statesmanlike insight into the pith and marrow of the historic past, which makes one of Scott's historical novels what it is—the envy of artists, the delight of young and old, the despair of formal historians. *Veranilda* is without a doubt a splendid piece of work; Gissing wrote it with every bit of the care that his old friend Biffen expended upon *Mr Bailey, grocer*. He worked slowly, patiently, affectionately, scrupulously. Each sentence was as good as he could make it, harmonious to the ear, with words of precious meaning skilfully set; and he believed in it with the illusion so indispensable to an artist's well-being and continuance in good work. It represented for him what *Salammbô* did to Flaubert. But he could not allow himself six years to write a book as Flaubert did. *Salammbô*, after all, was a magnificent failure, and *Veranilda*,—well, it must be confessed, sadly but surely, that *Veranilda* was a failure too. Far otherwise was it with *Ryecroft*, which represents, as it were, the *summa* of Gissing's habitual meditation, aesthetic feeling and sombre emotional experience. Not that it is a pessimistic work,—quite the contrary, it represents the mellowing influences, the increase of faith in simple, unsophisticated English girlhood and womanhood, in domestic pursuits, in innocent children, in rural homeliness and honest Wessex landscape, which began to operate about 1896, and is seen so unmistakably in the closing scenes of *The Whirlpool*. Three chief strains are subtly interblended in the composition. First that of a nature book, full of air, foliage and landscape—that English landscape art of Linnell and De Wint and Foster for which he repeatedly expresses such a passionate tendre, refreshed by 'blasts from the channel, with raining scud and spume of mist breaking upon the hills' in which he seems to crystallise the very essence of a Western winter. Secondly, a paean half of praise and half of regret for the vanishing England, passing so rapidly even as he writes into 'a new England which tries so hard to be unlike the old.' A deeper and richer note of thankfulness, mixed as it must be with anxiety, for the good old ways of English life (as lamented by Mr Poorgrass and Mark Clark), old English simplicity, and old English fare—the fine prodigality of the English platter, has never been raised. God grant that the leaven may work! And thirdly there is a deeply brooding strain of saddening yet softened autobiographical reminiscence, over which is thrown a light veil of literary appreciation and topical comment. Here is a typical *cadenza*, rising to a swell at one point (suggestive for the moment of Raleigh's famous apostrophe), and then most gently falling, in a manner not wholly unworthy, I venture to think, of Webster and Sir Thomas Browne, of both of which authors there is internal evidence that Gissing made some study.

[The final paragraph from Autumn XII is quoted.]

And in this deeply moving and beautiful passage we get a foretaste, it may be, of the euthanasia, following a brief summer of St Martin, for which the scarred and troublous portions of Gissing's earlier life had served as a preparation. Some there are, no doubt, to whom it will seem no extravagance in closing these private pages to use the author's own words, of a more potent Enchanter: 'As I close the book, love and reverence possess me.'

Whatever the critics may determine as to the merit of the stories in the present volume, there can be no question as to the interest they derive from their connection with what had gone before. Thus 'Topham's Chance' is manifestly the outcome of material pondered as early as 1884. 'The Lodger in Maze Pond' develops in a most suggestive fashion certain problems discussed in 1894. Miss Rodney is a re-incarnation of Rhoda Nunn and Constance Bride. 'Christopherson' is a delicious expansion of a mood indicated in *Ryecroft* (Spring XII.), and 'A Capitalist' indicates the growing interest in the business side of practical life, the dawn of which is seen in *The Town Traveller* and in the discussion of Dickens's potentialities as a capitalist. The very artichokes in *The House of Cobwebs* (which, like the kindly hand that raised them, alas! fell a victim to the first frost of the season) are suggestive of a charming passage detailing the retired author's experience as a gardener. What Dr Furnivall might call the 'backward reach' of every one of these stories will render their perusal delightful to those cultivated readers of Gissing, of whom there are by no means a few, to whom every fragment of his suave and delicate workmanship 'repressed yet full of power, vivid though sombre in colouring,' has a technical interest and charm. Nor will they search in vain for Gissing's incorrigible mannerisms, his haunting insistence upon the note of 'Dort wo du nicht bist ist das Glück,' his tricks of the brush in portraiture, his characteristic epithets, the *dusking* twilight, the *decently ignoble* penury, the *not ignoble* ambition, the *not wholly base* riot of the senses in early manhood. In my own opinion we have here in 'The Scrupulous Father,' and to a less degree, perhaps, in the first and last of these stories, and in 'A Poor Gentleman' and 'Christopherson,' perfectly characteristic and quite admirable specimens of Gissing's own genre, and later, unstudied, but always finished prose style.

But a few words remain to be said, and these, in part at any rate, in recapitulation. In the old race, of which Dickens and Thackeray were representative, a successful determination to rise upon the broad back of popularity coincided with a growing conviction that the evil in the world was steadily diminishing. Like healthy schoolboys who have worked their way up to the sixth form, they imagined that the bullying of which they had had to complain was become pretty much a thing of the past. In Gissing the misery inherent in the sharp contrasts of modern life was a far more deeply ingrained conviction. He cared little for the remedial aspect of the question. His idea was to analyse this misery as an artist and to express it to the world.

One of the most impressive elements in the resulting novels is the witness they bear to prolonged and intense suffering, the suffering of a proud, reserved, and over-sensitive mind brought into constant contact with the coarse and brutal facts of life. The creator of Mr Biffen suffers all the torture of the fastidious, the delicately honourable, the scrupulously high-minded in daily contact with persons of blunt feelings, low ideals, and base instincts. 'Human cattle, the herd that feed and breed, with them it was well; but the few born to a desire for ever unattainable, the gentle spirits who from their prisoning circumstance looked up and afar, how the heart ached to think of them!' The natural bent of Gissing's talent was towards poetry and classical antiquity. His mind had considerable natural affinity with that of Tennyson. He was passionately fond of old literature, of the study of metre and of historical reverie. The subtle curiosities of Anatole France are just of the kind that would have appealed irresistibly to him. His delight in psychological complexity and feats of style are not seldom reminiscent of Paul Bourget. His life would have gained immeasurably by a transference to less pinched and pitiful surroundings: but it is more than doubtful whether his work would have done so.

The compulsion of the twin monsters Bread and Cheese forced him to write novels the scene of which was laid in the one milieu he had thoroughly observed, that of either utterly hideous or shabby genteel squalor in London. He gradually obtained a rare mastery in the delineation of his unlovely *mise en scène*. He gradually created a small public who read eagerly everything that came from his pen, despite his economy of material (even of ideas), and despite the repetition to which a natural tendency was increased by compulsory over-production. In all his best books we have evidence of the savage and ironical delight with which he depicted to the shadow of a hair the sordid and vulgar elements by which he had been so cruelly depressed. The aesthetic observer who wanted material for a picture of the blank desolation and ugliness of modern city life could find no better substratum than in the works of George Gissing. Many of his descriptions of typical London scenes in Lambeth Walk, Clerkenwell, or Judd Street, for instance, are the work of a detached, remorseless, photographic artist realising that ugly sordidness of daily life to which the ordinary observer becomes in the course of time as completely habituated as he does to the smoke-laden air. To a cognate sentiment of revolt I attribute that excessive deference to scholarship and refinement which leads him in so many novels to treat these desirable attributes as if they were ends and objects of life in themselves. It has also misled him but too often into depicting a world of suicides, ignoring or overlooking a secret hobby, or passion, or chimaera which is the one thing that renders existence endurable to so many of the waifs and strays of life. He takes existence sadly—too sadly, it may well be; but his drabs and greys provide an atmosphere that is almost inseparable to some of us from our gaunt London streets. In Farringdon Road, for example, I look up instinctively to the expressionless upper windows where Mr Luckworth Crewe spreads his baits for intending advertisers. A tram ride through Clerkenwell and its leagues of dreary, inhospitable brickwork will take you through the heart of a region where Clem Peckover, Pennyloaf Candy, and Totty Nancarrow are multiplied rather than varied since they were first depicted by George Gissing. As for the British Museum, it is peopled to this day by characters from *New Grub Street*.

There may be a perceptible lack of virility, a fluctuating vagueness of outline about the characterisation of some of his men. In his treatment of crowds, in his description of a mob, personified as 'some huge beast purring to itself in stupid contentment,' he can have few rivals. In tracing the influence of women over his heroes he evinces no common subtlety: it is here probably that he is at his best. The *odor di femmina*, to use a phrase of Don Giovanni's, is a marked characteristic of his books. Of the kisses—

by hopeless fancy feigned
On lips that are for others—

there are indeed many to be discovered hidden away between these pages. And the beautiful verse has a fine parallel in the prose of one of Gissing's later novels.

> Some girl, of delicate instinct, of purpose sweet and pure, wasting her unloved life in toil and want and indignity; some man, whose youth and courage strove against a mean environment, whose eyes grew haggard in the vain search for a companion promised in his dreams; they lived, these two, parted perchance only by the wall of neighbour houses, yet all huge London was between them, and their hands would never touch.

The dream of fair women which occupies the mood of Piers Otway in the opening passage of the same novel, was evidently no remotely conceived fancy. Its realisation, in ideal love, represents the author's *Crown of Life*. The wise man who said that Beautiful Woman was a heaven to the eye, a hell to the soul, and a purgatory to the purse of man, could hardly find a more copious field of illustration than in the fiction of George Gissing.

Gissing was a sedulous artist; some of his books, it is true, are very hurried productions, finished in haste for the market with no great amount either of inspiration or artistic confidence about them. But little slovenly work will be found bearing his name, for he was a thoroughly trained writer; a suave and seductive workmanship had become a second nature to him, and there was always a flavour of scholarly, subacid and quasi-ironical modernity about his style. There is little doubt that his quality as a stylist was better adapted to the studies of modern London life, on its seamier side, which he had observed at first hand, than to stories of the conventional dramatic structure which he too often felt himself bound to adopt. In these his failure to grapple with a big objective, or to rise to some prosperous situation, is often painfully marked. A master of explanation and description rather than of animated narrative or sparkling dialogue, he lacked the wit and humour, the brilliance and energy of a consummate style which might have enabled him to compete with the great scenic masters in fiction, or with craftsmen such as Hardy or Stevenson, or with incomparable wits and conversationalists such as Meredith. It is true, again, that his London-street novels lack certain artistic elements of beauty (though here and there occur glints of rainy or sunset townscape in a half-tone, consummately handled and eminently impressive); and his intense sincerity cannot wholly atone for this loss. Where, however, a quiet refinement and delicacy of style is needed as in those sane and suggestive, atmospheric, critical or introspective studies, such as *By the Ionian Sea*, the unrivalled presentment of *Charles Dickens*, and that gentle masterpiece of softened autobiography, *The Private Papers of Henry Ryecroft* (its resignation and autumnal calm, its finer note of wistfulness and wide human compassion, fully deserve comparison with the priceless work of Silvio Pellico) in which he indulged himself during the last and increasingly prosperous years of his life, then Gissing's style is discovered to be a charmed instrument. That he will *sup late*, our Gissing, we are quite content to believe. But that a place is reserved for him, of that at any rate we are reasonably confident. The three books just named, in conjunction with his short stories and his *New Grub Street* (not to mention *Thyrza* or *The Nether World*), will suffice to ensure him a devout and admiring group of followers for a very long time to come; they accentuate profoundly the feeling of vivid regret and almost personal loss which not a few of his more assiduous readers experienced upon the sad news of his premature death at St Jean-de-Luz on the 28th December 1903, at the early age of forty-six.*

* Actually Gissing died at Ispoure, near St Jean-Pied-de-Port, and was buried at St Jean-de-Luz.

189. James Joyce on Gissing

November 1906

These extracts may be found in *The Letters of James Joyce*, edited by Richard Ellmann, Faber, London, 1966.

(*a*) Extract from a letter to Stanislaus Joyce, 6 November 1906: 'I read Gissing's *Demos: A Story of English Socialism*. Why are English novels so terribly boring? I think G. has little merit. The socialist in this is first a worker, and then inherits a fortune, jilts his first girl, marries a lady, becomes a big employer and takes to drink. You know the kind of story. There is a clergyman in it with searching eyes and a deep voice who makes all the socialists wince under his firm gaze. I am going to read another book of his. Then I will try Arthur Morrison and Hardy; and finally Thackeray. Without boasting I think I have little or nothing to learn from English novelists. . . . I am labouring at the end of *Demos*. Gissing's effort to be just to his socialist protagonist is very distressing.'

(*b*) Extract from a letter to Stanislaus Joyce, 13 November 1906: 'I am reading another book by Gissing *The Crown of Life*. Here are two samples of his way of writing " 'Arry, in fact, to use a coarse but expressive phrase, was a hopeless blackguard" "When he left, which he did later in the day (to catch a train) the conversation resumed its usual course &c." His books remind me of what Effore calls *Pastefazoi*.* I perceive that my first opinion of him was founded on pure good nature, nothing else.'

(*c*) Extract from a letter to Stanislaus Joyce, 20 November 1906: 'With great difficulty I finished Gissing's *The Crown of Life*, this crown being love according to G.G. What irritates me most in him is when he begins to write eloquently about nature.'

* Noodles and beans, a favourite Triestine dish.

190. Paul Elmer More, 'George Gissing', *Shelburne Essays* (Fifth Series)

1908, 45–65

Paul Elmer More (1864–1937), a leading American critic of conservative leanings, was the author of the eleven volumes of *Shelburne Essays* (1904–21). This piece first appeared in the *Nation* (New York), 17 January 1907, 53–5. It was reprinted in *Selected Shelburne Essays* (Oxford University Press, World's Classics, 1935), 80–96.

When Gissing died at St Jean-de-Luz, in 1903, broken down at the age of forty-six by years of toil and privation, he had begun to acquire in the world at large something of the reputation he had long possessed among a select circle. But it is to be feared that the irony of his later works, such as the posthumous volume of tales recently published,* may create a wrong impression of his genius among these newly won friends. For Gissing, more than most writers, underwent a change with the progress of time. His work in fact may be divided into three fairly distinct periods. Passing over the immature *Workers in the Dawn* (1880), we may mark off the first group of novels as beginning with *The Unclassed* (1884), and ending with *Born in Exile* (1892); between these two are *Isabel Clarendon, Demos, Thyrza, A Life's Morning, The Nether World, The Emancipated,* and *New Grub Street.* The second group, starting with *Denzil Quarrier* (1892), may be limited by *The Crown of Life* (1899), although the transition here to his final manner is more gradual than the earlier change. This second division embraces what are perhaps the best known of Gissing's novels—*In the Year of*

* *The House of Cobwebs and Other Stories.* By George Gissing. To which is prefixed *The Work of George Gissing,* an introductory study, by Thomas Seccombe. New York: E. P. Dutton & Co., 1906. Several of the most important of Gissing's earlier novels are not to be found in New York, either in bookshop or library; and, indeed, he cannot be said ever to have been properly published at all. By getting together a complete and decently printed edition of his works some enterprising publisher might benefit himself and the community.

Jubilee and *The Whirlpool*—and here again there is danger of misunderstanding. These are books of undeniable power, comparable in some ways to Hardy's *Jude the Obscure*, but pointed in the wrong direction, and not truly characteristic. One feels a troubling and uncertain note in all this intermediate work, done while the author, having passed beyond his first intense preoccupation with the warfare for existence, was still far from the fair serenity of his close. The greater Gissing is not to be found here, but in those tales which embody his own experiences in the cruel and primeval nether world of London—tales which together make what might be called the Epic of Poverty.

Poverty, the gaunt greedy struggle for bread, the naked keen reality of hunger that goads the world onward—how this grim power reigns in all Gissing's early novels, crushing the uninured dreamers and soiling the strong. It is the guiding power of *The Unclassed*. It casts its spume of disease and misery on the path of *Thyrza*,* † that fragile Madonna of the slums, yet finds even here its pathetic voice of song:

[A quotation from ch. ix, evoking the significance of London children dancing to the sounds of a street organ, follows.]

A superb piece of imaginative prose, indeed, as Mr Seccombe calls it, and significant of the music which Gissing himself wrested from the pathos of the London streets. The note rises in *A Life's Morning* to tragic shrillness, making of it one of the most passionate stories in English of love striving against degraded associations. Again, in *New Grub Street*, it sinks to the forlorn plea of genius baffled by unremunerative toil and starved into despair. Those who care to know the full measure of agony through which the writer himself struggled, may find it portrayed here in the lives of the two unrecognised novelists. Only Gissing could tell how much of his own experience was poured into those 'dwellers in the valley of the shadow of books'; how much of his fierce aspiration to paint the world as it really exists was expressed by the garret-haunting, hunger-driven Biffen; how often his breast, like Reardon's, swelled with envy of the prosperous, com-

* It is a curious comment on the manufacture of books that *Thyrza*, which was published in 1887, has never been reprinted. I had to wait many months before I could pick up a second-hand copy, but my reward was great. It is a book of rare, poignant beauty. To the beginner in Gissing I should recommend this novel first.

† It is interesting to note that George Orwell, writing in London forty years later, still had cause to lament the non-availability of Gissing's novels. Orwell's assessment, entitled 'George Gissing' is reprinted in *Collected Articles on George Gissing*, edited by Pierre Coustillas, Frank Cass, London, 1968, 50–7.

mercialised man of letters. 'He knew what poverty means. The chilling of brain and heart, the unnerving of the hands, the slow gathering about one of fear and shame and impotent wrath; the dread feeling of helplessness, of the world's base indifference. Poverty! Poverty!' I am not sure that it is good to know these things even by hearsay, but for those who are strong in pity and fortified by resolve they have been written out once for all, ruthlessly, without mitigation.

More general, gathering up all the suffering and foulness and crime of want, embracing too the clear-eyed charity of strength that asks for no reward, is that terrible story of *The Nether World*. Here, most of all, Gissing is conscious of his grave theme. We have seen the pathetic joy of the children dancing to the simple music of the street organ; it may be well to compare with it a fragment of the chapter 'Io Saturnalia!' which describes a holiday of revelling at the Crystal Palace:

[Several paragraphs from *The Nether World*, Bk I, ch. xii, follow.]

It is not strange that the witness and recorder of these things should have interposed the question: Did the world ever exhibit a sadder spectacle? Only one is surprised that to his memory, steeped as it was in classic history, the words of Pericles did not involuntarily arise: 'Poverty is no bar. . . . And our laws have provided for the mind an ever-recurring respite from toil by the appointment of public recreations and religious ceremonies throughout the year, performed with peculiar elegance, and by their daily delight driving away sordid care.' How far we of the modern world have progressed from the philosophy of joy! We are not now at Athens, at the graves of those who died in battle for their native land, but in the harsher warfare of industrial London. And as a chorus above all the sounds of defeat and consternation rises the clamorous cry of 'Mad Jack,' like the prophesying of some Jeremiah of the slums:

[A quotation from *The Nether World*, Bk III, ch. x, follows.]

It has seemed worth while to quote thus at length, because Gissing is one of the few English novelists whose trained and supple language makes itself felt in such extracts, and because his first lesson of life is shown in them so clearly. 'Put money in thy purse,' might seem to be the upshot of it all; 'and again, put money in thy purse; for as the world is ordered, to lack current coin is to lack the privileges of humanity, and indigence is the death of the soul.' It is a dubious philosophy, one which the writer's own heroic culture rebuked, and yet, what is it more than the modern rendering of Homer's

> Jove fix'd it certain, that what ever day
> Makes man a slave, takes half his worth away?

But, waiving the point in ethics, there still remains the question of art: what profit is it, one asks, to paint in all its hideous colours this death of the soul, to forget the glad things of the world for its shadows, to deny Agamemnon and Achilles and choose Thersites for the hero of our tale? 'Art, nowadays,' Gissing replies boldly, 'must be the mouth-piece of misery, for misery is the key-note of modern life.' It is not entirely easy to reconcile such a theory with the judgment of Gissing's own riper years; for art, he came in the end to think, is 'an expression, satisfying and abiding, of the zest of life.' Certainly, it is this contrast between the misery and the zest of life, derived from the same materials, that makes the comparison between Dickens and Gissing so inevitable. Gissing felt it, and his *Critical Study* of Dickens is, as a result, a curiously ambiguous piece of writing; his intention is to praise, but he can never quite overcome his surprise and annoyance at the radical difference of Dickens' attitude toward poverty. And the same feeling crops out again and again in the earlier novels. Inextinguishable laughter were fittest, he says, musing on his own terrible nether world and thinking of the elder writer's gaiety, but the heart grows heavy. And elsewhere he blames the shallowness of Dickens, and calls on fiction to 'dig deeper' into the substratum of life. The question thus posed exhibits one of the irreducible differences of artistic method. In my last essay I tried to show how Dickens tended to portray his characters from the outside, without identifying himself with their real emotions. Here, on the contrary, we have a man whose ambition it was to strip off to the last rag those veils of melodrama and humour, which prevented Dickens from becoming a realist, and which, it may be added, he himself by native right possessed in large measure. He would not be waylaid and turned from his purpose by the picturesque grimaces of poverty, but would lay bare the sullen ugliness at its core; he would, in a word, write from the inside. The result of this difference of methods is too obvious to need attention here, but one rather curious detail I may point out. It has been observed that the people of Dickens indulge in a superhuman amount of drinking; wine and gin are elements of Gargantuan exhilaration. In Gissing's world, drunkenness is only a blind desire to escape from pain; and liquor, the rich man's friend, is the enemy always lying in wait to drag the needy to destruction.

Only by taking account of the sordid realities of Gissing's life can we understand the mingled attraction and repulsion exercised on him by the large joyousness and exulting pathos of Dickens in dealing with the nether world. Nothing, to be sure, in his career, was more depressing than the slavery of Dickens under 'Murdstone and Grinby,' but whereas Dickens rose almost at a bound to enormous prosperity, the life of Gissing was one of the tragedies of literature. Hints of that story are scattered through all his novels,—a youth cast from the country into the streets of London to earn a living as best he could, a period of storm and stress including a frantic attempt on fortune in the United States, years of starving at literary work, followed by years of broken health. He came out at the last into the light, but almost his friends might have pointed to him, as the people of Verona pointed to Dante, saying: 'There goes one who has been in hell.' Naturally a tone of bitterness, something of his own lack of vitality, if you will, crept into his work. He always wavered between the pathetic fallacy on the one hand of ascribing to the poor the distress of his own over-wrought sensitiveness and on the other hand hatred of a Destiny that inures its victims to their lot. 'The man who laughs,' he said, reproachfully, 'takes the side of a cruel omnipotence.' The words are suggestive. Not 'cruel,' but *unimplicated*, let us say, and accept the phrase as a mark of the greater art. It is because Dickens stands with the powers above and is not finally implicated in his theme, that he could turn it into an expression satisfying and abiding, of the zest of life. And it is, on the other hand, just because Gissing cannot entirely rise above the 'misery' he describes, that all his marvellous understanding of the human heart and his chastened style do not quite save his art in the end.

And yet, if his theory and practice must from the highest standard be condemned, it would be unfair to overlook the reservations that should go with even so strict a judgment. For though the zest of life be lacking in these novels, there is something in them that strangely resembles it. 'How'—he exclaims in one of his latest works—'how, in the name of sense and mercy, is mankind content to live on in such a world as this?' The question obtrudes itself upon the reader again and again, and slowly he becomes aware of the vast, dumb, tumultuous *will to live* that is struggling into consciousness through all these horrors and madnesses. The very magnitude of the obstacles, the unreason of endurance, is witness to the unconquerable energy of this blind will.

What, after all, has been the substance of great literature, from the days when Sarpedon heartened Glaucus on the plains of Troy to the most modern singer of some soul divided against itself, but warfare, and again renewed war? And as one reads on in these novels of Gissing's, their plot begins to unfold itself as another and darker picture of the same battle. It is almost as if we were listening to the confused lamentation of a city besieged and captured by night, wherein the enemy is no invading army of Greece, but the more treacherous powers of hunger, and vice, and poverty:

Diverso interea miscentur moenia luctu.

And there is another element which helps to relieve the depressing nature of Gissing's theme. Literature of the slums is not lacking in these latter days. Young men and women whose standards of life have been unsettled turn thitherward for some basis of reality and some reflected seriousness of emotion. In each of our large cities you will find a college settlement where a band of prurient souls sit at type-writing machines glutting a morbid ambition on the sorrows of the poor. Now, Gissing did not learn the meaning of poverty in any such fashion; there is, at all events, nothing of the dilettante in his work. He wrote, not from callow sympathy or patronising observation, but from his own deep experience; and, writing thus, he put into his account of the nether world the one thing commonly wanting to these pictures—the profound sense of morality. Through all these graphic, sometimes appalling, scenes one knows that the writer is still primarily concerned with the inner effects of poverty, and his problem is the ancient, insoluble antinomy of the one and the many, the individual and the mass. Taken as a whole, the society he describes is the victim of circumstances. His philosophy is summed up in a gloomy determinism: 'indigence is the death of the soul,' and 'misery is vice.' And even where the instincts remain unsoiled, some hideous chance steps in to stunt the soul's growth:

It strengthened his growing hatred of London, a huge battlefield calling itself the home of civilisation and of peace. Battlefield on which the wounds were of soul, no less than of body. In these gaunt streets along which he passed at night, how many a sad heart suffered, by the dim glimmer that showed at upper windows, a hopeless solitude amid the innumerable throng! Human cattle, the herd that feed and breed, with them it was well; but the few born to a desire forever unattainable, the gentle spirits who from their prisoning circumstance looked up and afar, how the heart ached to think of them! Some girl, of delicate instinct, of purpose sweet and pure, wasting her unloved life in toil and want and indignity; some man, whose youth and courage strove against a mean environment, whose eyes grew haggard in the vain search for a companion promised in his dreams; they lived, these two, parted perchance only by the wall of neighbour houses, yet all huge London was between them, and their hands would never touch.

That is the philosophy of circumstance that rules over Gissing's world as a whole. But even here, as in that chorus of 'Mad Jack' already quoted, the contradictory and less comprehensible law of morality makes itself heard at times; and when he touches the individual the sure insight of the artist asserts itself, and he orders his people not as automatons, but as characters moved by their own volition, and, though it may be in unaccountable ways, reaping as they have sown. The knot of fate and free-will is not always disentangled, there is no conventional apportioning of rewards and penalties such as Dickens indulged in at the end of his novels; but always, through all the workings of heredity and environment, he leaves the reader conscious of that last inviolable mystery of man's nature, the sense of personal responsibility. Had not he, George Gissing, been caught in the cruel network of circumstances, and had he not preserved intact the feeling that he was personally accountable? It is thus he attains by another road to something of the liberal enlargement of Dickens: the greatest art, it need scarcely be said, would combine both the free outlook of the older writer and the moral insight of the younger.

Those are the principles—the instinctive will to live and the law of moral responsibility—that saved the writer's tragic stage from insupportable dreariness; they furnished, also, the clue that in the end led the writer himself out of the labyrinth of doubtful questionings. But for a while it seemed as if they were to be lost, for it is not so much any lowering of literary skill as a change in these essential points that marks the transition from his first to his second period. Just what caused the alteration I cannot say. Possibly the long years of defeat began to shake his moral equilibrium; possibly the growing influence upon him of French and Russian fiction was to blame. Certainly the pride of English, what raises it, despite its deficiencies of form and ideas, to be the first of modern literatures, is the deep-rooted convention of moral responsibility. It is that which through all its romantic divagations joins English so closely to Greek; which would have made Socrates more at home with Dr Johnson than with any other man of our world, and would have rendered Aeschylus the most appreciative listener of Shakespeare—if such associations are not too fanciful. No one can sprinkle himself with the scented water of Anatole France or dabble in the turbid Slavic pool without hazarding the loss of that traditional sense, and there are signs that Gissing's mind for a time was bewildered by ill-digested reading.

The new spirit may be defined by a comparison of such novels as *The Nether World* from his first period and *The Whirlpool* from his second (the very names are significant), or as *A Life's Morning* and *The Crown of Life*. In place of human nature battling with grim necessity, we now have a society of people contending against endless insinuations o tedium and vanity; in place of the will to live we meet a sex-consciousness, always strong in Gissing, but now grown to morbid intensity. And with this change comes a certain relaxing of moral fibre. The unconscious theme is no longer self-responsibility, or character in the strict meaning of the term, but a thousand vexatious questions of the day—anti-vivisection, anti-racing, anti-gambling, anti-hunting, anti-war, imperialism, the education of children, the emancipation of women, and, above all and more persistent than all, the thrice-dreary theories of marriage. The beginning of these may be traced back to *The Emancipated* (1890), written after he had been enabled by momentary success to visit Italy, the dream of his life. In that release from pressure his mind seems to have been left free to dwell on these problems resulting from the breakup of traditional obligations. But the core of the book is sound. 'An educated woman, this,' says Mallard, drawing the lesson of the heroine's life; 'one who has learnt a good deal about herself and the world. She is "emancipated," in the true sense of the hackneyed word; that is to say, she is not only freed from those bonds that numb the faculties of mind and heart, but is able to control the native passions that would make a slave of her.' And, indeed, it would be wrong to infer that the moral of his books is ever at bottom any other than this. In the full swing of his middle period he could close a novel with the ejaculation of his hero: 'Now I understand the necessity for social law!' But one is aware, nevertheless, that conventions have grown irksome to him, and that his interest turns too much on the thronging, ambiguous problems of emancipation.

If the reading of modern Continental literature may be suspected ot unsettling his inherited canons, his home-coming in the end was surely due in large measure to his devoted study of the classics. Strange as it may seem when one considers the topics he treated, there is scarcely a writer of the last century more thoroughly versed in Greek and Latin than Gissing, and that no doubt is the reason why the names of antiquity come to mind involuntarily when one tries to characterise his work. Through his struggle with poverty he commonly kept free of the pawnshop a few chosen books, Homer, Tibullus, Horace, Gibbon, Shakespeare. Writing the memoirs of his life, at ease, and with a library at his command, he recalls his difficulties:

[A quotation from *The Private Papers of Henry Ryecroft*, Spring X, follows.]

What a picture of the new Grub Street. One thinks of the deal table in Thoreau's hut at Walden on which a Homer lay, and one thinks, too, of Dickens in his comfortable study with his shelves of sham books. For most of his reading Gissing had to depend on public convenience:

[A quotation from *The Private Papers of Henry Ryecroft*, Spring XVII, follows.]

And Homer and Ancient Philosophy won the day. There was little occasion in the earlier novels to display this learning, yet here and there the author's longing for Rome and Italy breaks through, as in the passion of the apothecary's apprentice in *The Unclassed.* Then came the intellectual whirlpool. The release from that dizziness of brain shows itself first in a growing lightness of touch and aloofness from passion of all sorts. The novels and tales of the third period are chiefly distinguished by a tone of gentle and amused irony, in place of the satire of the middle group, and it is significant that the theme of *Will Warburton*, his last novel, is the same as that chosen by Biffen in the *New Grub Street* for the pronunciamento of rebellious realism—the life of a retail grocer. Only in the actual novel there is no realism at all as Biffen would have understood it, but the witty and mock-heroic story of a man of good birth who begins by selling groceries over the counter under an assumed name and ends by accepting his lot in all *gaieté de coeur*—so far had Gissing travelled from being at loggerheads with destiny. *Warburton* was written in Southern France when a moderate success had freed him from the hardest slavery of the pen, and when ill health had driven him from England. Here, too, he absolved himself from an ancient vow by composing, with all the artistry he possessed, a story of classical life—his *Veranilda*—and here he wrote that restrained and every way beautiful piece of self-revelation, *The Private Papers of Henry Ryecroft.*

There is nothing in the language quite like this volume of half-veiled autobiography. In the imagined quiet of a home in Devon, the part of England Gissing so passionately loved, he writes out his memories of toil and the reflections that come to him as the sum of his experiences. Here is no bitterness, no complaining; all the lesser problems that harassed him have solved themselves by simply vanishing; he returns to his early convictions, with the added ripeness of long meditation. He had used the life of the poor for his greatest creative work, and the question of the growing democracy is the only one that still abides with him in his repose. Everywhere he sees the decay of that natural instinct on which the morality of the world at large must always depend, and in its place an ever-widening spirit of interrogation which only unsettles and sets adrift. 'I am no friend of the people,' he exclaims, and the words come with a strange insistence from such a man. 'As a force, by which the tenor of the time is conditioned, they inspire me with distrust, with fear. . . . Every instinct of my being is anti-democratic, and I dread to think of what our England may become when Demos rules irresistibly. . . . Nothing is more rooted in my mind than the vast distinction between the individual and the class.' This doubt alone remained to annoy him, but with it he connected the other great movement of the day: 'I hate and fear "science" because of my conviction that, for long to come, if not for ever, it will be the remorseless enemy of mankind.' To science he attributed the spread of that half-education which increases the powers of action while lessening the inhibitions of self-knowledge. It was from his close reading of the classics, I think, though he himself does not say so, came his notion of the one only salvation through the aristocratic idea, the essential idea of Greek literature:

The task before us is no light one. Can we, whilst losing the class, retain the idea it embodied? Can we English, ever so subject to the material, liberate ourselves from that old association, yet guard its meaning in the sphere of spiritual life? Can we, with eyes which have ceased to look reverently on worn-out symbols, learn to select from among the grey-coated multitude, and place in reverence even higher, him who 'holds his patent of nobility straight from Almighty God'? Upon that depends the future of England.

The business of the novelist is with the realities of life, and not with hypotheses; yet one cannot leave Gissing without wishing that he had found strength and occasion to express in fiction these fundamental ideas of his maturity.

191. Virginia Woolf, 'The Novels of George Gissing', *The Times Literary Supplement*

11 January 1912, 9–10

The authorship of this unsigned appreciation, published on the occasion of the reissue of eight Gissing novels by Sidgwick & Jackson in 1911, is established by J. Kirkpatrick's bibliography of Virginia Woolf in the Soho Bibliographies.

Let any one who has spent his life in writing novels consider the day which has now arrived for George Gissing. The fruit of his life stands before us—a row of red volumes. If they were biographies, histories, books about books even, or speculations upon money or the course of the world there would be no need for the peculiar shudder. But they bear titles like these—*Denzil Quarrier*, *Born in Exile*, *New Grub Street*; places and people that have never existed save in one brain now cold. They are only novels. It seems that there is genuine cause for shuddering when one's work takes this form. Dead leaves cannot be more brittle or more worthless than things faintly imagined—and that the fruit of one's life should be twelve volumes of dead leaves! We have one moment of such panic before the novels of George Gissing, and then we rise again. Not in our time will they be found worthless.

An interesting letter to Mr Clodd was printed the other day. In it Gissing wrote:—*

By the bye, Pinker has suggested to me that he should try to get all my books into the hands of some one publisher. I should like this, but I have a doubt whether the time has come yet; there is a curious blending of respect and contempt in the publishers' mind towards me, and I should like to see which sentiment will prevail. If the respect, one ought to be able to make decent terms with a good house; if the contempt, one must relinquish ambitions proved to be idle, and so attain a certain tranquillity—even if it be that of the workhouse. I was always envious of workhouse folk; they are the most independent of all.

* George Gissing to Edward Clodd, 7 November 1899. See *The Letters of George Gissing to Edward Clodd*, edited by Pierre Coustillas, Enitharmon Press, London, 1972.

Respect has prevailed; Messrs Sidgwick and Jackson reprint the eight later works both well and cheaply. One, *Born in Exile*, is to be bought upon railway bookstalls for sevenpence. Nevertheless it is his own word 'respect' that seems to describe the attitude of the public towards him; he is certainly not popular; he is not really famous. If we may guess at the destiny of this new edition, we can imagine that it will find its way to houses where very few novels are kept. Ordinary cultivated people will buy them of course; but also governesses who scarcely ever read; mechanics; working men who despise novels; dons who place him high among writers of English prose; professional men; the daughters of farmers in the North. We can imagine that he is the favourite novelist of a great many middle-aged, sceptical, rather depressed men and women who when they read want thought and understanding of life as it is, not wit or romance. In saying this we are saying also that Gissing does not appeal to a great multitude; the phrase 'life as it is' is always the phrase of people who try to see life honestly and find it hard and dreary. Other versions of life they reject. They are not, perhaps, in the majority, but they form a minority that is very respectable, and perhaps increasing.

If this is at all true of his readers, what shall we say of the writer himself? There is a great difference between writing and reading, and Gissing was a born writer. When a novelist has been dead for some years and his books are gathered together we want as far as possible to stand where he stood; not to be moved by one character or one idea, but to grasp his point of view. His books are very sad; that is the first thing that strikes the reader. The ordinary excitement of guessing the end is scarcely to be indulged in. Conceive the most gloomy, yet natural, conclusion to every complexity, and you are likely to be right. He had, as most novelists have, one great theme. It is the life of a man of fine character and intelligence who is absolutely penniless and is therefore the sport of all that is most sordid and brutal in modern life. He earns, perhaps, a pound a week. He has thrown up his job in an office because an editor has accepted one of his stories. He marries a woman of some refinement; they live in a couple of rooms somewhere off the Tottenham Court-road. In a short time they cannot pay the rent; they move; they sell pieces of furniture; they live off tea and bread and butter; then his books go; all day long, in spite of headache and sore throat, in bitter fog and clinging mist, the wretched man has to spin imaginary loves and imaginary jests from his exhausted brain. He has the additional agony of loving good writing; he can lose himself still in dreams of the Acropolis or in argument about Euripides. His wife leaves him, for the dirt repels her; at last his stuff has become too poor even to sell, and he dies knowing himself beaten on every hand.

Many readers, happily, rebound from their depression when the end is reached, exclaiming, 'After all, this is only one side.' There are quantities of people who have enough money to avoid these horrors; a few who can command luxury. But what Gissing proves is the terrible importance of money, and, if you slip, how you fall and fall and fall. With learning, sensitive feelings, a love of beauty both in art and in human nature—all the qualities that generally (one hopes) keep their possessor somehow afloat—he descended to the depths where men and women live in vast shoals without light or freedom. What a strange place it is—this Nether World! There are women as brutal as savages, men who are half animals, women still preserving some ghost of love and pity, men turning a stunted brain upon the problems of their lot. All the things that grow fine and large up here are starved and twisted down there; just as the squares and parks, and the houses standing separate with rooms measured off for different occupations, are shrivelled into black alleys, sooty patches of green, and sordid lodging-houses, where there is shelter, but only the shelter that pigs or cows have, not room for the soul. Without money you cannot have space or leisure; worse than that, the chances are very much against your having either love or intelligence.

Many writers before and after Gissing have written with both knowledge and sympathy of the poor. What, after all, is more stimulating to the imagination than the sight of great poverty or great wealth? There was Mrs Gaskell, for instance, and Dickens; a score of writers in our own day have studied the conditions of their lives. But the impressive part about Gissing is that knowing them as he did he makes no secret of the fact that he hated them. That is the reason why his voice is so harsh, so penetrating, so little grateful to the ears. Can any one hate poverty with all their soul who does not hate the poor? 'Some great and noble sorrow,' he writes, 'may have the effect of drawing hearts together, but to struggle against destitution, to be crushed by care about shillings and sixpences . . . that must always degrade.' There is no sentimentalism about the fundamental equality of men in his works. Adela Mutimer in *Demos*, gazing at her husband's face opposite her, ponders thus; Gissing must often have thought the same:—

It was the face of a man by birth and breeding altogether beneath her . . . Perhaps for three generations her ancestors could claim so much gentility; it was more than enough to put a vast gulf between her and the Mutimers. Favourable circumstances of upbringing had endowed her with delicacy of heart and mind not inferior to that of any woman living; mated with an equal husband, the children born of her might hope to take their place among the most beautiful and the most intelligent. And her husband was a man incapable of understanding her idlest thought.

It would have been so much easier to lessen the gulf; so much more graceful to waive the advantages of three generations of gentle birth. But to hate the vices of the poor is the way to incite the best kind of pity. The measure of his bitterness is the measure of his love of good.

But there is nothing surprising in the fact that Gissing was never popular. However harsh and censorious people are in their daily actions, they do it unofficially as it were; they shrink from any statement of the creed that makes them act thus. In fiction particularly, which is a relaxation, like golf, they detest anything severe. It is part of their enjoyment to see others looking rosy and thus to feel somewhat rosier themselves. Gissing had no sympathy whatever with this common weakness. 'No, no,' he makes Biffen say in *New Grub Street*, 'let us copy life. When the man and woman are to meet for the great scene of passion, let it all be frustrated by one or other of them having a bad cold in the head, and so on. Let the pretty girl get a disfiguring pimple on her nose just before the ball at which she is going to shine. Show the numberless repulsive features of common decent life. Seriously, coldly; not a hint of facetiousness, or the thing becomes different.' The novel that Biffen wrote on these lines is, of course, a failure, and eventually he takes his own life upon Putney Heath.

The reader, then, whose pleasure it is to identify himself with the hero or heroine, and to feel in some strange way that he shares their virtues, is completely baffled. His natural instinct is to find fault with the cynicism of the writer. But Gissing is no cynic; the real cynics are the writers who have a trivial merry view of life, and make people easily content and drugged with cheap happiness. What good Gissing finds in human beings is absolutely genuine, for it has stood such tests; and the pleasures he allows them, the pleasures of reading, companionship, and a few comfortable evenings, glow with a warmth as of redhot coals. His work has another quality that does not make for popularity either. His men and women think. When we seek the cause of his gloom is it not most truly to be found there? Each of the people who from one cause or another has to suffer the worst bruises in the Nether World is a thinking creature, capable not only of feeling, but of making that feeling part of a view of life. It is not gone when the pain is over, but persists in the form of melancholy questionings. What is to be said for a world in which there is so much suffering? By itself this peculiarity is enough to distinguish Gissing's characters from those of other novelists. There are characters who feel violently; characters who are true types; witty characters, bad ones, good ones, eccentric ones, buffoons; but the thinking man has seldom had justice done to him. The great advantage of making people think is that you can describe other relationships besides the great one between the lover and the beloved. There is friendship, for instance; the relationship that is founded on liking the same books, or sharing the same enthusiasms; there is a relationship between one man and men in general. All these, it seems to us, Gissing has described with extraordinary fineness. It is out of these relationships that he makes the texture of his works. Loves have exploded; tragedies have fired up and sunk to ashes; these quiet, undemonstrative feelings between one man and another, one woman and another, persist; they spin some kind of thread across the ravages; they are the noblest things he has found in the world.

Naturally Gissing practised what is generally called the English method of writing fiction. Instead of leaping from one high pinnacle of emotion to the next, he filled in all the adjoining parts most carefully. It is sometimes very dull. The general effect is very low in tone. You have to read from the first page to the last to get the full benefit of his art. But if you read steadily the low almost insignificant chapters gather weight and impetus; they accumulate upon the imagination; they are building up a world from which there seems to be no escape; violence would have the effect of an escape. But thus it comes about that it is difficult to point to any scene or passage and demand admiration. Do we even single out one character among all his men and women to be remembered? He has no Jane Eyres, no Uncle Tobys. But here is a passage that is characteristic of his terse workmanlike prose, glowing at the heart with a kind of flameless fire:—

[Gissing's description of Manor Park Cemetery in *Demos* follows.]

We are in the habit of throwing faults upon the public as though it were a general rubbish heap, for it cannot bring an action for libel. But to be unpopular is a sign that there is something wrong, or how have the classics come to be the classics? Gissing's public we believe to be a very good public, but it leaves out much that is good in the great public. The reason is that he wrote his best only when he was describing struggles and miseries and noble sufferings like those we have dwelt upon above. Directly he dealt with men and women living at ease he lost his grip; he did not see; directly he changed his sober prosaic prose for a loftier style he was without merit. He had a world of his own as real, as hard, as convincing as though it were made of earth and stone—nay, far more so—but it was a small world. There is no such place as 'the' world; no such life as 'life as it is.' We need only consider the result of reading too much Gissing; we want another world; we take down *Evan Harrington*. Which is true—that misery, or this magnificence? They are both true; everything is true that can make us believe it to be true. Beauty beyond all other beauty, horror beyond all other horror still lie hidden about us, waiting for some one to see them. The thing that really matters, that makes a writer a true writer and his work permanent, is that he should really see. Then we believe, then there arise those passionate feelings that true books inspire. Is it possible to mistake books that have this life for books without it, hard though it is to explain where the difference lies? Two figures suggest themselves in default of reasons. You clasp a bird in your hands; it is so frightened that it lies perfectly still; yet somehow it is a living body, there is a heart in it and the breast is warm. You feel a fish on your line; the line hangs straight as before down into the sea, but there is a strain on it; it thrills and quivers. That is something like the feeling which live books give and dead ones cannot give; they strain and quiver. But satisfactory works of art have a quality that is no less important. It is that they are complete. A good novelist, it seems, goes about the world seeing squares and circles where the ordinary person sees mere storm-drift. The wildest extravagance of life in the moon can be complete, or the most shattered fragment. When a book has this quality it seems to us to possess both these essential qualities—life and completeness—and for these reasons we cannot imagine that they will perish. There will always be one or two people to exclaim, 'This man understood!'

Bibliography

This short select bibliography is intended to suggest both a more detailed knowledge of Gissing's thought and different scholarly approaches to his art and period.

COUSTILLAS, P. (ed.), *Collected Articles on George Gissing*, Frank Cass, London, 1968.

COUSTILLAS, P. (ed.), *Gissing's Writings on Dickens, A bio-bibliographical survey*, Enitharmon Press, London, 1969.

English Fiction (afterwards: *Literature*) *in Transition*, vol. iii, No. 2, 1960, 3–33, 'George Gissing: an annotated bibliography of writings about him'; vol. vii, No. 1, 1964, 14–26, 'George Gissing: an annotated bibliography of writings about him, foreign journals'; vol. vii, No. 2, 1964, 73–92, 'George Gissing: an annotated bibliography of writings about him'.

GISSING, G., *Commonplace Book*, edited by J. Korg, New York Public Library, 1962.

GISSING, G., *Letters of George Gissing to Members of his Family*, edited by A. and E. Gissing, Constable, London, 1927.

GISSING, G., *George Gissing and H. G. Wells*, edited by R. A. Gettmann, Hart-Davis, London, 1961.

GISSING, G., *The Letters of George Gissing to Eduard Bertz*, edited by A. C. Young, Constable, London, 1961.

GISSING, G., *The Letters of George Gissing to Gabrielle Fleury*, edited by P. Coustillas, New York Public Library, 1964.

GRAHAM, K., *English Criticism of the Novel, 1865–1900*, Clarendon Press, Oxford, 1965.

HOWARD, D., LUCAS, J. and GOODE, J., *Tradition and Tolerance in Nineteenth-Century Fiction*, Routledge & Kegan Paul, London, 1966.

KORG, J., *George Gissing, A critical biography*, University of Washington Press, Seattle, 1963.

LUCAS, J. (ed.), *Literature and Politics in the Nineteenth Century*, Methuen, London, 1971.

SPIERS, J. and COUSTILLAS, P., *The Rediscovery of George Gissing, A reader's guide*, National Book League, London, 1971.

The following section lists contemporary reviews and surveys of Gissing's work from 1880 to 1912 which have not been reprinted in the present collection. Where possible, all details of publication have been given.

Workers in the Dawn

Graphic, 19 June 1880, 627; *Court Circular and Court News*, 19 June 1880, 588; *Whitehall Review* (*Literary Supplement*), 15 July 1880, iv; *Daily News*, 29 July 1880, 6; *Illustrated London News*, 31 July 1880, 110; *Weekly Dispatch*, 15 August 1880; *St. James's Gazette*, 28 August, 1880, 13–14; *World*, 6 October 1880.

The Unclassed

Athenaeum, 28 June 1884, 820–1; *World*, 30 July 1884, 22; *Morning Post*, 7 August 1884, 6; *Daily Telegraph*, 21 August 1884, 6; *Spectator*, 31 January 1885; *Daily News*, 19 October 1885, 2; *Literary World* (London), 3 January 1896, 8; *Speaker*, 4 January 1896, 23; *World*, 12 February 1896, 31; *Outlook* (New York), 23 May 1896, 940; *World* (New York), 31 May 1896, 6; *New York Times*, 21 June 1896, 27.

Demos

Daily News, 1 April 1886, 3; *Public Opinion*, 2 April 1886, 422; *Vanity Fair*, 3 April 1886, 196; *Bookseller*, 6 April 1886, 321; *Daily Telegraph*, 13 April 1886; *St. Stephen's Review*, 17 April 1886, 34; *John Bull*, 17 April 1886, 255–6; *Court Journal*, 17 April 1886, 443; *Echo*, 21 April 1886; *Morning Post*, 22 April 1886, 3; *Weekly Dispatch*, 25 April 1886, 6; *World*, 28 April 1886, 19; *Graphic*, 1 May 1886, 482; *Daily Chronicle*, 22 May 1886, 6; *Literary World* (London), 28 May 1886, 507–8; *Scotsman*, 29 May 1886, 12; *Nation* (New York), 1 July 1886, 14; *Manchester Guardian*, 29 July 1886, 8; *Queen*, 31 July 1886, 143; *Westminster Review*, July 1886, 291; *Saturday Review*, 21 August 1886, 261; *Nouvelle Revue*, 1 May 1890, 220–1 (Ad. Badin).

Isabel Clarendon

St. James's Gazette, 5 June 1886, 7; *Daily Telegraph*, 10 June 1886, 2; *Athenaeum*, 19 June 1886, 808; *Court Journal*, 26 June 1886, 753; *Vanity Fair*, 10 July 1886, 27; *Illustrated London News*, 10 July 1886, 50; *Morning Post*, 28 July 1886, 2; *Queen*, 28 August 1886, 247; *Graphic*, 2 October 1886, 370; *Spectator*, 23 October 1886, 1420.

Thyrza

Scotsman, 2 May 1887, 4; *Publishers' Circular*, 2 May 1887, 455; *Court Journal*, 7 May 1887, 550; *Morning Post*, 11 May 1887, 2; *Public Opinion*, 13 May 1887, 582; *Illustrated London News*, 14 May 1887, 561; *Daily Telegraph*, 19 May 1887, 2; *The Times*, 21 May 1887, 17; *Glasgow Herald*, 24 May 1887, 10; *Bookseller*, 4 June 1887, 544; *Spectator*, 25 June 1887, 869; *Scottish Review*, July 1887, 196–7; *Graphic*, 6 August 1887, 147; *Vanity Fair*, 20 August 1887, 120; *Queen*, 20 August 1887, 246; *Publishers' Circular*, 4 July 1891, 16; *Saturday Review*, 17 October 1891, 450.

A Life's Morning

Scotsman, 26 November 1888, 3; *Public Opinion*, 7 December 1888, 722; *Manchester Guardian*, 10 December 1888, 6; *Pall Mall Gazette*, 12 December 1888, 5; *Whitehall Review*, 13 December 1888, 20; *Glasgow Herald*, 20 December 1888, 9; *Daily Telegraph*, 25 December 1888, 7; *Standard*, 28 December 1888, 2; *Graphic*, 5 January 1889, 19; *Morning Post*, 30 January 1889, 2; *Vanity Fair*, 15 June 1889, 454.

The Nether World

Public Opinion, 12 April 1889, 455; *Scotsman*, 15 April 1889, 3; *Queen*, 20 April 1889, 541; *Glasgow Herald*, 22 April 1889, 9; *Manchester Guardian*, 30 April 1889, 4; *Scottish Review*, April 1889, 446; *Daily Chronicle*, 6 May 1889, 6; *Morning Post*, 27 May 1889, 5; *Illustrated London News*, 1 June 1889, 694; *Pall Mall Gazette*, 4 June 1889, 3; *Graphic*, 15 June 1889, 667; *Standard*, 17 June 1889, 2; *New York Daily Tribune*, 18 June 1889, 8; *Vanity Fair*, 22 June 1889, 474; *World*, 22 June 1889, 22; *Critic* (New York), 6 July 1889, 5; *Athenaeum*, 27 July 1889, 126; *Scottish Review*, July 1889, 218.

The Emancipated

Athenaeum, 12 April 1890, 466; *Vanity Fair*, 19 April 1890, 352–3; *Graphic*, 26 April 1890, 488; *Morning Post*, 30 April 1890, 2; *St. James's Gazette*, 8 May 1890, 6; *Guardian* (London), 28 May 1890, 882; *Daily News*, 30 May 1890, 6; *Spectator*, 21 June 1890, 875; *Star*, 20 December 1893, 1; *Manchester Guardian*, 2 January 1894, 7; *Saturday Review*, 20 January 1894, 71; *Literary Era* (Philadelphia), October 1895, 272; *Dial* (Chicago), 1 November 1895, 255; *Nation* (New York), 6 February 1896, 124–5.

New Grub Street

Daily Telegraph, 11 April 1891, 3; *Scotsman*, 13 April 1891, 3; *Daily Graphic*, 13 April 1891; *Manchester Guardian*, 14 April 1891, 10; *Public Opinion*, 17 April 1891, 486; *Speaker*, 18 April 1891, 473; *Globe*, 23 April 1891, 6; *Glasgow Herald*, 23 April 1891, 9; *Athenaeum*, 9 May 1891, 601; *Vanity Fair*, 9 May 1891, 402; *National Observer*, 9 May 1891, 643; *Morning Post*, 11 May 1891, 2; *Daily Chronicle*, 13 May 1891, 7; *Queen*, 23 May 1891, 843; *Guardian* (London), 27 May 1891, 851; *Pall Mall Gazette*, 1 June 1891, 3; *London Figaro*, 13 June 1891, 4; *Graphic*, 20 June 1891, 707; *New Review*, June 1891, 564–5; *Scottish Review*, July 1891, 256; *Publishers' Circular*, 21 November 1891, 596; *Publishers' Circular*, 6 August 1892, 131; *Mercure de France*, May 1901, 557–9 (Henry-D. Davray); *La Nouvelle Revue*, 1 September 1902, 142; *Mercure de France*, September 1902, 748 (Rachilde).

Denzil Quarrier

Globe, 10 February 1892, 3; *Publishers' Circular*, 13 February 1892, 183; *Glasgow Herald*, 20 February 1892, 9; *World*, 24 February 1892, 24; *Bookseller*, 4 March 1892, 210b; *Literary World* (London), 12 March 1892, 88; *New York Times*, 13 March 1892, 19; *Whitehall Review*, 19 March 1892, 18–19; *New York Daily Tribune*, 27 March 1892, 18; *National Review*, March 1892, 131–2; *Bookman* (London), March 1892, 215; *Review of Reviews*, March 1892, 308; *New Review*, March 1892, 378 (H. D. Traill); *Academy*, 9 April 1892 (George Cotterell), 347; *Athenaeum*, 9 April 1892, 466; *Graphic*, 23 April 1892, 528; *Nation* (New York), 28 April 1892, 327; *Illustrated London News*, 28 May 1892, 659.

Born in Exile

Scotsman, 23 May 1892, 3; *Literary World* (London), 27 May 1892, 510–11; *Athenaeum*, 28 May 1892, 663; *Publishers' Circular*, 28 May 1892, 621; *Bookseller*, 3 June 1892, 515; *World*, 8 June 1892, 871; *Spectator*, 25 June 1892, 883; *Daily News*, 27 June 1892, 3; *Pall Mall Gazette*, 1 July 1892, 3; *Graphic*, 23 July 1892, 102; *Standard*, 27 July 1892, 6; *Review of Reviews*, July 1892, 83; *Westminster Review*, November 1892, 571–2; *Glasgow Herald*, 9 March 1893, 9; *Black and White*, 3 June 1893, 671; *Mercure de France*, May 1901, 557–9 (Henry-D. Davray); *T.P.'s Weekly*, 23 July 1909, 113–14 (F. H. Martin).

The Odd Women

Daily Chronicle, 19 April 1893, 3; *National Observer*, 22 April 1893, 579; *Globe*, 24 April 1893, 6; *Scotsman*, 24 April 1893, 3; *Manchester Guardian*, 25 April 1893, 10; *Daily Telegraph*, 22 May 1893, 2; *Guardian* (London), 24 May 1893, 839; *Spectator*, 27 May 1893, 707–8; *Queen*, 3 June 1893, 941; *Morning Post*, 12 June 1893, 2; *Woman's Herald*, 22 June 1893, 281–2; *Academy*, 24 June 1893, 542; *Review of Reviews*, July 1893, 99; *World*, 27 September 1893, 28; *Speaker*, 14 October 1893, 417–18; *Bookman* (New York), March 1896, 48–50 (Annie Nathan Meyer).

In the Year of Jubilee

Glasgow Herald, 6 December 1894, 10; *Scotsman*, 10 December 1894, 4; *World*, 19 December 1894, 32; *Daily News*, 27 December 1894, 6; *Morning Post*, 28 December 1894, 2; *Standard*, 28 December 1894, 2; *Globe*, 31 December 1894, 6; *Literary World* (London), 4 January 1895, 10–11; *To-Day*, 12 January 1895, 295; *National Observer*, 19 January 1895, 275; *Saturday Review*, 19 January 1895, 99–100; *Pall Mall Gazette*, 30 January 1895, 5; *Review of Reviews*, January 1895, 81; *Academy*, 2 March 1895, 189 (William Sharp); *Queen*, 2 March 1895, 392; *The Times*, 9 March 1895, 4; *Bookman* (New York), March 1895, 122–3; *Guardian*, 3 April 1895, 510; *Bookman* (London), May 1895, 54–5; *New York Times*, 28 July 1895; *Wave* (San Francisco), 10 August 1895; *Dial* (Chicago), 16 August 1895, 92 (William Morton Payne); *Literary Era* (Philadelphia), August 1895, 215; *Outlook* (New York), 14 September 1895, 432; *Book Buyer*, September 1895, 452–3; *Critic* (New York), 4 January 1896, 5.

Eve's Ransom

Glasgow Herald, 11 April 1895, 9; *Speaker*, 13 April 1895, 416–17; *Scotsman*, 15 April 1895, 3; *Daily Telegraph*, 19 April 1895, 6; *Publishers' Circular*, 20 April 1895, 427; *Daily News*, 23 April 1895, 6; *Sketch*, 24 April 1895, 697; *Literary World* (London), 26 April 1895, 386; *Saturday Review*, 27 April 1895, 531 (H. G. Wells); *New York Times*, 27 April 1895, 3; *Globe*, 29 April 1895, 3; *Woman*, 1 May 1895, 7; *World*, 1 May 1895, 27; *Athenaeum*, 11 May 1895, 605; *Pall Mall Gazette*, 14 May 1895, 4; *National Observer*, 18 May 1895, 4; *Guardian* (London), 22 May 1895, 765; *Morning Post*, 24 May 1895, 7; *Wave* (San Francisco), 25 May 1895; *Bookman* (London), May 1895, 54–5; *Literary Era* (Philadelphia), May 1895; *Bookseller*, 8 June, 1895, 509; *Nation* (New York), 11 July 1895, 32; *New York Daily Tribune*, 21 July 1895, 24; *Spectator*, 14 September 1895, 344–5; *Critic* (New York), 19 October 1895, 248; *Journal des Débats Politiques et Littéraires* (Edition hebdomadaire), 17 December 1898, 1183; *Athenaeum*, 28 January 1899, 111.

Sleeping Fires

Scotsman, 16 December 1895, 4; *Sketch*, 25 December 1895, 474; *Whitehall Review*, 28 December 1895, 12; *Glasgow Herald*, 2 January 1896, 2; *Publishers' Circular*, 11 January 1896, 53; *Literary World* (London), 17 January 1896, 47; *Speaker*, 18 January 1896, 81; *Globe*, 22 January 1896, 3; *Bookman* (London), January 1896, 130; *Woman*, 5 February 1896, 7 (Barbara); *Pall Mall Gazette*, 17 February 1896, 4; *The Times*, 22 February 1896, 10; *Graphic*, 22 February 1896, 224; *Bookseller*, 6 March 1896, 296; *New York Times*, 5 April 1896, 31; *Outlook* (New York), 25 April 1896, 772; *Westminster Review*, April 1896, 472; *Bookman* (New York), June 1896, 367; *Godey's Magazine*, August 1896; *Current Literature*, August 1896, 185.

The Paying Guest

Scotsman, 13 January 1896, 3; *Glasgow Herald*, 16 January 1896, 7; *Weekly Sun*, 19 January 1896, 2; *Daily Chronicle*, 21 January 1896, 3; *Star*, 21 January 1896, 1; *Globe*, 22 January 1896, 3; *Public Opinion*, 24 January 1896, 112; *Athenaeum*, 25 January 1896, 116; *Sketch*, 29 January 1896, 44; *Publishers' Circular*, 1 February 1896, 130; *To-Day*, 1 February 1896, 409; *Bookseller*, 7 February 1896, 124; *Illustrated*

London News, 7 March 1896, 302; *Book Buyer*, March 1896, 88–9; *Overland Monthly*, April 1896, 468; *Bookman* (New York), June 1896, 367.

The Whirlpool

Daily Chronicle, 10 April 1897, 3; *Saturday Review* (Supplement), 10 April 1897, 363 (Harold Frederic); *Scotsman*, 12 April 1897, 3; *Glasgow Herald*, 15 April 1897, 9; *Weekly Sun*, 18 April 1897, 2; *Morning Post*, 22 April 1897, 2; *Spectator*, 24 April 1897, 596; *National Observer and British Review*, 24 April 1897, 140–1; *Daily Telegraph*, 29 April 1897, 9; *Illustrated London News*, 1 May 1897, 600; *Sketch*, 5 May 1897, 66; *World*, 5 May 1897, 38; *Globe*, 7 May 1897, 6; *Bookseller*, 7 May 1897, 446; *Daily News*, 17 May 1897, 6; *Publishers' Circular*, 22 May 1897, 619; *Literary World* (London), 28 May 1897, 506–7; *Review of Reviews*, May 1897, 498–9; *Mercure de France*, June 1897, 584–5 (Henry-D. Davray); *Guardian* (London), 4 August 1897, 1217; *Graphic*, 21 August 1897, 259; *Literary News*, November 1897, 327; *New York Tribune Illustrated Supplement*, 6 February 1898, 18; *Outlook* (New York), 19 February 1898, 488; *Book Buyer*, February 1898, 38–40 (Hamlin Garland); *Bookman* (New York), March 1898, 64–6 (Harry Thurston Peck); *New York Times Saturday Review of Books and Arts*, 23 April 1898, 268; *Nation* (New York), 26 May 1898, 408; *Sewanee Review*, July 1898, 360–70 (Greenough White); *Dial* (Chicago), 1 August 1898, 78 (William Morton Payne).

Human Odds and Ends

Globe, 1 November 1897, 6; *Scotsman*, 1 November 1897, 3; *Glasgow Herald*, 4 November 1897, 10; *Manchester Guardian*, 9 November 1897, 9; *Sketch*, 24 November 1897, 206; *Daily News*, 26 November 1897, 9; *St. James's Gazette*, 26 November 1897, 5; *World*, 1 December 1897, 34; *Literature*, 11 December 1897, 243; *Spectator*, 11 December 1897, 863; *Graphic*, 11 December 1897, 776; *Literary World* (London), 7 January 1898, 8; *Guardian* (London), 19 January 1898, 98; *Athenaeum*, 22 January 1898, 116.

Charles Dickens, A Critical Study

Scotsman, 21 February 1898, 3; *Echo*, 26 February 1898, 1 (N.O.B.); *Glasgow Herald*, 26 February 1898, 9; *Aberdeen Journal*, 28 February 1898, 7; *Manchester Guardian*, 1 March 1898, 4; *Morning Post*, 3 March 1898, 2; *Bookseller*, 4 March 1898, 251; *Publishers' Circular*, 5 March 1898, 282; *Court Journal*, 5 March 1898, 350; *Saturday Review*, 5 March 1898, 330; *Pall Mall Gazette*, 7 March 1898, 10; *Nottingham Daily Express*, 8 March 1898, 7; *Manchester Courier*, 9 March 1898; *Methodist Times*, 10 March 1898, 150; *Academy*, 12 March 1898, 280–1; *Globe*, 14 March 1898, 3; *Glasgow Evening Times*, 15 March 1898; *Sketch*, 16 March 1898, 342; *Independent*, 17 March 1898, 174 (S. G. Warner); *Inquirer*, 19 March 1898, 182 (E. W. Lummis); *News of the Week*, 26 March 1898, 4 (W. M.); *Cosmopolis*, March 1898, 705; *Daily Graphic*, 2 April 1898, 12; *Sun* (New York), 3 April 1898, 2; *The Times*, 4 April 1898, 9; *Athenaeum*, 9 April 1898, 467; *Outlook* (New York), 9 April 1898, 929; *Nottingham Daily Express*, 11 April 1898, 4; *Spectator*, 30 April 1898, 603; *New Century Review*, April 1898, 325–6; *Literary World* (London), 6 May 1898; *Critic* (New York), 7 May 1898, 313–14; *Queen*, 7 May 1898, 793 (Walter Besant); *New York Times Saturday Review of Books and Arts*, 14 May 1898, 326 (E. Iraneus Stevenson); *Evesham Standard*, 14 May 1898; *Nation* (New York), 19 May 1898, 388; *Liverpool Post*, 19 May 1898; *Clarion*, 21 May 1898, 162; *Westminster Review*, May 1898, 591; *Literary News*, May 1898, 148; *Literary World* (Boston), 11 June 1898, 186; *Harper's Magazine*, June 1898, 3–4; *Mercure de France*, June 1898, 909–10 (Henry-D. Davray); *Nottingham Guardian*, 5 July 1898; *Guardian* (London), 20 July 1898, 1134; *East Anglian Daily Times*, 8 August 1898; *Forum*, August 1898, 758–9 (Brander Matthews); *Current Literature*, September 1898, 217; *Longman's Magazine*, September 1898, 467–71 (Andrew Lang); *Dial* (Chicago), 1 November 1898, 297–9; *Academy*, 22 April 1899, 461 (Lionel Johnson).

The Town Traveller

Westminster Gazette, 30 August 1898, 3; *Scotsman*, 1 September 1898, 7; *St. James's Gazette*, 1 September 1898, 12; *Spectator*, 3 September 1898, 312–13; *Whitehall Review*, 3 September 1898, 25; *Globe*, 7 September 1898, 6; *Vanity Fair*, 8 September 1898, 173; *Daily News*, 9 September 1898, 6; *Athenaeum*, 10 September 1898, 346; *Academy*

(Supplement), 10 September 1898, 245; *Glasgow Herald*, 10 September 1898, 7; *Critic* (London), 10 September 1898, 31; *Daily Chronicle*, 13 September 1898, 3; *Standard*, 13 September 1898, 2; *Daily Mail*, 13 September 1898, 3; *World*, 14 September 1898, 29; *Saturday Review*, 17 September 1898, 387; *Literature*, 17 September 1898, 255–6; *Truth* (London), 22 September 1898, 736; *Outlook* (London), 24 September 1898, 242; *Manchester Guardian*, 27 September 1898, 7; *Literary World* (London), 7 October 1898, 233; *Illustrated London News*, 8 October 1898, 514; *Bookseller*, 12 October 1898, 949; *New York Times Saturday Review*, 15 October 1898, 686; *Outlook* (New York), 15 October 1898, 446; *Sketch*, 19 October 1898, 566; *Cosmopolis*, October 1898, 84; *Bookman* (London), October 1898, 19; *The Times*, 23 November 1898, 13; *Literary Era* (Philadelphia), November 1898; *Bookman* (New York), November 1898, 256–7; *Life* (New York), 22 December 1898 (Droch); *Cosmopolitan*, December 1898 (Louis Zangwill); *English Illustrated Magazine*, January 1899, 460; *Literary World* (Boston), 18 February 1899, 54.

The Crown of Life

Academy, 28 October 1899, 485; *Spectator*, 4 November 1899, pp. 661–2 (C. L. Graves); *Publishers' Circular*, 4 November 1899, 498; *Manchester Guardian*, 7 November 1899, 4; *Globe*, 8 November 1899, 4; *Scotsman*, 9 November 1899, 3; *Daily Chronicle*, 10 November 1899, 4; *Speaker*, 11 November 1899, 153; *Pall Mall Gazette*, 11 November 1899, 4; *Morning Post*, 16 November 1899, 3; *Literary World* (London), 17 November 1899, 377; *Daily News*, 17 November 1899, 9; *Glasgow Herald*, 17 November 1899, 4; *Athenaeum*, 18 November 1899, 683; *World*, 22 November 1899, 31; *Author*, 1 December 1899, 164; *Saturday Review*, 2 December 1899, 712; *Outlook* (London), 9 December 1899, 626; *Queen*, 9 December 1899, 1006 (M.C.B.); *New York Times Saturday Review*, 23 December 1899, 898; *Westminster Gazette*, 30 December 1899, 3; *Bookman* (London), December 1899, 89; *Guardian* (London), 17 January 1900, 103; *Critic* (New York), January 1900, 91; *Mercure de France*, February 1900, 551 (Henry-D. Davray); *San Francisco Newsletter*, 19 May 1900.

Our Friend the Charlatan

Daily Telegraph, 31 May 1901, 11 (W. L. Courtney); *Spectator*, 1 June 1901, 809; *Globe*, 5 June 1901, 4; *Glasgow Herald*, 6 June 1901, 9; *Scotsman*, 6 June 1901, 2; *Morning Post*, 7 June 1901, 2; *Guardian* (London), 12 June 1901, 806; *St. James's Gazette*, 19 June 1901, 5; *Athenaeum*, 22 June 1901, 783–4; *Outlook* (New York), 22 June 1901, 460; *Illustrated London News*, 29 June 1901, 942; *World*, 3 July 1901, 31–2; *Saturday Review*, 6 July 1901, 20; *Outlook* (London), 13 July 1901, 762; *Graphic*, 27 July 1901, 128–30; *Fortnightly Review*, July 1901, 166–7 (Stephen Gwynn); *Das Litterarische Echo*, July 1901, 1430 (Elizabeth Lee); *Literary World* (Boston), 1 August 1901, 115; *Truth* (London), 15 August 1901, 446 (Desmond O'Brien); *La Revue*, 15 August 1901, 421–3; *Queen*, 21 August 1901, 306–7; *Literary World* (London), 23 August 1901, 127; *Sphere*, 24 August 1901, 226 (C. K. Shorter); *Bookman* (London), August 1901, 152–4 (A. Macdonell); *Book Lover* (Melbourne), September 1901, 98; *Literary News*, September 1901, 260; *Bookman* (New York), September 1901, 95–6; *Overland Monthly*, October 1901, 314–15.

By the Ionian Sea

Daily Chronicle, 13 June 1901, 3; *Scotsman*, 17 June 1901, 2; *Daily Telegraph*, 21 June 1901, 6; *Westminster Gazette*, 27 June 1901, 3; *The Times*, 15 July 1901, 8; *Athenaeum*, 27 July 1901, 121; *La Revue*, 15 August 1901, 421–3; *Sphere*, 24 August 1901, 226 (C. K. Shorter); *Outlook* (New York), 13 May 1905, 137–8; *Dial* (Chicago), 1 June 1905, p. 385; *Nation* (New York), 8 June 1905, 464–5; *Literary World* (London), 15 June 1905, 214; *Critic* (New York), August 1905, 190; *New York Tribune Weekly Review*, 22 October 1905, 11.

Forster's Life of Dickens

The Times Literary Supplement, 17 October 1902, 310; *Academy and Literature*, 18 October 1902, 407; *Daily News*, 21 October 1902, 8; *World*, 22 October 1902, 665; *Pilot*, 25 October 1902, 426; *Guardian* (London), 29 October 1902, 1552; *Athenaeum*, 1 November 1902, 585; *Literary World* (London), 7 November 1902, 365; *Revue des Deux Mondes*, 15November 1902, 458–68 (T. de Wyzewa); *Book Lover* (Melbourne), December 1902, 285; *T.P.'s Weekly*, 26 December 1902, 193–4;

Manchester Guardian, 1 January 1903, 4; *Speaker*, 10 January 1903, 381; *Current Literature*, February 1903, 244; *Pall Mall Gazette*, 20 February 1903, 4.

The Private Papers of Henry Ryecroft

Outlook (London), 31 January 1903, 763; *Daily Mail*, 3 February 1903, 2; *To-Day*, 4 February 1903, 51–2; *Scotsman*, 5 February 1903, 2; *Daily Chronicle*, 7 February 1903, 3; *Glasgow Herald*, 12 February 1903, 9; *Illustrated London News*, 14 February 1903, 236; *Globe*, 16 February 1903, 8; *Westminster Gazette*, 20 February 1903, 4; *Literary World* (London), 20 February 1903, 166–7; *Manchester Guardian*, 20 February 1903, 4; *World*, 24 February 1903, 322; *Daily News*, 27 February 1903, 8; *T.P.'s Weekly*, 27 February 1903, 489; *Litterarische Echo*, 1 March 1903, 771 (Elizabeth Lee); *Morning Post*, 5 March 1903, 2; *Methodist Times*, 5 March 1903, 154; *Speaker*, 7 March 1903, 559; *Spectator*, 14 March 1903, 418; *Liverpool Daily Post*, 18 March 1903, 7; *Observer*, 22 March 1903, 7; *Truth* (London), 26 March 1903, 833 (Desmond O'Brien); *Publishers' Circular*, 28 March 1903, 360; *Bookman* (London), March 1903 (A. St John Adcock); *Author*, 1 April 1903, 188–90 (V.E.M.); *Book Lover* (Melbourne), April 1903, 325–6; *Bookseller*, 8 April 1903, 330; *Independent* (Boston), 9 April 1903, 853–4; *Contemporary Review*, April 1903, 599–601; *World's Work*, April 1903, 582–3; *New Liberal Review*, April 1903, 451–3; *Bookman* (New York), April 1903, 198; *Nation* (New York), 11 June 1903, 478; *Mercure de France*, June 1903, 843–4 (Henry-D. Davray); *Dial* (Chicago), 1 July 1903, 16; *Clarion*, 25 March 1904, 3 (A.L.S.).

Veranilda

Morning Post, 28 September 1904, 6; *Pall Mall Gazette*, 1 October 1904, 5; *Daily News*, 3 October 1904, 4 (C. F. G. Masterman); *Scotsman*, 6 October 1904, 2; *Globe*, 7 October 1904, 8; *Academy*, 8 October 1904, 311–12; *Glasgow Herald*, 15 October 1904, 11; *Illustrated London News*, 15 October 1904, 540; *World*, 18 October 1904, 636; *Athenaeum*, 22 October 1904, 544; *Speaker*, 22 October 1904, 88; *Week's Survey*, 22 October 1904, 33; *Literary World* (London), 28 October 1904, 326; *Litterarische Echo*, 15 November 1904, 273 (Elizabeth Lee); *Guardian* (London), 16 November 1904, 1931; *Bookman* (London), November 1904, 81 (William Barry); *Book Lover* (Melbourne), December 1904,

145; *Spectator*, 3 December 1904, 902–3; *Publishers' Circular*, 10 December 1904, 660; *Independent Review* (London), December 1904, 479–80 (D. McCarthy); *Litterarische Echo*, 1 January 1905, 475 (Max Meyerfeld); *Mercure de France*, 15 January 1905, 304–6 (Henry-D. Davray); *New York Tribune Weekly Review*, 18 February 1905, 11; *New York Times Saturday Review*, 25 February 1905, 118; *Nation* (New York), 1 June 1905, 441.

Will Warburton

Evening Standard and St James's Gazette, 23 June 1905, 13; *Morning Post*, 23 June 1905, 9; *Scotsman*, 26 June 1905, 2; *Daily Chronicle*, 28 June, 1905, 3 (C.E.L.); *Graphic*, 1 July 1905, 806; *Outlook* (London), 1 July 1905, 951–2; *Spectator*, 1 July 1905, 19–20; *Daily News*, 5 July 1905, 4; *Daily Telegraph*, 5 July 1905, 12; *Glasgow Herald*, 5 July 1905, 10; *Bookseller*, 6 July 1905, 576; *T.P.'s Weekly*, 7 July 1905, 17; *Academy*, 8 July 1905, 710 (Edward Thomas); *Outlook* (New York), 8 July 1905, 644; *Pall Mall Gazette*, 8 July 1905, 4; *New York Tribune Weekly Review*, 8 July 1905, 11; *Globe*, 10 July 1905, 4; *Westminster Gazette*, 15 July 1905, 14; *Literary World* (London), 15 July 1905, 250; *Guardian* (London), 19 July 1905, 1224; *Illustrated London News*, 22 July 1905, 128; *New York Times*, 22 July 1905, 487; *Week's Survey*, 29 July 1905, 523; *Litterarische Echo*, 15 August 1905, 1645–6 (Elizabeth Lee); *Bookman* (New York), August 1905, 654; *Review of Reviews*, August 1905, 208; *Bookman* (London), August 1905, 162 (A. St John Adcock); *Critic* (New York), September 1905, 284–5; *Book Lover* (Melbourne), October 1905, 110–11; *Publishers' Circular*, 9 December 1905, 669.

The House of Cobwebs

Morning Leader, 16 May 1906, 3; *Scotsman*, 17 May 1906, 2; *Daily Telegraph*, 18 May 1906, 14; *Academy*, 19 May 1906, 479; *Globe*, 23 May 1906, 4; *Spectator*, 26 May 1906, 835–6; *Outlook* (London), 16 June 1906, 817; *Evening News*, 18 June 1906, 2 (H. Hamilton Fyfe); *Gentleman's Magazine*, June 1906, 527–31 (Noel Ainslie); *Review of Reviews*, June 1906, 651; *Athenaeum*, 7 July 1906, 10; *Bookseller*, 10 July 1906, 546–7; *Mercure de France*, 15 July 1906, 295–7 (Henry-D. Davray); *Guardian* (London), 25 July 1906, 1253; *Bookman* (London), July 1906, 141–2 (William Barry); *New York Daily Tribune*, 4 August 1906, 5; *Argonaut*, 25 August 1906; *New York Times Saturday Review of Books*, 25 August

1906, 519; *Outlook* (New York), 1 September 1906, 44; *Literary World* (London), 15 September 1906, 395.

GENERAL SURVEYS

(*listed chronologically*)

Zotov, *Nabliudatiel*, 15 November 1889, 1–2.

Anon., *Russkaia Myusl*, February 1891, 110–11.

Collet, Clara E., 'George Gissing's Novels. A First Impression', *Charity Organization Review*, October 1891, 375–80.

A.R.O., 'George Gissing', *Labour Leader*, 14 November 1896, 392 and 21 November 1896, 400.

Michaelis, Kate Woodbridge, 'George Gissing', *Boston Evening Transcript*, 10 November 1898.

Courtney, W. L., 'George Gissing', *English Illustrated Magazine*, November 1903, 188–92.

Hubert, 'A Note on George Gissing', *Sunday Chronicle* (Manchester), 3 January 1904, 2.

Bateson, Margaret (Mrs W. E. Heitland), 'Mr George Gissing', *Guardian* (London), 6 January 1904, 34–5.

Beswick, Harry, 'George Gissing', *Clarion*, 8 January 1904, 3.

Sturmer, Herbert, and Ransome, Arthur, 'George Gissing. Two Appreciations', *Week's Survey*, 9 January 1904, 173–4.

Waugh, Arthur, 'George Gissing', *Fortnightly Review*, 1 February 1904, 244–56. Reprinted in Waugh's *Reticence in Literature and Other Papers*, J. G. Wilson, London, 1915, 161–82.

Zangwill, Israel, 'Without Prejudice: George Gissing', *To-Day*, 3 February 1904, 433–4.

Mimnermus, 'George Gissing 1857–1903', *Literary Guide*, 1 March 1904, 36–7.

Richardson, J. J., 'George Gissing', *Manchester Quarterly*, July 1904, 236–43.

Wells, H. G., 'George Gissing: An Impression', *Monthly Review*, August 1904, 160–72. Reprinted in *George Gissing and H. G. Wells*, ed. Royal A. Gettmann, Rupert Hart-Davis, London, 1961, 260–77.

[Roberts, Morley], 'The Exile of George Gissing', *Albany Magazine*, Christmas 1904, 24–31.

[Ainslie, Noel], 'Some Recollections of George Gissing', *Gentleman's Magazine*, February 1906, 11–18.

Harrison, Austin, 'George Gissing', *Nineteenth Century*, September 1906, 453–63.

Rzewuski, Stanislas, 'Georges Gissing', *Figaro* (Supplémen t Littéraire) 13 October 1906, 4.

Schaefer, August, *George Gissing: Sein Leben und Seine Romane*, Marburg, 1908.

Bonnier, Charles, *Milieux d'Art*, Liverpool, [1910], 28–31.

Swinnerton, Frank, *George Gissing: A Critical Study*, Martin Secker, London, 1912. New editions in 1924 and 1966.

Index

The Index is divided into four sections: I. George Gissing: writings; II. Characteristics of Gissing and aspects of his work and career; III. Persons; IV. Newspapers and periodicals.

I. GEORGE GISSING: WRITINGS

II. CHARACTERISTICS OF GISSING AND ASPECTS OF HIS WORK AND CAREER

III. PERSONS

IV. NEWSPAPERS AND PERIODICALS

THE CRITICAL HERITAGE SERIES

GENERAL EDITOR: B. C. SOUTHAM

Volumes published and forthcoming

JANE AUSTEN	B. C. Southam
BROWNING	Boyd Litzinger and Donald Smalley
BURNS	Donald A. Low
BYRON	Andrew Rutherford
THOMAS CARLYLE	Jules Paul Seigel
CLOUGH	Michael Thorpe
COLERIDGE	J. R. de J. Jackson
CONRAD	Norman Sherry
CRABBE	Arthur Pollard
DEFOE	J. P. W. Rogers
DICKENS	Philip Collins
DRYDEN	James and Helen Kinsley
GEORGE ELIOT	David Carroll
HENRY FIELDING	Ronald Paulson and Thomas Lockwood
FORD MADOX FORD	Frank MacShane
GEORGE GISSING	Pierre Coustillas and Colin Partridge
THOMAS HARDY	R. G. Cox
HAWTHORNE	J. Donald Crowley
IBSEN	Michael Egan
HENRY JAMES	Roger Gard
JOHNSON	James T. Boulton
JAMES JOYCE (in 2 vols)	Robert H. Deming
KEATS	G. M. Matthews
KIPLING	Roger Lancelyn Green
D. H. LAWRENCE	R. P. Draper
MEREDITH	Ioan Williams
MILTON (in 2 vols)	John T. Shawcross
WILLIAM MORRIS	Peter Faulkner

Continued